43D CONGRESS, 2d Session. } HOUSE OF REPRESENTATIVES. { REPORT No. 134.

# THE

# LAW OF CLAIMS AGAINST GOVERNMENTS,

INCLUDING

## THE MODE OF ADJUSTING THEM

AND

## THE PROCEDURE ADOPTED IN THEIR INVESTIGATION.

---

PUBLISHED BY ORDER OF THE CONGRESS OF THE UNITED STATES OF AMERICA.

---

WASHINGTON:
GOVERNMENT PRINTING OFFICE.
1875.

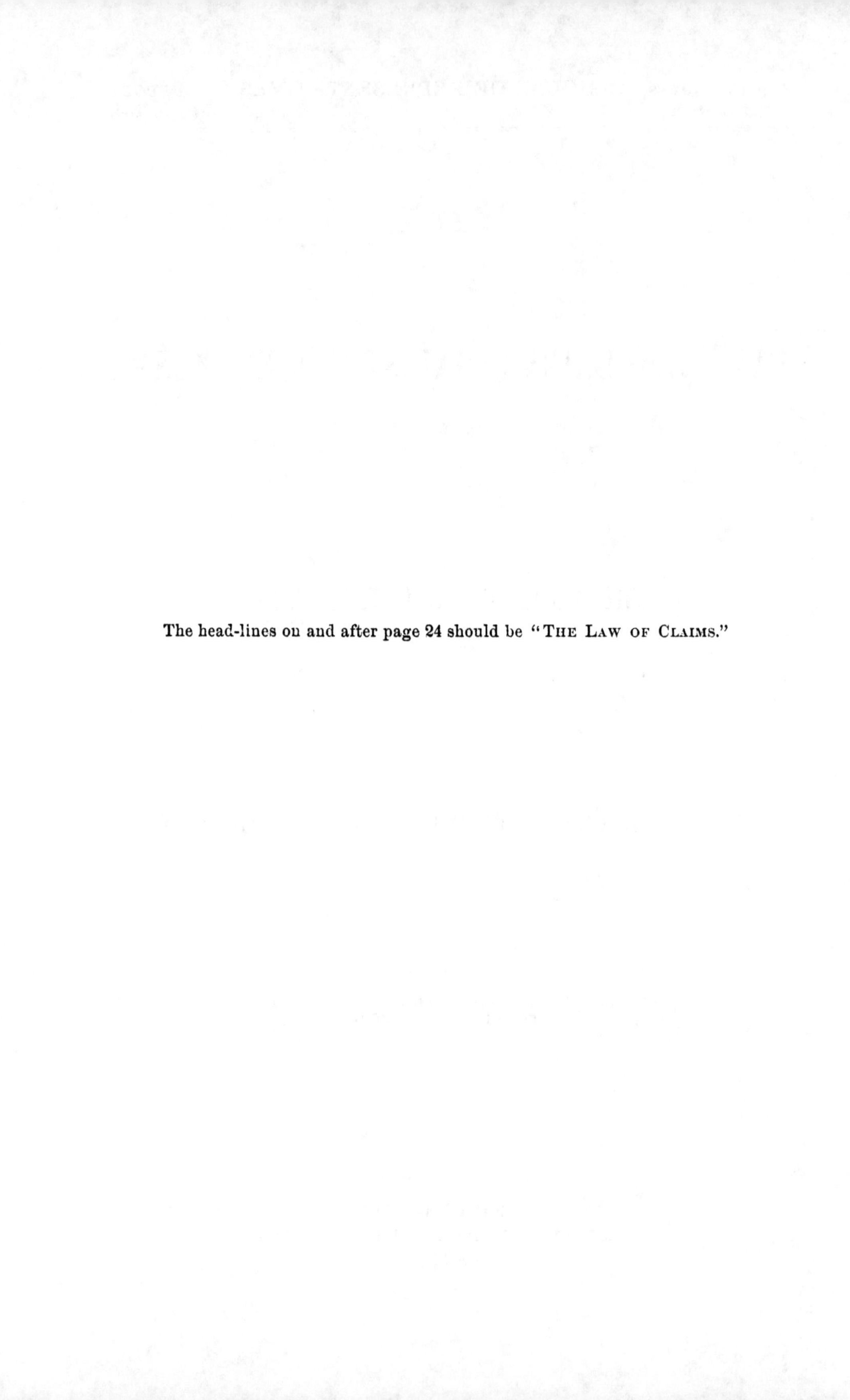

The head-lines on and after page 24 should be "The Law of Claims."

# PREFACE.

There were two principal objects in preparing the following pages: first, to show that the whole business of examining claims by committees of Congress should be abandoned, and appropriate tribunals created for that purpose, having judicial powers, with all the machinery now exercised by the commissioners of claims for ascertaining the truth; and, second, to state some principles of law which seemed necessary to secure justice for honest claimants and to protect the Government against demands which find no sanction in sound precedent or public law.

Some of the reasons in favor of withdrawing from Congress the consideration of claims were presented in a speech in the House of Representatives June 3, 1874, (Congressional Record, vol. 2, part 5, (vol. 6,) p. 4511,) and still more appear in the following pages.

Since that time the writer has found a valuable discussion of the subject at the second session of the Thirtieth Congress, which is well worthy of attentive perusal. (Globe, vol. 20, pp. 38, 139, 144, 159, 163, 172, 178, 188, 198, 203, 302, 303, 307, 378, 492, 543.)

A report made at the same Congress on the same subject is also very instructive. (See House Report 441, vol. 2, first session 29th Congress; House Report 498, vol. 3, first session 30th Congress; House Report 937, vol. 4, second session 27th Congress; House Report 295, vol. 1, first session 28th Congress; House Report 442, vol. 2, first session 30th Congress; House Report 10, vol. 1, first session 39th Congress.)

Some of the earlier debates in Congress are equally deserving attention. (Annals of Congress, 14th Congress, second session, 1816–'17, pp. 245, 299, 382, 426, 462, 1028, 1035, 1040, 1051, 1211.)

Some of the reforms which are believed to be just, salutary, and desirable are indicated in the following pages.

The vast increase of population and business in the United States is such that it is believed there should be a tribunal of claims, the members of which should be selected from the best talent of the country, and have a tenure of office like that of the judges of the courts, with power to make awards to be reported to Congress for payment. Their opinions on questions of law should be subject to revision by the Supreme Court. This tribunal should have all the powers now exercised by the commissioners of claims, and their conclusions of law and fact on every claim should be printed.

Their awards, when not taken to the Supreme Court for review, should be final.

Either this tribunal or a bureau of claims in the Department of Justice would seem to be necessary to secure the rights of honest claimants and protection to the Government.

The following pages were not designed as a full statement of the law of claims or the procedure applicable to them. The *right* to relief and a mode of *procedure* to attain it in the many classes of claims which have hitherto appealed to Congress, because in many, if not most of them, there was no other tribunal having jurisdiction, should be recognized, and provision made by law for securing justice to every claimant having a meritorious claim.

The future cannot fail to give rise to claims which will always require a tribunal such as is suggested.

The Court of Claims has a jurisdiction well defined, and its continued existence is a necessity.

Its jurisdiction may be properly enlarged.

That portion of the following pages which relates to the law of claims in the United States is a revision and enlargement of House Report No. 262, made by the Committee on War-Claims March 26, 1874, at the first session of the Forty-third Congress.

That report was reprinted entire in "The Forum Law Review" for April, 1874, pp. 213–291, then published at Baltimore, (now New York,) and the substance of it in an elementary form was published in the (Philadelphia) American Law Register for May, June, and July, 1874, and February, 1875, (vols. 13 and 14, N. S.)

The secretary of legation of the Japanese embassy procured copies of the report and forwarded to the international-law adviser of the Japanese government, who was formerly a citizen of the United States.

Many claims were presented to and urged upon that government, growing out of a rebellion there. It is believed the revised work now presented may be found useful as furnishing a reference to authorities on some questions of international and constitutional law.

There are some references in the following pages to the justice and necessity of fixing a limitation on thepresentation of claims, not only in the courts, but in the Departments of Government, and in all tribunals having jurisdiction of them. (See pp. 13, 18, 238, 242, 318, 324.)

This is more fully discussed in sundry reports made to the House of Representatives during the Forty-third Congress by the Committee on War-Claims, to which reference can be had; and the reports of other committees in this and preceding Congresses doubtless present the subject in a more forcible light.

The experience of all time has shown the necessity for applying a limitation on the prosecution of actions in courts. The common law raises a presumption of the payment of claims after a given time. (House Rep. Com. War-Claims No. 784, 1 sess. 43 Cong., p. 17.)

There is greater necessity for applying a limitation in favor of the Government in many, if not most cases, than between individual citizens.

The officers of Government who may be cognizant of facts necessary to protect it from unjust claims are too frequently changed, and thus go out of position where duty or interest so strongly requires them to watch its interests, or where opportunity may exist for doing so. It is even possible for some, by employment or otherwise, to become adversely interested.

Even officers do not always exercise the same vigilance for the public interest that private citizens do for theirs. These and other considerations no less weighty render this subject worthy of consideration. (See Index, "Fraudulent Claims.")

In the examination of war-claims, there is one important principle of law which is liable to be overlooked—that which relates to the *measure of damages*. War generally furnishes the occasion for demanding exorbitant prices for property sold to, or used by, the Government. The presence of an army often makes such demands for some kinds of property, that holders of it take advantage of the situation to extort enormous prices. When the Government takes property in time of war, under circumstances which require "just compensation" to be made, *the measure of damages* is not the fictitious prices so often asked, but only "a fair price, without regard to the enhanced value resulting from the presence of" an army. (See *post* 236—House Rep. No. 497, 1 sess. 43d Cong., Com. War-Claims; House Rep. No. 748, 1 sess. 43d Cong.; Halleck Int. Law 460, sec. 17.) During the rebellion, on the theater of war, in localities alternately occupied by the contending armies, property was so insecure that it could be scarcely said to have any real value.

A practice has grown up, to some extent, which is often injurious to claimants and prejudicial to the Government. Officers in the Departments, and even the courts, when rejecting claims upon the ground that no law authorizes payment, sometimes take occasion to say that *a remedy may be sought in Congress*. (House Rep. No. 673, part 2, 1 sess. 43d Cong., Com. War-Claims; 8 Wallace, 275.)

It is no part of the duty of these officers, or courts, to advise claimants as to the means by which they may obtain relief in opposition to the established law, nor is it within the sphere of their appropriate duties to make recommendations to Congress. The Constitution devolves on the President the duty of recommending to Congress such measures as justice and the public interest require.

Congress can with no more propriety disregard law, settled on correct principle, than courts, or officers in the Departments. Unauthorized suggestions to appeal to Congress for relief often involve claimants in expense and disappointment.

The following pages are perhaps the first attempt by a report in Congress to discuss at considerable length some of the subjects therein considered, and they are submitted in the hope that they may be of some value.

# CONTENTS.

# ALIEN CLAIMS.

FEBRUARY 10, 1875.—Ordered to be printed and recommitted to the Committee on War-Claims.

Mr. LAWRENCE, from the Committee on War-Claims, submitted the following

# REPORT:

[To accompany bill H. R. 3916.]

*The Committee on War-Claims, to whom was referred the bill (H. R. 3916) to provide for the adjudication of the claims of aliens, have considered the same, and report:*

The bill, in the form in which the committee have agreed upon the same, is as follows:

A BILL to provide for the adjudication of the claims of aliens.

*Be it enacted by the Senate and House of Representatives of the United States of America in Congress assembled,* That the claims of subjects or citizens of a foreign state against the United States may be referred to the Court of Claims by the Secretary of State, with the concurrence of the foreign government presenting them; and the Court of Claims shall then have jurisdiction to hear and determine the same in accordance with the principles of international law, or in pursuance of any treaty stipulation or agreement between the United States and such foreign state. Claims may be prosecuted in the name of the claimant by petition, in the nature of a petition of right. All cases shall proceed according to the rules and practice of the Court of Claims. Either party shall have the right of appeal from the final judgment of said court. Judgments, if against the United States for damages in money, shall be satisfied in like manner as other judgments of said court, unless otherwise provided by treaty or other stipulation between the United States and the government presenting the claim.

The committee have agreed to recommend the passage of this bill in this form. There are many reasons which might be urged in support of the bill.

The President, in his annual message of December, 1873, said to Congress:

I recommend legislation to create a special court, to consist of three judges, who shall be empowered to hear and determine all claims of aliens upon the United States arising out of acts committed against their persons or property during the insurrection. The recent reference under the treaty of Washington was confined to claims of British subjects arising during the period named in the treaty; but it is understood that there are other British claims of a similar nature arising after the 9th of April, 1865, and it is known that other claims of a like nature are advanced by citizens or subjects of other powers. It is desirable to have these claims also examined and disposed of.

There are many reasons why some court should have jurisdiction of alien claims. Almost from the foundation of the Government mixed commissions have been created, by diplomatic arrangements, to make awards on the claims of our citizens against other nations, and those of subjects of other powers against this nation. The result shows a necessity for a permanent court.

The rapidly increasing population and commerce of the United States, and the multiplied means of and necessity for intercourse with foreign nations, must necessarily add to the number and magnitude of claims and questions arising on international law.

While the awards of these commissions have been valuable in many respects, they have not resulted in giving to the world a well defined and authoritative system or uniform rules of international law. Their decisions have sometimes been contradictory in principle.

A court regularly clothed with jurisdiction to pass upon questions of international law and of all claims of aliens would secure a degree of learning and uniformity scarcely attainable by temporary commissions composed of different persons selected for an occasion.

Heretofore the awards of these commissions have been final.

If a court shall be given jurisdiction, from whose decision an appeal may be taken to the Supreme Court of the United States, the great learning and ability of that court will aid in securing a settled system of international law which will not reach it in any other mode. A court will also be more economical than the plan of a mixed commission.[1]

---

[1] TREASURY DEPARTMENT, *Washington, D. C., February* 14, 1874.

SIR: Referring to your letter of the 19th ultimo, I transmit herewith an amended statement of the expenses of the several commissions held during the last ten years, showing the total expenditures to the close of the last fiscal year, the detailed items of expenditure, the annual expenditure, and the salaries of the principal officers.

I am, very respectfully,

F. A. SAWYER, *Assistant Secretary,*

Hon. WM. LAWRENCE, *House of Representatives.*

| | Expenditures in detail. | Total expenditures. | Annual expenditures for the fiscal year ending— | | Salaries. |
|---|---|---|---|---|---|
| *Salaries and expenses of the United States and Spanish Claims Commission from July* 1, 1871, *to June* 30, 1873. | | | | | |
| Salary of advocate | [2, 780 55 | | June 30, 1872 | $12, 647 35 | Advocate....*$5, 000 |
| Salary of secretary, ($5 per diem) | 3, 860 00 | | June 30, 1873 | 16, 451 19 | Secretary... †5 |
| Salary of counsel | 3, 043 50 | | ............ | ......... | Counsel ..... *5, 000 |
| Salary of arbitrator | 10, 810 44 | | ............ | ......... | Arbitrator.. *5, 000 |
| Salaries of messenger and porters | 1, 300 00 | | ............ | ......... | Messenger.. *300 |
| Copying and translating | 715 25 | | | | |
| Contingent expenses, including freight, postage, stationery, &c | 6, 588 80 | | | | |
| | | $29, 098 54 | | 29, 098 54 | |
| *Commission for the settlement of claims of the United States against the United States of Colombia, from September* 18, 1865, *to October* 10, 1866. | | | | | |
| Salary of Thomas Biddle, commissioner | 2, 500 00 | | June 30, 1865 | 12, 953 42 | Commiss'ner. ‡2, 500 |
| Salary of Charles W. Davis, sec'y | 10, 453 42 | | June 30, 1867 | 1, 000 00 | Secretary ... ‡2, 000 |
| Salary of G. Dean, counsel | 1, 000 00 | | | | |
| | | 13, 952 42 | | 13, 953 42 | |
| *Expenses of carrying into effect the convention with the republic of Venezuela, from October* 26, 1867, *to October* 6, 1868. | | | | | |
| Salary of J. W. Macado, umpire | 1, 500 00 | | June 30, 1869 | 4, 193 42 | Commiss'ner. ‡2, 500 |
| Salary of D. M. Talmage, commissioner | 2, 693 42 | | ............ | ......... | Umpire..... §1, 500 |
| | | 4, 193 42 | ............ | 4, 193 42 | |

The whole subject of the necessity and value of giving this jurisdiction to some court has been fully considered by the learned and able

| | Expenditures in detail. | Total expenditures. | Annual expenditures for the fiscal year ending— | | Salaries. |
|---|---|---|---|---|---|
| *Compensation of commissioner, and contingent expenses of the commission, to adjust claims of citizens of United States against New Granada and Costa Rica, from November 7, 1865, to January 30, 1867.* | | | | | |
| Allowance to John Lewis, heir-at-law of Moses Lewis, killed at Panama | $5,406 15 | | June 30, 1866 | $5,406 15 | .................. |
| Allowance by commissioners | 1,586 66 | | June 30, 1867 | 3,088 66 | Umpire.... §$1,500 |
| Moiety paid by the United States as compensation to umpire to New Granada | 1,500 00 | | | | |
| | | $8,494 81 | .............. | 8,494 81 | |
| *Commission on the part of the United States to carry into effect the treaty, &c., between the United States and Hudson Bay and Puget Sound Agricultural Company.* | | | | | |
| Salary of counsel from January 1, 1865, to November 30, 1869, and expenses | 19,178 21 | | June 30, 1865 | 7,570 00 | Commiss'ner *5,000 |
| Salary of clerk (same date) and expenses | 12,656 00 | | June 30, 1866 | 9,872 70 | Counsel..... †2,500 |
| Witness and other fees | 10,979 63 | | June 30, 1867 | 20,333 00 | Clerk....... †2,500 |
| Messengers and porters | 3,247 00 | | June 30, 1868 | 18,667 18 | |
| Copying | 793 40 | | June 30, 1869 | 9,452 79 | |
| Contingent expenses | 20,109 27 | | June 30, 1870 | 8,526 20 | |
| | | 66,963 51 | | | |
| Amount for which no vouchers have been rendered, and with which the parties stand charged | .......... | 7,458 36 | | | |
| Total amount expended | .......... | 74,421 87 | .............. | 74,421 87 | |
| *Salaries and expenses of the Mixed Commission on American and Briitsh claims, from April 17, 1871, to June 30, 1873.* | | | | | |
| Salary and expenses of E. R. Hoar, commissioner | 6,000 00 | | June 30, 1871 | 20,000 00 | 2 commiss'ers ‡6,000 |
| Salary and expenses of G. H. Williams, commissioner | 6,000 00 | | June 30, 1872 | 56,493 13 | 1 commiss'er's exp's. |
| Expenses of Samuel Nelson, commissioner | 1,440 00 | | June 30, 1873 | 197,179 81 | Agt. & couns'l †10,000 |
| Salary and expenses of R. S. Hale, agent and consul | 6,083 23 | | | | 1 commiss'r. †10,000 |
| Salary and expenses of James S. Frazer, commissioner, from July 29, 1871, to June 30, 1873 | 20,117 87 | | | | Secretary... ‡3,000 |
| Salary of T. C. Cox, secretary, from October 1, 1871, to June 30, 1873 | 5,032 61 | | | | |
| Contingent expenses, including messengers, furniture, refreshments, stationery, clerk-hire, printing, newspapers, carpets, telegraphing, labor, &c | 132,631 84 | | | | |
| Legal services, witness fees, and of stenographer | 4,312 60 | | | | |
| | | 181,618 15 | | | |
| Amount for which no vouchers have been rendered, and with which the parties stand charged | ......... | 92,054 79 | | | |
| Total amount expended | .......... | 273,672 94 | .............. | 273,672 94 | |

Secretary of State, whose enlightened labors have added so much luster to our diplomatic history. His conclusions on this subject are submitted herewith.[2]

| | Expenditures in detail. | Total expenditures. | Annual expenditures for the fiscal year ending— | | Salaries. | |
|---|---|---|---|---|---|---|
| *Expenses of American and Mexican Commission, from July* 1, 1869, *to June* 30, 1873. | | | | | | |
| Salary of George H. Gaither, secretary | $1,801 76 | | June 30, 1870 | $20,981 03 | Commiss'ner | ‡$4,500 |
| | | | | | Umpire | †3,000 |
| Salary of R. Coyle, secretary | 9,193 74 | | June 30, 1871 | 27,048 65 | Agent | †4,000 |
| Pay of clerks, messengers, and porters | 22,448 90 | | June 30, 1872 | 28,381 45 | Secretary | †2,500 |
| | | | | | Asst. to agent | †3,000 |
| Contingent expenses, rent, fuel, stationery, &c | 19,938 69 | | June 30, 1873 | 20,212 20 | 2 clerks | ‖1,400 |
| | | $53,383 09 | | | 2 translators | ‖1,500 |
| | | | | | 1 messenger. | †600 |
| Amount for which no vouchers have been rendered, and with which the parties stand charged | | 43,240 24 | | | 1 asa't mess. | †300 |
| Total amount expended | | 96,623 33 | | 96,623 33 | | |

* Per annum. ‖† Per diem. † In full for services. § Moiety paid by United States.
* In full for services and expenses. † Per annum. ‡ Each, for salary and expenses. ‖ Each, per annum.

[2] They are as follows:

DEPARTMENT OF STATE, *Washington, February* 27, 1874.

SIR: Referring to my previous letters respecting the "bill to establish a court of alien claims," I have now the honor to inclose a memorandum, showing the several amendments to the bill (H. R. 1739) which have been proposed or suggested by such gentlemen as I have had *time to consult upon it;* and *the views of this Department* in respect of *their suggestions.*

I also take advantage of this opportunity to present for your consideration sundry reasons (1) why it is desirable that Congress should pass an act for disposing of "alien war-claims;" (2) why the provisions of the bill introduced by you, amended by such suggestions as are adopted by the Department of State, should be enacted; (3) why, should it be enacted, the results will be favorable to the United States; and (4) why we may hope that such results will be accepted by other interested powers.

I.—*Reasons why a law should be enacted for disposing of alien war-claims.*

During and after the late war many claims were presented by representatives of foreign powers, for injuries alleged to have been suffered by citizens or subjects of such powers, arising out of acts committed against their persons or property during the war. Especially were such claims presented on behalf of citizens or subjects of Great Britain, France, Germany, and Italy.

No recognition has been made of any possible liability for the claims advanced by the representatives of France, Germany, or Italy. But by the treaty known as the treaty of Washington it was agreed that the British claims arising out of such acts committed between April 13, 1861, and April 9, 1865, should be submitted to arbitration. The result of this arbitration is thus described in the last annual message of the President:

"It was awarded that the Government of the United States should pay to the government of Her Britannic Majesty, within twelve months from the date of the award, the sum of $1,929,819 in gold. The commission disallowed all other claims of British subjects against the United States. The amount of the claims presented by the British government, but disallowed or dismissed, is understood to be about $93,000,000."

These proceedings practically worked a preference of this class of British claims over all others It left unrecognized, and without means provided for adjudicating upon, first the claims of other governments, (as France, Germany, and Italy,) and, second, British claims later than April 9, 1865.

It cannot be doubted that the United States rightfully exercised acts of war after the 9th of April, 1865. That was the date of Lee's surrender. A state of war continued after that time which rendered necessary many or all of the acts which are complained of, and those acts, when sifted, will probably prove to constitute as little foundation for claims against the United States as the acts committed within the date named in the treaty of Washington.

The powers whose subjects have had their claims deferred to those of British sub-

It cannot be doubted that such a court would be a great agency for

---

jects, as well as Great Britain herself, on behalf of British subjects whose claims arose after April 9, 1865, stand ready to ask us to decide upon the validity of their claims. What answer can the Department of State make to such a request?

This bill proposes to furnish an answer. If passed, it will enable us to say, "It is true that British claimants between April, 1861, and April, 1865, had a commission to establish such claims as might be found valid. The United States had then no court in which such claims could be examined. Now, we offer to all such claimants a court of law, and invite them to submit their claims to judicial investigation. We thus avoid a number of simultaneous mixed commissions, with possible conflicting decisions, and we render substantial justice to all who shall prove substantial injuries."

II.—*Reasons for the provisions of the proposed act.*

In the intercourse of nations it is an admitted principle of comity that where the local courts afford a remedy, and where there is no reason to distrust the firmness and sense of equity of those courts, a claim will not be urged diplomatically until the local remedies shall be exhausted, unless good and satisfactory reasons can be shown for not pursuing the remedy to the highest court of appeal.

The proposed bill aims to give such complete remedies to the foreign claimants, that substantially nothing will be left for diplomatic discussion.

In order to secure such completeness, it has been thought essential to confer upon claimants the right of appeal, to the Supreme Court, from the court of alien claims, in case of adverse decisions.

This has made it necessary to make the tenure of the judges "during good behavior." No other court is recognized by the Constitution as entitled to be "vested" with "the judicial power of the United States," in such a way as to confer upon the Supreme Court "appellate jurisdiction" from its decisions. In order, therefore, to secure the right of appeal, the bill proposes to create a permanent court.

It has been suggested that jurisdiction should be conferred upon this court over claims of citizens of the United States as well as of aliens for torts committed by the United States. Should the House think best to so widen its jurisdiction, the Department of State would not feel disposed to question the wisdom of the act.

It has also been suggested that jurisdiction over this class of cases might be conferred upon existing tribunals.

If the jurisdiction should be conferred upon the United States district or circuit courts, it would greatly increase the expense to the United States, and would make it almost impossible for one person to supervise all the proceedings in defense. I need not say to so intelligent a lawyer as yourself how advantageous, how absolutely necessary, in fact, it will be to the United States to put their defense against these claims under one guidance. This advantage would be lost should claimants be allowed to sue in circuit or district courts. And, further, the crowded state of the calendars of those courts in the large towns, where probably most of the suits would be conducted, would prolong the proceedings beyond what would be desirable.

It has also been suggested that the present Southern Claims Commission should be empowered to hear and determine upon this class of claims. But this commission is not a court from which appeals can be taken to the Supreme Court; and although greatly respected here, where its members are best known, it could not be expected to command abroad the weight and confidence which would induce foreign governments to accept its decisions as final.

The Court of Claims has also been mentioned as a body justly entitled, by its high character for learning and for patient investigation, to be clothed with the power of deciding these claims. Although the Court of Claims is not so well known abroad as at home, and although foreign governments might, therefore, feel more disposed to question its decisions than would be just, yet this objection might, perhaps, be overlooked if the state of the calendar of that court promised an early settlement of these claims. But, unfortunately, such is not the case. I annex a statement of the condition of the calendar of that court, prepared by the examiner of claims of this Department, which shows that the court is already overburdened with business, and would not be able to perform the great additional labor of deciding these claims.

There seems, therefore, to be no escape from the necessity of creating a court for the purpose and endowing it with the necessary powers.

The proposed bill recognizes the fact that this court is to be the creature of a diplomatic necessity; that it is to take the place of diplomatic action; and that its results may be set up hereafter, diplomatically, as a bar against claims of foreign governments, advanced on behalf of their citizens or subjects. It therefore proposes to have the proceedings conducted with the knowledge of, and in some respects under, the supervision of the Secretary of State.

In order to prevent purely speculative or fictitious claims from being advanced, it equires claimants to print, at their own expense, all documents and evidence put into he case by them; but, lest a *bona-fide* claimant should suffer from this necessity, it

good in preserving a good understanding between nations and in securing the relations of peace.

---

will, as amended, authorize such claimant to recover, with an award for his claim, the expenses he may have been put to for such printing.

It guards against surprises on either side, by requiring claimants to furnish to the Government a full statement of the claim, with the names of all the witnesses relied upon to establish it, and by obliging the Government to set forth in its answer all the grounds of law and fact upon which it relies for its defense.

It guards against perjury by provisions for the punishment of the perjurer, and for the disallowance of the claim sought to be maintained by such evidence.

It provides for an appeal to the Supreme Court of the United States. And, in order that such appeal may not unreasonably prolong the term of the court below, it provides that such appeal shall be heard upon the original papers, including the arguments, and that final judgment shall be rendered in the Supreme Court without a remitter; and, in order that claimants may not be vexed by appeals that ought not to be taken, it requires the written assent of the Attorney-General to an appeal by the United States.

It is believed that such a system would work out justice and give satisfaction to all concerned.

III.—*Reasons why a favorable result may be looked for.*

It may be assumed that the claims which it is proposed to adjust through the instrumentality of the proposed act are similar in all respects to those which were adjusted through the instrumentality of the British and American Mixed Claims Commission under the treaty of Washington.

In view, also, of the intimate commercial and social relations between Great Britain and the United States which existed at the outbreak of the war, and of the magnitude of the British-American commerce as compared with the commerce of any other nation with the United States, it may be asumed that that commission passed upon a large majority of the claims of aliens growing out of the war.

It may also be assumed that the rules of proof which it is proposed to adopt will deter persons from presenting purely speculative claims.

Assuming these facts, let us examine the results of the American-British Mixed Commission. Four hundred and seventy-eight cases against the United States were presented and tried, and judgment entered within two years from the organization of the commission; of these, 259 included claims for property taken by the United States forces, 181 for property destroyed by the United States forces; 7 for property destroyed by the rebels, 100 for alleged unlawful arrests or imprisonments, 76 for unlawful capture or condemnation of vessels, 3 for unlawfully warning off vessels, and 34 for other matters.

All the expenses of printing in these cases were borne by the two governments jointly—5 per cent. retained from the award being applied toward re-imbursing them. Under the proposed court, this expense will be much reduced, but no percentage is deducted.

The aggregate amount of the claims presented was about $96,000,000. The amount allowed was a little less than $2,000,000, the exact sum being, as already stated, $1,929,819.

There is no reason to suppose that, in the cases which remain, there would be a larger proportion of valid claims.

But whether the proportion would be greater or less, it is evident that the opportunities for a judicial examination into the facts and merits in each case would be greater in a court such as it is proposed to establish than in a mixed commission, composed of commissioners trained under different systems of law, and accustomed to different modes of investigating facts.

IV. *Reasons why the judgments of such a court would probably be accepted by other governments.*

It might be enough under this head to say that there is a probability, amounting almost to a certainty, that the judgments of the proposed court as revised by the Supreme Court will be in entire harmony with the recognized principles of international law, and will therefore not be questioned. I believe that such would be the case.

The bill proposes to give the right of appeal to all who feel themselves aggrieved by the decision of the court below.

No claimant who did not exercise that right could properly claim the assistance of his government in a diplomatic prosecution of his claim. And I am persuaded that such is the respect in which the Supreme Court is held throughout the civilized world, that no government would feel disposed to question its decision.

It appears from the report of the Navy Department that the total number of vessels captured and sent to the courts for adjudication between the dates named in the treaty

It is manifestly just that there should be some tribunal clothed with the power to hear the claims of aliens against our Government.

The committee have concluded that the Court of Claims can properly be clothed with the jurisdiction of alien claims arising not only during the rebellion but at any time hereafter, and the foregoing bill proposes to give this jurisdiction.

---

of Washington was eleven hundred and forty-nine; and that three hundred and fifty-five vessels were burned, sunk, or otherwise injured.

In the proceedings before the late British-American Mixed Commission, seventy-six memorials were filed, advancing claims against the United States for vessels and cargoes captured, detained, or warned away from blockaded ports. Awards against the United States were made in the case of eleven vessels.

The injuries complained of in the cases of the Boyne and the Monmouth were received in consequence of being illegally warned off the coast. This was an injury for which our courts afforded no remedy; consequently the cases were never brought before our courts.

The injuries in the case of the Tubal Cain and the Labuan were caused by an illegal detention in a port of the United States, for which, also, our laws afforded no remedy.

The Madeira was a collision case, and was never before the Supreme Court.

The York was burned on the coast of North Carolina, consequently no proceedings could be taken *in rem* against the vessel and cargo.

The Circassian, the Hiawatha, the Science, the Sir William Peel, the Springbok, and the Volant were decided adversely to the United States, in whole or in part, after a hearing and decision in the Supreme Court.

In the case of the Circassian there was a dissenting opinion by the late Mr. Justice Nelson. The mixed commission, by a majority vote, sustained the conclusions of the dissenting justice.

In the case of the Hiawatha, there were dissenting opinions by Chief-Justice Taney and Justices Nelson, Catron, and Clifford. The mixed commission, by a majority vote, agreed in the results reached by the dissenting justices.

The Science and the Peel were ordered by the Supreme Court to be restored, as not being subject to capture. The mixed commission, by a majority vote, decided that there was no probable cause to justify the seizure, and awarded damages in addition to restitution.

In the cases of the Springbok and the Volant, the commission sustained the decision of the Supreme Court on all the main issues, but rendered in each a trifling award against the United States on collateral issues.

Thus, out of 449 captures sent to the courts for adjudication, the adjudications have been shaken in but six cases—two of which decisions were rendered by a divided court, two of which were sustained by the mixed commission in principle, and reversed only on the question of fact as to the probable cause; and two of which were sustained in principle, and reversed only on unimportant collateral points.

Such a record fully justifies the language used by the late Lord Palmerston, in the House of Commons, during the war: "We have no reason to mistrust the equity and independence of the tribunals of the United States, which have to try questions such as those now under discussion."

It also authorizes the expression of a confident opinion that foreign powers, whose subjects or citizens may be claimants before the court which your bill proposes to establish, will acquiesce in the decisions which that court may make.

I have the honor to be, sir, your obedient servant,

HAMILTON FISH.

Hon. WM. LAWRENCE, *Chairman of Committee on War-Claims, House of Representatives.*

And see article in the (Boston) American Law Review, July, 1867, vol. 1, pp. 655–657.

At the first session of the Forty-third Congress a bill was introduced into the House by Mr. Lawrence, as follows:

A BILL to establish a Court of Alien and War Claims.[a]

*Be it enacted by the Senate and House of Representatives of the United States of America in Congress assembled*, That, for the purpose of providing a tribunal to hear and determine the claims of citizens of the United States and aliens against the United States for compensation for alleged torts suffered through the acts of persons for whose doings it may be asserted that the United States should be held responsible, there shall be

---

[a] The commissioners of claims have no jurisdiction over alien claims of any kind. The Court of Claims has no jurisdiction of *torts*.

Under its provisions there may be an appeal to the Supreme Court of the United States, whose final decisions will make valuable rules of international law. The usage heretofore prevailing in this Government has been to organize special tribunals to pass upon claims of aliens. These have been found expensive, and the long delay required by diplomatic arrangements to secure the organization of such tribunals, fol-

established in the city of Washington a court to be called "The Court of Alien and War Claims," to consist of three judges, with power to hear and determine all claims on the part of citizens of the United States, who during the rebellion were not citizens of any State[a] proclaimed in rebellion, and who remained loyal to the Government of the United States, or corporations under the authority of and located in any State not proclaimed in rebellion, or citizens or subjects or corporations of any foreign power, upon the United States, arising out of acts committed against the persons or property of such citizens or subjects during a period of recognized war between the United States and a belligerent not the sovereign of the claimant or claimants, which may be brought before it, as hereinafter provided. The said court shall consist of a chief-justice and of two associate justices, to be appointed by the President, by and with the advice and consent of the Senate, and to hold office during good behavior. Any two of the justices of the court hereby established shall constitute a quorum, and may hold a court for the transaction of business. The compensation of the members of the said court shall be as follows: For the chief-justice, for the term during which the court is occupied in the transaction of business, including adjournments, at the rate of thousand dollars a year; and for the associate justices for such period, at the rate of thousand dollars a year. The compensation shall cease when such term ceases, as hereinafter provided, and shall be revived whenever said court shall be again continued by order of the President, and shall then, and in each case, be convened for such time as said court may be occupied in determining the matters for which it may be convened.

SEC. 2. That the first meeting of the said court shall be held on the first Monday of December next, (which shall be the commencement of the first term,) for the purpose of hearing and determining all claims which may be brought before it on the part of said corporations, citizens of the United States, or citizens or subjects of any foreign power, against the United States, arising out of acts committed against the persons or properties of such claimants during the period which intervened between the commencement and the close of the late rebellion, except such claims as are barred by the provisions of the treaty of the eighth of May, eighteen hundred and seventy-one, between Her Britannic Majesty and the United States. It shall be lawful to present said claims, which are to be submitted to the adjudication of said court, up to and including the thirty-first day of December, which will be in the year eighteen hundred and seventy-five, but not later; all claims so presented must be adjudicated and determined by the said court before the first day of January, which will be in the year eighteen hundred and seventy-eight, and the close and determination of such adjudications, and the final adjournment of the court, shall be regarded as the close of the first term. Thereafter the said court may be again convened at the pleasure of the President, as there may be occasion for its services. It shall, in term time, have authority to establish rules and regulations for its government not inconsistent with the provisions of this act; to perform such acts as may be necessary to carry into effect the powers hereby conferred upon it; to administer oaths; to punish for contempt in the manner prescribed by law; to appoint commissioners to take testimony to be used in evidence; to prescribe the fees they shall receive for their services; to issue commissions for the taking of such testimony; and to issue subpœnas for witnesses, either before the court or before such commissioners, which shall have the same force and effect as if issued from a circuit or district court of the United States, and compliance therewith shall be compelled under such rules and orders as the court hereby created may establish. Said court may have a seal, with such device as it may order. It may on its organization appoint the following officers, who shall serve during the pleasure of the court, but not later than its dissolution when the business for which it is organized shall be completed; namely, a reporter, with a compensation at the rate of thousand dollars a year; one stenographer, with a compensation at the rate of thousand dollars a year; a bailiff, with a compensation at the rate of thousand dollars a year; and such other officers as Congress may make appropriations for. Said court may, when again convened by the President, make new appointments to such offices, for the term for which it may be convened, and with like compensation.

SEC 3. That upon the organization of said court, and whenever the same shall be convened by the President as hereinbefore provided, the court shall appoint a clerk of

[a] Provision is made for allowing claims for military supplies by act March 3, 1871, to loyal citizens of *rebel States*, but not in favor of such citizens in loyal States. (See House Ex. Doc. No. 121, 1st sess. 43d Cong.) Alien claims are not within the jurisdiction of the Commissioners of Claims.

lowed by the further delay necessary to secure a final adjudication, has not only long postponed but often defeated the ends of justice.

These tribunals have rarely ever given written opinions, at any considerable length, announcing the principles on which their decisions have been based; they have, therefore, furnished no settled principles of international law, and are rarely ever quoted or looked to as author-

---

said court, who shall receive a compensation at the rate of thousand dollars a year for the time for which he shall serve, and who shall, for such period, have the custody of the seal and records of the court, and shall be authorized to administer oaths and affidavits. The said clerk shall disburse, under the directions of the court, the contingent fund which may at any time be appropriated for the use of the court; but he shall, in each case, first give bond in such an amount and in such form as may be approved by the court, and his accounts shall be settled by the proper accounting officers of the Treasury in the same way as those of clerks of courts of the United States are or may be settled. An assistant clerk may also be appointed by the court for a like term, if necessary, with a compensation at the rate of thousand dollars per annum.

SEC. 4. That, on or before the organization of the said court, an agent for the United States to represent the Government before the said court, until its business shall be transacted, shall be appointed by the President, by and with the advice and consent of the Senate. And as often as the said court shall be convened by the President, an agent shall in like manner be appointed. He shall receive a compensation at the rate of thousand dollars a year. With the consent of the Secretary of State, he may employ an assistant, with a compensation at the rate of thousand dollars a year. It shall be the duty of the agent to prepare all cases on the part of the Government for hearing before said court, and to argue the same orally or in writing, as may be ordered by the court; to cause testimony to be taken when necessary in order to protect the interests of the United States; to prepare forms, file interrogatories, and superintend the taking of testimony in the manner prescribed by said court; and, generally, to render such services as may be required of him from time to time in the discharge of the duties of his said office. Neither such agent nor such assistant agent shall receive any fee or compensation for services rendered in said court, except the salary herein-before provided.

SEC. 5. That, as soon as possible after the passage of this act, it shall be the duty of the Secretary of State to give notice thereof to all foreign governments who have presented, or shall hereafter present, on behalf of their corporations, citizens, or subjects, claims against the United States arising out of acts committed against their persons or property during the late rebellion, and to invite each to appoint an agent to present such claims to said court. And whenever and so often as the President shall hereafter convene the said court, it shall be the duty of the Secretary of State to give a similar notice and invitation to each government which may, at the time of such notice and invitation, have diplomatically presented, on behalf of its subjects or citizens, claims against the United States of the character for the settlement of which the said court is created. All claimants whose governments are not represented before said court, and who are not themselves represented by an attorney or attorneys qualified to practice in the Supreme Court of the United States, must, on filing their petitions, notify the clerk of the court, in writing, of some address in the city of Washington where orders and notices in the cause may be served upon them.

SEC. 6. No claim which might have been heard and determined in a district or circuit court of the United States, or in the Court of Claims, shall be heard and determined by the court hereby created, unless it shall appear that such claim was heard and determined in such district or circuit court, or in such Court of Claims, and either that no appeal lay by law to the Supreme Court, or that on an appeal to the Supreme Court and hearing therein the claimant avers that there has been a miscarriage of justice, or that the claimant shall satisfy the court that there was good and sufficient reason why no appeal was taken to the Supreme Court. And all cases shall be heard and determined according to the rules and canons of international law, as accepted in practice by the civilized powers.

Proceedings by claimants in said courts shall be commenced by a memorial presented on behalf of the claimant by the agent of the government of which the claimant is a citizen or subject, or, if there be no agent of such government, presented with the assent of the principal diplomatic representative of such government at Washington. The memorial shall set forth a full statement of the claim, with references to dates and places, with the names and residences of the witnesses who are relied upon to establish the claim, and with a reference to any action which may have been had on the claim either in Congress or in any Department. It shall also specify by name each and every person interested in the claim, either directly or indirectly, and shall state when, and upon what consideration, such person became so interested; and it shall declare

ity. They may sometimes lack that training in international law and other experience which could be secured by a court devoted for life to such inquiries.

Other nations, almost without exception, have given to all aliens, including our own citizens, the right to go into their courts, and have an adjudication of their claims upon such nations. This is shown by the following extract from a note to the report No. 262, made by this committee March 26, 1874, to wit:

In Fichera *v.* U. S., 9 Court Claims R., decided in 1873, Nott, J., said:

"The only question presented by this case is whether, under the Italian law, an American citizen may maintain an action against the government of Italy. As we have before found, the perfected justice of the civil law made the government, in matters of ordinary obligation, subject to the suit of the citizen, in the ordinary tribunals of the country. We have found this right to be preserved under modern codes in Prussia, Hanover, and Bavaria, (*Brown's Case*, 5 C. Cls. R., p. 571;) in the republic of Switzerland, (*Lobsiger's Case*, id., p. 687;) in Holland, the Netherlands, the Hanseatic Prov-

---

affirmatively that no other person is interested therein, either directly or indirectly. Such memorial shall be verified by the oath or affirmation of the claimant or party in interest. The memorial, and all other papers offered on behalf of the claimant, shall be printed by him for the use of the court and the other party, in such form as the court may by rule require.

SEC. 7. That the United States shall be allowed such time as the court may direct, not more than six nor less than two months, to answer each petition, in which shall be set up fully and specifically all matters of law and fact which are relied on. The answer shall not be required to be under oath. The answer, and all other papers offered by the United States, shall be printed by the Government for the use of the court and the other party in such form as the court may order; and the same regulation shall apply to any subsequent pleadings which the court may permit either party to file.

SEC. 8. That evidence shall be taken at the expense of the party offering it on such notice by each party to the other, and in such manner as the court shall direct; except that the court may, if the interests of justice require it, order any witness whose deposition is offered in evidence to appear personally for examination, and also may, on the motion of the United States, make an order in any case pending in said court, directing that the claimant or claimants in such case, or any one or more of them, shall appear upon reasonable notice, either before the court, or before any commissioner thereof, and be examined, on oath or affirmation, touching any or all matters pertaining to said claim. If any claimant, after such order shall have been made, and due and reasonable notice thereof shall have been served according to the rules of the court and the requirements of the order, shall, without just excuse, fail to appear, or shall refuse to testify or answer fully as to all matters within his knowledge material to the issue, or if it shall appear that any claimant has corruptly practiced, or attempted to practice, fraud against the United States touching his claim, or any part thereof, the said court is hereby empowered to find specifically that the claimant has so failed to appear, or has so refused to testify or answer fully, or has so practiced, or attempted to practice, fraud, and thereupon the said court shall give judgment in favor of the United States, and the claimant shall thereupon be forever barred from prosecuting his claim in said court.

SEC. 9. That no evidence shall be received on either side on the trial of the main questions, in any case pending in said court, which is taken *ex parte*, without notice to the other party in such manner as may be required by the rules of said court. In taking any testimony to be used in support of any claim before said court, opportunity shall be given to the United States to file interrogatories, or by attorney to examine witnesses, under such regulations as said court shall prescribe, and like opportunity shall be afforded the claimant in cases where testimony is taken on behalf of the United States under like regulations. If any person shall knowingly or willfully swear falsely before said court, or in proceedings therein, or before any person or persons commissioned by them, or authorized by law to administer oaths or take testimony in a case pending before said court at the time of taking such oath or affirmation, or in a case thereafter to be submitted to said court, such person shall be deemed guilty of perjury, and on conviction thereof shall be subjected to the same pains, penalties, and disabilities which now are, or hereafter shall be, prescribed for willful and corrupt perjury. All evidence shall be printed at the expense of the party at whose request it is taken.

SEC. 10. That the said court shall have power to call upon any of the Departments for any information or papers it may deem necessary, and shall have the use of all recorded and printed reports made by committees of each House when deemed to be

inces, and the Free City of Hamburg, (*Brown's Case*, 6 C. Cls. R., p. 193;) in France, (*Dauphin's Case*, id., p. 221;) in Spain, (*Molina's Case*, id., p. 269;) and in Belgium, (*De Gives's Case*, 7 C. Cls. R., p. 517.)

It was also shown in *Brown's Case*, (5 C. Cls. R., p. 571,) by a distinguished historical writer who was examined as a witness, Mr. Frederick Kapp, that this liability of a government under the civil law is not a device of modern civilization, but has been deemed inherent in the system, and has been so long established that, to use the phrase of the common law, the memory of man runneth not to the contrary. Therefore, it is to be expected that in Italy, the seat and fountain of the civil law, this same liability of government is to be found existing. The "Civil Code of the Kingdom of Italy" of 1866 recognizes, rather than establishes, the fundamental principle of liability; but it expressly provides (article 10) that, "in suits pending before the judicial authority between private persons and the public administration, the proceedings shall always take place formally at the regular session."

It is also provided, by the third article of the same code, that "the alien is admitted to enjoy all the civil rights granted to citizens." These provisions establish the right of an Italian citizen to maintain his action in this court, within the meaning of the *Act July* 27, 1868, (15 Stat., p. 243, § 2,) which prohibits the subject of a foreign gov-

---

necessary in the prosecution of the duties prescribed by this act; but the head of no Department shall be required to answer any call for information or papers if, in his opinion, it would be injurious to the public interests.

SEC. 11. That, within thirty days after entry of final judgment in any case pending in said court, either party may appeal therefrom to the Supreme Court of the United States; but the agent of the United States shall not in any case give notice of appeal, except under written instructions from the Attorney-General. It shall be the duty of the party appealing to cause to be printed, for the use of the justices of the Supreme Court, all the papers in the case, including the memorials, the answers, the evidence, the arguments, all interlocutory motions and orders, the judgment, the opinions of the judges, (if any are given,) and the record or judgment-roll. The appeal shall be entered at the first term of the Supreme Court held in Washington after the entry of final judgment in the court below, within ten days after the opening of the term. If not entered within that time, the judgment of the court below shall stand. If entered within that time, the case shall be heard upon the printed papers without further argument, unless the Supreme Court shall order an argument, and shall give notice thereof to the Secretary of State. Final judgment may be rendered by the Supreme Court in all such appealed cases; and in each case the clerk of that court shall give notice thereof to the Secretary of State.

SEC. 12. That at the close of their labors at the first term of the court as hereinbefore provided, and at the close of any term for which the court may be hereafter convened, the said judges shall transmit to the Secretary of State, under their hands and seals, a statement showing in detail the decisions and awards made by them, with the nationality of each claimant, and the amount awarded to each; also, showing in like detail, and with like statements, the claims which were presented for allowance, and which were not allowed; also, showing, in like detail, and with like statements, the cases in which appeals may have been taken to the Supreme Court of the United States. They shall also deposit in the Department of State the original records and other papers of the court (including all original papers on file and the seal of the court) during the period for which it may have been in session, which shall thereafter constitute a part of the archives of that Department. And it shall be the duty of the Secretary of State in each case, as soon thereafter as may be, to transmit to Congress a copy of the said statement, and to notify each government whose citizens or subjects may have presented claims for adjudication by said court, of the judgments made in favor of or against such citizens or subjects. And it shall also be the duty of the Secretary of State to give similar notice to Congress and to foreign governments of judgments rendered by the Supreme Court of the United States on appeals taken from the judgments of the court established by this act. And the result of the proceedings of the said courts are to be regarded as a full, perfect, and final settlement of all claims of aliens which were, or which might have been, presented before the court established by this act.

SEC. 13. That whenever and as often as said court may be convened, the Secretary of State shall provide proper rooms and accommodations for the transaction of its business.

SEC. 14. Said court shall have jurisdiction of and power to hear and determine all claims and rights of action against the United States which shall be presented to the Secretary of State, by petition, in the nature of a petition of right, and which shall be by him referred to said court, and all claims and rights of action which shall be referred to said court by the President of the United States or by either House of Congress. And the provisions of this act shall, so far as applicable, govern the proceedings on such claims and rights of action.

SEC. 15. That this act shall take effect upon its passage.

ernment from maintaining a suit for captured property, unless "the right to prosecute claims against such government in its courts is reciprocal, and extends to citizens of the United States."

In England aliens have a remedy by "petition of right," regulated by act 23 and 24 Victoria, July 3, 1860. (U. S. *v.* O'Keefe, 11 Wallace, 179; Carlisle *v.* U. S., 16 Wallace, 148. See Whiting's War-Powers of the President, 51; The Venus, 8 Cranch; The Hoop, 1 Robinson, 196; The Army Warwick, Sprague, J.)

See Whiting's "War-Claims," affixed to 43d ed. of "War-Powers," p. 333, ed. of 1871; Perrin *v.* U. S., 4 Court Claims 547.[3]

---

[3] In addition to the reasons in favor of a court of alien claims, it may be stated that it is provided by act of Congress as to the Court of Claims, that—

"The jurisdiction of the said court shall not extend to any claim against the Government not pending therein on December one, eighteen hundred and sixty-two, growing out of, or dependent on, any treaty stipulation entered into with foreign nations or with the Indian tribes."

In Brown *vs.* The United States, decided in the Court of Claims May 22, 1871, Nott, J., said:

"Our popular orators and writers have impressed upon the public mind the belief that in this republic of ours private rights receive unequalled protection from the Government; and some have actually pointed to the establishment of this court as a sublime spectacle to be seen nowhere else on earth. The action of a former Congress, however, in requiring (act 27 July, 1868, 15 Stat. L., p. 243) that aliens should not maintain certain suits here unless their own governments accorded a corresponding right to citizens of the United States, has revealed the fact that the legal redress given to a citizen of the United States against the United States is less than he can have against almost any government in Christendom. The laws of other nations have been produced and proved in this court, and the mortifying fact is judicially established that the Government of the United States holds itself, of nearly all governments, the least amenable to the law.

"First in this high civilization that protects the individual and assures his rights stands the great empire of the German states. 'The state,' says a lawyer, also distinguished as a writer, who was examined as a witness in this court, 'represented in its pecuniary capacity as the representative of money and property affairs, is called the *fiscus*. For the purpose of maintaining suits against the government, the fiscus stands in the place of the government; for the purpose of compelling the payment of demands against the state, the fiscus is substituted for the state itself. I know of no restriction of the rights of the subjects of Prussia to maintain any suit against the fiscus; foreigners as well as subjects, any man, can sue the fiscus: the power to maintain a suit against the fiscus is a matter of absolute right. Suits in relation to state property, in which the fiscus is either plaintiff or defendant, are treated and decided like suits among private parties, and all the consequences of defaults and executions take place against the fiscus. The fiscus is brought into court by the service of summons and complaint upon the fiscal attorney. The fiscal attorney has to answer just like any other party and bring his proof. *Judgment rendered against the fiscus may be satisfied and discharged in the usual way, by execution.' Brown's Case*, (5 C. Cls. R., p. 271.)

"In Hanover and Bavaria the redress is substantially the same. *Muller's Case*, (6 id., p. —.) In the republic of Switzerland the 'federal tribunal takes cognizance of suits between the confederation on the one side and corporations or individuals on the other when these corporations or private citizens are complainants and the object of litigation is of the value of at least 3,000 francs.' *Law 5th June*, 1849; (*Lobsiger's Case*, 5 id., p. 687.) In Holland, the Netherlands, the Hanseatic Provinces, the free city of Hamburg, and probably in all countries which have inherited the perfected justice of the civil law, the government is in legal liability thus subject to the citizen. Even in France, under the late empire, there was a less circumscribed means of redress, a more certain judicial remedy, a more effective method of enforcing the judgment recovered, than has been given to the American citizen, notwithstanding the pledge of the Constitution. Of all the governments of Europe, it is believed that Russia alone does not hold the state amenable in matters of property to the law. Of all the countries whose laws have been examined in this court, Spain only resembles the United States in fettering the judicial proceedings of her courts by restrictions and leaving the execution of their decrees dependent upon the legislative will. Yet, even in Spain, we know historically, back in the time of Ferdinand and Isabella, that the son of Columbus '*did not succeed to his father's dignities till he had obtained a judgment in his favor against the Crown from the council of the Indias, an act*,' adds Prescott, '*highly honorable to that tribunal, and showing that the independence of the courts of justice, the greatest bulwark of civil liberty, was well maintained under King Ferdinand*.' (Ferd. and Isabella, 3d vol., p. 245.) The records of this court also show that, within the present century, an American citizen recovered a judgment against Spain, in a Spanish tribunal, to the very large amount of $373,879.88, and that he elected to retain Spain as his debtor when

Much valuable information has been obtained since the last session of Congress through the State Department at the instance of a member of the committee from foreign governments in relation to the mode of adjudicating claims under their authority.[4]

---

the decree was about to be transferred to, and assumed by, the United States, and that his choice was judicious, for though thus transferred and assumed, the debt has never been paid. *Meade's Case*, (2 C. Cls. R., p. 225)."

The jurisdiction of the Court of Claims is also limited to actions *ex contractu*.

The jurisdiction of this and, to some extent, other courts is also limited or regulated both as to contracts and torts and as to aliens and citizens by act of March 3, 1863, 12 Stat., 755; act of May 11, 1866, 14 Stat., 46; act July 4, 1864, chap. 240, 13 Stat., 381; joint resolution June 18, 1866, No. 50, 14 Stat., 360; joint resolution July 28, 1866, No. 99, 14 Stat., 370; act February 21, 1867, chap. 57, 14 Stat., 397; joint resolution March 2, 1867, No. 50, 14 Stat., 572; act July 27, 1868, 15 Stat., 243, sec. 2; Planters' Bank *vs.* Union Bank, 16 Wallace, 483.

[4] The whole subject of claims against the Government is one of great difficulty. There can be but little difficulty as to the payment of salaries and claims arising on express written contract. The proper Departments of the Government are authorized to audit and allow these generally; and in cases of doubt, as to claims arising on contracts, &c., the Court of Claims has jurisdiction, subject to a six years' statute of limitations.

But there are claims in great numbers and of immense magnitude, as the journals of Congress show, growing out of the rebellion, out of contracts, and in various forms, for the consideration of which there is no tribunal but Congress.

The many fraudulent claims presented to Congress, and sometimes paid under special acts, show that the relief in this form is exceedingly slow and unsatisfactory.

One great danger to the Treasury is, that claims are presented long after they arose, and when the Government has no means of meeting and refuting the plausible evidence often furnished in support of them, but which might be shown to be false or susceptible of explanation if earlier presented.

The President, in his annual message of December, 1873, said:

"There is a still more fruitful source of expenditure, which I will point out later in this message. I refer to the easy method of manufacturing claims for losses incurred in suppressing the late rebellion. * * * * * *

"Your careful attention is invited to the subject of claims against the Government, and to the facilities afforded by existing laws for their prosecution. Each of the Departments of State, Treasury, and War have demands for many millions of dollars upon their files, and they are rapidly accumulating. To these may be added those now pending before Congress, the Court of Claims, and the southern claims commission, (Commissioners of Claims,) making in the aggregate an immense sum. Most of these grow out of the rebellion, and are intended to indemnify persons on both sides for their losses during the war; and *not a few of them are fabricated and supported by false testimony*. Projects are on foot, it is believed, to induce Congress to provide for new classes of claims, and to revive old ones through the repeal or modification of the statute of limitations, by which they are now barred. I presume these schemes, if proposed, will be received with little favor by Congress, and I recommend that persons having claims against the *United States cognizable by any tribunal or department thereof, be required to present them at an early day, and that legislation be directed, as far as practicable, to the defeat of unfounded and unjust demands upon the Government;* and I would suggest, as a means of preventing fraud, that witnesses be called upon to appear in person to testify before those tribunals having said claims before them for adjudication. *Probably the largest saving to the National Treasury can be secured by timely legislation on these subjects, of any of the economic measures that will be proposed.*"

This subject has been somewhat discussed elsewhere. (Congressional Record, Forty-third Congress, first session, June 3, 1874, vol. 6, p. 4514; 20th vol. American Law Register, p. 189; note by Judge Redfield on decision of Court of Claims in Brown's case.)

Case of Charles J. Davis, administrator of John Davis, a claim for $58,000, passed twice at different times by both Houses of Congress, then referred to the Court of Claims, which developed the fact, by decision made January 18, 1875, that the claim had already been paid. (Davis' speech in Senate May 13, 1874; Congressional Record, vol. 5, p. 3832; House Report No. 91, Committee on War-Claims, first session Forty-third Congress, February 9, 1874.)

Among the measures which are believed to be reforms in the matter of claims introduced, recommended, or acted on during the Forty-third Congress, are the following:

I. A bill relating to the Commissioners of Claims, and for other purposes. (See Congressional Record, vol. 6, p. 4514, June 3, 1874.) This bill passed the House. If to this could be added a provision by which the Commissioners of Claims should be converted *into a court*, with power to report their conclusions to Congress, it would add to their

It is deemed of so much importance that it is hereto appended and made a part of this report.

---

independence, and tend to secure justice. The machinery which these commissioners have, by which they send agents into the locality where claims arose, enables them to defeat many unjust claims.

It seems remarkable that for so many years claims have been examined by committees of Congress and acted on with no counsel to represent the interests of the Government, and no officer clothed with the duty to procure evidence. If committees must examine claims, they should act as judges, and should never be approached with personal solicitations, or hear private communications. Whatever is heard or said should be to the whole committee. Claims often involve great questions of law. Claimants very generally present able arguments on the law and the facts. Members of committees are not generally all lawyers; and if they were, they are often not so well qualified to judge of facts as other persons. But if they *had the time* and the *qualifications* to investigate both law and fact, they should not be required to examine arguments of claimants with a view to see if they could be answered. This involves the danger of acquiring a habit of taking sides against claimants. The judge should never become the lawyer on either side. In courts the State is always represented by counsel. If a similar usage is not applied before committees, the Government is almost certain to suffer for want of as full a presentation of the proper view of the law and facts which may exist *against* as well as in favor of claims. The Commissioners of Claims should be converted into a court, with proper counsel for the Government.

The bill above referred to would, it is believed, effect a reform in the mode of investigating claims.

The following is the bill as it passed the House, with amendments proposed in the Senate:

[H. R. 1565, 43d Congress, 2d Session.]

IN THE SENATE OF THE UNITED STATES.

JUNE 17, 1874.—Read twice and referred to the Committee on Claims.

JANUARY 21, 1875.—Reported with amendments, viz: Strike out the parts within brackets [ ] and insert the parts printed in *italics*.

AN ACT relating to the Commissioners of Claims, and for other purposes.

*Be it enacted by the Senate and House of Representatives of the United States of America in Congress assembled*, That the time within which petitions for the allowance of claims may be presented to the Commissioners of Claims be, and hereby is, extended to the [fourth day of July, eighteen hundred and seventy-five] *first day of January, eighteen hundred and seventy-six;* and that all claims within the jurisdiction of the Commissioners of Claims which shall not be filed in their office on or before the [fourth day of July, eighteen hundred and seventy-five] *first day of January, eighteen hundred and seventy-six*, shall be, and hereby are, forever barred, and the commissioners shall not examine the same.

SEC. 2. That every petition or memorial, *filed after the passage of this act*, for the allowance of a claim, shall contain a statement, by items, of the several amounts claimed on account of the matters set forth in such petition or memorial; *and all petitions or memorials already filed which do not contain such statement shall, if the commissioners so order, be amended to furnish the same within such time and under such rules as shall be prescribed by the Commissioners;* and the aggregate amount so claimed shall not thereafter be increased for any cause. Every such petition or memorial, *or the amendment thereof*, shall also contain an explicit statement of any payments already made by or in behalf of the United States on account of property taken, furnished, or used by the forces of the United States during the late rebellion, and a declaration that the said petition or memorial, *or the amendment thereof*, embraces every just item and cause of claim against the United States for property so taken, furnished, or used.

SEC. 3. That in [lieu of] *addition to* the three agents now provided by law, the said commissioners shall be authorized to employ [five] *two* agents to investigate and report upon claims; and *all* the said agents shall have power to administer oaths and take depositions[; and, in addition to the clerks now authorized by law, the said commissioners may employ each one clerk, at a salary not exceeding one thousand eight hundred dollars per annum].

SEC. 4. That whenever the commissioners are satisfied [that a claim is fraudulent in whole or in part, or] that the claimant is attempting to procure, by fraud, false evidence, or conclusion, *or by the willful concealment of payment or other material fact*, the allowance of a claim, in whole or in part, it shall be their duty to disallow the entire claim.

SEC. 5. That every person who knowingly and willfully swears falsely in any oath or affidavit which is or may be authorized by law, or in any oath taken or affidavit made, to be used as evidence in any court, "or before either House of Congress, or any com-

This confirms the statement already made, that foreign governments

mittee or officer thereof," or before any officer or person acting under the authority of the Constitution or law, shall be deemed guilty of perjury, and shall be punished by fine not more than two thousand dollars, or imprisoned at hard labor not more than five years, or both, in the discretion of the court. And in every case where such oath or affidavit is subscribed by the person making the same, proof of such fact shall be sufficient evidence of the official authority of the person before whom the same purports to be made or taken to administer and certify said oath or affidavit. All offenses heretofore committed may be prosecuted or punished in the same manner as if this act had not passed.

SEC. 6. That every person who procures, or endeavors to procure, or counsels or advises, another to commit perjury, shall be punishable as if guilty of perjury.

[SEC. 7. That the Commissioners of Claims shall receive, examine, and consider the justice and validity of such claims, growing out of the late war of the rebellion, as may be referred to them by either House of Congress; and said commissioners shall make report of their proceedings, and of each claim considered by them, with the evidence in relation thereto, and their conclusions of law and fact thereon, at the commencement of each session of Congress, to the Speaker of the House of Representatives, who shall lay the same before said House.]

[SEC. 8. That the President of the United States be, and is hereby, authorized to nominate, and, by and with the advice and consent of the Senate, to appoint, in addition to the Commissioners of Claims now authorized, two Commissioners of Claims, who shall continue in office until the tenth day of March, eighteen hundred and seventy-seven, with like power and duties and compensation as the Commissioners of Claims now in office. Any two commissioners, with the approval of the president of the board of commissioners, shall be competent to make a report, and the president of the board shall assign to the commissioners the claims, to be by them examined, considered, and reported on.]

SEC. [9] 7. That the provisions of an act to prevent and punish frauds upon the Government of the United States, approved March second, eighteen hundred and sixty-three, are extended and made applicable to a time of peace, and to persons who shall make or cause to be made, or presented to the Commissioners of Claims, or to either House of Congress, any claim upon or against the Government of the United States, or any Department or officer thereof, or any evidence in support thereof; and if any person shall fraudulently withdraw or abstract from the files of said commissioners, or from the files of either House of Congress, or of any committee thereof, any document or evidence, every person so offending shall suffer the penalties and be liable to punishment as in said act provided.

SEC. [10] 8. That every petition presented to either House of Congress for the payment of claims [may] *shall* be verified by oath or affidavit.

Passed the House of Representatives June 16, 1874.

Attest: EDWARD MCPHERSON, *Clerk.*

II. The bill to provide for the adjudication of the claims of aliens.

The Committee on War-Claims have decided to report this bill to the House, with a recommendation that it do pass.

III. A bill as follows:

[H. R. 3862. 43d Congress, 2d session.]

"IN THE HOUSE OF REPRESENTATIVES.

"DECEMBER 8, 1874.

"Read twice, referred to the Committee on War-Claims, and ordered to be printed.

"Mr. LAWRENCE, on leave, introduced the following bill:

"A BILL to limit the time for the allowance of claims.

"*Be it enacted by the Senate and House of Representatives of the United States of America in Congress assembled,* That after the first day of January, eighteen hundred and seventy-five, no claim against the United States shall be presented to, audited, allowed, or paid, by any Department or officer of the United States, unless the same shall have been filed in the proper Department, or with the proper officer, within six years after the claimant had the legal capacity and right to so file or present such claim. Nothing herein shall limit the time for filing any claim where by existing law the time is fixed for filing such claims."

The Committee on War-Claims have decided to recommend the House to pass this bill.

give to our citizens the right to go into their courts to have an adjudication of their claims against such governments.

---

IV. A bill which passed the House as follows:

"[H. R. 3478. 43d Congress, 1st session.]

"IN THE HOUSE OF REPRESENTATIVES.

"MAY 25, 1874.

"Read twice, referred to the Committee on Revision of the Laws of the United States and ordered to be printed.

"Mr. LAWRENCE, on leave, introduced the following bill:

"A BILL in relation to parties in the Court of Claims.

"*Be it enacted by the Senate and House of Representatives of the United States of America in Congress assembled*, That in all cases pending in the Court of Claims, where a new or additional party or parties may be necessary to a complete determination of the case, or necessary to protect the interests of the United States, the court shall have power to order any such person or corporation to be made a party or parties, and to issue process to the marshal of any district or Territory in which such corporation may be located, or such person reside, or be found; and it shall be the duty of such marshal to serve and return the same as other process. And if any such person or corporation be a non-resident of the United States, service may be made by publication of notice in such manner as the court may order."

V. A joint resolution, as follows:

"[H. Res. 131, 43d Congress, 2d session.]

"IN THE HOUSE OF REPRESENTATIVES.—*December* 21, 1874.—Read twice, referred to the Committee on War-Claims, and ordered to be printed.

"Mr. Lawrence, on leave, introduced the following joint resolution:

"JOINT RESOLUTION proposing an amendment to the Constitution.

"*Resolved by the Senate and House of Representatives of the United States of America in Congress assembled, (two-thirds of each House concurring therein,)* That the following article is hereby proposed as an amendment to the Constitution of the United States, and when ratified by the legislatures of three-fourths of the several States shall be valid to all intents and purposes as a part of the Constitution, to wit:

"ARTICLE —. No claim against the United States shall be paid unless presented in pursuance of law by the claimant within ten years after having the legal right and capacity to do so, or within such less period as may be prescribed by law. A claim rejected by any authorized officer, or reported on adversely by a committee of either House of Congress, shall not be re-examined or paid unless within six years after such rejection or adverse report."

The following, explanatory of this subject, is from the Chicago Daily Tribune, December 28, 1874:

## LIMITATION OF CLAIMS.

### LETTER FROM THE HON. WILLIAM LAWRENCE.

HOUSE OF REPRESENTATIVES, *Washington, D. C., December* 25.

*To the Editor of the Chicago Tribune:*

I notice an article in the Tribune of the 23d instant, on "The limitation of claims," in which you refer to a proposition I submitted in the House to amend the Constitution so that no claim against the United States shall be paid unless presented by the claimant, in pursuance of law, within ten years after having the legal right and capacity to do so.

You do me the honor to say, "The proposition is a good one;" but you say you "fail to see the necessity for a constitutional amendment," because a law of Congress would serve the practical end to be attained, and that "Congress itself will be bound thereby."

You forcibly point out the difficulty of procuring an amendment of the Constitution, the delay, and the fact that "it is doubtful whether such an amendment would not be opposed by the democratic party and the Southern States as an effort to undermine their pet schemes for the future." This, I believe, would be the case to a considerable extent; and yet if public attention could be aroused to the necessity of an amendment, I believe it could be secured.

I hope, therefore, you will permit me briefly to call attention to the necessity of it.

You say the whole object can be accomplished by law.

I have introduced a bill, and have been directed by the Committee on War-Claims to report it to the House and recommend its passage, which provides:

"That, after the 1st day of July, 1875, no claim against the United States shall be presented to, audited, allowed or paid, by any Department or officer of the United States, unless the same shall have been filed in the proper Department or with the

We cannot hope to preserve the entire good will and respect of for-

---

proper officer within six years after the claimant had the legal capacity and right to so file or present such claim."

Your theory is, that a limitation in the presentation of claims to Congress can be provided by law, and that "Congress itself can be bound thereby."

The Constitution, Art. I of amendments, provides that "Congress shall make no law respecting an establishment of religion, or prohibiting the free exercise thereof; or abridging the freedom of speech or of the press; or the right of the people peaceably to assemble, and to petition the Government for a redress of grievances."

It is now generally conceded that, where there is a right to petition, there is a corresponding duty to hear and act on the petition.

A practice has prevailed, from the foundation of the Government, to petition Congress for the payment of claims. Can the right of the citizen thus to petition, or the duty of Congress to hear and act on such petition, be prohibited or abridged by law? The language of the Constitution cited would certainly seem to prohibit any such law.

The only theory on which such a law could be passed would be, that the investigation of claims is a judicial duty—not legislative; that Congress may by law limit the time within which there may be a judicial investigation in courts; and that hence the right to ask of Congress the performance of a duty not legislative in its character may be denied and its exercise prohibited by law.

I had the privilege of discussing this question somewhat in a speech in the House, June 3, 1874, in which I said:

"The Constitution provides that 'the judicial power shall extend to controversies to which the United States shall be a party.'

"At the time this was adopted, the 'petition of right' was a recognized common-law mode of reaching the courts of England with claims against the Government. It is fair to presume the Constitution was designed to give an equivalent remedy.

"It has been urged with much force that the Government is composed of three co-ordinate branches, the legislative, judiciary, and executive, to each one of which are delegated certain powers and duties. It is the duty of the legislative department to provide the means or remedies by which the right of parties may be determined, but not to pass upon or determine such rights. This latter power is exclusively vested in the judiciary. It is therefore not within the power of the legislative body to pass any act of a judicial nature. Jones *vs.* Perry, 10 Yerger, 59; Holden *vs.* Jarvis, 11 Massachusetts, 400; Picquet's Appeal, 5 Pickering, 65; Lewis *vs.* Webb, 3 Greenleaf, 326; Ex parte to Bedford, Jurist and Law Magazine for October, 1833, page 301, 4 New Hampshire, 572; Lane *vs.* Dorman, 3 Scammon, 235; Davenport vs. Wood, 11 Illinois, 551."

But the practice of investigating claims, and ascertaining their amount, by committees of Congress, has been so long exercised that it may be regarded as too late now to call it in question. This view was taken in a speech in the House on the 21st instant, in which it was said:

"There are two classes of powers; those which are conferred by express provisions of the Constitution and those which are incidental. No man doubts but each House of the British Parliament has power to punish for contempt. It is a power long exercised, declared by all writers on the British constitution, and denied by no one. When our Constitution confers upon Congress, as it does in the very first section of the first article, all legislative powers therein granted, there is given to Congress the incidental power to ascertain every fact necessary to enable it to legislate intelligently on every subject within its constitutional jurisdiction. Among the powers necessary to accomplish this purpose is the power to summon witnesses and to compel them to testify. That power has been exercised from the foundation of the Government up to this time, and it has never been doubted or denied."

Congress clearly has the power to appropriate money to pay claims; and whatever theory might be presented as to the duty of Congress to examine and ascertain their amount, Congress will continue to do so, especially with the democratic party and the Southern States, so largely interested in claims, fully represented in Congress.

A law would, therefore, be utterly ineffectual, so far as Congress is concerned.

This may be shown by an example. Congress established a Court of Claims to get rid of the evils of examining claims in Congress. These evils are numerous.

I quote again from my speech of June 3, 1874, as follows:

"The act of March 3, 1863, amending the act establishing the Court of Claims sought to avoid all these evils by providing (12 Statutes, 765, sec. 2) as follows:

"'That all petitions and bills praying or providing for the satisfaction of private claims against the Government, founded upon any law of Congress, or upon any regulation of an Executive Department, or upon any contract, express or implied, with the Government of the United States, shall, unless otherwise ordered by resolution of the House in which the same are presented or introduced, be transmitted by the Secretary of the Senate or the Clerk of the House of Representatives, with all the accompanying documents, to the court aforesaid.'

"But this in practice has failed for two reasons. The jurisdiction only extends to

eign nations whose citizens have just claims on our Government, if we

---

three classes of claims; and as to this it has been a failure, because the provision 'unless otherwise ordered' has totally defeated its object. It is always 'ordered' that claims when presented shall go to committees."

I respectfully submit, therefore, that your proposition that a sufficient remedy may be provided by law, and that "Congress itself would be bound thereby," is not correct. Each Congress would have the right to repeal any such law.

That there is a great and urgent necessity for some means to protect the Government against enormous and fraudulent claims, especially those arising in the Southern States, and growing out of the war, would seem to be certain. Without this there will be no end of them. I might illustrate this by many examples. The celebrated "Fisher claim" is one.

In 1812, the Florida Indians, or our troops, or both, committed some depredations on Fisher's corn-fields, in that State. He made a claim originally for $8,000. Congress has already paid on it $66,803.33, and yet there is a demand in this Congress for $66,848 more; and on the 27th of March last the Committee on Military Affairs in the House reported in favor of paying $16,848.

There are now pending before the Committee on War-Claims of the House more than 1,300 claims, demanding over $20,000,000, besides other claims in the Senate to an enormous amount.

Those who were rebels during the war can now prove loyalty that cannot now be met by proof of the truth. Claims can and will be multiplied indefinitely, and hundreds of millions will not satisfy them, if the democratic party comes into power. The recent "Sugg Fort claim," which was hurried through the Commissary Department and the Treasury Department, and which is now, on investigation, reported a fraud, is sufficient to show that claims which have been kept a dozen years and now come to the front, when the evidence against them is lost or inaccessible, are entitled to but little favor, if any. One claimant can exert more power and influence than half the population of a State. The claimant is vigilant, and so are his friends and his lobby. They can enlist powerful influences, political, personal, social, newspapers, and otherwise. There are no such influences, or but few, and rarely ever so active and vigilant, on behalf of the Treasury and the people. Now, if the Tribune will give the power of its great influence to aid in the good work of doing justice to honest claimants, and of cutting off those fraudulent claims which dare not come forth while memories are fresh to defeat them, I believe it will be a public service rightly performed.

Respectfully, &c.,

WM. LAWRENCE.

VI. The Committee on War-Claims adopted the following:

"ROOM OF COMMITTEE ON WAR-CLAIMS,
"HOUSE OF REPRESENTATIVES, *Washington, D. C., January* 9, 1874.

"The following resolution, adopted by the Committee on War-Claims of the House of Representatives of the Forty-third Congress, is published for the information of all concerned:

"*Resolved*, That the claimant in each claim which now is, or may be hereafter, referred to this committee, other than those from the Commissioners of Claims, shall be and is required to furnish, with the papers relating to the claim, information on the following points:

"1st. Whether the claim, or any part of it, has been presented to any Department or officer of the Government.

"2d. If so, when, and what Department or officer, and what action has been taken thereon.

"3d. Whether the claim, or any part of it, has been presented to either House of Congress, or to any committee of either House of Congress.

"4th. If so, when, and what action has been taken on the same.

"The above information to be furnished by affidavit of the claimant or his attorney.

"A true copy.

"HENRY H. SMITH, *Clerk*."

It might be salutary to require all this *by law* in *all cases* and *in all Departments* of the Government. And as to claims presented more than two years after they arose, or other fixed period, the claimant should be required, on presenting his claim, to give notice in a prescribed form of the filing thereof in one or more leading newspapers in the capital of the State or Territory where he resides, stating the office or tribunal having jurisdiction to consider it. This would often elicit information which would secure justice. The Commissioners of Claims say the publication of the claims filed before them has in many cases enabled them to procure very valuable evidence.

[From the Washington Chronicle, Monday, December 21, 1874.]

PRIVATE CLAIMS BEFORE CONGRESS.

We call attention to an article printed in the Chronicle this morning from the pen of an able and experienced member of Congress, on the subject of the proper disposi-

refuse or delay to make provision for them. Nor indeed can we hope

tion of private claims pending before the two Houses, which is well worth careful perusal on the part of his fellow-members.

It was not our purpose, in the article to which our honorable friend refers, to censure the members generally for inattention to this branch of their public duty. No doubt it now receives an equitable share of the time of the hard-working members, of whom the writer is known to be one of the most indefatigable. It is to be regretted that all do not, perhaps cannot, work with the same degree of effectiveness. The capable and industrious ought not, certainly, to be condemned on account of the incapacity or indolence of others of their associates.

And it is a truth, that the most capable Senators and Representatives of experience will heartily indorse, that a committee of Congress is, in many respects, an unfit and unsafe place for the adjudication of such causes. Unfit, because the members of committees will not all attend and give their attention to the business. The whole work, consequently, devolves on a few persons, who cannot carefully examine all the cases of this description sent to them for investigation. And the small part which is reported cannot, as the writer shows, secure the deliberate consideration of the House and Senate, so that the bulk of the work performed by the committees is not finally acted on by the Congress to which it is submitted, and must be abandoned by the claimants, or continue to be presented from Congress to Congress, constantly accumulating in magnitude.

It is an unfit place, because an adverse decision does not necessarily terminate the application of the claimant for redress. He is almost certain to attribute his defeat to the stupidity or inattention of committeemen, rather than the badness of his cause. And if not broken down in his finances, he is almost certain to return in person or by agent, or through the interposition of his Representative or Senator, year after year, with the hope of better luck. Hence, it has become a sort of axiom at the national capital that no claim presented to Congress can ever be effectually disposed of except by its payment; while an adverse decision by a court, after a full hearing, would end it forever.

A committee of Congress is an unfit tribunal because the testimony submitted is nearly always *ex parte*, and in favor of the applicants for relief, no one being interested who has facilities for taking testimony in favor of the Government. This, being well known to Senators and Representatives, has induced a habit with many of systematically voting against all private claims, however just they may appear on their face and well supported by evidence, believing that the Government side has not been fully represented.

It would, therefore, be far better for honest and meritorious claimants, as well as for the Government, to have them all referred to a court properly constituted, which appears to the committees of Congress to possess intrinsic merits.

*To the Editor of the Washington Chronicle:*

In the Chronicle of the 18th instant you discuss with much force and justice the subject of "private claims before Congress." You allude to the fact that these are very numerous, often fraudulent in character or amount, or both, and that the general impression that this is so, "no doubt often results in the greatest injustice to honest" claimants.

You say also, "it is the duty of Senators and Representatives to either take time to examine them, [claims,] carefully winnowing the chaff from the grain, and provide, with reasonable promptness, for the payment of those found to be just, or to provide a judicial tribunal for their adjudication."

I think it fortunate that attention has been called to the subject from a source which is entitled to and will command respect.

I wish to correct one inference which might, by possibility, be drawn from your article; that is, that members or committees of Congress have been negligent in examining and disposing of just claims, or have done less than they might.

If this were even so, it is by no means a chief source of the great evil and wrong of justice, long delayed.

By the rules of the House of Representatives Fridays are "private-bill days;" that is, these days are set apart for the consideration of private bills as the regular business of those "unfortunate" days.

Experience has shown that the demands upon the time of Congress are so numerous, pressing, and great, that it is not practicable to devote more time to private bills than the rules now prescribe. It is often found, indeed, that the general business of Congress requires that Friday be devoted to that, as was the case last Friday in the House. The private bills include not only claims for money, but for land, and relief in various forms, as for pensions, &c.

There are now on the private calendar of the House one hundred and seventy-six private bills, many of them claims for money, nearly all of which came over from the last session.

to preserve our own self-respect in case of a denial of justice to any

---

During the last session of Congress Mr. Speaker Blaine said, from the chair, that the private calendar had received more attention during that session than during any preceding session since he had been in Congress.

After the first of January next, there are only seven Fridays during this session, requiring about twenty-five bills to be disposed of for each day, or one for every twelve minutes, allowing the sessions to be five hours each, to clear the calendar. It is not very probable that Congress could dispose of much more than this even if the committees were to crowd the calendar with a hundred or five hundred more bills.

The committees of Congress can act on and report more private bills than Congress can act on, and this has always been so. This inability of Congress to act on all claims and private bills is the real and chief source of the delay, and consequent injustice done to honest claimants.

And as the country increases in population, wealth, and business, this evil is to become greater, for the general public business will require still more of the time of Congress. Even if Congress should continue in session as nearly all the time as might be practicable, (as I believe it should during the whole year,) the private claims and bills could never receive the requisite time and attention.

This must be apparent from the number and character of the claims and the amounts involved. Those before the Committees of Claims, both of the Senate and House, are very numerous.

There are now before the Committee of War-Claims of the House about thirteen hundred claims, involving, as estimated by the clerk of the committee, about $20,000,000. This number does not fully represent the claimants, for one claim, or bill, frequently includes the claims of numerous persons. The committees have not been negligent in the work assigned to them.

The Committee of War-Claims at the last session of Congress reported on one hundred and thirteen claims, and, besides, examined many on which reports could have been made if Congress could have acted on them. Many of the claims were argued at much length by able counsel, consuming much of the time of the committee. The reports made have settled principles which, if adhered to, are decisive of the questions involved in a majority of the claims now pending.

The committee reported seven general bills, one covering appropriations for one thousand and eighty-six claims, reported allowed by the Commissioners of Claims, reaching, in the aggregate, $575,000. These claims required a general examination to an extent sufficient to test their correctness. One of the general bills reported by the committee required much consideration, as it proposed to confer jurisdiction on the Commissioners of Claims to examine and report on claims which might be referred to them by either House of Congress. (See Congressional Record, vol. 2, part 5, [vol. 6,] p. 4511, June 3, 1874.)

The committee during the last session of Congress performed more labor in relation to claims than the whole work of any one of the highest State courts in a year in many of the States. I refer more especially to this committee because I am more familiar with its work than of any other. But other committees, having other classes of claims and private bills, did an immense amount of work—all that could be done.

There are grave difficulties in the way of examining and allowing claims by committees of Congress. There are still graver objections to adopting this mode as the general plan of passing on claims. But it is not the purpose of this article to discuss these now. They have been considered somewhat elsewhere. (Congressional Record, vol. 6, p. 4511.)

Your article says it is the duty of Congress either to examine claims, "or to provide a judicial tribunal for their adjudication." The act of Congress of March 3, 1871, created the Commissioners of Claims to examine and report on certain claims for stores and supplies furnished or taken for Union military forces during the rebellion in the insurrectionary States.

The bill (H. R. No. 1565) already referred to, reported by the Committee on War-Claims, giving the Commissioners jurisdiction of claims which might be referred by either House of Congress, passed the House, and is now before the Committee on Claims of the Senate.

If this bill should pass, and become a law, it would remedy the whole evil to which you have so well and so properly called attention. It would require but little labor to examine claims in Congress sufficiently to see if they had such merit as to require a full examination by the Commissioners.

These Commissioners are clothed with the best means yet devised to thoroughly ascertain the true merits of claims.

If this bill shall pass it will relieve the whole difficulty.

I would regard it as an improvement that this tribunal should be created into a court, with all its present powers. The Government will always need such a tribunal. It would be well if claims before the Departments could be referred to it also.

citizen or alien, however humble. The committee therefore recommend the passage of the bill.

---

Now, if you can examine this subject and give the aid of the Chronicle in the direction of the needed reform, you will contribute much to secure justice for honest claimants, and protect the Government from fraudulent claims.

If this reform is secured there will be a tribunal, accessible at all times, where claimants can be heard, and justice done without denial or delay.

W. L.

VII. The following bill has been introduced in the House of Representatives and is now pending:

[H. R. 4569. 43d Congress, 2d Session.]

"IN THE HOUSE OF REPRESENTATIVES.

"FEBRUARY 6, 1875.

"Read twice, referred to the Committee on War-Claims, and ordered to be printed.

"Mr. LAWRENCE, by unanimous consent, introduced the following bill:

"A BILL to prevent abuses in the prosecution of claims against the Government.

"*Be it enacted by the Senate and House of Representatives of the United States of America in Congress assembled,* That no account or claim against the United States exceeding one hundred dollars, which shall not have been presented to the proper officer authorized to receive, audit, and examine the same, or which, having been so presented, has not been paid within two years after the same accrued, shall be audited, examined, or paid until the claimant, his agent, or attorney, shall have given public notice, in a newspaper in general circulation in the locality where the account or claim accrued, of the presentation thereof, with the title of the officer authorized to examine the same, in such form and with such other particulars as may be prescribed by the head of the Department in which the same may be presented; and no such account or claim shall be paid until at least four months after the same has been examined and the balance duly certified.

"SEC. 2. That no account or claim against the United States shall be received, audited, or examined by any officer thereof until the claimant, his agent, or attorney, shall present therewith an affidavit stating that said account or claim is just and is justly due or owing to the claimant from the United States; that there is no set-off against the same, and that no payment has been made thereon except as thereon credited, and showing whether such account or claim, or any part thereof, has ever previously been presented to any Department or officer of the Government, or to either House of Congress, and, if so, when, and what action has been taken thereon; and that the same has never been otherwise or at any other time so presented. Said affidavit shall only be made by the agent or attorney when, for some reason shown by affidavit satisfactory to the officer charged with the duty to receive, audit, or examine such account or claim, it is not practicable that it should be made by the claimant personally.

"SEC. 3. That it shall be unlawful for any Senator, Representative, or Delegate in Congress, or other officer, clerk, or employé of the Government, or any clerk or employé in any Department or Bureau, or in any Office authorized by law, or the clerk of any committee of either House of Congress, or of any joint committee of the two Houses, otherwise than in the performance of a duty authorized or required by act of Congress, either while in office or within four years thereafter, to counsel, advise, advocate, or urge the payment or allowance of any account or claim or other action or proceeding in favor thereof against the United States, either before or to any member or committee of either House of Congress, or any joint committee of the two Houses, or any officer of the Government. But nothing herein shall apply to pension-claims, or deny to any such Senator, Representative, officer, or clerk the right to give testimony in writing as to any account or claim, or to give an opinion in writing on the request of the head of any Department in which any such account or claim may be pending, or to any member of any committee in the performance of any duty as such; nor to any account or claim held by any such Senator, Representative, Delegate, officer, or clerk in his own right. Every person who shall offend against or violate any provision of this section shall be deemed guilty of a crime, and, on conviction thereof, shall be fined in any sum not exceeding two thousand dollars, or imprisoned at hard labor, for a term not exceeding five years, or both, at the discretion of the court. And if any officer authorized by law to receive, examine, or certify the amount of any account or claim shall so certify or recommend or advise payment thereof, without a careful examination thereof, and of all evidence filed or presented in support thereof, he shall in like manner be liable to fine and imprisonment as aforesaid."

# THE LAW OF CLAIMS ON FOREIGN GOVERNMENTS.

THE MODE OF ADJUSTING CLAIMS AGAINST FOREIGN GOVERNMENTS, AND THE PROCEDURE ADOPTED IN THEIR INVESTIGATION.

## DOCUMENTS TRANSMITTED BY HON. HAMILTON FISH, SECRETARY OF STATE, TO THE CHAIRMAN OF THE COMMITTEE ON WAR-CLAIMS OF THE HOUSE OF REPRESENTATIVES IN THE YEAR 1874.

---

DEPARTMENT OF STATE,
*Washington, September* 21, 1874.

SIR: Referring to your letter of the 5th of June last, requesting that the diplomatic officers of the United States might be instructed to obtain certain information in regard to the adjustment of war-claims by the governments to which they are accredited, I have now the honor to inclose, herewith, for your information, a copy of a dispatch of the 21st ultimo, No. 281, and of its accompaniment, upon the subject, from Mr. Peirce, minister resident of the United States to the Hawaiian Islands.

I have the honor to be, sir, your obedient servant,

JOHN L. CADWALADER,
*Acting Secretary.*

Hon. WILLIAM LAWRENCE,
*Bellefontaine, Ohio.*

*Inclosure.*

Mr. Peirce to Mr. Fish, August 21, 1874, No. 281, with an accompaniment.

---

[Inclosure.]

No. 281.] LEGATION OF THE UNITED STATES OF AMERICA,
*Honolulu, August* 21, 1874.

SIR: In reply to the inquiries propounded by the honorable J. C. B. Davis, Acting Secretary of State, in his circular of date June 23, 1874, in regard to the course pursued by the Hawaiian government in relation to the adjustment of claims presented against it, whether held by its own subjects or by aliens, and as to the mode of procedure adopted in the investigation of such claims, I have to inform you that the subject-matter was fully presented by me in a note addressed to the minister of foreign affairs *ad interim*, of date July 29, and inclosing a copy of the schedule of inquiries referred to by Mr. Davis. The minister requested the Hawaiian attorney-general to reply to the schedule of inquiries. A copy of his answers the former has this moment sent to me, and I herewith inclose the same as received, the immediate departure of the mail for San Francisco not permitting a copy to be taken by the legation.

With great respect, your obedient servant,

HENRY A. PEIRCE.

Hon. HAMILTON FISH,
*Secretary of State, Washington, D. C.*

[Inclosure.]

*Copy of His Hawaiian Majesty's attorney-general's reply to Mr. Davis's schedule of inquiries, dated August 20, 1874; signed R. H. Stanley.*

HONOLULU, *August* 20, 1874.

SIR: The schedule of inquiries which I have the honor to receive at your hands has received careful consideration, and I beg to submit my replies thereto.

First. Claims against the government may be investigated, determined, and, if allowed, their payment directed and provided for by the legislature. Heretofore such claims have been instituted in the courts of the kingdom by the consent of the government.

Second. No mode of procedure is pointed out by the rules of the legislative assembly; but should a claim against the government be presented to the legislature it would be referred to either the finance or judiciary committee, and evidence would be procured by the committee sending for persons, books and papers, as authorized by the rules of the assembly.

Third. No provision is made for the examination and determination of claims by the executive department. In the enforcement of claims by the executive department, suit is brought in the courts of the kingdom and evidence procured by subpœna, depositions, and letters rogatory. There is no mode of procedure established for the investigation of claims by or before executive officers.

Fourth. The government cannot be sued without its consent, and it is expressly provided that no suit can be instituted against the government unless by permission of the king in privy council.

The privilege of maintaining an action against the government, *i. e.*, with its consent, extends to aliens.

Fifth. The status of aliens before the courts of this kingdom is the same as subjects, and all aliens can maintain an action in such courts against citizens or subjects.

Sixth. In the adjudication of claims, the same rule applies to the government as to individuals in regard to evidence, whether in law or equity side of the court; and the government has no privilege in relation to evidence in its behalf, and the same means are used in procuring evidence as noted in third reply.

Seventh. In common-law actions, the plaintiff or defendant of record, or the real plaintiff or defendant in interest, is not allowed to testify in his own behalf.

In bringing an action before the courts of this kingdom by non-resident aliens, it is necessary that full power be given the attorney, the same to be acknowledged of before an Hawaiian consul or a notary public; if before a notary, then to be authenticated by a consul for Hawaii.

Very respectfully submitted by your excellency's obedient servant,

R. H. STANLEY,
*Attorney-General.*

His Excellency WILLIAM L. GREEN,
*His Hawaiian Majesty's Minister of Foreign Affairs ad interim, &c.*

---

DEPARTMENT OF STATE,
*Washington, December* 12, 1874.

SIR: Referring to your letter of the 5th of June last, requesting that the diplomatic representatives of the United States be instructed to procure information respecting the mode of adjustment, &c., of the claims of private persons against the governments to which they are accredited, I have the honor to transmit herewith a copy of the instructions and schedule of inquiries addressed to the several ministers of the United States, and copies of all correspondence, together with the original printed papers and books which have been received from them by the Department in answer to those instructions, except a dispatch from Mr. Peirce, the minister of the United States at Honolulu, of the 21st of August, 1874, (No. 281,) a copy of which was sent to you with the letter of this Department of the 21st of September last.

I have the honor to be, sir, your obedient servant,

HAMILTON FISH.

Hon. WILLIAM LAWRENCE,
*Chairman of the Committee on War-Claims, House of Representatives.*

*List of accompaniments.*

1. Mr. Davis to United States ministers, June 23, 1874.
2. Mr. Jones to Mr. Fish, July 18, 1874, (two inclosures.)
3. Mr. Rublee to Mr. Fish, No. 177, August 1, 1874, (five inclosures.)
4. Mr. Delaplaine to Mr. Fish, No. 773, August 3, 1874, (six inclosures.)
5. Mr. Boker to Mr. Fish, No. 210, August 11, 1874, (two inclosures.)
6. Mr. Hoffman to Mr. Fish, No. 1018, August 13, 1874, (thirteen inclosures.)
7. Mr. Wing to Mr. Fish, No. 410, August 13, 1874, (three inclosures.)
8. Mr. Gorham to Mr. Fish, No. 149, August 20, 1874, (one inclosure.)
9. Mr. Scruggs to Mr. Fish, No. 56, August 27, 1874, (three inclosures.)
10. Mr. Turner to Mr. Fish, No. 147, September 11, 1874, (three inclosures.)
11. Mr. Williamson to Mr. Fish, No. 235, September 12, 1874, (one inclosure.)
12. Mr. Russell to Mr. Fish, No. 18, September 21, 1874, (three inclosures.)
13. Mr. Andrews to Mr. Fish, No. 241, September 26, 1874, (four inclosures.)
14. Mr. Davis to Mr. Fish, No. 18, September 28, 1874, (two inclosures.)
15. Mr. Marsh to Mr. Fish, No. 521, October 7, 1874, (two inclosures.)
16. General Schenck to Mr. Fish, No. 624, October 17, 1874, (four inclosures.)

---

DEPARTMENT OF STATE,
*Washington, June* 23, 1874.

SIR: For the purpose of facilitating the adjustment and determination of claims presented against the Government of the United States, whether held by its own citizens or by the subjects or citizens of foreign governments, and with a view of establishing, as far as may be practicable, a general and uniform system and mode of procedure for the investigation and determination of these classes of claims, the Department is desirous of obtaining exact and trustworthy information in regard to the course pursued by the government of ——— in relation to the adjustment of claims of a similar character against that government, and the mode of procedure adopted in the investigation and determination of such claims.

It is, therefore, desired that you will, at your earliest convenience, avail yourself of such opportunities as your position may afford to procure this information, and that you will also, with as little delay as the nature of the required service will allow, transmit the result of your inquires to the Department.

Accompanying this instruction is a list of inquiries, numbered from 1 to 7, inclusive, pointing more directly to the particular information sought and the specific points upon which it is most desired. While it is supposed these may aid you in your researches, it is not intended either to limit your inquiries to these particular questions nor to confine you to the manner thus indicated in obtaining the desired information.

It is especially desirable that the information be derived from the most trustworthy and authentic sources, and that when it is based upon legislative enactments or public and general regulations by the executive departments, copies of such laws and published regulations should, as far as practicable, accompany your report.

I am, sir, your obedient servant,

J. C. B. DAVIS,
*Acting Secretary.*

*Inclosure.*

Schedule of inquiries.

---

[Inclosure.]

SCHEDULE OF INQUIRIES.

1st. Are claims against the government investigated, determined, and, if allowed, their payment directed and provided for by the legislative branch of the Government?

2d. If the legislative authority does entertain such claims, what is the mode of procedure, by committee or otherwise, and what means, if any, are provided for procuring evidence on behalf of the government?

3d. What provision, if any, is made for the examination and determination of claims by the executive department? What is the mode of procedure in the investigation of claims by or before executive officers, and what means are provided for procuring evidence on behalf of the government?

4th. Is there any provision of law allowing a citizen or subject to sue the Government in the regularly-established courts, or in any special tribunal, and does the privilege of maintaining an action against the Government (if it exists) extend to aliens?

5th. What is the status of aliens before the regularly-established courts of the country? Can they maintain an action in such courts against a citizen or subject, and, if so, does the privilege extend to all aliens, or is it confined to resident aliens only?

6th. If different systems of adjudication exist as regards different classes of claims, what is the system with reference to each class, and what the mode of procedure, and the privileges of the Government in relation to evidence in its behalf and the means of procuring such evidence?

7th. Add any other information, general or special, of which you may be possessed bearing on the subject.

---

*Mr. Jones to Mr. Fish.*

LONDON, *July* 18, 1874.

SIR: Just as I was leaving Brussels I received yours of the 23d June, requesting information for the purpose of facilitating the adjustment and determination of claims, &c. I gave Mr. Jottrand, père, a memorandum of what I required, and he now sends me the inclosed. Mr. J. is a lawyer of forty years' practice at Brussels; has a son in congress, and was himself a member of the first congress. I inclose his note to me, by which it will be seen that I shall have to pay him 150 francs.

I must apologize for sending the document in its present form, but am constantly on the go, and have deemed it better to send it now than to retain it until my return, which I trust will be satisfactory.

Your obedient servant,

J. R. JONES.

Hon. HAMILTON FISH,
*Secretary of State.*

---

[Inclosure No. 1.]

JULY 14, 1874.

MY DEAR MR. JONES: As I intend to start before long, in some journeying to enjoy my holidays in the next recess of business in the courts of law, and everywhere generally, I have lost no time in satisfying to your demand. Here is my paper on the inquiries wanted by you; and I hope you will find them satisfactory for the use you have to make of them. I dare recommend to you the mending of my broken English, when used for your purpose.

The question of my fees is very difficult to be solved by me. I would not charge you like an ordinary client; that is to say, I must take in consideration the kind services you have obliged me with, and owe to make a compensation for them. If you would find fault in my charging you with 150 francs for fees, pray tell it me frankly, and I will settle the matter according to your best judgment, after your and my return to home in October next.

Faithfully, your friend,

L. JOTTRAND, PÈRE.

---

[Inclosure No. 2.]

First. Are claims against the Belgian government investigated, determined, and, if allowed, their payment directed and provided for by the legislative branch of the government?

Claims against the Belgian government must be directed to the king, at Brussels, by a request on stamped paper, of the size called *grand papier* in the law; the cost of each sheet being 1 franc 20 centimes. The language to be used is commonly the French—albeit, according to article 23, of the Belgian constitution, both the Dutch (Flemish) and German may be used also, at will.

The object of the claim, its cause or origin, the facts and circumstances whereon established must be exposed; and the documents pertaining to the matter annexed, with an inventory index or succinct description of them at the foot of the request; the whole to be deposited at the royal palace or sent thither by post, duly franked, under the plain subscription, *Au Roi à Bruxelles.*

On receiving such request, the King taking or not taking knowledge of it, as the case may be, the chief secretary of the King's cabinet causes a summary examination of the matter to be made by a clerk, in order to know the ministerial department to which the matter may be related—foreign affairs, interior, justice, public works, finances, or war—the request is sent from the King's cabinet to the competent department in the six. The claimant is made aware of it by a cabinet dispatch; and from that time he must apply for his claim directly to that department under address of the minister, or by calling on him or the chief clerk intrusted with the matter. The department investigates the case, determines on it; and, the claim being found just and allowable, the minister orders the payment on the special chapter of his department's budget which the matter is related to, and causes a bond for payment to be delivered. This bond, called a *mandat de paiement,* is submitted to the Belgian court of public accounts, *la cour des comptes,* at Brussels, which verities of the chapter of the budget designed is the one properly charged with the expense whereof question; and, if so found, puts on the *mandat à visa* authorizing payment; and this takes place then at the treasury public (the national bank at Brussels or anywhere at its delegates in the provinces) on show of the paper.

If no chapter of the said ministerial department's budget, in run for the year, can be charged with the expense; or if that chapter is already exhausted by previous payments, or if the court of public accounts does not agree with the minister on the question that such or such chapter is the proper one to be charged with the payment, the ministerial department would propose, in the next budget, an allocation for the payment. But the legislative authority may then debate the question, "Is the payment to be allowed, yea or nay?" The competent minister would, of course, sustain his proposition, the claimant at leisure to petition to the legislative power, in the house of representatives and in the senate, successively, in order to make his rights evident. The said claimant could get representatives or senators to his party, the public press being called, too, in the discussion. The matter then publicly debated, in both houses of representatives and senators, like all matters in the budget, would succeed or not, in the sense of the claim. If succeeding, the payment would take place in the way as aforesaid; if not, the claim would drop and be set aside. But in such case yet, like in case of rejection of the claim by the minister at the beginning, the claimant would be admitted to bring the matter in the regular courts of law, by a suit for his rights against the government; because he could not be debarred in his claim otherwise than by sentence of regular justice, the legislative authority, no more than the ministerial or governmental one, being competent to decide definitely in matters of civil obligations between particulars and government any more than between particulars and particulars, as such. Indeed the Belgian constitution provides, in its article 92, "Contestations having for their objects civil rights, are exclusively under the competence of the courts of law."

If a claim against the government, on a question of *mine or thine,* is proved good in the courts of law, it must be settled by the public budget of the proper ministerial department; and nobody in the legislative nor administrative authorities has power to the contrary.

Second. If the legislative authority does entertain such claims, what is the mode of procedure, by committee or otherwise, and what means, if any, are provided for procuring evidence on behalf of the government?

From what has been said hereabove, it follows that no claims of particulars in matter of obligations can be brought directly before the legislature; and, consequently, no procedure, by committee or otherwise, can be kept. In case of discussion in the legislature, between the ministers and the houses, about matters to be brought or not in the budget, and related to particular interests which a minister admits to be claimable on his department, and the legislature would not allow, the debate takes place on the documents only procured by the party interested, and which the minister himself has admitted as doing sufficiently. The debaters in both the legislative houses do object only from these documents. No further evidence is offered; no investigation by inquiry before committee or otherwise may happen. If the credit asked by the minister is allowed, the minister will pay the claim; if not, the minister will not pay, and the matter may then be brought by the claimant before the courts of law, with the consequences aforesaid.

3d. What provision, if any, is made for the examination and determination of claims by the executive department? What is the mode of procedure in the investigation of claims by or before executive officers, and what means are provided for procuring evidence on behalf of the Government?

As it has been seen, all debatable matter between a claimant and the government, like debatable matter between particulars, must be brought before the courts of law, and settled thither only. Thus, it cannot happen that a discussion whatever takes place between a claimant and the government to be settled by way of a procedure before the government itself, and its officers. The claimant must make his claim good, from the beginning, by documents satisfactory to the government. It may happen that, in the investigation of the documents, the government would require from the claimant more documents than those furnished in the beginning, and determine that such or such documents are wanted, and may, perhaps be procured; which the claimant is at leasure to do, in a certain time allowed to him therefor. But the government will at the end settle the matter according to the documents procured. If the claim is allowed, the payment takes place, as said here above; if rejected, the matter drops there; and the courts of law are the only recourse for the claimant.

4th. Is there any provision of law allowing a citizen or subject to sue the government in the regularly-established courts, or in any special tribunal; and does the privilege of maintaining an action against the Government, if it exists, extend to aliens?

Perfectly. According to article 92 of the Belgian constitution, already quoted, the regular courts of law are the judges exclusive in all questions of *mine or thine* between all kinds of litigants. During the French domination Belgium had what the French call *la jurisdiction administrative, le contentieux administratif*, which they yet enjoy. In suits between the particulars and the government, their *conseil d'état* is the judge. The Belgian have no *conseil d'état*, no more than the American of the United States. After the French domination Belgium had the Dutch one, during about fifteen years, in the beginning of which no *contentieux administratif*, no *jurisdiction administrative* existed. But, at the end of his reign, the king, William First of Orange, endeavored to establish that detested *jurisdiction* again, and had a *conseil d'état* for judging the *contentieux administratif*, of his own arbitrary reinstallment. This was, in 1830, not the least of the griefs of the Belgian against William's government; and caused, for a large part, the eversion of that government, by the Belgian revolution of that epoch. Under the Belgian national institutions before the French and Dutch domination in their country, it was a rule that Brabancons, Flemish, Liegeois, etc., could not be governed otherwise than *par droit et sentences des tribunaux*. The rule was re-established by the Belgian constitution of February, 1831, in article 92 aforesaid. The regularly-established courts are the judges in all suits, as well between particulars and government as between citizen and citizen. No special tribunal does exist; and the right and by no means the privilege of maintaining an action against the government in the ordinary courts of law extends to aliens, by force of this other article of the Belgian constitution, article 128, which provides that an alien being on Belgian ground enjoys the benefit of the Belgian laws, (1.) The Belgian civil code provides further, article 15, that a Belgian may be sued before a Belgian court of law for obligations contracted in Belgium, or abroad, with an alien, (2.)

5th. What is the status of aliens before the regularly-established courts of the country? Can they maintain an action in such courts against a citizen or subject; and, if so, does the privilege extend to all aliens, or is it confined to resident aliens only?

The above quoted articles answer the question. An alien not resident in Belgium can sue a Belgian before Belgian courts, like an alien resident, who has nevertheless a peculiar privilege; that is, to sue a Belgian without procuring the *cautio judicatum solvi*, whereof question in article 16 of the civil code, as here (3) mentioned.

6th. If different systems of adjudication exist as regards different classes of claims, what is the system with reference to each class, and what the mode of procedure and the privilege of the government in relation to evidence on its behalf, and the means of procuring such evidence?

The claims may properly be divided in three classes, according to civil rights in matter of obligations.

A. Rights peculiarly civil, resulting of civil contracts or obligations, as, selling and buying; borrowing and lending, (in matters non-commercial;) leasing, and taking in lease, houses, lands, furniture, etc.; wills in matter of succession and heirs, and the like.

B. Rights related to contracts or obligations in commercial matters; matters of societies or partnerships for commercial enterprises; matters of commercial navigations, and the like.

C. Damages to be recovered in consequence of crimes, misdemeanors, or delinquencies of all kind in penal law, (*droit pénal.*)

In the first class, and in suits for a value above 150 francs, no evidence whatever is admitted, nor for the claimant, nor for the defendant, which is not by written deeds or documents. Verbal testimony is not allowed. Every action must be preceded, (excepting the cases of great urgency,) by an experience to be made before a magistrate called *juge de paix*, in order to know if the to-be plaintiff and the to-be defendant could not be conciliated about the matter to sue for. That experience does not take place in suits where minors, lunatics, partners above two in number, government, and all kind of public establishment are concerned. An alien suitor must furnish *cautio judicatum solvi*, as said before; and would get no hearing by the court, without the deposit of cash in the hands of a public officer thereto appointed, for a value to fix by the court, when thus required by the defendant.

In the second class, all kind of evidence, by verbal testimony, pro and con, can be admitted; no preliminary experience for conciliation is wanted; no *cautio judicatum solvi* is required. The procedure is summary; at less expenses than in the first class; and the parties may plead their cases themselves, without attorneys or barristers, who are indispensable in the first class.

In the third class the damages may be recovered before the court judging the delinquent for his detect, and by a summary procedure peculiar to the criminal courts which it seems useless to explain here.

The government has no privilege in relation to evidence in its behalf; the procedure is quite the same for itself and the private suitor.

7th. Add any other information, general or special of which you may be possessed, bearing on the subject.

As a general information, it can be said that the fees of attorneys and barristers are less than in England and the United States; except in the second and the third classes aforesaid the suits can be protracted long enough, in civil matters properly sued; longer than in France, but not so long, as one is generally told, as in England and the United States of America.

It is now question to abridge the law-suits by a reform in the laws of procedure; but the legislative authority has not yet been seized with the intended prospect of law, thereabout.

---

## *Mr. Rublee to Mr. Fish.*

No 177.] LEGATION OF THE UNITED STATES,
*Berne, August* 1, 1874. (Received August 28.)

SIR: Upon receipt of the dispatch, not numbered, of Mr. J. C. B. Davis, Acting Secretary of State, dated June 23, 1874, asking me to obtain and transmit to the Department of State, exact and trustworthy information respecting the course pursued by the government of Switzerland relative to the adjustment of claims against that government, and the mode of procedure adopted in regard to the investigation and determination of such claims, I addressed a note to the President of the confederation, inclosing with it a copy of the series of questions accompanying the aforesaid dispatch.

Copies of this note, and of the response of the President thereto, with copies of the federal constitution of Switzerland, and of such laws of Switzerland as relate to the adjustment of claims against the government, are herewith inclosed.

The note of the President with the accompanying documents, will be found to contain the information desired.

I have, &c.,

HORACE RUBLEE.

---

[Inclosure 1 in No. 177.]

*Mr. Rublee to the President of the Swiss Confederation.*

LEGATION OF THE UNITED STATES,
*Berne, July* 13, 1874.

The undersigned, minister resident of the United States, has been requested by his Government to obtain as full information as possible in regard to the course pursued by the government of Switzerland in regard to the adjustment of claims presented against it, whether held by its own citizens or by the citizens of other states, and the mode of procedure adopted in the investigation and determination of such claims.

This information is desired in view of the circumstance that the Government of the United States is contemplating a revision of its regulations regarding such claims, with the object of establishing a uniform system and mode of procedure.

The undersigned, in order to obtain exact and trustworthy information upon the subject in question, incloses herewith a series of inquiries, and respectfully asks that your excellency will be pleased to cause the same to be referred to the appropriate department, and the answers thereto to be prepared and transmitted to the undersigned at the earliest convenient period.

The undersigned, &c.

HORACE RUBLEE.

---

[Inclosure 2 in No. 177.—Translation.]

*The High Federal Council to Mr. Rublee.*

BERNE, *July* 29, 1874.

The federal council has received a note of the 13th instant from the minister resident of the United States, in which he asks, in the name of his Government, information concerning the modes of procedure of the federal government in cases of claims, either on the part of its own citizens or of the refugees from other States.

The federal council is obliged to infer from the contents of this note, and the questions subjoined to it, that the subject is not of collisions of public rights but of question of civil rights. It is, then, starting from this point of view, that it has the honor to reply to the questions propounded to it.

In this instance it will commence by calling to mind that, as was the case under the régime of the federal constitution of 1848, so the new federal constitution of 29th May, 1874, and the federal law concerning the federal judiciary of 27th June, 1874, have applied rigorously the principle of the division of power for claims of civil rights brought up by the confederation, or against it. It follows from this that neither legislative nor executive authority are competent to pronounce on claims of this kind, only the competent tribunals, which have the prerogative of pronouncing upon the text of the laws and the principles of right generally obligatory, and that without calling in question the constitutionality of these laws.

Concerning the question, Which are the competent tribunals? it is necessary to cite the following cases:

1. Questions of civil right between the confederation (or a special branch of its administration) and one or more of the cantons.

All proceedings of this kind, whether the confederation or an administration be plaintiff or defendant, whether the question is a personal claim or a real suit, and whatever may be the value of the disputed objects, must be brought before the federal tribunal. (Article 110, No. 1, of the federal constitution, and article 27 of the federal law on the organization of the federal judiciary, of 27th June, 1874.)

2. The civil suit between the confederation or a federal administration and a corporation or an individual.

Suits of this category appeal also to the federal tribunal, provided always that the corporation or the individual are the plaintiffs and that the object under litigation is worth at least 3,000 francs. (Article 110, No. 2, of the federal constitution, and article 27 of the aforementioned federal law.)

On the contrary, in a suit where the confederation or one of its administrations is plaintiff, or if the value of the object under litigation is less than 3,000 francs, it is necessary to observe—*a*, if the object of litigation concerns a personal claim; or, *b*, if it is of real nature.

Ad. *a*. A suit of this kind must be brought by the plaintiff (corporation or individual) according to the tenor of article 59 of the federal constitution, before the proper tribunal of the canton in which the administration of the confederation sued or held to account has its legal seat.

In a contrary case, when an administration of the confederation is the plaintiff, the suit should, according to the tenor of article 59 of the federal constitution, be brought before the competent tribunal of the canton in which the defendant (corporation or individual) lives.

Ad. *b*. A real suit should, in the two cases mentioned under *a*, be opened before the tribunal for the place in which the object of the suit is situated.

The federal council believes thus far to have answered questions I, II, and III.

IV. Concerning the question of knowing if it is admissible for a citizen to bring suit against the federal constitution, directly or indirectly, by a special branch of administration, it must reply in the affirmative. This case is also provided for by article 110 of the federal constitution. As regards foreigners, Switzerland has concluded with several states treaties of settlement which assure to the refugees of these states the same rights as those due to Swiss citizens, so that they also may be treated upon the same footing as the latter in the mode of procedure.

Refugees from other states may also plead, before the competent tribunal, their cause against the confederation, but in that case they are usually obliged to give bail sufficient to indemnify the cost of proceedings.

Generally, it is admitted, in Switzerland as a principle, that a foreigner, as such, cannot be excluded from the right of pleading, but that he can plead his cause, before the proper tribunal, toward all individuals living on Swiss territory, and this, whether the foreigner plaintiff live in the country or no.

VI. It makes no difference in the proceedings (except the contingent fees.) The federal law of 22d November, 1850, on the course to be followed before the federal tribunal in civil cases makes the rule, and in the cantons it is the special laws on the civil suit.

The government has no privilege as to means; it is assimilated to all other parties to the suit.

VII. To conclude the observations, the federal council has the honor to transmit, subjoined, to the minister resident of the United States, the new federal constitution of the 29th May, 1874, the federal law on the organization of the judiciary, of the 27th June, 1874, and the provisional federal law of the 22d November, 1850, on the course to be followed before the federal tribunal in civil suits, which went into force definitely on the 13th July, 1855.

I seize, &c.

In the name of the federal Swiss council. For the president of the confederation.

(Signed) CÉRÉSOLE.

The chancellor of the confederation,

(Signed) SCHISSS.

---

[Inclosure 3 in No. 177.]

*Loi fédérale provisoire sur la procédure à suivre par devant le Tribunal fédéral en matière civile.*

L'ASSEMBLÉE FÉDÉRALE DE LA CONFÉDÉRATION SUISSE:

En exécution de l'art. 107 de la Constitution fédérale

Dans le but de fixer légalement, la procédure à suivre par devant le Tribunal fédéral pour les contestations civiles, conformément à l'art. 87 de la loi du 5 juin 1849 sur l'organisation judiciare fédérale (Voir le nouveau Recueil officiel I, page 65);

Vu le projet présenté par le Conseil fédéral,

DÉCRÈTE:

## DISPOSITIONS GÉNÉRALES.

### CHAPITRE PREMIER.—FONCTIONS DES JUGES.

ARTICLE PREMIER. Les dispositions de la présente loi relatives aux tribunaux eux-mêmes doivent être suivies autant que possible par les présidents des tribunaux et les juges d'instruction, lorsqu'ils agissent isolément.

Art. 2. Le tribunal ne doit pas prendre en considération les faits qui ne sont pas mentionnés dans les actes; cependant, lorsque les exposés ou les écritures des parties sont incomplets, vagues ou confus, il peut d'office prendre les mesures nécessaires pour qu'il y soit porté remède.

Art. 3. Le droit fédéral est appliqué d'office par le tribunal.

Les principes de droit autres, cantonaux ou locaux dont les parties veulent faire état doivent être indiqués par elles; au besoin elles doivent en justifier.

Art. 4. Le tribunal ne doit accorder à une partie ni plus ni autre chose que ce qu'elle a demandé, ni moins que ce que sa partie adverse a reconnu devoir.

## Chapitre II.—Des parties.

### I.—*Capacité pour introduire des actions juridiques.*

Art. 5. Tout personne capable d'agir civilement peut faire valoir ses droits devant le tribunal fédéral soit comme demandeur soit comme défendeur.

### II.—*Débat collectif.*

Art. 6. Les personnes qui ont en commun un droit ou une obligation ou dont le droit ou l'obligation dépend d'un seul et méme acte juridique peuvent se porter conjointement demandeurs ou défendeurs.

Art. 7. Chacune des parties peut suivre au procès (§ 147) indépendamment des autres, pourvu qu'elle ne soit pas liée par des engagements juridiques particuliers. Cependant elles doivent agir ensemble pour ce qu'elles ont de commun dans la demande et dans la défense. (Art. 53.)

Art. 8. Le défendeur (ou les défendeurs) ne peut tirer une fin de non-recevoir de ce que la demande n'est pas formée au nom de tous ceux qui étaient en droit de la faire, ou lorsque tous les co-obligés ne sont pas mis en cause; mais dans ce cas le juge doit, lors du prononcé du jugement, ou partager l'objet en litige, ou, si cela n'est pas possible, ajouter au jugement une réserve en faveur du défendeur ou enfin suivant les circonstances repousser momentanément la demande.

Le demandeur peut dans ces circonstances mettre subséquemment en cause les co-obligés que lui désigne le défendeur. S'il en est ainsi ou s'il réussit à décider d'autres personnes, fondées en droit, à s'associer subséquemment à la demande, la procédure doit être immédiatement continuée, comme si toutes ces personnes avaient été mises en cause dès le commencement du procès.

### III. *Participation d'un tiers au procès.*

#### A.—Dénonciation d'instance.

Art. 9. Celui qui veut exercer un recours contre un tiers, en cas de condamnation, peut lui donner connaissance du procès par l'entremise du juge en indiquant préalablement les motifs du recours en garantie et en laissant le tiers libre de prendre part au procès pour le soutenir.

Art. 10. Dès le moment où l'instancée a été dénoncée, le tiers dénoncé doit être mis en état de faire valoir tous ses moyens en faveur du dénonçant pour la demande ou pour la défense, et recevoir à cet effet communication de toutes les demandes et autres pièces juridiques. Cette disposition n'est pas applicable lorsque le tiers dénoncé a formellement refusé de prendre part au procès.

Les frais occasionnés sont supportés provisoirement par le dénonçant.

Art. 11. Le dénonçant peut, lorsqu'il ne veut pas accepter ou continuer le procès, en donner connaissance au dénoncé et lui faire fixer par le juge un délai pour déclarer s'il veut également renoncer au procès ou le poursuivre à ses risques et périls.

Le dénoncé ne doit point être considéré comme partie ou comme partie jointe au dénonçant, par cela même qu'il continue le procès mais seulement comme remplaçant le dénonçant.

Le jugement est prononcé, dans l'affaire principale, nominativement contre le dénonçant, et le dénoncé doit seulement acquitter les amendes disciplinaires auxquelles il a été condamné ainsi que les frais et dépens causés par lui.

Art. 12. Le dénoncé peut dénoncer à son tour, conformément à l'art. 9, une autre personne qu'il veut appeler en garantie.

Art. 13. Toute personne menacée de la possibilité d'un recours peut spontanément offrir son intervention à la partie intéressée. Si son offre est acceptée elle doit être considérée, comme la personne à qui le procès a été dénoncé.

Art. 14. L'intervention au procès n'équivaut point à la reconnaissance de l'obligation d'indemniser soit que cette intervention ait lieu *après* (art. 9) ou *sans* (art. 13) invitation préalable.

Art. 15. Les rapports qui peuvent exister entre le dénonçant et le dénoncé ne doivent point faire le sujet de la délibération ou du jugement, sauf dans le cas où la partie adverse du dénonçant contesterait au dénoncé le droit d'intervenir au procès.

B.—Intervention accessoire.

ART. 16. Un tiers dont le droit ou l'obligation, dépend de l'affaire en litige peut en tout état de cause s'associer à la partie que cela concerne. Il doit cependant prendre le procès dans l'état où il le trouve. Il devient en réalité par la partie jointe (art. 7) à celui qu'il soutient.

C.—Intervention principale.

ART. 17. Un tiers qui croit avoir sur l'objet litigieux un droit supérieur, excluant totalement ou partiellement les deux parties, ne peut intervenir dans le procès, mais il est libre d'intenter également une action.

ART. 18. Le tribunal peut, selon qu'il le juge convenable, ordonner que les deux affaires soient menées séparément jusqu'à la fin de la procédure principale ou simultanément. En tout cas un seul et même jugement doit statuer sur les deux demandes.

ART. 19. Les contestations sur la question de savoir si et comment un tiers peut prendre part au procès, soit par une intervention principale, soit par une intervention accessoire, sont jugées pendant la procédure préparatoire par le juge d'instruction et plus tard par le tribunal lui-même.

IV.—*Droits et devoirs des parties.*

ART. 20. Les parties peuvent en tout temps consulter les procès-verbaux et les actes. Des copies leur sont délivrées sur leur demande et moyennant finance.

Tout écrit présenté au tribunal ainsi que toute ordonance judicaire doit être communiqué sans délai aux deux parties.

Ces communications ont lieu d'après le mode prescrit pour la communication des citations. (Art. 56–58.)

ART. 21. Les parties doivent avoir une égale faculté de prendre part à toutes les délibérations.

ART. 22. Les parties doivent observer dans leurs exposée le respect dû aux juges et ménager leur adversaire et les tiers autant que la défense de leur propre droit le permet. Celui qui viole cette prescription ou qui nie ou dénature malicieusement la vérité, ou qui attaque son adversaire d'une manière inconvenante, ou qui traîne méchamment le procès en longueur, est possible d'une peine disciplinaire, à teneur de l'art. 76 de la loi sur l'organisation judiciaire fédérale.

ART. 23. Chaque partie doit avancer le montant des frais occasionnés par ses actes et toutes deux ensemble la valeur des frais causés par des propositions communes ou par les actes faits d'office par le tribunal.

Les parties y sont invitées sous peine d'omission de l'acte dont les frais doivent être couverts et au détriment de la partie qui devait faire l'avance.

ART. 24. La partie qui succombe est tenue de rembourser à la partie adverse tous les frais occasionnés par le procès.

Les frais sont répartis proportionnellement lorsque le jugement n'est pas exclusivement en faveur de l'une des parties ou lorsqu'une partie a restreint elle-même sa demande primitive.

ART. 25. Chacune des parties, avant le commencement de la procédure définitive (art. 170 et suiv.) remet au président du tribunal et a son adversaire une note des frais aussi détaillé que possible avec les pièces à l'appui. La question des frais est traitée et jugée en même temps que la question principale.

ART. 26. Le demandeur qui n'a pas de domicile fixe dans la Confédération ou qui est dans un état d'insolvabilité notoire peut, pendant tout le cours du procès, être sommé de donner des sûretés, par consignation de la somme, par gages ou cautions, soit pour le montant des émoluments du tribunal, soit aussi, sur la demande du défendeur, pour les frais du procès. L'autorité qui a prononcé la sommation, que ce soit le président du tribunal ou le juge d'instruction (art. 95), est juge de la validité de ces sûretés.

La procédure est suspendue jusqu'à ce que le demandeur ait satisfait à la sommation.

ART. 27. Le tribunal peut accorder le *bénéfice du pauvre* aux personnes qui prouvent qu'elles sont trop pauvres pour pouvoir acquitter les frais du procès. Ces personnes sont libérées de l'obligation de fournir caution (art. 26) et les frais de justice leur sont remis, en tout ou en partie, qu'ils soient dus à la caisse fédérale, ou à un fonctionnaire ou employé de la Confédération.

Le tribunal peut refuser le bénéfice du pauvre, lorsqu'il ressort de l'exposé des faits joints à la demande que le procès est sans aucun fondement et fait à plaisir.

Les personnes qui ont joui du bénéfice du pauvre sont tenues de rembourser les frais dont il leur a été fait remise, lorsqu'elles se trouvent plus tard en état de le faire.

CHAPITRE III.—DES PERSONNES ADJOINTES AUX PARTIES.

ART. 28. Toute personne capable d'agir civilement peut diriger elle-même son procès ou se faire représenter par une personne capable d'agir civilement.

Art. 29. Le même droit appartient aux personnes, telles que tuteurs, conseils, curateurs, qui sont suffisamment autoriseés d'après les lois de leur canton, á demander et à défendre en justice pour d'autres personnes.

Art. 30. Les personnes chargées d'un procès au nom d'une autorité d'une corporation, ou d'une société peuvent également se faire représenter par un mandataire.

Art. 31. Plusieurs personnes ne peuvent dans un seul et même débat prendre la parole au nom d'une seule et même partie.

Art. 32. Celui qui veut faire pour autrui des actes juridiques doit justifier de sa qualité par une procuration écrite.

Art. 33. La procuration doit contenir une désignation suffisante des parties, du mandataire, du sujet du procès, du temps et du lieu où elle est faite, et la signature propre du mandant. Si celui-ci ne sait pas écrire, la déclaration de sa volonté doit être constatée par un acte authentique.

Art. 34. L'authenticité de la signature doit être certifiée conformément aux dispositions des lois de l'endroit. Il doit y être joint, comme attestant l'exécution légale de cette formalité, légalisation de la Chancellerie d'Etat du canton, ou, lorsque la procuration est faite à l'étranger, la légalisation d'une autorité administrative supérieure du pays. Lorsque le mandant n'est lui-même que mandataire d'une personne incapable d'agir civilement, d'une société, ou d'une personne morale, la légalisation doit contenir la declaration que le mandant est autorisé d'après les lois du pays à intenter ou à soutenir le procès pour la partie qui fait ou soutient réellement le procès.

Art. 35. Le mandataire d'un canton est accrédité par le gouvernement cantonal, le mandataire de la Confédération par le Conseil fédéral. Les procurations sont expédiées sous le sceau de l'autorité respective et signées par le président et le secrétaire d'icelle..

Art. 36. Pendant tout le cours du procès, la partie adverse peut exiger ou le juge ordonner d'office la production ou la rectification de la procuration.

Art. 37. Une procuration produite postérieurement doit, dans le doute, être considérée comme une approbation des actes déjà faits dans l'affaire par le mandataire.

Art. 38. Une procuration générale pour conduire un procès autorisé le fonde de pouvoirs à faire tous les actes qui ont pour but la solution de l'affaire par voie juridique; elle ne l'autorise point à signer un accommodement, à accepter un tribunal arbitral, à modifier la demande (art. 47) à se désister de la demande ou à recevoir des paiements.

Art. 39. Le mandataire ne peut transmettre la procuration, à moins que le droit de substitution ne lui soit formellement accordé.

Art. 40. Les actes et omissions du mandataire obligent le mandant comme s'ils avaient été faits par le mandant lui-même.

Les peines disciplinaires encourues par le mandataire l'atteignent seul.

## Chapitre IV.—Principes généraux de la procédure.

### I.—*Interdiction de provocation à former une demande.*

Art. 41. Nul ne peut être forcé à faire valoir contre sa volonté ou plutôt qu'il ne veut, le droit réel ou probable qu'il possède.

### II.—*Cumulation de demandes.*

Art. 42. Le demandeur ou le défendeur peut simultanément et dans la même procédure faire valoir plusieurs demandes contre le même adversaire, pourvu toutefois que le tribunal soit compétent à l'égard de chacune d'elles.

Art. 43. Lorsque plusieurs personnes ne sont pas parties à un seul et même procès (art. 6), ces personnes peuvent cependant, par exception et dans le but de diminuer les frais, se porter ensemble comme demandeurs ou défendeurs au procès, si leurs demandes ou les demandes adverses se fondent sur le même fait et que les motifs de droit soient les mêmes.

Est réservée la disposition de la loi sur les heimathloses (art. 9) qui déroge au présent article.

Art. 44. Dans les deux cas mentionnés aux art. 42 et 43 le tribunal peut pour des raisons spéciales, ordonner en tout état de cause, d'office ou sur la demande d'une des parties la disjonction du procès.

### III.—*Production simultanée des moyens de la demande et de la défense.*

Art. 45. Tous les moyens à l'appui de la demande ou de la défense doivent être présentés d'une seule fois. Les moyens qui n'ont pas été présentés ne peuvent plus être produits postérieurement à moins que la loi ne permette une exception.

### IV.—*Modification de la plainte.*

Art. 46. Les parties ne peuvent modifier postérieurement au détriment de leur adversaire, le contenu de leurs exposés, quant à ce qui concerne les faits. Elles sont liées à la demande telle qu'elle a été formulée primitivement. Celle-ci peut cependant, en tout temps être restreinte ou rectifiée dans les fautes d'écriture ou de calcul seulement.

ART. 47. Chacune des parties peut pendant le cours du procès, et tant que la procédure principale n'a pas été close déclarer *une fois* la réforme.

ART. 48. La réforme anéantit toute la procédure jusqu'au point indiqué par la partie qui la réclame.

Cependant la réforme laisse intactes les parties suivantes du procès:

*a.* Les compromis conclus par les parties;

*b.* Le serment déféré ou référé en tant que la partie adverse s'est déclarée prête à l'accepter;

*c.* Les déclarations faites sous serment par les parties;

*d.* Les dépositions des témoins et les rapports d'experts.

ART. 49. Celui qui déclare la réforme doit, dans un délai fixé par le juge rembourser à son adversaire les frais de la procédure mise à néant et commencer la nouvelle procédure; dans le cas contraire la réforme reste sans effets.

Le juge d'instruction se fait présenter la note des frais avec les pièces nécessaires et décide des contestations qui pourraient s'élever à ce sujet, après avoir entendu les deux parties et sous réserve de l'action en réclamation (art. 173).

### V.—*De la fixation du temps dans le procès.*

ART. 50. Les parties doivent procéder aux actes qui leur incombent à un jour fixe ou dans un délai déterminé.

#### A.—Jours fixes.

ART. 51. Le juge prononce d'office ou sur la demande d'une partie la citation à comparaître à jour fixe.

Les parties présentes à l'audience du tribunal peuvent être assignées oralement pour la séance suivante. Le protocole du tribunal fait preuve de cette citation.

Toute citation qui n'est pas faite à l'audience du tribunal doit être faite par écrit.

ART. 52. La citation doit indiquer d'une manière exacte l'autorité judiciaire, les parties, la procédure à faire, l'époque et le lieu de la comparution, les conséquences du défaut; la citation par écrit doit en outre être datée et signée par le secrétaire de l'autorité judiciaire dont elle émane.

ART. 53. La citation est adressée à la partie elle-même ou à son mandataire.

Lorsqu'il y a plusieurs personnes en cause, ces personnes doivent désigner un mandataire commun auquel toutes les citations et communications sont valablement remises; toute personne demeurant hors de la Confédération doit désigner dans le même but un mandataire résidant en Suisse.

ART. 54. Tout changement de domicile, soit des parties, soit de leurs mandataires, pendant le cours du procès, doit être immédiatement porté à la connaissance du juge.

ART. 55. Toute violation des deux articles qui précèdent est passible d'une amende disciplinaire (art. 76 de la loi sur l'organisation judiciaire fédérale) et peut entraîner, suivant les cas, une condamnation en dommages et intérêts envers la partie adverse ou envers la caisse fédérale en réparation du préjudice causé. Cette disposition n'exclut point les autres conséquences auxquelles les contrevenants sont exposés d'après la présente loi.

ART. 56. Les citations sont remises en deux doubles à la poste, qui remet l'un au destinataire et retourne l'autre à l'autorité judiciaire.

Le Conseil fédéral est autorisé à publier, si cela est nécessaire, un règlement relatif aux citations.

ART. 57. Lorsque la citation n'est pas acceptée ou que la signature du double est refusée, le juge invite l'autorité cantonale compétente à procéder à la citation conformément aux lois du lieu.

Ce refus, non-justifié, entraîne outre les frais une amende disciplinaire de 20 francs.

ART. 58. Les citations qui, pour un motif quelconque, ne peuvent être transmises à la personne qu'elles concernent, doivent être insérées dans la Feuille fédérale, dans la Feuille officielle du canton respectif et dans deux autres feuilles publiques désignées par l'autorité judiciaire. Les citations doivent en outre, lorsque cela est possible, être affichées dans la commune d'origine du cité et dans la commune où il a demeuré en dernier lieu.

ART. 59. La citation n'est pas valable si la personne cité n'a pas pour y satisfaire un délai de huit jours à dater de la réception, ou d'un mois à dater de la dernière publication de la citation publique (art. 58).

ART. 60. Le jour fixe dure depuis le moment fixé par la citation jusqu'à celui où le juge lève la séance.

ART. 61. La partie valablement citée qui ne comparaît pas à l'appel au jour fixe est passible d'une amende disciplinaire. Elle peut cependant comparaître postérieurement tant que la séance n'a pas été levée.

ART. 62. Si les deux parties ne comparaissent pas au jour fixe, le juge doit les condamner à des dommages et intérêts envers la caisse fédérale pour le préjudice causé et fixer un nouveau jour de comparution, excepté dans le cas où elles auraient conclu un accommodement et qu'elles l'auraient annoncé au plus tard au jour fixe. Si l'une des parties seule est absente, la partie qui comparaît peut procéder à tous les actes qui lui incombent et faire déclarer forfaits, par le juge, tous les actes que sa partie adverse aurait été en droit de faire.

B.—Des délais.

ART. 63. Les délais sont fixés par la loi ou par le juge (délais légaux ou judiciaires).

ART. 64. Dans le calcul des délais légaux, le mois est compté pour trente jours, et le jour de l'évènement à partir duquel le délai court n'est pas compté.

Au dernier jour du délai il peut être procédé à l'acte dont il s'agit, jusqu'à six heures du soir.

ART. 65. Les délais légaux ne peuvent être prolongés que du commun accord des parties. Celui qui les laisse expirer perd le droit dont l'exercice était attaché par la loi à ces délais mêmes.

ART. 66. Les délais judiciaires sont fixes par l'indication du temps auquel ils expirent. Lorsque le dernier jour et non l'heure est indiqué, il y a lieu à appliquer la disposition de l'art. 64 deuxième alinéa.

ART. 67. Tant que le délai judiciaire n'est pas écoulé, le juge peut, pour motifs importants, le prolonger sur la demande de la partie intéressée.

ART. 68. Lorsq'une partie laisse expirer le délai judiciaire, le judge donne cours aux conséquences qu'il avait expressément indiquées pour ce cas, dans les limites de la loi.

C.—Restitution des parties dans le cas d'expiration des jours fixes ou des délais.

ART. 69. La restitution contre l'expiration des délais peut toujours avoir lieu du consentement de la partie adverse.

ART. 70. En cas d'opposition de la partie adverse, la restitution n'est admissible que sous les conditions suivantes :

*a.* La demande doit être présentée, par écrit, au juge dans les dix jours à dater du moment où le requérant a été averti des conséquences qu'entraînerait sa négligence (art. 62 68 et 23) ;

*b.* Les actes de procédure négligés, tels que l'avance des frais (art. 23), l'indication d'une caution (art. 26), etc., doivent être exécutés en méme temps, ou du moins on doit fournir la preuve qu'ils ont été exécutés dans l'intervalle ;

*c.* Le requérant doit prouver que lui ou son mandataire ont été empêchés par des obstacles indépendants de leur volonté de paraître au jour fixe ou d'agir dans le délai indiqué. Les moyens de preuve sont joints à la demande, ou lorsque cela n'est pas possible, ils sont indiqués préalablement d'une manière précise (art. 158, 159).

ART. 71. Si la partie adverse du requérant persiste dans son refus, le juge cite par devant lui les deux parties et leurs témoins, et après les avoir ouïs, statue immédiatement sur cette question incidente.

ART. 72. Il n'y a lieu à restitution contre le délai de dix jours mentionné à l'article 70 que dans le cas ou le requérant n'a pu en profiter, par suite d'obstacles indépendants de sa volonté, et s'il présente sa demande dans les dix jours à dater de la cessation de l'obstacle.

D.—Jours fériés.

ART. 73. Il n'y a pas d'audiences les dimanches et les jours fériés.

Si un délai expire à l'un de ces jours, il pourra encore être valablement procédé, le jour suivant, à l'acte dont il s'agit.

Ne sont considérés comme jours fériés que ceux qui sont reconnus comme tels par la loi du lieu où se fait la procédure.

E.—Suspension du procès.

ART. 74. Sur la demande commune des parties, le juge peut suspendre le cours du procès pour un temps déterminé. La suspension ne peut excéder six mois.

La demande en suspension peut être renouvelée après l'expiration du temps déterminé.

ART. 75. Lorsqu'une partie perd la capacité d'agir civilement, ou lorsque ses droits passent à autrui par mort ou par insolvabilité, un délai est accordé aux tuteurs, héritiers, créanciers, etc., pour déclarer s'ils veulent continuer le procès ou se désister.

VI.—*Désistément.*

ART. 76. Le désistement au procès produit les mêmes effets qu'un jugement de condamnation envers celui qui s'est désisté. Celui qui se désiste doit payer tous les frais et émoluments judiciaires, si les parties ne conviennent du contraire.

Art. 77. Le désistement sous réserve de pouvoir intenter plus tard le même procès contre la même personne no doit être admis que dans le cas où le défendeur déclare que la demande n'est pas encore fondée à ce moment, où bien lorsque le demandeur a fait spontanément la même déclaration et motivé ainsi son désistement conditionnel. Même dans ce cas celui qui se désiste doit indemniser son adversaire pour tous les frais et payer les émoluments judiciaires.

Dans les cas mentionnés aux art. 76 et 77, le juge d'instruction se fait présenter la note des frais avec les pièces nécessaires à l'appui et statue après avoir ouï les parties et sous réserve de l'action en réclamation, conformément à l'art. 171.

Art. 78. Les contestations sur des droits dont les parties ont la libre disposition peuvent être abandonnées par elles momentanément ou definitivement, au moyen d'une transaction à leur gré.

La transaction n'est valable qu'autant qu'elle est faite par écrit et signée par les parties ou par leurs mandataires munis à cet effet d'une procuration spéciale (art. 38).

Une transaction valable a force de jugement rendu. L'émolument judiciaire est supporté en commun par les deux parties sauf stipulation contraire dans la transaction.

### Chapitre V.—De la forme des audiences du Tribunal

Art. 79. La procédure est orale et publique, en tant que la loi n'exige pas ou permet la remise de pièces écrites.

Art. 80. Le juge et les parties peuvent se servir à leur gré des trois langues principales de la Suisse (article 109 de la Constitution fédérale).

Lorsque cela sera nécessaire, la délibération orale et les pièces écrites devront être traduites par un expert nommé par le juge.

Art. 81. Il est dressé procès-verbal des delibérations orale. Le procés-verbal est écrit pendant l'audience et en présence des parties.

Il contient : la désignation du lieu et du temps de l'audience, les noms des personnes qui y ont pris part d'une manière quelconque, les assertions de fait importantes, les demandes de droit des parties, les dépositions des témoins et des experts et les ordres du juge.

Art. 82. Le procès-verbal est lu aux personnes qui ont été agissantes à l'audience ; il doit être signé par elles. Si quelqu'un refuse de signer, il sera fait mention du refus et de ses motifs.

Art. 83. Les rectifications de fait présentées à la lecture du procès-verbal doivent être insérées textuellement à la suite et suivies de la signature de celui que cela concerne.

Art. 84. S'il s'élève des doutes lors de la lecture du procès-verbal sur son exactitude relativement à la déposition d'un témoin ou au préavis d'un expert, ces doutes doivent être levés par une nouvelle audition du témoin ou de l'expert.

Les éclaircissements donnés par une partie relativement à ses propres exposés lors de la signature du procès-verbal doivent être insérés.

Le procès-verbal ne peut être modifié que par le juge lui-même pour ce qui concerne es ordonnances judiciaires.

Une fois le protocole signé, aucune modification n'est admise sans le consentement des deux parties.

Art. 85. Les pièces écrites sont signées par les parties ou par les mandataires et mentionnées dans le procès-verbal et dans un registre spécial.

Les parties reçoivent sur leur demande des récépissés pour tout ce qu'elles déposent.

Art. 86. Les actes qui ont été perdus doivent autant que possible être remplacés au moyen des actes doubles ou des copies qui se trouveraient entre les mains des parties. Les frais sont supportés par celui qui a perdu l'acte.

Art. 87. Les actes déposés par les parties ne peuvent leur être rendus, à elles ou à leurs mandataires, qu'après à fin du procès et contre reçu. Pendant le cours du procès le juge ne peut en ordonner la remise que pour des raisons spéciales et en prenant les mesures nécessaires pour prévenir tout préjudice.

Art. 88. Les actes qui resteront après la fin du procès, les reçus pour les actes rendus et le procès-verbal seront réunis en un dossier par ordre de date et déposés dans les archives fédérales.

## PARTIE SPECIALE.

### Titre I. —Introduction du procès.

Art. 89. La demande est faite par écrit; elle doit désigner en abrégé mais d'une manière précise:

*a.* Les parties;

*b.* Les faits qui motivent la demande ou qui sont relatifs à la légitimation des parties, y compris les principes de droit soit étrangers, soit cantonaux, soit locaux, mentionnés à l'art. 3;

*c.* L'objet de la demande ;

*d.* Lorsque cela est nécessaire, la valeur de l'objet litigieux (art. 47, n°. 2 et 4 de la loi sur l'organisation judiciaire fédérale);

*e.* La désignation exacte et détaillée des moyens de preuve à l'appui des faits mentionnés.

Les demandes qui se basent sur des comptes doivent être accompagnées d'un compte courant détaillé.

ART. 90. Dans les contestations entre plusieurs cantons ou entre la Confédération et un canton, la demande accompagnée des pièces nécessaires est remise au président du Tribunal fédéral par l'intermédiaire du Conseil fédéral. Dans tous les autres cas, la demande est remise directement au président du Tribunal fédéral (art. 101 de la Const. fed.). La demande doit être accompagnée d'un double qui est remis au défendeur par le Conseil fédéral ou respectivement par le président du Tribunal fédéral.

ART. 91. La remise de la demande au défendeur l'autorise à former une demande reconventionelle, le rend responsable de tout retard, lui enlève le droit de disposer librement de l'objet litigieux et interrompt toute prescription acquisitive ou libératoire.

ART. 92. Le défendeur a un délai de trois semaines à dater du jour de la réception de la demande pour contester auprès de l'autorité qui la lui a transmise la compétence du Tribunal fédéral.

ART. 93. Dans le cas de divergence sur la question de competence, les actes sont retournés au demandeur, qui est mis en demeure de réclamer la décision de l'Assemblée fédérale.

ART. 94. Lorsque la valeur de l'objet litigieux est importante pour la question de compétence (art. 47 de la loi sur l'organisation judiciaire fédéral) le président du Tribunal fédéral peut, sur la demande de l'une des parties, faire expertiser la valeur de l'objet par des hommes de l'art, dont le rapport est soumis à l'Assemblée fédérale.

Les intérêts et les frais de procès ne doivent pas être pris en considération. La valeur de la jouissance d'une année se représente par vingt fois la valeur de la moyenne du revenu.

ART. 95. Lorsque la compétence du Tribunal fédéral n'est pas niée dans le délai de trois semaines (art. 92), ou lorsqu'elle a été réglée par l'Assemblée fédérale, le président du Tribunal fédéral charge l'un des membres de ce corps de diriger la procédure préparatoire et donne communication aux parties de cette nomination.

ART. 96. Le juge d'instruction nomme lui-même son secrétaire.

## TITRE II.—PROCÉDURE PRÉPARATOIRE.

ART. 97. Le juge d'instruction doit préparer la procédure soit par la fixation des faits qui se rapportent à la cause, soit par l'audition de la preuve de manière que l'affaire soit en état d'être terminée dans une seule et même audience du tribunal.

### CHAPITRE PREMIER.—FIXATION DES FAITS.

ART 98. Le juge d'instruction indique avant tout au défendeur un jour dans lequel ou jusqu'auquel il devra:

*a.* Présenter toute demande incidente;

*b.* Déclarer d'une manière formelle et complète s'il admet ou s'il n'admet pas la demande principale ou incidente du demandeur, s'il reconnaît ou s'il ne reconnaît pas les faits avancés par ce dernier (art. 89, *b.*);

*c.* Présenter tous ses moyens de défense et les raisons de fait à l'appui;

*d.* Indiquer d'une manière détaillée et précise les preuves à l'appui de ses moyens;

*e.* Former s'il y a lieu une demande reconventionnelle.

ART. 99. L'expiration du jour fixe ou du délai entraîne les conséquences suivantes:

*a.* En cas de retard dans la présentation d'une demande incidente ou dans l'énonciation d'un moyen de défense, le défendeur peut être condamné au paiement des frais occasionnés et à une amende disciplinaire;

*b.* Les assertions de fait avancées par le demandeur et qui n'ont pas été contestées pendant le délai ou au jour fixe, sont considérées comme reconnues;

*c.* Les preuves qui n'ont pas été indiqués par les parties ou qui ne l'ont été que d'une manière confuse, doivent être exclues, sous réserve des dispositions contenues aux art. 164 et 165;

*d.* Aucune demande reconventionnelle ne peut être formée après l'expiration du délai ou du jour fixe.

ART. 100. Le demandeur est tenu de se prononcer, au jour fixe ou dans un délai qui lui sera fixé, sur les faits qui servent de base à la réponse du défendeur; toutes les assertions qu'il n'aura pas contestées formellement, et chacune spécialement, doivent être considérées comme reconnues.

ART. 101. Lorsque le demandeur cherche par une réplique à affaiblir un moyen présenté par le défendeur, mais sans dénier le moyen lui-même, le défendeur pourra s'expliquer de la même manière que le demandeur l'a fait à son égard sur les faits qui servent de base á la réplique.

Les dispositions applicables à l'énonciation des moyens aux répliques, etc., sont respectivement applicables aux dupliques, etc.

Les moyens de preuve à l'appui des répliques, dupliques etc., doivent être présentés en même temps, comme pour la demande et la réponse (art. 89 *e*, 98 *d*, 99 *c*).

ART. 102. La demande reconventionnelle est dans la règle traitée dans une procédure spéciale, de la même manière que la demande principale.

Les discussions orales devant le juge d'instruction et qui sont relatives soit à la demande principale, soit à la demande reconventionnelle, doivent, autant que possible avoir lieu le même jour.

Dans des causes tout à fait simples on peut admettre une seule et même procédure.

## CHAPITRE II.—PROCÉDURE PROBATOIRE.

ART. 103. Dès que la distinction est établie entre les faits admis et les faits non admis, le juge applique à ces derniers la procédure probatoire.

ART. 104. Est regardé comme reconnu tout fait qui dans le cours du procès est affirmé par l'une des parties et n'a pas été contesté formellement par l'autre.

Les restrictions et additions faites par une partie à son aveu, ne doivent point en être séparées, sauf dans le cas où elles ont le sens d'un moyen de défense.

### I.—*Moyen de preuve.*

#### A.—L'aveu.

ART. 105. Un aveu constant, quoique extrajudiciaire a les mêmes effets que s'il avait eu lieu par déclaration devant le tribunal, lorsqu'il a été fait en termes formels en vue de la partie adverse ou de son mandataire, et dans le but de mettre un certain fait hors de doute.

Si l'un de ces caractères manque, le tribunal apprécie librement la déclaration extrajudiciaire.

#### B.—Documents.

ART. 106. Les documents faits dans la forme légale par un fonctionnaire jouissant de la confiance publique, dans les affaires de son ressort et dans les limites de ses pouvoirs, font preuve complète contre chacun.

ART. 107. Les documents émanant de particuliers font preuve complète contre leur auteur.

Les tiers dont les droits sont subordonnés aux actes de l'auteur ou qui en sont responsables de toute autre manière, sont liés par sa signature, à moins qu'on puisse démontrer comme probable qu'il y a eu entente frauduleuse, au préjudice du tiers, entre l'auteur et celui en faveur de qui le document est fait.

ART. 108. Dans la règle, le document qui est aux mains de son propre auteur, ne prouve rien en faveur de celui-ci.

Par exception à cette disposition, le juge apprécie librement la force probatoire de livres tenus régulièrement.

ART. 109. Les documents émanant de tiers méritent d'autant plus de confiance que les auteurs sont plus irréprochables et impartiaux, et qu'ils se sont trouvés en état de connaitre les faits dont il est question.

Cependant les déclarations par écrit, faites pour le procès par des particuliers qui auraient pu être entendus oralement, ne doivent pas être prises en considération.

ART. 110. L'original même des documents doit être présenté au juge.

Sont admis comme l'original:

*a.* La copie reconnue par les parties;

*b.* L'extrait de livres ou registres publics certifié par le fonctionnaire compétent.

ART. 111. La partie qui fait la preuve, et qui ne peut, par une cause indépendante de sa volonté, présenter le document lui-même, est admise à le remplacer par une copie dûment vidimée pourvu que l'authenticité de la signature ne soit pas contestée ou qu'elle soit spécialement démontrée.

ART. 112. Tout document doit être présenté au complet; on doit y joindre tous les autres documents sur lesquels le premier s'appuie.

ART. 113. L'authenticité d'un document public (art. 106) est établie en cas de contestation, par le témoignage de l'autorité compétente.

ART. 114. Est présumée l'authenticité d'un document particulier qui se trouve depuis dix ans au moins dans des archives publiques, ou dont la date et le caractère spécial indique qu'il existe vraisemblablement depuis plus de quarante ans.

Les copies vidimées établissent, sous la même supposition, la présomption d'existence antérieure d'un document identique; les copies non vidimées peuvent dans les mêmes suppositions, former tout au moins un indice.

ART. 115. L'authenticité de la signature d'un document particulier motive la présomption juridique de l'authenticité de ce qui précède la signature et la date.

Cependant si des modifications ont été apportées à ces dernières parties du document, et que la partie adverse de celui qui fait la preuve ne veuille pas les reconnaître, on doit prendre en considération le texte primitif, et si celui-ci ne peut plus être établi d'une manière certaine, le document perd sa force probatoire.

ART. 116. L'authenticité d'un document contesté est établie :

1. Par la preuve de la reconnaissance extrajudiciaire par la partie adverse ;
2. Par la déposition de témoins qui ont assisté à la signature du document ;
3. S'il s'agit de documents émanant d'un tiers, par la reconnaissance même de ce tiers ;
4. Par la comparaison des écritures.

ART. 117. S'il manque d'écritures pour la comparaison, la personne qui a écrit la document contesté, sera tenue, sous la menace des peines encourues, à écrire quelques lignes qui lui seront dictées en présence du juge ou d'experts.

ART. 118. Chaque partie doit, lorsqu'elle en est requise par son adversaire, présenter les documents qui se rapportent au procès ou attester par serment qu'elle ne les possède pas réellement, qu'elle n'en a pas transmis la possession à autrui, intentionellement et au préjudice de le partie adverse, et qu'elle ignore où ils se trouvent dans le moment.

ART. 119. Les tiers sont tenus, sous peine d'être traités comme des témoins défaillants (art. 134) de prêter le serment ci-dessus, ou de déposer les documents qui sont entre leurs mains ou d'indiquer le lieu où ils se trouvent.

Cette obligation est soumise aux mêmes restrictions que l'obligation de déposer comme témoin (art. 133 et 136).

La partie qui s'appuie sur un document doit en indemniser le possesseur sous tous les rapports et avancer provisoirement les frais de procédure qui pourraient être nécessaires.

Les passages d'un tel document qui, d'après l'attestation par serment du possesseur, ou d'après l'opinion même du juge, ne se rapportent pas au procès, ne doivent pas être anéantis, mais peuvent être passés sous silence.

ART. 120. Les dispositions relatives aux documents écrits sont aussi applicables, autant que la nature des choses le permet, aux monuments d'un autre genre (bornes de frontière, pierres et médailles commémoratives, etc.).

## C.—Des descentes sur les lieux et expertises.

ART. 121. Le juge peut d'office, ou sur la demande de l'une des parties, se transporter dans l'endroit où se trouvent des objets dont il serait important pour le procès de connaître la nature par la vue même, et dont le transport serait difficile.

ART. 122. Il est dressé un procès-verbal détaillé de cette descente sur les lieux et de tout ce qui s'y rattache (art. 81) et pour plus grande clarté il y est joint, si cela est nécessaire, des dessins et des modèles.

ART. 123. Le juge peut, d'office ou sur la demande de l'une des parties, appeler des experts lorsqu'il s'agit d'une descente sur les lieux ou de tous autres faits dont le jugement ou l'appréciation exigent des connaisances spéciales. Les experts sont nommés dans la règle au nombre de trois, à moins que les parties ne s'accordent sur un nombre inférieur.

ART. 124. Le juge nomme les experts. Nul ne doit être nommé s'il manque des connaissances nécessaires ou s'il peut être récusé comme juge. (Organization judiciaire féd. art. 56 et 57.)

ART. 125. Nul n'est tenu d'accepter les fonctions d'expert, mais celui qui s'en est une fois chargé, peut être forcé par des amendes disciplinaires successives et de plus en plus élevées, à les remplir dûment.

ART. 126. Le mandat des experts leur est conféré par écrit et d'une manière précise. Lorsque les experts ne sont pas déjà assermentés, en raison même de leur vocation, il peut être exigé d'eux, sur la demande d'une des parties, le serment "de remplir consciencieusement le mandat qui leur est confié et de n'agir ni par haine, ni par faveur pour personne."

ART. 127. Les experts donnent leur préavis avec leur motifs, soit par écrit pour les actes du procès, soit de vive voix, pour être inséré au procès-verbal.

Le tribunal apprécie librement ce préavis.

ART. 128. Si le tribunal ne trouve point dans le rapport les éclaircissements suffisants, il peut ordonner qu'il soit complété par les mêmes experts, ou en nommer de nouveaux.

## D.—Témoins.

ART. 129. Il n'y a pas lieu à entendre des témoins sur des faits sans importance.

ART. 130. La preuve testimoniale n'est pas admise contre le texte formel d'un document fait par les intéressés, pour une affaire juridique.

Il peut être fait exception à cette règle :

*a.* Pour démontrer l'incapacité d'agir, l'absence de consentement, la fraude, et la violence ;

*b*. Pour remplacer un document fait postérieurement pour la même affaire et qui a été perdu;

*c*. Pour compléter des documents postérieurs qui indiquent que le document primitif a été modifié.

ART. 131. Le juge apprécie librement les dépositions des témoins et le degré de confiance qu'elles méritent.

ART. 132. Sont incapables de déposer comme témoins et doivent, en conséquence, être exclus d'office :

1. Les personnes en état d'imbécilité ou d'aliénation mentale ;
2. Les personnes dépourvues des organes nécessaires à l'appréciation des faits en question ou à leur communication ;
3. Les enfants qui n'ont pas atteint l'âge de 14 ans.

Doivent être exclus sur la demande de la partie adverse :

1. Les plus proches parents de son adversaire, à savoir : les ascendants, les descendants, et leurs conjoints ; les frères et sœurs, beaux-frères et belles-sœurs ;
2. Les personnes condamnées pour crime.

ART. 133. Les ecclésiastiques, les médecins, et les avocats, procureurs ou avoués, ne doivent pas être entendus sur des secrets qui leur ont été confiés en raison de leur fonction ou de leur vocation.

ART. 134. Le témoin qui, sans excuse, n'obtempère pas à l'assignation qui lui est faite, doit être condamné au paiement d'une amende disciplinaire et au remboursement des frais causés par son absence. En outre une nouvelle citation peut être lancée contre lui.

ART. 135. Celui qui se refuse sans motif légal, à déposer ou à prêter serment comme témoin, doit indemniser la partie qui fait la preuve pour le dommage que ce refus lui cause. Pour calculer le montant de ce dommage, le tribunal partira de la présomption que le témoignage refusé, aurait été en faveur de celui qui fait la preuve.

ART. 136. Ne sont pas obligés de déposer contre une partie et sont, par conséquent, exceptés des dispositions des articles 134 et 135 :

1. Les plus proches parents de cette partie, à savoir : les ascendants, les descendants et leurs conjoints ; les frères et sœurs, beaux-frères et belles-sœurs ;
2. Les personnes qui compromettraient leur honneur ou leurs droits par leurs propres dépositions.

ART. 137. Chaque témoin reçoit d'avance, sur sa demande, l'indemnité à laquelle il a droit.

ART. 138. Pour l'audition des témoins qui demeurent à l'étranger, une demande est faite au tribunal étranger compétent.

Tous les autres témoins sont entendus soit par le juge d'instruction lui-même, soit sur l'ordonnance de ce magistrat, par le tribunal compétent (celui du domicile du témoin).

ART. 139. L'audition a lieu en général dans le lieu où se fait la procédure préparatoire ou au siége du tribunal requis.

Les témoins qui pour des motifs graves sont empêchés de comparaître devant le juge, peuvent être entendus dans leur demeure.

Le même mode est aussi autorisé lorsqu'il est plus avantageux pour l'intelligence des dépositions que les témoins soient interrogés dans le lieu auquel ont trait leurs dépositions.

ART. 140. Toutes facilités doivent être accordées aux parties, lorsque cela est possible, pour assister à l'audition des témoins.

Les parties ont le droit d'indiquer d'avance les points sur lesquels elles désirent obtenir des explications des témoins, ainsi que de leur faire adresser des questions subséquentes ; le juge décide si ces dernières sont admissibles ou non.

ART. 141. Le juge avertit les témoins par lecture de la formule du serment, qu'ils ont à affirmer leur dire par serment, puis il procède à leur audition pour chacun séparément et en l'absence des autres. Nul, sauf le juge ou respectivement le président du tribunal, ne peut adresser directement des questions aux témoins.

ART. 142. Les dépositions des témoins sont consignées au procès-verbal dans leur teneur substantielle, lues en leur présence et signées par eux. (Art. 81 et suiv.)

ART. 143. Les témoins prêtent, sur la demande d'une des parties, le serment suivant, une fois l'interrogatoire terminé :

"J'ai répondu selon la vérité aux questions qui m'ont été posées, et je n'ai rien caché de ce qui m'était connu. Je le jure devant Dieu qui sait tout, aussi vrai que je souhaite que sa grâce me soit en aide."

Lorsque d'après la religion du témoin, l'efficacité du serment est subordonnée à certaines formes extérieures, ces formes doivent être observées.

ART. 144. Pour les personnes qui appartiennent à une secte religieuse d'après les croyances de laquelle le serment est défendu, il sera remplacé par une confirmation solennelle équivalente au serment d'après ces mêmes croyances.

ART. 145. Les employés publics peuvent donner par écrit leurs dépositions, lorsqu'elles se basent sur leurs procès-verbaux ou actes ; ils ne sont pas appelés à les attester par serment.

### E.—Du serment déféré.

ART. 146. Celui qui fait la preuve peut, lorsqu'il s'agit de faits importants qui sont contestés, déférer le serment à son adversaire, s'il n'a pas d'autre moyen de preuve. Néanmoins l'inculpation d'un crime ou d'un délit ne peut jamais être l'objet d'un serment. Le serment ne peut non plus être déféré à une personne atteinte de folie, ou faible d'esprit, ou muette, ou qui n'a pas encore accompli sa seizième année.

ART. 147. Celui qui fait la preuve ne peut déférer le serment à une tierce-personne, mais seulement à sa partie adverse et celle-ci doit prêter le serment elle-même.

Cependant cette règle subit les exceptions suivantes :

1. Celui qui fait la preuve peut, à son gré, déférer le serment au tuteur ou au pupille, pourvu que celui-ci ait la capacité requise pour prêter serment ;
2. Quand il s'agit de corporations, celui qui fait la preuve désigne deux chefs de la corporation pour prêter serment ;
3. Lorsque plusieurs individus se trouvent impliqués dans la même affaire, chacun d'eux prête serment (art. 7). Cependant le même serment d'un seul suffit dans le cas où par sa position il oblige les autres.

ART. 148. La partie à qui le serment est déféré, peut, ou le prêter ou le référer à son adversaire ou entreprendre elle-même la preuve contraire.

Si elle ne fait ni l'un ni l'autre, le fait avancé par son adversaire est considéré comme établi.

ART. 149. La partie qui doit prêter un serment (soit déféré soit référé) est entendue et assermentée de la même manière que les témoins (art. 138–144). Elle ne peut mettre en avant aucun prétexte d'ignorance pour ce qui se rapporte à ses propres actions, et si elle prétexte d'ignorance pour d'autres faits, elle doit en outre jurer qu'elle s'est appliquée à rechercher la verité et qu'elle n'a pas connaissance d'autres faits que ceux qu'elle a indiqués.

ART. 150. Les faits sur lesquels, contrairement aux dispositions de l'article précédent la partie assermentée s'est prononcée d'une manière obscure ou détournée, doivent être considérés comme avérés. Dans tous les autres cas, la déposition faite sous serment doit être admise en droit comme vraie et la preuve contraire est interdite.

### F.—De la preuve complexe.

ART. 151. La preuve, faite seulement par des indices, est appréciée librement par le juge, toutefois dans les limites des présomptions établies par la loi.

ART. 152. Chaque indice doit être établi d'après les mêmes règles que les faits sur lesquels la demande ou la défense se base directement.

### G.—Du serment supplétoire et du serment purgatoire.

ART. 153. Lorsqu'un fait important et contesté ne peut être établi d'une manière convaincant ni par témoins, ni par documents, ni par indices, mais qu'il a acquis pour le tribunal un certain degré de vraisemblance, le tribunal lui-même, mais non pas le juge d'instruction, peut, soit d'office, soit sur requête de l'une des parties, déférer le serment à celui qui fait preuve ou à son adversaire dans le but de suppléer ou d'infirmer la preuve commencée.

ART. 154. Le serment est prêté de la même manière que le serment déféré (art. 148).

### H.—Dispositions générales.

ART. 155. Les deux parties peuvent également utiliser tout moyen de preuve qui n'a pas été seulement indiqué, mais réellement développé dans les actes.

ART. 156. Lorsqu'un moyen de preuve périt par la faute de la partie adverse, la preuve offerte est considérée comme ayant été faite. Sont réservées les pénalités que les faits pourraient entraîner.

## II.—*Procédure probatoire.*

### A.—Introduction de la preuve.

ART. 157. Le juge fixe, avant tout, un jour auquel ou jusqu'auquel les parties ont à présenter tous les moyens de preuve à l'appui de leurs propres assertions ou pour combattre le dire de leur adversaire.

Toute négligence sous ce rapport entraînera l'exclusion des moyens de preuves apportés ou énoncés trop tard.

ART. 158. Celui qui fait la preuve remet au juge (art. 110 et 111) les pièces écrites qui sont en sa possession ; quant aux documents qui se trouvent entre les mains de la partie adverse ou d'un tiers, il les désigne d'une manière aussi précise que possible et demande au judge d'en ordonner la production.

Le juge obtempère immédiatement à cette demande en se référant aux art. 118 et 119 et en indiquant les conséquences du refus.

ART. 159. La preuve par témoins commence par la dénomination précise des témoins et par l'indication des faits qui doivent être établis.

ART. 160. Celui qui demande une descente sur les lieux ou la nomination d'experts, doit se référer à ce moyen de preuve et en indiquer l'objet et le but.

ART. 161. Celui qui veut déférer le serment à son adversaire, désigne les faits qui doivent être établis par serment ainsi que les personnes qui doivent prêter le serment (art. 147).

B.—Débat préalable.

ART. 162. Après l'expiration des délais fixés pour l'introduction de la preuve, le juge cite les parties, sous les peines mentionnées aux art. 62 et 166 à comparaître par devant lui à un jour fixe pour ouvrir le débat sur les moyens de preuve produits ou seulement annoncés.

Lorsqu'il n'a pas été fixé de délai, mais bien un jour fixe pour l'introduction de la preuve (art. 50 et 51), le débat sur les moyens de preuve produits ou seulement annoncés peut, selon les circonstances, avoir lieu le jour même ou être renvoyé à un autre jour fixe.

Les tiers qui nient la possession d'une pièce qui leur est demandée ou qui refusent de s'en dessaisir (art. 119) doivent aussi être cités à cette audience sur la demande de la partie intéressée.

ART. 163. Au jour fixe chaque partie doit se prononcer sur l'authenticité des documents produits par son adversaire ; ce dernier est libre de commencer aussitôt la preuve sur les points contestés (art. 113–116) ou de se faire fixer un délai pour cela.

ART. 164. Les parties doivent aussi s'expliquer contradictoirement au jour fixe sur les points sur lesquels elles sont en désaccord quant à l'importance des faits pour lesquels la preuve est demandée ou quant à l'admissibilité des moyens de preuve indiqués.

Quant à la personne des témoins, il faut produire non-seulement les motifs de leur incapacité, mais encore énoncer toutes les circonstances qui peuvent infirmer la confiance en leur témoignage et si cela est nécessaire, en fournir immédiatement la preuve ou du moins demander un délai pour la faire.

Celui qui fait la preuve peut renoncer aux témoins reprochés et les remplacer par d'autres, s'il prouve qu'il a été dans l'impossibilité de les désigner plus tôt.

ART. 165. En général, celui qui a perdu un moyen de preuve déjà invoqué, peut encore, à ce moment de la procédure, le remplacer par un autre et faire valoir avant la fin de la procédure préparatoire, les moyens de preuve que, d'après son assertion confirmée par serment, il n'a découverts qu'après l'expiration du temps fixé pour l'introduction de la preuve.

ART. 166. Celui qui ne signale pas en temps opportun, conformément à l'article précédent, les vices de forme de la preuve produite ou offerte par son adversaire, ne peut plus faire état plus tard des dits vices.

C.—Admissiou de la preuve.

ART. 167. Les juge désigne, en indiquant ses motifs, les moyens de preuve qu'il estime admissibles, ainsi que ceux qu'il croit devoir repousser.

Les moyens de preuve admis sont immédiatement consignés au procès-verbal d'après les prescriptions des articles 106–150.

Cependant le serment ne peut être prêté par une partie pendant la procédure préparatoire que dans le cas où il n'y a de contestation, ni sur légitimité de ce moyen de preuve en soi, ni sur la personne de celui à qui le serment est déféré.

D.—Preuve à futur.

ART. 168. Le juge d'instruction peut, sur la demande de l'une des parties, faire appeler des témoins ou des experts à tout instant de la procédure ou ordonner une vue de lieux pour prévenir la perte d'un moyen de preuve. Il ne doit pas y avoir de délibération intermédiaire sur l'admissibilité de la preuve, ni sur les moyens de preuve invoqués. En revanche, sont réservées les exceptions que celui qui fait la preuve pourrait présenter pour la procédure préparatoire ordinaire. On devra du reste suivre, autant que possible, dans l'admission de la preuve, les prescriptions contenues dans les articles qui précèdent.

ART. 169. Celui qui veut faire une preuve à futur dans un procès qui n'est pas encore pendant, ou pour lequel un juge d'instruction n'a pas encore été désigné, doit présenter une demande à cet effet à l'autorité judiciaire compétente du canton.

CHAPITRE III.—FIN DE LA PROCÉDURE PRÉPARATOIRE.

ART. 170. Le juge doit déclarer la procédure préparatoire close aussitôt que le but de cette procédure est atteint et transmettre tous les procès-verbaux et actes au président du tribunal.

ART. 171. Le Tribunal fédéral statue sur les réclamations relatives aux mesures prises par le juge d'instruction. Ces réclamations n'ont pas d'effet suspensif et doivent, dans la règle, être présentées et traitées seulement au commencement de la procédure finale (art. 172 et suiv.).

## TITRE III.—PROCÉDURE PRINCIPALE.

ART. 172. Les procès-verbaux et les actes dressés par le juge d'instruction servent de base pour la procédure principale.

ART. 173. Une partie est fondée à réclamer le complément ou la rectification de ces actes;

1. Par de nouveaux moyens de preuve, si elle atteste par serment qu'elle ne les a découverts qu'après la clôture de la procédure préparatoire (art. 165);
2. Par des moyens de preuve dont le juge d'instruction a rejeté l'admission sans motifs suffisants ;
3. Par la rectification de fautes commises par le juge d'instruction dans l'admission de la preuve;
4. Par l'annulation de preuves inadmissibles au point de vue de la forme et que le juge d'instruction avait fait insérer au procès-verbal malgré une opposition fondée ;
5. Par l'annulation d'ordonnances qui auraient été rendues dans la procédure préparatoire au préjudice de la partie intéressée et sans motifs suffisants.

ART. 174. Une requête de cette nature doit être présentée au président du Tribunal fédéral dans la quinzaine à dater du jour où la procédure a été déclarée close, et aussitôt que possible, s'il s'agit de présenter des moyens de preuve découverts postérieurement (art. 173, chiffre 1). Les moyens de preuve dont il s'agit dans ce cas, doivent être joints à la requête, ou si cela n'est pas possible, tout au moins indiqués (arts. 158, 160).

ART. 175. Le président du tribunal communique la requête à la partie adverse, et lui fixe un délai pour faire la preuve contraire, s'il y a lieu.

ART. 176. Lorsque la réclamation d'une partie porte sur le procès-verbal de descente sur les lieux ou sur ce qu'il n'y a pas eu de descente sur les lieux, le président du tribunal peut déléguer un ou deux autres juges pour opérer une descente sur les lieux (art. 121 et suivants) ou bien, selon les circonstances, ordonner que le débat final ait lieu sur place, (art. 18, *b*, de la loi sur l'organisation judiciaire fédérale).

ART. 177. Il doit être fait droit, à moins d'obstacles tout particuliers, à toute requête tendant à ce que le président du tribunal nomme des experts et les fasse paraître dans la procédure finale, ou à ce qu'il cite des témoins qui n'auraient pas été entendus ou qui ne l'auraient été que d'une manière défectueuse.

Les témoins qui, pour un motif quelconque, ne peuvent se présenter devant le Tribunal fédéral, doivent être interrogés par le tribunal du lieu de leur domicile; cet interrogatoire est ordonné provisoirement par le président du Tribunal fédéral.

ART. 178. Les demandes et requêtes tendant à faire compléter ou rectifier la procédure préparatoire, ainsi que les contestations sur la prestation d'un serment déféré ou référé (art. 162) doivent être éclaircies avant tout dans la procédure finale et vidées par un jugement motivé, les deux parties entendues.

ART. 179. Les preuves apportées subséquemment et que le tribunal déclare admissibles, sont produites de suite, si cela est possible. Dans le cas d'une déclaration contraire, les témoins ou les experts cités, doivent être immédiatement renvoyés.

ART. 180. Il est ensuite procédé à la discussion juridique de l'affaire litigieuse, dans toute son étendue.

Dans ce but la parole est accordée deux fois à chacune des parties.

ART. 181. La délibération ainsi que la votation du tribunal est publique.

ART. 182. Le président invite à leur tour les membres du tribunal à présenter leur opinion. Le président parle le dernier.

Une fois cette préconsultation terminée, chaque membre peut demander librement la parole.

Le vote a lieu à mains levées; si les voix sont égales, le président départage.

ART. 183. Il est voté séparément sur chaque point litigieux.

Les questions doivent être posées de telle sorte que la première présentée soit toujours celle par laquelle la suivante est éliminée ou préparée. La question principale doit aussi être jugée avant les points accessoires.

ART. 184. L'arrêt doit être rendu sous une forme conditionnelle, si l'issue du procès dépend de la prestation du serment supplétoire ou purgatoire; l'arrêt doit déterminer dans ce cas, quelle sera la conséquence de la prestation ou de la non-prestation du serment, tant à l'égard des points principaux qu'à l'égard des points accessoires.

Après la prestation du serment ou le refus de le prêter, le tribunal lui-même ou le juge commis pour recevoir le serment, attestera qu'il a été ou qu'il n'a pas été prêté, et prononcera sous une forme absolue le jugement qui n'était que conditionnel.

ART. 185. L'expédition du jugement doit contenir:

1. La désignation du tribunal, des juges présents ainsi que des parties

2. Les points de fait les plus essentiels, et les demandes des parties d'une manière sommaire ;
3. Les motifs de l'arrêt ;
4. L'arrêt lui-même ;
5. La signature du président et du greffier avec l'indication du lieu et du temps où l'arrêt a été rendu et l'apposition du sceau du tribunal ;

ART. 186. Le jugement est prononcé oralement ; une expédition écrite en est remise aux parties ;

Le jugement acquiert forces de chose jugée dès le moment où il a été prononcé ;

## TITRE IV.—DE L'EXÉCUTION.

ART. 187. Le débiteur est poursuivi conformément aux lois du canton dans lequel il habite, lorsque le jugement le condamne à payer une certaine somme ou à fournir une caution. Si le débiteur s'est réfugié à l'étranger, s'il est absent ou inconnu, son patrimoine devra être immédiatement saisi par le juge du lieu, sur la demande de la partie intéressée, et vendu à l'enchère jusqu' à concurrence de la somme réclamée. La saisie devra aussi avoir lieu lorsque le débiteur présent ne paie pas après poursuit ou dissimule l'existence de ce patrimoine.

ART. 188. La partie condamnée à livrer certains objets tels que de l'argent ou à faire certains actes aura un délai qui ne pourra excéder un mois pour exécuter le jugement ; ce délai lui sera fixé, sur la demande de la partie intéressée, par le gouvernement où elle a son domicile, ou par celui du lieu où se trouve l'objet litigieux.

ART. 189. La partie condamnée qui ne se soumettra pas à cette mesure, sera renvoyée devant le tribunal de son domicile pour être punie pour désobéissance et l'exécution du jugement aura lieu à ses frais par le gouvernement cantonal.

Si les objets à livrer n'existent plus ou si l'exécution du jugement ne peut plus avoir lieu pour d'autres motifs, le patrimoine de la partie condamnée sera saisi jusque'à concurrence de la somme nécessaire pour garantir les intérêts de la partie adverse; les actes seront remis à cette dernière pour qu'elle puisse demander au Tribunal fédéral de convertir en une somme d'argent la prestation ordonnée.

ART. 190. Aucune autorité ne doit entraver l'exécution ni prolonger un délai, si ce n'est pas ordre du Tribunal fédéral, ou de son président, ainsi qu'il est dit aux articles 196 et 198, ou bien lorsqu'il ressort évidemment d'une preuve écrite, que l'exécution a déjà eu lieu.

ART. 191. Les réclamations sur l'exécution défectueuse des jugements du Tribunal fédéral, sont adressées au Conseil fédéral qui prend les mesures nécessaires.

Le Conseil fédéral peut aussi surveiller d'office l'exécution de ces jugements.

## TITRE V.—A.—DE LA RÉVISION.

ART. 192. La révision d'un jugement civil rendu par le Tribunal fédéral est admissible dans les cas suivants :

1. En cas d'annulation. Il y a annulation :

*a.* Lorsque les prescriptions de la loi sur l'organisation judiciaire fédérale n'ont pas été suivies dans la composition du tribunal ;

*b.* Lorsque les dispositions des articles 2, 4 et 181 de la présente loi sur la procédure civile n'ont pas été observées ;

*c.* Lorsque le tribunal n'a pas apprécié ou n'a apprécié que d'une manière erronée des faits importants contenus dans les procès-verbaux ;

*d.* Lorsqu'il n'a pas été statué sur certains points de la demande ou de la reconvention.

2. Lorsque le réclamant trouve des moyens de preuves concluants dont la production lui avait été impossible dans la procédure précédente.

3. S'il est prouvé par la voie d'un procès pénal qu'un juge qui a pris part au jugement était corrompu, ou que la partie adverse de l'appelant, ou un individu agissant en sa faveur, a commis un crime ou délit pour obtenir le jugement en question.

ART. 193. La demande en révision doit être présentée devant le tribunal, sous peine de déchéance, dans un délai d'un mois à dater de la réception de l'expédition écrite du jugement pour les cas prévus à l'art. 192, chiffre 1, et pour les autres cas, dans un délai de trois mois à dater de la découverte du motif de révisions.

ART. 194. Après un délai de cinq ans, la révision d'un jugement ne peut plus être demandée que pour les cas prévus à l'article 192, chiffre 3.

Un débat oral a lieu sur l'admissibilité de la demande en révision devant le tribunal qui a rendu le jugement. Si la demande en révision est admise, le requérant á un délai de trois mois pour introduire sa demande en révision du précédent jugement et en restitution contre les suites du dit jugement.

ART. 196. La demande en révision ne suspend point l'exécution du jugement attaqué, à moins que le tribunal n'en ait ordonné autrement en admettant la révision.

### B.—De l'interprétation du jugement.

Art. 197. Le tribunal doit, sur la demande d'une partie, ordonner l'interprétation ou la rectification du jugement dont les dispositions seraient obscures, incomplètes, a deux sens ou contradictoires, ou qui contiendraient des fautes de redaction ou de calcul.

Art. 198. Une demande semblable doit être communiquée à la partie adverse et un délai lui est accordé pour répondre, a défaut de quoi elle sera considérée comme consentante.

Ensuite la tribunal statue, dans la règle, sur la base de cette communication de pièces.

En tout cas, il n'y a pas lieu à un débat oral.

Dans ces occasions, le président du tribunal peut, provisoirement, par écrit, suspendre l'exécution du jugement.

## Titre VI.—Mesures provisionnelles.

Art. 199. Les mesures provisionnelles ont pour but:

*a.* De protéger une possession menacée;

*b.* D'empêcher qu'il soit apporté des changements à l'objet litigeux;

*c.* Pour écarter un dommage difficile à réparer, qui menace le requérant.

Les mesures provisionnelles sont ordonnées par le juge d'instruction pendant la procédure préparatoire, ou par le Tribunal fédéral avant ou après la procédure préparatoire et lorsque le tribunal n'est pas réuni, par son président.

Art. 200. Les mesures provisionnelles n'ont pour but que de maintenir l'état des choses existant et ne doivent pas par conséquent aller au-delà de ce qu'exige strictement ce but.

Le requérant doit être tenu de fournir des sûretés pour le dommage qui pourrait résulter des mesures provisionnelles, pour celui contre qui elles doivent être prises.

Art. 201. Lorsqu'il n'y a pas péril en la demeure, les mesures provisionnelles ne doivent pas être ordonnées avant que celui contre qui elles sont dirigées ait pu se prononcer à leur égard.

Art. 202. Les mesures provisionnelles ne doivent pas avoir d'influence sur la decision du procès même et ne doivent pas modifier la position juridique des parties. Elles peuvent en tout état de cause être annulées ou modifiées s'il n'y a plus de danger, ou si les circonstances sont différentes.

Les mesures provisoires prises par le juge d'instruction ou par le président du tribunal, doivent être soumises à la première occasion à l'approbation du tribunal; cependant le tribunal ne sera pas réuni extraordinairement dans ce but.

Art. 203. Le Conseil fédéral est chargé de l'exécution de la présente loi.

### L'Assemblée fédérale suisse,

Vu le projet de loi présenté par le Conseil fédéral sur la procédure à suivre par devant le Tribunal fédéral pour les contestations de droit civil,

### Arrête:

Art. 1. Le projet est adopté, pour le moment, dans son entier comme loi provisoire;

Art. 2. Ce projet ne sera adopté définitivement qu'après avoir été soumis avant deux ans expirés à une discussion détaillée dans les deux Conseils.

Ainsi décrété par le Conseil national suisse.

Berne, le 20 novembre 1850.

*Le Président,*

Dr. KERN.

*Le Secrétaire,*

SCHIESS.

Ainsi décrété par le Conseil des États suisse.

Berne, le 22 novembre 1850.

*Le Président,*

J. RUTTIMANN.

*Le Secrétaire,*

N. von MOOS.

### Le Conseil fédéral suisse,

Vu le décret pris les 20 et 22 novembre 1850, par l'Assemblée fédérale concernant le projet de loi qui lui a été présenté, sur la procédure à suivre par devant le Tribunal fédéral pour les contestations de droit civil, décret conçu comme suit:

Art. 1. Le projet est adopté, pour le moment, dans son entier comme loi provisoire;

Art. 2. Ce projet ne sera adopté définitivement qu'après avoir été soumis avant deux ans expirés à une discussion détaillée dans les deux Conseils;

ARRÊTE :

La présente loi sur la procédure à suivre par devant le Tribunal fédéral pour les contestations de droit civil sera communiquée à tous les gouvernements cantonaux pour être publiée par le dépôt qui en sera fait dans les communes, et sera insérée dans la Feuille fédérale et dans le Recueil officiel des lois de la Confederation.

Berne, le 28 novembre 1850.

Au nom du Conseil fédéral suisse :

*Le Président de la Confédération,*

H. DRUEY.

*Le Chancelier de la Confédération,*

SCHIESS.

---

[Inclosure 4 n No 177.]

*Loi fédérale sur l'organisation judiciaire fédérale* (*du* 27 *juin* 1874).

L'ASSEMBLÉE FÉDÉRALE DE LA CONFÉDÉRATION SUISSE,

En exécution des articles 106 à 114 de la Constitution fédérale du 29 mai 1874 et en modification de la loi fédérale du 5 juin 1849, sur la matière ;

Vu le message du Conseil fédéral du 23 mai 1874,

ARRÊTE :

## I.—DISPOSITIONS GÉNÉRALES.

ART. 1er. Le Tribunal fédéral se compose de *neuf membres et d'autant de suppléants.*

ART. 2. Les membres et les suppléants du Tribunal fédéral sont nommés par l'Assemblée fédérale, qui aura égard à ce que les trois langues nationales y soient représentées (art. 107 de la Constitution fédérale).

ART. 3. Peut être nommé au Tribunal fédéral tout citoyen suisse éligible au Conseil national.

Les membres de l'Assemblée fédérale et du Conseil fédéral et les fonctionnaires nommés par ces autorités ne peuvent en même temps faire partie du Tribunal fédérale (art. 108 de la Constitution fédérale).

ART. 4. Les membres du Tribunal fédérale ne peuvent, pendant la durée de leurs fonctions, revêtir aucun autre emploi, soit au service de la Confédération, soit dans un Canton, ni suivre d'autre carrière ou exercer de profession, (art. 108 de la Constitution fédérale).

En conséquence ils ne peuvent remplir les fonctions de directeur ou de membre du conseil d'administration d'une société qui a pour but un bénéfice.

ART. 5. Les parents ou alliés en ligne ascendante ou descendante a l'infini, ou en ligne collatérale jusqu'au degré de cousin germain inclusivement, ainsi que les maris de sœurs, ne peuvent être ensemble membres ou suppléants du Tribunal fédéral.

Deux personnes qui se trouvent dans l'un des cas d'incompatibilité prévus dans le présent article ne peuvent non plus fonctionner ensemble près le tribunal fédéral ou l'une de ses sections, soit comme juge, soit comme greffier, soit comme juge d'instruction ou comme officier du ministère public.

Le fonctionnaire judiciaire qui, en contractant mariage, donne lieu à un cas d'incompatibilité avec un autre fonctionnaire judiciaire, se démet, par ce fait, de ses fonctions.

ART. 6. La durée des fonctions des membres et des suppléants du Tribunal fédéral est fixée à *six ans.*

La première nomination aura lieu immédiatement après l'entrée en vigueur de la présente loi et de l'arrêté fédéral prévu à l'art. 11.

Les membres qui font vacance dans l'intervalle des six ans sont remplacés à la première session de l'Assemblée fédérale pour le reste de la durée de leurs fonctions.

ART. 7. Le *Président* et le *Vice-Président* du Tribunal fédérale sont nommés par l'Assemblée féderale, pour deux ans, parmi les membres du corps.

Lorsque le Président et le Vice-Président sont empêchés de siéger, ils sont remplacés par le membre du Tribunal fédéral premier élu.

ART. 8. Le Tribunal fédéral nomme deux *greffiers,* dont l'un de la Suisse allemande et l'autre de la Suisse romande. Tous deux doivent savoir l'allemand et le français. L'un des deux au moois doit connaître la langue italienne, les nominations se font au scrutin secret, pour la durée de six ans.

Les greffiers tiennent le protocole du Tribunal fédéral et de ses sections. Le Tribunal fédéral désigne d'ailleurs à chacun des greffiers ses attributions. Lorsqu'un greffier est empêché de fonctionner, le Président lui désigne un remplaçant.

ART. 9. Dans les limites du crédit qui lui est assigné pour cela, le Tribunal fédéral nomme le personnel de chancellerie dont il a besoin et les huissiers nécessaires pour son service.

ART. 10. Pour procéder à une élection, ainsi que pour prendre toute décision dans les causes de droit civil et de droit public placées dans le compétence du Tribunal fédéral, la *présence de sept membres au moins* est nécessaire.

Pour toutes ces décisions, le nombre des membres, y compris le Président, doit être impair. Le President prend part à la délibération et à la votation.

ART. 11. Le *siége* du Tribunal fédéral et de sa chancellerie sera désigne par un arrêté fédéral special.

La ville qui aura été désignée pour le siége du Tribunal fournira gratuitement, en quelque temps que ce soit, meublera et entretiendra les locaux nécessaires pour les audiences du Tribunal fédéral et de ses sections, pour sa chancellerie et pour ses archives. Les dispositions qui auront été prises dans ce but seront soumises à l'approbation du Conseil fédéral.

ART. 12. Les membres du Tribunal fédéral et les greffiers sont tenus de demeurer au siége du Tribunal.

Les dispositions de la loi fédérale du 23 décembre 1851 (III. 33) sur les garanties politiques et de police (art. 1 et 6), concernant les rapports personnels des membres du Conseil fédéral et du chancelier, sont applicables aux membres du Tribunal fédéral et aux greffiers.

ART. 13. Les dispositions des art. 3 (alinéa 2), 4 et 12 ne sont pas applicables aux suppléants du Tribunal fédéral.

ART. 14. Les membres du Tribunal fédéral reçoivent un traitement de fr. 10,000, le Président un traitement de fr. 11,000 et les greffiers un traitement de fr. 6–8,000. Les suppléants et les autres fonctionnaires judiciaires recevront des jetons de présence dont le montant sera fixé par un arrêté spécial.

ART. 15. Pour autant que les affaires le permettent, le Tribunal fédéral peut une ou deux fois par an ordonner des *vacances*, pendant lesquelles tous ses membres, sauf le Président ou le Vice-Président, pourront quitter le siége du tribunal. La durée de ces vacances ne pourra cependant dépasser quatre semaines par année.

En outre, et lorsqu'il existe des motifs suffisants, le Tribunal fédéral peut accorder un *congé* à l'un de ses membres ou aux greffiers.

ART. 16. Il est *interdit* à un membre ou suppléant du Tribunal fédéral *de fonctionner comme juge:*

1° Dans toute cause où lui-même, sa femme, sa fiancée, ses parents ou alliés en ligne directe à l'infini et en ligne collatérale jusqu'au degré de cousin germain inclusivement, ou le mari de la sœur de sa femme, a un intérêt direct ou indirect;

2° Dans la cause d'une personne dont il est le tuteur ou curateur;

3° Dans les affaires où il a déjà procédé étant dans l'exercice d'autres fonctions, soit comme membre d'une autorité administrative ou judiciaire de la Confédération ou d'un Canton, soit comme fonctionnaire judiciaire, soit comme arbitre, soit comme fondé de pouvoir ou agent d'une parti, soit comme expert ou comme témoin;

4° Dans la cause d'une personne morale à laquelle il appartient, dans celle où son Canton d'origine ou sa commune apparaît comme partie au procès et dans les recours qui sont formés contre les autorités législatives ou contre le Gouvernement de son Canton.

Si un juge ou suppléant du Tribunal fédéral se trouve dans l'un des cas prévus par le présent article, il doit en avertir en temps utile le Président du Tribunal fédéral ou de la section compétente.

ART. 17. Tout juge ou suppléant du Tribunal fédéral *peut être recusé*, par les parties, ou *peut demander lui-même sa récusation:*

1° S'il se trouve avec l'une des parties dans un rapport qui donne naissance à une inimitié ou à une dépendance particulière;

2° S'il a exprimé, depuis que le procès est pendant devant le Tribunal fédéral, son opinion sur le cas soumis au Tribunal.

Les demandes en récusation, qu'elles soient presentées par un juge ou par les parties, doivent être remises en temps utile au Président du Tribunal fédéral ou à son remplaçant. Si la demande émane d'une des parties, le Président la communique au membre que cela concerne, ainsi qu'a la partie adverse, en les invitant á y répondre. Dans les cas contestés, le Tribunal prononce sur la demande en récusation.

ART. 18. Le Tribunal fédéral ne peut être récusé en corps.

Si, dans un cas spécial, le nombre des membres et des suppléants dont la récusation est proposée est tel qu'aucune opération valide ne puisse avoir lieu, le Président du Tribunal fédéral tirera au sort, parmi les Présidents des Tribunaux suprêmes des Cantons, le nombre nécessaire de *suppléants extraordinaires* pour prononcer sur la demande en récusation et même, le cas échéant sur l'affaire au fond.

ART. 19. Avant d'entrer en fonctions, les fonctionnaires judiciaires fédéraux doivent prêter serment de remplir fidèlement leur devoir.

Le Tribunal fédéral est assermenté par l'Assemblée fédérale; les membres et les suppléants qui ne sont pas présents à cette solennité prêtent serment à la première audience à laquelle ils assistent.

Les greffiers et leur substitut, les juges d'instruction et leurs greffiers sont assermentés par le Président du Tribunal fédéral ou par l'un des membres commis par lui à cet effet. Les officiers du ministère public fédéral prêtent serment entre les mains du Conseil fédéral.

Il est chaque fois dressé procès-verbal de l'assermentation.

Pour les fonctionnaires judiciaires auxquels leurs convictions défendent de prêter ce serment, une promesse solennelle peut en tenir lieu.

ART. 20. Les délibérations et les votations du Tribunal fédéral et de ses sections sont publiques.

Cette disposition n'est pas applicable aux délibérations des jurés et de la chambre d'accusation.

ART. 21. Les *Présidents* du Tribunal fédéral et de ses diverses sections reçoivent les pièces adressées à ces autorités et tiennent un protocole de leur entrée et des dispositions prises par eux.

ART. 22. Le Président organise les audiences du Tribunal suivant que les affaires l'exigent et prend dans ce but les mesures nécessaires. Il dirige les débats et veille au maintien de la tranquillité et de l'ordre. Il peut faire sortir de la salle des séances et, au besoin, faire détenir pendant 24 heures au plus les personnes qui résistent à ses ordres.

ART. 23. Le Président surveille dans l'accomplissement de leur devoir les juges d'instruction, les greffiers et les employés inférieurs.

ART. 24. Chaque année le Tribunal fédéral adresse à l'assemblée fédérale un *rapport* circonstancié sur toutes les branches de l'administration de la justice fédérale.

ART. 25. Les autorités et les fonctionnaires établis pour l'administration de la justice fédérale accomplissent tous les actes de leur compétence dans toute l'étendue de la Confédération, sans avoir besoin du consentement préalable des autorités du Canton où ils procèdent.

Les autorités cantonales doivent, chacune dans leur ressort, faire droit aux réquisitions que les fonctionnaires judiciaires fédéraux leur adressent dans l'intérêt de l'administration de la justice.

ART. 26. Le Conseil fédéral fait les *avances* necessaires à la caisse du Tribunal. La chancellerie du Tribunal tient un compte exact des recettes et des dépenses.

## II.—ADMINISTRATION DE LA JUSTICE CIVILE.

ART. 27. Le Tribunal fédéral connait de différends de droit civil:

1° entre la *Confédération* et un ou plusieurs *Cantons;*

2° entre des *corporations* ou des *particuliers* comme demandeurs et la *Confédération* comme défenderesse, pour autant que le litige atteint une valeur en capital de 3,000 francs au moins;

3° entre *Cantons;*

4° entre des *Cantons* d'une part et des *corporations* ou des *particuliers* d'autre part, quand le litige atteint une valeur en capital de 3,000 francs au moins, et que l'une des parties le requiert.

Il connait de plus des différends concernant le *heimathlosat*, d'après la loi du 3 décembre 1850 (II. 130), ainsi que des contestations qui surgissent entre communes de différents Cantons, touchant le *droit de cité* (art. 110 de la Constitution fédérale).

ART. 28. Le Tribunal fédéral connait en outre de toutes les causes que la législation fédérale place dans la compétence du Tribunal fédéral par des lois spéciales (art. 114 de la Constitution fédérale).

Le Tribunal fédéral connnaît notamment, en vertu des lois fédérales existantes:

*a.* Des contestations en matière d'*expropriations* pour la construction des chemins de fer ou d'autres travaux d'utilité publique, auxquels l'Assemblée fédérale déclare que la loi fédérale du 1er mai 1850 (I. 319) est applicable, et d'après les dispositions de cette loi, ainsi que de celle du 18 juillet 1857;

*b.* Des *divorces* de *mariages mixtes,* en application de la loi fédérale du 3 février 1862 (VII. 129);

*c.* De toutes les contestations de droit privé entre la *Confédération* et une *Compagnie de chemins de fer,* en exécution de l'article 39 de la loi fédérale du 23 décembre 1872 (XI. 1) sur les chemins de fer, et spécialement des actions en dommages et intérêts prévues aux articles 14, 19, 24 et 33 de la dite loi;

*d.* Des actions en dommages et intérêts des *administrations de chemins de fer* contre des *particuliers,* dans les cas prévus à l'art. 15, alinéa 2, de la dite loi;

*e.* Des actions en dommages et intérêts des *administrations de chemins de fer entre elles,* dans les cas prévus à l'art. 30, alinéa 3, de la dite loi;

*f.* De toutes les contestations qui surgissent à l'occasion de la *liquidation forcée de Compagnies de chemins de fer,* en exécution de la loi fédérale du 24 juin 1874 sur la matière.

ART. 29. Dans les causes où il s'agira de l'application des lois fédérales par les tribunaux cantonaux, et lorsque l'object du litige sera d'une valeur d'au moins fr. 3000, ou non susceptible d'estimation, chaque partie a le droit de recourir au Tribunal fédéral pour obtenir la réforme du jugement au fond rendu par la dernière instance judiciaire cantonale.

La valeur en capital est déterminée par la somme en litige devant la dernière instance cantonale.

Les parties peuvent convenir que dans ces causes le jugement au fond d'une première instance cantonale sera soumis directement au Tribunal fédéral sans recourir à la seconde instance cantonale.

ART. 30. Pour ce recours, il est accordé un délai péremptoire de 20 jours dès la communication du jugement contre lequel il est dirigé. La partie qui voudra en faire usage doit le déclarer dans le même délai au siége du tribunal cantonal qui a rendu le jugement dont est recours. Dans ce cas, le tribunal cantonal en question devra adresser au Président du Tribunal fédéral, dans un délai de 14 jours à partir de celui où cette déclaration est intervenue, le jugement et les actes des parties.

Après avoir reçu les actes, le Président du Tribunal fédéral fixe le jour où l'affaire sera portée devant le Tribunal fédéral et en informe les parties.

Les parties ont le droit de comparaître au jour fixé devant le Tribunal fédéral et de plaider leur cause oralement ou de la faire plaider par des fondés de pouvoirs.

Le Tribunal fédéral devra baser son jugement sur l'état des faits tel qu'il aura été établi par les tribunaux cantonaux. Cependant lorsque devant les instances cantonales la preuve de faits contestés de nature à exercer une influence prépondérante sur le jugement à rendre n'aurait pas été admise, le Tribunal fédéral pourra faire compléter les actes du dossier par l'instance qui a rendu ce jugement et statuer ensuite, definitivement, sans une nouvelle audition des parties.

ART. 31. Le Tribunal fédéral est tenu de juger, outre les causes prévues aux articles 27 à 29:

1° celles que la *Constitution* ou la *législation* d'un Canton placent d'avance dans la compétence du Tribunal fédéral. De pareilles dispositions ne sont valables que moyennant la ratification de l'Assemblée fédérale;

2° celles qui sont portés devant lui par *convention des parties* et dont l'objet atteint une valeur en capital de 3000 francs au moins (art. 111 de la Constitution fédérale).

## III.—ADMINISTRATION DE LA JUSTICE PÉNALE.

ART. 32. Le Tribunal assisté du Jury, lequel statue sur les faits, connaît en matière pénale:

1° des cas de *haute trahison* envers la Confédération, de *révolte* ou de *violence* contre les autorités fédérales;

2° des crimes et des délits contre le *droit des gens;*

3° des crimes et des délits politiques qui sont la cause ou la suite de troubles par lesquels une *intervention* fédérale armée est occasionée;

4° des faits relevés à la charge de *fonctionnaires* nommées par une autorité fédérale, quand cette autorité en saisit le Tribunal fédéral (art. 112 de la Constitution fédérale).

Les dispositions altérieures concernant la compétence des assises fédérales sont renfermées aux articles 73 à 77 du Code pénal fédéral du 4 février, 1853 (III. 335).

ART. 33. Le tribunal fédéral est obligé de statuer aussi sur d'autres cas que ceux mentionnés à l'art. 32, si la Constitution ou la législation d'un Canton les fait rentrer dans la compétence de ce Tribunal et si l'Assemblée fédérale y a consenti.

ART. 34. Pour l'administration de la justice pénale, le Tribunal fédéral se divise: en Chambre d'accusation, en Chambre criminelle et en Tribunal de cassation. Ces trois Chambres sont nommées au commencement de chaque année pour la durée d'un an.

Aucun juge ne peut connaître de la même affaire dans plus d'une section du Tribunal fédéral.

ART. 35. La *Chambre d'accusation* se compose de trois membres et d'un nombre égal de suppléants qui sont appellés à siéger en cas d'empêchement des premiers. Le membre premier élu est Président.

ART. 36. La Chambre d'accusation a sous sa direction et sa surveillance deux *juges d'instruction*, que le Tribunal fédéral nomme pour six ans. Ils désignent eux-mêmes leurs greffiers, sous réserve de la ratification de ces nominations par le Président de la Chambre d'accusation.

En cas d'empêchement des juges d'instruction ordinaires, le Tribunal fédéral ou, s'il n'est pas réuni, le Président peut nommer et appeler des juges d'instruction extraordinaires.

ART. 37. Le Conseil fédéral nomme dans chaque cas spécial le Procureur-général de la Confédération.

ART. 38. La *Chambre criminelle*, qui prend part à toutes les sessions des assises fédérales, se compose de trois membres et de trois suppléants pour les cas d'empêchement. Les trois langues nationales doivent être representées au sein de ce corps. Le Président de la Chambre criminelle est nommé par le Tribunal fédéral pour chaque session.

Lorsqu'un membre ou un suppléant de la Chambre criminelle est empêché par des circonstances imprévues d'assister à une session des assises, le Président de celles-ci peut nommer et appeler, pour le remplacer, un suppléant extraordinaire, qu'il choisit parmi les membres d'une autorité judiciaire cantonale.

ART. 39. Les assises fédérales se composent de la Chambre criminelle et de douze *jurés*, élus dans les cantons par le peuple et tirés au sort dans la liste de l'arrondissement.

ART. 40. Le territoire de la Confédération est divisé en cinq arrondissements d'assises.

Le premier comprend les cantons de Genève, de Vaud, de Fribourg (à l'exception des communes où prédomine la langue allemande), de Neuchâtel et les communes des cantons de Berne et du Valais, où la langue française est prédominante.

Le second comprend les Cantons de Berne (à l'exception des localités comprises dans le premier arrondissement), de Soleure, de Bâle, de Lucerne, ainsi que les communes des Cantons de Fribourg et du Valais, où l'on parle allemand.

Le troisième comprend les Cantons d'Argovie, de Zurich, de Schaffhouse, de Thurgovie, de Zoug, de Schwyz, et d'Unterwalden.

Le quatrième comprend les Cantons d'Uri, de Glaris, d'Appenzell, de Saint-Gall, et des Grisons (à l'exception des communes où la langue italienne prédomine).

Le cinquième comprend le Canton du Tessin et les communes italiennes du Canton des Grisons.

Seront nommés et portés sur la liste de l'arrondissement dans les quatre premiers arrondissements un juré sur 1,000 habitants, et, dans le cinquième arrondissement, un juré sur 500 habitants.

ART. 41. *Peut être nommé juré* tout Suisse ayant le droit de voter d'après l'art. 74 de la Constitution fédérale. Sont toutefois exceptes :

1° Les membres des autorités judiciaires cantonales supérieures, tous les présidents de tribunaux, juges d'instruction et officiers du ministère public, ainsi que tous les fonctionnaires fédéraux et cantonaux de l'ordre administratif, non compris les employés communaux ;

2° Les ecclésiastiques;

3° Les employés dans les maisons d'arrêt et de détention ;

4° Les employés de police.

ART. 42. Tout citoyen appelé aux fonctions de juré *est tenu d'accepter*. Sont exceptés :

1° Tous ceux qui ont atteint l'âge de 60 ans révolus ;

2° Ceux dont le nom a été porté sur la dernière liste des jurés ;

3° Ceux qui sont empêchés de remplir les fonctions de juré pour cause de maladie ou d'infirmité.

ART. 43. Les questions relatives à l'éligibilité aux fonctions de juré et à l'obligation de les accepter sont du ressort des *Gouvernements* cantonaux.

Ils transmettent les listes de jurés des Cantons au Tribunal fédéral, qui en forme les listes d'arrondissement et les publie (art. 40).

Les noms des jurés qui, pour une cause quelconque, ont perdu cette qualité, ou qui sont décédés, sont transmis par le Gouvernement cantonal au Tribunal fédéral pour qu'ils soient rayés de la liste.

ART. 44. Les listes de jurés sont *renouvelées* tous les six ans. Le Conseil fédéral pourvoit à ce que les nouvelles listes soient formées en temps utile.

ART. 45. Avant l'ouverture de chaque session des assises, la Chambre criminelle fait déposer, en séance publique, dans une urne, les noms des jurés de l'arrondissement dans lequel les débats devront avoir lieu; elle en fait ensuite tirer au sort cinquante-quatre noms, qui sont lus et enregistrés.

Des copies de la liste spéciale ainsi formée sont immédiatement communiquées au Procureur-Général désigné par le Conseil fédéral, ainsi qu'à l'accusé ou à son défenseur.

ART. 46. Chaque fois qu'une affaire est renvoyée aux assises, le Procureur-Général de la Confédération et l'accusé peuvent *recuser* chacun vingt jurés.

Si, dans la même affaire, il y a plusieurs accusés, ils peuvent exercer conjointement leurs récusations, ou faire usage de leur droit séparément. Dans l'un et l'autre cas, ils ne peuvent, pris ensemble, dépasser le nombre de récusations accordé à un accusé seul. Si les accusés ne se concertent pas pour exercer conjointement leurs récusations, le sort décide entre eux dans quel ordre chacun exerce ses récusations. Les jurés qui, de cette manière, sont récusés par l'un des accusés, le sont alors pour tous les autres accusés, jusqu'à ce que le nombre des récusations accordées soit épuisé.

ART. 47. Les récusations sont annoncés, verbalement ou par écrit, au Président de la chambre criminelle, dans les quatorze jours dès la réception de la copie mentionée à l'art. 45. Celui qui ne fait pas usage de son droit dans le délai prescrit est censé y avoir renoncé.

ART. 48. Lorsque quarante jurés ont été récusés, les *quatorze* restants sont *convoqués* aux assises.

Si le nombre des récusations ne s'élève pas à quarante, la Chambre criminelle désigne par le *sort*, parmi les jurés non récusés, les quartorze qui devront être appelés aux assises.

Dans les deux cas, le sort désigne pareillement les deux jurés qui, parmi les quatorze, doivent être adjoints au jury pour fonctionner en qualité de *suppléants*.

ART. 49. Toutefois, lorsque dans une session des assises il y a un grand nombre d'accusés à juger, ou pour tout autre motif grave, le Président de la Chambre criminelle peut appeller les cinquante-quatre jurés portés sur la liste spéciale et ne faire procéder aux récusations qu'à *l'overture des débats*.

ART. 50. L'invitation de se rendre aux assises est addressée aux jurés au moins six jours avant l'ouverture de la session.

ART. 51. La Chambre criminelle désigne dans chaque cas le lieu où les assises doivent se réunir.

Dans les cas ordinaires, un crime ou délit est juge dans l'arrondissement d'assises où il a été commis. Cependant dans l'intérêt d'une justice impartiale ou de la sûreté publique il peut être fait exception à cette règle.

ART. 52. Pour chaque session des assises fédérales, le Gouvernement cantonal du lieu où elles sont appelées à siéger met à leur disposition un *local* convenable. Les frais causés par ces arrangements sont supportés par la caisse du Tribunal. Les loyers ne sont cependant pas portés en compte.

ART. 53. Les gardes, les escortes, et les geôliers sont fournis, sur réquisition du Président des assises ou du juge d'instruction, par les autorités cantonales du lieu de la poursuite de l'affaire. Les frais en sont supportés par la caisse du Tribunal.

ART. 54. Les *personnes mises en état d'arrestation* sont écrouées dans les prisons cantonales. Leur entretien est bonifié par la caisse du Tribunal d'après les tarifs du Canton. En ce qui touche la surveillance et le traitement des détenus, le geôlier se conforme aux ordres du juge d'instruction fédéral ou, le cas échéant, du Président des assises.

ART. 55. La *Cour de cassation* connaît soit des recours en cassation, des demandes de révision et de réhabilitation dans les causes criminelles (articles 135–168, 175–182 du Code de procédure pénale fédérale, II. 735), soit des recours contre des jugements de Tribunaux cantonaux qui portent sur des transgressions des lois fiscales fédérales (art. 18 de la loi fédérale du 30 juin 1849, I. 87).

Le Tribunal de cassation se compose du Président du Tribunal fédéral, qui en est d'office le président, de quatre juges et de trois suppléants. Pour rendre des arrêts valables, la Cour de cassation doit toujours être au complet, c'est-à-dire composée de cinq juges. Cas échéant, elle pourra être complétée suivant leur tour de rôle au moyen des autres juges et suppléants ayant le droit de voter d'après l'article 34. Si leur nombre ne suffit pas il sera procédé conformément à l'art. 18.

## IV.—DES CONTESTATIONS DE DROIT PUBLIC.

ART. 56. Le Tribunal fédéral connaît des *conflits de compétence* entre les autorités fédérales d'une part et les autorités cantonales d'autre part. (Art. 113, § 1, de la Constitution fédérale.)

Lorsqu'une partie prétend qu'une contestation dont le Tribunal fédéral a été nanti est du ressort exclusif de l'autorité cantonale, ou doit être jugée par une autorité étrangère ou un tribunal arbitral, le Tribunal fédéral statue lui-même sur sa compétence.

L'Assemblée fédérale connaît des contestations entre le Conseil fédéral et le Tribunal fédéral, sur la question de savoir si un cas est du ressort de l'une ou de l'autre de ces autorités (art. 85, § 13, de la Constitution fédérale).

ART. 57. Le Tribunal fédéral connaît en outre des différends *entre Cantons*, lorsque ces différends sont du domaine du droit public.

Sont compris spécialement dans cette catégorie: les rectifications de frontières intercantonales, les questions d'application de traités intercantonaux et les questions de compétence entre les autorités de Cantons différents, lorsque dans ces divers cas c'est un Gouvernement cantonal lui-même qui nantit le Tribunal fédéral de l'affaire.

ART. 58. Le Tribunal fédéral statue sur les demandes *d'extradition* qui sont formulées en vertu des traités d'extradition existants, pour autant que l'application du traité en question est contestée. Les mesures préliminaires restent dans la compétence du Conseil fédéral.

ART. 59. Le Tribunal fédéral connaît enfin des recours présentés par les particuliers et les corporations, concernant:

*a.* La violation des droits qui leur sont garantis soit par la Constitution, soit par la législation fédérale, soit par la Constitution de leurs Cantons;

*b.* La violation de conventions et de concordats intercantonaux, ainsi que des traités avec l'étranger,

lorsque ces recours sont dirigés contre des décisions d'autorités cantonales et qu'ils ont été déposés dans les soixante jours dès leur communication aux intéressés.

Sont réservées, à teneur de l'art. 113, alinéa 2me, de la Constitution fédérale, les contestations administratives ayant trait aux dispositions suivantes de la Constitution fédérale et dont la solution rentre, aux termes des art. 85, chiffre 12, et 102, chiffre 2, dans la compétence soit du Conseil fédéral, soit de l'Assemblée fédérale:

1° Art. 18, alinéa 3, concernant la gratuité de l'equipement du soldat;

2° Art. 27, alinéas 2 et 3, concernant les écoles primaires publiques des Cantons;

3° Art. 31, concernant la liberté de commerce et d'industrie;

4° Art. 31 et 32, concernant les droits de consommation et les droits d'entrée sur les vins et les autres boissons spiritueuses encore reconnus;

5° Art. 43, 45 et 47, concernant les droits des suisses établis;

6° Art. 49, 50 et 51, concernant la liberté de conscience et de croyance et le libre exercice des cultes, etc. Restent néanmoins dans la compétence du tribunal fédéral: les contestations relatives aux impôts (art. 49, alinéa 6) et les contestations de droit privé auxquelles donne lieu la création de communautés religieuses nouvelles ou une scission de communautés religieuses existantes (art. 50, alinéa 3);

7° Art 53, concernant l'état civil et le droit de disposer des lieux de sépulture, dans la mesure où la loi défèrera au Conseil fédéral la compétence sur ces matières;

Sont également soumis à la décision soit du Conseil fédéral, soit de l'Assemblée fédérale:

8° Les recours concernant l'application des lois fédérales prévues aux art. 25, 33, 34, 39, 40 et 69 de la Constitution fédérale;

9° Les recours contre la validité d'élections et votations cantonales;

10° Les contestations provenant des dispositions des traités avec l'étranger concernant le commerce et les péages, les patentes, l'établissement, l'affranchissement de la taxe militaire et la libre circulation.

Art 60. Le Tribunal fédéral appliquera dans tous les cas mentionnés aux art. 56, 57, 58 et 59 les lois votées par l'Assemblée fédérale et les arrêtés de cette Assemblée qui ont une portée générale. Il se conformera également aux traités que l'assemblée fédérale aura ratifiés (art. 113 de la Constitution fédérale).

Art. 61. Le Tribunal fédéral ne prononce dans la règle sur des contestations de droit public qu'à la suite d'une *procédure écrite.*

Les recours sont transmis pour rapport à la partie adverse ou, à son défaut, à l'autorité contre laquelle ils sont dirigés. Une fois la réponse reçue, le juge d'instruction peut, s'il le juge convenable, prescrire une réplique et une duplique. Il ordonne en même temps la production des moyens de preuve nécessaires.

Exceptionnellement, sur la demande d'une des parties, et lorsqu'il existe des motifs particuliers pour le faire, le Tribunal fédéral peut ordonner des *débats oraux.*

Art. 62. Dans les procès qui portent sur des contestations de droit public, il ne peut, dans la règle, ni être demandé d'émoluments, ni être alloué d'indemnités aux parties.

Cependant le Tribunal peut faire des exceptions dans les cas ou elles seraient justifiées par l'origine ou la cause de la contestation, ou par la manière dont le procès a été instruit par les parties.

Art. 63. Le President du Tribunal peut, sur la demande d'une partie, ordonner les mesures nécessaires pour le maintien de l'état de fait.

Ces mesures doivent être ratifiées par le Tribunal dans sa première audience.

## DISPOSITIONS FINALES.

Art. 64. Sont abrogées par la présente loi:

1° La loi fédérale sur l'orginasation judiciaire fédérale, du 5 juin 1849 (i. 65);

2° La loi fédérale sur les attributions et le traitement du procureur-général, du 20 décembre 1850 (ii. 163);

3° La loi fédérale concernant une modification à l'art. 30 de l'organisation judiciair, du 16 juillet 1862 (vii. 295),

ainsi que toutes les dispositions des autres lois fédérales qui pourraient se trouver en contradiction avec celles de la présente loi.

Art. 65. La présente loi entrera en vigueur, sous réserve de l'exercice des droits populaires, conformément à l'art. 89 de la Constitution fédérale, après un délai de quatre-vingt-dix jours dès celui de sa promulgation.

Le Conseil fédéral est chargé de la publication et de l'execution de la présente loi.

Ainsi arrêté par le Conseil national.

Berne, le 26 juin 1874.

*Le Président:* FEER-HERZOG.

*Le Secrétaire:* SCHIESS.

Ainsi arrêté par le Conseil des États.

Berne, le 27 juin 1874.

*Le Président:* KŒCHLIN.

*Le Secrétaire:* J.-L. LÜTSCHER.

LE CONSEIL FÉDÉRAL ARRÊTE :

La loi fédérale ci-dessus sera publiée dans la Feuille fédérale.
Berne, le 1er juillet 1874.
*Le Président de la Confédération :*
SCHENK.
*Le Chancelier de la Confédération :*
SCHIESS.

*Arrêté fédéral concernant le siége du Tribunal fédéral.* (*Du* 26 *juin* 1874.)

L'ASSEMBLÉE FÉDÉRAL DE LA CONFÉDÉRATION SUISSE,

En exécution des dispositions des articles 106 et 107 de la Constitution fédérale et de l'art. 11 de la loi fédéral sur l'organisation judiciaire fédérale,

ARRÊTE :

1. La ville de Lausanne est, sous réserve de l'entrée en vigueur de la nouvelle loi sur l'organisation judiciaire fédéral, désignée comme siége du Tribunal fédéral.

2. Les autorités compétentes du Canton de Vaud, soit de la ville de Lausanne, devront, dans le délai d'un mois à compter du jour ou la loi fédérale sur l'organisation judiciaire fédérale sera entrée en vigueur, faire parvenir au conseil fedéral les engagements, constatant qu'elles sont en mesure de se charger d'une manière définitive des obligations qu'impose l'art. 11 de cette loi.

Ainsi arrêté par le Conseil national.
Berne, le 26 juin 1874.
*Le Président :*
FEER-HERZOG.
*Le Secrétaire :*
SCHIESS,

Ainsi arrêté par le Conseil des États.
Berne, le 26 juin 1874.
*Le Président :*
KŒCHLIN,
*Le Secrétaire :*
J.-L. LÜTSCHER,

LE CONSEIL FÉDÉRAL ARRÊTE :

L'arrêté fédéral ci-dessus sera inséré dans la Feuille fédérale.
Berne, le 1er juillet 1874.
*Le Président de la Confédération :*
SCHENK.
*Lu Chancelier de la Confédération :*
SCHIESS.

NOTE.—Par l'arrêté ci-dessus il a été donné suite au postulat que le conseil a adopté le 23 et le Conseil des États le 25 juin 1874, comme suit :

" La question du siége du Tribunal fédéral devant être tranchée dans le cours de la présente session, le Conseil fédéral est invité à communiquer à l'Assemblée fé érale les demandes qui lui ont été adressées à ce sujet en les accompagnant de son préavis s'il juge à propos de le donner."

---

[Inclosure 5 in No. 177.]

*Constitution fédérale de la Confédération suisse du* 29 *mai* 1874.

AU NOM DE DIEU TOUT PUISSANT ! LA CONFÉDÉRATION SUISSE,

Voulant affermir l'alliance des Confédérés, maintenir et accroître l'unité, la force, et l'honneur de la Nation suisse, a adopté la Constitution fédérale suivante :

*Constitution fédérale de la Confédération suisse.*

## CHAPITRE I.

### DISPOSITIONS GÉNÉRALES.

ARTICLE PREMIER. Les peuples des vingt-deux Cantons souverains de la Suisse, unis par la présente alliance, savoir : *Zurich, Berne, Lucerne, Uri, Schwyz, Unterwalden* (le Haut et le Bas), *Glaris, Zoug, Fribourg, Soleure, Bâle,* (Ville et Campagne), *Schaffhouse, Appenzell* (les deux Rhones), *St. Gall, Grisons, Argovie, Thurgovie, Tessin, Vaud, Valais, Neuchâtel* et *Genève,* forment dans leur ensemble la CONFÉDÉRATION SUISSE.

ARTICLE 2. La Confédération a pour but d'assurer l'indépendance de la patrie contre l'étranger, de maintenir la tranquillité et l'ordre à l'intérieur, de protéger la liberté et les droits des Confédérés et d'accroître leur prospérité commune.

ARTICLE 3. Les Cantons sont souverains en tant que leur souveraineté n'est pas limitée par la Constitution fédérale, et, comme tels, ils exercent tous les droits qui ne sont pas délégués au pouvoir fédéral.

ARTICLE 4. Tous les Suisses sont égaux devant la loi. Il n'y a en Suisse ni sujets, ni priviléges de lieu, de naissance, de personnes ou de familles.

ARTICLE 5. La Confédération garantit aux Cantons leur territoire, leur souveraineté dans les limites fixées par l'article 3, leurs Constitutions, la liberté et les droits du peuple, les droits constitutionnels des citoyens, ainsi que les droits et les attributions que le peuple a conférés aux autorités.

ARTICLE 6. Les Cantons sont tenus de demander à la Confédération la garantie de leurs Constitutions.

Cette garantie est accordée, pourvu :

*a.* Que ces Constitutions ne renferment rien de contraire aux dispositions de la Constitution fédérale ;

*b.* Qu'elles assurent l'exercice des droits politiques d'après des formes républicaines, représentatives ou démocratiques ;

*c.* Qu'elles aient été acceptées par le peuple et qu'elles puissent être révisées lorsque la majorité absolue des citoyens le demande.

ARTICLE 7. Toute alliance particulière et tout traité d'une nature politique entre Cantons sont interdits.

En revanche, les Cantons ont le droit de conclure entre eux des conventions sur des objets de législation, d'administration ou de justice; toutefois, ils doivent les porter à la connaissance de l'autorité fédérale, laquelle, si ces conventions renferment quelque chose de contraire à la Confédération ou aux droits des autres Cantons, est autorisée à en empêcher l'exécution. Dans le cas contraire, les Cantons contractants sont autorisés à réclamer pour l'exécution la coopération des autorités fédérales.

ARTICLE 8. La Confédération a seule le droit de déclarer la guerre et de conclure la paix, ainsi que de faire avec les États étrangers des alliances et des traités, notamment des traités de péage (douanes) et de commerce.

ARTICLE 9. Exceptionnellement, les Cantons conservent le droit de conclure avec les États étrangers des traités sur des objets concernant l'économie publique, les rapports de voisinage et de police ; néanmoins ces traités ne doivent rien contenir de contraire à la Confédération ou aux droits d'autres Cantons.

ARTICLE 10. Les rapports officiels entre les Cantons et les Gouvernements étrangers ou leurs représentants ont lieu par l'intermédiaire du Conseil fédéral.

Toutefois, les Cantons peuvent correspondre directement avec les autorités inférieures et les employés d'un État étranger, lorsqu'il s'agit des objets mentionnés à l'article précédent.

ARTICLE 11. Il ne peut être conclu de capitulations militaires.

ARTICLE 12. Les membres des autorités fédérales, les fonctionnaires civils et militaires de la Confédération, et les représentants ou les commissaires fédéraux ne peuvent recevoir d'un Gouvernement étranger ni pensions ou traitements, ni titres, présents ou décorations.

S'ils sont déjà en possession de pensions, de titres ou de décorations, ils devront renoncer à jouir de leurs pensions et à porter leurs titres et leurs décorations pendant la durée de leurs fonctions.

Toutefois les employés inférieurs peuvent être autorisés par le Conseil fédéral à recevoir leurs pensions.

On ne peut, dans l'armée fédérale, porter ni décoration ni titre accordés par un gouvernement étranger.

Il est interdit à tout officier, sous-officier ou soldat d'accepter des distinctions de ce genre.

ARTICLE 13. La Confédération n'a pas le droit d'entretenir des troupes permanentes.

Nul Canton ou demi-Canton ne peut avoir plus de 300 hommes de troupes permanentes, sans l'autorisation du pouvoir fédéral ; la gendarmerie n'est pas comprise dans ce nombre.

ARTICLE 14. Des différends venant à s'élever entre Cantons, les Etats s'abstiendront de toute voie de fait et de tout armement. Ils se soumettront à la décision qui sera prise sur ces différends conformément aux prescriptions fédérales.

ARTICLE 15. Dans le cas d'un danger subit provenant du dehors, le Gouvernment du Canton menacé doit requérir le secours des États confédérés et en aviser immédiatement l'autorité fédérale, le tout sans préjudice des dispositions qu'elle pourra prendre. Les Cantons requis sont tenus de prêter secours. Les frais sont supportés par la Confédération.

ARTICLE 16. En cas de troubles à l'intérieur, ou lorsque le danger provient d'un autre Canton, le Gouvernement du Canton menacé doit en aviser immédiatement le Conseil fédéral, afin qu'il puisse prendre les mesures nécessaires dans les limites de sa compétence (Article 102, chiffres 3, 10 et 11) ou convoquer l'Assemblée fédérale. Lorsqu'il y a urgence, le Gouvernement est autorisé, en avertissant immédiatement le Conseil fédéral, à requérir le secours d'autres États confédérés, qui sont tenus de le prêter.

Lorsque le Gouvernement est hors d'état d'invoquer le secours, l'autorité fédérale compétente peut intervenir sans réquisition; elle est tenue de le faire lorsque les troubles compromettent la sûrete de la Suisse.

En cas d'intervention, les autorités fédérales veillent à l'observation des dispositions prescrites à l'article 5.

Les frais sont supportés par le Canton qui a requis l'assistance ou occasionné l'intervention, à moins que l'Assemblée fédérale n'en décide autrement, en considération de circonstances particulières.

ARTICLE 17. Dans les cas mentionnés aux deux articles précédents, chaque Canton est tenu d'accorder libre passage aux troupes. Celles-ci seront immédiatement placées sous le commandement fédéral.

ARTICLE 18. Tout Suisse est tenu au service miltaire.

Les militaires qui, par le fait du service fédéral, perdent la vie ou voient leur santé altérée d'une manière permanente, ont droit à des secours de la Confédération, pour eux ou pour leur famille, s'ils sont dans le besoin.

Chaque soldat reçoit gratuitement ses premiers effets d'armement, d'équipement, et d'habillement. L'arme reste en mains du soldat aux conditions qui seront fixées par la législation fédérale.

La Confédération édictera des prescriptions uniformes sur la taxe d'exemption du service militaire.

ARTICLE 19. L'armée fédérale est composée:

*a.* Des corps de troupes des Cantons;

*b.* De tous les Suisses qui, n'appartenant pas à ces corps, sont néanmoins astreints au service militaire.

Le droit de disposer de l'armée, ainsi que du matériel de guerre prévu par la ioi, appartient à la Confédération.

En cas de danger, la Confédération a aussi le droit de disposer exclusivement et directement des hommes non incorporés dans l'armée fédérale et de toutes les autres ressources militaires des Cantons.

Les Cantons disposent des forces militaires de leur territoire, pour autant que ce droit n'est pas limité par la Constitution ou les lois fédérales.

ARTICLE 20. Les lois sur l'organisation de l'armée émanent de la Confédération. L'exécution des lois militaires dans les Cantons a lieu par les authortés cantonales, dans les limites qui seront fixées par la législation fédérale et sous la surveillance de la Confédération.

L'instruction militaire dans son ensemble appartient à la Confédération; il en est de même de l'armement.

La fourniture et l'entretien de l'habillement et de l'équipement restent dans la compétence cantonale; toutefois, les dépenses qui en résultent sont bonifiées aux Cantons par la Confédération, d'après une règle à établir par la législation fédérale.

ARTICLE 21. A moins que des considérations militaires ne s'y opposent, les corps doivent être formés de troupes d'un même Canton.

La composition de ces corps de troupes, le soin du maintien de leur effectif, la nomination et la promotion des officiers de ces corps appartiennent aux Cantons sous réserve des prescriptions générales qui leur seront transmises par la Confédération.

ARTICLE 22. Moyennant une indemnité équitable, la Confédération a le droit de se servir ou de devenir propriétaire des places d'armes et des bâtiments ayant une destination militaire qui existent dans les Cantons, ainsi que de leurs accessoires.

Les conditions de l'indemnité seront réglées par la législation fédérale.

ARTICLE 23. La Confédération peut ordonner à ses frais ou encourager par des subsides les travaux publics qui intéressent la Suisse ou une partie considérable du pays.

Dans ce but, elle peut ordonner l'expropriation moyennant une juste indemnité. La législation fédérale statuera les dispositions ultérieures sur cette matière.

L'Assemblée fédérale peut interdire les constructions publiques qui porteraient atteinte aux intérêts militaires de la Confédération.

ARTICLE 24. La Confédération a le droit de haute surveillance sur la police des endiguements et des forêts dans les régions élevées.

Elle concourra à la correction et à l'endiguement des torrents, ainsi qu'au reboisement des régions où ils prennent leur source. Elle décrétera les mesures nécessaires pour assurer l'entretien de ces ouvrages et la conservation des forêts existantes.

ARTICLE 25. La Confédération a le droit de statuer des dispositions législatives pour régler l'exercice de la pêche et de la chasse, principalement en vue de la conservation du gros gibier dans les montagnes, ainsi que pour protéger les oiseaux utiles à l'agriculture et à la sylviculture.

ARTICLE 26. La législation sur la construction et l'exploitation des chemins de fer est du domaine de la Confédération.

ARTICLE 27. La Confédération a le droit de créer, outre l'École polytechnique existante, une Université fédérale et d'autres établissements d'instruction supérieure ou de subventionner des établissements de ce genre.

Les Cantons pourvoient à l'instruction primaire, qui doit être suffisante et placée exclusivement sous la direction de l'autorité civile. Elle est obligatoire et, dans les écoles publiques, gratuite.

Les écoles publiques doivent pouvoir être fréquentées par les adhérents de toutes les confessions, sans qu'ils aient à souffrir d'aucune façon dans leur liberté de conscience ou de croyance.

La Confédération prendra les mesures nécessaires contre les Cantons qui ne satisferaient pas à ces obligations.

ARTICLE 28. Ce qui concerne les péages relève de la confédération. Celle-ci peut percevoir des droits d'entrée et des droits de sortie.

ARTICLE 29. La perception des péages fédéraux sera réglée conformément aux principes suivants:

1. Droits sur l'importation :

*a.* Les matières nécessaires à l'industrie et à l'agriculture du pays seront taxées aussi bas que possible.

*b.* Il en sera de même des objets nécessaires à la vie.

*c.* Les objets de luxe seront soumis aux taxes les plus élevées.

A moins d'obstacles majeurs, ces principes devront aussi être observés lors de la conclusion de traités de commerce avec l'étranger.

2. Les droits sur l'exportation seront aussi modérés que possible.

3. La législation des péages contiendra des dispositions propres à assurer le commerce frontière et sur les marchés.

Les dispositions ci-dessus n'empêchent point la Confédération de prendre temporairement des mesures exceptionnelles dans les circonstances extraordinaires.

ARTICLE 30. Le produit des péages appartient à la Confédération.

Les indemnités payées jusqu'à présent aux Cantons pour le rachat des péages, des droits de chaussée et de pontonage, des droits de douane et d'autres émoluments semblables, sont supprimées.

Les Cantons d'Uri, des Grisons, du Tessin et du Valais reçoivent, par exception et à raison de leurs routes alpestres internationales, une indemnité annuelle dont, en tenant compte de toutes les circonstances, le chiffre est fixé comme suit :

| | Francs. |
|---|---|
| Uri | 80,000 |
| Grisons | 200,000 |
| Tessin | 200,000 |
| Valais | 50,000 |

Les Cantons d'Uri et du Tessin recevront en outre pour le déblaiement des neiges sur la route du St.-Gothard, une indemnité annuelle totale de 40,000 francs, aussi longtemps que cette route ne sera pas remplacée par un chemin de fer.

ARTICLE 31. La liberté de commerce et d'industrie est garantie dans toute l'étendue de la Confédération.

Sont réservée :

*a.* La régale du sel et de la poudre de guerre, les péages fédéraux, les droits d'entrée sur les vins et les autres boissons spiritueuses, ainsi que les autres droits de consommation formellement reconnus par la confédération, à teneur de l'article 32 ;

*b.* Les mesures de police sanitaire contre les épidémies et les épizooties ;

*c.* Les dispositions touchant l'exercice des professions commerciales et industrielles, les impôts qui s'y rattachent et la police des routes.

Ces dispositions ne peuvent rien renfermer de contraire au principe de la liberté de commerce et d'industrie.

ARTICLE 32. Les Cantons sont autorisés à percevoir les droits d'entrée sur les vins et les autres boissons spiritueuses prévus à l'article 31, lettre *a*, toutefois sous les restrictions suivantes :

*a.* La perception de ces droits d'entrée ne doit nullement grever le transit ; elle doit gêner le moins possible le commerce, qui ne peut être frappé d'aucune autre taxe.

*b.* Si les objets importés pour la consommation sont réexportés du Canton, les droits payés pour l'entrée sont restitués sans qu'il en résulte d'autres charges.

*c.* Les produits d'origine suisse seront moins imposés que ceux de l'étranger.

*d.* Les droits actuels d'entrée sur les vins et les autres boissons spiritueuses d'origine suisse ne pourront être haussés par les Cantons où il en existe. Il n'en pourra être établi sur ces produits par les Cantons qui n'en perçoivent pas actuellement.

*e.* Les lois et les arrêtés des Cantons sur la perception des droits d'entrée sont, avant leur mise à exécution, soumis à l'approbation de l'autorité fédérale, afin qu'elle puisse, au besoin, faire observer les dispositions qui précèdent.

Tous les droits d'entrée perçus actuellement par les Cantons, ainsi que les droits analogues perçus par les communes, doivent disparaître sans indemnité à l'expiration de l'année 1890.

ARTICLE 33. Les Cantons peuvent exiger des preuves de capacité de ceux qui veulent exercer des professions libérales.

La législation fédérale pourvoit à ce que ces derniers puissent obtenir à cet effet des actes de capacité valables dans toute la Confédération.

ARTICLE 34. La Confédération a le droit de statuer des prescriptions uniformes sur le travail des enfants dans les fabriques, sur la durée du travail qui pourra y être imposé aux adultes, ainsi que sur la protection à accorder aux ouvriers contre l'exercice des industries insalubres et dangereuses.

Les opérations des agences d'émigration et des entreprises d'assurance non instituées par l'État sont soumises à la surveillance et à la législation fédérales.

ARTICLE 35. Il est interdit d'ouvrir des maisons de jeu. Celles qui existent actuellement seront fermées le 31 décembre 1877.

Les concessions qui auraient eté accordées ou renouvelées depuis le commencement de l'année 1871, sont déclareés nulles.

La Confédération peut aussi prendre les mesures nécessaires concernant les loteries.

ARTICLE 36. Dans toute la Suisse, les postes et les télégraphes sont du domaine fédéral.

Le produit des postes et des télégraphes appartient à la caisse fédérale.

Les tarifs seront fixés d'après les mêmes principes et aussi équitablement que possible dans toutes les parties de la Suisse.

L'inviolabilité du secret des lettres et des télégrammes est guarantie.

ARTICLE 37. La Confédération exerce la haute surveillance sur les routes et les ponts dont le maintain l'intéresse.

Les sommes dues aux Cantons désignés à l'article 30, à raison de leurs routes alpestres internationales, seront retenues par l'autorité fédérale si ces routes ne sont pas convenablement entrenues par eux.

ARTICLE 38. La Confédération exerce tous les droits compris dans la régale des monnaies.

Elle a seule le droit de battre monnaie.

Elle fixe le système monétaire et peut édicter, s'il y a lieu, des prescriptions sur la tarification de monnaies étrangères.

ARTICLE 39. La Confédération a le droit de décréter par voie législative des prescriptions générales sur l'émission et le remboursement des billets de banque.

Elle ne peut cependant créer aucun monopole pour l'émission des billets de banque, ni décréter l'acceptation obligatoire de ces billets.

ARTICLE 40. La Confédération détermine le système des poids et mesures.

Les Cantons exécutent, sous la surveillance de la Confédération, les lois concernant cette matière.

ARTICLE 41. La fabrication et la vente de la poudre de guerre dans toute la Suisse appartiennent exclusivement à la Confédération.

Les compositions minières impropres au tir ne sont point comprises dans la régale des poudres.

ARTICLE 42. Les dépenses de la Confédération sont couvertes:

*a.* Par le produit de la fortune fédérale;

*b.* Par le produit des péages fédéraux perçus à la frontière suisse;

*c.* Par le produit des postes et des télégraphes;

*d.* Par le produit de la régale des poudres;

*e.* Par la moitié du produit brut de la taxe sur les exemptions militaires perçue par les Cantons;

*f.* Par les contributions des Cantons, que réglera la législation fédérale, en tenant compte surtout de leur richesse et de leurs ressources imposables.

ARTICLE 43. Tout citoyen d'un Canton est citoyen suisse.

Il peut à ce titre, prendre part, au lieu de son domicile, à toutes les élections et votations en matière fédérale, après avoir dûment justifié de sa qualite d'électeur.

Nul ne peut exercer des droits politiques dans plus d'un Canton.

Le Suisse établi jouit, au lieu de son domicile, de tous les droits des citoyens du Canton et, avec ceux-ci, de tous les droits des bourgeois de la commune. La participation aux biens des bourgeoisies et des corporations et le droit de vote dans les affaires purement bourgeoisiales sont exceptés de ces droits, à moins que la législation cantonale n'en décide autrement.

En matière cantonale et communale il devient électeur après un établissement de trois mois.

Les lois cantonales sur l'etablissement et sur les droits électoraux que possèdent en matière communale les citoyens établis sont soumises à la sanction du Conseil fédéral.

ARTICLE 44. Aucun Canton ne peut renvoyer de son territoire un de ses ressortissants, ni le priver du droit d'origine ou de cité.

La législation fédérale déterminera les conditions auxquelles les étrangers peuvent être naturalisés, ainsi que celles auxquelles un Suisse peut renoncer à sa nationalité pour obtenir la naturalisation dans un pays étranger.

ARTICLE 45. Tout citoyen suisse a le droit de s'établir sur un point quelconque du territoire suisse, moyennant la productien d'un acte d'origine ou d'une autre pièce analogue.

Exceptionnellement, l'établissement peut être *refusé* ou *retiré* à ceux qui, par suite d'un jugement pénal, ne jouissent pas de leurs droits civiques.

L'établissement peut être de plus *retiré* à ceux qui ont été à réitérés fois punis pour des délits graves, comme aussi à ceux qui tombent d'une manière permanente à la charge de la bienfaisance publique at auxquels leur commune, soit leur Canton d'origine, refuse une assistance suffisante après avoir été invitée officiellement à l'accorder.

Dans les Cantons où existe l'assistance au domicile, l'autorisation de s'établir peut être subordonnée, s'il s'agit de ressortissants du Canton, à la condition qu'ils soient en état de travailler et qu'ils ne soient pas tombés, à leur ancien domicile dans le Canton d'origine d'une manière permanente à la charge de la bienfaisance publique.

Tout renvoi pour cause d'indigence doit être ratifié par le gouvernement du Canton du domicile et communiqué préalablement au Gouvernement du Canton d'origine.

Le Canton dans lequel un Suisse établit son domicile ne peut exiger de lui un cautionement, ni lui imposer accune charge particulière pour cet établissement. De même les communes ne peuvent imposer aux Suisses domicilés sur leur territoire d'autres contributions que celles qu'elles impossent à leurs propres ressortissants.

Une loi fédérale fixera la maximum de l'émolument de chancellerie à payer pour obtenir un permis d'établissement.

ARTICLE. 46. Les personnes établies en Suisse sont soumises, dans la règle, à la juridiction et à la législation du lieu de leur domicile en ce qui concerne les rapports de droit civil.

La législation fédérale statuera les dispositions nécessaires en vue de l'application de ce principe, et pour empêcher qu'un citoyen ne soit imposé à double.

ARTICLE 47. Une loi fédérale déterminera la différence entre l'établissment et le séjour et fixera en même temps les règles auxquelles seront soumis les Suisses en séjour quant à leurs droits politiques et à leurs droits civils.

ARTICLE 48. Une loi fédérale statuera les dispositions nécessaires pour régler ce qui concerne les frais de maladie et de sépulture des ressortissants pauvres d'un Canton tombés malades ou décédés dans un autre Canton.

ARTICLE 49. La liberté de conscience et de croyance est inviolable.

Nul ne peut être contraint de faire partie d'une association religieuse, de suivre un enseignement religieux, d'accomplir un acte religieux, ni encourir des peines, de quelque nature qu'elles soient, pour cause d'opinion religieuse.

La personne qui exerce l'autorité paternelle ou tutélaire a le droit de disposer, conformément aux principes ci-dessus, de l'éducation religieuse des enfants jusqu'à l'âge de 16 ans révolus.

L'exercice des droits civils ou politiques ne peut être restreint par des prescriptions ou des conditions de nature ecclésiastique ou religieuse, quelles qu elles soient.

Nul ne peut, pour cause d'opinion religieuse, s'affranchir de l'accomplissement d'un devoir civique.

Nul n'est tenu de payer des impôts dont le produit est spécialement affecté aux frais proprement dits du culte d'une communauté religieuse à laquelle il n'appartient pas. L'exécution ultérieure de ce principe reste réservée à la législation fédérale.

ARTICLE. 50. Le libre exercice des cultes est garanti dans les limites compatibles avec l'ordre public et les bonnes mœurs.

Les Cantons et la Confédération peuvent prendre les mesures nécessaires pour le maintien de l'ordre public et de la paix entre les membres des diverses communautés religieuses, ainsi que contre les empiétements des autorités ecclésiastiques sur les droits des citoyens et de l'Etat.

Les contestations de droit public ou de droit privé auxqelles donne lieu la création de communautés religieuses ou une scission de communautés religieuses existantes, peuvent être portées par voie de recours devant les autorités fédérales compétentes.

Il ne peut être érigé d'évêchés sur le territoire suisse sans l'approbation de la confédération.

ARTICLE 51. L'ordre des Jésuites et les sociétés qui lui sont affiliés ne peuvent être reçus dans aucune partie de la Suisse, et toute action dans l'Église et dans l'École est interdite à leurs membres.

Cette interdiction peut s'étendre aussi, par voie d'arrêté fédéral, à d'autres ordres religieux dont l'action est dangereuse pour l'État ou trouble la paix entre les confessions.

ARTICLE 52. Il est interdit de fonder de nouveaux couvents ou ordres religieux et de rétablir ceux qui ont été supprimés.

ARTICLE 53. L'état civil et la tenue des registres qui s'y rapportent est du ressort des autorités civiles. La législation fédérale statuera à ce sujet les dispositions ultérieures.

Le droit de disposer des lieux de sépulture appartient à l'autorité civile. Elle doit pourvoir à ce que toute personne décédée puisse être enterrée décemment.

ARTICLE 54. Le droit au mariage est placé sous la protection de la Confédération.

Aucun empêchement au mariage ne peut être fondé sur des motifs confessionnels, sur l'indigence de l'un ou de l'autre des époux, sur leur conduite ou sur quelque autre motif de police que ce soit.

Sera reconnu comme valable dans toute la Confédération le mariage conclu dans un Canton ou à l'étranger conformément à la législation qui y est en vigeur.

La femme acquiert par le mariage le droit de cité et de bourgeoisie de son mari.

Les enfants nés avant le mariage sont légitimés par le mariage subséquent de leurs parents.

Il ne peut être perçu aucune finance d'admission ni aucune taxe semblable de l'un ou de l'autre époux.

ARTICLE 55. La liberté de la presse est garantie.

Toutefois les lois cantonales statuent les mesures nécessaires à la répression des abus; ces lois sont soumises à l'approbation du conseil fédéral.

La Confédération peut aussi statuer des peines pour réprimer les abus dirigés contre elle ou ses autorités.

ARTICLE 56. Les citoyens ont le droit de former des associations, pourvu qu'il n'y ait dans le but de ces associations ou dans les moyens qu'elles emploient rien d'illicite ou de dangereux pour l'État. Les lois cantonales statuent les mesures nécessaires à la répression des abus.

ARTICLE 57. Le droit de pétition est garanti.

ARTICLE 58. Nul ne peut être distrait de son juge naturel. En consequence, il ne pourra être établi de tribunaux extraordinaires.

La jurisdiction ecclésiastique est abolie.

ARTICLE 59. Pour réclamations personnelles, le débiteur solvable ayant domicile en Suisse doit être recherché devant le juge de son domicile; ses biens ne peuvent en conséquence être saisis ou séquestrés hors du Canton ou il est domicilié, en vertu de réclamations personnelles.

Demeurent réservées, en ce qui concerne les étrangers, les dispositions des traités internationaux.

La contrainte par corp est abolie.

ARTICLE 60. Tous les Cantons sont obligés de traiter les citoyens des autres États confédéres comme ceux de leur État en matière de législation et pour tout ce qui concerne les voies juridiques.

ARTICLE 61. Les jugements civils définitifs rendus dans un Canton sont exécutoires dans toute la Suisse.

ARTICLE 62. La traite foraine est abolie dans l'intérieur de la Suisse, ainsi que le droit de retrait des citoyens d'un Canton contre ceux d'autres États confédérés.

ARTICLE 63. La traite foraine à l'égard des pays étrangers est abolie sous réserve de réciprocité.

ARTICLE 64. La législation:

Sur la capacité,

Sur toutes les matières du droit se rapportant au commerce, et aux transactioes mobilières (droit des obligations, y compris le droit commercial et le droit de change),

Sur la propriété littéraire et artistique,

Sur la poursuite pour dettes et la faillite,

est du ressort de la Confédération.

L'administration de la justice reste aux Cantons, sous réserve des attributions du Tribunal fédéral.

ARTICLE 65. La peine de mort est abolie.

Sont réservées toutefois les dispositions du code pénal militaire, en temps de guerre.

Les peines corporelles sont abolies.

ARTICLE 66. La législation fédérale fixe les limites dans lesquelles un citoyen suisse peut être privé de ses droits politiques.

ARTICLE 67. La législation fédérale statue sur l'extradition des accusés d'un Canton à l'autre; toutefois l'extradition ne peut être rendue obligatoire pour les délits politiques et ceux de la presse.

ARTICLE 68. Les mesures à prendre pour incorporer les gens sans patrie (*Heimathlosen*) et pour empêcher de nouveaux cas de ce genre, sont réglées par la loi fédérale.

ARTICLE 69. La législation concernant les mesures de police sanitaire contre les épidémies et les épizooties qui offrent un danger général, est du domaine de la Confédération.

ARTICLE 70. La Confédération a le droit de renvoyer de son territoire les étrangers qui compromettent la sûreté intérieure ou extérieure de la Suisse.

## CHAPITRE II.

### AUTORITÉS FÉDÉRALES.

#### I.—*Assemblée fédérale.*

ARTICLE 71. Sous réserve des droits du peuple et des Cantons (articles 89 et 121) l'autorité suprême de la Confédération est exercée par l'Assemblée fédérale, qui se compose de deux Sections ou Conseils, savoir:

A. le Conseil national;

B. le Conseil des Etats.

A.—Conseil national.

ARTICLE 72. Le Conseil national se compose des députés du peuple suisse, élus à raison d'un membre par 20,000 âmes de la population totale. Les fractions en sus de 10 mille âmes sont comptées pour 20 mille.

Chaque Canton et, dans les Cantons partagés, chaque demi-Canton élit un député au moins.

ARTICLE 73. Les élections pour le Conseil national sont directes. Elles ont lieu dans des colléges électoraux fédéraux, qui ne peuvent toutefois être formés de parties de différents Cantons.

ARTICLE 74. Á droit de prendre part aux élections et aux votations tout Suisse ágé de vingt ans révolus et qui n'est du reste point exclu du droit de citoyen actif par la législation du Canton dans lequel il a son domicile.

Toutefois, la législation fédérale pourra régler d'une manière uniforme l'exercice de ce droit.

ARTICLE 75. Est éligible comme membre du Conseil national tout citoyen suisse laïque et ayant droit de voter.

ARTICLE 76. Le Conseil national est élu pour trois ans et renouvelé intégralement chaque fois.

ARTICLE 77. Les députés au Conseil des États, les membres du Conseil fédéral et les fonctionnaires nommés par ce Conseil ne peuvent être simultanément members du Conseil national.

ARTICLE 78. Le Conseil national choisit dans son sein, pour chaque session ordinaire ou extraordianire, un Président et un vice-Président.

Le membre qui a été Président pendant une session ordinaire ne peut, à la session ordinaire suivante, revêtir cette charge ni celle de vice-Président.

Le même membre ne peut être vice-Président pendant deux sessions ordinaires consécutives.

Lorsque les avis sont également partagés, le Président décide; dans les élections, il vote comme les autres membres.

ARTICLE 79. Les membres du Conseil national sont indemnisés par la Caisse fédérale.

B.—Conseil des États.

ARTICLE 80. Le Conseil des États se compose de quarante-quatre députés des Cantons. Chaque Canton nomme deux députés; dans les Cantons partagés, chaque demi-État en élit un.

ARTICLE 81. Les membres du Conseil national et ceux du Conseil fédéral ne peuvent être députés au Conseil des États.

ARTICLE 82. Le Conseil des États choisit dans son sein, pour chaque session ordinaire ou extraordinaire, un Président et un vice-Président.

Le Président ni le vice-Président ne peuvent être élus parmi les députés du Canton dans lequel a été choisi le Président pour la session ordinaire qui a immédiatement précédé.

Les députés du même Canton ne peuvent revêtir la charge de vice-Président pendant deux sessions ordinaires consécutives.

Lorsque les avis sont également partagés, le Président décide; dans les élections, il vote comme les autres membres.

ARTICLE 83. Les députés au Conseil des États sont indemnisés par les Cantons.

C.—Attributions de l'Assemblée fédérale.

ARTICLE 84. Le Conseil national et le Conseil des États délibèrent sur tous les objets que la présente Constitution place dans le ressort de la Confédération et qui ne sont pas attribués à une autre autorité fédérale.

ARTICLE 85. Les affaires de la compétence des deux Conseils sont notamment les suivantes:

1. Les lois sur l'organisation et le mode d'élection des autorités fédérales;

2. Les lois et arrêtés sur les matières que la Constitution place dans la compétence fédérale;

3. Le traitement et les indemnités des membres des autorités de la Confédération et de la Chancellerie fédérale; la création de fonctions fédérales permanentes et la fixation des traitements;

4. L'élection du Conseil fédéral, du Tribunal fédéral et du Chancelier, ainsi que du Général en chef de l'armée fédérale;

La législation fédérale pourra attribuer à l'Assemblée fédérale d'autres droits d'élection ou de confirmation;

5. Les alliances et les traités avec les États étrangers, ainsi que l'approbation des traités des Cantons entre eux ou avec les États étrangers; toutefois les traités des Can-

tons ne sont portés à l'Assemblée fédérale que lorsque le Conseil fédéral ou un autre Canton élève des réclamations;

6. Les mesures pour la sûreté extérieure ainsi que pour le maintien de l'indépendance et de la neutralité de la Suisse; les déclarations de guerre et la conclusion de la paix.

7. La garantie des Constitutions et du territoire des Cantons; l'intervention par suite de cette garantie; les mesures pour la sûreté intérieure de la Suisse, pour le maintien de la tranquillité et de l'ordre; l'amnestie et le droit de grâce.

8. Les mesures pour faire respecter la Constitution fédérale et assurer la garantie des Constitutions cantonales, ainsi que celles qui ont pour but d'obtenir l'accomplissement des devoirs fédéraux.

9. Le droit de disposer de l'armée fédérale.

10. L'établissement du budget annuel, l'approbation des comptes de l'État et les arrêtés autorisant des emprunts.

11. La haute surveillance de l'administration et de la justice fédérales.

12. Les réclamations contre les décisions du Conseil fédéral relatives à des contestations administratives (art. 113.)

13. Les conflits de compétence entre autorités fédérales.

14. La révision de la Constitution fédérale.

ARTICLE 86. Les deux Conseils s'assemblent, chaque année une fois, en session ordinaire, le jour fixé par le règlement.

Ill sont extraordinairement convoqués par le Conseil fédéral, ou sur la demande du quart des membres du Conseil national ou sur celle de cinq Cantons.

ARTICLE 87. Un Conseil ne peut délibérer qu'autant que les députés présents forment la majorité absolu du nombre total de ses membres.

ARTICLE 88. Dans le Conseil national et dans le Conseil des États les délibérations sont prises à la majorité absolue des votants.

ARTICLE 89. Les lois fédérales, les décrets et les arrêtés fédéraux ne peuvent être rendus qu'avec l'accord des deux Conseils.

Les lois fédérales sont soumises à l'adoption ou au rejet du peuple, si la demande en est faite par 30,000 citoyens actifs ou par huit Cantons. Il en est de même des arrêtés fédéraux qui sont d'une portée générale et qui n'ont pas un caractère d'urgence.

ARTICLE 90. La législation fédérale déterminera les formes et les délais à observer pour les votations populaires.

ARTICLE 91. Les membres des deux Conseils votent sans instructions.

ARTICLE 92. Chaque Conseil délibère séparément. Toutefois, lorsqu'il s'agit des élections mentionnées à l'article 85, chiffre 4, d'exercer le droit de grâce ou de prononcer sur un conflit de compétence (article 85, chiffre 13,) les deux Conseils se réunissent pour délibérer en commun sous la direction du Président du Conseil national, et c'est la majorité des membres votants des deux Conseils qui décide.

ARTICLE 93. L'initiative appartient à chacun des deux Conseils et à chacun de leurs membres.

Les Cantons peuvent exercer le même droit par correspondance.

ARTICLE 94. Dans la règle, les séances des Conseils sont publiques.

## II.—*Conseil fédéral.*

ARTICLE 95. L'autorité directoriale et exécutive supérieure de la Confédération est exercée par un Conseil fédéral composé de sept membres.

ARTICLE 96. Les membres du Conseil fédéral sont nommés pour trois ans, par les Conseils réunis, et choisis parmi tous les citoyens suisses éligibles au Conseil national. On ne pourra toutefois choisir plus d'un membre du Conseil fédéral dans le même Canton.

Le Conseil fédéral est renouvelé intégralement après chaque renouvellement du Conseil national.

Les membres qui font vacance dans l'intervalle des trois ans sont remplacés, à la première session de l'Assemblée fedérale, pour le reste de la durée de leurs fonctions.

ARTICLE 97. Les membres du Conseil fédéral ne peuvent, pendant la durée de leurs fonctions, revêtir aucun autre emploi, soit au service de la Confédération, soit dans un Canton, ni suivre d'autre carrière ou exercer de profession.

ARTICLE 98. Le Conseil fédéral est présidé par le Président de la Confédération. Il a un vice-Président.

Le Président de la Confédération et le vice-Président du Conseil fédéral sont nommés pour une année, par l'Assemblés fédérale, entre les membres du Conseil.

Le Président sortant de charge ne peut être élu Président ou vice-Président pour l'année qui suit.

Le même membre ne peut revêtir la charge de vice-Président pendant deux années de suite.

ARTICLE 99. Le Président de la Confédération et les autres membres du Conseil fédéral reçoivent un traitement annuel de la Caisse fédérale.

ARTICLE 100. Le Conseil fédéral ne peut délibérer que lorsqu'il y a au moins quatre membres présents.

ARTICLE 101. Les membres du Conseil fédéral ont voix consultative dans les deux sections de l'Assemblée fédérale, ainsi que le droit d'y faire des propositions sur les objets en délibération.

ARTICLE 102. Les attributions et les obligations du Conseil fédéral, dans les limites de la présente constitution, sont notamment les suivantes :

1. Il dirige les affaires fédérales, conformément aux lois et arrêtés de la Confédération.

2. Il veille à l'observation de la constitution, des lois et des arrêtés de la Confédération, ainsi que des prescriptions des concordats fédéraux; il prend, de son chef ou sur plainte, les mesures nécessaires pour les faire observer, lorsque le recours n'est pas du nombre de ceux qui doivent être portés devant le Tribunal fédéral à teneur de l'art. 113.

3. Il veille à la garantie des constitutions cantonales.

4. Il présente des projects de lois ou d'arrêtés à l'Assemblée fédérale et donne son préavis sur les propositions qui lui sont adressées par les Conseils ou par les Cantons.

5. Il pourvoir à l'exécution des lois et des arrêtés de la Confédération et à celles des jugements du Tribunal fédéral, ainsi que des transactions ou des sentences arbitrales sur des différends entre cantons.

6. Il fait les nominations qui ne sont pas attribuées à l'assemblée fédérale ou au tribunal fédéral ou à une autre autorité.

7. Il examine les traités des cantons entre eux ou avec l'étranger, et il les approuve, s'il y a lieu (article 85, chiffre 5).

8. Il veille aux intérêts de la confédération au dehors, notamment à l'observation de ses rapports internationaux, et il est, en général, chargé des relations extérieures.

9. Il veille à la sûreté extérieure de la Suisse, au maintien de son indépendance et de sa neutralité.

10. Il veille à la sûreté intérieure de la Confédération, au maintien de la tranquillité et de l'ordre.

11. En cas d'urgence et lorsque l'Assemblée fédérale n'est pas réunie, le Conseil fédéral est autorisé à lever les troupes nécessaires et à en disposer, sous réserve de convoquer immédiatement les conseils, si le nombre des troupes leveés dépasse deux mille hommes ou si elles restent sur pied au delà de trois semaines.

12. Il est chargé de ce qui a rapport au militaire fédéral, ainsi que de toutes les autres branches de l'administration qui appartiennent à la confédération.

13. Il examine les lois et les ordonnances des Cantons qui doivent être soumises à son approbation; il exerce la surveillance sur les branches de l'administration cantonale qui sont placées sous son contrôle.

14. Il administre les finances de la confédération, propose le budget et rend les compte des recettes et des dépenses.

15. Il surveille la gestion de tous les fonctionnaires et employés de l'administration fédérale.

16. Il rende compte de sa gestion à l'Assemblée fédérale, à chaque session ordinaire, lui présente un rapport sur la situation de la Confédération tant à l'intérieur qu'au dehors, et recommande à son attention les mesures qu'il croit utiles à l'accroissement de la prospérité commune.

Il fait aussi des rapports spéciaux lorsque l'Assemblée fédérale ou une de ses Sections le demande.

ARTICLE 103. Les affaires du Conseil fédéral sont réparties par départements entre ses membres. Cette répartition a uniquement pour but de faciliter l'examen et l'expédition des affaires; les décisions émanent du Conseil fédéral comme autorité.

ARTICLE 104. Le Conseil fédéral et ses départements sont autorisés à appeler des experts pour des objets spéciaux.

### III.—*Chancellerie fédérale.*

ARTICLE 105. Une chancellerie fédérale, à la tête de laquelle se trouve le Chancelier de la Confédération, est chargée du secrétariat de l'Assemblée fédérale et de celui Conseil fédéral.

Le Chancelier est élu par l'Assemblée fédérale pour le terme de trois ans, en même temps que le Conseil fédéral.

La chancellerie est sous la surveillance spéciale du Conseil fédéral.

Une loi fédérale détermine ce qui a rapport à l'organisation de la chancellerie.

### IV.—*Tribunal fédéral.*

ARTICLE 106. Il y a un Tribunal fédéral pour l'administration de la justice en matiére fédérale.

Il y a, de plus, un Jury pour les affaires pénales (article 112).

ARTICLE 107. Les membres et les suppléants du Tribunal fédéral sont nommés par l'Assemblée fédérale, qui aura égard à ce que les trois langues nationales y soient représentées.

La loi détermine l'organisation du Tribunal fédéral et de ses sections, le nombre de ses membres et des suppléants, la durée de leurs functions et leur traitement.

ARTICLE 108. Peut être nommé au Tribunal fédéral tout citoyen suisse éligible au Conseil national.

Les membres de l'Assemblée fédérale et du Conseil fédéral et les fonctionnaires nommés par ces autorités ne peuvent en même temps faire partie du Tribunal fédéral.

Les membres du Tribunal fédéral ne peuvent, pendant la durée de leurs fonctions, revêtir aucun autre emploi, soit au service de la Confédération, soit dans un Canton, ni suivre d'autre carrière ou exercer de profession.

ARTICLE 109. Le Tribunal fédéral organise sa chancellerie et en nomme le personnel.

ARTICLE 110. Le Tribunal fédéral connaît des différends de droit civil:

1. Entre la Conféderation et les Cantons;
2. Entre la Confédération d'une part et des corporations ou des particuliers d'autre part, quand ces corporations ou ces particuliers sont demandeurs et quand le litige atteint le degré d'importance que déterminera la législation fédérale;
3. Entre Cantons;
4. Entre des Cantons d'une part et des corporations ou des particuliers d'autre part, quand une des parties le requiert et que le litige atteint le degré d'importance que déterminera la législation fédérale.

Il connaît de plus des différends concernant le *heimatlosat*, ainsi que des contestations qui surgissent entre communes de différents Cantons, touchant le droit de cité.

ARTICLE 111. Le Tribunal fédéral est tenu de juger d'autres causes, lorsque les parties s'accordent à le nantir et que l'objet en litige atteint le degré d'importance que determinera la législation fédérale.

ARTICLE 112. Le Tribunal fédéral assisté du Jury, lequel statue sur les faits, connaît en matière pénale:

1. Des cas de haute trahison envers la Confédération, de révolte ou de violence contre les autorités fédérales;
2. Des crimes et des délits contre le droit des gens;
3. Des crimes et des délits politiques qui sont la cause ou la suite de troubles par lesquels une intervention fédéral armée est occasionnée;
4. Des faits relevés à la charge de fonctionnaires nommés par une autorité fédéral, quand cette autorité en saisit le Tribunal fédéral.

ARTICLE 113. Le Tribunal fédéral connaît, en outre:

1. Des conflits de compétence entre les autorités fédérales, d'une part, et les autorités cantonales, d'autre part;
2. Des differends entre Cantons, lorsque ces differends sont du domaine du droit public.
3. Des réclamations pour violation de droits constitutionnels des citoyens ainsi que des réclamations de particuliers pour violation de concordats ou de traités.

Sont réservées les contestations administratives, à déterminer par la législation fédérale.

Dans tous les cas prémentionnés, le Tribunal fédéral appliquera les lois votées par l'Assemblée fédéral et les arrêtés de cette assemblée qui ont une portée générale. Il se conformera également aux traités que l'Assemblée fédérale aura ratifiés.

ARTICLE 114. Outre les cas mentionnés aux articles 110, 112 et 113, la législation fédérale peut placés d'autres affaires dans la compétence du Tribunal fédéral; elle peut, en particulier, donner à ce tribunal des attributions ayant pour but d'assurer l'application uniforme des lois prévues à l'article 64.

*V.—Dispositions diverses.*

ARTICLE 115. Tout ce qui concerne le siége des autorités de la Confédération est l'objet de la législation fédérale.

ARTICLE 116. Les trois principales langues parlées en Suisse, l'allemand, le français et l'italien, sont langues nationales de la Confédération.

ARTICLE 117. Les fonctionnaires de la Confédération sont responsables de leur gestion. Une loi fédérale détermine ce qui tient à cette responsabilité.

## CHAPITRE III.

### RÉVISION DE LA CONSTITUTION FÉDÉRALE.

ARTICLE 118. La Constitution fédérale peut être révisée en tout temps.

ARTICLE 119. La révision a lieu dans les formes statuées pour la législation fédérale.

ARTICLE 120. Lorsqu'une section de l'Assemblée fédérale décrète la révision de la

Constitution fédérale et que l'autre section n'y consent pas, ou bien lorsque cinquante mille citoyens suisses ayant droit de voter demandent la révision, la question de savoir si la Constitution fédérale doit être révisée est, dans l'un comme dans l'autre cas, soumise à la votation du peuple suisse, par oui ou par non.

Si, dans l'un ou l'autre de ces cas, la majorité des citoyens suisses prenant part à la votation se prononce pour l'affirmative, les deux conseils seront renouvelés pour travailler à la révision.

ARTICLE 121. La Constitution fédérale révisée entre en vigueur lorsqu'elle a été acceptée par la majorité des citoyens suisses prenant part à la votation et par la majorité des etats.

Pour établir la majorité des États, le vote d'un demi-Canton est compté pour une demi-voix.

Le résultat de la votation populaire dans chaque Canton est considéré comme le vote de l'État.

DISPOSITIONS TRANSITOIRES.

ARTICLE PREMIER. Le produit des postes et des péages sera réparti sur les bases actuelles jusqu'à l'époque où la Confédération prendra effectivement à sa charge les dépenses militaires supportées jusqu'à ce jour par les Cantons.

La législation fédérale pourvoira en outre à ce que la perte que pourraient entraîner dans leur ensemble les modifications résultant des articles 20, 30, 36, 2e alinéa, et 42 *e*, pour le fisc de certains Cantons, ne frappe ceux-ci que graduellement et n'atteigne son chiffre total qu'après une période transitoire de quelques années.

Les Cantons qui n'auraient pas rempli, au moment où l'article 20 de la Constitution entrera en vigueur, les obligations militaires qui leur sont imposées par l'ancienne Constitution et les lois fédérales seront tenus de les exécuter à leurs propres frais.

ARTICLE 2. Les dispositions des lois fédérales, des concordats et des Constitutions ou des lois cantonales contraires à la présente Constitution cessent d'être en vigueur par le fait de l'adoption de celle-ci, ou de la promulgation des lois qu'elle prévoit.

ARTICLE 3. Les nouvelles dispositions concernant l'organisation et la compétence du Tribunal fédéral n'entrent en vigueur qu'après la promulgation des lois fédérales y relatives.

ARTICLE 4. Un délai de cinq ans est accordé aux Cantons pour introduire la gratuité de l'enseignement public primaire (article 27).

ARTICLE 5. Les personnes qui exercent une profession libérale et qui, avant la promulgation de la loi fédérale prévue à l'article 33, ont obtenu un certificat de capacité d'un Canton ou d'une autorité concordataire représentant plusieurs Cantons, peuvent exercer cette profession sur tout le territoire de la Confédération.

Ainsi arrêté par le Conseil national, pour être soumis à la votation du peuple suisse et des cantons.

Berne, le 31 janvier 1874.

*Le Président :*

ZIEGLER.

*Le Secrétaire :*

SCHIESS.

Ainsi arrêté par le Conseil des États, pour être soumis à la votation du peuple suisse et des Cantons.

Berne, le 31 janvier 1874.

*Le Président :*

A. KOPP.

*Le Secrétaire :*

J.-L. LÜTSCHER.

*Arrêté fédéral corcernant le résultat de la votation sur le projet de Constitution fédérale révisée du* 31 *janvier* 1874 (*du* 29 *mai* 1874).

L'ASSEMBLÉE FÉDÉRALE DE LA CONFÉDÉRATION SUISSE,

Vu les procès-verbaux de la votation à laquelle le peuple suisse a procédé dans toute la Confédération le dimanche 19 avril 1874, sur le projet de Constitution fédérale révisée, du 31 janvier 1874 ;

Après avoir pris connaissance des déclarations des autorités cantonales compétentes, touchant le vote des États ;

Vu le message du Conseil fédéral, du 20 mai 1874, duquel il résulte ce qui suit :

*a. Relativement au vote du peuple*, les opérations du 19 avril ont donné les résultats suivants :

| Cantons. | Acceptants. | Rejetants. |
|---|---|---|
| Zurich | 61,779 | 3,516 |
| Berne | 63,367 | 18,225 |
| Lucerne | 11,276 | 18,188 |
| Uri | 332 | 3,866 |
| Schwyz | 1,988 | 9,298 |
| Unterwalden-le-Haut | 562 | 2,807 |
| Unterwalden-le-Bas | 522 | 2,235 |
| Glaris | 5,196 | 1,643 |
| Zoug | 1,797 | 2,740 |
| Fribourg | 5,568 | 21,368 |
| Soleure | 10,739 | 5,746 |
| Bâle-Ville | 6,821 | 1,071 |
| Bâle-Campagne | 9,236 | 1,428 |
| Schaffhouse | 6,596 | 219 |
| Appenzell Rh.-E | 9,858 | 2,040 |
| Appenzell Rh.-I | 427 | 2,558 |
| St-Gall | 26,134 | 19,939 |
| Grisons | 10,624 | 9,492 |
| Argovie | 27,196 | 14,558 |
| Thurgovie | 18,232 | 3,761 |
| Tessin | 6,245 | 12,507 |
| Vaud | 26,204 | 17,362 |
| Valais | 3,558 | 19,368 |
| Neuchâtel | 16,295 | 1,251 |
| Genève | 9,674 | 2,827 |
| | 340,199 | 198,013 |

En conséquence, le projet de constitution révisée a été adopté par 340,199 citoyens et rejeté par 198,013, de sorte que le nombre des acceptants est de 142,186 supérieur à celui des refusants.

*b. Relativement au vote des Etats*, les Cantons suivants ont formulé des votes spéciaux :

Uri ........ le 5 mai 1874.
Unterwalden-le-Bas ........ le 6 avril 1874.
Glaris ........ le 12 avril 1874.
Grisons ........ le 1 mai 1874.
Tessin ........ le 5 mars 1874.
Genève ........ le 19 avril 1874.

Les États de Glaris, des Grisons, du Tessin et de Genève se sont prononcés pour l'acceptation, et ceux d'Uri et d'Unterwalden-le-Bas pour le rejet.

Tous les autres Etats ont déclaré qu'ils considéraient le résultat du vote populaire comme étant le vote de l'État.

Il en résulte que le projet de Constitution révisée a été adopté par 14½ Etats, savoir: Zurich, Berne, Glaris, Soleure, Bâle, Schaffhouse, Appenzell Rh.-E., St-Gall, Grisons, Argovie, Thurgovie, Tessin, Vaud, Neuchâtel et Genève; et qu'il a été rejeté par 7½ états, savoir: Lucerne, Uri, Schwyz, Unterwalden, Zoug, Fribourg, Appenzell Rh.-I., et Valais;

*Déclare ce qui suit :*

1°. La Constitution fédérale révisée, telle qu'elle se trouve renfermée dans la loi fédérale du 31 janvier 1874, a été acceptée soit par la majorité des citoyens suisses ayant pris part à la votation, soit par la majorité des Cantons; en conséquence, elle est, par le présenté arrêté, solennellement declarée en vigueur à dater du 29 mai 1874.

2°. La présente déclaration est transmise au Conseil fédéral pour qu'il pourvoie à ce qu'elle reçoive la publicité nécessaire et qu'il prenne les mesures ultérieures d'exécution.

Ainsi arrêté par le Conseil national,
Berne, le 28 mai 1874.
*Le Président :*
ZIEGLER.
*Le Secrétaire :*
SCHIESS.

Ainsi arrêté par le Conseil des États,
Berne, le 29 mai 1874.
*Le Président :*
A. KOPP.
*Le Secrétaire :*
J.-L. LÜTSCHER.

LE CONSEIL FÉDÉRAL ARRÊTÉ:

L'arrêté fédéral ci-dessus sera, avec la Constitution fédérale elle-même, inséré au Recueil officiel des lois de la Confédération et communiqué aux Gouvernements cantonaux pour qu'ils lui donnent la publicité convenable en le faisant afficher.

Berne, le 30 mai 1874.

*Le Président de la Confédération :*

SCHENK.

*Le Chancelier de la Confédération :*

SCHIESS.

---

*Mr. Delaplaine to Mr. Fish.*

No. 773.]

AMERICAN LEGATION,
*Vienna, August* 3, 1874. (Received August 18.)

SIR: In compliance with the Department circular-dispatch of the 23d of June last I have endeavored to obtain reliable and authentic information in regard to the course pursued by the government of Austria-Hungary, in relation to the adjustment of claims presented against it. I have mainly consulted in this matter with the Count Revertera, the chief of the legal section of the imperial and royal ministry for foreign affairs. The report and general observations with special reference to the schedule of inquiries forwarded by the Department in the dispatch alluded to, which I have drawn and herewith append, have been obligingly revised by him, and have been pronounced correct in every respect. I shall transmit through Mr. Consul Robinson, via Hamburg, certain volumes for reference, containing more detailed and copious information, as well as full statements of the laws and ordinances upon the subject. The titles of such volumes being as follows:

1. Das allgemeine bürgerliche Gesetzbuch für das Kaiserthum Oesterreich.
2. Die Civil- und Militair-Jurisdictionsnorm. The formula of civil and military jurisdiction.
3. Staatsgrundgesetze der österreichischen Monarchie. State fundamental laws of the Austrian monarchy.
4. Supplement to same.
5. The universal citizens' law-books for the Austrian empire.
6. Katechismus der österreichischen Staatsverfassung. Catechism of the Austrian state constitution.

I have, &c.,

J. F. DELAPLAINE.

---

*Report and general observations upon the subject referred to in Department circular-dispatch of 23d June, 1874.*

1. It is not within the province of either legislative branch of the government to investigate or entertain the examination of claims against the government, with the possibly single exception, that in the case of the omission or refusal of any official to perform administrative acts incumbent upon him under his duty or obligations as such, then a petition by the party aggrieved may be made to either branch of the reichsrath for relief. In such case there is no investigation or trial, but the petition will be transmitted to the president of the ministry, with the injunction to cause justice to be done in the matter.

2. The matter is referred to a committee for examination and subsequent report, but no special means are afforded for obtaining evidence on behalf of the government, other than by a simple citation of witnesses to appear before the committee.

3. The executive department is in no case whatever authorized or empowered to examine or determine claims of any class; but in matters purely administrative, the ministry may be called to give decisions under its responsibility in case any party con-

siders himself aggrieved, as in the case, for instance, of an excessive tax or contribution being imposed, &c. There exists a draught of law for the establishment of a court of administration, to be called "Verwaltungsgericht," which has, however, not yet been voted upon in the reichsrath. This court is intended to correct any erroneous decision of the ministry, but only in reference to matters purely administrative.

4. Every citizen having any claim, either pecuniary or for damages, against the government, is entitled to prosecute the same by suit at law, equally as against an individual, but before the landesgericht, (provincial court,) excepting when the subject of the claim has reference to the right of the occupation of landed property, or to the rents or income arising from real estate, in which case the suit must be prosecuted before the bezirksgericht, or district court, within the district where such property is situated, and this privilege extends to aliens alike as to citizens.

5. Aliens, whether resident or non-resident, are entitled to maintain actions in all the courts of law of the empire, and stand upon the same footing as citizens, with the single exception of an absence of reciprocity existing on the part of the native country of such alien being a fact, which might, if proved, exclude him from the privilege.

Further, a non-resident alien can, before prosecuting a suit at law, be required to furnish security for costs to be paid by him if so adjudged by the court; but only when such security in similar cases is required in his country.

6. The two classes of claims may be distinguished as those having reference to political rights, and those founded upon contract, or private rights. The adjudication under the former is properly appertaining to the reichs gericht, composed of members nominated by the Crown and elected by the reichsrath; but in all cases of private right, the procedure in complaints against the government consists in the presentation by the prosecutor of his complaint to the respective court having jurisdiction, which orders the same to be served upon the finanz procuratur, whose duty it is to defend the government, which possesses no privileges, in regard to evidence in its behalf or in procuring same, but stands in the same position as an ordinary defendant.

It may be further remarked that the sovereign himself is amenable to the ordinary courts of justice, as any private person in matters affecting his private domain, personal property, or rights. In the former case, the customary legal process is served upon the I. & R. verwalter, or manager of the domain, otherwise, upon the hofmeisterant.

The simple privilege possessed by the state in the matter of bringing actions for real property, consists in the right of prescription being in its favor for a period of forty years instead of thirty, in the case of individuals.

---

*Mr. Boker to Mr. Fish.*

No. 210.] LEGATION OF THE UNITED STATES,
*Constantinople, August* 11, 1874. (Received September 2.)

SIR: I have the honor to acknowledge the receipt of a dispatch, unnumbered, under date of June 23, 1874, together with a "schedule of inquiries," the object of which dispatch is to obtain exact information regarding the practice of the Ottoman government in the adjudication of claims against that government, in order that the information thus sought may be used "for the purpose of facilitating the adjustment and determination of claims presented against the Government of the United States, whether held by its own citizens or by the subjects or citizens of foreign governments, and with a view of establishing, as far as may be practicable, a general and uniform system and mode of procedure for the investigation and determination of these classes of claims" by the Government of the United States.

The underlying principles, which pervade public affairs in the United States and in the Ottoman Empire, are so antagonistic that, save in the way of contrast, I doubt whether the governmental practices of the latter country could be made to serve as a basis for either theory or action in the former country. As this essential difference in the spirit and the form of the two governments is well known to the Department,

I shall proceed, without further preliminary remarks, to reply to the questions contained in the "schedule of inquiries," adding thereto such information as the subject may seem to demand.

Question 1. "Are claims against the government investigated, determined, and, if allowed, their payment directed and provided for by the legislative branch of the government?"

Question 2. "If the legislative authority does entertain such claims, what is the mode of procedure, by committee or otherwise, and what means, if any, are provided for procuring evidence on behalf of the Government?"

Both the above questions are answered by saying that the constitutional distinction between the legislative and the executive branches of the government, which prevails in all civilized countries, does not exist in the absolute monarchy of Turkey. In that country the legislative and the executive functions of the government are but one, and their administration is lodged in the same hands.

Question 3. "What provision, if any, is made for the examination and determination of claims by the executive department? What is the mode of procedure in the investigation of claims by or before executive officers; and what means are provided for procuring evidence on behalf of the government?"

Claims on behalf of or against the Ottoman government are, by the regulation which defines the constitution and the functions of the council of state, submitted for investigation to the appropriate section of that body, which, sitting as a tribunal, has the same power as any court of law to summon witnesses and to procure evidence on either side.

The council of state consists of about fifty members, notables of the empire, who are appointed by the Sultan. This body is divided into five sections of ten members each, each section having cognizance of a particular department of the public administration. Section 1 is charged with the interests of the interior, the war, and the marine departments. Section 2 with the finance and the *evcaf* departments; the latter department being that which regulates the vast and complicated questions of the *vacoufs*, or religious establishments of the empire, which hold, either in fee-simple or by lien, a hand upon a great body of the real estate of Turkey. Section 3 is charged with the legislative department in all its branches. Section 4 with the public works, the commercial and the agricultural departments. Section 5 with the department of public instruction.

On a claim being made by or presented against the Ottoman government, the claim is delivered for investigation to that section of the council of state to which the question properly belongs. The section, after trying the case by the ordinary rules of evidence, reports to the whole body of the council, which latter in turn submits its views as to the merits of the affair, in the form of a report, to the grand vizier. It must be borne in mind that the council of state is an advisory body merely, having no executive functions whatever. Should the grand vizier be satisfied with the report of the council of state, its advice is put in force by his decree, which is final. Should the grand vizier and the counsel of State differ in opinion, the question is recommitted to the latter, with instructions from the former to alter its judgment in accordance with the supreme will; a means of arriving at absolute truth and justice which, so far, has never been neglected.

Should a claim, treated as above stated, be one between the government and an Ottoman subject, it would be terminated by the execution of the decree of the grand vizier, from which there is no appeal save by the rare and difficult means of a petition to the Sultan himself; a mode of redress which the government takes care to render it next to impossible to obtain.

The mode of procedure, in the case of claims for or against foreigners, differs entirely from that above described, as will hereafter be shown.

Question 4. "Is there any provision of law allowing a citizen or subject to sue the government in the regularly-established courts, or in any special tribunal, and does the privilege of maintaining an action against the government (if it exists) extend to aliens?"

Claims on the part of Ottoman subjects against the government are not triable by the ordinary courts of Turkey, but must be prosecuted by petition to the grand vizier, who refers such claims to the council of state, at his discretion. Foreign governments have never recognized this procedure as applicable to their subjects or citizens, but claim to bring suits, to which the Ottoman government is a party, before the *tidjaret*, or mixed commercial court. This claim, although it has been and is now disputed by the government, has never been positively denied in practice. The usual way, however, of presenting claims of any importance against the Ottoman government is by means of direct diplomatic intervention. The grand vizier then advises with the council of state, as before mentioned, and afterward renders his decision to the foreign embassy or legation. In the unusual event of a settlement not being arrived at as the result of one of those prolonged negotiations between a foreign representative and the Ottoman government, I judge that the ambassador would insist either that the government should agree to an arbitration or answer to a citation before the *tidjaret*, and I do not think that the government could avoid submitting to one of these alternatives, such is the influence of diplomacy in this imperfectly-organized and self-distrustful state.

Question 5. "What is the status of aliens before the regularly-established courts of the country? Can they maintain an action in such courts against a citizen or subject; and if so, does the privilege extend to all aliens, or is it confined to resident aliens only?"

The status of aliens before all the Ottoman courts, with the single exception of the *chér'i*, or real-estate court, is the same as that of Turkish subjects. In the *chér'i* the testimony of Christian witnesses is not admitted. Considering how readily and at what low rates oral testimony is purchasable in Turkey, the above provision seems to be a wise one, although it is but a half measure, for in order to render the course of justice as to testimony perfectly pure and unsuspected, Mussulman witnesses, by an extension of the system, should also be excluded. The court might then rely, as it generally does at present, upon documentary evidence; or, lacking the latter, might hear both sides of the cause, and settle it scientifically, according to what philosophers call the "antecedent probabilities."

Non-resident aliens, properly represented by counsel, have the same privileges before the Ottoman courts as resident aliens.

Here, setting theory aside, it may be well to say something as to the practice which exists in Turkey regarding suits between foreigners of different nationalities and between foreigners and Ottoman subjects. Causes between foreigners of different nationalities are always tried in the consular court of the defendant. Of course, in anticipation of a law-suit, there is always a struggle on each side to secure the position of defendant—a supposed necessity for success that sometimes leads to actions of which I fear rigid moralists would not always approve.

Suits between foreigners and Ottoman subjects are invariably brought before the *tidjaret*, or mixed court of commerce, with the exception only of such suits as relate to real estate, which latter are under the exclusive jurisdiction of the *chér'i*. Trial by jury does not exist in the Ottoman Empire. The *tidjaret* is a court composed of five judges; the president and two members of which are Ottoman subjects, not necessarily Mussulmans, and the other two judges are of the nationality of the foreign party to the suit. The procedure before the *tidjaret* is the same as that before any court, composed solely of judges, in our own country. It should also be added, in justice to the character of the *tidjaret*, that its decisions may sometimes be respected.

The saddest exhibition which a Turkish court presents is the taking of oral testimony. As I have before said, testimony as to any conceivable state of the so-called facts of a case can easily be purchased, and is used with the most reckless profusion, even by the parties to a suit who have justice upon their side. At the doors of all the courts, particularly, by some irony of Heaven, before the doors of the semi-ecclesiastical court of the Sheik-ul-Islám, at all hours of the day, squat men whose sole business it is to be employed as witnesses in causes about which they know nothing at the outset. The character of these men depends upon the intelligence with which they can receive a lie, and the plausibility with which they can afterward utter it. To hear the Oriental volubility and vehemence with which these false witnesses will hurl their opposing lies into one another's teeth, the auditor might readily mistake the testimony for the argument, and the deponent for the advocate; so circumstantial is the statement and so fee-zealous and passionate is the style of its delivery. In consequence of this state of things, oral testimony goes for little before a Turkish court when opposed by documentary proof or the probabilities of common sense, provided always the court itself be inclined to render justice.

Question 6. "If different systems of adjudication exist as regards different classes of claims, what is the system with reference to each class, and what the mode of procedure and the privileges of the Government in relation to evidence in its behalf and the means of procuring such evidence?"

The system of adjudicating all classes of claims, for or against the Ottoman government, is theoretically the same in all cases. The procedure before the council of state, and the rules as to testimony and the means of procuring it, are the same as those before an ordinary tribunal.

That which has already been written will perhaps render needless any further expansion of the subject, as suggested in section 7 of the "schedule of inquiries." I shall inclose with this dispatch a copy of all that has been so far published of a work entitled *Legislation Ottomane*, by his excellency Aristarchi Bey, the present Ottoman minister at Washington, which work may be of interest to the Department, as it contains the only codification of Ottoman law in a foreign language that has yet been attempted, and its successful execution does great honor to its distinguished author. The volumes which are to follow, I shall forward to the Department on their completion. The theory of Turkish legal organization, as set forth in the pages of *Legislation Ottomane*, cannot fail to attract attention when read in correlation with the practice which I have briefly indicated in this dispatch.

I have the honor, &c.,

GEO. H. BOKER.

[1 inclosure, "Legislation Ottomane," 2 volumes.]

*Mr. Hoffman to Mr. Fish.*

No. 1018.] LEGATION OF THE UNITED STATES,
*Paris, August* 13, 1874. (Received August 28.)

SIR: Referring to your circular letter of June 23, 1874, I have now the honor to forward to you herewith a copy of a letter received this morning from the French government, giving the information required by you as to the mode of prosecuting claims against the government in France, the means of procuring testimony for the government, &c.

Accompanying the letter will be found a number of documents, printed and written.

There has been some delay in communicating this information, which the Duke Decazes regrets. Whether, now that it is communicated, it will be found to be thorough and comprehensive, and covering the point, much insisted on in the questions, of the manner of procuring testimony for the government, you can better judge than I. One thing strikes me, however, the great prominence given in this dispatch to the liberality of the French government in making provisions for indemnities to sufferers from civil war, and this without the slightest distinction between the citizen and the foreigner. A captious spirit might suggest that this was intended as a hint to us to do likewise.

I shall write to the Duke Decazes to thank him for the trouble he has taken in the matter.

I have the honor to be, very respectfully, your obedient servant,
WICKHAM HOFFMAN.

Hon. HAMILTON FISH,
*Secretary of State.*

---

VERSAILLES, *August* 12, 1874.

SIR: You did me the honor to address me on the 7th ultimo, for the purpose of expressing to me the desire, on behalf of the Government of the United States, to be informed as to the mode of procedure adopted in France in the case of claims against the state.

I should have been happy to comply with your request sooner, but just as your letter reached me the National Assembly was about to enter upon the consideration of an important measure connected with the same subject, and as the adoption of said measure seemed probable, I preferred to await the vote of the assembly, in order to be able to send you full information.

The measure proposed by M. Denormandie and his colleagues has now become a law of the country, having been promulgated in the official journal of the 7th instant. I therefore hasten to answer the various questions propounded by you, in the order observed in your communication.

Question 1. "When claims brought against the government have been examined and admitted, does the legislative branch of the government regulate and provide for payment of the same?"

According to the laws of France an action may be brought against the state by a private individual either before the civil or administrative tribunals, according to the nature of the case. If the state is sentenced to pay a sum of money, such sum is taken from the budget of expenditures, and as it is the duty of the legislative branch to vote the budget, it follows that the legislative branch really provides for the payment.

Claims against the state brought before the courts constitute what it is customary to call "*actions contentieuses;*" *i. e.*, actions in which it is presumed that a right, in the judicial sense of the word, is claimed.

In other cases—and your request for information probably refers to claims of this kind—it happens that individuals *whose interests have suffered some detriment* bring claims against the state, either addressing the administration directly or the legislative branch. If the admission of these claims involves the payment of pecuniary indemnities, it is the duty of the legislative branch to provide for the payment in case no appropriation has previously been made to meet these expenditures.

Question 2. "When the legislative branch receives such claims, what is the mode of procedure? Are commissions appointed for their settlement? What means are provided for the establishment of proof?"

There is no special mode of procedure. Claimants may present petitions, or deputies, either in their own name or in the name of the parties interested, may introduce measures before the legislative branch; or the government itself may bring in a bill.

If a petition is presented, the assembly, in case of its admission, refers it to the ministry having jurisdiction in the matter to which the petition refers. If a motion is made or a bill presented, the examination thereof is referred to a commission, which makes its report, and the assembly passes a vote of approval or rejection. In the first case the law which is passed regulates the fundamental points of the right to indemnity and the details of execution. In general, the legislative branch does not decide as to the admission or rejection of the claims which the parties interested may have to present in execution of the law; the legislative branch generally leaves this to be done by administrative commissions, after it has prescribed the principal rules or mentioned the general conditions which are to be fulfilled.

The events which have taken place in France since the last war have given rise to several legislative provisions of this kind. The following is an enumeration of them according to their respective dates:

Law of June 15, 1871, on requisitions.

Law of September 6, 1871, granting the sum of 106,000,000 to the sufferers by the war.

Law of April 7, 1873, providing for an additional grant of 260,000,000.

Law of July 28, 1874, (passed on motion of Denormandie and others,) granting still another sum of 26,000,000 to a special class of sufferers.

The first of these laws (that of June 15, 1871, inclosure No. 1) was designed to reimburse in full such persons as had been obliged to meet requisitions ordered by the French authorities, civil or military. The measure was not limited to the bearers of regularly-issued certificates. Persons who had not received regular requisitions were, in spite of that fact, allowed to present their claims to the proper authorities.

The law of September 6, 1871, (inclosure No. 2,) established the principle of solidarity, in accordance with which the legislator designed to cause the whole nation to aid in making good the material damages of all kinds caused by the war. This law allowed, provisionally, the sum of 100,000,000 to be distributed among the invaded departments; and also, the sum of 6,000,000, which latter was specially appropriated to the payment of damages caused by the re-instatement of the lawful power in Paris after the insurrection of the commune. The most liberal spirit presided over the application of the principle of indemnification. No distinction was made on account of the causes of the damages. All persons who had suffered material losses in consequence of the war were allowed to present their claims, whether for war-contributions, fines, or anything of the kind.

Contributions in money which had been levied as imposts by the German authorities were refunded (article 5 of the law) to the municipalities and individuals who had paid them.

For the examination of the claims two kinds of commissions were appointed, viz, cantonal commissions, which decided in the first place, and departmental commissions, appointed for the purpose of revising the decisions of the former, (article 2 of the law.)

All the details of the execution of the law were prescribed in decrees published in a series of circulars from the ministry of the interior, (inclosure No. 3.)

The law of April 7, 1873, (inclosure No. 4,) consists of two parts, having for their object, the one the repayment to the city of Paris of the amount levied by the Germans as a war-contribution; the other the payment of the indemnities remaining due for the reparation of material war-damages. For the sum of 140,000,000, which was allowed to it, the city of Paris obligated itself to pay the indemnities for the reparation of the damages caused by the insurrection of the commune and by the return of the troops to Paris. The details of execution are nearly the same as those prescribed for the preceding law. (Inclosures 5 and 8—there are two inclosures marked 8.)

The law of July 28, 1874, (inclosure No. 9,) requires a special explanation.

The National Assembly, in passing the two indemnity laws of September 6, 1871, and April 7, 1873, intended to grant relief to all persons who, having suffered from the war, could not, in strictness, base an appeal for indemnity upon any right thereto. These measures had thus left certain classes of losses unprovided for, for the reparation of which it was thought that the parties interested had ground for an action before the courts. Such especially were the losses occasioned by the preventive measures adopted in certain localities at Paris, Lyons, Belfort, &c., for the requirements of the national defense, which had caused the destruction of a considerable amount of property. Experience having shown, however, that jurisprudence was far from being fixed in this manner, [matter ?] that on a certain number of points the right was doubtful, and that consequently respectable interests would suffer, since, if rejected by the courts, they could receive no part of the indemnities granted by the previous laws, the assembly, wishing to do justice to all, decided to make a further appropriation of 26,000,000 designed especially for the relief of persons who, during the war, had suffered material and direct losses resulting from the defensive measures adopted by the French military authorities.

The law of the 28th of July last closes the series of relief measures which the assembly and the government were led by a spirit of justice and a humane policy to adopt. After the passage of these three laws, it may be said that there is no kind of damage resulting from war for which relief has not been granted, if not in full, at least in a certain measure, and that without respect of persons. Foreigners, Germans as well as others, were allowed to receive a share of the indemnities granted, whether these had been appropriated to the reparation of losses resulting from the war, properly so called, or to that of losses caused by the insurrection of the commune.

France has always taken the most liberal standpoint in granting indemnities after civil wars. Thus it was that a law of December 13, 1830, supplementary to the law of the 30th of August preceding, placed the sum of 2,400,000 francs to the credit of the government for the purpose of indemnifying the sufferers by the July revolution. Another law, of December 24, 1851, (inclosure No. 11,) appropriated 5,600,000 francs to the relief of the persons who had suffered damages to their property in consequence of the revolution of February, and the revolution of June, 1848. In all these cases, foreigners, as well as French citizens, were permitted to enjoy the benefits of the measures of relief which were adopted.

This note would not be complete if mention were not made of a law which, without comprising the responsibility of the state, nevertheless enters into the same order of ideas.

The law of the 10th of Vendémiaire, year IV, (inclosure No. 12,) renders the communes responsible for acts of violence committed in their territories by mobs and armed or unarmed assemblages, as well as for reparation of the damages resulting therefrom. The benefits of this law may be claimed by foreigners as well as native citizens.

Question 3. "What methods are adopted for the examination and settlement of claims by the executive branch of the government? What is the mode of procedure for the examination of claims by or before the agents of the executive, and what are the means prescribed for the establishment of proof?"

When claims are brought against the government, each department examines such matters as are within its province, and the claims are acted upon or not, according as they are deemed well founded or inadmissible. There is no special procedure for this examination. The minister or his representatives decide with perfect freedom, and if the claimant is not satisfied with their adverse decision, he may carry his claim, according to the nature of the case, either before the ordinary courts or before the administrative jurisdiction.

When the claims are such that the legislative branch of the government is called to act upon them, as was seen in the case of war damages, the mode of procedure and the methods of proof are prescribed by the laws referred to under No. 2 of the questions, and the administrative circulars (see inclosure No. —) give all information on this head.

Question 4. "Are there any legal provisions which permit a citizen or a subject to bring an action against the government in the regularly-established courts of justice, or in a special court; and if a privilege is necessary in order to bring suit against the government, is this privilege extended to foreigners?"

As was seen under No. 1, any citizen may bring an action against the government in the courts of justice, if he considers that his rights have suffered any detriment.

In principle the ordinary courts are incompetent when the case to be decided depends upon the interpretation of administrative acts. In this case it is proper to address the administrative tribunals, (councils of prefecture, councils of state.) Formerly no action could be brought against public functionaries unless the authorization of the council of state had previously been obtained. This provision has been abolished since 1870.

There is no special tribunal in France for foreigners. These have access to the courts the same as native citizens, except that a foreigner who brings an action is obliged to furnish the security *judicatum solvi*. This is required by way of provision for the sentence that may be pronounced against him.

Question 5. "What is the status of foreigners before the regularly-established courts of the country? Can they bring an action before these courts against a citizen or a subject; and, if so, is this privilege extended to all foreigners, or is it confined to resident foreigners?"

The explanations given for the fourth question are, in a great measure, applicable to the fifth.

Foreigners may bring suit against a *citizen of the country* in all courts; the formality of security is, however, required. No distinction is made between the resident and the transient foreigner. Neverthelesss, it is proper to observe that, regularly, in order to enjoy civil rights in France, a foreigner must have been authorized to fix his domicile there.

Question 6. "If various systems of admission exist for different classes, what system is observed in reference to each class? What is the mode of procedure, and the privilege of the government in reference to the proof? What are the means of establishing this proof?"

By the explanations already given, it is seen that there is, properly speaking, no special system of admission according to the kind of claims. Either the claims are within the province of the tribunals, and then they must be brought in the ordinary form, before the civil courts or before the courts of administrative litigation; or the claims are not within the province of the tribunals, and then they are matters for purely administrative decision. There is no special procedure. The agents of the executive examine them, forming their conclusions by the aid of all the means in their power, without being restricted to particular forms.

Finally, if a special law is passed, as in the case of war damages, provision is therein made for the mode of procedure, and the method of establishing proof.

Such is, sir, recapitulated as succinctly as possible, the information which seems suitable in reply to the series of questions in relation to which you have done me the honor to consult me. Should these explanations, which relate to a subject of so wide a range, seem to you insufficient, or obscure on certain points, I shall be most happy to complete them, or to elucidate their meaning.

Accept the assurances, &c.

DECAZES.

Mr. WASHBURNE,
*Minister of the United States.*

---

[Inclosure No. 1.]

*A law relative to requisitions made upon private citizens, since the commencement of the war, by the civil and military authorities.*

(June 15, 1871. Published in the Official Journal of June 22, 1871.)

The National Assembly has adopted, the president of the council, chief of the executive power of the French Republic, promulgates, the following law:

ARTICLE 1. The bearers of requisition certificates given by the French authorities, civil or military, since the beginning of the war, shall be obliged, under penalty of forfeiting all claim upon the treasury. to deposit, within two months, at the office of the prefect of the department, or at that of the sub-prefect of the district in which such requisitions were made, the said certificates, with a statement of the amounts claimed by them, and the documentary evidence in support of their claims, if the delivery thereof has not yet been made to the proper authorities.

All persons thinking themselves entitled to indemnity, on account of the furnishing of articles of any kind, which they may have been compelled to furnish or deliver to the French troops without having received regular requisitions, must likewise deposit, under penalty of forfeiting their right to indemnity, at the places and within the period of time above mentioned, a statement of the sums to which they claim that they are entitled, together with the documentary evidence in their possession.

A receipt shall be given to depositors.

2. The provisions of this law shall be conveyed to the knowledge of the parties interested by means of special handbills, and the fact of the posting of such bills shall be shown by a report of the mayor.

The period of two months, which is specified in the foregoing article, shall not commence until these bills shall have been posted.

3. Within the three months following the expiration of the term granted for the depositing of requisition certificates, the proper authorities shall decide upon all claims presented by the depositors.

Done in open session at Versailles, May 19 and 17, and June 15, 1871.

The president,

JULES GRÉVY.

The secretaries:

PAUL BETHMONT,
MIS DE CASTELLANE,
VTE. DE MEAUX,
PAUL DE RÉMUSAT,
BON DE BARANTE.

The president of the council, chief of the executive power of the French Republic,
A. THIERS.

The keeper of the seals, minister of justice,

J. DUFAURE.

[Inclosure No. 2.]

*A law providing that contributions, requisitions, and material damages of all kinds, caused by the invasion, shall be paid by the French nation at large.*

SEPTEMBER 6, 1871.

The National Assembly has adopted, and the President of the French Republic promulgates, the following law:

Whereas, in the late war, the portion of the territory invaded by the enemy suffered numberless burdens and underwent numberless devastations; and, whereas, the sentiments of nationality which are in the hearts of all Frenchmen impose upon the state the obligation of indemnifying those who have suffered these exceptional losses in the common struggle;

The National Assembly, without intending any violation of the principles laid down in the law of July 10, 1791, and the decree of August 10, 1853, decrees:

ARTICLE I. An indemnity shall be granted to all those upon whom, during the invasion, contributions have been levied or requisitions made, either in money or in goods, or who have paid fines or suffered material damages.

ARTICLE II. The amounts of these contributions, requisitions, fines, and damages shall be verified by the cantonal commissions now acting under the direction of the minister of the interior.

A departmental commission shall revise the labor of the cantonal commissions, and shall finally fix the sum of the losses of which evidence may be furnished. This commission shall be composed of the prefect, president, of four councilors-general, designated by the council-general, and of four persons representing the minister of the interior and the minister of finance.

ARTICLE III. When the extent of the losses shall have been thus verified, a law shall fix the amount which the condition of the public treasury shall permit to be granted for their payment, and shall provide for its distribution. The sum of one hundred millions of francs shall be placed immediately at the disposal of the minister of the interior and of the minister of finance to divide among the departments according to the losses suffered by them, in order to be distributed by the prefect, assisted by a commission to be appointed by the council-general, among the most needy victims of the war and the communes which are most involved in debt. This first appropriation shall form a part of the sum total allotted to each department in order to be distributed among all those having well-founded claims.

ARTICLE IV. The sum of six millions of francs shall likewise be placed at the disposal of the minister of finance and of the minister of the interior, in order to be (unless in case some other provision shall be made) distributed among those who have suffered most from the operations of attack made by the French army for the purpose of re-entering Paris.

ARTICLE V. Independently of the foregoing provisions, contributions in money collected by way of taxes by the German authorities shall be repaid as follows:

SECTION I. Those communes which have paid sums by way of taxes shall be re-imbursed by the treasury.

SEC. II. Tax-payers who shall furnish evidence of the payment of sums in the same manner, either to the Germans or to the French municipal authorities, shall be permitted to deduct such amount from their taxes for 1870 and 1871. They shall be obliged to produce, within one month, their documentary evidence.

SEC. III. The above regulation shall comprise—

First. The amount of the direct French tax;

Second. Double this amount, representing the indirect tax claimed by the Prussians.

All that in these payments shall exceed the double direct tax shall be considered as a simple war-contribution, and governed by the principles laid down in the foregoing articles.

Done in public session at Versailles, July 3, August 8, and September 6, 1871.

The president,

JULES GRÉVY.

The secretaries:

PAUL BETHMONT,
VTE. DE MEAUX,
PAUL DE RÉMUSAT,
BON DE BARANTE,
MIS. DE CASTELLANE,
N. JOHNSTON.

The President of the French Republic,

A. THIERS.

The minister of the interior,

F. LAMBRECHT.

[Inclosure No. 3.]

*Occurrences prior to the 3d of March.*

It has been asked whether the law of September 6 was applicable both to damages caused by the German army and those caused by the French army. No doubt can be entertained upon this head; the law is explicit. It appears, in fact, from the discussion which took place in the National Assembly, and especially from the declaration made by the minister of commerce in the name of the government, that the law of September 6 is applied in a general way *to all those who have suffered material damages* from the war, without distinguishing whether these damages were caused by the French army or by the enemy.

A desire has also been expressed to know whether this general expression to all those was applied without distinction to all persons, whether French or of foreign birth, who have suffered from the effects of the war. In principle, the doctrine which consists in allowing foreigners to participate in the measures of reparation granted to French citizens is entirely in accordance with the law of nations and with the spirit of justice of modern society. This doctrine, moreover, has not only the merit of being liberal; in a political point of view it has its advantages also. We often have to claim indemnities in foreign countries in favor of our citizens who have suffered in consequence of internal or external wars. By admitting foreigners in our country to enjoy the benefit of these indemnities, we give to our own claims in their countries a strength of which our diplomatic agents can usefully avail themselves, and to which they have already given their attention since the passage of the law of September 6.

I therefore beg you, Mr. Prefect, to consider the claims of foreigners in the work of revision which is to be done. Nevertheless, as we have with certain foreign powers treaties which have created a particular conventional right in favor of our respective citizens, and as with others the application of the principle of indemnity involves a question of reciprocity, it will be your duty to inform me beforehand of each affair concerning a foreigner, since the regulation which is to concern him must preserve a provisional character until its final decision by my department and that of foreign affairs.

---

[Inclosure No. 4.]

*A law appropriating the sum of* 140,000,000 *to the city of Paris and the sum of* 120,000,000 *to the invaded departments.*

(April 7, 1873.—Published in the official journal of April 3, 1873.)

The National Assembly has passed, the President of the French Republic promulgates, the following law:

ARTICLE I. There shall be granted from the funds of the treasury, first, to the city of Paris the sum of 140,000,000 of francs; second, to the departments invaded the sum of 120,000,000 of francs, for the purposes hereinafter specified.

ARTICLE II. The sum of 140,000,000 of francs granted to the city of Paris by Article I shall be paid in twenty-six annuities, in half-yearly payments of 4,840,424 francs 40 centimes each, comprising the amortization and the interest at five per cent.

A first sum of 9,680,848 francs 80 centimes is inscribed in the budget of the minister of the interior for 1873.

In view of this appropriation, the city of Paris shall be responsible:

1st. For the payment of the balance of the indemnities remaining due for the reparation of material damages caused either within Paris or in its environs by the military operations of the second siege.

2d. For the reparation of the material damages suffered by property, whether movable or immovable, in Paris and its environs, and resulting from the insurrection of March 18, 1871.

These two indemnities shall be definitively determined by commissions, presided over by the prefect of the Seine.

The payment shall take place as follows:

For the first category, in fifteen equal annuities with interest at five per cent.

For the second category, in fifteen equal annuities without interest, the whole, according to the resolution of the municipal council dated July 19, 1872.

ARTICLE III. In order to facilitate the operations of discount which may be agreed upon by the city and the parties receiving indemnities, the city of Paris is authorized to conclude with loan societies agreements for discount at the minimum rate of six per cent., not including a commission of two per cent. once paid. It may also commence them, if deemed expedient, with the aid of its funds in the treasury and the resources of its floating debt.

ARTICLE IV. The balance which shall remain unexpended in the hands of the city after the above payments shall have been made, shall represent the indemnity granted to it for the surplus of its claims.

ARTICLE V. In view of the appropriation granted in Article I, the city of Paris shall raise no claim against the state, either for re-imbursement of the balance of the war-contribution of 200,000,000 of francs, or for the re-imbursement of its war-expenses and the loss suffered by it in consequence of the insurrection of March, 1871.

ARTICLE VI. It is authorized for the term of fifteen years, on the conditions established by the resolution of the municipal council at Paris, dated March 22, 1873, to collect 17 centimes on the principal of the tax on landed, personal, and movable property, and on doors and windows, and of five centimes on the license-tax.

ARTICLE VII. The appropriation of 120,000,000 of francs granted from the funds of the treasury to the departments invaded, according to Article I of this law, shall be applied as follows: 8,049,280 francs 65 centimes to the balance of the re-imbursement of taxes paid to the Germans; 111,950,719 francs 35 centimes to the reparation of all losses and all damages suffered, in consequence of the invasion, by individuals, cities, communes, and departments, during the war of 1870-'71.

The sum of 8,049,280 francs 65 centimes shall be paid on the same terms as the sums appropriated by the law of May 27, 1872, and a like sum is placed at the disposal of the minister of finance during the year 1872.

The sum of 111,950,719 francs 35 centimes shall be paid in twenty-six annuities, in equal half-yearly payments of 3,870,635 francs 70 centimes each, comprising the amortization and the interest at 5 per cent.

The sum of 7,741,271 francs 40 centimes is placed at the disposal of the minister of the interior for this purpose during the year 1873.

The distribution shall be made by the minister of the interior among the invaded departments, according to the losses verified by the departmental commissions for revision, account being kept of the sums allotted in the first distribution of one hundred millions of francs.

The sums allotted to the departments, according to the provision of the present article, shall be divided among the parties interested, namely, departments, communes, or individuals, by a decision of the council-general.

This decision shall be given in accordance with the recommendations of the commission for distribution, to be appointed according to article III of the law of September 6, 1871, and to be presided over by the prefect.

Nevertheless, the decisions of the councils-general shall only be executed after having been approved by the minister of the interior.

ARTICLE VIII. The sums contributed to the communes shall be paid to them by annuities in the manner specified in the fifth paragraph of Article VII.

The amounts granted to individuals may be paid to them in cash. The departments or the communes shall to this effect be authorized to convert into money, by way of discount, the portion of the annuity corresponding to the private claims. To this effect, they are authorized to make such financial operations as shall be judged most expedient. Nevertheless, the discount paid by them shall not exceed 6 per cent. without including a commission of 2 per cent., once paid.

ARTICLE IX. A decree, issued in the form of public regulations, shall determine in what proportion it may be expedient to deliver to the departments, to the communes, or to individuals, certificates of liquidation representing the annuities granted by the present law.

The same decree shall determine the form and the conditions of delivery of titles to those having well-founded claims.

Done in public session, at Versailles, April 7, 1873.

*The President,*

L. BUFFET.

*The secretaries,*

FELIX VOISON.
L. GRIVART.
E. DE CAZENOVE DE PRADINE.
ALBERT DESJARDINS.

*The President of the Republic,*

A. THIERS.

*The minister of the interior,*

E. DE GOULARD.

---

[Inclosure No. 5.]

MINISTÈRE DE L'INTÉRIEUR.—DIRECTION DE L'ADMINISTRATION DÉPARTEMENTALE ET COMMUNALE.—PREMIÈRE DIVISION.—PREMIER BUREAU.—INDEMNITÉS POUR DOMMAGES DE GUERRE. (RÉPARTITION DEFINITIVE.)—CIRCULAIRE.

VERSAILLES, *le* 15 *mai* 1873.

MONSIEUR LE PRÉFET, l'article 3 de la loi du 6 septembre 1871, relative à la réparation des dommages résultant de l'invasion, portait:

"Lorsque l'étendue des pertes aura été ainsi constatée, une loi fixera la somme que l'état du Trésor public permettra de consacrer à leur dédommagement et en déterminera la répartition."

Dans sa séance de 7 avril dernier, l'Assemblée nationale a voté le nouveau subside promis. Je vous envoie ci-joint le texte de la loi.

L'article 1er accorde à la ville de Paris une somme de 140 millions et aux départements envahis une somme de 120 millions.

Cette allocation complétera l'œuvre de réparation que l'Assemblée nationale et le Gouvernement ont résolue de concert.

Les articles 2, 3, 4, 5, et 6 concernent le mode de payement de l'allocation attribuée à la ville de Paris; je n'ai pas aujourd'hui à m'en occuper.

Aux termes de l'article 7, il est fait deux parts de la somme de 120 millions accordée aux départments envahis: la première, s'élevant à 8,049,280 fr. 65 cent., servira à par faire le crédit de 53,658,759 francs ouvert par la loi du 27 mai 1872, et destiné au remboursement des impôts payés aux Allemands, conformément aux dispositions de l'article 5 de la loi du 6 septembre 1871; c'est à M. le Ministre des finances à en régler la répartition. La seconde, s'élevant à 111,950,719 fr. 35 cent., sera affectée à la réparation de toutes les pertes et tous les dommages subis, du fait de l'invasion, par les départements, les communes et les particuliers. C'est à mon administration qu'est dévolu le soin d'en assurer le partage. La presente circulaire a pour but de faire connaître les règles générales auxquelles il sera soumis.

Les payements auront lieu en vingt-six annuités par termes semestriels égaux comprenant l'amortissement et l'intérêt à 5 p. % (art. 7, § 5). Je traiterai cette question à l'occasion de l'article 9 de la loi dans une circulaire speciale qui suivra le règlement d'administration publique dont je me réserve de vous parler tout à l'heure.

Dès maintenant j'appelle votre attention sur les paragraphes 6, 7, 8, 9, et 10 de l'article 7.

BASES DE LA RÉPARTITION DE L'INDEMNITÉ ENTRE LES DÉPARTEMENTS.

Un décret de M. le Président de la République arrêtera la distribution de l'allocation de 111,950,719 fr. 35 cent. entre les départements envahis, au prorata des pertes constatées paréles Commissions, de révision dont l'article 2 de la loi du 6 septembre 1871 avait prescript la formation. Le gouvernement, en y procédant, tiendra compte des sommes attribuées dans la répartition du crédit primitif de 100 millions (Décret du 27 octobre 1871).

Pour opérer sur des bases équitables, mon intention est de rendre autant que possible uniforme le travail des Commissions de révision. Or, vous le savez, Monsieur le Préfet, dans tous les départements elles n'ont pas agi en se plaçant au même point de vue: quelques-unes ont admis certains dommages que d'autres ont rejetés; des omissions ont eu lieu dans plusieurs départements; dans d'autres on a écarté comme tardives certaines réclamations, bien que la loi du 26 septembre 1871 n'ait fixé aucun délai à peine de forclusion.

Enfin des dommages résultant de vols, d'incendies et de faits d'occupation de troupes postérieurs au 2 mars 1871, constatés cependant parédes procès-verbaux, n'ont pas été admis partout, les commissions de révision étant alors autorisées à croire que le gouvernement allemande en accepterait le remboursement intégral. Or, soit que les demandes n'aient pas été produites dans le délai d'un mois accordé, pour cette catégorie de dommages, par l'article 5, § 2, de la loi du 6 septembre 1871, soit qu'elles n'aient pas été accueillies par la Chancellerie allemande, les Commissions de révision les ont écartées; il ne serait cependant ni juste ni équitable que les intéressées fussent privés aujourd'hué d'une réparation quelconque.

Les états, d'ailleurs très-sommaires, que j'ai sous les yeux, présentent donc dans leur composition des variations nombreuses qui, si elles étaient maintenues, porteraient atteinte à des droits légitimes et fausseraient la répartition générale.

Chargé par la loi de corriger ces inégalités et de restituer au travail définitif ce caractère de justice et ces conditions d'harmonie et de régularité qu'il ne pouvait avoir, alors que les commissions locales jugeaient isolément et se déterminaient par des appréciations consciencieuses sans doute, mais auxquelles manquait un lien général, je dois aujourd'hui, Monsieur le Préfet, faire appel à votre concours pour être mis à même de statuer, comme l'a voulu le législateur, en appliquant le même traitement aux situations similaires et en rétablissant, par conséquent, entre les états d'origine diverse, une uniformité devenue indispensable.

Voici les dispositions que je vous recommande dans ce but:

ÉTAT GÉNÉRAL DES PERTES.

Vous ferez d'abord examiner par la Commission de révision toutes les demandes écartées comme tardives, celles que je vous ai adressées et qui vous parviendront directement. Mais comme il est nécessaire de clore au plus tôt les états de perte, vous préviendrez les intéressés, par tous les moyens de publicité possible, que toutes les demandes présentées postérieurement au 8 juin prochain seront considérées comme nulles et non avenues.

Sans attendre que la Commission ait achevé son travail, vous devrez former un dossier spécial de chaque réclamation et des piéces qui l'accompagnent.

Ces piéces seront renfermées dans un bordereau sur lequel on indiquera le numéro d'ordre, les noms de la commune, du canton, de l'arrondissement et celui du pétitionnaire.

Lorsque les dossiers seront ainsi disposés, vous les classerez par commune et suivant l'ordre alphabétique. Les dossiers de chaque commune formeront une liasse; ces liasses seront également classées suivant l'ordre alphabétique des communes dans une chemise comprenant tous les articles du canton; ces chemises seront elles-mêmes rangées suivant l'ordre alphabétique des cantons de l'arrondissement.

Enfin les dossiers de chaque arrondissement seront à leur tour classés par ordre alphabétique.

Ainsi distribuées, les réclamations seront analysées dans un tableau dont je vous envoie les formules avec la présente circulaire.

Les dommages inscrits au compte personnel du départment feront l'objet du premier article et le dossier portera le numéro 1. On écrira le mot "département" à la 3e colonne.

Dans la même colonne on portera successivement, en descendant d'une ligne:

1° Le nom du premier arrondissement (ordre alphabétique);

2° Le nom du premier canton, et enfin le nom de la première commune qui recevra le numéro 1 (dans la 1re colonne).

Si la commune a éprouvé des dommages, elle formera un article spécial désigné par le mot "commune." Les noms des particuliers viendront ensuite dans l'ordre du classement et recevront un numéro qui sera porté sur la chemise.

Vous n'éprouverez pas de difficulté pour remplir la colonne 4 (montant des impôts, contributions et amendes payés); les chiffres ayant été arrêtés par les Commissions de révision, il vous suffra de les inscrire en ayant soin d'arrondir le nombre en francs. Si le nombre des centimes est inférieur à 50, vous le négligerez; s'il est supérieur, vous augmenterez de 1 franc la partie entière. Par exemple, si les contributions payées par une commune ou un particulier s'élèvent à 105 fr. 45 cent., vous inscrirez 105 francs; si, au contraire, elles s'elèvent à 105 fr. 75 cent., vous inscrirez 106 francs.

Pour remplir la colonne 5 (montant des sommes payées en exécution de l'article 5 de la loi du 6 septembre, 1871), vous aurez à vous concerter avec M. le Trésorier-général, qui devra mettre à votre disposition tous les renseignements nécessaires. M. le Ministre des finances m'a assuré tout son concours. Les chiffres de la colonne 6 représenteront en nombres ronds les différences entre les chiffres de la colonne 4 et ceux de la colonne 5; ils devront aussi être portés en francs, ainsi que je l'ai indiqué plus haut. Il en sera de même pour les inscriptions des colonnes 7 à 24.

Lorsque le tableau aura ainsi été préparé, vous me le transmettrez accompagné de tous les dossiers; j'y ferai les additions ou retranchements destinés à le mettre en harmonie avec celui des autres départements, et j'arrêterai la répartition dans les termes prévus par le paragraphe 7 de la loi du avril. Il serait à désirer qu'elle pût avoir lieu avant la prochaine session du conseil général.

J'insiste donc pourque le tableau et les documents annexés que le décret visera me parvienment au plus tard le 20 juin.

### RÉPARTITION ENTRE LES INTÉRESSÉS.

Aux termes des paragraphes 8 et 9 de l'article 7 de la loi, les sommes allouées aux départements seront distribuées entre les intéressés (départements, communes ou particuliers) par une décision du conseil général rendue sur les propositions de la commission instituée sous votre présidence.

Dès que je vous notifi rai le décret de réartition, vous réunirez la Commission, et votre premier soin sera de lui faire remarquer que le travail actuel n'a pas le même caractère que celui de 1872.

Vous le savez, en effet, la première allocation était destinée aux victimes les plus nécessiteuses et aux communes les plus obérées. C'est donc avec raison que la plupart des commissions locales se sont attachées d'abord à pourvoir aux besoins les plus pressants; mais toutes n'ont pas suivi la même règle, et si, au début, pour des motifs dont je ne conteste pas la valeur, des personnes dont la situation n'était pas réellement nécessiteuse ont été admises à l'indemnité, les mêmes raisons de les y faire participer n'existeraient plus, aujourd'hui, qu'il s'agit d'un solde. En regard de ces situations, les unes définitivement satisfaites, les autres appellées à recevoir un nouveau dédommagement, il en est, Monsieur le Préfet, qui n'avaient pas d'abord été prévues et auxquelles l'Assemblée nationale a voulu également venir en aide.

Ainsi, le gouvernement a pris l'engagement à la tribune d'étendre les secours de l'État, par mesure exceptionelle, à quelques établissements et communes, heureusement en petit nombre, sur qui semblent s'être plus particulièrement abattus les désastres de la guerre. Il y a là des ruines qui, faute de ressources, n'ont pas encore été relevées. La Commission devra en tenir grand compte dans son travail. Je devance ses sympathies et les vôtres, Monsieur le Préfet, en vous rappelant, à cet égard, le désir de l'Assemblée.

À quelque catégorie de droits ou d'infortunes que doivent s'appliquer les propositions de la Commission ou même les décisions du conseil général, il ne vous échappera pas, Monsieur le Préfet, que ces évaluations n'auront que le caractère d'un travail préparatoire. La répartition ne deviendra définitive qu'après avoir été approuveé par le Ministre de l'intérieur (article 7, § 10).

Vous aurez, en conséquence, à me faire parvenir, dés la clôture de la session d'août, le tableau dûment rempli par les soins du conseil général; je reviserai, s'il y a lieu, l'opération et je fixerai les droits de chacun.

Le rôle des indemnitaires sera immédiatement établi dans mes bureaux et je vous en adresserai un exemplaire que vous notifierez par extrait aux intéressés dans la forme qu'indiqueront mes instructions ultérieures.

PAYEMENT DES INDEMNITÉS.

Conformément à l'article 8, § 1er, les sommes attribuées aux départements et aux communes seront payées en vingt-six annuités par termes semestriels égaux. L'ordonnancement aura lieu suivant les règles ordinaires de la comptabilité publique.

Quant aux indemnités dues aux particuliers, la loi prévoit (art. 8, § 2) que les payements pourront être faits comptant; elle autorise à cet effet les départements et les communes à convertir en argent, par voie d'escompte, la portion de l'indemnité correspondant aux réclamations privées, et à se procurer les ressources au moyen des opérations financières que seront jugés les meilleures.

Cette substitution des d 'partements et des communes aux particuliers est soumise à une condition essentielle; l'escompte à supporter par ces derniers ne devra pas dépasser 6 p. %, non compris un droit de commission de 2 p. % une fois payé.

Pour assurer l'exécution de cet article de la loi, vous inviterez le conseil général à se prononcer sur la question de savoir s'il entend faire profiter les indemnitaires de la faculté d'un remboursement immédiat. Vous joindrez une copie du procès-verbal de sa délibération aux propositions de répartition présentées par l'assemblée départementale. Suivant les résolutions qui seront prises par le conseil, je vous inviterai à demander une délibération analogue aux conseils municipaux des communes intéressées. Mon administration sera ainsi en mesure de préparer le décret qui déterminera, conformément aux prescriptions de l'article 9, dans quelle proportion il y aura lieu de remettre aux départements, aux communes et aux particuliers les bons de liquidation représentatifs des annuités, et qui réglera la forme des titres et les conditions de leur remise aux aya..ts droit.

Je vous transmettrai, quand le moment sera venu, des instructions au sujet de cette liquidation.

Quant à présent, je me borne à vous recommander l'exécution scrupuleuse et prompte des instructions qui précédent. Le sujet est digne de votre sollicitude, et, en vous demandant de m'aider à réaliser les généreuses intentions des représentants du pays, je suis assuré de ne pas faire un vain appel à votre dévouement et au patriotisme des commissions locales et du conseil général.

Recevez, Monsieur le Préfet, l'assurance de ma considération très-distinguée.

Le Ministre de l'Intérieur, E. DE GOULARD.

---

*Loi portant allocation à la ville de Paris d'une somme de 140 millions, et aux départements envahis d'une somme de 120 millions.*

L'Assemblée nationale a adopté, le Président de la Republique Française promulgue la loi dont la teneur suit:

ARTICLE PREMIER. Il est accordé sur les fonds du Trésor: 1° à la ville de Paris une somme de cent quarante millions de francs (140,000,000f); 2° aux départements envahis une somme de cent vingt millions de francs (120,000,000f), pour être appliquées aux emplois qui seront ci-après indiqués.

ART. 2. La somme de cent quarante millions de francs (140,000,000f) accordée à la ville de Paris par l'article 1er ci-dessus sera payée en vingt-six annuités en deux termes semestriels de quatre millions huit cent quarante mille quatre cent vingt-quatre francs quarante centimes (4,840,424f 40c) chacun, comprenant l'amortissement et l'intérêt à 5 p. %.

Une première somme de neuf millions six cent quatre-vingts mille huit cent quarante-huit francs quatre-vingts centimes (9,680,848f 80c) est inscrite au budget du ministére de l'intérieur, exercice 1873.

Moyennant cette allocation, la ville de Paris supportera: 1° le payement des soldes

des indemnités restant dues pour la réparation des dommages matériels causés à l'intérieur ou à l'entour de Paris par le fait des opérations militaires du second siége ;

2° La réparation des dommages matériels soufferts par les propriétés mobilières et immobilières de Paris et de ses alentours, et résultant de l'insurrection de 18 mars, 1871.

Ces deux ordres d'indemnités seront définitivement réglés par des commissions administratives présidées par le Préfet de la Seine.

Le payement aura lieu comme suit :

Pour la première catégorie, en quinze annuités égales, avec intérêt à 5 p. %.

Pour la seconde catégorie, en quinze annuités égales, sans intérêt. Le tout conformément à la délibération du conseil municipal en date du 19 juillet 1872.

ART. 3. Pour faciliter les opérations d'escompte qui pourraient être convenues de gré à gré entre la ville et les indemnitaires, la ville de Paris est autorisée à conclure avec des sociétés de crédit des traites d'escompte au taux maximum de 7 p. %, non compris un droit de commission de 2 p. % une fois payé.

Elle pourra également les commencer, s'il y a lieu, à l'aide de ses fonds de trésorerie et des ressources de sa dette flottante.

ART. 4. Le solde qui restera libre aux mains de la ville, après que les payéments ci-dessus auront été effectués, représentera le dédommagement qui lui est accordé pour le surplus de ses réclamations.

ART. 5. Au moyen de l'allocation votée dans l'article 1er, la ville de Paris ne pourra exercer contre l'État aucune réclamation tant à raison du remboursement du solde de la contribution de guerre de 200 millions de francs que du remboursement de ses dépenses de guerre et des pertes qu'elle a subies par suite de l'insurrection du 18 mars 1871.

ART. 6. Est autorissée pour la durée de quinze ans, aux conditions réglées par la délibération du conseil municipal de Paris en date du 22 mars 1873, la perception de dix-sept centimes (0f 17c) sur le principal des contributions foncière, personnelle et mobilière et des portes et fenêtres, et de cinq centimes (0f 05c) sur la contribution des patentes.

ART. 7. L'allocation de cent vingt millions de francs (120,000,000f), accordée sur les fonds du Trésor aux départements envahis en vertu de l'article 1er ci-dessus, s'appliquera, savoir :

Pour huit millions quarante-neuf mille deux cent quatre-vingts francs soixante-cinq centimes (8,049,280f 65c) au solde des remboursements pour impôts payés aux Allemands.

Pour cent onze millions neuf cent cinquante mille sept cent dix-neuf francs trente-cinq centimes (111,950,719f 35c) à la réparation de toutes les pertes et de tous les dommages subis, par le fait de l'invasion, par les individus, les villes, les communes et les départements, pendant la guerre de 1870–1871.

La somme de huit millions quarante-neuf mille deux cent quatre-vingts francs soixante-cinq centimes (8,049,280f 65c) sera payée dans les mêmes conditions que les sommes allouées par la loi du 27 mai 1872, et un crédit de pareille somme est ouvert au Ministre des finances sur l'exercice 1872.

La somme de cent onze millions neuf cent cinquante mille sept cent dix-neuf francs trente-cinq centimes (111,950,719f 35c) sera payée en vingt-six annuités, par termes semestriels égaux de trois millions huit cent soixante-dix mille six cent trente-cinq francs soixante-dix centimes (3,870,635f 70c) chacun, comprenant l'amortissement et l'intérêt à 5 p. %.

Un crédit de sept millions sept cent quarante et un mille deux cent soixante et onze francs quarante centimes (7,741,271f 40c) est ouvert pour cet objet au Ministre de l'intérieur.

La répartition se fera par les soins du Ministre de l'intérieur, entre les départements envahis, au prorata des pertes constatées par les commissions départementales de révision, en tenant compte des sommes attribuées dans la premiére répartition de cent millions de francs (100,000,000f).

Les sommes attribuées aux départements conformément aux dispositions du présent article seront réparties entre les intéressés, à savoir : le département, les communes ou les particuliers, par une décision du conseil général.

Cette décision sera prise sur les propositions de la commission de répartition établie par l'article 3 de la loi du 6 septembre 1871, présidée par le préfet.

Toutefois les décisions des conseils généraux ne seront exécutées qu'après avoir été approvées par le Ministre de l'intérieur.

ART. 8. Les sommes attribuées aux communes leur seront réglées par annuités, dans les conditions indiquées au paragraphe 5 de l'article 7 ci-dessus.

Les sommes attribuées aux particuliers pourront être payées comptant. Les départments ou les communes sont à cet effet, autorisés à convertir en argent, par voie d'escompte, la portion de l'annuitè correspondant aux réclamations particulières. A cet effet, ils sont autorisés à faire les opérations financières qui seront jugées les meilleures.

Toutefois l'escompte par eux supporté ne pourra excéder 6 p. %, non compris un droit de commission de 2 p. % une fois payé.

ART. 9. Un décret rendu dans la forme des réglements d'administration publique determinera dans quelle proportion il pourra y avoir lieu de remettre aux départements, aux communes et aux particuliers, les bons de liquidation représentant les annuités accordées par la présente loi.

Le même décret réglera la forme et les conditions de la remise des titres aux ayants droit.

Délibéré en séance publique, à Versailles, le 7 avril 1873.

*Le Président :* L. BUFFET.
*Les Secrétaires :* FÉLIX VOISIN, L. GRIVART, E. DE CAZENOVE DE PRADINE, ALBERT DESJARDINS.

*Le Président de la Republique:* A. THIERS.
*Le Ministre de l'Intéreur,*
E. DE GOULARD.

---

[Inclosure No. 6.]

*Report to the President of the French Republic.*

VERSAILLES, *August* 23, 1874.

MR. PRESIDENT: The law of April 7, 1873, granted an appropriation of 140 millions of francs to the city of Paris, on condition that the city should pay, in fifteen years, the indemnities for the damages caused by the second siege and the insurrection of March 18, 1871. This sum is to be paid in fifty-two semi-annual payments of 4,840,424 francs 40 centimes, comprising the amortization and the interest at five per cent.

As so long a time is granted for these payments, the city could not procure the funds which it needed, in order to pay in full those persons who, according to article III, desire to realize immediately the indemnities which are due them.

You have desired to remedy this difficulty by submitting to the assembly the bill which was passed during its session of July 26, 1873. This law will facilitate the performance of the obligations which are imposed upon the city. To this end, it authorizes the city to create bonds of liquidation, which the municipal administration will place in circulation, or which it will deliver directly to the parties entitled to indemnity, if the latter prefer.

This combination, which was proposed May 23, 1873, by the prefect of the Seine, and adopted on the 31st of the same month by the municipal council of Paris, consists in offering to parties entitled to indemnity, in exchange for the bonds which are payable in fifteen years, to which the law of April 7 entitles them, bonds of liquidation yielding 5 per cent. interest, payable at par in twenty-six years, by way of semi-annual drawings, and having an approximatively equal value in cash.

Such is the system established by the law of July 26, the enforcement of which will be provided for by decree, according to Article II.

NUMBER OF TITLES.

We have the honor to propose to you, Mr. President, to limit the issue of bonds to 277,300, representing a capital of 138,650,000 francs. This capital is inferior to the active debt (*créance*) of the city; but as it has not seemed possible to admit notes smaller than 500 francs each, although on the one hand a certain number of persons entitled to indemnity have a claim only to sums inferior to this amount; on the other, the delivery of the bonds could not take place before the expiration of the first half year of the period of re-imbursement. The department of the interior and the department of finance have recognized the necessity of ordering the payment for the benefit of the city of the amount of the first half annuity, 4,840,424 francs 40 centimes, which will serve to pay in full the indemnities amounting to less than 500 francs and the differences of indemnities amounting to more than that sum.

This sum consists of the first half year of the interest of the debt of the state (3,500,000 francs) and of the amortization corresponding to that half year, or 1,310,424 francs 40 centimes. It now remains, therefore, only to amortize a principal of 138,659,575 francs 60 centimes, which exceeds the amount of the issue by 9,575 francs.

We will explain, as regards Article VII, why this difference cannot be covered by bonds.

EXEMPTION FROM DUTIES AND FROM THE INCOME-TAX.

The financial combination authorized by the law will result in favoring the circulation of the new values created by the city. Hence it became necessary to render them payable at all the pay-offices of the treasury, and this is prescribed by the second article. The decree submits them, moreover, to the examination of the central paying-cashier, and of the central controller of the public treasury; and, in consequence, it exempts the bonds from the payment of the duties of transmission and of the income-tax, but it leaves untouched the obligation to stamp them.

FORM OF THE BONDS.

The third article regulates the form of the bonds. This form shall be similar to the model appended to the decree.

The bonds shall have but a single series, numbered from 1 to 277,300. They shall comprise 51 coupons, the value of which shall be 12½ francs each.

DELIVERY OF THE BONDS.

The municipal receiver of the city of Paris shall be instructed to deliver the bonds to the parties interested on the presentation of, and in exchange for, provisional bonds.

METHODS OF AMORTIZATION AND TIMES OF PAYMENT.

Articles V and VI approve the plan of amortization prepared by the prefect of the Seine. This plan indicates—1. The dates of the drawings; 2. The number of the series of 100 bonds to be drawn from the wheels, to be used as the portion of the annuity which is left disposable after the payment of the interest; 3. The principal amortized at each drawing; 4. The sum necessary for the payment of the half year's interest; 5. The dates of the payments.

By reason of the amount of labor which has to be performed by the central pay-office during the first days of each quarter of a year, it was necessary to postpone the payments until the 20th of the months of April and October. In consequence, the drawings were to take place at such dates as should render it possible to give the necessary publicity to the numbers drawn. We propose to fix them at the 20th of March and the 20th of September.

In order to lighten the expense of the manufacture of the wheels, the drawings shall take place by series of 100 bonds. This mode of procedure naturally causes irregularities in the amount of the annuities, consequently the sum to be inscribed in the budget of the state suffers slight variations; but it will be possible to remedy this inequality, which is not in accord with the law of April 7, which provides for fixed annuities by carrying forward credits from one year to the other, and by causing the annual sum to be inscribed each year in the budget to vary.

SUM LEFT OVER AND ABOVE THE AMORTIZATION.

The plan of amortization not comprising, and not being able to comprise, in consequence of the obligation of making series of 100, more than 277,300 bonds, for a principal of 138,650,000, and the half annuity received by the city, amortizing only a capital of 1,340,424 francs 40 centimes, the amount of which sums is 139,990,420 francs 40 centimes, there remains, over and above the amortization of the entire sum of 140 millions, a capital of 9,575 francs 60 centimes.

The service of the interest and of the amortization of this complementary capital would impose upon the Treasury, according to the law of April 7, the obligation of paying to the city of Paris two half annuities of 334 francs 27 centimes during twenty-six years. It has seemed to us proper not to allow to remain in the budgets of the state, as in those of the city, during twenty-six years an article of so little importance, and we propose to add the payment of this sum of 9,575 francs 60 centimes and the interest (239 francs 90 centimes) to that of the first half annuity, which the treasury has already paid in coin. This mode of regulation is the more acceptable, since the amount in principal and interest of the 51 half annuities, calculated with an amortization by series of 100 bonds, must secure at the end of the period to the treasury, as compared with the results of the amortization provided by law of April 7, a saving of 33,070 francs 41 centimes.

EXPENSE OF THE OPERATION.

The advantages reaped by the city are of such a nature that it is just to make it responsible for all the expenses of the operation. In order to settle any subsequent difficulty, and although on this head the city makes no objections, it has seemed proper to us to make it an object of special provision, (Article VIII.) If you approve these suggestions, Mr. President, we sha'l have the honor to beg you to be pleased to affix your signature to the following decree.

Be pleased to accept, Mr. President, the assurances of our respect.

The minister of the interior,

BEULÉ.

The minister of finance,

P. MAGNE.

The President of the French Republic—

On report of the minister of the interior and minister of finance:

In consideration of the law of April 7 and that of July 26, 1873;

In consideration of the memorial presented May 23, 1873, by the prefect of the Seine to the municipal council of Paris;

In consideration of the resolutions of this council dated May 31 and July 1, 1873;

In consideration of the plan of amortization of the bonds of liquidation authorized by the law of July 26, 1873—

DECREES:

ARTICLE I. The number of bonds of liquidation of 500 francs each which the city of Paris is authorized to issue according to the law of July 26, 1873, is hereby fixed at 277,300.

ARTICLE II. These bonds shall be delivered by the prefect of the Seine, and examined by the central paying cashier and by the central controller of the public treasury. They are exempt from the payment of transmission duties and of the income-tax, but they shall pay a stamp-duty of 1 per 1,000, established for commercial purposes.

ARTICLE III. Each bond shall bear a number, from 1 up to 277,300, and a numbered series of 51 coupons, value 12 francs 50 centimes each. The form shall be similar to the model appended to the present decree.

ARTICLE IV. The delivery of the bonds to the parties entitled to indemnity shall be made by the municipal receiver of Paris, on presentation and in exchange for the certificate of distribution delivered to each person interested.

ARTICLE V. On the 20th of the months of March and of September of each year, the bonds payable at par shall be drawn by round series of 100 each, in accordance with the plan of amortization appended to the present decree. The first drawing shall take place on the 20th September, 1873, and the last on the 20th September, 1898.

ARTICLE VI. After the 20th of the months of April and of October, the payment of the coupons and of the bonds drawn by law shall be made at Paris, at the central pay-office of the treasury, and in the departments at the pay-offices of the paying treasurers-general and of the receivers of finance.

ARTICLE VII. The sum of 9,575 francs 60 centimes, exceeding the number which will be amortized by the issue of 277,300 bonds, shall be repaid to the city of Paris in a single payment, together with the interest due thereon, viz, 239 francs 39 centimes. These two sums shall be deducted from the amount inscribed in the budget of the minister of the interior, viz, 9,680,848 francs 80 centimes, (year 1873, chapter 35.)

ARTICLE VIII. The city of Paris shall bear all expenses resulting from the payment of the coupons and of the bonds, and, in general, expenses caused by the execution of the present decree.

Done at Versailles, August 23, 1873.

MARSHAL DE MACMAHON,
*Duke of Magenta.*

By the President of the Republic:
The minister of the interior,

BEULÉ.

The minister of finance,

P. MAGNE.

---

[Inclosure No. 7.]

MINISTRY OF THE INTERIOR,
*Versailles, September* 5, 1873.

An order issued by the minister of the interior, under date of November 29, 1871, provided for the appointment of a committee, (to be presided over by the prefect of the Seine,) whose duty it should be to appraise the damage caused by the operations of attack of the French army on re-entering Paris, and to distribute a first installment of six millions, appropriated by the national assembly September 6, 1871.

A ministerial decision, rendered in pursuance of article 2, of the law of April 7, 1873, instructed this commission definitely to settle the amount of the sum to be paid by the city of Paris in fifteen annual payments, with interest at five per cent. This commission, after having met thirty-two times, has just concluded its labors. It has fixed the number of persons entitled to indemnity at 8,146, and has caused to be prepared for delivery to each one of these persons a provisional certificate which furnishes evidence of his rights. The sum total of the damages has been fixed at 29,385,980 francs 14 centimes. The sum of six millions, distributed in the course of the year 1872, to the amount of 5,974,605 francs 47 centimes, has rendered it possible to give to the needy claimants from 30 to 35 per cent. or thereabouts, and to all others 17 per cent.

The difference, amounting to about 25,394 francs 53 centimes, was used for the payment of experts, and for payment of salary of clerks, printing of warrants, titles, &c.

The total amount to be paid by the city of Paris is, therefore, 23,411,374 francs 67 centimes, divided as follows:

| | Number of certificates delivered. | Amount of claims for losses allowed by the commission. | Amount of allowances from the appropriation of six millions. | Amount of sums still to be paid by the city of Paris. |
|---|---|---|---|---|
| Eighth arrondissement | 65 | 249, 279. 79 | 30, 832. 34 | 218, 447. 45 |
| Fourteenth arrondissement | 234 | 399, 227. 40 | 112, 334. 28 | 286, 893. 12 |
| Fifteenth arrondissement | 300 | 450, 701. 20 | 88, 049. 96 | 362, 651. 24 |
| Sixteenth arrondissement | 1, 452 | 7, 285, 823. 00 | 1, 568, 496. 55 | 5, 717, 326. 45 |
| Seventeenth arrondissement | 609 | 1, 277, 939. 25 | 270, 309. 09 | 1, 007, 630. 16 |
| CANTON OF COURBEVOIE. | | | | |
| Asnières | 580 | 1, 734, 641. 00 | 356, 364. 13 | 1, 378, 276. 87 |
| Colombes | 59 | 45, 203. 00 | 13, 440. 30 | 31, 762. 70 |
| Courbevoie | 559 | 1, 286. 400. 00 | 278, 634. 76 | 1, 007, 765. 24 |
| Gennevilliers | 62 | 40, 521. 00 | 13, 726. 00 | 26, 795. 00 |
| Nanterre | 6 | 3, 570. 00 | 813. 20 | 2, 756 80 |
| Suresnes | 54 | 28, 835. 00 | 6, 412. 45 | 22, 422. 55 |
| Puteaux | 274 | 274, 273. 00 | 60, 326. 85 | 213, 946. 15 |
| CANTON OF NEUILLY. | | | | |
| Boulogne | 148 | 254, 251. 00 | 50, 268. 26 | 203, 982. 74 |
| Clichy-la-Garenne | 104 | 327, 535. 00 | 68, 409. 10 | 259, 125. 90 |
| Levallois-Perret | 339 | 396, 062. 00 | 83, 437. 17 | 312, 624. 83 |
| Neuilly | 1, 654 | 10, 026, 039. 00 | 2, 063, 188. 92 | 7, 962, 850. 08 |
| CANTON OF SAINT DENIS. | | | | |
| Saint Ouen | 1 | 250. 00 | 175. 00 | 75. 00 |
| CANTON OF SCEAUX. | | | | |
| Antony | 3 | 900. 00 | 210. 00 | 690. 00 |
| Bagneux | 43 | 120, 790. 00 | 21, 552. 60 | 99, 237. 40 |
| Bourg-la-Reine | 6 | 10, 042. 00 | 1, 320. 00 | 8, 722. 00 |
| Chatenay | 19 | 14, 713. 00 | 3, 887. 30 | 10, 825. 70 |
| Chatillon | 123 | 382, 524. 00 | 83, 849. 50 | 298, 674. 50 |
| Clamart | 353 | 535, 289. 50 | 141, 859. 40 | 393, 430. 10 |
| Fountenay-aux-Roses | 32 | 67, 680. 00 | 14, 275. 75 | 53, 404. 25 |
| Issy | 541 | 2, 290, 412. 00 | 484, 451. 41 | 1, 805, 960. 59 |
| Montrouge | 107 | 45, 339. 00 | 9, 611. 45 | 35, 727. 55 |
| Plessis-Piquet | 19 | 25, 060. 00 | 5, 759. 60 | 19, 300. 40 |
| Sceaux | 1 | 1, 000. 00 | ............ | 1, 000. 00 |
| Vanves | 332 | 522, 030. 00 | 140, 130. 10 | 381, 899. 90 |
| CANTON OF VILLEJUIF. | | | | |
| Arcueil | 1 | 57, 625. 00 | ............ | 57, 625. 00 |
| Ivry | 3 | 2, 455. 00 | 130. 00 | 2, 325. 00 |
| Rungis | 2 | 3, 650. 00 | ............ | 3, 650. 00 |
| Thiais | 3 | 630. 00 | ............ | 630. 00 |
| Vitry | 1 | 400. 00 | ............ | 400. 00 |
| DEPARTMENT OF SEINE-ET-OISE. | | | | |
| Saint Cloud | 47 | 111, 190. 00 | 2, 350. 00 | 108, 840. 00 |
| Bellevue | 3 | 32, 000. 00 | ............ | 32, 000. 00 |
| Meudon | 4 | 92, 000. 00 | ............ | 92, 000. 00 |
| Sèvres | 1 | 4, 000. 00 | ............ | 4, 000. 00 |
| Compagnie du Chemin de fer de l'Ouest | 2 | 985, 700. 00 | ............ | 985, 700. 00 |
| General totals | 8, 146 | 29, 385, 980. 14 | 5, 974, 605. 47 | 23, 411, 374. 67 |
| Amount paid to experts | ........ | ............ | 7, 000. 00 | ............ |
| Amount paid for clerk-hire and printing | ........ | ............ | 14, 097. 27 | ............ |
| Reserve, August 21, 1873 | ........ | ............ | 4, 297. 26 | ............ |
| Total | ........ | ............ | 6, 000, 000. 00 | ............ |

Persons who have not applied for the provisional certificate prepared in their name, may apply to the minister of the interior, rue Cambacérès No. 7, from 2 to 4 o'clock.

The exchange of the provisional certificates for bonds payable to bearer will soon take place at the *palais du Luxembourg*. An advertisement in the Journal Officiel will announce the day of such exchange.

[Inclosure No. 8.]

*Report to the President of the French Republic.*

VERSAILLES, *November* 5, 1873.

Mr. PRESIDENT: The National Assembly has appropriated the sum of 211,950,719 francs 35 centimes to the reparation of all damages suffered, in consequence of the invasion, by individuals, cities, communes, and departments during the war of 1870–1871. This sum is divided into two appropriations, one of 100,000,000, granted September 6, 1871, for the benefit of the most needy victims and the communes most involved in debt; the other of 111,950.719 francs 35 centimes, which, in the view of the National Assembly, represents a final balance.

I shall have the honor, Mr. President, to make a report to you to-day concerning the distribution of this second appropriation. But in order to enable you generally to appreciate this work in its entirety, I must go further back and place before your eyes a summary analysis of the various operations to which it has given rise.

Immediately after the war, when the country was beginning to be reconstructed, the minister of the interior appointed, in all the departments invaded, cantonal commissions, to which was confided the difficult and painful task of examining the damages suffered, of verifying them, and of preparing a general statement concerning them. This preparatory examination was speedily accomplished, and if it was not always irreproachable, I will presently state why.

Toward the close of August, 1871, all the elements thereof were collected. Actuated by patriotic solicitude for so much misery, which had as yet in no wise been relieved, the National Assembly adopted a series of measures intended to pay the debt of France to that portion of the population which had suffered most cruelly.

At the same time that the first appropriation of 100,000,000 was made, the assembly appointed on the 6th of September, 1871, departmental commissions, whose duty it was made to distribute and to decide without appeal. To the minister of the interior was only reserved the care of distributing this payment on account among the thirty-four departments invaded, according to the damage suffered. The law instructed the minister of finance to repay to the communes and individuals, to the amount of double the direct tax for the period of occupation, all taxes collected by the German army. As to the expenses of lodging, board, and various requisitions made subsequently to the 2d of March, 1871, when preliminaries of peace were ratified, the management was to assure the regulation thereof.

In order to be really efficacious, it was necessary for the relief to arrive speedily for those who awaited it with such legitimate impatience. This consideration induced the Government to take, as the basis of the first division, the estimates made by the cantonal commissions. These were, it is true, only provisional allotments which were subsequently to be corrected. It was the object of the decree of October 27, 1871, the execution of which, notwithstanding all the activity of the departmental commissions of the prefects, and of the mayors, was postponed until the last days of the year 1872. The proposed decree which I have the honor to submit to you to-day is the complement thereof.

Like my honorable predecessor, M. de Goulard, I should have been very glad, Mr. President, to be able speedily to carry out the generous intentions of the National Assembly. When suffering exists, and when the government has obtained from the representatives of the country the means of alleviating it, it is its duty not to lose a day, nor even an hour. The various agents whose assistance I have invoked, have acted with the most commendable zeal. But considerable obstacles hampered my work. While it was important to perform it rapidly, it was not less essential to place it above all well-founded criticism, and it was my duty to devote the more care to that object since a special provision of the law of April 7, 1873, rendered subordinate the decisions of the cantonal commissions, of the departmental commissions, and of the councils-general themselves, to the definitive sanction of the minister of the interior.

The statement which is about to follow will give you an idea, Mr. President, of these difficulties, and will point out the course which I adopted in order to reach the best result.

The cantonal commissions had confounded in their evaluations the occurrences which took place prior to the 2d of March, which entitled the sufferers only to a partial indemnity, and the occurrences which took place subsequently to that date, which, on the contrary, entitled the sufferers to full reparation. This error occurred not only in the case of material damages. Yielding to the same idea, the communes had established no distinction between the taxes whose payment in full could be required, and the contributions, fines, &c., which could be repaid only in part, and some of them had thought proper to set aside certain classes of losses which were admitted by others; their estimates, being based only upon vague data, were generally lacking in exactness for want of rules and uniform bases. They had viewed damages of the same nature in a very different light. Hence there were singular and unjust disparities in the various cantons, which result was the more unfortunate, since the cantons, whose loss had been the object of the most conscientious estimates, were injured for the benefit of districts whose claims had been subjected to a less severe examination.

Struck by these inequalities, one of my predecessors addressed, December 12, 1871, precise and detailed instructions to the departmental commissions appointed by the law. He recommended to examine each claim produced, to verify its legitimacy, and to reduce it to its just value. He indicated the principal points to be examined, and made known the method of evaluation and the tariffs to be applied to each class of claims. From 821,087,980 francs 52 centimes, which was the sum shown by the returns prepared by the cantonal commissions, the amount of losses was reduced to 659,339,770 francs 42 centimes. The final indemnity of 111,950,719 francs 35 centimes which was granted April 7, 1873, was calculated according to this latter sum.

As regards the budget, a first result, very important without doubt, was also reached. But when it became my duty to undertake the revision with which I was charged by the law of April 7, 1873, it was not long before I discovered that the work of the departmental commissions, like that of the cantonal commissions, still left much to be desired.

After a first examination I discovered variations and differences such that I no longer doubted the necessity of reviewing the elements thereof in detail. Moreover, the payments in liquidation bonds provided by the law rendered indispensable the preparation of lists of names comprising all persons having a right to participate in the distribution. The preparation of these lists revealed facts to me which were still more to be regretted.

Some communes of revision had thought that they must take as their standard, for the want of sufficient elements to base their calculations upon, the evaluations of the cantonal commissions which they had reproduced exactly. Now, being pressed by time, the latter had been obliged to adopt, without examination in a great number of cases, the statements of the parties interested and of the municipalities.

It is readily seen that serious errors must have occurred in the work so hastily done, and which circumstances rendered still more difficult.

Often, moreover, the mayors interpreting improperly the instructions received from the ministers, or being too much occupied with the interests of their communes, had prepared a general statement of the war contributions, of the requisitions in money and in goods, of fines, of thefts, of fires, and of expenses incurred for lodging, board, &c., without giving the names of the persons who had suffered them, without furnishing any claim of the parties interested, without furnishing evidence of any kind, and based upon estimates which were almost always exaggerated.

The cantonal commissions, in the first place, the communes of the revision next, had approved these reports, or had confined themselves, without stating any reasons, to making gross reductions in the amounts presented by the municipalities, so that the most just claims were treated in the same manner as were those which had little or no foundation.

Such was the situation when I required the production of lists of names. After the lapse of more than two years, the prefects naturally found serious difficulties in presenting such lists. They were furnished to me, however, and I have not regretted the laborious investigations which they caused; for soon afterward I obtained proof that, by the side of claimants who, although worthy of interest, had had no part in the first division, there were persons who had received indemnities superior to their losses, however great the latter had been. This arose from the fact that the commissions of distribution, being unable to assign the indemnities individually, had been obliged to confine themselves to a distribution by communes, leaving to the mayors the care of proceeding to the subsequent distribution among parties having claims.

I have regretted to find that in place of making a proportionate distribution, and of assigning to the parties in their jurisdiction having claims, the amounts which properly belong to them, the members of certain municipalities had retained for their personal emolument the entire amount appropriated to their commune, and had thus indemnified themselves for the whole of their loss, the estimation of which had been examined by no one.

I could not allow such facts in the final distribution to exist, and in order surely to reach them, I required that by the side of the name of each person should be placed the amount of the loss and that of the indemnity in the first appropriation of one hundred millions.

Irregularities of another kind were also found.

Most of the communes took it upon themselves to make payment for the requisitions, expenses of boarding the troops, &c. The commissions of revision had justly permitted them to share the benefits of an indemnity; but they had failed to strike out from the claims of the inhabitants the sums which had already been repaid by the communes. It was the duty of my administration to rectify these mistakes, which were formerly serious. In a single canton of one of our richest departments, the difference amounted to nearly three millions.

Some reports included on the one hand the price of provisions for which requisition had been made by the Germans and consumed in the interior of the commune, and on the other an indemnity for board; the parties interested would thus have received for the same thing a double indemnity.

It has been necessary to reduce the expenses of lodging invariably to 1 franc 40 centimes per man, and 2 francs 15 centimes per horse, (lodging and board included.) Calculated in the lump, and on statements which were always doubtful, these expenses have sometimes been carried to the personal account of the communes, either because the inhabitants had raised no claims on this head, or because the municipalities were unable to furnish lists of names. When presented in this form, these claims have not seemed to me sufficiently well founded; and, although in certain cases appropriations have been granted, I have been obliged to set them aside, in order to prevent the municipalities (which has sometimes occurred) from having recourse to fictitious names in order to secure for the communes sums to which they were not at all entitled.

If in some departments the calculation of the expenses of lodging and board has given rise to the irregularities to which I have just referred, in others, on the contrary, the commissions of revision have not thought proper to admit these expenses, although they were justified. I have rectified this.

You see, Mr. President, control has been extended to all elements and all details.

This revision has been long and laborious; it has imposed much labor upon the offices of the prefects and the central administration, but its effect will be to secure a uniform treatment and an equitable appropriation to each department and to each person interested.

I have just succeeded in reducing the total amount of the losses from 659,339,770 francs to 657,256,923 francs.

The difference is more than 2,000,000. But any one would form a very incomplete idea of the labor who should consider this amount as being all. In order to form a correct idea of the matter it is necessary to examine the differences which, in consequence of the rectifications made, exist from one department, from one canton, from one commune, to the other. One department which presented a claim of 24,000,000 saw that claim reduced to 6,000,000; the claim of another, on the other hand, was increased by 2,000,000. In other words, what the National Assembly desired is now realized; justice is equal for all.

The proposed decree, Mr. President, will secure these results. You will observe that, while the two appropriations granted by the laws of September 6, 1871, and April 7, 1873, amount to 211,950,719 francs 35 centimes, I confine myself to suggesting to you to distribute only 200,000,000 now, and to reserve the sum of 10,950,719 francs 35 centimes. According to the express desire of the National Assembly, a part of this remainder shall be appropriated to relieve those communes and those public establishments which have suffered most from pillage and fire. The other part shall serve to make good the material damages caused to the railroad companies, which damages are estimated at not less than 8,000,000. It will be, moreover, applied to the correcting of isolated errors which may have occurred in fixing the loss and final payment of the administrative expenses of the operation. These expenses will be relatively considerable; they comprise, in fact, the salaries of persons employed, and payment for the preparation and for the distribution of the liquidation-bonds. The number of these bonds will exceed 2,000,000. It has been necessary to examine that number of particular situations.

If you approve these suggestions, Mr. President, I beg you to be pleased to affix your signature to the accompanying decree.

Be pleased to accept, Mr. President, the assurances of my respect.

The minister of the interior,

BEULÉ.

The President of the French Republic—

In consideration of the law of September 6, 1871, and that of April 7, 1873;

In consideration of the decree of October 27, 1871,

On the report of the minister of the interior—

DECREES:

ARTICLE I. The sum of 2,000,000 of francs shall be distributed among the invaded departments, according to the statements appended to the present decree, which sum represents, with the exception of 1,000,000 authorized by the decree of October 27, 1871, and the reserve hereinafter mentioned, the appropriations granted by way of indemnity of losses resulting from material damages, fines, war contributions, and requisitions in money and goods.

ARTICLE II. The sum of 10,950,719 francs 35 centimes is reserved to be appropriated: 1st, to the relief of the communes and public establishments which have suffered most from fire and pillage; 2d, to the reparation of material damages suffered by railroad companies; 3d, to the correction of errors which may have occurred in fixing the amount of losses; 4th, to the payment of the material expenses of the operation.

ARTICLE III. The minister of the interior is charged with the execution of the present decree.

Done at Versailles, October 31, 1873.

MARSHAL DE MACMAHON,
*Duke of Magenta.*

By the President of the Republic:
The minister of the interior,

BEULÉ.

*Répartition d'une somme de* 200 *millions entre départements envahis.*

Exécution des lois des 6 Septembre, 1871, et 7 Avril, 1873.

| | Départements. | Nombre de communes. | Montant des pertes constatées. | Indemnité proportionnelle. | Allocation fixée par le décret du 27 october 1871. | Indemnité arrêtée par le présent décret. |
|---|---|---|---|---|---|---|
| 1 | Aisne | 804 | 17, 267, 522 | 5, 254, 400 | 3, 748, 800 | 1, 505, 600. 00 |
| 2 | Ardennes | 487 | 41, 487, 309 | 12, 624, 400 | 4, 883, 000 | 7, 741, 400. 00 |
| 3 | Aube | 446 | 6, 741, [illegible]67 | 2, 051, 400 | 1, 261, 300 | 790, 100. 00 |
| 4 | Calvados | 78 | 674, 164 | 205, 100 | 97, 200 | 107, 900. 00 |
| 5 | Cher | 15 | 108, 416 | 33, 000 | 13, 000 | 20, 000. 00 |
| 6 | Côte-d'Or | 715 | 15, 884, 781 | 4, 833, 700 | 1, 461, 800 | 3, 371, 000. 00 |
| 7 | Doubs | 605 | 5, 945, 659 | 1, 809, 200 | 951, 700 | 857, 500. 00 |
| 8 | Eure | 604 | 13, 095, 199 | 3, 984, 800 | 1, 538, 700 | 2, 446, 100. 00 |
| 9 | Eure-et-Loir | 426 | 25, 706, 397 | 7, 822, 300 | 3, 381, 800 | 4, 440, 500. 00 |
| 10 | Indre-et-Loire | 212 | 4, 485, 296 | 1, 364, 800 | 838, 100 | 526, 700. 00 |
| 11 | Jura | 426 | 8, 580, 612 | 2, 611, 000 | 1, 111, 200 | 1, 499, 800. 00 |
| 12 | Loir-et-Cher | 275 | 20, 269, 890 | 6, 167, 400 | 2, 528, 800 | 3, 638, 600. 00 |
| 13 | Loiret | 339 | 38, 808, 128 | 11, 809, 100 | 5, 047, 400 | 6, 761, 700. 00 |
| 14 | Marne | 567 | 19, 985, 830 | 6, 081, 600 | 4, 098, 000 | 1, 983, 600. 00 |
| 15 | Marne (Haute-) | 516 | 7, 395, 288 | 2, 250, 300 | 1, 330, 700 | 919, 600 00 |
| 16 | Mayenne | 50 | 637, 350 | 193, 900 | 105, 500 | 88, 400. 00 |
| 17 | Meurthe-et-Moselle | 669 | 28, 737, 124 | 8, 744, 600 | 4, 868, 900 | 3, 875, 700. 00 |
| 18 | Meuse | 586 | 20, 189, 571 | 6, 143, 600 | 4, 211, 300 | 1, 932, 300. 00 |
| 19 | Nièvre | 2 | 5, 617 | 1, 700 | 700 | 1, 000. 00 |
| 20 | Nord | 89 | 1, 258, 025 | 382, 800 | 270, 100 | 112, 700. 00 |
| 21 | Oise | 700 | 12, 283, 248 | 3, 737, 700 | 2, 313, 500 | 1, 424, 200. 00 |
| 22 | Orne | 288 | 3, 539, 525 | 1, 077, 100 | 604, 400 | 472, 700. 00 |
| 23 | Pas-de-Calais | 122 | 2, 028, 469 | 617, 300 | 301, 100 | 316, 200. 00 |
| 24 | Belfort, (Territoire de) | 106 | 7, 410, 772 | 2, 255, 100 | 800, 600 | 1, 454, 500. 00 |
| 25 | Saône (Haute-) | 583 | 15, 078, 787 | 4, 588, 400 | 2, 058, 300 | 2, 530, 100. 00 |
| 26 | Saône-et-Loire | 6 | 31, 370 | 9, 500 | 3, 700 | 5, 800. 00 |
| 27 | Sarthe | 325 | 17, 618, 941 | 5, 361, 400 | 2, 928, 800 | 2, 432, 600. 00 |
| 28 | Seine | 71 | 72, 408, 000 | 22, 033, 400 | 11, 651, 200 | 10, 382, 200. 00 |
| 29 | Seine-Inférieure | 706 | 13, 708, 977 | 4, 171, 600 | 3, 551, 600 | 620, 000. 00 |
| 30 | Seine-et-Marne | 526 | 46, 416, 345 | 14, 124, 300 | 6, 646, 400 | 7, 477, 900. 00 |
| 31 | Seine-et-Oise | 685 | 152, 884, 447 | 46, 522, 000 | 20, 186, 400 | 26, 335, 600. 00 |
| 32 | Somme | 832 | 23, 509, 753 | 7, 153, 900 | 3, 936, 700 | 3, 217, 200. 00 |
| 33 | Vosges | 531 | 7, 899, 971 | 2, 403, 900 | 1, 144, 100 | 1, 259, 800. 00 |
| 34 | Yonne | 432 | 5, 176, 773 | 1, 575, 300 | 1, 125, 200 | 450, 100. 00 |
| | Totaux | 13, 924 | 657, 256, 923 | 200, 000, 000 | 99, 000, 000 | 101, 000, 000 00 |
| | Réserve | ........ | ........ | ........ | 1, 000, 000 | 10, 950, 719 35 |
| | | ........ | ........ | ........ | 100, 000, 000 | 111, 950, 719 35 |

Vu pour être annexé au décret du 31 octobre 1873.

*Le ministre de l'intérieur.*

BEULÉ.

---

[Inclosure No. 8, *bis*.]

The President of the French Republic—

In consideration of the law of September 6, 1871, and that of April 7, 1873;

In consideration of the estimates of damages prepared by the departmental commissions of revision:

In accordance with the suggestion of the vice-president of the council, minister of the interior,

DECREES:

ARTICLE 1. There shall be distributed among the invaded departments, according to the table appended to the present decree, the sum of two hundred and eight millions seven hundred thousand francs, (208,700,000 francs,) representing, with the exception of the deduction of one million (1,000,000 francs) authorized by the decree of October

27, 1871, and the reserve which will be referred to hereafter, the allowances granted, by way of indemnity for losses resulting from material damages, from the imposition of fines, from war contributions, and from requisitions of money and goods.

ART. 2. The sum of two millions two hundred and fifty thousand seven hundred and nineteen francs 35 centimes shall be reserved, so as to be appropriated: 1st, to the payment of the material expenses of the operation; 2d, to the reparation of the damages caused by the Germans to the railway lines.

ART. 3. The decree of October 31, 1873, is hereby revoked.

ART. 4. The vice-president of the council, minister of the interior, is instructed to enforce the execution of the present decree.

Done at Versailles, February 7, 1871.

MARSHAL DE MACMAHON,
*Duke of Magenta.*

By the President of the Republic:
BROGLIE,
*Vice-President of the Council and Minister of the Interior.*

*Distribution of the sum of* 208,700,000 *francs among the invaded departments, in pursuance of the law of September* 6, 1871, *and that of April* 7, 1873.

| Number. | Departments. | Number of communes. | Amount of bona-fide losses. | Proportional indemnity. | Allowance made by the decree of October 27, 1871. | Indemnity fixed by the present decree. |
|---|---|---|---|---|---|---|
| | | | *Francs.* | *Francs.* | *Francs.* | *Francs.* |
| 1 | Aisne | 804 | 22, 640, 847 | 6, 878, 400 | 3, 748, 800 | 3, 129, 600. 00 |
| 2 | Ardennes | 487 | 41, 487, 309 | 12, 604, 000 | 4, 883, 000 | 7, 721, 000. 00 |
| 3 | Aube | 446 | 6, 744, 056 | 2, 048, 900 | 1, 261, 300 | 787, 600. 00 |
| 4 | Calvados | 78 | 674, 164 | 204, 800 | 97, 200 | 107, 600. 00 |
| 5 | Cher | 15 | 108, 416 | 32, 900 | 13, 000 | 19, 900. 00 |
| 6 | Côte-d'Or | 715 | 16, 048, 674 | 4, 875, 600 | 1, 461, 800 | 3, 413, 800. 00 |
| 7 | Doubs | 605 | 5, 945, 659 | 1, 806, 300 | 951, 700 | 854, 600. 00 |
| 8 | Eure | 704 | 13, 364, 598 | 4, 060, 200 | 1, 538, 700 | 2, 521, 500. 00 |
| 9 | Eure-et-Loir | 426 | 25, 720, 571 | 7, 814, 000 | 3, 381, 800 | 4, 432, 200. 00 |
| 10 | Indre-et-Loire | 212 | 4, 485, 296 | 1, 362, 700 | 838, 100 | 524, 600. 00 |
| 11 | Jura | 426 | 8, 842, 960 | 2, 686, 500 | 1, 111, 200 | 1, 575, 300. 00 |
| 12 | Loir-et-Cher | 275 | 20, 273, 690 | 6, 159, 200 | 2, 528, 800 | 3, 630, 400. 00 |
| 13 | Loiret | 339 | 39, 363, 352 | 11, 958, 700 | 5, 047, 400 | 6, 911, 300. 00 |
| 14 | Marne | 567 | 26, 310, 429 | 7, 993, 200 | 4, 098, 000 | 3, 895, 200. 00 |
| 15 | Marne (Haute-) | 516 | 7, 547, 787 | 2, 293, 000 | 1, 330, 700 | 962, 300. 00 |
| 16 | Mayenne | 50 | 637, 350 | 193, 600 | 105, 500 | 88, 100. 00 |
| 17 | Meurthe-et-Moselle | 669 | 29, 095, 189 | 8, 839, 200 | 4, 868, 900 | 3, 970, 300. 00 |
| 18 | Meuse | 586 | 27, 486, 587 | 8, 350, 500 | 4, 211, 300 | 4, 139, 200. 00 |
| 19 | Nièvre | 2 | 5, 617 | 1, 700 | 700 | 1, 000. 00 |
| 20 | Nord | 89 | 1, 258, 025 | 382, 200 | 270, 100 | 112, 100. 00 |
| 21 | Oise | 700 | 12, 306, 158 | 3, 738, 700 | 2, 313, 500 | 1, 425, 200. 00 |
| 22 | Orne | 288 | 3, 540, 525 | 1, 075, 600 | 604, 400 | 471, 200. 00 |
| 23 | Pas-de-Calais | 122 | 2, 028, 469 | 616, 300 | 301, 100 | 315, 200. 00 |
| 24 | Belfort (Territoire de) | 106 | 7, 982, 546 | 2, 425, 100 | 800, 600 | 1, 624, 500. 00 |
| 25 | Saône (Haute-) | 583 | 15, 097, 275 | 4, 586, 600 | 2, 058, 300 | 2, 528, 300. 00 |
| 26 | Saône-et-Loire | 6 | 31, 370 | 9, 500 | 3, 700 | 5, 800. 00 |
| 27 | Sarthe | 325 | 17, 618, 941 | 5, 352, 700 | 2, 928, 800 | 2, 423, 900. 00 |
| 28 | Seine | 71 | 72, 870, 000 | 22, 138, 200 | 11, 651, 200 | 10, 487, 000. 00 |
| 29 | Seine-Inférieure | 706 | 13, 754, 977 | 4, 178, 800 | 3, 551, 600 | 627, 200. 00 |
| 30 | Seine-et-Marne | 526 | 46, 481, 799 | 14, 121, 300 | 6, 646, 400 | 7, 474, 900. 00 |
| 31 | Seine-et-Oise | 685 | 159, 646, 188 | 48, 501, 000 | 20, 186, 400 | 28, 314, 600. 00 |
| 32 | Somme | 832 | 23, 580, 893 | 7, 164, 000 | 3, 936, 700 | 3, 227, 300. 00 |
| 33 | Vosges | 531 | 7, 910, 921 | 2, 403, 400 | 1, 144, 100 | 1, 259, 300. 00 |
| 34 | Yonne | 432 | 6, 067, 117 | 1, 843, 200 | 1, 125, 200 | 718, 000. 00 |
| | Totals | 13, 924 | 686, 957, 755 | 208, 700, 000 | 99, 000, 000 | 109, 700, 000. 00 |
| | RESERVE. | | | | | |
| | Inhabitants of Alsace and Lorraine | | | | 1, 000, 000 | |
| | Railway companies | | | | | 1, 000, 000. 00 |
| | Material expenses | | | | | 1, 250, 719. 35 |
| | Grand total | | | | 100, 000, 000 | 111, 950, 719. 35 |

The above table is an appendix to the decree of February 7, 1874.

The vice-president of the council, minister of the interior,

BROGLIE.

The President of the French Republic—

In consideration of the report of the vice-president of the council, minister of the interior, and of the minister of finance;

In consideration of the law of April 7, 1873, appropriating the sum of 111,930,719 francs for the benefit of the invaded departments, and especially of article 9, which is as follows:

"A decree, issued in the form of the regulations of public administration, shall determine in what proportion the liquidation bonds, representing the annuities granted by the present law, shall be delivered to the departments and communes and to individuals.

"The same decree shall determine the manner and the conditions of the delivery of bonds to persons having well-founded claims;"

In consideration of the decree of February 7, 1874, providing for the distribution of the sums appropriated by the national assembly;

The council of state having been heard,

DECREES:

ARTICLE 1. Liquidation bonds representing a sum equal to the amount of the indemnities fixed by the minister of the interior in accordance with the suggestion of the general councils of the departments, shall be delivered to such departments, communes, and individuals as suffered losses during the war of 1870–1871.

ART. 2. The liquidation bonds shall be of 500 francs each. They shall each yield, after January 1, 1873, 25 francs per annum as interest, payable semi-annually; they shall be redeemed at par by lot, in accordance with the plan of amortization annexed to the present decree.

The drawing shall take place at Paris, at such time and on such conditions as may be fixed by the minister of finance.

ART. 3. All fractions less than five hundred francs (500 francs) shall be paid in provisional bonds, bearing interest from January 1, 1873; nevertheless, the interest on these provisional bonds shall not be paid until after their conversion into permanent bonds of 500 francs each.

The provisional bonds shall be in denominations of 5 francs, 10 francs, 15 francs, 20 francs, 25 francs, 50 francs, 100 francs, 200 francs, 300 francs, and 400 francs.

ART. 4. The final five hundred franc bonds and the provisional bonds shall be payable to bearer, and negotiable.

ART. 5. The final liquidation bonds shall be issued by the minister of the interior, countersigned by the central paying-cashier, and visaed by the central comptroller.

ART. 6. Both the provisional and the final bonds shall conform to the models annexed to the present decree. Each final bond shall bear fifty-two interest coupons, numbered from 1 to 52.

ART. 7. The amount to which each person is entitled shall be stated in a list which shall be prepared by the minister of the interior.

In the said list shall be stated the full name of each party entitled to indemnity, together with the amount allowed him.

ART. 8. The delivery of the bonds to persons entitled to indemnity shall be performed at Paris, by the central cashier of the public treasury, and in the departments by the paying treasurers-general, the private receivers of finance, or the collectors, on the presentation of letters of advice signed by the prefect, and for discharge by the party receiving.

If a person entitled to indemnity is unable to write, evidence of the delivery shall be furnished by the signatures of two witnesses, and by that of the accounting-agent, whatever may be the amount of the bonds.

ART. 9. The certificates designed to establish the identity or the quality of parties receiving may, at the request of the parties, be delivered on free paper and without charge, by the justice of the peace, whose attestation as to the facts therein stated shall be sufficient to exempt the accounting-agent from responsibility.

ART. 10. Liquidation bonds, to be delivered to departments and communes, either by way of indemnification for their own losses, or of repayment of such indemnities as the municipal or general councils, according to the law of April 7, 1873, (art. 8) may have consented to pay to private individuals, shall remain deposited until the time when they shall be negotiated, in the central paying-office of the public treasury; the central cashier shall deliver to the paying treasurer-general, or to the municipal receiver, certificates of deposit, stating the numbers of the bonds; the form of these certificates shall be determined hereafter by the minister of finance.

Provisionally, and until the time which shall hereafter be fixed by the minister of finance, the bonds deliverable to the communes may be deposited at the offices of the paying treasurers-general, who shall likewise deliver certificates to the municipal receivers.

ART. 11. After the 15th of January and the 15th of July of each year, the payment of the half-yearly coupons and the redemption of the bonds drawn by lot shall take place at Paris, at the central paying-office of the treasury, and in the departments, at the offices of the paying treasurers-general, and of the private receivers of the finances.

Nevertheless, payment shall be made for the half years ending July 15, 1873, January 15 and July 15, 1874, at such time as shall be fixed hereafter by a decree of the minister of finance.

ART. 12. The vice-president of the council and the minister of finance are charged, each in his own province, with the enforcement of the present decree.

Done at Versailles, March 20, 1874.

MARSHAL DE MACMAHON,
*Duke of Magenta.*

By the president of the republic:

The vice-president of the council, minister of the interior,
BROGLIE.

The minister of agriculture and commerce, minister of finance *ad interim*,
DESEILLIGNY.

---

[Inclosure No. 9.]

*A law providing for an indemnity to those who have suffered loss from destruction of property for the national defense.*

The National Assembly has passed the following law:

ARTICLE I. In derogation of existing legislation, and by way of exception, an indemnity shall be allowed to all who shall furnish evidence that they have, as proprietors or occupants, suffered material and direct damages resulting from the measures of defense which were taken by the French military authorities during the war of 1870–1871, in fortified towns or elsewhere, either within or without any military zone.

ARTICLE II. The following persons shall be excluded from the benefits of this law:

1st, those who shall not renounce any action before the judicial or administrative tribunals;

2d, those who shall not have addressed or renewed their claims to the administration, according to the first paragraph of the fourth article of this law;

3d, those who have signed an agreement to demolish at the first requisition, or whose immovable property has been constructed in violation of law.

ARTICLE III. A commission, whose duty it shall be to examine all claims, shall be appointed by decree of the president of the republic, issued in accordance with the suggestion of the minister of war and of the minister of the interior.

Claims already made must be renewed and the new claims must be addressed:

For Paris, to the department of the Seine and the minister of the interior;

For the departments, to the prefects.

ARTICLE IV. These renewals and the presentation of new claims must take place within two months from the promulgation of this law.

The mere fact of the presentation of a claim, or the renewal of one already made, shall involve the acceptance of the decision which shall be rendered by the commission.

Any person who shall not have made or renewed his claim, according to the provisions of the present article, within two months, shall forfeit the same.

As regards persons who have not the control of their property, these renewals, or the presentation of these new claims, shall be exempt from special authorization and from all judicial formalities.

ARTICLE V. The commission shall examine these claims, with the existing documents, or by the aid of any means which they may think proper to employ.

In case those who have suffered damages coming under the classes provided for and above referred to shall have enjoyed the benefit of the indemnities granted by the assembly by the law of September 6, 1871, and that of April 7, 1873, the sums received by them shall be deducted from the amount which would be granted to them by the present law.

The commission shall decide finally and without appeal the amount to which each claimant shall be entitled.

ARTICLE VI. Al ldisputes which may arise from the d·livery of the bonds, or the verification of the identity and the rights of parties interested, either in consequence of error in the names or for any other cause, shall be similarly judged, without appeal and without expense, by the justice of the peace of the canton, who shall deliver a certificate to parties entitled to indemnity, on free paper, establishing their rights.

This certificate shall take the place of the documentary evidence required by the regulations concerning public accounts.

ARTICLE VII. When total or partial liquidations shall have been approved by the administrative commission, certificates shall be issued in favor of the parties receiving indemnity, which certificates shall be paid either in liquidation bonds to the bearer, five per cent. at par, or in specie, or partly in bonds and partly in specie, on the terms and in the proportions which shall be determined by the minister of finance.

In case of the total or partial payment in specie, a deduction shall be made, at the expense of those receiving the indemnity, which deduction shall repay the expenses and the loss in the negotiation of the liquidation bonds, if any such loss shall have occurred.

ARTICLE VIII. The minister of finance is authorized to create and to negotiate, at the highest price obtainable, 52,000 liquidation bonds, payable to bearer, of 500 francs each, bearing 25 francs interest, the first payment of interest to be made January 1, 1875, and the bonds to be payable at par in twenty-five years from the latter date.

The amount of these bonds shall be devoted to the payment of indemnities for all losses, of whatever nature they may be, redress for which has been or might be demanded before the civil or administrative tribunals, or which shall form the object of claims addressed to the commission appointed by the third article of the present law.

The first allotment of thirty per cent. of these bonds may be made immediately by the commission, for the benefit of persons whose claims it may have admitted.

ARTICLE IX. A credit of 1,848,000 francs shall be opened to the minister of finance. This shall be deducted from the budget for 1875, and shall be devoted to the payment of the first annuity.

Also a credit of 200,000 francs on account, for the expenses of the operation, which shall be deducted from the budget for 1874.

ARTICLE X. Any action which may be brought before the judicial or administrative tribunals for damages caused by the military authorities for the purposes of the national defense, during the war of 1870, must be brought within one year from the promulgation of the present law.

Done in public session at Versailles, May 22, June 26, and July 28, 1874.

The President,

L. BUFFET.

The Secretaries,

FRANCISQUE RIVE,
E. DE CAZENOVE DE PRADINE,
LOUIS DE SÉGUR,
FÉLIX VOISIN.

The President of the Republic promulgates the present law.

MARSHAL DE MACMAHON,
*Duke of Magenta.*

The vice-president of the council, minister of war,

GENERAL E. DE CISSEY.

---

[Inclosure No. 10.]

*Law of August* 30, 1830.

ARTICLE 1. Rewards shall be granted to all those who were wounded while defending the national cause on the glorious days of the 26th, 27th, 28th, and 29th of July last.

The fathers, mothers, widows, and children of those who fell at that time, or who have since died in consequence of their wounds, shall receive pensions or assistance.

ART. 2. All persons whose property has been injured in consequence of these events shall be indemnified at the expense of the state.

ART. 3. A medal shall be struck in commemoration of these events.

ART. 4. A commission appointed by the King shall make the necessary investigations for the purpose of establishing the titles of those who have a right according to the foregoing articles to rewards, pensions, assistance, and indemnity. The report of the commission shall be communicated to the chambers in support of the request for the appropriation which shall be needed. The names of the citizens who have merited rewards, and a general list of those who have fallen, shall be inserted in the Bulletin of the Laws, and published in the Moniteur.

NOTE.—An appropriation of 2,400,000 francs was, in accordance with the provisions of this law, placed at the disposal of the minister of the interior by a law dated December 13, 1830.

[Inclosure No. 11.]

*Law of December 24, 1851.*

ARTICLE 1. The sum of 5,600,000 francs shall be placed at the disposal of the minister of the interior, to be applied to the payment of the indemnities to be granted to individuals whose property has suffered material injury in consequence of the events of February and June, 1848.

ARTICLE 2. These indemnities shall be apportioned under the supervision of the minister of the interior, in accordance with the decisions of the commission appointed by the decree of September 2, 1850.

---

[Inclosure No. 12.]

*Law of the 10th of Vendémiaire, in relation to the internal police of the communes of the republic.*

TITLE IV.

*Of the kinds of offenses for which the communes are civilly responsible.*

ART. 1. Each commune shall be responsible for offenses committed by open force or by violence within its territory, by mobs or assemblages, whether armed or unarmed, either against persons or property, whether the latter belong to the nation or to individuals. They shall also be responsible for the damages which may be caused by such mobs or assemblages.

* * * * * * *

ART. 3. If the mobs or assemblages have been formed by inhabitants of several communes, they shall all be responsible for the offenses which shall have been committed, and all shall be obliged to contribute both to the payment of the damages and that of the fine.

* * * * * * *

ART. 6. When any person, whether domiciled or not, in a commune shall have been robbed, maltreated, or murdered, all the inhabitants shall be held responsible for the payment of damages to him, or, in case of his death, to his widow and children.

* * * * * * *

TITLE V.

*Of civil damages and redress*

ART. 1. When, in consequence of assemblages or mobs, a citizen shall have been forced to pay; when he shall have been robbed or plundered within the territory of a commune, all the inhabitants of the commune shall be held to make restitution in hand of the articles stolen or taken by force, or to make payment therefor at the rate of double their value on the day when the robbery shall have taken place.

ART. 2. When an offense of the nature of those mentioned in the foregoing articles shall have been committed in a commune, the municipal officers or the municipal agent shall be required to obtain proof thereof within twenty-four hours, and to send a report, within three days at most, to the commissioner of the executive power near the civil tribunal of the department. Police officers shall, nevertheless, be required to fulfill, in this respect, all the obligations imposed upon them by law.

ART. 3. The commissioner of the executive power near the administration of the department in the territory of which injuries have been done by open force and by violence to the property of the nation, shall prosecute the parties who have committed such injuries for reparation and damages before the civil tribunal of the department.

ART. 4. The damages which the communes are held to pay by the terms of the preceding articles shall be fixed by the civil tribunal of the department, after an examination of the reports and other documents proving the acts of violence, excesses, and offenses.

ART. 5. The civil tribunal of the department shall fix the amount to be paid for reparation and damages within ten days, at furthest, after the sending of the reports.

ART. 6. The amount to be paid as damages shall never be less than the full value of the articles stolen or carried off.

ART. 7. The decision of the civil tribunal fixing the amount to be paid as damages shall be sent, within twenty-four hours, by the commissioner of the executive power to the departmental administration, which shall be required to send it, within three days, to the municipality or the municipal administration of the canton.

*Mr. Wing to Mr. Fish.*

No. 410.] UNITED STATES LEGATION, QUITO, ECUADOR,
*August* 13, 1874. (Received September 9.)

SIR: Herewith I have the honor to forward my note to Minister Leon, (1,) to which were appended the six interrogatories contained in dispatch of June 23, 1874, of the Department, not numbered. Nos. 2 and 3 are copy and translation of Minister Leon's answer; Nos. 4 and 5 are copy and translation of the inclosure referred to in the communication of Minister Leon.

For any further information in regard to the subject, the codes hitherto forwarded to the Department will afford it. Practically speaking, however, the answer and inclosure cover the whole matter, so far as Ecuador is able to do so under existing enactments.

I have, &c.,

RUMSEY WING.

*List of Inclosures.*

No. 1. My note to Minister Leon.
No. 2. Minister Leon's reply thereto.
No. 3. Translation thereof.
No. 4. Inclosure in Minister Leon's note.
No. 5. Translation thereof.

---

[Inclosure 1.]

UNITED STATES LEGATION,
*Quito, Ecuador, August* 1, 1874.

SIR: I have the honor to forward to your excellency a schedule of certain inquiries relative to the course pursued by the government of Ecuador in regard to the adjustment of claims presented against it, whether held by its own citizens or by the subjects and citizens of foreign governments, and concerning other matters bearing thereon.

May I beg that your excellency will furnish me with the desired information at your earliest convenience; and that, if practicable, your excellency will kindly supply me with copies of such legislative enactments and public and general regulations of the executive department as may pertain to the inquiries in question.

With assurance of my very distinguished consideration, I have, &c.,

RUMSEY WING.

His Excellency Señor FRANCISCO JANVIER LEON,
*Minister for Foreign Affairs, &c.*

---

[Inclosure 2.—Translation.]

FOREIGN OFFICE, *Quito, August* 8, 1874.

I have had the honor to receive the esteemed communication of your excellency of date 1st of the present month; and confining myself to the different points contained therein, I am happy to give your excellency the following answer:

Claims against the government, according to Ecuadorian legislation, may be made in two ways: some proceeding from contracts made by the executive power *per se*, or through its agents with a private party; and others arise from exactions committed by bodies of troops, or by damage caused in virtue of an order from the government.

In the first case, the action brought against the government must be initiated in the supreme court, which will try the cause in the ordinary way as established by the code of civil suits, and the government, as well as private parties, have the same privilege to prove their rights.

In the second case, the claim must be presented to the board of finance of the province where the exaction was made and the damage received, or to the district judge of the province, according to the time passed and the nature of the documents which prove it, as is laid down in the special law of indemnification of September 27, 1852 which your excellency will find published in the annexed copy, No. 78, of *El Nacional;* and in neither case does the government enjoy any privilege.

This right the laws concede not only to Ecuadorians, but also to resident or transient foreigners, who, in this respect, are assimilated to natives, for they are only considered exempt from certain duties, which, according to the law of nations, is not imposed upon them by an uncertain residence in the republic; and they can carry on their own suits *per se*, or by an agent empowered in the legal form.

Should the payment or indemnification be decreed by the judicial power in virtue of the collection as set forth, it is incumbent upon the legislature to authorize the expense of the sum determined in the sentence, because the executive power is not empowered to order any payment that does not appear in the general estimates of the nation or some other law.

With assurances, &c.,

FRANCISCO JANVIER LEON.

---

[Inclosure 3.—Translation.]

The National Assembly of Ecuador, considering that it is necessary to establish fixed rules, so that, according to them, such as may have reclamations against the public treasury may present their rights for the payment of money, or for forced and voluntary loans, or for supplies, or for any damage caused by commissioned authorities, or by troops, and to prevent in this wise any run upon the national income by illegal debts,

DECREES:

ARTICLE 1. When any person or corporation cannot present legal proofs to evidence forced or voluntary loans that may have been made to the republic, or supplies, or damages caused by troops, commanders of corps, or civil or military authorities, from the 1st of January, 1830, they will establish them by supplementary evidence in the time and in the conditions required by law.

ART. 2. The following will be regarded as legal proofs:

1st. The certificates of the officers of the treasury and commissaries of war, inserting also the entry in the books where the supplementary evidence may have been made;

2d. The original contracts, provided that the creditor makes it appear that, on his part, he has fulfilled the stipulations contained therein;

3d. The obligations or bills of credit given to the creditors by public functionaries and military leaders, which through public notoriety or competent proof appears, or is assured, that they were authorized to ask or demand the supplies;

4th. The vouchers of the erogations that those deputed may have given to those concerned therein through competent authority to demand them, but not those signed afterward, provided that the commission referred to is accredited and carries with it the signature of the commissioner; and

5th. The documents that assure the supplies, which, through force by troops, or by bands of armed men representing a political party, or by foreign troops in case of invasion, and that may have produced damage to the interests of any person whatsoever.

ART. 3. The proofs to accredit the authorization of the commissioners and the acknowledgment of their signatures will be presented in a verbal suit before the judge of finance of the province in which the supplies or loans were made, or the damage was suffered, previously citing the fiscal agent in the provinces where there may be one; and where not, the treasurer, or he who is acting in his stead.

ART. 4. When the reclamation is made, with the legal proofs set forth in article 2, the creditor will repair to the board of finance of the respective province; which, should they consider the evidence as sufficient, will order it to be sent to the treasury with this declaration, for the liquidation of the debt; but should they declare it insufficient, and the creditor, not conforming thereto, should insist in his reclamation through litigation, he will repair to the district judge of finance within the absolute term of thirty days, counted from the one in which the board of finance returned the proceedings for this effect, and being in the same place, it must be done in the term of eight days. The said district will try the cause in the primary court, and the matter will afterward take the ordinary course.

ART. 5. Should the board of finance not certify to any part of the amount that is asked for, with legal proofs, on account of its being insufficiently proved, the creditor may apply, in this case, to the expressed judge of finance, in the same terms and for the same effects set forth in the preceding article.

ART. 6. When the reclamation is begun with supplementary evidence, the creditor must present it to the district judge of finance of the province where the supply was given, and in lieu thereof, to the judge of the primary court who may be his substitute.

ART. 7. At the time of soliciting the supplementary proof before the district judge of finance, the creditor must name the amount that he claims if it was in money advanced, the fixed number if it were in cattle, or the maximum that he estimates that he has a right to demand in the event of his not being able to make the specification referred to.

ART. 8. The judge of finance, or his substitute, will receive himself the affidavits of the witness that the creditor may present, but when, on account of the distance from whence it is necessary to bring the evidence, he cannot comply with this matter, or have the witnesses brought into his presence, he will give the respective order to the municipal parochial authorities to receive the evidence.

ART. 9. The fiscal agent, or in lieu thereof the treasurer, or the one acting in his stead, will defend the suit against the national treasury until its definite conclusion; and all will be null that is done without summoning him or in his absence.

ART. 10. It is an obligation of the fiscal agent, treasurer, or he who may be acting in his stead, or for lack and inability of their attending, the lawyer that the district judge may name, or, in default of a lawyer, an intelligent citizen, to further all the writs, and counter affidavits conducing to the clearing up the reality of the debt which is demanded, as also to sanction the appeal that may be desired to the respective tribunals, provided that without resolution the national treasury may not have been incumbered.

ART. 11. Concluded the brief of the supplementary evidence, the judge will send them to the fiscal agent or treasurer, or their substitute, to examine them and agree thereto, but without his advancing anything thereto. The judge will approve them, should he deem them sufficient, and order the appointment of appraisers as the representatives of the fiscal agent and the creditor, should it be necessary to value the things that are claimed. But should he decide the evidence insufficient, he will so assert by writ.

ONLY SECTION. Should the appraisers spoken of in the preceding article not agree, the judge will officially name a third party to adjust the matter at issue.

ART. 12. The appraisement finished, the opinion will be presented for both sides, and appearing just and arranged, the judge will so declare, informing the amount due according to the merits as set forth by the evidence produced, and from his decision an appeal may be taken to the superior court, or a consultation had therewith, as also in the principal part of the question.

ART. 13. The following will not be held as sufficient proof, nor the evidence of witnesses as conclusive in these cases:

1st. Should the witnesses not have been present at the supply, or that which was taken or seized, or had positive information thereof.

2d. Having been present thereat, or having had positive information thereto, they are unable to determine the time or date, and the person or persons, or the body of troops that did it.

ART. 14. If the authorities or commanders are living by whom or by whose order it is declared that the exactions were make, the commissioners will make them appear; and any other persons who are said to have seen the act, the judge will take the steps essential to an inquiry into the truth, or by affidavits from those who may be authorized to give them, or by evidence. To this end, the judge will question the witnesses on the points expressed, although there may have been no previous indication in regard thereto.

ART. 15. The witnesses will in all cases be questioned, and they must declare or inform, under oath, in the following form, if they were authorities:

1st. If they know what the amount or effects which are reclaimed were demanded as a forced contribution, imposed by a pre-existing law, and distributed by a competent authority among the inhabitants of a town occupied by troops.

2d. If they know, or not, whether the claimants have been paid in all or part of the debt which they try to prove.

3d. If the exactions were used for the support of the troops or in other public matters.

ART. 16. In cases first and second of the former article no claim will be considered when in the second case it has been entirely paid; but in the third the wrong inversion of the exactions will not prejudice the right of the creditor as against the national treasury, provided that they may have been done by competent authority, or by bodies of troops, or by other bodies, as set forth in the fifth part of article 2, remaining open a fiscal action against the employé or commissioner who made bad use of the exaction.

ART. 17. The value of cattle, horses, and other effects that may have been given for the service of the state will be the same as they were at the time of their delivery, unless a certain price had been determined on, or that it is known that of the class in general, computing its value according to the time and place where the supply was made.

ART. 18. To the judge of finance, before whom the supplementary proofs were adduced, belongs the classification of the debt in litigation.

ONLY SECTION. This enactment does not take away the duty of the authorities or the parishes to return to their respective owners the furniture or animals which are reclaimed, as enacted by an officer in commission or agent of the government, before the loss of the property is effectuated.

ART. 19. From the sentence pronounced by the district judge of finance in the cases under this law there may be an appeal to the respective tribunals, but should the fiscal agent, or his substitute, not appeal, on account of its being apparently arranged, the tribunal will be consulted, provided that through it the national treasury is declared responsible, and thence the action will follow the same course as the others against the treasury, according to law.

ART. 20. The creditor who may have maliciously reclaimed any illegal sums, will be condemned in costs and punished with the penalty of falsification, should he have produced false documents; and with that of a public thief, if, in virtue thereof, he may have obtained the payment of the supposed debt, besides losing what was legitimately owing him.

ART. 21. Those who give certificates of illegal debts, or the witnesses who swear falsely in favor of the creditors, will both be responsible for the costs and damages to the national treasury, but in case of having avoided damage to the national treasury that might have been occasioned, be what it may, a fine of from fifty to five hundred dollars will be imposed, and in lieu thereof, for not being able to pay it, the criminal will be condemned to an arrest of from three months to one year, without detriment in both cases to the penalty imposed by law for the crime of falsification.

ART. 22. The district judges of finance, the notaries, the fiscal agents, the treasurers, or collectors, each one, as it may happen, and the ministers of the courts who may supervise as is laid down in the present law of these cases of debt, are also responsible for the damages that occur to the national treasury, through their omission, connivance, or malice, suffering also, each one of them, a fine of from fifty to five hundred dollars, without prejudice to the penalties established by law to make them responsible.

ART. 23. The suit finished and judgment rendered, it will be delivered to the creditors, (leaving an authentic copy,) so that they may apply to the respective treasuries with the object of obtaining liquidation, all of which will be done according to the present law.

ART. 24. Every creditor of the republic of which article 1 speaks will present his claim within one year exactly, counted from the promulgation of the present law, but those who in future may have claims by actions arising after the publication of this law, must present them within one year exactly, counted from the time the damage took place, for any of the mentioned causes, and respectively passing these periods, no claim can be presented, nor can any claim be admitted in any other time.

ART. 25. No person who directly or indirectly has taken or may take part in the revolutions or invasions that may occur against the nationality of the republic, or may have fought, or may fight, will have the right to be indemnified for damages that in this wise he may have suffered or suffers, provided that his criminality is notorious or is legally proved.

ART. 26. To the creditors absent in the service of the republic the time designated in article 24 is prorogued six months.

Let it be communicated to the executive power, for its information and compliance.

Given in the hall of sessions, in Guayaquil, September 24, 1852, eighth year of liberty

The president of the assembly,

PEDRO MONCAYO.

The secretary,

PEDRO FERMIN CEVALLOS.

The secretary,

PABLO BUSTAMANTE.

GOVERNMENT HOUSE OF GUAYAQUIL,
*September 25, 1852, Eighth Year of Liberty*

Let it be executed.

JOSÉ MARIA URBINA.

Interior secretary *ad interim*.

JANVIER ESPINOSA.

Copy.

JOSÉ LETAMENDI,
*Chief Clerk.*

---

## *Mr. Gorham to Mr. Fish.*

No. 149.] LEGATION OF THE UNITED STATES,
*The Hague, August* 20, 1874. (Received September 9.)

SIR: In order to procure through the most reliable source the information called for in Acting Secretary Davis's communication of the 23d of June last, relative to the treatment of claims presented against the government of the Netherlands, I applied to the minister of foreign affairs, and have this day received the statement of which the following is a translation.

I am, &c.,

CHARLES T. GORHAM.

---

[Inclosure.]

THE HAGUE, *August* 19, 1874.

His Excellency the MINISTER: In answer to your letter of the 20th of July last, and after having consulted the minister of justice, I have the honor to communicate to you herewith, in the order of the questions that you have addressed to me, answers as follows:

1. Suits against the state and the execution of judgments pronounced on account of them do not come within the sphere of legislative power.

2. As the first question is resolved negatively, there is no occasion to examine the second.

3. Suits commenced against the state are not under the control of the administration.

4. Foreigners as well as citizens of the country may bring an action against the state before the civil tribunals. The real actions, and those that have for object reclamations in matter of contributions, must be brought before the ordinary tribunals; all others before the high court of the Netherlands, (court of cassation.)

5. With few exceptions, the civil rights of the kingdom are the same to foreigners, whether domiciled in the country or not, as to native citizens, both in that which concerns rights material or formal. These exceptions are as follows:

*a.* Every foreign plaintiff, principal or agent, is bound, if required by the defendant, and before the latter is obliged to make known his defense, to secure the payment of damage and interest to which he might be condemned. This obligation is incumbent on a foreigner, domiciled in the kingdom or not.

*b.* While in regard to Dutchmen a writ of arrest may only issue in certain cases determined by law, it may be pronounced against foreigners who have not their domicile in the kingdom for every debt, without exception, contracted with a Dutchman.

*c.* Foreigners having no domicile in the kingdom, before judgment is pronounced against them, may be imprisoned by order of the president of the tribunal of the district for any past-due obligation, if contracted with a Dutchman.

*d.* An indigent foreigner is only admitted to proceed gratuitously, either as complainant or defendant, when the favor of the *Pro Deo* has been stipulated by agreement.

1. There are no special or particular dispositions on the mode of proceeding against the state before the civil tribunals. The common right is equally applicable in matters of proof.

Hoping that the preceding information will be satisfactory,

I seize, &c.,

L. GERICKE.

Monsieur GORHAM, *Minister, &c.*

---

## *Mr. Scruggs to Mr. Fish.*

No. 56.]

LEGATION OF THE UNITED STATES,
*Bogotá, August* 27, 1874.

SIR: Your circular of the 23d of June last, inclosing a list of inquiries relative to the mode of procedure recognized or provided by the Colombian government for citizens and foreigners preferring claims against it, has been received.

In answer to the same, I have the honor to state, first, that the Colombian Congress has no constitutional authority for investigating and determining such claims. Only the executive and judicial departments of the government have cognizance of such cases.

3d and 4th. Aliens and denizens, equally with citizens, may have recourse directly to the executive branch of the government for presenting claims on account of loans, forced loans, expropriations, violations of contracts, and for other acts for which the government may be responsible. Should the executive entertain the claims, he may enter into an agreement for their settlement. If the reclamation be for a large sum, or should involve important international or political questions, he must, in the absence of previous authority of Congress, submit his action to that body for approval, or, as the case may be, simply ask for an appropriation for the payment of the reclamation allowed. In every case the claimant may avail himself of all the means of proof recognized by common law.

5th. All aliens or denizens, of whatever class or condition, may, equally with citizens, enter suit against the government before the local tribunals. The procedure and rules of evidence in such cases are prescribed in the *Código Judicial* of Colombia of 1872, a copy of which, with the sections marked therein, has been forwarded to you by this mail.

6th. The law in force defining the status, rights, privileges, and duties of foreign residents is that of June 21, 1866, a copy of which, up to this time, I have been wholly unable to procure. I am, however, under obligations to the minister of foreign affairs for the loan of his office-copy of the volume containing it. Reclamations and claims by foreign residents are divided into two classes—

1st. Those made by citizens of such foreign powers as, by treaty or practice, extend reciprocity to Colombia. If citizens of such nations resident here have not forfeited their neutral character and rights, the reclamations awarded them must be paid in coin (*pesos de ley*) of Colombia.

2d. Those made by resident citizens of such foreign powers as do not grant reciprocity, or by other foreign residents who may be adjudged as having lost their neutral character and rights, are, when allowed, paid in the old bills of credit or bonds of the government.

It seems to have been the policy of this government during the past few years to refer, as far as possible, all indemnity claims, whether made by citizens or aliens, to the decision of the federal supreme court. Cases thus adjudicated, especially when foreign residents were interested, have generally resulted in decisions adversely to the claimants, so much so, that resident foreigners now go to that tribunal under protest. Instances are not uncommon where this class of claimants, after voluntarily submitting their cases to the court of last resort, have sought appeal from adverse decisions to the legations of their respective governments. But it has, I believe, been the practice of the English and French legations here, in the absence of strong mitigating circumstances, to refuse to take them up.

The practice with the German legation has been less uniform in this respect. It has made reclamation for indemnity in exceptional cases of this kind. In one instance it has been successful. That case is briefly as follows:

Simmons, a resident German citizen, had his goods and effects seized by, and he also made a loan of money to, the successful party in the revolution of 1861. When that party became established in possession of the government, he made a demand for reclamation. With his consent, tacitly or formally given, the case went before the federal supreme court. That tribunal awarded indemnity in amount less than the proven value of the money and articles furnished, and, moreover, ordered its payment in government securities, then worth less than forty cents on the dollar. The claimant appealed from the decision to his diplomatic representatives in Bogota, who took it up. Indemnity was finally admitted by the executive department, and the Congress of 1873 voted an appropriation for its payment in legal coin of the country. The money has not yet been paid, but I presume it will be during the present year.

I have the honor to be, sir, your obedient servant,

WM. L. SCRUGGS.

Hon. HAMILTON FISH,
*Secretary of State.*

---

[Inclosures.]

Translations, from the *Codigo Fiscal* of Colombia of 1873, of articles 2166, 2167, and 2168.

Separately by this mail:

One copy of the *Codigo Judicial* (Judicial Code) of Colombia of 1872, with the law of May 19, 1873, amending certain sections thereof.

---

[Inclosure No. 1.—Translation.]

*From the Fiscal Code of Colombia of* 1873.

ART. 2166. Imposts, taxes, loans, expropriations, &c., on account of civil war, which are payable in old bonds, are those recognized against the national treasury by sentence of the supreme federal court in favor of Colombian citizens or foreigners with whose nations there may not be treaties of reciprocity, or who may have lost their neutral character by express declaration of the same tribunal.

ART. 2167. In favor of the same [class of] foreigners, dues may be recognized administratively, payable in old bonds, provided there be an adverse decision [of the courts] in which it is shown and established that they had [previously] lost their neutral character.

ART. 2168. Other foreigners are paid in money for expropriations, taxes, and loans, or other claims arising from civil war, when the sentence of the supreme federal court is in their favor, declaring that they were neutral in the strife, and that they did not make the loans or permit the supplies voluntarily.

UNITED STATES LEGATION,
*Bogotá, August* 27, 1874.

The above is a faithful translation of the original, now in the library of this legation.

WM. L. SCRUGGS,
*United States Minister Resident.*

---

[Inclosure No. 2.]

*Chapter* 5 *of the Judicial Code of the United States of Colombia, adopted by the Congress of that republic in* 1872.

WITNESSES.

ART. 529. Any person, male or female, who gives testimony in a court of justice in relation to matters which are being examined by such court, is a witness.

ART. 530. In order that a witness may be considered properly qualified, and his testimony receivable, it is necessary that he be not liable to objection on the ground of lack of knowledge, uprightness, or impartiality.

ART. 531. A lack of knowledge is presumed, 1st, in an insane person, an imbecile, and an intoxicated person, so long as the state of insanity, imbecility, or intoxication lasts; 2d, in any one who, for any other cause, is not in possession of his reason at the time of testifying; 3d, in a person less than fourteen years of age; one who has attained that age, however, may testify in regard to facts which occurred previously, if he states that he remembers them well. The deposition of a person under fourteen and over ten years of age may serve as the basis of a conjecture of more or less weight, according to the development of the intellectual faculties of the deponent.

ART. 532. The testimony of the following persons cannot be received, on the ground of lack of uprightness: 1st, one who has once borne false testimony; 2d, a forger; 3d, one who is not known to the judge, or to the party in litigation with the person presenting him, unless evidence shall be furnished that he is a person of good reputation.

ART. 533. The following persons cannot give testimony, on the ground of lack of impartiality: 1st, a child in favor of a parent, or ancestor, or *vice versa*, except in matters of age or relationship; 2d, a wife for a husband, or a husband for a wife, or one brother or sister for another, so long as both are living under paternal authority; 3d, one who is a party to the suit and his servants; 4th, a mortal enemy; 5th, an attorney, defender, or patron for his client or *protégé;* 6th, a guardian or trustee for his pupil or ward, or *vice versa;* 7th, one who has sold a thing in a suit concerning the same thing, and in favor of the purchaser; 8th, a partner or joint owner in a suit concerning the common property or business.

ART. 534. The voting members of municipal corporations, and the individuals belonging to congregations, colleges, or universities, may give testimony in suits which only concern their respective corporations or societies.

ART. 535. Witnesses who are disqualified by reason of lack of knowledge cannot be presented by either of the parties, except minors, who may be presented for the purposes referred to in the second part of article 531.

ART. 536. Witnesses disqualified by lack of uprightness cannot be presented in court by either of the parties.

ART. 537. Witnesses disqualified by lack of impartiality may be presented by the party in litigation with that party in whose favor the law presumes that they have an interest in testifying, and their entire testimony shall be considered admissible from this fact alone, unless the party who presented such witnesses protested, on doing so, that only the favorable portion of their testimony was unexceptionable.

ART. 538. Notwithstanding the provisions of the foregoing article, a husband can never be required to testify against a wife, or *vice versa,* nor can a child be required to testify against a parent, or *vice versa.*

ART. 539. Testimony cannot be required, 1st, of a lawyer or attorney concerning the confidential disclosures of his clients in regard to a case of which he may have charge; 2d, of a confessor concerning revelations made by a penitent; 3d, of the judge who is trying a case, when his testimony is unnecessary on account of their being other proofs of the same fact which are sufficient.

ART. 540. The testimony of one witness cannot of itself furnish satisfactory proof, but, when the witness is unexceptionable, it may furnish strong presumptive evidence.

ART. 541. The testimony of two unexceptionable witnesses who agree in their statements concerning the fact, and concerning the circumstances of manner, time, and place, furnishes satisfactory proof.

ART. 542. The testimony of a witness who deposes with regard to any fact from hearsay, is valueless, except when the deposition is concerning an occurrence which took place very long ago, or when it is sought to show what common report has been.

ART. 543. Sworn statements with regard to words never furnish evidence concerning facts, although they do so concerning words, whenever the witness declares that he has heard them uttered, and in this case the uniformity of the testimony of the two witnesses must refer both to the words and the circumstances which may be capable of altering or modifying its import.

ART 544. The statement of a witness who notably contradicts himself in the same deposition, as to the manner, place, time, and other circumstances of the occurrence, is of no value. The deposition of a witness who testifies under the influence of bribery or seduction is likewise valueless.

ART. 545. When the testimony of the witnesses presented by the same party or by both parties is contradictory, credit shall be given to that of the majority whose statements agree.

In case of equality in the number of witnesses, credit shall be given to the statements of those whose uprightness and intelligence is best known, and if there shall also be equality in this respect, credit shall be given to none of the witnesses.

ART. 546. When there is a discrepancy between the contents of a public document and the statements of the witnesses who were parties to its preparation, the instrument shall be believed if it agrees with the protocol or register, and if the notary was or is a man in good repute; but if the notary shall not be or shall not have been in good repute, and the instrument shall have been recently drawn up, the witnesses must be believed, although the instrument agrees with the register.

ART. 547. In order to prove the falsity of a document drawn up before a notary, the testimony of four unexceptionable witnesses shall be required who depose that the party was at another place on the day when the instrument was drawn up; but if the latter shall be of a private nature, the concurrent testimony of two witnesses shall be sufficient.

ART. 548. In order to prove that a debt has been paid, when evidence of its existence is furnished by a public document, the testimony of five witnesses who declare that they witnessed the payment shall be necessary.

ART. 549. In order that the testimony of witnesses may be considered as evidence in ordinary trials, it is necessary that it be received and ratified by the judge having jurisdiction in the case within the time allowed for the presentation of proof, the other party to the suit having been previously summoned, save in the cases provided for in article 553.

ART. 550. When in the course of a trial statements of witnesses are presented which were made before another judge or in relation to another case, it will be necessary that, within the time allowed for the presentation of proof, they be ratified, the opposite party being summoned, without which requisite they cannot be regarded as evidence when judgment is rendered.

ART. 551. When, after an informal inquiry (*informacion sumaria*) has been held, a suit shall be instituted, in which a certain time is allowed for the presentation of proof, the witnesses shall ratify their statements, the opposite party having been first summoned, without which requisite the statements of such witnesses shall not be regarded as evidence when the final sentence is pronounced.

ART. 552. When by reason of the death of a witness who has made an informal declaration, such declaration cannot be ratified, the party presenting the statement of the witness may demand that, the opposite party having been notified, accredited witnesses may declare with regard to the veracity and good faith of the deceased witness, and that the judge or the clerk of the court in which the declaration was made may certify whether such declaration was really made by the witness in question. This having been done, the declaration shall be considered as legally ratified.

ART. 553. The testimony asked for within the time allowed for the presentation of proof may be received by a deputy judge, when the witness, by reason of advanced age, sickness, absence, or a distance of more than fifteen kilometers, or any other serious hinderance, is unable to appear before the judge who is trying the case.

ART. 554. When the cause of examining a witness by proxy is his absence, one of the judges of the place where the witness resides shall be deputed to take his testimony, or, in case of the inability or refusal of the judges, one of their legal substitutes, the series of questions presented being sent to him, which questions must first be laid before the opposite party, together with the order for their transmission, so that if the opposite party shall present any counter-questions, they may be transmitted likewise.

ART. 555. In case of the absence of the witnesses, the judge who is trying the case may, if he thinks proper, or at the request of either of the parties, summon the witnesses to appear before him to give their testimony at the expense of the party who has asked for the same in the former case, and of the one who has solicited the appearance in the latter.

The witnesses in such cases must have their traveling-expenses paid as well as their expenses in the place where they give their testimony, for such time as may be strictly necessary.

ART. 556. When witnesses reside in a foreign country, letters rogatory shall be sent, through the secretary of foreign relations of the union, to one of the judicial authorities of such country, who, by the laws thereof, is empowered to take testimony, in order that he may receive the required evidence and transmit the same to the secretary aforesaid, through the diplomatic or consular agent of Colombia, or through a similar agent residing in that country, representing some friendly nation.

Testimony may also be received, in the case provided for by this article, by the diplomatic or consular agent of the Colombian Union, if the witnesses shall be willing to testify before them, and if there shall be any obstacle to their going before the authorities of the foreign country in which the witnesses reside.

The expense of procuring testimony in the case provided for by this article shall be paid by the party soliciting it.

The testimony, when received by foreign authorities, must be authenticated by a diplomatic or consular agent of the Colombian Union or of a friendly nation.

ART. 557. The judge of first instance shall send the request, in the case provided for by the foregoing article, to the president or governor of the state in which he resides, to the end that the latter may transmit it to the secretary of foreign relations of the union.

ART. 558. The testimony of persons prevented by sickness or any other cause, of matrons or other respectable ladies, shall be taken at their own houses or dwellings by the judge who is trying the case, or by a deputy. In such cases the parties to the suit shall be notified of the day and hour when the testimony is to be taken, so that they may be present if they desire; but their failure to be present shall be no obstacle to the taking of the testimony.

ART. 559. Witnesses or experts whose evidence is needed shall be summoned by a notice signed by the judge, in which shall be stated the day, hour, and place at which they are to appear, together with the object of the summons, which shall be for the same day or for one of the three following, according to distance and urgency.

ART. 560. The notice shall be delivered to the witness by the clerk of the court, or by a messenger employed by the court, and for its delivery the clerk shall be responsible; whoever shall deliver the notice shall require the party summoned to sign it, and in case of his inability to appear, to state the fact.

If he shall be unwilling or unable to sign, the bearer of the summons, if he be a subaltern employé of the court, shall summon a witness, by whose testimony the fact of the witness's having been summoned may be accredited, and if the clerk of the court shall have been the bearer of the summons, his testimony alone, in writing, shall furnish sufficient proof of the delivery of the summons.

ART. 561. Any person summoned in due form as a witness or as a judicial expert must appear and make the declaration that is required of him. If he shall not do so, he shall be punished by fines until he does appear, or shall be placed under arrest for disobedience to the judge's order. Such fines may be as high as ten dollars.

The following persons shall be exempted from this requirement: senators and representatives, so long as they enjoy immunity; the President of the republic and the secretaries of state, the judges of the supreme federal court, the attorney-general of the nation, generals while in service, prelates, and any judge of a higher grade than the one before whom his testimony is required. All these persons shall testify by means of a sworn statement, for which purpose the judge or magistrate who is trying the case shall notify them, transmitting to them copies of the necessary papers, or the original papers themselves, if there shall be no obstacle thereto and no risk of loss.

ART. 562. Diplomatic agents or ministers whose testimony is required shall be requested, in writing, to testify, a copy of the necessary papers being sent them, and if the agent or minister so requested shall consent to give his testimony, he shall do so by means of a written statement.

This provision shall be applicable to persons belonging to the suite and to the members of the family of foreign diplomatic agents or ministers.

When the testimony solicited shall be that of a servant or domestic of such diplomatic agents, it shall be received in the ordinary form, with the consent of such agent or minister, which shall be asked by means of a note.

Both in the case provided for in the foregoing paragraph and in the one provided for in the first paragraph of this article, the note referred to shall be sent through the secretary of foreign relations of the union.

ART. 563. Witnesses, before testifying, must make oath before the judge and clerk of the court that they will not fail to tell the truth.

ART. 564. After the witness has been sworn, the articles of the penal law which relate to perjury and false witnesses in civil cases shall be read to him.

ART. 565. Persons under twenty-one and over fourteen years of age need no guardian in order to testify; the judge will take care that they be not annoyed by captious questions.

ART. 566. Witnesses shall be examined separately, and their depositions shall be taken down in the same manner; these must be signed by the judge or the clerk of the court, and by the deponent, or a witness, in case the deponent shall be unable or unwilling to sign.

ART. 567. A witness shall not be interrupted while testifying, and his statements shall be written as he makes them; each statement must be read to him after it is written, and the entire deposition must be read to him when finished, which fact shall be stated in the deposition itself.

ART. 568. When an answer of the witness has been written, the judge shall immediately put to him the following questions, unless the replies thereto shall be evident from the answer already made:

How do you know the fact which you state? Is it because you were an eye-witness of the occurrence, or because you have heard an account of it, or how? On what day, at what hour, and in what place did the occurrence to which you refer take place?

ART. 569. A statement made by a witness shall not be regarded as evidence if, when asked by the judge, or by the party, how the facts came to his knowledge, he shall be unwilling or unable to give the reasons for his statement, or shall give no reason except that such is his *belief*. The statement of a witness is valid, however, although he may not state the manner in which the fact concerning which he is testifying came to his knowledge, if he shall not be questioned upon this point, and the judge shall be responsible for the omission.

ART. 570. The judge shall also require the witness to state, if the latter shall fail to do so, the day and hour when, and the place where, the occurrence in question took place.

ART. 571. The ratifications of evidence which has been received extrajudicially shall not be valid, unless the statements made shall be repeated; that is to say, if the witnesses shall confine themselves to stating that they affirm and ratify, without having anything to add or retract.

ART. 572. If a witness shall say that, in order to answer a question, he needs to call to mind the facts or to examine documents, and shall ask time to do so, the judge shall grant his request, if, in his judgment, it shall be necessary.

ART. 573. The reply that "the contents of the question are true" shall not be admitted, but the contents of the same question shall be taken down for a reply, if nothing else shall be added.

ART. 574. When witnesses give ambiguous or evasive answers, or refuse to reply to proper questions, the judge may force them to give proper answers, by means of fines or arrest, or even by solitary confinement, if the gravity of the case, the maliciousness of the answers given, or the audacity of the refusal shall require it.

ART. 575. The provisions of the foregoing article shall not prevent a witness from answering that he does not know or does not recollect the facts concerning which he is questioned; or from refusing to reply in cases in which it is not lawful to force him to reveal the facts which it is desired to elicit.

ART. 576. Statements made by witnesses shall be written out without leaving blanks, and without abbreviations; corrections and interlinings shall be avoided, if possible; but, if it shall be necessary to correct or interline any word or words, the fact shall always be stated at the end, after which those who are to sign shall do so.

ART. 577. When a deposition is finished, and is read to the witness, he may make such corrections, explanations, and additions as he may think proper, which shall be stated with all clearness at the end of the deposition; but what is already therein written shall not be altered.

ART. 578. Witnesses who are unable to write have the right to get a person in whom they have confidence to sign for them and to read their deposition to them, that they may be certain that it is an accurate statement of what they have said.

ART. 579. A witness, before leaving the room in which he has testified, and without having spoken with another person, may correct or elucidate a deposition which he has already signed; and the judge may, at any time, summon a witness to explain any ambiguous or obscure passage in his deposition.

ART. 580. Either party may object to the witnesses presented by the other, and cross-examine them either in writing or orally; but no objection can be made to witnesses save for one or more of the disqualifying causes specified in articles 531 to 533.

ART. 581. When the ground of objection is lack of impartiality, this must be stated and proved by the party interested, that it may be considered when the evidence is weighed.

ART. 582. The questions for cross-examination shall remain in possession of the presiding or of the deputy judge, who shall be strictly responsible for their due custody, until the moment of the examination of the witnesses; the cross-questions shall be read as soon as they have answered the principal questions, or after each question has been answered, according to the desire of the party represented.

---

[Inclosure No. 3.]

*Lei 76 de 1873 (19 de mayo) adicional i reformatoria del Código Judicial de la Union*

El Congreso de los Estados Unidos de Colombia

DECRETA:

ART. 1.° Se hacen las siguientes adiciones i reformas al "Código Judicial de la Union" sancionado el 7 de junio de 1872:

1.ª Los incisos 7.°, 9.° i 11. del artícuclo 18, seccion 1.ª, quedan reemplazados con los siguientes:

"Inciso 7. De las causas criminales que por delitos o culpas puramente militares se siguen en tiempo de paz a los jefes de la fuerza armada al servicio de la Union, desde Sarjento mayor inclusive hasta el mas alto grado de la milicia."

Inciso 9. Se le agrega el siguiente parágrafo:

"Parágrafo. Para el cumplimiento de esta atribucion se reputarán jefes superiores de oficinas de Hacienda, además de los que la lejislacion fiscal califique como táles, el Tesorero jeneral de la Union, el Administrador de las salinas de Cipaquirá, los Administradores de Aduanas, los de Casas de moneda, el Director jeneral de Correos, el Ajente jeneral de Bienes desamortizados i los funcionarios o empleados que hayan de subrogar a éstos, cualquiera que sea la denominacion que les dé la lei."

"Inciso 11.° De las c usas i negocios contenciosos sobre presas marítimas."

2.ª Los incisos 1. , 2.ª i 5. de la seccion 2.ª del artículo 18 se reemplazan con los que iguen:

"Inciso 1.° De todos los negocios contenciosos que se refieran a bienes, rentas o cualesquiera otros derechos de la Hacienda de la Union, i los cuales se hayan decidido en 1.ª instancia por los Juzgados i Tribunales de los Estados o de los Territorios.

"Inciso 2.° Se deroga este inciso.

"Inciso 5. De las apelaciones o consultas de las sentencias definitivas pronunciadas por los Jueces nacionales en causas criminales por delitos o culpas puramente militares que se siguen en tiempo de paz contra individuos de la fuerza armada, desde soldado hasta Capitan inclusive."

Los incisos 8. i 9. de la seccion 3.ª del artículo 18 se reemplazan así:

"Inciso 8.° Admitir, en receso del Congreso, las renuncias que le presenten de sus destinos el Presidente de la Union i los Designados para ejercer el Poder Ejecutivo de la misma, i conceder al Encargado de dicho Poder licencia hasta por sesenta dias en un año, tambien en receso del Congreso."

"Inciso 9.° Llamar, conforme a la Constitucion de la República, al ciudadano que deba reemplazar al Encargado del Poder Ejecutivo, en los casos del inciso anterior."

3.ª El inciso 14 del artículo 46 queda derogado.

4.ª Despues del 54 se coloca el siguiente:

"Artículo. Son tambien Jueces nacionales de primera instancia, en los negocios criminales, los Tribunales o Cortes superiores de justicia de los Estados, para conocer de las causas por delitos comunes de la competencia de la Union, cometidos por funcionarios públicos que, segun la lejislacion del respectivo Estado, deban ser juzgados en primera instancia por dichos Tribunales o Cortes."

5.ª Artículo 56. Se deroga este artículo.

6.ª Artículo 62. Se deroga el incise 4.°, i se reemplaza el 8.° con el siguiente:

"Inciso 8.° Conocer en primera instancia, en tiempo de paz, de las causas criminales que por delitos o culpas puramente militares se siguen a los individuos de la fuerza armada, desde soldado hasta Capitan inclusive."

7.ª Artículo 63. Se reemplaza su inciso 10 con el siguiente:

"Inciso 10. Conocer en segunda instancia, cuando haya lugar a ella, de las causas civiles i criminales de que conocen en primera instancia los Correjidores, segun la lei."

8.ª Despues del artículo 68 se coloca el siguiente capítulo:

"Capítulo V.

*"Atribuciones de los Consejos de guerra.*

"Artículo. Todos los delitos que se cometan en tiempo de guerra por los individuos de la fuerza armada al servicio de la Union, serán juzgados i castigados por los Consejos de guerra, con arreglo a lo dispuesto en el Tratado 5. de las 'Ordenanzas para el réjimen, disciplina, subordinacion i servicio de la Guardia colombiana,' en cuanto no se opongan a la Constitucion i leyes de la República."

9.ª Artículo 115. Se le reemplaza con el siguiente.

"Artículo 115. El Procurador jeneral de la Nacion tendrá dos jefes de seccion i dos escribientes, de su libre nombramiento i remocion."

10. Artículo 155. Se le reemplaza de este modo:

"Artículo 155. Al Secretario i al Oficial mayor de la Corte les está prohibido patrocinar a los particulares i ejercer sus poderes en asuntos judiciales, sean éstos de la competencia de la Union o de la de los Estados."

11. Al artículo 187 se le agrega este inciso:

"Se esceptúan de lo dispuesto en la primera parte de este artículo los autos interlocutorios i los de pura sustanciacion, que podrán ser suscritos con media firma. Los Jueces nacionales de primera instancia, sus Secretarios i los Ajentes del Ministerio público, usarán firma entera en el primer acto en que intervengan, sea cual fuere, en cada negocio judicial; i lo mismo se observará siempre que ocurra variacion en el personal de dichos empleados."

12.ª El artículo 287 se adiciona con el siguiente:

"En los juicios sumarios i en todos los demás en que no haya contestacion de la demanda, el poder termina por la muerte del poderdante antes de la notificacion de la demanda al demandado."

13.ª Se deroga el artículo 428.

14.ª El artículo 484 queda reemplazado con éste:

"La disposicion del artículo anterior no impide que las pruebas demoradas se practiquen apesar de estar trascurrido el término probatorio, i que se agreguen a los autos en cualquier estado de ellos, con tal que no se haya citado para sentencia."

"Pero para que se agreguen las pruebas, en el caso de este artículo, es preciso que recaiga sobre el particular auto espreso del Juez, a peticion de parte, la que ha de justificar que ella no ha sido culpable por la demora. Este incidente se sustanciará como las demás articulaciones, i se suspenderá la citacion para sentencia hasta que se decida el punto i se agreguen las pruebas en cuestion, si así se resolviere."

15 Suprímese el inciso 3.° del artículo 532.

16.ª Artículo 561. Se le reemplaza del modo siguiente:

"Todo el que fuere llamado en la forma legal como testigo o como perito judicial, deberá comparecer a dar la declaracion que se le pide; si no lo hiciere así, será apremiado con multas hasta que comparezca, o con arresto por la desobediencia a la órden del Juez. Dichas multas podrán ser hasta de diez pesos."

"Se esceptúan de esta disposicion: los Senadores i Representantes, miéntras gozan de inmunidad, el Presidente de la República i los Secretarios de Estado, los Majistrados de la Corte Suprema federal, el Procurador jeneral de la Nacion, los Gobernadores o Presidentes de los Estados, los Jenerales en servicio i todo Juez superior respecto de aquel ante quien deba declarar: todas estas personas declararán por medio de certificacion jurada, a cuyo efecto el Juez o Majistrado de la causa les pasará oficio, acompañando copia de lo necesario, o bien las dilijencias orijinales, si no hubiere inconveniente o riesgo de pérdida."

17.ª El artículo 579 se reforma así:

"El testigo, ántes de salir de la pieza donde dió su declaracion, i sin haber hablado con otra persona, puede mejorar o aclarar la declaracion que ya hubiere firmado; i el Juez tiene la facultad de llamar en cualquier tiempo al testigo para que aclare cualquier pasaje dudoso u oscuro de su declaracion, a menos que ya se haya citado para sentencia."

18.ª El artículo 580 queda reformado así:

"Cada parte puede tachar a los testigos que la otra haya presentado, i repreguntarlos por escrito o de palabra; pero los testigos no pueden ser tachados sino por alguna de las causas que invalidan el testimonio segun este capítulo."

19.ª Antes del inciso último del artículo 651 se intercala éste:

"Despues de dictada la sentencia de última instancia, la solicitud de devolucion no podrá hacerse sino ante el Juzgado de primera instancia."

20.ª Despues del artículo 755 se agrega el siguiente:

"Las sentencias de la Corte Suprema federal i de los Juzgados nacionales no necesitan de la formalidad de rejistro para producir todos sus efectos."

21.ª Entre la primera parte i la segunda del artículo 827 se intercala este inciso:

"Del mismo modo procederán los Prefectos de los Territorios para admitir o negar los recursos de hecho que ante ellos se interpongan."

22.ª Entre los artículos 859 i 860 se intercala el siguiente:

"Cuando la demanda se conteste por defensor o curador, i en los juicios de divorcio por el cónyuje o su representante legal, aunque éstos convengan en los hechos o no contesten de una manera espresa, o de ningun modo, no se tendrá por confeso al demandado, sino que se abrirá el juicio a prueba como si hubiera contradiccion."

23.ª El artículo 866 se reemplaza con el siguiente:

"Desde que el actor entable la demanda i desde que el reo la conteste, hasta que concluya la primera mitad del término probatorio, tienen uno i otro el derecho de denunciar el pleito a quien crean está en el deber de salir a la defensa de la cosa que se litiga, por estar obligado al saneamiento por cualquiera razon. En los juicios en que no haya término probatorio, la denuncia debe hacerse dentro de los seis dias siguientes a la notificacion de la demanda o de la providencia dirijida contra la cosa que pueda o deba ser saneada."

24.ª Al artículo 873 se le agrega el siguiente inciso:

"Lo dispuesto en este artículo no comprende a los Ajentes del Ministerio público que representen a la Nacion en los negocios judiciales."

25.ª El capítulo 2.°, título 9.° del libro 2.°, se adiciona con el siguiente artículo, colocado después del 888:

"Despues de concluido el término probatorio, i antes de la citacion para sentencia, la Corte Suprema puede dictar autos para mejor proveer en todos los negocios de que conozca i en cualquier instancia, para el esclarecimiento de los puntos que juzgue dudosos; i las pruebas que en consecuencia se practiquen se recibirán previa citacion de las partes."

26.ª Entre los artículos 890 i 891 se agrega el siguiente:

"Son comunes a este capítulo las disposiciones de los artículos 873, 874 i 876, en cuanto se trate de pruebas que hayan de practicarse en país estranjero o dentro de la República a una distancia mayor de cincuenta miriámetros de la residencia de la Corte; pero la peticion de término en esos casos debe hacerse durante la primera mitad del término probatorio en segunda instancia."

27.ª El artículo 893 se reemplaza con éste:

"Las demandas sobre intereses particulares, en que no média el interes de la Nacion, i de las cuales conocen los Prefectos i los Correjidores de los Territorios nacionales, se dividen en demandas de mayor i de menor cuantía. Las primeras son aquellas que en su accion principal pasan de trescientos pesos; i las segundas aquellas que no pasan de dicha cantidad. Se considerará como accion principal el total de la cantidad líquida que se demande."

28.ª Se deroga el inciso 2.°, artículo 895, i se reemplaza con éste:

"En los espresados juicios entre particulares no hai lugar a consulta en ningun caso, ni intervendrá en ellos el Ministerio público."

29.ª El artículo 940 queda reformado en estos términos:

"Si los bienes manifestados o denunciados por el ejecutante o el ejecutado se hallaren en poder de un tercer poseedor que los reclame como suyos en el acto en que vayan a embargarse, se dejarán en su poder embargados, siempre que dé una fianza a satisfaccion del Juez ejecutor, de entregarlos tales como se hallaban cuando se procedió al embargo, i con todos sus frutos, si se declarare que no le pertenecen. Lo mismo se hará si las dilijencias de embargo i depósito no se entienden con el tercer poseedor en persona, i éste hace la reclamacion de que se ha hablado, en cualquier estado del juicio antes del remate, dentro de tercero dia de notificársele personalmente la providencia de embargo. La cuestion de propiedad se ventilará en juicio de tercería, sin perjuicio de embargarse otros bienes del ejecutado a solicitud o por denuncio del ejecutante."

30.ª Al artículo 980 se le añade este inciso:

"La copia de que trata este artículo se equipara a una escritura pública; i, por consiguiente, no hai necesidad de otorgamiento de ésta para la trasmision de la propiedad. Cuando el remate haya sido de bienes inmuebles, bastará que ese título se rejistre en la oficina respectiva, si la lei exije esa formalidad en los instrumentos públicos sobre trasmision de esa clase de bienes."

31.ª El artículo 1002 se adiciona con este inciso:

"Dichos empleados actuarán en estos casos con alguno de los subalternos de sus oficinas, i si no tuvieren subalternos, con un Secretario *ad hoc*, que prestará juramento de desempeñar fielmente su encargo."

32.ª El artículo 1046 se reforma así:

"Si los bienes manifestados por el concursado o denunciados por los acreedores se hallaren en poder de una tercera persona que los reclame como suyos, al tiempo de embargarse, si se entendieron con ella las dilijencias de embargo i depósito, o dentro de tres dias de notificársele personalmente dicho embargo, siempre que no se haya hecho el remate cuando tales dilijencias no se entienden con ella; se dejarán en su poder, con tal que dé fianza, a satisfaccion del Juez, de devolverlas tales como se hallaban cuando se procedió al embargo i con todos sus frutos, siempre que se declare que dichos bienes pertenecen al deudor concursado.

"Si los bienes de que se trata son funjibles, la fianza será de devolverlos en la misma cantidad i de la misma calidad que los embargados."

33.ª Entre los artículos 1094 i 1095 se intercalan los dos que siguen:

"Artículo A. Los Tribunales i Juzgados nacionales, en los juicios de concurso de acreedores cuyo conocimiento les corresponda, graduarán los créditos de los acreedores, en lo que no tengan relacion con el Fisco, aplicando la lejislacion sustantiva vijente en el Estado respectivo al tiempo de adquirirse el crédito."

"Artículo B. Las formalidades exijidas por la lejislacion de los Estados para la validez de los documentos con que se comprueben los créditos, se tendrán tambien en cuenta para decidir sobre la existencia de dichos créditos."

34.ª El artículo 1100 queda reformado así:

"Si ninguna de las partes pidiere que la causa se reciba a prueba, el Secretario lo informará, como tambien el hecho de haber espirado el término probatorio en el caso del artículo anterior; i el Majistrado sustanciador proveerá auto mandando citar a las partes para sentencia, i señalando uno de los cinco dias siguientes para oir a las partes en los estrados de la Corte, en los cuales pueden aquéllas alegar de palabra o presentar sus alegatos escritos."

35.ª El artículo 1120 se reforma de este modo:

"Es Juez competente para decretar la apertura i publicacion de un testamento, el de primera instancia del lugar donde tuvo su último domicilio el testador; sin perjuicio de usar de las escepciones legales, i salvas siempre las disposiciones especiales."

36.ª El artículo 1204 se reforma así:

"Son comunes a este juicio las disposiciones de los artículos 1183 a 1194."

37.ª Antes del artículo 1270 se colocan los dos siguientes:

"Artículo A. Cuando un ciudadano haya de pedir ante la Corte Suprema federal la suspension de un acto lejislativo de alguno de los Estados de la Union, dirijirá previamente su memorial al Poder Ejecutivo del Estado, quien ordenará en el acto que el funcionario encargado del Ministerio público de dicho Estado informe dentro de un término que no excederá de seis dias."

"Artículo B. Siempre que el Procurador o encargado del Ministerio público del Estado apoye su concepto en actos lejislativos del mismo Estado, diferentes de aquel cuya suspension o nulidad se pide, acompañará copia de ellos a su informe, a no ser que el peticionario los haya acompañado a su memorial."

38.ª El artículo 1315 queda reemplazado con éste:

"Los casos de divorcio o de nulidad de matrimonio se calificarán i apreciarán segun las leyes sustantivas nacionales.

"Sinembargo, todo caso de separacion de los cónyujes, por divorcio o nulidad, se decidirá en los Territorios cedidos o que se cedan a la Nacion con arreglo a las leyes del Estado a que antes pertenecia el Territorio respectivo, si con arreglo a esas mismas leyes fué celebrado el matrimonio de que se trata.

"Los matrimonios celebrados en cualquier Estado que no sea aquel a que antes pertenecia un Territorio, pueden ser en éste anulados, i los cónyujes separados por divorcio, por las causas que autorizan la disolucion i el divorcio, segun las leyes del Estado donde se contrajo el matrimonio.

"La disposicion del inciso anterior es aplicable a los matrimonios contraidos en país estranjero i respecto de los cuales se pida la nulidad o el divorcio en alguno de los Territorios nacionales.

"La existencia de las leyes que deban aplicarse, en los casos de los tres incisos anteriores, deberá probarse en el juicio con copia auténtica de las disposiciones que se aleguen, espedida por el Poder Ejecutivo o el Tribunal Superior de la respectiva Nacion o Estado, i certificacion de los mismos sobre su vijencia a tiempo de celebrarse el matrimonio."

39.ª El artículo 1368 queda derogado, i en su lugar queda el siguiente:

"Cuando un guardador pretenda enajenar o gravar con hipoteca o servidumbre los bienes raíces de la persona que esté a su cargo, o enajenar o empeñar los muebles preciosos o que tengan un valor de afecto, ocurrirá por escrito al Juez de primera instancia del Territorio donde existan los bienes, solicitando la autorizacion necesaria segun las leyes sustantivas."

40.ª Al artículo 1373 se le agrega este inciso:

"Esta resolucion es apelable en ambos efectos."

41.ª En el artículo 1381 se pondrá "Título 1.º" en donde dice: "Título 2.º"

42.ª El artículo 1408 se reforma así:

"La accion civil i la criminal pueden intentarse a un mismo tiempo, e intentadas así deben sustanciarse i decidirse en un mismo juicio, observando la tramitacion correspondiente al juicio criminal. Si no se han intentado juntas, la accion civil no podrá promoverse miéntras no haya concluido el juicio criminal con la condenacion del delincuente."

43ª. Al artículo 1414 se le agrega este inciso:

"Los funcionarios de instruccion de los Estados lo serán tambien para todos los delitos de la competencia de la Union que se cometan en los lugares donde no residan jueces nacionales de primera instancia."

44ª. Se adiciona el artículo 1445 con el inciso siguiente:

"Si en el respectivo establecimiento no hai ocho presos o detenidos, se presentarán los que hubiere para el reconocimiento, i si no hai mas que el indiciado, solo éste se presentará a la vista del agraviado o testigo, previas en todo caso las demás formalidades prevenidas en este artículo."

45.ª El artículo 1496 queda reformado así:

"De todos los actos que se practiquen se estenderán dilijencias, que serán firmadas por el funcionario de instruccion i las demás personas que concurran a ellas por llamamiento de la lei, i autorizadas por el Secretario de dicho funcionario, i además se foliará cada hoja que se vaya agregando al espediente."

46.ª El artículo 1497 se modifica poniendo las palabras "Título VII" en lugar de "Título II."

47.ª El último inciso del artículo 1513 se reforma de este modo:

"Se entenderá que un acusador deserta del juicio cuando se ausenta o rehusa admitir las citaciones o notificaciones que se trate de hacerle o no formaliza su acusacion oportunamente."

48.ª El artículo 1534 será reemplazado con éste:

"Luego que el Juez competente haya concluido o recibido las dilijencias correspondientes para comprobar el cuerpo del delito i descubrir los culpables, examinará si la averiguacion está perfecta, en cuyo caso dará vista de ella al Ministerio público; pero si no lo estuvieren, dispondrá lo conveniente a la perfeccion del sumario.

"Si encontrare que hai plena prueba de la existencia del delito, i por lo menos un testigo idóneo o graves indicios contra alguno o algunos, declarará que hai lugar al seguimiento de causa contra éstos, previa audiencia del Ministerio público.

"Con escepcion de los juicios de responsabilidad, en que el cargo contra el procesado debe deducirse citando espresamente la disposicion o artículo infrinjido, en los demás se formulará el cargo mencionando el delito en términos jenerales con la denominacion que le dé la lei, como homicidio, heridas, hurto, &c., sin calificar desde el auto de formacion de causa si el homicidio fué premeditado, involuntario o de otra especie, o señalar algun artículo especial en el capítulo o seccion correspondiente de la lei penal que trate del delito materia del proceso."

49.ª El artículo 1598 se modifica así:

"Cada parte puede tachar los testigos que la otra haya presentado, por carecer de las cualidades de que habla el artículo 1577, o por alguna de las causas que se espresan en los artículos 1578, 1585 i 1586. La lista de los testigos con que se pretenda probar las tachas, se presentará dentro de las cuarenta i ocho horas de entregada a la parte que tacha la lista de los testigos a quienes la tacha se refiera."

50.ª El artículo 1616 se adiciona con estas palabras:

"La no concurrencia de las partes o de cualquiera de ellas no impide la celebracion del juicio, siempre que se les haya notificado en debida forma el auto en que se señaló dia para dicha celebracion."

51.ª El artículo 1722 se reforma así:

"En las apelaciones i consultas de autos interlocutorios procederá la Corte Suprema del mismo modo establecido para esa especie de autos en negocios civiles."

52.ª Al artículo 1783 se le añade este inciso:

"Tambien deberá procederse de oficio, sea cual fuere la pena que haya de imponerse, siempre que en el juicio esté la Nacion interesada."

53.ª El capítulo 4.º, título 10.º, libro 3.º, se adiciona con este artículo, que seguirá al 1833:

"El principio establecido en el artículo 1783 no obsta para la aplicacion de las disposiciones consignadas en este capítulo."

54.ª El artículo 1848 queda modificado en estos términos:

"Cuando el reo o reos fueren aprehendidos, i el valor del contrabando, es decir, del jénero i efectos confiscables, no pasare de cien pesos, con solo el sumario se procederá a celebrar el juicio con arreglo al artículo 1616, en cuyo acto se oirá verbalmente al reo, a su defensor si lo hubiere nombrado, al respectivo Ajente del Ministerio público i a los testigos que presentaren ambas partes, poniéndose de todo una dilijencia sucinta pero clara i exacta"

55.ª Al capítulo 8.º, título 10, libro 3.º, se le agregan los siguientes artículos despues del 1877:

"Artículo A. Cuando a las autoridades judiciales de Colombia se les reclame directamente la entrega de un reo, por las de igual carácter de un país estranjero, a virtud de lo estipulado en las Convenciones sobre estradicion, examinarán los documentos que se acompañan a la solicitud, practicarán las demás dilijencias prevenidas en dichas Convenciones, i, previa audiencia del respectivo Ajente del Ministerio público, decidirán si debe o nó accederse a la estradicion, conforme a los Tratados.

"Artículo B. Si la reclamacion se dirije a algun Majistrado o Juez que no sea del órden jeneral, se pasará al Juez nacional respectivo, para que decida con arreglo al artículo anterior.

"Artículo C. Cuando la estradicion se pida directamente al Poder Ejecutivo de la Union por un gobierno estranjero, i, segun los pactos internacionales vijentes, deban practicarse dilijencias de carácter judicial, como las de hacer comparecer al presunto reo, oir sus descargos i tomar en consideracion las pruebas de su criminalidad, dicha solicitud se pasará, con los documentos anexos, al Juez nacional de primera instancia de la jurisdiccion donde resida i se crea que reside la persona reclamada para los efectos de los artículos anteriores.

"Si los pactos sobre estradicion no exijen la práctica de las espresadas dilijencias, no se hará necesaria la intervencion judicial, i el negocio se decidirá administrativamente."

"Artículo D. Las resoluciones sobre estradicion de reos que dicten los jueces nacionales de primera instancia son apelables por el Ministerio público i por el presunto reo; i en todo caso se consultarán con la Corte Suprema federal, la que procederá como está dispuesto para los autos interlocutorios, i dará aviso de la resolucion definitiva al Poder Ejecutivo de la Union."

56.ª El título del citado capítulo 8.º se reforma en estos términos:

"Modo de proceder en los casos de estradicion de reos."

57.ª Queda derogada la seccion 2.ª, capítulo 10.º, título 10.º, libro 3.º, i se reemplaza con la siguiente:

"SECCION 2.ª

"*Procedimiento para declarar que se ha perdido o recobrado el carácter de colombiano.*

"Artículo A. Corresponde a la Corte Suprema federal declarar quiénes han perdido el carácter de colombianos, en los casos de los artículos 32 i 88 de la Constitucion.

"Artículo B. La Corte procederá a virtud de pedimento del Procurador jeneral o de cualquier ciudadano.

"Artículo C. El procedimiento para hacer la declaratoria de que se trata será el siguiente:

"Dentro de tercero dia despues de darse a la Corte el denuncio, o de presentado el pedimento del Procurador jeneral o del solicitante, i de oido este funcionario si él no hubiere hecho el pedimento, se exijirá informe a la persona a quien el denuncio se refiera, fijándole un plazo para contestar, que será igual al tiempo que se calcule necesario para recorrer de ida i regreso la distancia a que se halle de la capital i quince dias más; i recibido el informe en que se reconozca el hecho denunciado, o trascurrido un término doble del señalado, sin que dicho informe se reciba, se dictará dentro de los quince dias siguientes la resolucion declaratoria de haber perdido la condicion de colombiano el individuo objeto del denuncio.

"Si en el informe espresado, oportunamente recibido, se negare el hecho denunciado, la Corte Suprema lo averiguará por medio de la Secretaría de Relaciones Esteriores, la que se dirijirá sobre el asunto al Ministro de la República acreditado ante el Gobierno mencionado en el denuncio, o a alguno de los Cónsules admitidos por el mismo Gobierno; i fallará en vista de los informes de dichos empleados, dentro de quince dias despues de recibidos.

"Artículo D. El fallo de la Corte Suprema federal será definitivo: i solo podrá reconsiderarse por ella misma en el caso de que se dicte sin haberse recibido el informe del individuo que haya sido objeto del denuncio, si este u otro en su nombre lo solicita comprobando que no llegó a sus mano el pliego con que se le notificó el auto en que se le pidió informe, o que llegó con retardo considerable.

"Artículo E. Tambien podrá la Corte reconsiderar su resolucion cuando el mismo individuo objeto del denuncio, u otro en su nombre, lo solicite acompañando una documentacion que contradiga el hecho que se habia declarado cierto. La solicitud de reconsideracion en este caso, lo mismo que en el del artículo anterior, deberá hacerse dentro de cuatro meses contados desde la fecha en que el fallo fuere publicado en el periódico oficial de la Nacion; i en ambos casos la Corte Suprema podrá adoptar las medidas conducentes al esclarecimiento de los hechos, i fallará dentro de quince dias después de trascurrido el tiempo que señale para la investigacion.

"Artículo F. En el pedimento del Procurador se indicarán los datos i los documentos i demás pruebas en que lo apoye, i los denuncios de los particulares deberán presentarse con iguales pruebas o indicaciones, sobre la existencia o realidad de las cuales procurará cerciorarse la Corte Suprema antes de pedir el informe. El espediente se remitirá orijinal, con las seguridades convenientes, al que debe informar, accompañando las pruebas que se hubieren presentado o adquirido; i en la Secretaría de la Corte se dejará copia de lo conducente para que se pueda fallar en caso de no rendirse el informe oportunamente.

"Artículo G. Los colombianos que hubieren perdido el carácter de táles en virtud de resolucion de la Corte Suprema, dictada en cumplimiento de esta seccion, lo recobrarán si fijan su residencia en el territorio de la Union, i declaran ante el Secretario de Relaciones Esteriores, o ante el Poder Ejecutivo del Estado en que residan, que quieren volver a ser colombianos. La manifestacion del interesado, con un informe del funcionario ante quien la haga, sobre la efectividad de la actual residencia de aquel, se remitirá a la Corte Suprema para que, con audiencia del Procurador jeneral, declare que el solicitante ha recobrado la calidad de colombiano.

"Parágrafo. Se esceptúan de esta disposicion los colombianos que hayan servido a otra Nacion contra la República, los cuales jamás podrán recobrar la nacionalidad perdida.

"Artículo H. Cuando, estando en receso el Congreso nacional, un colombiano admita empleos, condecoraciones, títulos o rentas de gobiernos estranjeros, de una manera condicional i a reserva de solicitar el permiso de aquella corporacion, no se reputará consumada la infraccion del artículo 88 de la Constitution, sino en uno de estos dos casos: 1º. Si el que aceptó con dicha reserva no solicita el permiso en la sessiones ordinarias del Congreso inmediatamente posteriores a la aceptation; 2º. Si pedido el permiso i rehusado por el Congreso, el aceptante persiste en los efectos de la aceptacion, como si tal permiso le hubiera sido otorgado."

58.ª Al artículo 1924 se le agregan estas palabras:

"Hai presuncion legal de que se ha delinquido a sabiendas, cuando la suposicion contraria de ignorancia se refiera a puntos de derecho, como sucede, por ejemplo, en las infracciones de lei que cometen los funcionarios públicos en el ejercicio de sus atribuciones i que dan oríjen a juicios de responsabilidad, tales como los abusos de autoridad, el exceso en las atribuciones del empleo, la usurpacion de facultades i otras semejantes."

59.ª El artículo 1927 se deroga, i en su lugar queda el siguiente:

"Desde que este Código empiece a rejir, quedarán derogadas todas las disposiciones anteriores sobre organizacion del Poder Judicial nacional, i sobre procedimiento en los negocios civiles i criminales de la competencia de los Tribunales i Juzgados de la Union."

Art. 2.ª Al hacer una nueva edicion del "Código Judicial," o formar la Recopilacion de leyes de la Union, se tendrán presentes las variaciones introducidas por esta lei, para refundirlas en dicho Código, dándoles la colocacion que les corresponda, i haciendo las enmiendas consiguientes en la numeracion de los artículos, i las rectificaciones en las citas de éstos que queden alteradas por la nueva numeracion.

Dadá en Bogotá, a diez i seis de mayo de mil ochocientos setenta i tres.

*El Presidente del Senado de Plenipotenciarios.* M. PLATA AZUERO.

*El Presidente de la Cámara de Representantes,* J. M. MALDOMADO NEIRA.

*El Secretario del Senado de Plenipotenicarios,* JULIO E. PÉREZ.

*El Secretario de la Cámara de Representantes,* JOSÉ MARIA QUIJANO OTERO.

Bogotá, 19 de mayo de 1873.

Publíquese i ejecútese.

*El Presidente de la Union,* M. MURILLO.

[L. S.]

*El Secretario de lo Interior i Relaciones Esteriores,* JIL COLUNJE.

*Mr. Turner to Mr. Fish.*

No. 147.] MONROVIA, *September* 11, 1874.

SIR: I have the honor, in compliance with instructions contained in the Department's unnumbered note, date June 23, 1874, to transmit herewith information relative to the mode or system employed by the government of Liberia for the investigation and adjustment of such claims as may from time to time be alleged against said government. It will be observed that in procuring the information desired, I have confined my inquiries to a correspondence with the Department of State; this course was especially necessary on account of the utter absence of all printed authentic documentary information bearing upon the important subject with reference to which the inquiries were submitted. It is true, that at the conclusion of each session of the legislative branch of the government, a pamphlet, containing the laws enacted at the session, is printed; it is equally true that the government has never caused a revision, collection, or compilation, in durable form, of the laws of this republic. This omission to preserve in print important historical facts is not alone confined to the laws enacted by the government, but extends to all matters of statistics, the publication and preservation of which would enable the government and people to judge of the benefit or injury resulting to the nation from the execution of the laws enacted. There are extant no printed documents or reports of the revenue, of the census, of finance, of education, of agriculture, &c.; and I have thus far been unable to obtain for my permanent possession a printed copy of the constitution itself. Because it may be of incidental or indirect relevancy to so much of the subject concerning which information is desired, as relates to aliens, I have determined to quote for the information of the Department sections 12 and 13 of article 5 of the constitution of Liberia. Those sections of the constitution read as follows:

SECTION 12. No person shall be entitled to hold real estate in this republic unless he be a citizen of the same. Nevertheless this article shall not be construed to apply to colonization, missionary, educational, or other benevolent institutions so long as the property or estate is applied to its legitimate purposes.

SECTION 13. The great effect of forming these colonies being to provide a home for the dispersed and oppressed children of Africa, and to regenerate and enlighten this benighted continent, none but persons of color shall be admitted to citizenship in the republic.

It will be noticed that while the "declaration of independence" declares the "courts of justice are open equally to the stranger and the citizen for the redress of grievances, for the remedy of injuries, and for the punishment of crime," the exclusiveness of the constitution renders it practically impossible for the alien to acquire any real substantial property-claim within the republic; and in the mean time positively debars a very large class of persons from ever attaining to citizenship. The above exclusive features are repugnant to, and complained of by, foreigners, and strenuously objected to by a few progressive Liberians; but there is no doubt of the popularity of these measures with the people of this republic. Whatever may have been the incentive to bind such unprogressive economy upon the organic system of the republic, it must be conceded that if the tendency of the nature of such laws is not to segregation, it is, to say the least, in the direction to dissimilitude to the liberal spirit of that economy now shaping the statesmanship and policy of the nations.

I have the honor to be, sir, with highest esteem, &c.,

J. MILTON TURNER.

Hon. HAMILTON FISH,
*Secretary of State, Washington, D. C.*

[Inclosure 1.]

*Mr. Turner to Mr. Moore.*

A.

LEGATION OF THE UNITED STATES,
*Monrovia, August* 22, 1874.

SIR: The Government of the United States, being desirous of obtaining accurate information upon the subject of the adjustment and determination of state claims, with a view of establishing, as far as practicable, a general and uniform system and mode of procedure for their investigation, &c., has instructed me to procure and transmit, with as little delay as possible, such replies as your government can furnish in reference thereto. I transmit herewith a copy of a list of inquiries, the purport of which is not intended to confine you specifically in furnishing information on the subject mentioned; and this legation will feel much obliged by your inserting in the blank space opposite each question, the information sought, and returning the same as early as may be in consonance with your convenience, together with any laws or other enactments bearing upon the matter in question.

I have the honor to be, sir, your obedient servant,

J. MILTON TURNER.

Hon. J. E. MOORE,
*Secretary of State, Liberia.*

---

[Inclosure 2.]

*Mr. Moore to Mr. Turner.*

B.

MONROVIA, *September* 11, 1874.

SIR: On the receipt of your communication of 22d ultimo, the schedule of your inquiries therein was submitted to Hon. W. M. Davis, attorney-general, and I now have the honor to transmit you herewith the replies thereto, prepared by him. I regret that I am unable to furnish you with a copy of the laws as requested, they being at present out of print.

I have the honor to be, sir, your obedient servant,

J. E. MOORE.

His Excellency J. MILTON TURNER,
*United States Minister Resident, &c., Monrovia.*

---

[Inclosure 3.]

| *Schedule of inquiries.* | *Answers.* |
|---|---|
| 1st. Are claims against the government investigated, determined, and, if allowed, their payment directed and provided for by the legislative branch of the government? | 1st. Claims against the republic of Liberia are sometimes investigated and determined by the legislative branch of the government, and if such claims are allowed their payment is directed and provided for by a special act of the legislature, or by the amount of the claim allowed being included in the general appropriation bill, and paid by the secretary of the treasury under the warrant of the President drawn for the amount. |
| 2d. If the legislative authority does entertain such claims, what is the mode of procedure, by committee or otherwise, and what means, if any, are provided for procuring evidence on behalf of the government? | 2d. When such claims are entertained by the legislative authority, the usual mode of procedure is, for that branch of the legislature to which the application first comes to appoint a committee to investigate the claim, and to give such committee full power to compel the attendance of witnesses, and such other evidence as they may require in behalf of the government. Sometimes a joint committee of both houses is appointed to investigate the matter; the report of the committee is then acted upon by the legislature. |

3d. What provision, if any, is made for the examination and determination of claims by the executive department? What is the mode of procedure in the investigation of claims by or before executive offices, and what means are provided for procuring evidence on behalf of the government?

3d. There is no constitutional nor legislative provision made in our government for the final determination of claims against the government to be made by the executive department. Executive officers do investigate such claims, and use such means as may be in their power and reach to procure evidence in behalf of the government; but if the claimant is not satisfied with the determination come to by such executive officer, he may resort to the courts of law, or to the legislature, with his claim.

4th. Is there any provision of law allowing a citizen or subject to sue the government in the regularly-established courts, or in any special tribunal, and does the privilege of maintaining an action against the government (if it exists) extend to aliens?

4th. By a provision of our laws, citizens may bring suits against the government for the breach of any contract made on behalf of government by any person whose duty it was to make such contracts, and who had the authority to make it; and citizens may also bring suits against the government for any damage they may sustain by reason of the application of their property to the use of the government. Such suits must be brought in the courts of quarter sessions and common pleas, in the several counties; and such suits must be brought against the republic of Liberia, as defendant, and the plaintiff must cause the county attorney to be notified to appear and defend such suit. Such suits may also be brought by aliens; and in all such suits appeals may be had, by either party, to the supreme court, either by bill of exceptions under our statutes, or by writ of error according to the common law.

5th. What is the status of aliens before the regularly-established courts of the country? Can they maintain an action in such courts against a citizen or subject, and, if so, does the privilege extend to all aliens, or is it confined to resident aliens only?

5th. Our declaration of independence declares that "Our courts of justice are open equally to the stranger and the citizen, for the redress of grievances, for the remedy of injuries, and for the punishment of crime," and the status of aliens before our regularly-established courts is, therefore, the same as that of citizens. Aliens may maintain actions in our courts against citizens and against aliens; and this privilege extends to all aliens, resident or non-resident aliens.

6th. If different systems of adjudication exist, as regards different classes of claims, what is the system with reference to each class, and what the mode of procedure and the privileges of the Government in relation to evidence in its behalf and the means of procuring such evidence?

6th. We do not have different systems of adjudicating claims, nor are claims against the Government classified, but all kinds of claims may be investigated by the legislature and the executive department, as above stated.

7th. Add any other information general or special, of which you may be possessed, bearing on the subject.

7th. The judicial power of this republic is vested in one supreme court, and such subordinate courts as the legislature may, from time to time, establish. The subordinate courts, at present, are the monthly courts of probate, in the several counties, which have also a limited jurisdiction in some civil and criminal cases; and the courts of quarter sessions and common pleas, which courts adjudicate cases both of law and equity, and also have original jurisdiction in all admiralty and maritime cases, and cases of fraud upon our revenue laws. Appeals may be had in all cases by either party from court to court up to the supreme court, which is the court of last resort.

*Mr. Williamson to Mr. Fish.*

No. 235.] UNITED STATES LEGATION AT CENTRAL AMERICA,
*Guatemala, September* 12, 1874. (Received Oct. 13.)

SIR: I have the honor to send you herewith a translated copy of the answer received from Mr. Brioso, minister of foreign affairs of Salvador, in reply to the letter addressed him by me, of which a copy was attached to my No. 209.

No other answer has been received up to this date.

I have, &c.,

GEORGE WILLIAMSON.

---

[Inclosure 1.—Translation.]

SAN SALVADOR, *September* 2, 1874.

SIR: I have been much pleased at receiving your esteemed favor of the 11th of last August, and influenced by the importance of its object, I hasten to give you the information you ask.

We do not have special laws as to the manner of making reclamations against the government. When these are made by foreigners, after having tried ordinary means, before the common tribunals, they have recourse to the minister of foreign affairs. In this office the necessary investigations are continued without any determined form, admitting every kind of evidence to obtain a conviction that the claim is good and just, or the contrary, and according to this result it is admitted or refused.

For natives there are no special laws. In particular cases, general directions are given for examining, liquidating, and paying the accounts against the government' caused by extortion, losses and damages caused in wars, and for resulting expenses for a small assembly that, with short sessions, and the assistance of an attorney who represents the interests of the nation, decides upon the legality or illegality of the claim. From this decision there is an appeal to the government, which decrees what it believes just, only reviewing the proceedings.

The persons, natives or foreigners, who have not been able to make good their claim for any reason, have recourse to the legislative body, which acts on it in the manner established for all business that it considers at the request of parties, and orders or refuses the payment of the claim in a resolution that is called an order, and that does not have the general character of law.

Foreigners in Salvador, resident or absent, have the right to be represented before the tribunals by attorneys, authorized by the court of justice to exercise these functions, and enjoy all the civil rights the natives possess. They can acquire property of all kinds and dispose of it by will or in any other legal manner.

I will not weary you with the form of diplomatic reclamations, for the principles of international law are followed in these negotiations.

This is a compend of what is practiced. I hope I may have satisfied your wishes with this information, but if there is anything wanting I will take much pleasure in giving you the data you may be pleased to ask of me.

I am, with much esteem, your obedient servant,

M. BRIOSA.

Señor Minister Don GEORGE WILLIAMSON.

---

*Mr. Russell to Mr. Fish.*

No. 18.] UNITED STATES LEGATION AT CARÁCAS,
*September* 21, 1874.

SIR: I have the honor to report, respectfully referring to Department circular of June 23, 1874, inquiring as to the mode of pursuing claims against this government:

1. Claims against government are not investigated or determined by its legislative branch, nor by the executive, but solely by the judiciary, viz, by the high federal court.

2. Citizens and aliens alike are allowed to sue the government in said

court, which is a regularly-constituted tribunal having jurisdiction of other cases.

3. Aliens and citizens have the same rights, whether as plaintiffs or as defendants in all the courts of the country, and this is true of suits in the high federal court against the government.

4. The equal right to sue citizens or the nation not only includes resident aliens; it applies as well to aliens non-resident.

5. The same system of adjudication exists in all classes of claims. The government has a double security as to evidence in its behalf: (1,) the representative of the treasury must always be notified of the prosecution of a claim; (2,) the judges are authorized to direct the production of any evidence which they regard as proper, of their own notion. Thus they are, to a certain extent, guardians of the rights of the public.

I give the law as it exists in theory and on the statute-book. As to its practical working, it is difficult to obtain trustworthy information.

Of course, the decree of the high federal court does not execute itself. Legislation is needed to provide funds to satisfy judgment. And it is well known that Venezuela is deeply indebted and unable to pay her debts.

My information as to the law is derived in part from Dr. J. M. Blanco, who was, when he wrote, acting minister of foreign relations, and who has also been an eminent judge. His letter, A, with a translation, B, is annexed. I also annex the constitutional clause, C, with translation, D, giving to the high federal court jurisdiction of suits against the nation; also, the decree or law, E, with translation, F, regulating the prosecution of claims against the nation. E is a printed copy from an official publication, being No. 549 of the "Cuenta," or report of General Guzman Blanco. Said Cuenta was sent to the Department by General Pile, with his No. 80, May 7, 1873. Some of its provisions have been discussed by the two governments.

I am, sir, very respectfully, your obedient servant,

THOMAS RUSSELL.

Hon. HAMILTON FISH,
*Secretary of State, Washington, D. C.*

---

[Inclosure 1.]

B.

CARÁCAS, *September* 10, 1874.

Gratifying in part the wishes expressed by your excellency in your note of August 8 last, I have the honor to state to your excellency that in the official gazette No. 48, of which I send a copy to the legation which is in your worthy charge, with date of February 22, 1873, will be found inserted the law of the 14th of said month and year, upon claims of citizens and aliens on the nation. This law, as your excellency will see, gives to the high federal court the cognizance of the matter, and establishes the mode of proceeding when such claims are to be commenced.

The high federal court is, moreover, the only tribunal competent in any case, in which the nation may be sued, in conformity with No. 6, article 89, of the constitution, and as aliens share in the republic the same civil rights with Venezuelans, the former and latter with equality of conditions can be actors against the government before the aforesaid body.

As for lawsuits between private parties they are carried on and decided by the ordinary courts respectively, and in such trials aliens, domiciled or transient, can be plaintiffs or defendants, since, as has been heretofore set forth, they share the same civil rights with Venezuelans.

Concerning the remaining questions contained in the paper inclosed by your excellency in the note to which I have replied, I will give the necessary instructions in order to furnish your excellency with the desired answer.

I take, with pleasure, &c.,

JESUS MA. BLANCO.

[Inclosure 2.—Translation.]

D.

*Clause in the constitution of Venezuela giving jurisdiction of claims to the high federal court.*

ART. 89. The subjects of jurisdiction of the high federal court are * * * *
6. To take cognizance of civil suits, when the nation is sued, and the law prescribes it.

---

[Inclosure 3.—Translation.]

F.

ARTICLE 1. Those who make claims against the nation, whether citizens or aliens, because of wrongs, injuries, or spoliation, on account of the acts of officers, national or of the States, whether in war, civil or national, or in time of peace, shall do so in the way which this law prescribes.

ART. 2. The claim shall be made by formal demand before the high federal court.

ART. 3. In these suits there shall be cited, besides the representative of the nation, the officer to whom the acts are imputed and the State to which said officer belongs, if such shall be the case.

ART. 4. Before trial of the claim the court shall publish in some newspaper, and at the cost of the plaintiff, an abstract of the claim in which shall be set forth the acts and other grounds on which the suit is founded, the name, surname, residence, and occupation of the demandant, and the sum demanded. This abstract shall be subscribed by the clerk of the court.

ART. 5. In these trials testimony *aliunde* shall not be admitted, except in case of its being shown that the officer who caused the wrong or spoliation has refused to give the proper proof in writing, or unless it appears in an evident manner, from the nature and circumstances of the case, that it was wholly impossible to obtain that proof.

ART. 6. The tribunal may direct that any evidence shall be furnished which it believes will lead to the discovery of the truth, whether at the request of the parties, or of any other person whatever, or officially [of its own motion.]

ART. 7. The nation shall have the right of re-imbursing itself through the responsible officer or through the State to which said officer belonged at the time of the wrong, for the sum which the national treasury expends by virtue of the condemnatory sentence.

ART. 8. Whoever appears manifestly to have exaggerated the amount of the injuries which he claims to have suffered, shall lose whatever right he might have had, and shall incur a fine of five hundred to three thousand venezolanos, or imprisonment from three to twelve months. If it appears that the claim is wholly false, the guilty party shall incur a fine of one thousand to five thousand venezolanos, or imprisonment from six to twenty-four months.

ART. 9. In no case shall it be pretended that the nation or the States shall pay for wrongs, injuries, or spoliations which were not done by the legitimate authorities acting in their public character.

ART. 10. The action to claim wrongs, injuries, or spoliations of which this law speaks is barred in two years.

ART. 11. All those who without public character decree contributions or forced loans, or direct acts of spoliation of whatever nature, as well as the executors, (or actors,) shall be responsible directly and personally with their estates for the damage.

ART. 12. In these suits the law shall be followed which directs the proceedings of the high federal court.

ART. 13. The law of March 6, 1854, as to the indemnification of aliens is repealed.

Done at Carácas, February 14, 1873. (Misprinted 1673.)

---

*Mr. Andrews to Mr. Fish.*

No. 241.] LEGATION OF THE UNITED STATES,
*Stockholm*, *September* 26, 1874. (Received October 16.)

SIR: In reply to your letter of June 23, relative to the course pursued in Sweden and Norway in the investigation and determination of claims against the state, whether held by citizens or aliens, I have the honor to inform you that I made inquiry of the matter through the foreign office by letter, of which a copy is inclosed, and have received an answer from the minister of foreign affairs *ad interim*, inclosing a statement of the law of Sweden and of Norway; from which it appears that in each country private parties, whether citizens or aliens, and whether residing in or out of the country, can sue the government in the regularly-established tribunals, and that the government or state has no privilege in the courts beyond what is enjoyed by individuals. Also, that the rule appears to be one of common law; and, further, that the legislative department does not occupy itself in determining claims.

I have the honor to inclose a copy of the letter of the minister of foreign affairs of the 21st instant, with translation; also, a copy of each statement, in Swedish, accompanying his letter, and translations of the same.

As the matter of execution of a judgment against the government was left to be implied in the statements from the foreign office, I have taken pains to inform myself from the best source on that point, and I have to inform you that, after an individual has obtained judgment in court against the state, he can, if it is necessary, on application to the chief executive officer of the proper county, procure such seizure and sale of the property of the state as will satisfy the execution. I do not find, however, that there has been any instance where execution has actually been taken out and served against the state. When judgment is obtained there is never delay in its satisfaction at the public treasury.

To show how firmly settled the principle and practice are in Sweden that the state may be brought into court to answer to the complaint of an individual, it may be stated that three hundred years ago, in the time of Gustavus I, and later, in the reign of Charles XII, both of which monarchs exercised dictatorial power, the crown or government submitted to the judgments which private individuals obtained against it in the courts of justice.

Up to within a very recent period a suit against Sweden for a considerable claim, in which the city of Stettin was plaintiff, was pending in one of the courts of Stockholm. It seems to have been pending about one hundred years, for what reason I know not, and was lately settled by the government paying the principal sum without interest.

In conformity with the same principle of liability, the Swedish law of 1830 made the state's bank liable to be sued by an individual.

There are two limitations to the government's liability to an action at law by an individual. The first is that any claim is barred unless action is brought within ten years from the date of its accruing. The second is that the government cannot be sued to recover back taxes which have been paid.

I have, &c.,

C. C. ANDREWS.

---

[Inclosure 1 in No. 241.]

*Mr. Andrews to General Björnstjerna.*

LEGATION OF THE UNITED STATES,
*Stockholm, July* 15, 1874.

SIR: We have in the United States, as you are probably aware, a national "Court of Claims," which sits in Washington, and is empowered to adjudicate upon claims against the United States growing out of contracts between private parties and the Government. But in respect to other claims against the Government, parties must have recourse to Congress by petition—a practice which imposes a great deal of labor on the legislative department.

My Government now has in view the establishment of a system of procedure for the investigation and determination not only of claims of its own citizens against itself, but also the claims which the subjects or citizens of foreign governments may wish to bring against it; and has instructed me to obtain exact information as to the course pursued by the governments of Sweden and Norway in the adjustment of claims of a similar character.

As the subject is important, and as it is but just the Swedish and Norwegian systems shall be presented in a proper light, I have felt that your excellency would permit me to lay before you, as I now have the honor to do, the inclosed two copies of inquiries which have been communicated to me by my government, and to request that the information called for under each may be furnished to me in respect to both Sweden and Norway; also, if practicable, that copies of legislative enactments or executive regulations on which the adjudication of claims of either class is based in each of the United Kingdoms may accompany such information.

In expressing to your excellency the belief that my Government will cheerfully reciprocate the favor herein desired, I seize the occasion to renew to you, sir, the assurances of my most distinguished consideration.

C. C. ANDREWS.

His Excellency General O. M. BJÖRNSTJERNA,
*Minister of State and Foreign Affairs.*

---

[Inclosure 2 in No. 241.—Translation.]

*Mr. C. F. Wærn to Mr. Andrews.*

STOCKHOLM, *September* 21, 1874.

SIR: In reply to your note of the 15th July last, I have the honor to transmit herewith a statement containing the information which you expressed a wish to obtain concerning the procedure followed in the United Kingdoms in regard to claims instituted by individuals against the government.

Please accept, sir, the assurances of my most distinguished consideration.

C. F. WÆRN.

Mr. ANDREWS,
*Minister Resident of the United States.*

---

[Inclosure 3 in No. 241.—Translation.]

*The law of Sweden as to adjudication of claims, accompanying Mr. C. F. Wærn's letter of September* 21, 1874.

## SWEDEN.

According to the Swedish law, claims against the royal majesty and crown (the government) are not (as in the memorandum is required) examined and determined by the riksdag or legislative power, but are prosecuted and adjudicated upon under the same regulations as are provided for suits in general, namely, before and by the regularly-established courts of justice. The government enjoys in such case no other rights or privileges nor has other obligations than its adversary. The legal process and practice provided in the general laws obtain with equally binding force for both, and it is open to the inhabitants of the country as well as aliens, according to competency, by summons to institute and maintain suits against the government. Likewise, foreigners, without regard to whether they are or are not residing in Sweden, are as fully empowered as the country's own inhabitants to solicit the Swedish courts of justice for the trial of their claims against Swedish citizens.

---

[Inclosure 4 in No. 241.—Translation.]

*Statement of the law of Norway on the adjudication of claims, accompanying Mr. C. F. Wærn's letter of September* 21, 1874.

## NORWAY.

Answer to mem. 1, 2. Private claims against the state are neither considered nor determined by the legislative power, which neither, in the event of their competency being acknowledged immediately, occupies itself with their satisfaction.

Answer to mem. 3, 4. Such claims are presented before the authorized department of the government, which, when the matter gives occasion, procures closer information and testimony concerning the competency or validity of the claim in question, whereafter it acknowledges the same and does equity in respect thereof. In the law, however, there is no special provision for this investigation. It does not proceed in form of process. If the claim is not acknowledged, the losing party, whether alien or not, is free to submit the matter to trial by the ordinary courts of justice, in which case the same rules are applicable that in general are valid for process between individuals.

Answer to mem. 5. Foreigners have equal right with Norwegian citizens to bring suits in the ordinary courts of justice, and without regard to whether they reside in the country or not.

Answer to mem. 6. What is stated above applies to all sorts of private claims. The government has no privilege in regard to testimony or procedure.

Answer to mem. 7. The foregoing is based partly on the determinations of the statute laws of the state concerning the authorities of the several powers of the state; partly on the construction (supposition) of the law; partly, and finally, on the fact that nothing to the contrary is prescribed in the law.

---

*Mr. Davis to Mr. Fish.*

No 18.] LEGATION OF THE UNITED STATES,
*Berlin, September* 28, 1874.

SIR: Referring to the Department's circular, dated the 23d of June last, respecting the mode of prosecuting claims against governments, I have now to inclose a copy of a note from the foreign office with the answers of this government to the queries of the Department.

I am, &c.,

J. C. B. DAVIS.

Hon. HAMILTON FISH,
*&c., &c., &c.*

[Inclosures.]

1. Note of Mr. v. Philipsborn to Mr. Davis, September 12, 1874. (Copy.)
2. Memorial accompanying the above. (Copy.)
3. Translation of inclosure 1.
4. Translation of inclosure 2.

---

[Inclosure 3.—Translation of inclosure 1.]

FOREIGN OFFICE,
*Berlin, September* 12, 1874.

The undersigned, referring to the note of Mr. Fish, of July 10, of this year, to Mr. von Bülow, respecting the mode of procedure with regard to claims of individuals against the German government, has the honor to transmit herewith to Mr. Bancroft Davis, envoy of the United States of America, a memorial indicating the rules which obtain in such cases.

The undersigned also profits by this occasion to renew to Mr. Bancroft Davis the expression of his most distinguished consideration.

v. PHILIPSBORN.

Mr. BANCROFT DAVIS,
*&c., &c., &c.*

---

[Inclosure 4.—Translation of inclosure 2.]

MEMORIAL.

FOREIGN OFFICE.

1. The legislation of the German Empire, with regard to the investigation, determination, and satisfaction of claims against the imperial government, contains no general directions uniformly applicable to all claims of this kind. Instructions which regulate the prosecution, determination, and satisfaction of certain kinds of claims

against the empire are, however, given in a number of special laws, for instance, in the law respecting the pensioning of military persons, of June 27, 1871, sections 113–116, (Imperial statutes, page 301.) In the law respecting postal affairs, of October 28, 1871, section 15, (Imperial Statutes, page 348.) In the law respecting the relations of the empire with regard to the use of certain articles by a branch of the administration, of May 25, 1873, section 1, (Imperial Statutes, page 113.) In considering and disposing of individual claims, presented in pursuance of these laws, the legislative power of the empire does not, however, act uniformly in all cases.

2. There is, therefore, no particular mode of procedure. In the procedure where claims against the government come up before the administrative or judicial tribunals for investigation, and in the procuring of evidence in such procedure, the same rules obtain, in general, as in the consideration, determination, and deciding of such claims when presented against other parties. In exceptional cases only are directions to be found prescribing a particular feature of the procedure in the case of a claim against the empire. For instance, the law concerning the prevention of the spread of the cattle-plague, of April 7, 1869, section 3, (Union Statutes, page 106,) contains the provision that when, pursuant to the same, claim is made against the imperial treasury for damages for cattle that have died or been killed on account of the cattle-plague, the value of the animals is to be determined by impartial appraisers.

3. Other than that noticed under 2, there is nothing of general applicability prescribed as to the procedure in examining and determining claims. The practice of this tribunal follows substantially the principle of determining, after hearing the parties, the questions of fact and law at issue in a procedure as simple and unhampered with formalities as possible.

4. In all cases in which legal proceedings against the empire are admissible, they are taken in the ordinary courts. The empire has no special court. A procedure by way of arbitration, however, sometimes takes place, both parties consenting thereto. It is immaterial in this connection whether the complainant be a German or an alien.

5. The question as to the conditions under which aliens are capable of maintaining actions before the courts, is to be determined for the entire empire, uniformly, by the civil-procedure regulation to be submitted to the Diet of the empire at its next session. The present laws of the German States contain different provisions on this subject. In the main this question may be thus answered: In case no exception is made on account of "*Rarizvorital*," aliens have the same right of complaint before German tribunals as citizens. They are, however, of course required to give security for costs.

6. As regards the system of adjudication there exist no special modes of procedure for the different classes of claims against the empire than those above indicated.

---

*Mr. Marsh to Mr. Fish.*

No. 52.] LEGATION OF THE UNITED STATES,
*Rome, October* 7, 1874.

SIR: On the receipt of your circular, not numbered, of June 23, 1874, Mr. Wurts, then in charge of legation, applied to the department of foreign affairs for the information desired in respect to the mode of adjustment of the claims of private persons against the government of Italy.

I have the honor to inclose herewith copies and translations of the reply of the ministry and the memoir therein referred to. The volumes and pamphlets accompanying these papers were inclosed in a case with other Italian public documents forwarded yesterday, via Leghorn, to the United States dispatch-agent at New York, who has been advised of the consignment.

I have the honor to be, sir, your obedient servant,

GEORGE P. MARSH.

Hon. HAMILTON FISH,
*Secretary of State.*

---

[Inclosure 1 in No. 52.—Translation.]

ROME, *September* 14, 1874.

MR. MINISTER: In reply to the request contained in the esteemed note from your legation, dated on the 14th of July last, I hasten to transmit to your excellency the subjoined copy of a memoir in which are amply developed the details concerning the legislation and the modes of procedure which in Italy determine the claims of private individuals against the government; a memoir to which are annexed the codes and the various laws cited in it.

I have the honor, in the mean time, to renew to you, Mr. Minister, the assurances of my high consideration.

For the minister.

PEIROLERI.

Hon. GEORGE P. MARSH,
*Minister of the United States of America at Rome.*

---

[Inclosure 2 in No. 52.—Translation]

*Memoir upon the inquiries proposed by the Government of the United States of America respecting the legislation and the modes of procedure in Italy for the determination of claims preferred by private persons against the Government.*

The laws of Italy contain no special provisions for deciding upon claims which citizens may prefer against the Government, nor is any particular mode of procedure ordained for that purpose.

If the claims (or complaints) relate to ministerial ordinances, or to the discharge of the appointed functions which public officers are called upon to fulfill in virtue of the organic or administrative laws, they may be presented in any form, and they are usually addressed to the immediate supervision of the officers against whom they may be preferred.

When recourse to administrative authorities has failed, and demands for reparation can no longer be made through official superiors, and, moreover, when there is a question as to the legality of the administrative proceedings against which the complaint is made, the law has reserved to the claimant an extraordinary remedy, which is an appeal to the King, according to No. 4, art. 9, of the law concerning the council of state. In such cases it is necessary to ask the opinion of the council of state, and when the decision which is asked upon the complaint proves contrary to the judgment of said council, it is always made to appear in the royal decree that the council of ministers has been consulted. In other cases appeals must be laid before the deliberative administrative bodies which are appointed by law in certain cases to pronounce their opinion in controversies which have arisen between individuals and public administrations.

For more special information on this subject reference may be made to the above-cited law upon the council of state of the 20th of March, 1865, No. 2248, annex D, and that of the court of accounts of the 14th of August, 1862, No. 800, annex B.

But the complaints upon which the court of accounts and the council of state are called upon to pronounce, are, as has been said above, not merely of an administrative nature but they concern more particularly the relation between the government and public officers, or those who are charged with a fixed duty or function, and not properly private citizens, who have no relations of dependence with the public administration.

If, on the other hand, the complaints refer to any grievance which the private citizen thinks he may urge against the government, and in general the assertion of any civil or political right which he thinks infringed, (such as appear to be the complaints referred to in the queries proposed,) they are adjudicated in the same way as are all questions which may arise between two private persons. The government has no privileges of forum, and any citizen can summon it before the ordinary tribunals and by the ordinary course of procedure, and can obtain against it in any case whatever an appropriate judgment.

Before the administrative unification accomplished in Italy in 1866, there existed special tribunals for the decision of legal controversies between the government and private persons, but since that time the law of the 20th of March, 1865, annex E, has been in full operation—a law which annuls all distinction of jurisdiction—and the spirit of which is that the government shall have no privilege over private individuals, and that, equally with private citizens, it is bound to respect the laws, and to be subject to the same tribunals, when contested questions arise, which belong to the competency of the ordinary magistrates.

Having, then, in deference to the principles of civil progress and the solidarity of nations, so settled Italian legislation that the foreigner is admitted to enjoy in Italy the civil rights belonging to the citizen, it follows as a consequence that the right above named of summoning the government before the common tribunals may be exercised equally by the citizen and the foreigner, without distinction of mode of procedure or limitation of any sort. (See Civil Code and Code of Civil Procedure.) And, finally, claims may be presented to the legislative authority in the form of a petition, and when they are of a character to come within the competency of the chambers, or as happens in the case where many private citizens are concerned, they may be presented to the legislative authority upon the motion of parliament, or of the government itself, in order that the parliament may make provision for them by suitable legislation.

Cases of this sort have occurred in relation to damage sustained from military operations by the citizens of the late governments of the peninsula in the war for the independence and unity of Italy; and for such damages a bill of relief, annex C, was introduced by the minister of finance on the 1st of April, 1871.

For further explanation of the various matters thus far treated of, we subjoin the principal laws above cited, as well as the above-mentioned bill of relief of 1871, and also the civil code of the kingdom of Italy and the national constitution of the 4th of March, 1848, annex F, G.

---

## CHAMBER OF DEPUTIES—KINGDOM OF ITALY.

*Extract from the report of the committee appointed to consider the bill presented by the minister of finance, April 1, 1871, in relation to claims for damages caused by acts of war.*

The ancient law of war made it allowable to kill the enemy, and also his wife and children, on one's own ground, on the ground of the enemy, on no man's ground, and at sea.

According to Cicero, victory rendered even sacred things profane. He wrote: "The graves of our enemies are not respected by us."

It was natural that all the property of an enemy, taken in war and enslaved, should be acquired by the conqueror or master. Immovable property fell to the conquering state, movable property to whomsoever got possession of it, either for himself, or to be divided with his companions.

Civilization has changed the law. As early as 1743, Montesquieu laid down the doctrine that the law of nations was founded on this principle: that the various nations ought to do each other the greatest possible good in peace and the last injury possible in war. War is not a relation between man and man, but between state and state; the individuals of two nations engaged in war, says Portalis, are enemies by accident; they are not so as men, or even as citizens, but only as soldiers.

To say nothing of the biblical record, or of the pagan law, of the inexorable enforcement of which by the Romans and the northern barbarians we have historical accounts, we have advanced, step by step, to the declaration of the principles of the congress of Paris of March 30, 1856, and to the instructions given to the armies in the field during the war of secession between the northern and southern sections of the United States. We are, moreover, constantly advancing, not yet having reached the goal toward which civilization is conveying us; and we are at a greater distance therefrom in naval warfare than in that which is conducted by land. Nations armed for the extermination of other nations have been succeeded by permanent armies against permanent armies, and desolation is now confined to the field of battle.

The Spaniard Ferdinand Vasquez, in his Celebrated Controversies, denies entirely that there is any obligation on the part of the state to compensate a citizen for damages suffered by him on account of war, "because the law of war permits such things." War, however, being a social act, society should make good the losses caused by war, or, the war being ended, should grant indemnity for its damages by a just equalization of burdens. The nation, which makes war at its own risk and for its own advantage, cannot leave the arbitration of the damages suffered to blind chance, but must divide these damages among all, since all share the benefits. So says Ahrens, in his Philosophy of Law; and so says Heffter, in his Law of the Nations of Modern Europe.

Vattel makes a distinction between damages of war occasioned by the state or the sovereign and those caused by the acts of the enemy. Of the former he says: "Some are done deliberately and by way of precaution, as when a field, a house, or a garden belonging to a private citizen is taken for the purpose of constructing the bastion of a city there, or a work of fortification, or when harvests or store-houses are destroyed to prevent their falling into the hands of the enemy. The state should make good damages of this kind to the citizen, who is only under obligations to bear his share of them. Other damages are caused by inevitable necessity; such are, for instance, those caused by artillery in a city which is retaken from the enemy. These are accidents and misfortunes of chance for the proprietors upon whom they fall. The sovereign should give them equitable consideration when the condition of his affairs will permit him to do so, but there is no ground of action against the state for misfortunes of this nature, for losses which it has caused, not deliberately, but of necessity, by accident, in the exercise of its rights.

"I say the same," continues Vattel, "of damages caused by the enemy. All the subjects are exposed to them, and woe to those on whom they fall! This risk may be run in a community as regards property, since it is run in regard to life. If the state were to indemnify all those who suffer loss in this way, the public treasury would be speedily exhausted. Each individual would then have to contribute of his substance in a just proportion, which would be impracticable. Such indemnities, moreover, would open the door to a thousand abuses and to a frightful amount of detail. Hence it is to be presumed that this was never contemplated by those who united for the purpose of living in a community.

"It is, however," says Vattel, in conclusion, "the duty of the state and of the sovereign, and therefore most equitable and most just, to relieve, so far as this may be possible, those unfortunate persons who have been ruined by the devastations of war; as, for instance, to take care of a family whose head and support has perished in the service of the state. There are many debts which are considered sacred by an upright man, although they may furnish no ground for an action against him."

Vattel does not lay down a doctrine different from that of Ahrens and Heffter; he only desires to have damages caused by war made good, with this difference: For damages deliberately caused by the authorities for military operations of offense or defense, Vattel thinks that there is ground for a civil action, but he denies the existence of any such ground for fortuitous damages, such as, for instance, those caused by a hostile invasion. For the latter damages he warmly recommends that indemnity should be granted, but he thinks it proper that the state of the public finances should be to some extent consulted.

The following decrees have become celebrated in history, namely, those promulgated in France by the national assembly, August 11, 1792, and by the convention of August 14, 1793, and the 16th of messidor, of the year 2. The national assembly decreed as follows: "Indemnities shall be granted to French citizens who, during the war, shall have lost their property, either in whole or in part, through the acts of foreign enemies." But if payment was to be made to all persons who had been injured in property by the enemy, or in the defense of the territory, indemnity was decreed in each particular case by the convention itself. Nor will we separate the bitter remembrance of the assignats from this generous record; in their case the result of excessive payments was that nobody was paid, or that payments were made in a kind of money that was valueless.

Count Cavour, in his celebrated orations to the chamber of deputies, in relation to the treaty of Zurich, during the session of May 21, 1860, had regard to the distinction drawn by Vattel.

The courts have enforced the same theory. Where there is deliberation and freedom of design, there is responsibility for the damage done. Where injuries have been caused by accident, over which the will had no control, the case was one which could not be foreseen, and there no responsibility exists.

In 1858 and 1860 the court of appeals of Lucca and the court of cassation at Florence in the case of Santarnecchi, in 1867 and 1868 the tribunal and the court of appeals of Milan in the case of Antona Traversi, and in 1866 the court of appeals of Messina and the court of cassation of Palermo in the case of Tripodo, raised that distinction of Vattel to a received maxim of jurisprudence among us.

There has been no difficulty in its enforcement when the point in question has been the felling of trees or the destruction of buildings in the neighborhood of fortresses not yet attacked by the enemy, or the occupation of ground for temporary fortifications during an armistice.

A difficulty has arisen with regard to the requisitions made by the enemy through the local authorities. As regards payment for requisitions made within the state by national troops, no one has ever doubted, and no one doubts. The royal orders of August 9, 1836, are in accord with the French law of April 26 and 29, 1792, in admitting the principle of payment; the urgency of a case may authorize seizure, but not grant exemption from the payment of indemnity, even *ex post facto*.

Count Cavour laid it down as a matter of law that the requisitions made by Austria in Lombardy constituted a real debt for Italy, but that the requisitions made on this side of the Ticino were not to be so considered. "In Lombardy, before the war, the Austrian government was a regular government; on this side of the Ticino, it was an enemy in arms." Such are his words. Deputy Cabella said in reply that the enemy, in occupied provinces, exercises sovereignty *de facto*, and has the right to live, and, consequently, if he makes requisitions in order to feed his troops, he imposes a debt upon the state.

It is true that requisitions were made instead of depredations, that they saved the country from rapine, and that they substituted rule and order for military license.

Dalloz calls attention to the law of September 23, 1814, which declared that the taxes, both direct and indirect, levied in 1813 and 1814, were to be appropriated to the payment of requisitions made by the armies; to the law of June 28, 1815, which authorized the government to secure subsistence and military transportation for its armies by way of requisitions, for which payment was to be made; to the ordinance of August 16, 1815, which, on the ground of urgent necessity, imposed a tax of

100,000,000, and divided it among the various departments in proportion to their resources, in order to diminish the burden of the requisitions, which weighed only upon the invaded departments; to the ordinance of October 5, 1815; and to the finance laws of April 28, 1816. Notwithstanding all this, it is found that an action was denied to persons who had suffered damage through requisitions made by the mayor for the benefit of hostile troops.

Blüntschli, speaking of the contributions which an army has a right to levy in hostile territory, endeavors to restrict them to those which are absolutely indispensable for the subsistence and movement of the army. He thinks that a hostile army may demand war-contributions only within the limits established by usage or by the laws of the country. He thinks it wrong for an enemy, who has ordered a requisition, to confine itself to giving a receipt therefor, and to creating the impression that payment will be made by the local government, which, having received nothing, does not desire to be held responsible; and, having observed that this subject is rarely mentioned in treaties of peace, Blüntschli concludes that the rights of communities and individuals toward a hostile state are then very gravely compromised, and that all that remains to them is to beg their government to aid them in the name of equity.

Jurisprudence has expressed itself in this sense also among us.

With regard to the requisitions made in 1859 by the Austrians in Lomellina, through the syndics, there is a learned decision of the court of cassation of Milan, bearing date of July 18, 1864, and given in the case between the commune of Sannazzaro and Peter Maggi. The concluding portion thereof is as follows: "The communal authorities who, during the foreign invasion, remained at their posts, and the citizens who listened to their voice, and now patiently await an equitable provision, fulfilled a patriotic duty and deserved well of their country; and, certainly, there are sacred debts for those who know their duty, although such debts may not give ground for judicial action. Nor is it to be feared that the nation will forget what is rendered advisable by the superior interests of the future, and, above all, by charity toward numerous families who have been despoiled, and perhaps reduced to a condition of misery. It is only denied that judicial action, with principles, methods, and proceedings not adapted to the case, may be substituted where legislative arbitration alone is competent and practicable."

Between persons who have suffered injury in war and the government there exists the relation of creditor and debtor where the damage has been caused by a deliberate design of the authorities, whereas there is no ground for action if the damage is fortuitous, although in the latter case it may be granted. Damage caused by an enemy is fortuitous; so likewise are requisitions made by an enemy, although made through the local magistrates of the country.

*The following is the bill proposed by the ministry:*

ARTICLE I. Landed property seized for military reasons by previous governments without payment of indemnity, during the wars which prepared and completed our national regeneration, and in those in which, at the commencement of the present century, the provinces of the then Italian Kingdom were desolated, if still held by the Italian government, shall be restored by it in the condition in which it now is, or it shall be duly appraised and payment therefor shall be made to those who, furnishing proper legal evidence of their ownership of such property, shall furnish evidence at the same time of the date and of the manner of the seizure, and also of the date of the claims for indemnity presented by them which shall have remained unsatisfied.

ART. II. From the obligation of 4,749,000 nominal florins delivered by the Austro-Hungarian government to the Italian government, in accordance with the terms of article 2, of convention A, of January 6, 1871, approved by law March 23, 1871, number 137, (second series,) a quota of 634,000 florins, also nominal, shall be deducted, to aid those citizens of the Lom-

*Bill proposed by the committee.*

ARTICLE I. Military or war debts of a public nature which, having been formed or contracted according to former ordinances, were left unsettled by the established governments of the former Italian states, which were succeeded in 1859, 1860, 1866, 1870, by the government of the kingdom of Italy, shall be paid by the government of the King in bonds bearing interest at the rate of five per cent. per annum, such bonds to be received at their par value except the debts provided for in the following article.

ART. II. Debts of like nature left by the provisional governments of 1848, and requisitions for which due evidence can be furnished, which were made either by the national troops in the wars of 1848 and 1849, or by Austria in the wars of 1859 and 1866 in Lombardy and in the Venetian and Mantuan territory, shall be paid in bonds bearing interest at the rate of three per cent. per annum, such bonds to be received at par.

ART. III. The government shall appoint suitable commissions to investigate and settle the claims provided for by the present law.

Persons having claims shall present the

bardo-Venetian provinces whose condition is now most indigent, and who may not have been indemnified for the requisitions and other damages suffered by them in consequence of the wars mentioned in the foregoing article, and who may be able to furnish proof of the damage, and to state the date of their claims presented without avail.

ART. III. A commission composed of delegates of the provinces of Lombardy and Venetia, one for each province, to be appointed by the provisional council, shall have charge of the distribution of the sum, as above provided for.

The commission shall be presided over by the prefect of the city of Verona, and shall sit there, and it may appoint one of its members to execute its orders.

same, with their documentary evidence, to the said commission within six months from the date of the appointment of said commission, which shall settle the same within one year from their presentation.

ART. IV. The present law shall not take effect in the case of those persons who may be unwilling to abide by the provisions of its first and second articles.

*Opinion of the Italian council of state in relation to war-damages.*

The section of finance, in its session of May 27, 1867, has considered:

That, in accordance with the jurisprudence already adopted by the former council of state of Turin and enforced in various cases also by the kingdom of Italy, war-damages which are caused by a direct act of war, and which therefore assume the character of an accidental act performed in obedience to immediate necessity, cannot be considered as giving a lawful title to claims for indemnity. This view has been accepted by the majority of writers on public law, and is founded upon the principle of *vis major* and of inability to do otherwise on the part of the state, which has caused the damage only of necessity and in the performance of its duty of self-defense, and therefore with a view of benefiting rather than of injuring.

The juridical principle of *vis major*, which exempts the state from all responsibility, does not interfere with the propriety of indemnities being granted by the state to those who have suffered injury. This may be done from motives of equity and of political expediency, but the two questions should not be confounded, and the idea is not to be entertained that, where citizens are obliged to risk their lives in defense of their country, proprietors who, for the benefit of the same defense, may have suffered material damages, can consider themselves as real creditors of the state and have ground to bring an action for indemnity.

The principle referred to brings with it its own limitation—the damage done deliberately by the state, not under the immediate pressure of attack and at the moment of the meeting of belligerent forces, when it may be said that there is no choice either of time or place, since the determination of the place and time is a necessary consequence of the movements of the enemy. All preparations which precede the war, and which are ordered at a distance from the real field of action and only by way of providing for the contingencies of war, have not in themselves that character of unavoidable necessity which justifies the exclusion of persons who have suffered damage from all compensation. Therefore, the injuries done by troops on the march, before the actual commencement of the war, the demolition of buildings and the felling of trees around fortresses not attacked by the enemy, the occupation of grounds and the erection of temporary fortifications during an armistice, and similar acts, cannot be considered as consequences of real acts of war; it will therefore be proper in these cases to proceed more cautiously and not to refuse offers looking to an equitable arrangement.

It is true that in some cases works of fortification and seizures made not under the urgency of attack by the enemy may, in view of the rapidity and the complication of strategical operations, assume a character of urgency and of inevitable necessity, but a sure decision as to the nature of these acts can only be reached by an examination of each individual case, and the council of state does not deem it possible to lay down an immutable juridical rule which would be of value in all contingencies of this kind. Therefore the fundamental principle has been kept in view which authorizes, nay, obliges, the state to refuse indemnities for real damages of actual war, this principle being one which contains in itself the reasons for the exceptions.

The ministry, in all cases in which the presence and the urgency of the act of war is not evident, which act leaves room neither for choice nor freedom nor responsibility, and which is to be considered in all respects as similar acts and disasters caused by nature, will be at liberty previously to collect such demands as may be of service in estimating the amount of the damage done; it may examine the intentions of the parties claiming indemnity; it may consider the uncertainty of the questions of law and of fact, and before coming to an arrangement it will find it prudent to consult its legal advisers or the council of state, which, examining the act in all its bearings, will be able to estimate the probabilities of a settlement or of a juridical condemnation, and to suggest in consequence the most convenient terms of an arrangement.

It is here proper to consider the method of estimating the damages. The ministry has already wisely provided that, wherever it may be possible, the officers of the engineer corps are to make a previous examination. The possibility of examining the conditions of the soil or of the buildings previously to their transformation by military operations, and to form an exact estimate of the nature of the works and the alterations made for military purposes, is in itself an indication that that urgency and that instantaneity which transforms an unwarlike act into a case of *vis major* were wanting.

At the same time, these official verifications furnish the means of freeing the State from the annoyances of exaggerated demands and fictitious claims.

There is, moreover, another consideration. Injuries done in the excitement of war, or by temporary works constructed in haste, are almost always of more immediate importance in appearance than in reality, and in all respects similar to the injuries done by a chance disaster, which only deprives the proprietor, in the majority of cases, of the temporary use of his property.

Very different are the damages done in pursuance of a premeditated design, as, for example, those which result from the erection of permanent fortifications, which necessarily attract acts of war, and subject the surrounding territory to a kind of perpetual servitude. It is true that the law with regard to military service has, in part, made provision for this, but it is no less true that, when the general provisions of war or the special provisions of strategy impose upon land-owners whose property is near, military sacrifices which are not imposed by the ordinary service, it is proper to pay greater regard to their claims, their situation being worse than that of the other proprietors of the state. For this reason the council of state of Turin was of the opinion that the claims of persons who had suffered injury in consequence of the felling of the trees around the fortresses of Casale and Alessandria might be considered, and, on this ground, the claims of property-owners, whose property was injured last year in the neighborhood of the fortress of Piacenza, might also be considered.

As to damages done by national troops on the march, these should certainly not be considered as war-damages, and therefore compensation therefor should not be made by those bodies and those commanders who, by not observing rigorous discipline, injured the lands or the habitations of the citizens. But on this point the council of state will speak more decidedly when all the facts shall have been laid before it, because, if the marches referred to took place when war was imminent, and under the urgency of extraordinary orders, especially in regard to the time of arriving and the direction to be taken, which orders were reasonably to be presumed to have been given in consequence of the attitude of the hostile forces, it might be said that there were not lacking some elements of *vis major* and of necessity, which might diminish the responsibility of those who caused the damages.

SAPPÀ,
*President of the Session.*

---

B.

No. 800.

*Legge per l'instituzione della Corte dei conti del Regno d'Italia,* 14 *agosto* 1862.

VITTORIO EMANUELE II,

PER GRAZIA DI DIO E PER VOLONTÀ DELLA NAZIONE RE D'ITALIA,

Il Senato e la Camera dei Deputati hanno approvato;
Noi abbiamo sanzionato e promulghiamo quanto segue:

## TITOLO I.

### DELL'INSTITUZIONE E COMPOSIZIONE DELLA CORTE DEI CONTI.

ART. 1. È instituita la Corte dei conti del Regno d'Italia.

ART. 2. La Corte ha sede nella città capitale del Regno; è divisa in tre Sezioni e composta di: Un Presidente, Due Presidenti di Sezione, Dodici Consiglieri, Un Procuratore generale, Un Segretario generale, Venti Ragionieri. Il Procuratore generale rappresenta presso la Corte il Pubblico Ministero.

ART. 3. Il Presidente della Corte, i Presidenti di Sezione e i Consiglieri sono nominati per Decreto Reale, proposto dal Ministro delle Finanze dopo deliberazione del Consiglio dei Ministri.

ART. 4. I Presidenti e Consiglieri della Corte non potranno essere revocati, nè collocati d'ufficio in riposo, nè allontanati in qualsiasi altro modo, se non per Decreto Reale, col parere conforme di una Commissione composta dei Presidenti e Vice-Presidenti del Senato e della Camera dei Deputati.

La Commissione è presieduta dal Presidente del Senato, e conserva il suo ufficio nell' intervallo delle sessioni e delle legislature.

Il parere della Commissione potrà essere provocato dal Presidente della Corte o dal Governo.

ART. 5. Le nomine, promozioni e rimozioni degli Impiegati della Corte e de'suoi Uffici di riscontro e di revisione sono fatte con Decreto Reale, a relazione del Ministro delle Finanze, sulla proposta della Corte a Sezioni riunite.

ART. 6. I Funzionari indicati nell'articolo 2 hanno gli stipendi determinati nella Tabella annessa alla presente Legge.

Per gli altri Impiegati della Corte sono applicate le norme stabilite per l'Amministrazione centrale.

ART. 7. La Corte delibera in via ordinaria per Sezioni separate.

Delibera a Sezioni riunite nei casi determinati dalla Legge e dai Regolamenti e quando il Presidente lo reputa opportuno.

ART. 8. Per le deliberazioni di ciascuna Sezione è necessario il numero dispari di votanti non minore di cinque.

Per le deliberazioni della Corte in Sezioni riunite è necessario il numero dispari di votanti non minore di nove.

La Corte e le Sezioni deliberano a maggiorità assoluta di voti.

ART. 9. I Ragionieri hanno voto deliberativo negli affari soltanto dei quali sono relatori.

Possono essere chiamati dal Presidente a supplire ai Consiglieri che sieno assenti od impediti, e in questo caso hanno pure voto deliberativo.

Il numero dei Ragionieri non sarà maggiore di due nelle singole Sezioni, nè di tre nelle Sezioni riunite.

## TITOLO II.

### DELLE ATTRIBUZIONI DELLA CORTE DEI CONTI.

ART. 10. La Corte, in conformità della Legge e dei Regolamenti:

Fa il riscontro delle spese dello Stato;

Veglia alla riscossione delle pubbliche entrate;

Veglia perche la gestione degli Agenti dello Stato in denaro o in materia sia assicurata don cauzione o col sindacato di speciali Revisori;

Accerta e confronta i conti dei Ministeri col conto generale dell'Amministrazione celle Finanze prima che sieno presentati alle Camere.

Giudica dei conti che debbono rendere tutti coloro che hanno manneggio di denaro o di altri valori dello Stato e di altre pubbliche Amministrazioni designate dalle Leggi.

ART. 11. La Corte liquida le pensioni competenti per Legge a carico dello Stato, e in caso di richiamo ne giudica definitivamente in Sezioni riunite colle forme prescritte per la sua giurisdizione contenziosa.

ART. 12. Oltre le attribuzioni conferite dalla presente Legge, la Corte dei conti esercita tutte quelle altre che le sono conferite da Leggi speciali.

ART. 13. Tutti i Decreti Reali, qualunque sia il Ministero da cui emanano e qualunque ne sia l'obbietto, sono presentati alla Corte perchè vi si apponga il *visto*, e ne sia fatta registrazione.

ART. 14. Ove la Corte riconosca contrario alle Leggi od ai Regolamenti alcuno degli atti o decreti che le vengono presentati, ricuserà il suo *visto* con deliberazione motivata. La deliberazione sarà trasmessa dal Presidente al Ministro cui spetta, e, quando questo persista, sarà presa in esame dal Consiglio dei Ministri.

Se esso risolverà che l'atto o decreto debba aver corso, la Corte sarà chiamata a deliberare, e qualora la medesima non riconosca cessata la cagione del rifiuto, ne ordinerà la registrazione e vi apporrà il *visto con riserva.*

ART. 15. La risponsabilità dei Ministri non viene mai meno in qualsiasi caso per effetto della registrazione e del *visto* della Corte.

ART. 16. La Corte ha diritto di chiedere ai Ministri, alle Amministrazioni ed agli Agenti che da esse dipendono, le informazioni e i documenti che si riferiscono alle riscossioni e alle spese, e tutte le notizie e i documenti necessari all'esercizio delle sue attribuzioni.

ART. 17. La Corte prende nota e dà avviso ai Ministri di tutte le infrazioni alle Leggi ed ai Regolamenti dell'Amministrazione dello Stato che le occorre di rilevare nel compiere le sue incombenze.

ART. 18. La Corte in gennaio di ogni anno communica agli Uffici di Presidenza del Senato e della Camera dei Deputati l'elenco delle registrazioni eseguite *con riserva*, accompagnato dalle deliberazioni relative.

### CAPITOLO I.

*Del riscontro delle spese.*

ART. 19. Sono presentati alla Corte dei conti, perchè vi apponga il *visto* e li faccia trascrivere nei suoi registri, tutti i Decreti coi quali si approvano contratti o si autorizzano spese, qualunque ne sia la forma e la natura, e tutti gli atti di nomina, promozione o trasferimento d'impiegati, e quelli coi quali si danno stipendi, pensioni od altri assegnamenti a carico dello Stato.

Sono eccettuati i decreti e gli atti coi quali si concedono indennità, o retribuzioni per una sola volta, non eccedenti le lire 2,000.

ART. 20. I mandati e gli ordini di pagamento debbono coi documenti giustificativi essere sottoposti alla registrazione e al *visto* debbano precedere il pagamento e i casi nei quali possano a quello succedere.

Determina il modo col quale la Corte fa il riscontro delle spese direttamente, o per mezzo di Uffici da essa dipendenti o da suoi Delegati.

ART. 21. La Corte vigila perchè le spese non superino le somme stanziate nel bilancio e queste si applichino alle spese prescritte, perchè non si faccia trasporto di somme non consentito per Legge e perchè la liquidazione e il pagamento delle spese sieno conformi alle Leggi e ai Regolamenti.

### CAPITOLO II.

*Della vigilanza sulla riscossione delle entrate e sui valori in denaro o in materie.*

ART. 22. I Ministri trasmettono alla Corte, dopo verificati dalle Amministrazioni, i prospetti delle riscossioni e dei pagamenti che si fanno dagli Agenti del Governo nel corso dell'esercizio.

ART. 23. Si trasmettono ancora alla Corte i conti delle Casse delle Stato colla indicazione dei valori e del modo col quale sono rappresentati.

ART. 24. Sono trasmesse alla Corte le relazioni degl'Ispettori o di altri Ufficiali incaricati del sindacato, e quelle colle quali ciascuna Amministrazione, nel rendere il conto annuale delle sue entrate, ne giustifica il risultamento.

ART. 25. Eguali trasmissioni debbono farsi alla Corte relativamente alle entrante ed uscite, alle situazioni ed alle ispezioni dei magazzini ed alla gestione degli Agenti del Governo che hanno il maneggio di materie o valori dello Stato.

### CAPITOLO III.

*Della vigilanza della Corte in ordine alle cauzioni.*

ART. 26. Per l'esercizio della vigilanza commessa alla Corte debbono le varie Amministrazioni trasmetterle l'elenco delle cauzioni dovute dagli Agenti dello Stato, come pure l'elenco degli Ufficiali sindacatori che debbono invigilare gli altri non tenuti a dare cauzione.

ART. 27. Gli atti coi quali si approvano le cauzioni sono sottoposti al *visto* della Corte.

È parimente necessario il *visto* della Corte per gli atti di riduzione, trasporto o cancellazione delle cauzioni stesse.

### CAPITOLO IV.

*Dell'esame dei conti dei Ministri.*

ART. 28. Il conto che ciascun Ministro deve rendere al termine di ogni esercizio e il conto generale dell'Amministrazione delle Finanze, prima che siano presentati all'approvazione delle Camere, sono dal Ministro di Finanza trasmessi alla Corte dei conti.

ART. 29. La Corte verifica il conto di ciascun Ministro e quello dell'Amministrazione generale delle Finanze, e ne confronta i risultamenti tanto per le entrate, quanto per le spese, ponendoli a riscontro colle Leggi del bilancio.

Verifica se i risultamenti speciali e generali dei conti corrispondono a quelli dei conti particolari di ciascuna Amministrazione e di ogni Agente incaricato delle riscossioni e dei pagamenti.

Verifica ancora, quando lo reputa necessario, i vari articoli e le partite dei conti, e domanda i documenti dei quali ha bisogno.

ART. 30. La Corte trasmette al Ministro delle Finanze i conti colla sua deliberazione.

ART. 31. Sarà unita alla deliberazione suddetta, e con essa presentata al parlamento a corredo del progetto di legge per l'assesto definitivo del Bilancio, una relazione della Corte, colla quale deve esporre:

Le ragioni per le quali ha apposto *con riservo* il suo *visto* a mandati o ad altri atti o decreti;

Le sue osservazioni intorno al modo col quale le varie Amministrazioni si sono conformate alle discipline d'ordine amministrativo o finanziario;

Le Variazioni o le riforme che crede opportune pel perfezionamento delle Leggi e dei Regolamenti sull'Amministrazione e sui conti del pubblico denaro.

ART. 32. La verificazione e l'accertamento dei conti dei ministri e del conto dell'Amministrazione generale delle finanze e la deliberazione per l'assesto definitivo del bilancio, come pure la relazione di cui all'articolo precedente, sono fatte dalla Corte a sezioni riunite.

## CAPITOLO V.

*Del giudizio sui conti.*

ART. 33. La Corte dei conti giudica con giurisdizione contenziosa dei conti dei Tesorieri, dei Ricevitori, dei Cassieri e degli Agenti incaricati di riscuotere, di pagare, di conservare e di maneggiare denaro pubblico, o di tenere in custodia valori e materie di proprietà dello Stato.

Giudica pure dei conti dei Tesorieri ed Agenti di altre pubbliche Amministrazione, per quanto le spetti, a termini di Leggi speciali.

ART. 34. La Corte giudica in prima ed ultima istanza dei conti dei Tesorieri, dei Ricevitori, dei Cassieri e degli altri Agenti dell'Amministrazione dello Stato.

Pronunzia in seconda istanza sopra gli appelli dalle decisioni dei Consigli di Prefettura intorno ai giudizi dei conti di loro competenza.

ART. 35. La presentazione del conto costituisce l'Agente dell'Amministrazione in giudizio.

Il giudizio può essere iniziato dietro istanza del pubblico ministero, per decreto della Corte da notificarsi all'agente dell'Amministrazione, con la fissazione di un termine a presentare il conto nei casi:

*a*) Di cessazione degli Agenti dell'Amministrazione dal loro ufficio;

*b*) Di deficienze accertate dall'Amministrazione;

*c*) Di ritardo a presentare i conti nei termini stabiliti per Legge o per Regolamento.

ART. 36. Spirato il termine stabilito dalla Corte, questa, citato l'Agente dell'Amministrazione, ad istanza del pubblico ministero, potrà condannarlo, a ragione della mora, ad una pena pecuniaria non maggiore della metà degli stipendi, degli aggi e delle indennità al medesimo dovute, e quando esso non goda di stipendi, di aggi e di indemnità potrà condannarlo al pagamento di una somma non maggiore di L. 2,000. Potrà pur anche, secondo la gravità dei casi, proporne al ministro da cui dipende la sospensione ed anche la destituzione.

Queste disposizioni s'intenderanno applicabili senza pregiudizio dei provvedimenti d'ordine, di vigilanza e di cautela, i quali competano ai Capi delle rispettive Amministrazioni.

Nel caso che l'Agente persista nella sua renitenza a dare il conto, questo, per Decreto della Corte, ad istanza del Pubblico Ministero, sarà fatto compilare a spese dell'Agente.

ART. 37. Le osservazioni della Corte intorno al conto saranno notificate all'Agente al domicilio reale o nel luogo della sua residenza, in conformità delle Leggi civili vigenti, per mezzo del Capo dell'Amministrazione da cui dipende.

Egli può presentare le sue giustificazioni nel modo e nei termini stabiliti nel Regolamento di procedura dei giudizi della Corte.

ART. 38. Se nell'esame del conto la Corte osservi che siano ad alcuno imputabili atti di concussione, di frode, o di falsificazione, ni referirà col mezzo del Procuratore generale al Ministro di Grazia e Giustizia ed a quello da cui dipende l'Amministrazione o l'Agente, affinchè si proceda, secondo le Leggi, per la punizione del reo.

ART. 39. I giudizi sui conti sono pubblici. Sarà sempre sentito il Pubblico Ministero.

ART. 40. Quando la Corte riconosca che i conti furono saldati, o si bilanciano in favore dell'Agente dell'Amministrazione, pronuncia il discarico del medesimo e la liberazione, ove occorra, della cauzione e la cancellacione delle ipoteche. Nel caso opposto, liquida il debito dell'Agente, e pronunzia, ove occorra, la condanna al pagamento.

ART. 41. L'Agente può opporsi alle decisioni della Corte nel termine di trenta giorni dalla notificazione in persona o al suo domicilio per mezzo dell'Amministrazione da cui dipende.

Non si ammettono opposizioni allorchè la condanna riguardi partite del conto, alle quali si riferiscono le osservazioni notificate all'Agente nel modo indicato all'articolo 37.

Il giudizio sulle opposizioni non sospenderà l'esecuzione della decisione, eccetto i casi nei quali la sospensione sia ordinata dalla Corte, sentito il Pubblico Ministero, prima di passare al giudizio del merito.

ART. 42. Le decisioni della Corte potranno essere impugnate soltanto coi rimedi straordinari:

*a*) Del ricorso per annullamento;

*b*) Del ricorso per rivocazione.

Essi si possono esperimentare tanto dall'Agente, quanto dal Pubblico Ministero.

In nessun caso sospendono l'esecuzione delle decisioni impugnate.

ART. 43. Il ricorso per annullamento è ammesso soltanto per motivo di eccesso di potere, o d'incompetenza per ragione di materia.

Esso si presenta al Consiglio di Stato nel termine di tre mesi dalla notificazione della decisione, con le forme stabilite dalla Legge e dai Regolamenti sul Consiglio di Stato.

La decisione del Consiglio sarà presa in Sezioni riunite e sarà dal suo Presidente partecipata alla Corte.

Se la decisione della Corte è annullata, questa si uniforma alle massime di diritto stabilite dal Consiglio.

ART. 44. L'Agente ha diritto di ricorrere alla Corte per revocazione nel termine di tre anni quando:

a) Vi sia stato errore di fatto o di calcolo;

b) Per l'esame di altri conti o per altro modo si sia riconosciuta omissione o doppio impiego;

c) Si siano rinvenuti nuovi documenti dopo pronunciata la decisione;

d) Il giudizio sia stato pronunziato sopra documenti falsi.

Il giudizio di rivocazione sarà sempre preceduto da deliberazione della Corte sull'ammissione del ricorso, sentito il Pubblico Ministero.

Negli ultimi tre casi, scorsi tre anni, il ricorso in rivocazione dovrà presentarsi nel termine di giorni 30 dal riconoscimento della omissione o doppio impiego, dalla scoperta di nuovi documenti, o dalla notizia venuta al ricorrente della dichiarazione di falsità dei documenti, salvi tuttavia gli effetti della prescrizione trentennaria.

ART. 45. Nel caso e nel termine indicati nell'articolo precedente, la rivocazione potrà anche aver luogo d'ufficio, o sulla istanza del Pubblico Ministero, in contradditorio dell'Agente contabile.

ART. 46. La rivocazione della decisione non ha effetto che per la parte del conto dichiarata erronea e per le conseguenti rettificazioni.

ART. 47. Le decisioni della Corte saranno trasmesse a cura del Pubblico Ministero, per la loro esecuzione, al Ministro dal quale dipende l'Agente.

ART. 48. Per l'esecuzione delle decisioni della Corte saranno applicabili le norme di competenza, i mezzi e le forme stabilite dalla Legge per la riscossione dei tributi diretti.

Spetterà tuttavia alla Corte il giudizio sulle questioni di interpretazione delle sue decisioni.

## TITOLO III.

### DISPOSIZIONI GENERALI E TRANSITORIE.

ART. 49. Con Regio Decreto a proposizione del Ministro delle Finanze, sentita la Corte dei conti, saranno stabilite:

a) Le forme del procedimento nei giudizi della Corte;

b) Le norme da seguirsi per la verificazione e per l'accertamento dei conti dell'Amministrazione.

ART. 50. La Corte dei conti a Sezioni riunite determinerà con Regolamento provvisorio le forme, con le quali essa deve procedere nell'esercizio delle sue attribuzioni non contenziose fino all'emanazione di una Legge sulla materia.

Il Presidente della Corte provvederà con Regolamento alla disciplina ed al servizio interno degli Uffici e della Segretaria della Corte, agli Uscieri, alle spese d'ufficio e a quanto altro sarà necessario per l'esecuzione della presente Legge.

ART. 51. Le Corti dei conti, attualmente sedenti in Torino, in Firenze, in Napoli ed in Palermo sono abolite. Nulla è innovato in riguardo alle Sezioni del Contenzioso amministrativo in Napoli ed in Palermo, finchè non sia proveduto con Legge generale sulla materia.

ART. 52. Commissioni temporanee nominate con Decreti Regi, a proposizione del Ministro delle Finanze, condurranno a termine in Torino, in Firenze, in Napoli ed in Palermo la revisione dei conti che riguardano gli anni 1861 e i precedenti.

Sarà nello stesso modo provveduto alla liquidazione e revisione dei conti arretrati che si riferiscono agli esercizi anteriori a quello del 1860, i quali erano di competenza della Camera dei conti sedente in Parma.

Le deliberazioni delle suddette Commissioni saranno depositate negli Archivi della Corte dei conti.

La trattazione degli affari in corso presso la Corte dei conti di Torino sàra, senza interruzione e senza che occorrano nuovi atti, ripresa e continuata dalla Corte dei conti del Regno, colle forme stabilite dalla presente Legge.

ART. 53. Finchè non sia pubblicata una Legge generale sulle pensioni, la Corte dei conti si atterrà per le medesime alle norme tuttora vigenti per le diverse Provincie del Regno.

ART. 54. La presente Legge andrà in vigore venti giorni dopo la sua promulgazione.

Ordiniamo che la presente, munita del sigillo dello Stato, sia inserta nella raccolta ufficiale delle Leggi e dei Decreti del Regno d'Italia, mandando a chiunque spetti di osservarla e di farla osservare come Legge dello Stato.

Dato a Torino addì 14 Agosto 1862.

VITTORIO EMANUELE.

[Luogo del sigillo.]
*V. Il Guardasigilli,*
R. CONFORTI.

QUINTINO SELLA.

*Tabella degli stipendi.*

| | |
|---|---|
| Presidente | *L.* 15,000 |
| Presidenti di Sezione | 12,000 |
| Consiglieri e Procuratore generale | 9,000 |
| Segretario generale | 8,000 |
| Ragionieri di 1ª classe | 6,000 |
| Ragionieri di 2ª classe | 5,000 |

Visto d'ordine di S. M.
*Il Ministro delle Finanze,*

QUINTINO SELLA.

---

No. 99.

SESSIONE 1871-72, SECONDA DELLA XI LEGISLATURA.—CAMERA DEI DEPUTATI.

*Progetto di legge presentato dal Ministro delle finanze (Sella) nella tornata del* 1° *aprile* 1871 *riprodotto nella tornata del* 17 *aprile* 1872.

## INDENNITÀ PER DANNI DI GUERRA.[1]

SIGNORI!—Risollevata in una discussione recente la questione dei danni di guerra, io prometteva di presentare su questa materia un progetto di legge, che fosse quale sarebbe risultato più conveniente dagli studi fatti dall'amministrazione. A tale promessa io confesso di non saper soddisfare in modo migliore, che portando nuovamente innanzi a voi il progetto di legge già presentato nella tornata del 1° aprile 1871.

La quistione pare a me molto ardua e molto grave per le sue conseguenze finanziarie. Io vi indico una soluzione la quale mentre da un lato soddisfa talune domande per ogni rispetto incontestabili, e dà modo di sopperire ai più stringenti bisogni di chi per danni patiti nelle guerre che prepararono e compirono il nazionale risorgimento, dall'altro circoscrive l'onere della fianza entro limiti che non possano comprometterne l'andamento. Resta ora al Parlamento alla cui sagacia niuno degli aspetti del gravissimo problema da risolversi sfuggirà, il vedere quale deliberazione sia a prendersi.

## PROGETTO DI LEGGE.

ART. 1. I fondi per ragioni militari dai precedenti Governi espropriati, senza pagamento d'indennità, nelle guerre che prepararono e compierono il nostro nazionale risorgimento, come in quelle onde furono funestate nell'entrare del secolo le provincie del primo regno italico, quando sieno tenuti tuttora dal Governo italiano, saranno da esso restituiti nello stato in cui si trovano attualmente, o ne sarà pagato il prezzo di stima a coloro che, giustificando nei modi legali la proprietà del fondo, dimostreranno insieme il tempo ed il modo dell'espropriazione, e la data della domanda o delle domande d'indennità rimaste insoddisfatte.

ART. 2. Dalla obbligazione di 4,749,000 fiorini nominali, rimessa dal Governo austro-ungarico al Governo italiano ai termini dell'articolo 2 della convenzione *A* del 6 gennaio 1871 approvata con legge del 23 marzo anno medesimo, numero 137 (serie seconda), sarà prelevata una quota parte di fiorini 634,000 del pari nominali, per sovvenire ai cittadini delle provincie lombardo-venete di più ristretta condizione di fortuna, che non fossero stati indennizzati delle requisizioni ed altri danni per essi sofferti a causa delle guerre menzionate nell'articola precedente, e che fossero d'altronde in grado di fornire la prova del danno e indicare la data dei reclami presentati senza risultato.

ART. 3. Del reparto della somma come sopra stabilita è incaricata una Commissione composta di delegati delle provincie della Lombardia e della Venezia, uno per ciascheduna provincia, nominato dal rispettivo Consiglio provinciale.

La Commissione sarà presieduta dal prefetto della città di Verona, dove avrà la sua sede; e potrà fra i suoi componenti, nominare un Comitato per la esecuzione delle sue deliberazioni.

---

No. 90.

SESSIONE 1870-71, PRIMA DELLA XI LEGISLATURA.—CAMERA DEI DEPUTATI.

*Progetto di Legge presentato dal Ministro delle Finanze (Sella) nella tornata del* 1° *aprile* 1871.

## INDENNITÀ PER DANNI DI GUERRA.

SIGNORI!—Le convenzioni finanziarie, concluse coll'impero austro-ungarico in esecuzione del trattato di pace del 3 ottobre 1866, richiamavano l'attenzione vostra all'arduo

[1] Vedi Sessione 1870-71, Stampati n° 90.

problema: se debba, o possa lo Stato, assumere l'onere gravissimo di restaurare ai cittadini, agli enti morali, ai comuni e alle provincie, che lo Stato compongono, i danni per essi sofferti nelle varie vicende militari e politiche che travagliarono il paese nostro, prima ch'egli potesse, per tale preparazione di calamità e di sacrifizi, conquistare le presenti sue condizioni di unità e d'indipendenza.

Il problema medesimo, se non nell'attuale integrità sua, pure parzialmente, ora per questa, ora per quella provincia, ed ora per una, ora per altra specie di danni, già più volte fu posto, e più volte fu argomento di discussione nel Parlamento subalpino e nel nostro; se non che mai ad altro fu possibile di prevenire, che a soccorrere alcuna volta, a titolo di umanità e di equità, quelli che più avevano sofferto e che più erano bisognosi di aiuto; e a dimostrare sempre come al desiderio vivissimo, manifestato dal Governo e dal Parlamento, di risarcire a tutti ogni danno, fosse impari la potenza di farlo.

Questo che fu il risultamento costante delle prove anteriori, due cose apertamente dimostra; la prima che per la massima parte, e quasi per la totalità di quei danni, non avevano i danneggiati diritto civilmente esperibile verso lo Stato per ottenerne il risarcimento; la seconda che siamo in tale materia, nella quale i rapporti che intercedono fra i danneggiati e il Governo, invece di essere privati rapporti da creditori a debitore, sono rapporti di indole pubblica da Governo a governati; rapporti che trovano la norma loro nei canoni di giustizia distributiva, come nelle ragioni di convenienza politica.

I quali due caratteri anche più manifesti appariscono per la estensione che acquista oggi il problema. Quando cioè gli obblighi dello Stato debbono considerarsi rispetto a tutte indistintamente le provincie del regno; e non soltanto pei danni cagionati dalle guerre del 1859 e 1866, ma anche per quelli che furono conseguenza della guerra e delle politiche vicende del 1848 e 1849; e per quelli più remoti ancora che le guerre del primo impero arrecarono alle provincie della Lombardia e della Venezia, e pei quali in ordine al trattato del 25 aprile 1818, furono dalla Francia pagati all'Austria 25 milioni di franchi.

E quando inoltre i medesimi obblighi dello Stato debbono considerarsi anche dal punto di vista della successione del Governo italiano all'austriaco, per cui convien definire da quale specie di vincolo obbligatorio possa il Governo italiano essere tenuto; sia a pagare quelle indennità che l'austriaco non pagava, comunque avesse ricevuto un compenso, dalla Francia per le guerre del primo impero, e dalla Sardegna per quelle del 1848 e 1849; sia a risarcire ad un tempo, per le guerre del 1859 e 1866; i danni direttamente inferiti dalle milizie proprie, come quelli inferiti dalle milizie del nemico che combatteva, ed al quale è dipoi succeduto.

Il complessivo ammontare di quei danni, per le indagini che sin qui è stato possibile di fare, ma che non potrebbero con assoluta certezza dichiararsi esaurite, importerebbe una somma superiore a 114 milioni di lire; e se non tutti, una buona parte però sarebbero danni accertati e liquidati per opera di Commissioni create in tempi diversi, le quali, per essere sopraffatte dal numero ognora crescente di reclami e di domande, cui parvero sempre inferiori le condizioni finanziarie dello Stato, dovettero cessare prima di avere condotto a termine i loro lavori.

Ciò apparisce dal prospetto unito alla presente relazione con tutti gli allegati di corredo; che sono appunto i rapporti delle menzionate Commissioni. Unire altri documenti sarebbe impossibile, a meno che non volesse darsi comunicazione della immensa congerie di carte giacenti in diversi archivi del regno, che contengono le domande colle annesse giustificazioni degl'interessati: comunicazione la quale, mentre riuscirebbe affatto illusoria per la impossibilità dell'esame in cui si troverebbe la Camera, sarebbe per essa anche inutile, potendo dagl'indicati rapporti raccogliere dati più che sufficienti a giudicare, così della origine, comme della indole dei proposti titoli d'indennità.

Una buona parte della somma dei danni che in quel prospetto figura, consta di quelli che avrebbe dovuto risarcire il Governo austriaco, o per avere già ottenuto somme a tale oggetto, o per esserne stato egli stesso l'autore. I titoli di questi danni, o che essi si riferiscano alle guerre del primo impero francese, o a quelle del 1848 e 1849, o alle ultime del 1859 e 1866, sono presso a poco i medesimi: forniture e somministrazioni di viveri, requisizioni militari, espropriazioni di terreni, occupazioni temporanee d'immobili, abbattimento di alberi e di fabbricati intorno alle fortificazioni, e danni di guerra in genere.

Ma quale che sia il titolo di questi danni, due cose principalmente conviene esaminare per riconoscere quale essere potrebbe il debito odierno del Governo italiano rispetto ai medesimi; conviene cioè esaminare che cosa avrebbero potuto attendere i danneggiati dal Governo austriaco se egli avesse durato nelle provincie della Lombardia e della Venezia; e di quale indole sia l'obbligazione che il Governo nazionale, come succeduto nella sovranità di quelle provincie, potrebbe avere di corrispondere le indennità dall'Austria non soddisfatte.

Al primo quesito risponde l'esperienza della lunga dominazione austriaca nelle dette provincie, che pur lasciava insoluta molta parte del debito, che per danni di guerra l'Austria aveva verso le medesime, in ordine alla convenzione del 25 aprile 1818 colla Francia, e quasi tutto ciò che era relativo al primo degli articoli addizionali al trattato di Milano del 6 agosto 1849 colla Sardegna. Alla quale mancata soddisfazione concorsero le norme giuridiche seguite dal Governo austriaco in tale materia.

Per l'Austria quei trattati, ed il pagamento delle somme nei medesimi convenute, avevano bensì esonerato la Francia come la Sardegna da qualunque responsabilità per titolo di danni di guerra verso i sudditi suoi delle provincie lombardo-venete, ma ad essa stessa nessun obbligo avevano imposto; mettendola unicamente in grado d'indennizzare i sudditi medesimi nel modo e nella misura che avesse creduto più conveniente. Per essa la materia dei danni di guerra era di competenza esclusivamente politica, rimessa in tutto al discreto arbitrio del Governo, non solo pei principii generali di gius pubblico, ma anche per esplicita disposizione del suo Codice civile, così formulata nell'articolo 1044: "La ripartizione dei danni di guerra viene regolata dalle autorità politiche dietro norme speciali."

Prevalendosi pertanto il Governo austriaco di un simile arbitrio nel reparto delle indennità di guerra ai sudditi delle provincie del regno lombardo-veneto, pose a carico delle provincie stesse, almeno per la guerra degli anni 1848 e 1849, la liquidazione come il pagamento della corrispondente indennità per le requisizioni di ogni specie fatte dalle truppe austriache; quanto poi alle altre categorie di danni poco avanti enunciate dettò tali norme, ora con decreti ministeriali, ora con ordinanze, ora con istruzioni amministrative, per le quali molte di quelle categorie rimanevano escluse da qualunque compenso; ed anche per le categorie ammesse si faceva distinzione da persona a persona, accogliendo le domande dei devoti alla dinastia ed al Governo, e respingendo quelle di coloro che di esser tali non avessero opinione. Da ciò provenne, che dell'immenso numero delle domande presentate alle Commissioni istituite dal Governo austriaco per la liquidazione delle indennità, la massima parte vennero respinte; e l'ammissione delle altre, se si eccettuano quelle di coloro che reclamavano per espropriazione d'immobili, fu piuttosto concessione di favore a persone benaffette, che recognizione di un giusto titolo d'indennità. Una parte poi di quelle domande rimase senza esame e senza liquidazione; imperocchè quelle Commissioni, che già da molto tempo avevano una vita piuttosto apparente che reale, furono disciolte prima che avessero completamente esaurito il com ito loro.

Pel Governo austriaco la partita dei danni cagionati dalle guerre del 1813 e 1814, e da quelle del 1848 e 1849, sarebbe stata dunque partita saldata. E dovendo argomentare dai fatti precedenti e dalle norme giuridiche, ormai stabilite, onde erano informati, non vi è ragione alcuna per supporre che nella ipotesi indicata avrebbe l'Austria tenuto diverso sistema rispetto ai danni delle guerre del 1859 e 1866. Quando pertanto si dovesse partire dal concetto che gli obblighi del Governo austriaco sieno passati per successione nel Governo nazionale, converrebbe proporre il quesito: se i sudditi delle provincie lombardo-venete, rivendicati in libertà, possano esigere dal secondo più di quello che avrebbero ottenuto dal primo, rimanendo in servitù dell'Austria.

Nel quale argomento, ancorchè voglia prescindersi dal compenso che essi avrebbero trovato nelle mutate condizioni politiche, è facile il concludere che il Governo nazionale, pur rifiutando la eredità in tutta quella parte che risguarda le norme direttive segnate dal Governo austriaco al reparto delle indennità, dovrebbe però accettarla, per necessità logica e giuridica, in quella parte che si riferisce al diritto pubblico vigente nell'impero; per il quale la materia dei danni di guerra era materia di competenza politica, rimessa all'arbitrio discrezionale delle politiche autorità, per essere regolata secondo i canoni di giustizia distributiva, tenuto conto ad un tempo delle ragioni di politica convenienza. Talchè la posizione dei reclamanti per danni di guerra, quale era rispetto al Governo austriaco, tale dovrebbe essere rispetto al Governo italiano che a quello è succeduto. E come rispetto al primo quei rapporti, invece di essere rapporti di diritto civile privato, erano rapporti politico-amministrativi da Governo a governanti, che non davano ai reclamanti stessi azione civilmente esperibile avanti i tribunali; tali dovrebbero essere rispetto al secondo, quando si consideri come erede degli obblighi che aveva il Governo austriaco.

L'unica eccezione potrebbe essere per quelli dei reclamanti che ripetessero un fondo, già occupato per ragioni militari e tuttora detenuto dal Governo, e che abbandonando qualunque pretesa che appellasse a danni di guerra, sia per frutti perduti, sia per deterioramenti dal fondo sofferti, limitassero la loro domanda alla restituzione del fondo o al pagamento del prezzo di stima; imperocchè in questo caso il rapporto di diritto civile, come l'azione corrispondente per farlo valere, sorgerebbero dal fatto stesso della detenzione. Ma questa sarebbe oggi una eccezione pel Governo italiano, perchè lo era ugualmente e per la medesima ragione rispetto al Governo austriaco; il quale da ciò appunto era mosso a dare più facile accoglienza alle domande di coloro che reclamavano per espropriazione di immobili.

Se non che per altro principio di ragione si verrebbe, rispetto al Governo italiano, alle conclusioni medesime: per un principio che sorgerebbe non più dalla indole speciale dell'obbligo per successione trasmesso, ma dal fatto stesso della successione del Governo italiano al Governo austriaco; che essendo successione di Stato a Stato, non importa necessariamente, come le successioni dei privati cittadini, la ricognizione di tutti indistintamente i debiti dello Stato antico. La regola che il nuovo Stato succede, come nei diritti, così nelle obbligazioni dell'antico, non è del giure privato, ma è una regola di diritto pubblico internazionale, subordinata nella sua applicazione alle supreme ragioni di necessità e di convenienza politica, delle quali i soli poteri sovrani dello Stato possono essere i giudici. Da ciò proviene che le obbligazioni dello Stato antico non divengono pel nuovo obbligazioni perfette contro di esso civilmente esperibili, finchè dal nuovo Governo non sieno state riconosciute, ed i creditori non abbiano acquistato, per la legge di ricognizione, quel titolo civile che verso il nuovo Stato ad essi mancava.

Questa massima che non è solamente di gius pubblico, ma che è passata ormai nella giurisprudenza dei tribunali nostri, è confermata inoltre solennemente dalle consuetudini del regno e del Parlamento; non pochi essendo gli atti governativi come gli atti legislativi emanati in diverse occassioni per riconoscere diversi debiti dei precedenti Governi; e principale fra gli altri la legge del 4 agosto 1861 che riconosceva e dichiarava debiti del regno d'Italia una parte dei debiti consolidati di quei Governi, riservando a leggi speciali lo statuire sugli altri che rimanevano, contratti sotto la medesima forma o sotto forma diversa.

Ciò dimostra come, non solo pei danni di guerra delle provincie lombardo-venete, ma anche per quelli delle altre provincie d'Italia, che figurano nel prospetto unito alla presente relazione, i rapporti dei reclamanti verso il Governo abbiano essi pure la medesima indole politica di rapporti da Govorno a governati, essi pure definibili secondo le norme di giustizia distributiva e secondo le ragioni di convenienza politica.

Evidente è un tale carattere per gl'imprestiti forzosi nazionali che figurano per somma ingentissima in quel prospetto e che furono decretati nei rivolgimenti politici del 1821 in Napoli, e in quelli del 1848 e 1849 in Napoli ugualmente, come lo furono del pari nella Lombardia e nella Venezia dai rispettivi Governi provvisori, e in Roma dal Governo della repubblica romana. Rispetto ai quali imprestiti conviene inoltre notare che, quando pure possibilità vi fosse di riconoscere, anche parzialmente, il debito, forse la massima parte del sacrifizio che per tal modo s'imporrebbe al paese, piuttosto che restaurare i danni di coloro che effettivamente li soffersero, potrebbe servire di premio a chi sui danni e sulla miseria altrui avesse speculato.

Il medesimo carattere è del pari evidente pei reclami che si riferiscono a confische di beni sofferte da condannati politici nelle provincie di Modena e Reggio durante il Governo del ducca, o a pensioni che sarebbero dovute ad impiegati ugualmente per causa politica destituiti, o se, non ad essi, ai figli ed alle vedove loro; essendo inoltre evidente come questa categoria di danni crescerebbe in grandi proporzioni, se il Governo nazionale dovesse oggi indennizzare quanti avessero per avventura avuto pregiudizio dai Governi anteriori. •

Quanto al credito di diversi comuni della Toscana pel mantenimento delle truppe austriache dal 1849 al 1855, ch'esso non dia ai detti comuni azione civilmente esperibile contro il Governo, e che la competenza di statuire e risolvere in proposito appartenga al potere legislativo anzichè al giudiziario, lo ha già deciso il Consiglio di Stato, pronunziando sul conflitto di attribuzione elevato in occasione delle liti che appunto contro il Governo alcuni di essi avevano promosso.

Nè diversa è la indole della competenza, comunque diverse sieno le ragioni che la determinano, pei danni gravissimi sofferti dalle provincie della Lomellina e di Novara invase dalle truppe austriache nella guerra del 1859; imperocchè, per quanto sia stato scritto e disputato sul tema dei danni di guerra refettibili per diritto, mai è stato detto che sieno tali quelli cagionati dal nemico.

Se si eccettua pertanto, fra le categorie dei danni che figurano nel prospetto più volte menzionato, quella delle espropriazioni di terreni, fatte per causa di guerra senza corrispondente pagamento d'indennità; rispetto alla quale, se i terreni sieno tuttora tenuti dal Governo, la ragione di diritto per ottenerne la restituzione o conseguirne il pagamento del prezzo risultante dalla stima, sorgerebbe dal fatto stesso della detenzione: per tutte le altre non siamo in materia di diritto, ma in materia d'interessi più o meno gravemente sacrificati ed offesi, a provvedere ai quali, non ragioni di obbligazione civile potrebbero costringere, ma solo ragioni di umanità e di equità potrebbero consigliare, quando ciò fosse compatibile collo stato della pubblica finanza.

Ma le presenti condizioni della finanza pubblica sono ellena tali che possano permetterci di risarcire tanto numero di danni? Comunque vivo possa essere il desiderio di riparare a tante perdite e a tanti sacrifizi di averi, spesso sopportati con virtù e costanza eroica, quanti ne furono imposti ai cittadini, agli enti morali, ai comuni e alle provincie d'Italia, dalle dolorose vicende che prepararano e maturarono il nazionale risorgimento, v'è forse alcuno che abbia serio convincimento della possibilità di riuscire a tanto nelle presenti nostre condizioni finanziarie? E quando pure voglia applicarsi la regola di giustizia distributiva, per la quale i danni sopportati per comune utilità della nazione sulla intera nazione dovrebbero ripartirsi: non é forse l'intera nazione, che d'una maniera o di un'altra questi danni ha sofferto? Coll'ammettere le domande d'indennità, che già per molte migliaia si trovano cumulate negli archivi, potrebbe, è vero, tentarsi un reparto diverso da quello che lo svolgersi successivo degli avvenimenti ha già operato di fatto; ma con ciò nuovi danni e nuove sofferenze sarebbero procurate all'Italia senza estinguere le antiche, seguendo anche noi l'esempio della inferma.

Che non può trovar posa in su le piume,
Ma con dar volta suo dolore scherma.

Se il problema del risarcimento dei danni cagionati dalle guerre d'indipendenza, come da altri politici eventi al conseguimento della indipendenza e della unità nazionale preordinati, fu posto altre volte parzialmente per alcuna provincia o per alcuna specie di danni, nè ad altro si pervenne che a qualche provvedimento di soccorso, come in ogni pubblica calamità, ai danneggiati più poveri; io credo che unicamente a questo risultato sia possibile di pervenire oggi che il problema, posto nella sua integrità, ha dimostrato come non vi sia provincia o comune d'Italia, che non abbiano a ripetere per danni sofferti; e come il peso di risarcirli, che oltremodo gravoso sarebbe in condizioni floride di finanza, si affatto insopportabile nelle condizioni presenti, quando lo stato della finanza potrebbe riassumersi nello sforzo constante di raggiungere un pareggio che sempre sfugge, malgrado i carichi gravissimi imposti al paese; e quando a crescerne il numero sopravviene la necessità, da tutti sentita, di provedere al riordinamento dell'esercito e alla difesa dello Stato per mantenerci in quel grado di nazione, al quale appunto ci condussero i passati sacrifizi di tute quante le provincie d'Italia.

In questo concetto ho dovuto apparecchiare il progetto di legge, che io già prometteva alla Camera, e che oggi ho l'onore di presentarle. Esso due provvedimenti contiene; provvede a soddisfare alle ragioni di diritto che hanno coloro, i quali senza indennità fossero stati espropriati di alcun loro fondo per causa di guerra; e destina a sovvenzione dei cittadini di piccolo censo dello provincie lombardo-venete, che non fossero stati per anco indennizzati dei danni sofferti per causa di guerra, una quota determinata in fiorini nominali 634,000 della obbligazione rimessa dal Governo austro-ungarico al Governo italiano, ai termini dell'articulo 2 della convenzione *A*, del 6 gennaio anno corrente, approvatta con legge del 23 del decorso mese di marzo.

Il primo provvedimento è abbastanza giustificato dalle cose di sopra discorse; imperocchè, se il Governo italiano, che abbia tuttora il materiale possesso di fondi espropriati per causa di guerra dai precedenti Governi senza pagamento d'indennità, può di quei Governi rifiutare la eredità per tutto ciò che ha rapporto ai frutti perduti e ai deperimenti del fondo, che sono danni da essi cagionati, non potrebbe però declinare del pari l'obbligo che gli viene dal fatto stesso della detenzione, di restituire quei fondi nello stato in cui si trovano attualmente, o di pagarne il prezzo di stima.

Il provvedimento secondo da doppia ragione è giustificato; in primo luogo dalla proporzione molto maggiore dei danni sopportati dalle provincie italiane; in secundo luogo dall'essere, come già ebbi occasione di dichiarare alla Camera in occasione degli ultimi trattati coll'Austria, cosa loro la somma che verrebbe destinata a sovvenire ai danneggiati di esse provincie più bisognosi di soccorso, come quella che nel sistema della transazione conclusa coll'Austria rappresentava il fondo di riserva *della guardia nobile lombardo-veneta*, che doveva rimaner sempre *una proprietà del paese* per dichiarazione formalmente espressa nello statuto col quale quella guardia era stata organizzata.

Io confido che la Camera, approvando col progetto di legge i proposti provvedimenti, vorrà per tal modo risolvere il problema spinoso e doloroso, ma pur troppo altrimenti insolubile, dei danni di guerra.

## PROGETTO DI LEGGE.

ART. 1. I fondi per ragioni militari dai precedenti Governi espropriati, senza pagamento d'indennità, nelle guerre che prepararono e compierono il nostro nazionale risorgimento, come in quelle onde furono funestate nell'entrare del secolo, le provincie del primo regno italico quando sieno tenuti tuttora dal Governo italiano, saranno da esso restituiti nello stato in cui si trovano attualmente, o ne sarà pagato il prezzo di stima, a coloro che, giustificando nei modi legali la proprietà del fondo, dimostreranno insieme il tempo ed il modo della espropriazione, e la data della domanda o delle domande d'indennità rimaste insoddisfatte.

ART. 2. Dalla obbligazione di 4,749,000 fiorini nominali, rimessa del Governo austro-ungarico al Governo italiano ai termini dell'articolo 2 della convenzione *A* del 6 gennaio 1871 approvata con legge del 23 marzo anno medesimo, numero 137 (serie seconda), sarà prelevata una quota parte di fiorini 634,000 del pari nominali, per sovvenire ai cittadini delle provincie lombardo-venete di più ristretta condizione di fortuna, che non fossero stati indennizzati delle requisizioni ed altri danni per essi sofferti a causa delle guerre menzionate nell'articolo precedente, e che fossero d'altronde in grado di fornire la prova del danno e indicare la data dei reclami presentati senza risultato.

ART. 3. Del reparto della somma come sopra stabilita è incaricata una Commissione composta di delegati delle provincie della Lombardia e della Venezia, uno per ciascheduna provincia, nominato dal respettivo Consiglio provinciale.

La Commissione sarà presieduta dal prefetto della città di Verona, dove avrà la sua sede; e potrà, fra i suoi componenti, nominare un Comitato per la esecuzione delle sue deliberazioni.

*Crediti di corpi morali e privati del regno, cagionati dai rivolgimenti politici e dalle guerre che hanno avuto luogo a tutto l'anno* 1866.

| | Somme. | | Totali. |
|---|---|---|---|
| | Presunte. | Accertate. | |
| | *Lire. Ct.* | *Lire. Ct.* | *Lire. Ct.* |
| Crediti a tutto l'anno 1821 | 5, 043, 687 33 | 1, 135, 024 06 | 6, 178, 711 39 |
| Crediti provenienti dai fatti degli anni 1848 e 1849 | 43, 353, 374 62 | 21, 331, 603 41 | 64, 684, 978 03 |
| Crediti provenienti dalle guerre degli anni 1859 e 1860 | 22, 216, 239 80 | 3, 482, 092 53 | 25, 698, 332 33 |
| Crediti provenienti dalla guerra del 1866 | 18, 007, 340 21 | .............. | 18, 007, 340 21 |
| Somma | 88, 620, 641 96 | 25, 948, 720 00 | 114, 569, 361 96 |

*Crediti a tutto l'anno* 1824.

| Provincie. | Cagioni del credito. | Somma. | | Osservazioni. |
|---|---|---|---|---|
| | | Presunta. | Accertata. | |
| | | *Lire. Ct.* | *Lire Ct.* | |
| Lombardia | Espropriazioni e somministrazioni militari durante il primo regno italico. | 56, 506 33 | .............. | Le controscritte somme rappresentano il montare di crediti reclamati da comuni e privati di Lombardia, che non erano stati ancora liquidati quando fu sciolta la commissione apposita presso il Monte Lombardo-Veneto, instituita in esecuzione dell'articola 97 dell'atto finale del Congresso di Vienna del 9 giugno 1815. |
| | Somministrazioni fatte all'armata nella campagna del 1809. | 200, 584 71 | .............. | |
| | Indebite appropriazioni di stabili fatte dalla Cassa di ammortizzazione del Governo italico. | 425, 494 45 | .............. | |
| Venezia | Espropriazioni e somministrazioni militari durante il primo regno italico. | 135, 407 17 | .............. | Come sopra. |
| | Somministrazioni fatte all'armata nella campagna del 1809. | 3, 562, 454 03 | .............. | |
| | Indebite appropriazioni di stabili fatte dalla Cassa di ammortizzazione del Governo italico. | 663, 240 64 | .............. | |
| Parma e Piacenza. | Somministrazioni fatte negli anni 1811, 1812, 1814 e 1815. | .............. | 6, 835 68 | La controscritta somma è dovuta all'amministrazione degli opifizi civili di Borgo San Donnino, per provvista di paglioricci e panni pei detenuti in quelle prigioni e per ispesa di mantenimento dei ricoverati in quel deposito di mendicanti. |
| Provincie napolitane. | Prestito forzoso nazionale del 1821. | .............. | 1, 128, 188 38 | Questo prestito, votato dal Parlamento napolitano ed ordinato con legge del 17 febbraio 1821, doveva ripartirsi fra i negozianti, i proprietari, e gl'impiegati. Il montare fu stabilito in ducati 3,000,000, pari a lire 12,750,000, diviso in 150,000 obbligazioni di ducati 20, pari a lire 85 ciascuna. L'interesse fu stabilito al 9 per cento all'anno, e l'ammortizzazione doveva esserne fatta in dieci anni. Con determinazione del 27 marzo 1821 fu sospesa l'esecuzione del prestito, che venne annullato con decreto del 6 aprile 1821. Dal 17 febbraio al 29 marzo la Tesoreria generale di Napoli riscosse la somma di ducati 268,123 59 in conto del detto prestito, dalla quale dedotti ducati 2,667 50 restituiti nel 1821, rimangono a restituire ducati 265,456 09, pari a lire 1,128,188 38. |
| | | 5, 043, 687 33 | 1, 135, 024 06 | |
| | | 6, 178, 711 39 | | |

*Crediti provenienti dai fatti del* 1848 *e del* 1849.

| Provincie. | Cagioni del credito. | Somma. | | Osservazioni. |
|---|---|---|---|---|
| | | Presunta. | Accertata. | |
| | | *Lire. Ct.* | *Lire. Ct.* | |
| Provincie ex-pontificie, annesse all Italia nel 1859 e 1860. | Prestazioni e somministrazioni alle milizie della repubblica romana e del Governo pontificio. | .............. | 124, 867 97 | La controscritta somma si compone di molte partite, di cui ve ne hanno di piccolissimo ammontare. Esse sono quasi interamente liquidate. |
| Lombardia..... | Prestiti fatti dal Governo provvisorio nel 1848. | .............. | 8, 497, 890 72 | In questa somma sono compresi i prestiti in danaro ordinati dal Governo provvisorio coi decreti 27 marzo, 1° giugno, e 28 luglio 1848, le ritenute fatte sugli stipendi e sulle pensioni per effetto dei decreti del 29 aprile e 19 maggio 1848, ed il prestito in oggetti d'oro e di argento, ordinato col decreto del 1° luglio 1848. |
| | Somministrazioni e lavori fatti da corpi morali e privati per conto del Governo provvisorio. | .............. | 1, 235, 763 63 | Questa somma si compone di 295 partite liquidate dalla Commissione speciale già esistente presso il Ministero della guerra. |
| | Requisizioni militari e danni della guerra del 1848. | 2, 237, 957 54 | .............. | Questa somma si compone di 327 partite che non furono liquidate dalla detta Commissione per mancanza dei necessari documenti. |
| | Incendio di case nel suburbio di Milano, avvenuto nei giorni 4 e 5 agosto 1848. | 648, 489 56 | .............. | Questa somma è quella reclamata dagl'interessati che avevano instaurato giudizio contro il Governo austriaco: si presume però che i danni salgano in totale a somma forse quintupla. |
| Parma e Piacenza. | Prestazioni e somministrazioni a truppe austriache. | 86, 067 11 | .............. | Questa somma è quasi intieramente dovuta al comune di Parma in rimborso delle spese fatte per provvedere di alloggio e vitto le truppe austriache. |
| | Prestazioni e somministrazioni a truppe nazionali. | .............. | 8, 150 83 | La controscritta somma è quella stata ammessa dalla Commissione di liquidazione presso il Ministero della guerra. Le domande ascendevano a lire 23,039 01. |
| Ex-Ducato di Modena. | Requisizioni e somministrazioni militari, e danni di guerra. | 69, 814 38 | .............. | Di questa somma la Commissione liquidatrice presso il Ministero della guerra liquidò sole lire 609 73, respingendo le altre domande, perchè non regolarmente giustificate. |
| Toscana ....... | Mantenimento delle truppe austriache dal 1849 al 1855. | .............. | 6, 039, 251 58 | L'occupazione austriaca in Toscana cominciò il 5 maggio 1849, e durò fino al 30 aprile 1855. I comuni toscani sostennero la spesa del mantenimento delle truppe austriache, e si rivolsero poi al Governo per esserne rifatti, invocando a loro favore la convenzione del 22 aprile 1850, stipulata tra la Toscana e l'Austria. Un'apposita Commissione, creata nel 1856, liquidò il credito dei comuni per questo titolo, diffalcate le somme ricevute in conto dal Governo, in toscane lire 7,189,585 43, pari alle controscritte italiane lire 6,039,251 58. Vivissime istanze sono state fatte sempre dai detti comuni per ottenere il pagamento di questa somma, ed i principali di essi adirono i tribunali; ma, elevato il conflitto di giurisdizione, il Consiglio di Stato, con decreto del 17 agosto 1870, ha dichiarato l'incompetenza del potere giudiziario. |

Segue *Crediti provenienti dai fatti del* 1848 *e del* 1849.

| Provincie. | Cagioni del credito. | Somma. | | Osservazioni. |
|---|---|---|---|---|
| | | Presunta. | Accertata. | |
| | | *Lire. Ct.* | *Lire. Ct.* | |
| Provincie napolitane. | Prestito forzoso dell'anno 1848. | .............. | 1, 946, 637 74 | Il prestito controscritto fu stabilito nella somma di ducati 3.000.000, pari a lire italiane 12,750.000, ma poco dopo venne annullato. La tesoreria generale di Napoli riscosse: Ducati......... 1,135,531 43 ne furono restituiti: Ducati......... 677,499 02 sicchè rimangono da restituire..Ducati.. 458,032 41 che corrispondono alle controscritte lire 1.946,637 74. |
| Sicilia ......... | Somministrazioni militari fatte negli anni 1847 e 1848. | .............. | 18, 283 28 | Le domande fatte per questo titolo ammontano a lire 32,876 28, ma furono ammesse solo per la controscritta somma dalla Commissione di liquidazione già esistente presso il Ministero della guerra. |
| | Requisizioni militari e danni di guerra. | 240, 008 63 | .............. | Questa somma è il montare dei reclami che non vennero ammessi dalla detta Commissione, perchè non debitamente giustificati. |
| Piemonte ...... | Requisizioni e danni di guerra durante la campagna di marzo 1849. | .............. | 1, 652, 392 48 | I controscritti crediti furono liquidati da una Commissione creata nel 1849, nella somma di lire 2.152,392 48. Ma, per effetto della legge del 15 giugno 1850, furono pagate lire 500,000 a titolo di sussidio a quei danneggiati che erano in *ristretta condizione di fortuna.* |
| Provincie venete e di Mantova. | Requisizioni e danni delle guerre del 1848 e 1849. | 11, 150, 059 35 | .............. | La controscritta somma rappresenta il montare complessivo delle indennità reclamate con le 3301 istanze giunte alla Commissione istituita col regio decreto del 26 maggio 1867. |
| Venezia ....... | Prestito ordinato dal Governo provvisorio di Venezia con decreto del 14 maggio 1848. | 3, 888, 900 00 | .............. | Questo prestito fu stabilito in 10 milioni di lire austriache; ma le condizioni politiche fecero sì che si potesse riscuotere la sola quota della provincia di Venezia in austriache lire 4,500,000, pari alle controscritte italiane lire 3,888,900. |
| | Prestito ordinato dal Governo provvisorio di Venezia con decreto del 20 giugno 1848. | 1, 296, 300 00 | .............. | Questo prestito fu stabilito in austriache lire 1,500,000, che corrispondono ad italiane lire 1,296,300. |
| | Prestito in effetti d'oro e d'argento e ritenuta sugli stipendi e sulle pensioni, ordinati coi decreti del Governo provvisorio del 19 luglio e del 16 agosto 1848. | 1, 129, 880 00 | .............. | Si calcola che il valore degli oggetti d'oro e d'argento sia approssimativamente di austriache lire 1,200,000, e quello delle ritenute sugli stipendi e sulle pensioni di austriache lire 200,000. |
| | *Buoni* della Banca di sconto emessi dal Governo provvisorio, giusta il decreto del 25 luglio 1848. | 1, 609, 875 00 | .............. | Questi Buoni erano garantiti dal comune di Venezia e dalla Lombardia. |
| | Prestiti ordinati dal Governo provvisorio coi decreti del 19 settembre, 14 ottobre, 15 novembre 1848 e 9 aprile 1849. | 2, 659, 834 76 | .............. | Questi prestiti montavano in complesso ad austriache lire 9,000,000; ma si è tenuto conto solamente della parte versata in danaro effettivo, che si calcola di austriache lire 3,077,800, mentre il rimanente fu rappresentato dalla moneta patriottica. |

Segue *Crediti provenienti dai fatti del* 1848 *e del* 1849.

| Provincie. | Cagioni del credito. | Somma. | | Osservazioni. |
|---|---|---|---|---|
| | | Presunta. | Accertata. | |
| | | *Lire. Ct.* | *Lire. Ct.* | |
| *Segue* Venezia.. | *Moneta patriottica* rimasta in circolazione dopo la notificazione del Governo austriaco del 2 ottobre 1849. | 1, 571, 136 22 | ............. | La *moneta patriottica*, emessa in occasione dei detti prestiti, fu di austriache ..... L. 5,922,200<br>ne fu ammortizzata dal Governo provvisorio per .......L. 3,333,482<br>ne fu ritirata dopo la capitolazione del 22 agosto 1849 per .......L. 769,537<br>——— 4,103,019<br>sicchè ne rimase in circolazione per austriache ................L. 1,819,181<br>che corrispondono alle controscritte italiane lire 1,571,136 22. |
| | *Moneta del comune di Venezie.*—Perdita per la riduzione a metà del valore della moneta stessa, giusta la convenzione del 22 agosto 1849. | 8, 973, 774 57 | ............. | La carta emessa dal comune di Venezia, giusta i decreti del Governo provvisorio del 22 novembre 1848, 28 maggio e 28 giugno 1849 ammontava ad austriache .......L. 21,165,943 78<br>da cui, diffalcate le ammortizzazioni fatte dal comune per austriache .L. 399,652 26<br>rimangono austriache ............L. 20,766,291 52<br>che furono ammesse per metà del valore dal Governo austriaco. La perdita fu dunque di austriache lire 10,383,145 76, che corrispondono alle controscritte italiane lire 8,973,774 57. Questa somma però è messa solamente per memoria; dappoichè, essendo stata la carta del comune di Venezia commutata con valuta austriaca, non sarebbe più possibile di rinvenirne i creditori. |
| Roma.......... | Perdita del 35 per cento sul valore dei Buoni emessi dal Governo della repubblica romana, giusta i decreti del 1° e 26 marzo, 5 e 11 aprile e 5 maggio 1849. | 7, 791, 277 50 | ............. | Una notificazione del Governo pontificio del 24 settembre 1849 dichiara che i Buoni del Governo provvisorio e della Repubblica trovati in corso, ridotti del 35 per cento, giusta la notificazione del 3 agosto dello stesso anno, ammontavano a 2,692,000 scudi romani. Da questo dato adunque si può calcolare che i Buoni ascendevano alla somma di scudi 4,141,540, e che la perdita del 35 per cento importò la somma di 1,449,540 scudi. |
| | Prestito forzoso ordinato dal governo della repubblica con decreto del 2 marzo 1849. | ............. | 1, 298, 932 98 | Il prestito fu stabilito in misura progressiva, secondo le rendite delle varie famiglie. La somma riscossa pel detto prestito fu di scudi 241,661 95. |
| | Requisizione degli argenti dei privati, ordinata dal governo della repubblica con decreto del 2 maggio 1849. | ............. | 509, 432 20 | Il valore degli argenti requisiti fu di scudi 94,778 08 4. |
| | Requisizione del numerario contro biglietti, ordinata dal governo della repubblica con decreto del 10 maggio 1849. | ............. | ............. | Non si hanno dati per riconoscere il montare del numerario requisito. |
| | Danni cagionati dalla guerra del 1849. | ............. | ............. | Non si hanno dati per riconoscere il montare dei danni di guerra. |
| | | 43, 353, 374 62 | 21, 331, 603 41 | |
| | | 64, 684, 978 03 | | |

*Crediti provenienti dalle guerre degli anni* 1859 *e* 1860.

| Provincie. | Cagioni del credito. | Somma. | | Osservazioni. |
|---|---|---|---|---|
| | | Presunta. | Accertata. | |
| | | *Lire. Ct.* | *Lire. Ct.* | |
| Provincie ex-pontificie annesse all'Italia nel 1859 e 1860. | Somministrazioni e requisizioni militari e forniture diverse. | 613,156 62 | .............. | Questa somma è composta di molte partite, non tutte liquidate, fra cui ve ne ha di piccolo montare. |
| Lombardia..... | Requisizioni e forniture militari, espropriazioni e danni della guerra del 1859. | 12,241,279 24 | .............. | Questa Somma è il montare delle indennità reclamate dagl'interessati, delle quali non fu fatta liquidazione. |
| Parma e Piacenza. | Requisizioni e somministrazioni militari nella guerra del 1859. | 100,502 39 | .............. | La controscritta somma è composta di molte partite non tutte definitivamente liquidate. |
| | Espropriazioni di terreni, taglio di piante, abbattimento di fabbricati e altri danni cagionati dall'ampliamento delle fortificazioni di Piacenza fatte dalle truppe austriache nel 1859. | .............. | 997,710 14 | Il Governo provvisorio del 1859 ordinò che si facesse subito la perizia dei danni controscritti, affinchè venissero indennizzati i danneggiati. La perizia fu fatta dall'ingegnere Perotta, che liquidò i danni pel montare complessivo di lire 2,518,257 11; ma il Governo non aveva mai dato le disposizioni pel pagamento di questa somma. Gli interessati ricorsero allora ai tribunali, i quali, avuto riguardo all'indole dei danni, che per la massima parte consistevano in espropriazioni eseguite in ordine alla convenzione del 1822 stipulata fra il Governo parmense e l'austriaco per l'ampliamento delle fortificazioni di Piacenza, pronunziarono parecchie sentenze contro lo Stato. Fu ravvisata dunque la necessità di venire a trattative con gl'interessati per un amichevole componimento, che ora sta per conchiudersi sulle basi di una nuova perizia dei danni fatta eseguire, e che li fa ascendere, invece che a lire 2,518,257 11, alla somma di sole lire 999,710 14. A questa somma però debbono aggiungersi gli interessi legali che il Governo deve pagare dal giorno 12 settembre 1867, in cui cominciò il giudizio, fino a quello in cui avrà luogo il pagamento. |
| Modena e Reggio. | Somministrazioni fatte alle truppe austriache fino al 1859. | .............. | 250,283 36 | I crediti dei comuni delle controscritte provincie furono riconosciuti con decreti del 9 luglio e del 4 dicembre 1859 del Governo provvisorio, e ne fu ordinato il pagamento. Questa disposizione però non ebbe effetto, e solamente fu fatto esattamente liquidare il montare dei detti crediti, che si riconobbe essere di lire 250,-283 36, in luogo della maggiore somma di lire 586,538 36, reclamata dai comuni. |
| | Confische ed arbitrarie donazioni di beni appartenenti a condannati politici dell'ex-ducato, e pensioni dovute ad impiegati licenziati per ragione politica, ovvero alle loro vedove e figli. | .............. | 494,994 86 | Un decreto del governatore Farini del 23 agosto 1859 ordinava che fossero indennizzati questi danni, ma esso non potè aver effetto, per la mancanza di un provvedimento legislativo. Una Commissione appositamente instituita nel 1867, tenuto conto che la maggior parte dei beni confiscati potrebbe venire restituita alle famiglie dei condannati, liquidò i danni da indennizzarsi in danaro a lire 494,994 86. |

Segue *Crediti provenienti dalle guerre degli anni* 1859 *e* 1860.

| Provincie. | Cagioni del credito. | Somma. | | Osservazioni. |
|---|---|---|---|---|
| | | Presunta. | Accertata. | |
| | | *Lire. Ct.* | *Lire. Ct.* | |
| Provincie napolitane. | Forniture fatte nell'anno 1860 agli eserciti meridionale e borbonico. | .............. | 1, 739, 104 17 | Questa somma è dovuta al già fornitore degli eserciti meridionale e borbonico signor Cassitto, col quale è in corso una lite, asserendo egli di essere creditore di somma assai maggiore. |
| Provincie venete e di Mantova. | Espropriazioni e somministrazioni militari avvenute nel 1859. | 1, 233, 189 14 | .............. | La controscritta somma rappresenta il montare complessivo delle domande pervenute alla Commissione instituita presso il Ministero della guerra col regio decreto del 26 maggio 1867. |
| Navara ........ | Requisizioni e danni di guerra nella campagna del 1859. | 1, 905, 570 98 | .............. | |
| Lomellina...... | Requisizioni e danni di guerra nella campagna del 1859. | 6, 122, 541 43 | .............. | |
| | | 22, 216, 239 80 | 3, 482, 092 53 | |
| | | 25, 698, 332 33 | | |

*Crediti provenienti dalla guerra del* 1866.

| Provincie. | Cagioni del credito. | Somma. | | Osservazioni. |
|---|---|---|---|---|
| | | Presunta. | Accertata. | |
| | | *Lire. Ct.* | *Lire. Ct.* | |
| Provincie venete e di Mantova. | Contratti d'appalto per lavori, provviste, prestazioni d'opera e simili. | 2, 877, 553 35 | .......... | Le controscritte somme rappresentano il montare delle domande pervenute alla Commissione instituita presso il Ministero della guerra col regio decreto del 26 maggio 1867 (Allegato n° 20). |
| | Espropriazioni ed acquisti di stabili. | 305, 061 18 | .......... | |
| | Abbattimento di piante e fabbricati intorno alle fortificazioni. | 8 280, 887 79 | .......... | |
| | Occupazioni temporanee d'immobili. | 336, 678 10 | .......... | |
| | Requisizioni militari .. | 2, 277, 767 46 | .......... | |
| | Danni di guerra......... | 3, 929, 392 33 | .......... | |
| | Totale ............ | 18, 007, 340 21 | .......... | |

N° 99—A.

SESSIONE 1871–72, SECONDA DELLA XI LEGISLATURA.—CAMERA DEI DEPUTATI.

*Relazione della Giunta, composta dei Deputati Finzi, presidente, Pissavini, segretario, Mandruzzato, Morpurgo, Guerzoni, Verga, e Mantellini, relatore sul progetto di legge presentato del Ministro delle Finanze del* 1° *aprile* 1871 *riprodotto nella tornata del* 17 *aprile* 1872.

## INDENNITÀ PER DANNI DI GUERRA.

Tornata del 26 aprile 1873.

### IL PROGETTO DI LEGGE E LA SUA STORIA.

SIGNORI!—In esecuzione al trattato di Vienna del 3 ottobre 1866, approva to con la legge del 25 aprile 1867, rimanevano fra l'Austria e l'Italia due liquidazioni da fare, l'una del Monte lombardo-veneto, l'altra dei crediti personali ai principi e alle principesse di casa d'Austria e principesse entrate nella famiglia imperiale.

L'Italia reclamava dall'Austria:

1° Il fondo del clero veneto;

2° Il fondo territoriale veneto;

3° Il fondo dell'Università di Padova per tasse e sovvenzione governativa;

4° Il fondo del comune di Cividale;

5° L'attivo della cassa d'ammortizzazione del Monte veneto;

6° e 7° Il conguaglio del valore degli immobili e dei titoli rimasti all'Austria, con gli arretrati sui titoli consegnati all'Italia, per la convenzione di Milano del 9 settembre 1860;

8° Il resto della ripartizione del Monte, secondo l'articolo 37 di essa convenzione;

9° Gli arretrati sui titoli del debito pubblico generale austriaco;

10. L'attivo della cassa dei depositi del Monte veneto;

11. Il fondo della guardia nobile lombardo-veneta (fiorini 634,059 in obbligazioni, 352,378 29 in denaro);

12. Un deposito fatto in Vienna nel 7 novembre 1866 dalla società delle strade ferrate meridionali austriache;

13. Il fondo degli stabilimenti termali di Abano e Battaglia;

14. Il fondo del magistrato degli Schiavi di Genova;

15. Le indennità per le requisizioni e i danni di guerra del 1813 e 1814, e del 1848–49 (lire 12,000,000);

16. Le indennità per le requisizioni e i danni delle guerre del 1859 e 1866 (lire 18.000,000).

L'Austria, che pure aveva le sue partite da contrapporre, ammesse a credito dell'Italia le partite 1, 2, 3, 4, 5, 6, 7, 8 e 9. Rifiutò le altre, sostenendo dopo la cessione del Lombardo-Veneto, ad essa non restati altri obblighi che i risultanti dai trattati di pace, dove non si legge disposizione da cui venga dato d'argomentare l'onere nel Governo austro-ungarico di pagare i danni di guerra, non stati ancora risarciti nelle provincie che più non gli appartengono.

Le trattative riuscirono a una transazione *generale*, in cui persistendo sempre i commissari imperiali nel non potere ammettere alcuna indennità di guerra, fu da essi offerta e dai commissari italiani accettata la somma, in compenso di ogni pretesa reciproca dell'Italia e dell'Austria, di fiorini 4,749,000 rappresentada da un obbligazione sul debito pubblico austriaco al 5 per cento alla pari[5].

A conti fatti, l'Italia veniva pagata di tutte le sue pretese, anche contestate dall'Austria, eccetto che pei danni di guerra. Donde la opinione, che allora e poi si ebbe, non essere la partita dei danni di guerra rimasta senza influenza sulla determinazione dell'Austria di offrire quanto offerse e che l'Italia accettò, in transazione di ogni reciproca pretesa.

Sottoscritte nel 6 gennaio 1871 in Firenze le due convenzioni, l'una sulle pendenze con l'impero, l'altra sulle pendenze con gli arciduchi e le arciduchesse, venero alla Camera dei deputati ambedue presentate dai ministri delle finanze e degli esteri nella tornata del 16 dello stesso mese di gennaio.

Nel 3 marzo la Giunta[6] incaricata di esaminarle, presentò la sua relazione. E in essa relazione la Giunta si trattenne sui danni di guerra, le trattative corse fra i commissari austriaci e italiani, le note cambiatesi fra i due ministri delle finanze e degli esteri sull'argomento, per riuscire, come riuscì, ad una conclusione e ad una riserva. La conclusione fu di approvare le convenzioni nel modo proposto dai due ministri. Ma nell'intendimento che *esse convenzioni non abbiano a produrre altra novazione nel rapporto dei privati che la sostituzione del Governo italiano all'austriaco*, propose d'aggiungere alla legge un terzo articolo del tenore che appresso: *Rimangono salvi i crediti e i diritti dei terzi derivanti dai trattati del* 1814, 1815, 1818, *e dalle guerre del* 1848, 1849, 1859 *e* 1866.

La discussione, che impiegò le tornate del 6, 7 e 8 marzo, cadde quasi esclusivamente su quest'aggiunta. Per alcuni, l'Austria era tuttora tenuta a saldare i danneggiati dalla guerra del 1813, pei quali nel trattato del 1818 ebbe dalla Francia circa 27 milioni e mezzo, e i danneggiati dalla guerra del 1848, pei quali ebbe dallo Sardegna 75 milioni nel trattato di Milano del 1849. Pei danni delle guerre del 1859 e del 1866, dei quali nessun trattato faceva per l'Austria obbligazione convenzionale, i debiti dell'Austria si dicevano col territorio trasferiti all'Italia; con aver trovati più sostenitori che opponenti la opinione della successione dell'Italia all'Austria a titolo universale nei debiti e nei crediti, e della universalità della transazione convenuta a Firenze.

L'articolo venne tuttavia ritirato di fronte all'impegno formale preso del ministro

---

[5] Toutes les réclamations présentées par les deux Gouvernements sont compensées, en voie de transaction, moyennant le paiement que le gouvernement austro-hongrois s'engage à faire au gouvernement italien, dans le terme de quatre semaines après la ratification de la présentée convention, d'une somme de 4.749,000 florins, représentée par une obligation de la dette publique autrichienne convertie, de la même valeur nominale, intérêt 5 pour cent, jouissance 1er novembre 1870; laquelle obligation sera inscrite au nom du government italien. (Art. 2. Convenzione *A* stipulata in Firenze nel 6 gennaio 1871, approvata con la legge del 23 marzo, n° 137, serie 2a.)

[6] Lacava, Finzi, Massari, Pioltide Bianchi, Pissavini, Puccioni, Ronchetti, Righi, Cortese, relatore

delle finanze di presentare dentro lo stesso mese di marzo un apposito progetto di legge sui danni di guerra. Ei non ascose la paura che, mentre l'Austria nulla volle consentire nè pei danni delle guerre del 1813 e 1848 nè per quelli delle guerre del 1859 e 1866, l'articolo non risvegliasse lusinghe sopite, o non conferisse diritti a chi o non li ebbe mai o li perdè, a detrimento della finanza italiana, tanto bisognosa di venir risparmiata.

Nel 1° aprile 1871 il ministro delle finanze presentava diffatti il progetto di legge, che intitolò: *Indennità per danni di guerra.*

LA RELAZIONE MINISTERIALE E IL SUO PROGETTO DI LEGGE.

Nella relazione che accompagnava il progetto si esordisce dal minstro col ricordare che, ora per questa, ora per quella provincia, per una o per altra specie di danni della guerra, dal subalpino e dal Parlamento italiano è stato discusso e si è venuti qualche volta in soccorso di quelli che più avevano sofferto e che apparivano più bisognosi di aiuto. Donde si argomenta che non si era e non si è in tema di credito civile; o che in tale materia, fra danneggiati e Governo, intercedono, non privati, ma rapporti d'indole pubblica, da regolare coi canoni della distributiva giustizia, e con le ragioni della convenienza politica.

Riguardo ai debiti derivanti dall'Austria, nella relazione si richiama all'esame la posizione dei danneggiati non soddisfatti, in presenza alle norme giuridiche seguite da quel Governo in tale materia, e alle applicazioni date dall'Austria stessa al § 1044 del suo Codice: "La ripartizione dei danni di guerra viene regolata dalle autorità politiche dietro norme speciali."

E in appoggio della conclusione che siamo in materia politico-amministrativa, dalla relazione stessa si dice la successione di Stato a Stato, non del giure privato, ma di diritto pubblico internazionale, e per la quale le obbligazioni dell'antico non divengono per lo Stato nuovo obbligazioni perfette se non dopo la legge di ricognizione, che dia quel titolo civile che verso lo Stato nuovo i creditori non hanno.

Giurisprudenza, consuetudini del regno e Parlamento si invocano per concordi in questa sentenza; e la legge del 4 agosto 1861 si allega come la legge principe fra queste leggi di ricognizione.

La qual mancanza di legge *recognitiva*, sempre a senso della relazione, non solo è da opporre pei debiti lasciati dall'Austria, ma altresì pei debiti dei Governi provvisori e per quelli dei già Stati italiani. Per la relazione con tutti questi creditori, i rapporti del Governo nazionale sono rapporti di natura politica, da Governo a governati, definibili, con le norme della giustizia distributiva e secondo le ragioni di convenienza politica; non obbligazioni civili, e per le quali i creditori abbiano verso l'italiana le azioni che avrebbero per avventura potuto esperimentare verso le passate amministrazioni di Napoli, Modena e Toscana.

Via dunque dal conto imprestiti nazionali del 1821, del 1848 e 1849; via le confische e i pregiudizi inferiti dai Governi anteriori; via i crediti dei comuni toscani per le somministrazioni austriache dal 1849 al 1855; via dal conto i danni patiti dalle provincie della Lomellina e di Novara per le invasioni del 1859.

La relazione non fa grazia che pei fondi già occupati per cagione di guerra e non pagati, sebbene tuttora tenuti dal Governo nazionale; dacchè l'obbligazione di lui *sorgerebbe allora dal fatto stesso della sua detenzione.* Ma per tutte le altre pendenze o pretese, essa conclude che non siamo in materia di diritto *ma d'interessi, più o meno gravemente sacrificati ed offesi, a provvedere ai quali non ragioni di obbligazione civile potrebbero costringere, ma solo ragioni d'umanità e di equità potrebbero consigliare, quando ciò fosse compatibile con lo stato della pubblica finanza.*

Informata da questi principii, la relazione scende pertanto a proporre una legge di *due* articoli. Col *primo* si compensano gli espropriati nelle guerre, non dei frutti perduti nè dei sofferti deperimenti del fondo, ma solo del prezzo di stima dei fondi che loro non si restituiscano. L'eredità dei passati Governi è così rifiutata recisamente, limitato l'obbligo del Governo nazionale alle conseguenze del fatto suo proprio della detenzione. E col *secondo articolo* si destina un fondo per sovvenire ai cittadini delle provincie lombardo-venete di più ristretta condizione di fortuna. Si vuol socorrere a provincie, al confronto delle altre, danneggiate in proporzione molto maggiore; e vi si destina il fondo di riserva della guardia nobile lombardo-veneta, dacchè questo fondo, per disposizione espressa nello statuto d'organamento di quella guardia, doveva restare permanente proprietà del paese.

La relazione è accompagnata da un prospetto dei crediti che si lascierebbero non soddisfatti. Poichè ogni provincia avendo i suoi, si consiglia di non mutarne il reparto, che già ne avvenne di fatto; intanto che si studia di mettere in rilievo il peso che, sempre gravoso anche in floride condizioni della finanza, diverrebbe insopportabile nelle condizioni presenti, nelle quali lo stato della nostra finanza potrebbe riassumersi *nello sforzo costante di raggiungere un pareggio che sempre sfugge, malgrado i gravissimi carichi imposti al paese,* e quando insta la suprema necessità di provvedere al riordinamento dell'esercito e alle difese nazionali.

### L'ALLEGATO ALLA RELAZIONE MINISTERIALE.

Nell'allegato alla relazione si hanno partite per lire 6,178,711 39 a tutto il 1821. Vi sono notate la Lombardia e la Venezia per somministrazioni fatte all'armata nella campagna del 1809, e per espropriazioni e somministrazioni, o appropriazioni sotto il primo regno italico: Parma e Piacenza per somministrazioni fatte nel 1811, 1812, 1814, e 1815; le provincie napoletane per una parte d'imprestito nazionale del 1821, che dicesi non per anche restituito.

Dai fatti degli anni 1848 e 1849 l'allegato tira fuori una somma di lire 64,684,978 03. E a formarla vi concorrono le provincie ex-pontificie per somministrazioni alle milizie della repubblica romana e del papa; la Lombardia pei prestiti, somministrazioni e requisizioni, e per l'incendio delle case del suburbio di Milano nella notte dal 4 al 5 agosto; Parma e Piacenza per prestazioni e somministrazioni a truppe austriache e nazionali; Modena per requisizioni e somministrazioni militari; Toscana pel mantenimento delle truppe austriache dal 1849 al 1855; le provincie napoletane pel prestito forzato; la Sicilia per somministrazioni, requisizioni e danni di guerra; il Piemonte per requisizioni e danni della campagna di marzo 1849; le provincie venete e di Mantova per le requisizioni e i danni della guerra; Venezia per gli imprestiti, i buoni, e la moneta patriottica e del comune; Roma per la perdita dei *buoni* repubblicani, prestito forzato, requisizioni.

Il contingente delle guerre del 1859 e 1860 risulta di lire 25,698,332 33. A formare il quale contingente contribuiscono le provincie ex-pontificie, allora annesse, per somministrazioni e requisizioni militari e forniture diverse; la Lombardia per requisizioni, forniture ed espropriazioni; Parma e Piacenza per requisizioni e somministrazioni militari, e specialmente per espropriazioni, taglio di piante, abbatimento di case, ed ampliamento delle fortificazioni di Piacenza; Modena e Reggio per somministrazioni fatte agli Austriaci, e per confische patite da condannati politici; le provincie napoletane per forniture agli eserciti meridionale e borbonico; le provincie venete e di Mantova per espropriazioni e somministrazioni militari; Novara e la Lomellina per requisizioni e danni di guerra.

Le provenienze della guerra del 1866 sommano a lire 18,007,340 21, tutte a credito delle provincie venete e di Mantova per lavori, espropriazioni, abbattimento di piante e case intorno ai forti, per requisizioni e danni di guerra.

Si ottiene così un totale di lire 114,569,361 96, costituito da partite in gran parte già liquidate. La quale è certo somma egregia e che pienamente giustifica le preoccupazioni del ministro per la finanza italiana.

### CONTINUA LA STORIA.

Relazione, progetto di legge e allegato, portati in Comitato, suscitarono una tempesta d'opposizioni, di raccomandazioni, di controprogetti per la Giunta che si nominò per riferirne alla Camera. Ma sopraggiunse la chiusura della Sessione prima che la Giunta avesse compiuti i suoi lavori.

La questione tornò a sollevarsi alla Camera nella tornata dell'11 marzo 1872 in occasione di due petizioni, l'una di nº 9065 del comune di Basiglio (provincia di Milano) per requisizioni austriache del 1859, l'altra di nº 11326 del comune e della Camera di commercio di Venezia pel riconoscimento dei debiti contratti dal Governo provvisorio nel 1848–1849. Ambedue le petizioni furono, per deliberazione della Camera, inviate al ministro delle finanze, il quale tornò a promettere di portare la questione al cospetto del Parlamento, dove si sarrebbe discusso di tutte le opinioni e deliberato con piena cognizione di causa sul partito che convenga adottare.

E nel 17 aprile 1872 ei si sdebitava dell'assunto impegnò col ripresentare *tale* e *quale* il primo progetto di legge, che a senso del ministro, mentre indica una soluzione, la quale soddisfa a talune domande per ogni rispetto incontestabili e soccorre ai più stringenti bisogni pei danni patiti nelle guerre nazionali, non compromette l'andamento della pubblica finanza. Resta ora, così chiude la succinta sua relazione il ministro, *resta ora al Parlamento alla cui sagacia niuna degli aspetti del gravissimo problema da risolversi sfuggirà, il vedere quale deliberazione sia da prendere.*

Il progetto ebbe nella seconda la stessa accoglienza della prima volta in Comitato, che con le stesse raccomandazioni lo passò alla medesima Commissione, sostituiti due nuovi commissari all'onorevole Andreucci, fatto senatore, e all'onorevole Tasca che dette la sua rinunzia.

### LA COMMISSIONE E IL SUO MANDATO.

La Commissione ha studiata con la cura voluta dalla gravità dell'argomento la questione su tutti i punti, e dopo lunghe e pazienti discussioni incaricava me sottoscritto di rendere conto dei suoi studi sulla relazione, sull'allegato e sul disegno di legge dell'onorevole ministro, non che delle proposte state da essa tradotte in un controprogetto di legge.

La Commissione penò poco ad accorgersi che il ministro si era ispirato a un solo sentimento, non aveva preso consiglio che dalle condizioni della nostra finanza, tanto bisognosa d'essere risparmiata: essa fu presto d'accordo non potersi accettare un progetto che non teneva conto di un interesse, anche più supremo, qual è quello della giustizia, che pur costituisce il fine d'ogni politica associazione, e alla quale l'Italia non è mai venuta e non verrà meno.

La Commissione ha dovuto altresì convincersi che il rigettare puramente e semplicemente il progetto ministeriale avrebbe lasciata insoluta una questione che la Camera aveva più volte manifestato il desiderio di sciogliere, che era nell'interesse di tutti che si sciogliesse, e sollevata da relazioni che dallo stesso ministro apparivano presentate meno per far passare quel suo progetto in legge, che nel proposito di provocare dal Parlamento una soluzione dell'intricato quanto delicato problema.

Per la Commissione, che non partecipava dei principii, e rifiutava le applicazioni ministeriali, si è dunque trattato di riuscire a un progetto di legge che si sostituisse al progetto del Ministero, e col quale si dia a chi ha da avere, pure studiando di non turbare le nostre finanze da quell'assetto per dove con tanta lode del ministro si vedono avviate, che pur troppo non hanno ancora raggiunto, e dal quale nessuno pensa di deviarle.

Il mandato in questi termini diventava sicuramente non facile, e la Commissione conta sul benevolo concorso della Camera per uscirne a seconda di propositi che reputa comuni a tutti.

### I PRINCIPII DELLA COMMISSIONE.

### I.

Demostene loda gli Ateniesi che, dopo la cacciata dei trenta tiranni, restituirono i denari che i trenta avevano accattatti, in pubblico nome, dagli Spartani. *Et tum quidem etiam illis, qui iniurii in vos fuerunt pecunias illas conferre voluistis, ne quid de rerum conventarum fide deperiret.*

Per cangiare di rappresentanti lo Stato non cangia *fortuna*, o non perde diritti nè si scioglie da obbligazioni, per poco che quei diritti si acquistarono, o queste obbligazioni si assunsero da chi aveva dello Stato la legittima rappresentanza. *Les actes de l'Etat obligent l'Etat, et obligent par conséquent les divers représentants que l'Etat peut avoir.* Se il Re di Sardegna e l'elettore di Hesse alla restaurazione del 1814 immaginarono di considerare la epopea napoleonica come non avvenuta, non si deve in ciò vedere la espressione d'un principio di diritto, ma un vano capriccio della reazione. Intanto che si ebbe ragione di rifiutare il carattere di veri rappresentanti dello Stato ai Governi provvisorii del dittatore Manin a Venezia, di Kossuth in Ungheria, e alle repubbliche romana e badese del 1849. Così il più moderno pubblicista il *Bluntschli* nel suo Codice di diritto internazionale.[7]

*Il Weaton* negli elementi del diritto internazionale è del suo parere.[8]

È col cessare dello Stato per estinzione, dispersione o emigrazione del suo popolo che ne cessano a un tempo con lui i diritti e le obbligazioni. Ma quando dello Stato rimane la parte essenziale, cioè *popolo e territorio*, la sua fortuna attiva e passiva, demanio pubblico e demanio privato, coi suoi crediti e coi suoi debiti, passa nel successore, sia pure a titolo di conquista. Così prosegue *Bluntschli*, e prima di lui il nostro LAMPREDI. *Non desinit debere populus . . . aut si in victoris transeat potestatem.*

Può lo Stato nuovo aver buone ragioni per rifiutarsi dal pagare tutti o parte dei debiti dello Stato anteriore; può, osserva Weaton, *il fatto prendere il loco del* DIRITTO, ma del suo rifiuto, legittimo o no, deve almeno constare *per atto positivo e non equivoco.* Anzichè di legge *recognitiva*, la quale muti in *civile* la obbligazione *morale* nel nuovo Stato, di fare onore agl'impegni del popolo rimasto lo stesso e sul medesimo territorio, bisogna invece una dichiarazione la quale venga ad arrestare questo trasferimento della fortuna *attiva* e *passiva* che altrimenti avverrebbe *ipso jure.*

Nazione per ragione geografica, il bel paese *che Appennin parte e il mar circonda e l'Alpe*, per comunione di origine, di lingua, di letteratura, di arti, di storia, l'Italia aspirava da secoli a costituirsi in nazione anche politicamente. I fatti militari di San Martino e di Solferino, di Calatafimi e del Volturno, di Castelfidardo, di Custoza e per ultimo di Porta Pia rimossero l'ostacolo alla libera manifestazione dei voti degl'Italiani, che riuniti nei comizi di libertà votarono a suffragio universale il plebiscito. La Lombardia aveva votato il suo plebiscito fino dal 1848. E nell'11 e 12 marzo 1860 la Toscana e l'Emilia, nel 21 ottobre le provincie napoletane e la Sicilia, nel 4 e 5 novembre dello stesso anno 1860 le Marche e l'Umbria, nel 21 e 22 ottobre 1866 le provincie della Venezia e di Mantova, e Roma nel 2 ottobre 1870, tutte votarono concordi *per l'unione alla monarchia costituzionale del Re Vittorio Emanuele, o che il popolo vuole l'Italia una e indivisibile con Vittorio Emanuele Re costituzionale e suoi legittimi discendenti.*

L'*unione*, per consentimento unanime dei pubblicisti, porta fra gli Stati uniti la *comunione* dei pesi e dei vantaggi, sia internazionali, sia e molto più, di ragione civile. Dico molto più; il pagamento dei debiti escendo affare di *buona fede* e non di politica, *ne quid de rerum conventarum fide deperiret.*

*Grozio* dopo avere scritto: *non desinit debere pecuniam populus, rege sibi imposito, quam liber debebat*, soggiunge: *quod si quando uniantur duo populi non amittentur jura sed com-*

[7] 44, 45.

[8] P. 1, cap. 2.

*municabuntur.* E, dopo lui, *Puffendorf: si duo populi uniantur, non per modum fœderis, aut per communem regem sed ut revera ex duabus civitatibus una fiat: quo casu, jura quæ singulæ civitates uniendæ habuerunt, non amitti, sed communicari, sicut et onera atque debita, ubi diversum non convenerit.*

La sola eccezione è di quei diritti od obbligazioni la di cui conservazione non riesca compatible col nuovo ordine di cose. Così *Weaton* e *Bluntschli.*[9]

Nell'unirsi potevano convenire diversamente, di riservarsi, cioè, qualche debito o qualche credito di ragione civile, come anche qualche prerogativa o privilegio di ragione politica. Nella formazione del regno d'Italia i popoli che vi concorsero vollero invece la fusione dei diritti e delle obbligazioni, l'uno dell'altro, senza limiti e senza riserve; la più assoluta uguaglianza civile e politica. Fu questa la condizione, questo il patto del voto dato all'unione.

I plebisciti furono *per la monarchia costituzionale di Re Vittorio Emanuele: per l'Italia una e indivisibile con Vittorio Emanuele Re costituzionale;* e Vittorio Emanuele è *Re costituzionale* per lo Statuto dal magnanimo Re Carlo Alberto *dato a Torino a dì quattro del mese di marzo l'anno del Signore milleottocento quarantotto* e del suo regno *il decimo ottavo.*

Lo Statuto nel suo articolo 31 garantisce il debito pubblico e dice inviolablile ogni impegno dello Stato verso i suoi creditori. *Il debito pubblico è guarantito. Ogni impegno dello Stato verso i suoi creditori è inviolabile.*

Non so se in tutte, ma certo in molte parti d'Italia, lo Statuto del 1848 col suo articolo 31, venne promulgato prima del plebiscito, nè mai ebbe, e non ha vigore in virtù d'altra promulgazione che quella d'allora. In ogni modo, il plebiscito, che certo a esso Statuto si riferiva, votò l'unione a condizione che non solo il debito pubblico, ma che ogni impegno dello Stato verso i suoi creditori fossero rispettati. Lo che è quanto dire, coloro che credono fosse *morale* la obligazione d'Italia di pagare i debiti dei già Stati italiani fino alla legge di *ricognizione* che l'avesse mutata in obbligazione *civile,* trovano questa nella legge che accolse i plebisciti.

"Visto il risultamento della votazione universale delle provincie..... dalla quale consta essere generale voto di quella popolazione di unirsi al nostro Stato:

"Art. 1. Le provincie..... faranno parte integrante dello Stato dal giorno della data del presente decreto.

"Art. 2. Il presente decreto verrà presentato al Parlamento per essere convertito in legge."

"Il Senato, ecc.

"*Articolo unico.* Il Governo del Re è autorizzato a dar piena ed intera esecuzione all'articolo 1 del regio decreto, ecc."

Ecco la formula con la quale furono accettati i plebisciti dei già Stati, ora provincie d'Italia, con le leggi del 15 aprile e 17 dicembre 1860, 18 luglio 1857 e 31 dicembre 1870.

Le quali sono pur leggi nostre, dello Stato italiano, che mentre non lasciano dubbioso avere nella sua formazione il regno d'Italia riconosciuto e guarentito ogni debito pubblico, e qualunque impegno dei già Stati italiani, aspettano la loro osservanza e la loro applicazione come ogni altra legge dello Stato.

Sicuramente, quando la Lombardia si staccò dalla Venezia, e poi la Venezia si liberava dall'austriaca dominazione, rimanevano da separare i debiti speciali al paese unito, i debiti che esso aveva in comune con la parte italiana ancora divisa, e i debiti di tutto l'impero. Le Marche e l'Umbria portarono nell'unione all'Italia una eredità divisibile col patrimonio di San Pietro, finchè a questo patrimonio non si estese la unione.

Bisognava liquidare e ripartire, come si liquidò e ripartì debito e credito fra l'Italia e la Francia dopo la cessione di Nizza e Savoia, col trattato di Torino del 24 marzo e la convenzione del 13 agosto 1860. Con l'Austria la liquidazione e il riparto si fecero per la Lombardia nel trattato di Zurigo del 10 novembre 1859, e nella convenzione di Milano del 9 settembre 1860, per la Venezia in quello di Vienna del 3 ottobre 1866, Susseguito dalle convenzioni di Firenze del 6 gennaio 1871 di generale liquidazione. Con la Santa Sede, o per la Santa Sede la convenzione si stipulò, a mediazione della Francia, nel 7 dicembre 1866 stata approvata con la legge del 27 maggio 1867, alla quale tenne dietro il protocollo sottoscritto in Firense nel 31 luglio, reso esecutorio col decreto reale del 18 agosto 1868, nº 4574.

Finchè la questione era *internazionale,* o che prima bisognava intendersi fra Stato e Stato, il creditore dell'Austriaco o del Pontificio, che impaziente cercasse d'esser pagato dall'Italia, si trovò dal Consiglio di stato, giudice del conflitto, allontanato dei tribunali, e spesso dagli stessi tribunali respinto dal giudizio. Ma non dopo le convenzioni di Firenze, e non dopo la riunione di Roma all'Italia.

Dell'Italia è politica e non civile la obbligazione di riparare i torti dei mali Governi passati, e morale o politica, non civile, è la sua obbligazione rispetto ai debiti dei Governi provvisori del 1848.

Furono leggi di riparazione quella del 30 giugno 1861; l'articolo 42 della legge sulle pensioni del 14 aprile 1864, la legge del 23 aprile 1865, la legge del 5 marzo 1868 e la

[9] *Grozio,* lib. II, cap. 9.—*Puffendorf,* lib. VIII, cap. 12, §6.—*Weaton,* p. i, cap. 2, §9.—*Bluntschli,* §50 e §288.

più recente del 2 luglio 1872 che agli impiegati, sia dei permanenti che dei Governi provvisorii, stati privati per causa politica, del grado, se militari, del posto, se civili, e riammessi dal Governo nazionale in servizio, si consentì di computare per la pensione il tempo della interruzione patita nel servizio.

L'Italia, che fu generosa fino a restituire una posizione a chi poteva dubitarsi se l'avesse conseguita mai, non potrà e non dovrà lasciare senza riparazione i danni delle *confische* politiche. Ma questa sì che è tale riparazione che solo può essere data in virtù d'una legge. Lo ha deciso il Consiglio di stato nel 16 marzo 1872 nella causa *Pezzini*, condannato nel capo e nella confisca dei beni dalla Commissione stataria di Modena del 1835; e nell'8 aprile 1873, in altro conflitto, nella causa *Faucitano*, che subì uguale condanna nel 1851 sotto i Borboni di Napoli.[10]

La Cassazione di Palermo disse non *civile* ma *politica* la obbligazione nel Governo d'Italia di pagare i debiti del Governo provvisorio siciliano del 1848.[11] E il Consiglio di stato allontanò dai tribunali i creditori dei Governi provvisorii della Lombardia e della Venezia, attesochè *il decidere se il Governo del regno d'Italia sia succeduto al Governo provvisorio di Milano (o della Venezia) del 1848, non può essere di competenza dell'autorità giudiziaria*.[12]

A ben considerare, tanto coloro i quali ebbero a patire dei torti da parte dei Governi permanenti, quanto coloro che rimasero ad avere dai Governi provvisorii, più che *creditori* con azione *civile*, si trovavano, all'epoca delle *annessioni*, nella condizione di *pretendenti* politici, col loro diritto manomesso o pregiudicato, e che una legge di *restaurazione* poteva e può ristabilire, non *riconoscersi* o dichiararsi per sentenza di giudice.

Invece non conosco esempio di decisione di tribunale ordinario dove si neghi al creditore d'esperimentare le sue azioni verso l'Italia, per fatti o contratti dell'amministrazione piemontese, lombarda, toscana, parmense o napoletana, solamente per difetto di legge *recognitiva* del debito da parte dei poteri dello Stato nuovo.

È a torto che si cita l'autorità della Cassazione di Palermo, la quale decideva sopra una domanda contro il Governo provvisorio di Sicilia del 1848;[13] come si cita senza ragione una decisione della Corte d'appello di Firenze che rigettò la istanza d'un creditore per contratto col Governo pontificio, stata promossa prima della riunione di Roma.[14] Più o meno corretti che ne appaiano i motivi, una buona ermeneutica non consentirebbe a esse decisioni un'*autorità*, sia pur *dottrinale*, all'infuori dei termini del caso deciso.

Le Corti di Macerata, d'Ancona e di Milano hanno scartata affatto questa eccezione. E notisi che esse pure non vi pronunziarono che per mera occasione. La Corte di Macerata aveva da decidere sulla restituzione d'un deposito fatto in Roma per un servizio pubblico di Città di Castello. Le Corti di Ancona e di Milano avevano da pronunziarsi sopra la portata della *servitù militare* nei rapporti dell'indennità, dovuta o no, al padrone del fondo che ne vada soggetto. Fu a guisa di premessa, o per farsi strada a decidere la vera questione della causa, che esse Corti toccarono della natura ed estensione degli obblighi dell'Italia di derivazione dalle amministrazioni pontificia od austriaca.[15]

Di tutto ciò la ragione è una sola. L'amministrazione italiana non ha opposto il difetto d'una legge italiana di ricognizione del debito toscano, parmense o napoletano, come non avrebbe pensato ad opporlo pel debito piemontese; ma ha pagato o transatto. La eccezione ha creduto diriservarla per alcuni debiti soltanto, o perchè ne riguardasse con qualche diffidenza l'origine, o perchè la causa del debito le comparisse *politica* più che civile; e sempre in questioni di competenza, o di conflitto d'attribuzioni.

Per tacere dei pareri più antichi ricorderò, del Consiglio di stato, quello dato a sezioni riunite nel 6 febbraio 1868, dove, interrogato se pel fatto della rioccupazione francese di Roma fosse venuta meno la convenzione del 1866 sul reparto del debito pontificio, il Consiglio opinò connaturale all'occupazione del territorio, e però indipendente da ogni convenzione l'acquisto delle attività, come l'accollo delle passività che vi si riportano.[16]

Come ricorderò tre decisioni proferite dal Consiglio di stato, due nel 31 dicembre 1872 nella causa *Trevisani*, l'altra nell'8 aprile 1873 nella causa *Ranucci*. In tutte e tre il conflitto era stato decretato sul principio che, trattandosi di debito dependente, nei primi due dall'austriaco, e nel terzo caso dall'amministrazione pontificia, non poteva venirne azione civile da esperimentare verso l'Italia se non dopo una legge di ricognizione. I tribunali avevano rigettata la eccezione d'incompetenza; e sul decreto del prefetto, il Consiglio di stato rinviò la causa ai tribunali.[17]

Invano con *Bluntschli* (articolo 54) si dice di *pubblico diritto la successione di Stato a*

---

[10] Vedi allegato nº 14.

[11] Decisione 15 gennaio 1870, nella causa Morgante.

[12] Decisioni nelle cause Riva, Cagnola, Borgia, Rossi, Padri Mechitaristi di Venezia, e Croce del 16 maggio, 12 giugno, 2 luglio, 6 novembre e 7 dicembre 1872.

[13] Citata decis. del 15 gennaio 1870.

[14] Decis. 14 maggio 1870 nella causa Forini.

[15] Decis. della Corte di Macerata del 14 gennaio 1865 nella causa Piersantelli; della Corte di Ancona del 31 marzo 1868 nella causa Perozzi; e della Corte di Milano del 3 maggio 1868 nella causa Antona-Traversi.

[16] Allegato nº 13.

[17] Vedi decisioni negli allegati 15 e 16.

*Stato, la quale se una certa analogia ha con la successione del diritto civile non deve esserle confusa;* e invano con *Heffter* (§ 25), a chi domandi, in caso di scioglimento di tutto o di parte di uno Stato se, e a chi e a qual titolo, *universale* o *particolare*, ne ricada la successione dei vantaggi e dei carichi, si risponde *che mescolando così i principii del diritto privato con quelli del diritto pubblico si è dovuta necessariamente turbare la semplicità e l'armonia di questi ultimi.*

Innanzitutto *Bluntschli* ed *Heffter* parlano dei rapporti pubblici che stabiliti in vista dell'antica associazione politica cessano con essa dove il conservarli non risulti compatibile con la nuova condizione di cose. *L'amministrazione del demanio privato*, traduco *l'Heffter* nello stesso paragrafo, *coi pesi che lo gravano appartiene, dopo lo scioglimento d'uno Stato, a quello che gli è succeduto. È ciò che fa dire che il nuovo fisco succede a titolo universale nei dirritti e nelle obbligazioni dell'antico. Non bisogna perder di vista la regola,* BONA NON INTELLIGUNTUR NISI DEDUCTO AERE ALIENO.

In ogni modo nè con *Bluntschli* nè con *Heffter* si riesce davvero a rendere *internaziondle* una questione che sia di diritto *interno*, come di diritto *interno* diventò la questione fra noi pel Lombardo-Veneto dopo disinteressata l'Austria per effetto delle convenzioni del 1871, lo fu sempre pel Napoletano, Parmense, Toscano, e ora lo è per l'ex-Pontificio. Cessato, o non mai esistito fra *Stato a Stato*, rimane un solo *rapporto* da definire, quello fra la pubblica amministrazione e il suo creditore, e questo è rapporte di materia *civile*, dipendente dal diritto, non *internazionale*, ma *interno*. Col creditore per *contratto*, cadrà in discussione il *contratto*, il suo adempimento o inadempimento, tenuto conto delle circostanze di fatto che lo accompagnarono e susseguirono. I politici avvenimenti porgeranno materia alla *causa*, o ne tesseranno la fattispecie, ecco tutto; e in caso di contestazione dovranno bene pronunziarvi i giudici del diritto *civile*, alla fattispecie applicando le regole del Codice, e dove bisogni, i principii generali del diritto sia *privato* che *pubblico*. È quanto il Consiglio di stato decise, e con tale gravità di motivi da non poterci tornare più sopra.

Giurisprudenza e consuetudini del regno stanno adunque per principii affatto opposti a quelli della relazione ministeriale che pur ne invoca l'autorità.

Non a proposito essa relazione cita la legge del 4 agosta 1861 come la principale fra le leggi di *ricognizione* fatte dall'Italia dei debiti dei precedenti Governi. Poichè quella legge non intese già ad attribuire azione *civile* ai creditori dei già Stati d'Italia, ma sibbene a unificare i debiti pubblici che si potevano unificare. Già per la legge del 10 luglio 1861, che istitui il Gran Libro del debito pubblico, nessuna rendita poteva esservi iscritta se non in virtù di una legge. E la legge del 4 agosto, guidata da un fine economico e politico a un tempo, iscrisse nel nuovo Gran Libro del debito pubblico del regno d'Italia il maggior numero dei debiti dei già Stati italiani. Basta ripercorrere le discussioni fatte alla Camera[18] su queste leggi, per convincersi che, anzichè riconoscerne alcuni e altri no, si unificarono debiti quanti più si poterono, con rinviare a leggi speciali la iscrizione di quelli che si tenevano fuori, e con eccetuare quelli soltanto che non si prestavano a essere unificati, attese le specialità loro di premi, d'ammortizzazione, di garantie che ne rendevano la condizione differente dalla condizione degli altri. Le eccezioni vennero motivate dal rispetto dei diritti quesiti, non per negare ai debiti eccetuati una ricognizione fatta per gli altri, e della quale ricorresse bisogno. Unificati o no, l'Italia li ha tutti pagati e li paga.

## II.

L'antico diritto della guerra faceva lecito l'uccidere il nemico *in solo proprio, in solo hostili, in solo nullius et in mari*, fino ai fanciulli e alle donne, *quod infantium quoque et fœminarum cœdes impune habetur, et isto belli jure comprehenditur.* Così il *Grozio*, ispirato nel suo capo IV del libro III, al verso di *Virgilio :*

*Tum certare odiis, tum res rapuisse licebit.*

Secondo una felice frase di Cicerone, la vittoria rendeva profane anche le cose *sacre*, e sono parole del testo: *Sepulchra hostium nobis religiosa non sunt.*

Del nemico preso in guerra fatto servo, era naturale che ogni bene si acquistasse dal vincitore e padrone, e gli stabili allo Stato che aveva vinto, le cose mobili ricadevano a chi se le pigliava per sè o per dividersi coi compagni.[19]

La civiltà ha mutato il diritto. Fino dal 1743 *Montesquieu* insegnava il *gius* delle genti fondarsi su questo principio, *che le diverse nazioni devono farsi nella pace il maggior bene e nella guerra il minor male possibile.* La guerra non è relazione d'uomo a uomo, ma *di Stato a Stato;* gli individui dell'una o dell'altra di due nazioni in guerra, diceva *Portalis*, sono nemici *per accidente, e non lo sono come uomini, e nemmeno come cittadini, ma solo come soldati.*

Per tacere dei ricordi biblici, dalla legge pagana, della quale le storie ci hanno lasciate memorie di inesorabili applicazioni da parte dei Romani, conquistatori del mon-

[18] Tornate del 5 giugno e 19 giugno 1861.

[19] LL. 3, in fin. Ad leg. Cornel. de sicariis, 1, § 1, 5, § 7, 51. De adquir. rer. dom. 20 § 1, De captivis; 4, De sepulchro violato; 36, De religiosis.

do, e di feroci da parte dei barbari del nord, che nella caduta dell'impero ne invasero le provincie, siamo di progresso in progresso giunti alla dichiarazione dei principii del congresso di Parigi del 30 marzo 1856, e alle istruzioni date per le armate in campagna nella guerra di separazione fra le provincie del nord e le provincie del sud degli Stati Uniti. E ci troviamo sempre in via, non per anche giunti dove la civiltà ne sospinge; tuttavia lontani meno nelle guerre di terra che nelle guerre di mare. A populi armati in esterminio di altri popoli, si sostituirono eserciti permanenti contro eserciti permanenti, la devastazione fu resa locale sul campo della zuffa, o dove si decide il conflitto; la stessa lotta ebbe le sue leggi.

Lo spagnuolo Ferdinando *Vasquez* nelle sue *Controversie celebri* negò affatto nella *città* l'obbligo di risarcire al *cittadino* il danno patito per causa di guerra, *eo quod jus belli talia permittat.* La guerra invece essendo un *fatto sociale*, la società dovrà riparare le perdite che la guerra cagiona, o compensarne i danni mediante giusta *perequazione* a guerra finita. La nazione, che la guerra a suo rischio e vantaggio, non puo lasciare il cieco caso arbitro dei danni, ma le bisogna repartire questi danni fra tutti, come su tutti ricadono i benefizi. Così l'*Ahrens* nella sua filosofia del diritto, e l'*Heffter* nel suo diritto delle genti dell'Europa moderna. A *Vasquez*, l'ultimo scrittore del diritto antico, *Grozio*[20] e i suoi commentatori *Puffendorff*, *Heineccio*, *Barbeyrac*, avevano già contrapposta la medesima ragione della legge *rhodia* sul getto dalla nave pericolante.

*Vattel* distingue i danni nella guerra prodotti dallo Stato o dal sovrano, e i fatti dal nemico.

"Dei primi, alcuni, ei dice, sono inferiti liberamente e per precauzione, come quando si prende il campo, la casa, o il giardino di un particolare per costruirvi il bastione d'una città, o un'opera di fortificazione, quando si distruggono le messi o i propri magazzini perchè non ne profitti il nemico. Lo Stato deve pagare queste speci di danni al particolare, il quale non deve sopportare che la sua quota parte. Altri danni vengono da una inevitabile necessità, tali sono per esempio, i guasti dell'artiglieria in una città che si riprenda al nemico. Questi sono accidenti, disgrazie della fortuna pei proprietari sui quali ricadono. Il sovrano deve avervi un equo riguardo, quando la condizione dei suoi affari a lui lo consenta, ma non si ha contro lo Stato azione per sciagure di questa natura, per perdite che non ha cagionate liberamente, ma per necessità, per accidente, usando dei suoi diritti.

"Io dico, prosegue *Vattel*, lo stesso dei danni cagionati dal nemico. Tutti i sudditi vi sono esposti, e disgrazia a coloro sui quali ricadono! Si può in una società correr pure questo rischio pei beni, dacchè lo si corre per la vita. Se dovesse lo Stato indennizzare a rigore tutti quelli che perdono in questo modo, le pubbliche finanze sarebbero ben presto esaurite; dovrebbe ognuno contribuire del suo in una giusta proporzione, ciò che sarebbe impracticabile. Queste indennizzazioni, del resto, darebbero luogo a mille abusi, e a un dettaglio spaventoso. Donde è a presumere che a ciò non intendessero quelli che si sono uniti in società.

"È tuttavia, conclude *Vattel*, assai conforme ai doveri dello Stato, e del sovrano, e per conseguenza equissimo e anche giustissimo sollevare, tanto che si può, i disgraziati rovinati dalle devastazioni della guerra, come prender cura di una famiglia, di cui il capo e il sostegno ha perduta la vita in servizio dello Stato. Vi sono bene dei debiti sacri per chi conosce i suoi doveri, sebbene essi non dieno azione contro di lui."[21]

*Vattel* piuttosto che insegnare una teoria diversa da quella dell'*Ahrens* e dell'*Heffter* è così che l'annunzia. Ei vuol riparati i danni della guerra con questa differenza:

Che pei danni deliberati dall'autorità in apparecchio di militare offesa o difesa, col proposito di munizioni o di cautele, *Vattel* riconosce azione civile a risarcimento, che nega pei danni *fortuiti* o *fatali* come son quelli d'una invasione nemica. Per questi ultimi ei raccomanda, e con calore, di venire in soccorso, ma consente che si consulti un po'anche lo stato della pubblica finanza.

Sono rimasti celebri nell'istoria i decreti promulgati in Francia dall'Assemblea nazionale nell'11 agosto 1792 e dalla Convenzione nel 14 agosto 1793, e nel 16 messidoro dell'anno II. L'Assemblea nazionale decretava: "Il serait accordé des secours ou des indemnités aux citoyens français qui pendant la durée de la guerre auront perdu par le fait des ennemis extérieurs tout ou partie de leurs propriétés." Ma se si vollero risarciti tutti i danneggiati nei loro beni dai nemici o nella difesa del territorio, era caso per caso dalla Convenzione stessa che si decretava la indennità. Nè pur troppo a questo generoso ricordo vuolsi disgiungere l'altro amaro ricordo degli *assegnati;* che cioè col pagare soverchio si finì col pagare nessuno o col pagare in una moneta che valse più nulla.

Alla distinzione del *Vattel* si attenne il conte di *Cavour* nelle sue celebrate orazioni alla Camera dei deputati sul trattato di Zurigo nella tornato del 21 maggio, e sulla interpellanza *Depretis* in quella del 22 giugno 1860. Nel 16 agosto 1860 il ministro Farini vi informava una circolare diramata ai prefetti.[22] Il Consiglio di stato ne professò in via di massima i principii nel voto del 27 maggio 1867;[23] e ne ha fatta l'applicazione ai danneggiati di Gaeta, d'Alessandria, di Casale, di Piacenza, del Bolognese,

[20] Lib. III. cap. 20. [21] § 232. [22] Allegato nº 2. [23] Allegato nº 12.

di Castiglion delle Stiviere e di Roma, coi pareri del 26 maggio, 10, 14 luglio e 21 ottobre 1865, 28 febbraio, 26 giugno, 16 luglio, e 3 dicembre 1868, 12 luglio 1870, 10 febbraio, 5 maggio e 29 settembre 1871, per tacere d'altri.

I tribunali hanno applicata la medesima teoria. Dov'è deliberazione, libertà di consiglio, ivi la responsibilità del danno; dove l'accidente è all'infuori della volontà, della libertà e della scelta, fu imprevedibile il caso, *divina la forza*, ivi il fortuito, il fatale di cui nessuno risponde.

Nel 1858 e 1860 la Corte d'appello di Lucca e la Cassazione di Firenze in una causa *Santernecchi;* nel 1867 e 1868 il tribunale e la Corte d'appello di Milano in una causa *Antona-Traversi;* e nel 1866 la Corte d'appello di Messina e la Cassazione di Palermo nel 1868 in un causa *Tripodo,* hanno quella distinzione del *Vattel* elevata fra noi a massima ricevuta di giurisprudenza.[24]

Nell'applicazione non si ebbe difficoltà, quando si è trattato d'abbattimento d'alberi e di case intorno alle fortezze non ancora attaccate dal nemico, o di occupazioni di terreni per fortificazioni passeggere durante l'armistizio.

Una difficoltà è sorta sulle *requisizioni* fatte dal nemico per mezzo dell'autorità locale. Poichè di rimborsare le requisizioni fatte dentro lo Stato per le truppe nazionali, nessuno ha mai dubitato e non dubita. Le regie patenti del 9 agosto 1836 si trovano d'accordo con la legge francese del 26 e 29 aprile 1792 nell'ammettere il principio del pagamento; l'urgenza potendo autorizzare l'occupazione e il modo, assolvere dalla preventiva, non dall'indennità, anche *ex post facto.*

Il conte di Cavour *sul terreno del diritto,* rispose recisamente, costituire un vero debito dell'Italia *le requisizioni fatte dall'Austria in Lombardia,* e non considerarsi per tali le requisizioni *fatte da questa parte del Ticino. In Lombardia prima della guerra il Governo austriaco era Governo regolare, di qua del Ticino era un nemico combattente.* Sono le sue parole. Gli rispose il deputato *Cabella* che *il nemico sulle provincie occupate esercita i diritti della sovranità di fatto ed ha il diritto di vivere, e per conseguenza se fa requisizioni per alimentare le sue truppe, impone un debito allo Stato.*[25]

Ed è vero che le requisizioni si sostituirono ai saccheggi e alle depredazioni, riscattarono dalle rapine il paese invaso, imposero regola e modo alla militare licenza.

Ricorda il Dalloz la legge del 23 settembre 1814, che dichiarò affette alle requisizioni e forniture fatte per le armate le contribuzioni dirette sì ordinarie che straordinarie dal 1813 e 1814; la legge del 28 giugno 1815 che autorizzò il Governo ad assicurare le sussistenze e i trasporti militari delle armate per via di requisizioni, a prezzi di tariffa; e l'ordinanza del 16 agosto 1815, che in via d'urgenza impose una contribuzione straordinaria di cento milioni e la ripartì sui diversi dipartimenti in proporzione delle loro risorse, *per diminuire il carico delle requisizioni che pesavano unicamente sui dipartimenti invasi;* l'ordinanza del 5 ottobre 1815; le leggi di finanza del 28 aprile 1816 e sul bilancio del 1821, relative allo stesso argomento.

Con tutto ciò si trova negata *azione* ai danneggiati da requisizioni del *maire* per fornire le truppe nemiche.[26]

---

[24] *Annali di giurisprudenza toscano*, anno 1858, 2, 891, anno 1860, 1, 243; DD. del tribunale civile di Milano, del 23 maggio 1867, e della Corte d'appello di Milano, del 3 maggio 1868; Corte d'appello di Messina, del 28 dicembre 1866, Cassazione di Palermo del 7 gennaio 1868.

In Toscana sono conosciute le due decisioni dell'antica Ruota, e del Magistrato supremo del 1° luglio 1806 e 22 settembre 1807, nella *Liburnen. prætensæ refectionis damnorum.* Anche allora si trattave d'un barone D'Aspre entrato nel 1799 in Livorno coi Tedeschi, che avevano depredato un livornese (Trouquy) d'alcuni quadri di provenienza francese; nonostante gli editti che risparmiavano dai sequestri, accesi sulle robe del Governo francese, le robe dei privati, non militari e non impiegati nelle armate. Una Commissione di prede nominata dal D'Aspre ordinò la restituzione al Trouquy dei suoi quadri, a patto che ei rinunziasse ai venduti o spediti a Vienna. Il Trouquy ne mosse lite contro il Governo del regno d'Etruria. E prima *Ubaldo Maggi*, poi il *Sermolli* e il *Puccini*, e per ultimo il *Salvetti*, il *Niccolini* e il *Fini* rigettarono la domanda dell'attore. Allora i motivi delle decisioni spaziavano in trattati della materia. Io trascrivo questo solo, che è del PUCCINI:

"Non considerata punto la detta sentenza (della Commissione delle prede nominata dal D'Aspre), lo spoglio predetto rimaneva un atto di privata violenza fatto da persone mancanti d'autorità per commetterlo in qualunque rappresentanza vogliono riguardarsi, e che obbliga esse solamente e non la universalità dei possessori dello Stato, innocenti e non partecipi in alcuna guisa del fatto.

"O vuol considerarsi questa sentenza, e le sentenze ingiuste danno luogo a ripari convenienti avanti altri giudici, ed in ulteriori istanze, ma giammai a indennità contro il Tesoro pubblico dello Stato nel cui territorio sono proferite.

"Non tutti i danni, non tutte le perdite che gli individui soffrono per la circostanza d'una guerra debbono risarcirsi dall'universalità dello Stato, sebbene accaduti nel suo territorio. Alcuni fra i quali *Grozio* e *Puffendorf*, col loro traduttore *Barbeyrac*, hanno creduto, è vero, che nel rigore dei doveri sociali vi sia quello di far risentire a tutti per la quota parte di ciaschedune i danni di qualsivoglia specie portati sui singoli cittadini dalla guerra, come derivanti da una casua universale. Ma hannovi in opposizione altri che non riconoscono alcuna obbligazione di rimborso nella società per le conseguenze qualunque della guerra risentite dai particolari; come *Herzio*, *Enrico Coccejo*, *Sam. Stykio*. Gli stessi poi di sopra citati scrittori hanno creduto ineseguibile la loro dottrina nella sua pienezza, e ne fanno poi dipendere la giusta estensione ed applicazione dal Governo civile. Ed oggimai la teoria comune presso gli scrittori di diritto pubblico e nella pratica delle nazionieè che non sia lo Stato tenuto alla rifazione di altri danni che di quelli cagionati dalla legittima rappresentanza dell'universale, o che dell'universale hanno ridondato in un certo vantaggio; e che tutti gli altri di diversa specie restino a carico dei particolari che li hanno sofferti, come accidenti parziali e mali inevitabili della fortuna." ZIEGLER, *De jure majestatico;* VATTEL, *Droit des gens, etc.*

[25] Tornata del 22 giugno 1860.

[26] Ordon. 16 novembre 1825 in aff. Schoengrün.

Il *Bluntschli*, parlando delle contribuzioni che un'armata ha diritto di levare sul territorio nemico, si studia di restringerle alle assolutamente indispensabili per mantenersi e pei suoi movimenti. Ei crede potere l'armata nemica reclamare gratuitamente dalle popolazioni le sole imposizioni e contribuzioni di guerra nei limiti stabiliti dall'uso o dalle leggi del paese. Lamenta che, al di là, il nemico che ha ordinata la requisizione si limiti a rilasciarne ricevuta e a farne *sperare* il rimborso dal Governo locale, il quale, nulla avendo ricevuto, non vuol nulla saperne E, osservato che nei trattati di pace se ne fa raramente questione, il *Bluntschli* conclude trovarsi allora i diritti dei comuni e dei particolari verso lo Stato nemico ben gravemente compromessi, e che tutto ciò che ad essi rimane è di chiedere al loro Governo di aiutarli in nome dell'equità.[27]

La giurisprudenza si è pronunciata in questo senso anche fra noi.

Sulle requisizioni del 1859 fatte dagli Austriaci nella Lomellina col mezzo dei sindaci, si ha una dotta decisione della Cassazione di Milano del 18 *luglio* 1864, proferita nella causa fra il comune di *Sannazzaro e Maggi Pietro.*

Ivi la Cassazione nega i termini del *mandato* per difetto di volontà; della *gestione di negozi* che trova il suo appoggio nel mandato legalmente presunto; e della legge *rhodia*, che ha per base l'uguaglianza dei rischi e dei vantaggi. Invoca la dottrina dei pubblicisti, dei quali, i più favorevoli al principio dell'indennità, lo applicano verso lo Stato e non verso i comuni, essi pure danneggiati, e anche verso lo Stato non consentono azione civilmente esperibile. Cita la Francia rivoluzionaria, che sospinse la *solidalità nazionale* fino all'esaltazione del sentimento, eppure negò *ogni azione* giudiziaria *per fatti e danni di guerra inflitti ai cittadini da violenza nemica, con o senza il ministero passivo dei sindaci.* E cassò *senza rinvio* la sentenza del tribunale di Vigevano contraria alla comunità, chiudendo la serie delle sue considerazioni con la seguente:

"Attesochè le autorità comunali che nell'invasione dello straniero pur rimasero al loro posto e i cittadini che ne ascoltarono la voce ed ora aspettano pazientemente un equo provvedimento, adempierono un patriottico ufficio e ben meritarono del paese; e certamente vi hanno debiti sacrosanti per chi conosce il dovere benchè non sanzionati da azione giuridica; nè è da dubitare che la nazione sia per dimenticare ciò che le consigliano gl'interessi superiori dell'avvenire, la giustizia ed in specie la pietà verso numerose famiglie spogliate e forse ridotte in misero stato. Questo solo si nega che un'azione giudiziaria con principii, con metodi e con procedimenti inetti al bisogno, possa sostituirsi colà dov'è solo competente e praticabile un arbitrato legislativo."

## III.

Secondo la vostra Commissione, *giuridica* è dunque per l'Italia la obbligazione di pagare i debiti lasciati dalle amministrazioni permanenti, che precedevano la sua formazione; è *civile* l'azione dei creditori; di diritto *interno* la questione.

Non ha invece che natura *politica* il rapporto dell'Italia verso i creditori dei Governi provvisori del 1848 e 1849; e però non d'azione da sperimentare utilmente ai tribunali, ma quel rapporto può solo e deve formare soggetto d'un provvedimento legislativo.

Fra *danneggiato* per la guerra e *Governo* intercede rapporto di *creditore* a *debitore* dove il danno venga prodotto da proposito deliberato dall'autorità, mentre al danno *fortuito* o *fatale*, se si viene o si può venire in soccorso, non si consente *azione*. *Fatale* è il danno che reca il nemico, *incursus hostium*;[28] e lo sono pertanto le sue *requisizioni* anche se fatte e regolate col mezzo dei sindaci. Nelle quali vuolsi tuttavia riconoscere al diritto della *forza* mescolarsi un po 'anche il diritto della *ragione*, o il caso assumere indole di caso misto, da conseguentemente reclamare un trattamento speciale.

Ecco i principii che la Commissione ha presi a guida delle sue proposte; è dei quali scendo in suo nome a discorrere delle applicazioni, a suo giudizio, convenienti a tutte, l'una dopo l'altra, le partite notate nell'*allegato* alla relazione ministeriale.

La Commissione ha dovuto avvertire che l'*allegato* mescola insieme e confonde partite di natura diversa e politicamente e giuridicamente. Essa una volta per tutte qui nota che l'allegato, se da un lato abbonda, dall'altro trascura partite che hanno lo stesso titolo, e però da sottoporre a ugual trattamento.

Se pertanto i principii della Commissione prevarranno, l'applicazione de'suoi principii sarà da estendere a ogni pendenza che rientri nella formola generale della loro definizione, e ciò quand'anche si tratti di partita, non contemplata nell'allegato, o non dalla relazione presente, che ha preso a seguirlo.

### LE APPLICAZIONI ALL'ALLEGATO DEI PRINCIPII DELLA COMMISSIONE.

### 1.—*Lombardia e Venezia.*

Espropriazioni e somministrazioni militari, appropriazioni di stabili fatte dalla cassa d'ammortizzazione del Governo italico.

Sommano a lire 5,043,687 33 i crediti, non regolati, sebben reclamati da comuni e privati di *Lombardia* avanti alla speciale Commissione presso il Monte lombardo-veneto,

[27] 653.

[28] Leg. 18, ff; commodati.

instituita in esecuzione all'articolo 97 dell'atto finale del Congresso di Vienna del 9 giugno 1815.

Nel trattato del 30 maggio 1814, stipulato fra la Francia che cedeva e l'Austria che acquistava il Lombardo-Veneto, all'articolo 19 *il Governo francese si impegnava di far liquidare e pagare le somme rimaste a suo debito nei paesi fuori del suo territorio per contratti o altre obbligazioni per forniture o somministrazioni verso privati o verso istituti.*

Dopo i cento giorni, per la convenzione finale del 25 aprile 1818, la Francia, in esecuzione all'articolo 19, pagò ai Governi sottoscritti al trattato 12 milioni e 40,000 lire di rendita, o 240 milioni e 800,000 lire di capitale, dei quali toccarono all'Austria pel Lombardo-Veneto 25 milioni, oltre 2,612,642 lire da essa ricevute prima.

Con la patente del 27 agosto 1820 l'Austria instituì una Commissione liquidatrice del debito arretrato dell'amministrazione del cessato regno italico, con intimazione ai creditori ad esibire i loro titoli a tutto il 1821, e tolta ogni relativa competenza ai tribunali, come ad ogni altra magistratura amministrativa.

Eppure nel 1859 e nel 1866 questa liquidazione non era peranche chiusa, nè saldati si trovarono i conti. La convenzione del 9 settembre 1860, stipulata al seguito del trattato di Zurigo del 10 novembre 1859, e il trattato di Vienna del 3 ottobre 1866, rimettevano a regolarsi *fra chi di diritto* queste antiche pendenze.

E tutte si riprodussero, e invocati gli stessi titoli dei trattati del 1814, del 1815 e del 1818, dai commissari italiani nelle discussioni coi commissari imperiali, le quali precederono e prepararono la convenzione del 6 gennaio, approvata con la legge del 23 marzo 1871.[29]

E attesochè si pattuiva in questa convenzione—*toutes les réclamations présentées par les deux Gouvernements sont compensées en voie de transaction, moyennant le paiement que le Gouvernement Austro-Hongrois s'engage à faire au Gouvernement italien dans le semestre d'une somme de* 4,749,000 *florins*—il debito non ancora liquidato e non pagato dall'Austria diventò debito da liquidare e da pagare dall'Italia.

Nella discussione alla Camera sulle convenzioni del 1871, principio e applicazione furono propugnati da più d'un oratore. E a ragione. Poichè l'Austria non ha mai impugnato il debito. Messe poca buona volontà nel liquidarlo e anche meno nel pagarlo, ma eccezioni non le oppose mai. E ora il Governo d'Italia, subentrato negli obblighi dell'Austria per ragioni territoriali e per convenzione, non solo non vorrà opporre eccezioni non opposte dall'Austriaco, ma è da contare che porterà nel compiere le liquidazioni e nel saldare i pagamenti una volontà migliore di quella già messa dall'Austria che allungò tanto le prime per differire i secondi.

### 2.—*Parma e Piacenza.*

Somministrazioni degli anni 1811, 1812, 1814 e 1815.

È questo un credito degli ospizi civili di Borgo San Donnino del 1814 e 1815 per mantenimento di ricoverati mendicanti, di lire 6419 66, per provvista di paglericci e panni pei detenuti in quelle prigioni, e di lire 416 02, in tutto lire 6835 68.

Ma come sia debito dello Stato, e meno che mai perchè figuri in un prospetto di danni di guerra, alla Commissione non è risultato. Ella sa che il Governo parmense non lo riconobbe, e che si ha per debito *prescritto*, e però passa oltre.

### 3.—*Provincie napoletane.*

Prestito forzato nazionale del 1821.

È l'imprestito votato in 3,000,000 di ducati dal Parlamento napoletano, decretato per legge del 17 febbraio 1821, stato nel 27 marzo sospeso e poi annullato per decreto del 6 aprile 1821. Sui versamenti avvenuti dal 17 febbraio al 27 marzo si dicono rimasti da restituire ducati 265,456 09, pari a lire 1,128,188 38. Ma si tace come e perchè non restituiti, non si dice se i titoli sono conservati ed esibiti, e dove e in quale giuridica condizione si siano trovati o si trovino, o dopo quali precedenti dei Governi provvisorii o permanenti del Napoletano.

La Commissione pertanto ha lasciata questa partita senza proposte nelle condizioni di diritto che ha.

Dalla natura del suo mandato essa si tenne invitata ad esordire i suoi lavori dal 1848, da quando spuntò l'aurora del nazionale risorgimento. Dei debiti del già regno italico ha dovuto occuparsi, perchè li trovò fatti suoi dall'Austria e ringiovaniti nelle conferenze diplomatiche del 1870 e dalla convenzione approvata con la legge del 1871. Mentre a saputa della Commissione nulla è sopraggiunto che revochi a nuova vita un fatto che sembra dall'amministrazione borbonica lasciato per *compiuto*, col sistema di governo che aveva. Male avvezza, avrà fatto male; la sua sarà stata opera di mal governo, e potrà essere venuto un *torto* da riparare dal Governo italiano; ma non saremmo in termini di civile obbligazione o di debito che questo abbia senz'altro a dimettere. Le quali cose si dicono quasi a modo di *divinazione*, e, anzichè per proferire giudizi sopra fatti accertati, per giustificare la riserva della Commissione.

[29] Vedasi la relazione presentata su quella convenzione dalla Giunta nel 3 marzo 1871.

4.—*Imprestiti dei Governi provvisorii del* 1848.

La Lombardia apparisce per lire 8,497,890 72, somma costituita da imprestiti in denaro ordinati coi decreti del Governo provvisorio dei 27 marzo, 1° giugno e 28 luglio 1848, da ritenute fatte sugli stipendi e le pensioni coi decreti dei 29 aprile e 19 maggio 1848, e dal prestito in oggetti d'oro e d'argento decretato nel 1° luglio 1848.

La Lombardia votò il suo plebiscito nell'8 giugno 1848, accettato da Re Carlo Alberto nel 13 giugno e dal Parlamento subalpino con legge dell'11 luglio. Nè la Lombardia fu chiamata nel 1859 a rinnovare il suo plebiscito. *Restaurato il diritto nazionale, i vostri voti raffermano l'unione col mio regno che si fonda nelle guarentigie del viver civile,* bandiva Vittorio Emanuele col proclama del 9 giugno quando, *ricondotto dalle armi liberatrici,* riprendeva il governo di Lombardia. È un fatto storico che l'*unione* non si fece allora, o che nel 1859 si ripristinò l'unione votata nel 1848.

Di consenso coi regi commissari *Montezemolo* e *Strigelli*, questi imprestiti ebbero carattere in parte volontario, e in parte coattivo. Si presero da quel Governo anche i depositi necessari, dei quali poi l'Austria non restituì che i necessari per necessità di legge o di contratto, non rimasti nella cassa un giorno più del prescritto ed esclusi quelli eseguiti nel *periodo del Governo di fatto.* Sono restrizioni imposte dall'Austria e pubblicate con risoluzione del 13 luglio 1852. Intanto i denari raccolti da quelli imprestiti come i presi dalla cassa dei depositi servirono ugualmente alla causa nazionale, stata inaugurata con le famose cinque giornate.

Fin dal dicembre 1859 il commissario straordinario *Vigliani* propose di questi debiti la iscrizione nel libro del debito pubblico dello Stato. Nè la prefettura di Milano trovò in aprile del 1860 da fare diverse proposte.

Il ministro *Bastogi* nella discussione alla Camera sul progetto di legge per l'*unificazione* dei debiti pubblici d'Italia, rispondendo al deputato *Allievi*, dichiarava in nome del Ministero, presieduto allora dal *conte di Cavour*, riconoscere *i generosi sforzi fatti dalla Lombardia nel* 1848, *essersi data ogni cura per raccogliere documenti, esaminarli accuratamente per poter quindi presentare una legge affinchè vengano posti in regola i prestiti che fece la Lombardia nel* 1848.

Il ministro *Minghetti* a identiche dichiarazioni, sulle interpellanze del deputato *Macchi*, nelle tornate del 4 marzo e 28 luglio 1863, aggiungeva che alla presentazione d'un progetto di legge non mancava oramai che il parere del Consiglio di stato.

E il Consiglio di stato dette il suo parere nella seduta del 3 settembre di quell'anno 1863 nel senso che il progetto avesse ad essere presentato, comunque *trattandosi d'obbligazione naturale a cui si deve restituire il carattere d'obbligazione civile per considerazioni di giustizia, d'equità e di convenienza politica spetti al Governo il giudicare della opportunità del tempo in cui la proposta debba esser fatta.*[30]

Il Consiglio di stato, che costantemente ha negato ai creditori dei Governi provvisorii del 1848 di far valere ai tribunali le loro ragioni, si è mantenuto pure costante nel sol[illegible] Governo a provocare dal Parlamento una legge, la quale restituisse ai ti[illegible]ditori la virtù giuridica che avevano perduta e togliesse le *inique restrizion[illegible]* [illegible]all'Austria alla restituzione dei depositi con la risoluzione del 1852.[31]

Un p[illegible]o di legge d'initiativa parlamentare nel gennaio del 1865 venne anche presentato da 52 deputati per cambiare i titoli di quelli imprestiti in tanta rendita consolidata del 5 per cento. E se quel progetto restò sorpreso dalla chiusura della Sessione, costituisce pur sempre un precedente da tenere in conto.

Passaggi da una ad altra mano per alienazione di questi titoli potranno essere, e saranno avvenuti. La Giunta non sa nè vuole escluderlo, come è certo che agli acquirenti non sono quei titoli costati il loro valore nominale. Ma nè si deve esagerare il fatto, avendosi prove che molti di quei titoli si conservano tuttora dagli originari sovventori; e non è il 5, ma il 3 per cento che la Giunta si è indotta ad offrire a questa specie di creditori, ai quali venne meno o restò interrotta la condizione *giuridica* del loro titolo di credito. E dentro questi limiti, il trattamento sembra veramente dover vincere ogni ritegno, disarmare ogni opposizione.

Venezia sta nella lista dell'*allegato :*

per 3,888,900 00 prestito del 14 maggio 1848:
1,296,300 00 per quello del 20 giugno 1848;
1,296,880 00 prestito in oggetti d'oro, d'argento e ritenute del 19 luglio e 16 agosto;
1,609,875 00 *Buoni* emessi dalla Banca di sconto, giusta il decreto del 25 luglio 1848;
2,659,834 76 prestiti dei 19 settembre, 14 ottobre, 15 novembre 1848 e 9 aprile 1849;
1,571,136 22 moneta patriottica rimasta in circolazione dopo la notificazione austriaca del 2 ottobre 1849;

---

[30] Vedi allegato n° 11.

[31] Pareri del 20 ottobre 1868 in aff. Eredità Labia, del 26 marzo 1869 in aff. Rossi e del 5 marzo 1873 in aff. Raffard.

per 8,973,774 57 scapito sulla *carta*, emessa dal comune di Venezia, e per lire austriache 20,766,291 52, *cambiata* contro a valuta austriaca al 50 per cento, per effetto della convenzione del 22 agosto 1849.

Su quest'ultima partita non è a trattenersi; il cambio fra carta veneta e carta austriaca essendosi *consumato* senza lasciar traccie sensibili dietro a sè, e per disposizione del Governo del tempo.

Ma gli imprestiti della Venezia hanno la medisima origine, ebbero lo stesso fine e meritano ugual trattamento degli imprestiti lombardi.

Venezia si unì con la Lombardia al Piemonte per plebiscito accettato con la legge del 27 luglio 1848, ebbe il suo regio commissario, proseguì i militari apprestamenti dopo l'armistizio Salasco, fu sovvenuta dal Piemonte d'un sussidio mensile di lire 600,000, delle quali in gennaio del 1849 toccò un primo acconto di lire 200,000, e dopo Novara sostenne da sola quella eroica *resistenza ad ogni costo*, che resterà memorabile nella storia.

Se per Venezia mancano le dichiarazioni che i ministri fecero tante volte per la Lombardia, fu perchè Venezia potè solo riunirsi all'Italia in ottobre del 1866: mentre fu la petizione del suo municipio e della sua Camera di commercio, che provocò quella discussione alla Camera, al seguito della quale venne ripresentato il progetto su cui si discute.

ROMA ebbe la sua predita di *buoni* emessi dalla repubblica coi decreti dei 1° e 26 marzo, 5 e 11 aprile e 5 maggio 1849, e ritirati con la riduzione del 35 per cento per notificazione del Governo pontificio del 24 settembre 1849. E di questa perdita non potrebbe ora farsi ragione, come non è fatta per la *veneta*, mutata in *valuta austriaca* col maggiore scapito del 50 per cento. Poichè in quella come in questa perdita il cambio si ordonò come e da chi allora poteva ordinarlo, nè, dopo il ritiro dei titoli, sono rimasti danneggiati accertabili.

Ma Roma ebbe pure il suo imprestito coattivo, ordinato dalla repubblica col decreto del 2 marzo 1849, e una requisizione di argenti decretata nel 2 maggio; con aver data il primo una somma di lire 1,298,932 98, la seconda di lire 509,432 20.

Se non che, di fronte agli argenti requisiti si consegnarono dalla Zecca dei buoni, *stati pagati in moneta d'argento plateale emessa dalla repubblica*, e la Zecca versò in depositeria in settembre del 1850, in moneta metallica, scudi 5549 61, valore di 17 *buoni*, restati insoluti, per argenti presentati alla Zecca dal Triumvirato, dal Ministero dell'interno e da varie Commissioni di requisizioni.[32] Apparisce insomma partita saldata.

Non rimane pertanto che l'imprestito per 1,298,932 lire e centesimi 98. E di questo la vostra Commissione vi propone il medesimo trattamento degli imprestiti degli altri Governi provvisorii del 1848. Se il romano non si ispirò, come gli altri Governi, al principio monarchico, s'ispirò, come gli altri, al principio nazionale, con averlo, nella difesa di Roma, propognato con valore, resistendo a soldati stranieri, stimati allora i migliori d'Europa.

NAPOLI.—Nelle PROVINCIE NAPOLETANE, con decreto reale del 26 apr[illegible]i-nato un imprestito *forzato* per *due* e *volontario* per *un* milione di ducati. [illegible]

Annullato e ritirato, pare che rimangano di esso imprestito non rimbo[illegible]oli per ducati 458,032 41, pari a lire italiane 1,946,637 74. E se di questi ti[illegible]estino ancora in corso, la Commissione non ha potuto appurare. Se ne restano, meritano sicuramente di essere ritirati e pagati come si ritirano e pagano gli altri di quell'epoca, della medesima causa e che si raccomandano a uno stesso ordine di considerazioni. Napoli non ebbe Governo *provvisorio* nel 1848, e *reale* fu il decreto che ordinò l'imprestito. La quale è tal circostanza da non dimenticare nel trattamento di questa partita.

SICILIA.—Chi manca nella lista è la SICILIA. Poichè ai debiti del Governo provvisorio della Sicilia provvide un decreto luogotenenziale del 31 dicembre 1860, con questo articolo: *I titoli dei debiti nazionali del* 1848 *e* 1849 *non ancora estinti sono commutati in iscrizioni di rendita* 5 *per cento da assegnarsi sul loro valor capitale, col godimento dal* 1° *gennaio* 1861.

E quanti ebbero titoli di quei debiti nazionali della Sicilia se li trovano ora convertiti in altrettanto consolidato 5 per cento italiano.

La quale sorte non può che solicitare a provvedere ai debiti degli altri Governi di ugual natura, se pur non vogliamo che la giustizia distributiva patisca più a lungo un'offesa, che non si è nemmeno disposti a riparare completamente.

### 5.—*Somministrazioni, requisizioni e danni de guerra del* 1848–49.

Le PROVINCIE EX-PONTIFICIE, annesse nel 1859 e 1860, per prestazioni e somministrazioni alle milizie della repubblica romana e del Governo pontificio hanno pressochè liquidato un credito di lire 124,867 97.

La LOMBARDIA per somministrazioni e lavori di corpi morali e privati, per conto del Governo provvisorio, ha un credito accertato di lire 1,235,763 63 per tacere d'altra partita presunta di lire 2,237,957 54 messa in nota per requisizioni e danni, non giustificati e però da eliminare dal conto.

---

[32] È quanto risulta da un attestato rilasciato dall'intendente della Zecca romana nel 28 marzo 1871.

PARMA è notata per un piccolo credito presunto di lire 86,067 11 per spese di vitto e alloggio di truppe austriache, e, insieme con PIACENZA, per altro credito di lire 8150 83 per prestazioni e somministrazioni a truppe nazionali.

Nell'EX-DUCATO DI MODENA per questo titolo si liquidò appena la insignificante somma di lire 609 73.

E la SICILIA per somministrazioni militari liquidò per lire 18,283 28, e nulla per requisizioni e danni pei quali si avevano reclami per lire 240,008 63.

Il PIEMONTE nella campagna del marzo 1849 patì requisizioni e danni di guerra che si dissero ascendere a lire 2,152,392 48.

Una legge del 15 giugno 1850 aprì un credito di lire 500,000 per sovvenire *gli abitanti delle provincie di Novara e di Lomellina, danneggiati in occasione della guerra del mese di marzo* 1849 *e che trovansi in ristrette condizioni di fortuna.*

Sono 500,000 lire che scemano d'altrettanta somma quella partita, o, per dir meglio, la soldano. Se infatti delle requisizioni e dei danni si teneva allora lo stesso criterio, tutti sanno che le requisizioni regolari o giustificate furono pagate, donde è una partita rimasta nella nota solo per figura.

E per figura vi stanno le PROVINCIE VENETE e di MANTOVA niente meno che per lire 11,150,059 35 a titolo di requisizioni e danni della guerra del 1848 e 1849.

Imperocchè è noto come per disposizione del Governo austriaco le somministrazioni dei generi di sussistenza, fornite dal 18 marzo 1848 al 31 dicembre 1849 alle truppe imperiali accampate nel Lombardo-Veneto *per combattere la insurrezione e l'armata italiana, più la tassa di guerra allora imposta, e i gravi danni arrecati dal militare in quelle circostanze,* si fecero gravare a tutto carico delle provincie stesse in proporzione del loro estimo.

Ed è noto del pari che un decreto del Ministero di Vienna del 17 novembre 1858 sanzionò la *perequazione* o il *conguaglio* fra le provincie lombarde e venete di un debito

| | |
|---|---|
| risultato per prestazioni, in natura e in denaro, di | L.55, 988, 741 66 |
| Per il fondo *sociale* costituito per corrispondere alle esorbitanti pretese del militare | 862, 853 96 |
| Per la tassa bellica | 36, 045, 100 59 |
| In totale austriache | 92, 896, 706 21 |

Nella perequazione stata approvata, la Lombardia risultò debitrice per conguaglio verso la Venezia di lire 3,800,000. E se ne restò ritardato il pagamento fu per le sopraggiunte vicende politiche, e anche per difficoltà di subreparto del debito, sorte fra le provincie interessate.

Il Ministero ha dovuto più volte mescolarsi e mescolare il Consiglio di stato nella questione, portata per ultimo dalla provincia di Cremona alla decisione dei tribunali ordinari. Nè opportuno, nè legale pare pertanto alla Commissione il turbare con sue proposte il co[illegible] ordinario di giustizia, stato preso dapendenze, che alcune provincie hanno con [illegible] provincie, quali persone giuridiche, costituite l'una verso l'altra in rapporti civ[illegible]i debito e credito.[33] Si augura tuttavia la Commissione che ogni pendenza verrà [illegible]nita sollecitamente; e che nè l'autorità giudiziaria nè l'autorità amministrativa, nella sfera delle rispettive competenze, mancheranno, ciascuna dal canto suo, di decidere e provvedere con la prontezza che è parte di quella giustizia o di quella buona amministrazione che spetta a loro di rendere.

6.—*Incendio delle case nel suburbio di Milano, nella notte dal* 4 *al* 5 *agosto* 1848.

A uno speciale ricordo richiamano le case del suburbio di Milano incendiate nella notte dal 4 al 5 agosto 1848 per ordine di Re Carlo Alberto, quando ripiegava gli avanzi del valoroso suo esercito per coprire una città risoluta a disperata difesa. Fumavano ancora le case incendiate, che le sorti della guerra costrinsero alla capitolazione di Milano, e l'esercito sardo a ripassare il Ticino. Ma quelli incendi non furono dimenticati nè dal vincitore nè dal vinto.

Il maresciallo Radetzki, nel 18 agosto con notificazione dell'intendenza generale dell'armata, nominò una speciale Commissione con l'incarico di rilevare e stimare i danni in contraddittorio dei proprietari delle case incendiate.

E il suo Governo nelle trattative di pace, per elevare a maggior somma la indemnità della guerra da imporre sullo Stato sardo, allegò bene l'impegno assunto con la notificazione del 18 agosto.

Il Governo sardo col primo degli articoli addizionali al trattato di Milano del 6 agosto 1849, si sobbarcò a pagare *in diverse rate a S. M. l'imperatore d'Austria la somma di* 75 *milioni a titolo d'indennità delle spese di guerra d'ogni maniera e dei danni sofferti durante la guerra, dal Governo austriaco e dai suoi sudditi, città, corpi morali, o corporazioni, senza alcuna eccezione come pure pei reclami che fossero Stati elevati per la medesima causa dalle LL. AA. RR. l'arciduca, duca di Modena, e l'infante di Spagna, duca di Parma e di Piacenza.*

A pace fatta, il Governo austriaco distribuì poco, e a chi volle, di quei 75 milioni; e

[33] Vedi allegati numeri 8, 9 e 10.

ciò anche dopo l'atteggiamento preso dal conte di Cavour nel congresso di Parigi del 1856; dopo il quale pur vennero da Vienna ordini di riassumere la liquidazione cominciata dalla Commissione del 1848, e, sopra una petizione del comune dei Corpi Santi, si compiè il lavoro e si ripresero perfino i pagamenti.

Sopraggiunto il 1859; i commissari di Re Vittorio Emanuele, nelle trattative che riuscirono al trattato di Zurigo mossero aperte lagnanze della incompiuta esecuzione data dall'Austria al trattato di Milano. Come è vero che i commissari austriaci si rifiutarono ad ogni relativa discussione, deducendo quanto all'Austria eseguito il trattato, e rispetto, alla Sardegna, essersi la medesima sdebitata coi 75 milioni. La questione rimasta sospesa, diventò *un conto di più da regolare con l'Austria*, secondo allora diceva il ministro dell'interno, il compianto Farini.

I danneggiati infatti anzichè arrendersi, in numero di 41, muniti d'un certificato di credito, rilasciato a loro dalla direzione del Tesoro di Milano, chiesero e ottennero per lire 645,004 67 la *prenotazione di suppegno* sui crediti iscritti a favore del Governo austriaco presso l'ufficio delle ipoteche di Castiglione delle Stiviere.

Tuttora pende in Cassazione il ricorso dai medesimi interposto contro la sentenza della Corte d'appello di Brescia del 24 luglio 1867, la quale accolse la eccezione d'incompetenza opposta dal Governo austriaco, rimasto soccombente sul merito in prima istanza.

Pratiche nel frattempo si fecero a Vienna per strappare un accomodamento, e pratiche si tornarono a fare dai commissari italiani nelle trattative dalle quali uscì fuori la convenzione del 1871. E qui pure torna l'argomento che per la transazione, allora conclusa, e per la somma sborsata dall'Austria in 4,749,000 fiorini, a compenso d'ogni pretesa dell'Italia, anche questa partita è oramai da ritenere fra quelle nelle quali l'Italia subentrava all'Austria a titolo correspettivo.

Il Consiglio di stato, dirimendo un conflitto di attribuzioni suscitato nella causa delle sorelle Nicolini, figlie ed eredi d'uno dei danneggiati, ricorso ai tribunali contro l'amministrazione italiana, decise per la competenza del potere amministrativo a risolvere la controversia.[34]

Ma questa decisione non toglie, nè scema nel Governo nazionale l'impegno di *riconoscere* un debito le tante volte da esso fatto valere come debito del Governo a cui è subentrato. È il caso di attribuire virtù giuridica al titolo che per avventura ne manchi. Poichè, se il debito ha conservata la natura che aveva, il Governo nazionale non lo può soddisfare con le restrizioni e la mala fede che rimproverava all'Austriaco; ma lo deve con quella larghezza con la quale esigeva che lo avesse pagato l'Austriaco, secondo le promesse fatte e i compensi ottenuti.

Oggi, richiesta dei danni non è altrimenti la Sardegna, che li pagò coi 75 milioni quando perdeva la Lombardia, ma è l'Italia; e lo è, ora che ha riscosso il saldo che potè riscuotere per ogni sua pendenza con l'Austria, e, quello che più rileva, dopo acquistata o annessa la Lombardia.

### 7.—*Toscana.*

### Mantenimento delle truppe austriache dal 1849 al 1855.

Ecco una partita che non poteva e che non doveva confondersi coi danni di guerra, coi quali non ha nulla di comune.

Il moto popolare, che nell'11 aprile insanguinò le vie e le piazze della città di Firenze non valse a trattenere i proclami del 5 e 24 maggio, coi quali, per ordine del maresciallo Radetzky, il barone d'Aspre entrava con gli Austriaci in Toscana, e nella stessa Firenze, *chiamato dalgranduca a rassicurarlo sul trono;* e non il manifesto del conte Serristori del 18 maggio 1849 per annunziare *indispensabile il temporaneo intervento di milizie ausiliari ad assicurare permanentemente il trionfo della legge.*

Per la convenzione del 22 aprile 1850, stipulata fra l'imperatore d'Austria e il granduca, restò regolato tutto ciò che si riferiva *al soggiorno in Toscana d'un corpo ausiliare di truppe austriache,* con addossarsi l'Austria *la paga e l'equipaggiamento* e la Toscana tutte *le spese di mantenimento,* dal giorno dell'ingresso delle truppe nel territorio toscano.

La liquidazione venne affidata ad una Commissione con decreto del Governo del 13 giugno; e un decreto granducale del 3 novembre 1850 incaricò la Commissione stessa di liquidare i crediti per queste spese fatte dagli spedali e dalle comunità, alle quali si

[34]La decisione fu proferita quando la presente relazione era in corso di stampa, nel 3 maggio 1873, sulle considerazioni: "Che la controversia di che si tratta si risolve in una questione di partecipazione al reparte dell'indennità assegnata al Governo austriaco col trattato di pace del 1849 a favore dei suoi sudditi danneggiati dalla guerra; che tale reparto per propria natura e nello spirito del trattato, era atto di Governo da compiersi con quei criteri e quelle forme di giustizia distributiva, che appartengono all'amministrazione, anzichè ai tribunali; che in questo senso la considerò lo stesso Governo austriaco, e non havvi ragione per cui possa credersi mutata, col passaggio della Lombardia sotto le leggi italiane."

Il Governo austriaco considerava la questione tanto poco giuridica, che il maresciallo Radetzsky, il quale, nel 18 agosto 1849, aveva nominata la Commissione per liquidare questi danni, negò poi di contemplarli nel reparto; dacchè *la città di Milano pel contegno tenuto nell'epoca della guerra non si è resa meritevole di nessun speciale riguardo.*

Sono parole della istruzione del 12 aprile 1852, letta dall'onorevole Sella nella tornata del 7 marzo 1871.

prometteva il rimborso in un coi frutti che avessero dovuto corrispondere sui capitali presi a imprestito per *supplire a quegli straordinari aggravi per un oggetto che interessa l'universalità dello Stato.*[35]

Gli Austriaci rimasero in Toscana dal 5 maggio 1849 al 30 aprile 1855. E fino a quel giorno dalla relazione presentata nel 17 maggio 1858 dalla Commissione liquidatrice si hanno gli appresso risultati:

| | |
|---|---|
| Somministrazioni fatte dai comuni | L. 8, 844, 052 35 |
| Frutti corrisposti sulle somme dai comuni prese a imprestito | 1, 341, 359 17 |
| Spese inerenti a detti imprestiti | 31, 190 15 |
| Spese d'amministrazione | 40, 789 08 |
| Totale | 10, 357, 390 75 |
| Acconti dati dal Governo | 4, 318, 139 32 |
| Resta da pagare ai comuni | 6, 039, 251 43 |

Noto in questo conto Arezzo per circa lire 200,000, Lucca per 300,000, Pisa per 500,000, Pistoia per 100,000, Prato per 150,000, Siena per 100,000, e, se Livorno per un milione e mezzo, la città di Firenze, essa sola, per 3,200,000 lire, a cifre tonde.

Caduto il Governo granducale, il procuratore generale della Corte dei conti, con rapporto del 10 settembre 1860 propose di portare in giorno quella liquidazione e di soddisfare i comuni con tanti buoni fruttiferi sulla depositeria. E il barone Ricasoli, allora governatore generale della Toscana, nel 29 settembre decretò ambedue le proposte del procuratore generale. Se non che una deliberazione presa in Consiglio dei ministri a Torino nel 22 ottobre sospese la esecuzione del decreto del Ricasoli.

Chiedeva il Governo centrale informazioni sulla posizione di quei crediti; intanto che sulla emissione dei *Buoni* sollevò la questione costituzionale.

Interrogato, il Consiglio di stato con voto del 16 marzo 1861 ammise in genere il credito dei comuni, ma dubitò sui frutti, sulle spese e anche sulle tariffe aplicate per gli alloggi, stallaggi, trasporti e vetture.

Non così la Commissione istituita col decreto del 7 settembre 1860 nel Ministero della guerra, non così l'avvocato patrimoniale regio, e non così il referendario al Consiglio di stato, commendatore Bruzzo che ne riferì, d'incarico dei due ministri dell'interno e della guerra. Poichè la Commissione con rapporto del 28 agosto 1861, l'avvocato patrimoniale col voto dell'8 giugno 1862 e il commendatore Bruzzo col parere del 1° dicembre 1864 conclusero concordemente, avere i comuni toscani sostenute le spese di mantenimento delle truppe austriache per ordine e conto dello Stato, doversi ai medesimi comuni il rimborso del capitale anticipato, più dei frutti corrisposti, e delle spese incontrate, comparir *disperato* pel Governo l'assunto di difendersi dalle azioni che da quei creditori si fossero cimentate ai tribunali.

Si trattò allora fra la direzione del contenzioso e i comuni più interessati un accomodamento e se ne combinarono le basi. Ma di nuovo sentito, il Consiglio di stato propose nuovi dubbi, articolò nuove incertezze e suggerì nuove difese sopra alcune partite della liquidazione.

Le difese suggerite si spiegarono per conto dello Stato contro il comune di Livorno che primo ricorse al tribunale civile di Firenze. E il tribunale civile di Firenze, con sentenza del 23 marzo 1869, dette causa vinta al comune di Livorno su tutti i punti, rigettate con le antiche le difese nuove della finanza. Dopo questa sentenza, sicuri del fatto loro, i comuni di Firenze e di Pisa riassunsero la lite, ella finanza, nella *disperazione* di vincere, finalmente si appigliò al conflitto.

Il prefetto di Firenze lo decretò sul fondamento, che obbligazione, nascente dal prin cipio di *gius pubblico internazionale*, pel nuovo di pagare i debiti dello Stato vecchio, è solo *morale*, ed aspetta per tradursi in *civile* una legge di ricognizione del debito da parte di esso Stato nuovo.

Era il principio che leggesi riprodotto dalla relazione e che la vostra Giunta rifiuta, d'accordo in ciò, con l'ultima giurisprudenza del Consiglio di stato. Il quale, se coi decreti del 17 agosto 1870 nella causa coi comuni di Firenze e di Pisa, accolse il *conflitto*, lo accolse per un *motivo* e con intendimenti diversi affatto da quelli per cui venne decretato dal prefetto.

Avvertì il Consiglio che nel decreto del 1850 il Governo granducale ordinò ai comuni di fornire alle truppe austriache viveri e casermaggio, riservandosi di provvedere a suo tempo al rimborso della spesa, o *con farvi contribuire tutti i comuni del granducato*, o con fondi della depositeria; e considerò che lo sciogliere questa espressa riserva o il compierre l'atto governativo non potendo competere che al Governo, si era sempre nel periodo del *disporre* e non per anche entrati in quello del *giudicare*.

Può essere stata intenzione del Governo granducale di accennare con la sua riserva

[35] Allegato n° 1.

anche al partito di *far contribuire tutti i comuni* a una spesa che non era giusto pesasse sopra pochi soltanto e in proporzioni tanto disuguali. Fatto è che nella riserva il decreto non contienne *parola* di allusione a questo *contributo* dei comuni o a questo modo di *perequazione*.

Al Consiglio di stato inoltre sfuggì che quella vaga riserva del decreto, dal Governo toscano era stata dimenticata o già sciolta c l *tempo*, col *fatto* e con gli spiegati *propositi*. *Col tempo;* dal 1850 in poi il Governo toscano nulla avend disposto per *distribuire o ripartire* la spesa, e avendo anzi tutto disposto per accollarla sull'erario, come voleva la qualità sua di spesa interessante la *universalità dello Stato*. *Col fatto;* dacchè il Governo toscano liquidò il debito come se fosse tutto suo, e vi pagò tanti acconti da eccedere i *quattro decimi* del debito risultato dalla sua liquidazione finale del 1858. E coi *propositi;* poichè tanto il pegno sulle miniere dell'Elba con la casa Bastogi del 1851, quanto i tre milioni di rendita consolidata al 3 per cento stata emessa nel 1852, dal Governo toscano si decretarono con la dichiarazione espressa di servirsene a saldare le spese per le truppe *ausiliari*.[36] Furono spese costate ben più che 25 milioni, dei quali non erano che un resto i sei a credito dei comuni, risultati dalla liquidazione del 1858. E notisi che molta parte del consolidato trovavasi tuttora invenduta quando nel 27 aprile del 1859 cadde il Governo, che lasciò non saldato quel resto.

Il Consiglio di stato ignorava le circolari del Governo toscano e i suoi carteggi coi comuni per regolare un debito dal Governo constantemente ritenuto debito erariale; il Consiglio di stato non sapeva che il comune di Firenze si forniva e fornisce le necessarie risorse sopra cambiali, nelle quali, per una somma che ora eccede le 700,000 lire, trovasi impegnata la firma del Governo nazionale, come prima lo era del Governo toscano. Erano cambiali firmate prima dal direttore dei conti della depositeria, che ora lo sono dall'intendente di finanza e che di mano in mano che scad no, si rinnovavano e rinnovano alla Banca Nationale toscana per una somma cresciuta dello *sconto*.

In ogni modo, non è punto esatto quanto afferma la relazione, che nei decreti del 17 agosto 1870 il Consiglio di stato negasse ai comuni toscani per questo credito *azione civilmente esperibile contro il Governo italiano*. Avrebbe allora professata una massima troppo apertamente disdetta dai motivi delle recenti sue decisioni sui conflitti nelle cause *Trevisani e Ranucci*. La verità è che i decreti del 17 agosto 1870 furono di *semplice effetto sospensivo*, interlocutori non definitivi, o intesi allo scioglimento di una riserva, nel falso supposto che fosse sempre da sci gliere, e relativa al modo del pagamento, non all'accertamento, e non alla ricognizione del credito dei comuni. Se per quei decreti rimaneva da provvedere al modo del pagamento, anzichè contraddire, si ammetteva che si era un debito da pagare. No, l'azione civile ai comuni toscani non è stata mai contraddetta da nessun consulente, e nemmeno dal Consiglio di stato, come è stata, per sentenza dei tribunali riconosciuta ed ammessa.

La pendenza dura infine da troppo tempo per lasciarsi più a lungo non sistemata; essa non rimane cagione ultima se i bilanci della città di Firenze, la quale avanza più che la metà della somma, si trovano come si trovano. Creditori sono i comuni, non l'imperatore d'Austria e non il già granduca di Toscana. A chi ami con le *giuridiche* di mescolare le considerazioni *politiche*, la storia contemporanea ricorda, non solo che le truppe austriache stanziarono in Toscana come *ausiliari*, non come truppe *nemiche*, per convenzione, non per *fatto di guerra*, ma di più che in quelli anni Austria e Toscano vissero in tanto pace che fu alleanza; e che quest'alleanza, costò alla casa di Lorena il granducato, e fruttò al paese l'annettersi al regno, diventato regno d'Italia.

In Toscano non si aveva questione amministrativa e non si ebbe *mal governo;* in Toscana la questione *politica* data dai proclami dei generali tedeschi del maggio 1849.

### 8.—*Requisizioni militari del* 1859.

Nella guerra del 1859 si hanno somministrazioni militari e requisizioni per molti milioni.

Le provincie *ex-pontificie* presentarono per questo titolo una nota, dall'*allegato* ridotta presuntivamente a lire 613,156 62.

La *Lombardia* vi è portata per lire 12,241,279 24, ma con le *requisizioni* e *forniture* militari vi sono mescolate da un lato le *espropriazioni* e dall'altro i *danni della guerra*.

Anche *Parma* la sua cifra di lire 100,502 39 la ottiene con aggiungere alle requisizioni partite da riferire a danni di guerra.

*Modena* ha una storia speciale. Poichè due decreti del Governo provvisorio del 9 luglio e 4 dicembre 1859 riconoscono il credito di quei comuni nella somma stata poi liquidata in lire 250,283 36, e ne ordinano il pagamento, che essi aspettano ancora.

Le provincie che patirono le più forti requisizioni e i più gravi danni nella guerra del 1859 furono le provincie di *Novara della Lomellina* e di *Vercelli*. Di Novara è calcolata di lire 1,905,570 98; della Lomellina dall'allegato si calcola una sofferenza di lire 6,122,541 43; Vercelli vi fu dimenticata.

---

[36] È un proposito espresso tanto nel decreto del 10 giugno 1851, col quale si costituì un debito di 12 milioni sulle miniere, quanto nella relazione che precedè l'altro decreto del 3 novembre 1852, col quale si costituì il debito di tre milioni di rendita (lire toscane).

La storia ha registrati i feroci proclami coi quali Zobel annunziava la invasione degli Austriaci nella Lomellina, nel Novarese e nel Vercellese, provincie lasciate senza impiegati e senza armi dal Governo sardo per accorgimento di guerra al rompersi delle ostilità.

Se vi sono danni che meritassero un'equa ripartizione su tutte le provincie dello Stato, sembrano veramente i patiti per la causa comune da provincie abbandonate per ragioni di strategia, e che pagarono le pubbliche imposte anche del tempo che invece di governo durò su loro la invasione nemica. È un caso dove la ragione politica s'intreccia con la equità giuridica, con quella equità che non è grazia ma trionfo della giustizia, in quanto tempera nell'applicazione quel sommo *gius* che, rigidamente applicato, diventerebbe ingiuria somma.

Se non i danni, le requisizioni almeno bisognerà pertanto pagarle. Anche perchè furono i sindaci, capi dei comuni e ufficiali del Governo, i quali si adoperarono a mitigare spesso la rapacità tedesca nelle richieste, e sempre il danno dei requisiti nel modo di corrispondervi. Com'è vero, che in gran parte ne diventarono creditori gli stessi comuni, i quali, per pagare i *buoni* ai requisiti, dovettero indebitarsi per forti somme. Se la legge del 28 luglio 1861, n° 140, venne in loro soccorso, con mettere, a carico dei proventi dello Stato sulla cassa dei depositi e prestiti, l'interesse, oltre il 2½ per cento, delle somme dalla cassa imprestate per questo titolo a quei comuni, questi rimangono tuttavia debitori del capitale.

*Confische.*

Tacerò delle confische del *tirannello* di casa d'Este, e delle quali una Commissione speciale nel 1867 liquidava i danni in lire 494,994 56, non contati i beni da potersi nella maggior parte restituire in natura alle famiglie dei condannati.

Un decreto del Farini del 23 agosto 1859, mentre ordinava la immediata restituzione dei beni confiscati al generale Zucchi, senza pagamento di frutti, questa massima voleva applicata nei casi in esame della Commissione, da lui stesso nominata a rivedere i processi politici e a *proporre i modi equi di riparare in qualche guisi i danni recati alle disgraziate famiglie dalle confische e dalle arbitrarie distribuzioni dei loro beni.* Nessun dubbio pertanto che nel concetto stesso di questi decreti solo un atto legislativo possa abolire condanne e restituir beni confiscati per sentenza, e riparare con modi equi i danni conseguenti.

La Commissione vostra, ciò non ostante ha creduto doversi astenere da un argomento che si discostava troppo dal soggetto di una legge sui danni di guerra. A lei è parsa questa, tale materia da rinviare ad una legge a parte, quale si fece per indennizzare gli impiegati civili e militari, stati interrotti nella loro carriera per ragione politica. Essa è scesa in questa sentenza anche perchè, meglio di una legge generale, o che per generali definizioni ripari alle confische politiche di Modena, e che bisognerebbe estendere a quelle dei Borboni di Napoli, potrebbe comparire conveniente il provvedere con tante leggi speciali, caso per caso. E che si provveda la Commissione sollecita col suo voto e ne muove le più calde raccomandazioni.

*Sicilia e Napoli.*

Non una parola si spende dall'allegato per la Sicilia. E la ragione è questa, che ivi i danneggiatti dalle truppe borboniche si risarcirono con le rendite delle opere pie, fidecommissarie e istituti di beneficenza, in virtù dei decreti di Garibaldi del 18 maggio e 9 giugno 1860. La legge del 2 aprile 1865, anzichè disdire, regolò la esecuzione di quei decreti, facendo versare le somme dovute dalle opere pie nell'erario, con imporre a carico del bilancio dello Stato il pagamento dei buoni e degli interessi dei buoni rilasciati in pagamento ai danneggiati, per effetto dei decreti reali del 31 agosto 1861 e 18 novembre 1862. Di questi buoni si rilasciarono per circa cinque milioni; e nel bilancio dell'entrata del 1872 si hanno trasporti sulla competenza del 1872 e per residui attivi del 1871 e retro, di lire 3,075,000. La Sicilia non poteva dunque figurare nel conto.

Se *Napoli* vi è notato, e per lire 1,739,104 17, non è per danni di guerra o requisizioni, ma per un credito accampato in maggior somma dal *Cassitto*, fornitore degli eserciti meridionali.

Era il Cassitto proveditore generale delle sussistenze militari nelle provincie napoletane e siciliane, per contratto del 30 novembre 1867, fatto col Governo borbonico, per sei anni, dal primo gennaio 1858 alla fine del 1863.

Nel 1860 il Cassitto si trovò a fornire e fornì truppe borboniche, truppe garibaldine e truppe regolari italiane, e dall'intreccio o passaggio dall'uno all'altro servizio ne sorsero contestazioni di liquidazione e di competenza passiva su molte partite di spese o di provviste.

Con legge del 25 gennaio 1865, n° 2118 si dichiarò bene che *le somministrazioni fatte alle truppe borboniche non sarano ammesse a pagamento se non in quanto furono anteriori al 14 maggio 1860 per ciò che riguarda la Sicilia, e al 7 di settembre 1860 per quelle che si effet-*

*tuarono nelle provincie napoletane.* Ma, nonostante questa dichiarazione, la lite non potè risparmiarsi.

La intendenza militare, sull'appoggio delle conclusioni della Commissione liquidatrice istituita in Torino, sosteneva il Cassitto debitore di lire 1,458,069 33 avanti il tribunale di commercio di Napoli, che dichiarò invece creditore il Cassitto di lire 983,883 92. Da questa sentenza appellarono tanto la intendenza quanto il Cassitto. E la Corte di Napoli, dicidendo sui due appelli, con sentenza del 16 dicembre 1867 ridusse il credito del Cassitto a lire 818,978 77. Neppure a questa decisione della Corte d'appello si acquietarono i contendenti, che ambi la denunziarono alla Corte suprema di cassazione di Napoli. La quale, con decreto pubblicato nel 13 febbraio 1873, rigettò il ricorso di tutti e due.

È dunque caso contenzioso, e portato a tali termini da non cercare altro che la esecusione del giudicato.

*Mantova e Piacenza.*

Delle somministrazioni militari e delle espropriazioni del 1859 nell'allegato scritte a *Mantova* per una somma presunta de lire 1,233,189 14, conviene meglio che io mi trattenga in un con quelle del 1866, alle quali discendo, dacchè sono dominate dagli stessi principii. E toccherò allora delle lire 997,710 14 per espropriazioni di *Piacenza*, e come sienno da cancellare dal conto.

9.—*Espropriazioni e somministrazioni militari nel Veneto e Mantovano del* 1859 *e* 1866.

Il Codice civile austriaco ha due articoli o paragrafi, il 365 sulle espropriazioni nel capo 2° *del diritto della proprietà*, e il 1044 sui danni di guerra nel capo 22 *del mandato e di altra specie d'amministrazione degli affari.*

"§ 365. Quando l'utilità pubblica lo essiga deve ciascun membro dello Stato cedere anche la sua piena proprietà contro una conveniente indennizzazione.

"§ 1044. La ripartizione dei danni di guerra viene regolata dalle attorità politiche dietro norme speciali."

Coi rescritti o risoluzioni del 5 aprile 1816, 19 febbraio 1819, 20 maggio 1820 l'Austria provvide ai danneggiatti dalle guerre del primo regno italico. Dopo la guerra del 1859 diramò le istruzioni del 9 agosto 1861, con le quali ammise *a compenso le effettive prestazioni militari e i danni derivati alle proprietà.*

Per esse istruzioni *le espropriazioni dei fondi a uso permanente, e così pure le servitù speciali addossate ai fondi privati per iscopi di strategia militare*, non che i *danni derivati dall'occupazione e dalla distruzione di edifizi, o per iscopi passeggeri di strategia militare* sono compensati ai proprietari; ai quali, a norma del § 935 del Codice civile e della risoluzione del 4 maggio 1837 vengono altresì corrisposti gli interessi di mora del 4 per cento, *decorribili dal momento dell'apprensione e rispettivamente da quello della occupazione passeggera della proprietà* fino al pagamento o al deposito giudiciale del compenso.

E nel § 16 è detto: "Le parti, che non si ritenessero soddisfatte delle decisioni emesse e dei compensi loro assegnati, saranno rimesse alla via civile."[37]

In Austria lo Stato compensa:

1° Le prestazioni militari per le imperiali e reali truppe, cioè, l'*acquartieramento, le vetture militari o carriaggi in uso nel paese, le somministrazioni, forniture e requisizioni d'oggetti in natura, viveri, foraggi, traghetti, lavori in generale*, ecc.;

2° Le espropriazioni di terreni per iscopi militari;

3° I danneggiamenti di beni privati, in causa ad ordini degli imperiali e reali comandanti di truppe o delle imperiali e reali autorità per iscopi strategici.

(*I danni causati dalle operazioni militari non vengono compensati sa avvenuti in seguito a combattimenti o movimenti di marcia. Così pure i danni fortuiti o causati da disordini non danno diritto a compenso.*)

*Dei danni commessi per petulanza è responsabile chi ne è l'autore.* (Decreto *aulico del* 10 *aprile* 1821.)

Sono i principii riassunti nella notificazione pubblicata a Trieste nel 16 ottobre 1866 dall'Austria, per essere applicati alle provincie rimaste a lei, al di là dell'Isonzo.[38] E sono, del resto, i principii del *Vattel*, ed amessi nella giurisprudenza di tutti i popoli civili.

L'Austria dopo la guerra del 1859, in applicazione di questi stessi principii, pagò nel VENETO e MANTOVANO 2,997,160 fiorini 44 e mezzo, sopra fiorini 3,496,602 04 e mezzo stati liquidati. E un dispaccio del Ministero viennese del 13 marzo 1866, n° 1138, aveva ordinato di saldare la partita, salvo pei proprietari il provare la proprietà e libertà dei fondi colpiti. Fu dopo la guerra che l'Austria dichiarò cessati *i suoi impegni* verso le popolazioni. Come fu dopo la pace che l'Italia concluse con l'Austria le convenzioni di Firenze.

*Nessuna obiezione può effettivamente sollevarsi riguardo ai danni di guerra del* 1859, *ove si consideri che essi furono liquidati senza eccezione alcuna ed ammessi a pagamento.* Così la direzione generale del Tesoro nel 21 dicembre 1869 scriveva alla Commissione liquida-

[37] Allegato n° 3. [38] Allegati numeri 4, 5, 6 e 7.

trice istituita in Firenze presso il Ministero della guerra col regio decreto del 26 maggio 1867. E le lire 1,233,189 14 dell'*allegato*, rappresentano appunto il montare complessivo delle domande pervenute a essa Commissione.

Della guerra del 1866 le *venete e mantovana* sono le sole provincie notate nell'allegato; e lo sono per lire 18,007,340 21, divise in sei partite.

Della *prima* partita di lire 2,877,553 35, per *contratti d'appalto per lavori, provviste, prestazioni d'opere e simili*, la Commissione istituita col regio decreto del 26 maggio 1867 non ritenne ammissibili le domande che per lire 177,804 64, rigetatte le altre o sospese.

Le lire 305,061 18 *per espropriazioni ed acquisti di stabili*, notate in secondo luogo, constituiscono forse la sola fra tutte le partite dell'*allegato* che potrebbe rientrare nell'articolo 1 del progetto di legge ministeriale, dato che gli espropriati riescano a provare, secondo ivi è prescritto, *il tempo e il modo dell'espropriazione patita, la data della domanda o delle domande d'indennità rimaste insoddisfatte;* e bene inteso che i fondi espropriati *sieno tenuti tuttora dal Governo italiano*, e che il Governo italiano non si decida a restituirli *nello stato in cui si trovano attualmente.*

Non così la *terza* partita di lire 8,280,887 79 *per abbattimento di piante e fabricati intorno alle fortificazioni.*

La guerra non era per anche dichiarata, che l'Austria, prevedendola, volle costruire nuovi, e munire i suoi forti, con allargarne il raggio delle zone, da lasciar libero all'azione dei fuochi dei canoni di nuovo modello.

Fu allora che si abbatterono le piante e i fabricati intorno alle fortezze; in esecuzione di ordini dell'imperiale e reale commissariato generale dell'armata del sud del 31 maggio 1866, dell'imperiale e reale comando della città e fortezza di Verona dell'11 agosto e dell'imperiale e reale direzione militare del genio del 15 di detto mese, i quali disposero per l'accertamento dei danni a cura della solita Commissione mista, civile e militare, in applicazione all'articolo 365 del Codice e delle istruzioni del 1861.

La Commissione mista cessò dai suoi lavori solamente il 22 ottobre, o 19 giorni dopo firmata la pace, e cessò dopo avere, ai più fra i danneggiati, rilasciato un protocollo intestato così: "In seguito alla rispettata ordinanza 11 agosto 1866, nº 3857, dell'imperiale e reale comando di città e fortezza, l'imperiale e reale direzione del genio, allo scopo di riconoscere i titoli d'indennizzo e di ventilare l'importo dei danni pegli effetti del paragrafo 365 dell'imperante Codice civile austriaco, radunò una Commissione mista, composta dei membri seguenti, ecc., ecc.

Nessun dubbio pertanto che per l'Austria non fosse questo un debito regolato dal paragrafo 365 del Codice civile, o al quale non si avessero ad applicare le istruzioni del 1861, con quel loro *paragrafo* 16: "Le parti che non si ritenessero soddisfatte delle del cisioni emesse e dei compensi loro assegnati, saranno rimesse alla via civile."

L'Austria, autorizzata dal Governo di Parma con la convenzione del 14 marzo 1822, aveva atterate case e piante intorno alla fortezza di Piacenza. E i Piacentini, che non furono in tempo a farsi pagare dall'Austria, chiesero pagamento all'Italia. Sono le loro domande che si trovano nell'allegato per lire 997,710 14; ma ho già detto che la è partita da cancellare, ed ora aggiungo il perchè.

I *Piacentini* ricorsero ai tribunali, e *Antona-Traversi* fra gli altri riportò sentenza di condanna a carico dell'amministrazione italiana. La quale, per non esporsi ad altre condanne, ha transatto e pagato, a ciò confortata dal Consiglio di stato.[39]

Gli atterramenti delle piante intorno Alessandria e Casale erano già stati pagati da un pezzo;[40] e se questi furono opera delle autorità italiane, si ordinarono dalle austriache gli atterramenti degli alberi intorno a Pavia, dall'amministrazione italiana risarciti appena da ieri.[41]

La eccezione della incompetenza dei tribunali, e poi il conflitto di attribuzioni, risparmiati ai Piacentini e ai Pavesi, si riservarono pei Veronesi e a quei di Rovigo. Ed è naturale che i Veronesi e quei di Rovigo non debbano saper buon grado all'amministrazione italiana di questo privilegio così odioso per loro. Tanto più naturale, che della nota del 15 giugno 1869, scritta dal Digny, ministro delle finanze, al ministro degli esteri, e dall'ufficio dell'11 settembre del Bertolè-Viale ai Veronesi, il credito ne pareva ed era riconosciuto dal ministero italiano.[42]

La *quarta* partita è notata in lire 2,277,767 46 per requisizioni militari; e, di queste, lire 88,888 40 per somministrazioni, non per anche regolate dall'amministrazione austriaca, fatte fra il 1859 ed il 1866; mentre la maggior somma, o lire 2,188,879 06, rientrano tutte nel periodo della guerra del 1866.

Per l'approvigionamento delle truppe mobilizzate trovasi disposto, *che le somministrazioni fatte in dipendenza di requisizioni militari, sia in tempo di pace che di guerra all'imperiale e reale esercito in territorio dello Stato, od in quello di potenza amica, devono essere pagate a coloro che le hanno effettuate.*

Infatti le somministrazioni non solo si sono sempre dall'Austria pagate, ma, mobiliz-

[39] V. Pareri del 10 luglio 1865, 28 febbraio 1868, 12 luglio 1870 e 5 maggio 1871, *Sezione di finanza.* E vedasi l'allegato nº 4, al capitolo 41 del bilancio definitivo della guerra del 1872.

[40] V. Pareri del Consiglio di Stato del 14 luglio e 21 ottobre 1865.

[41] V. Parere dell'11 aprile 1873.

[42] Al momento che scrivo, il Consiglio di stato non si e ancora pronunziato sui conffitti avanti a lui pendenti nelle cause coi veronesi e quei di Rovigo.

zata appena l'armata, con notificazione luogotenziale del 25 giugno 1866 si provvide a *meglio garantire i comuni e gli individui chiamati a prestare somministrazioni a vantaggio del militare, e a metterli immediatamente in possesso d'un titolo legalmente valido e trasmissibile anche a terze persone, e con circolare dello stesso giorno si prescrissero norme per ovviare alle difficoltà incontrate nelle liquidazioni delle prestazioni fatte al militare nella guerra del* 1859.

Con la notificazione del 16 ottobre 1866, tredici giorni dopo sottoscritta la pace, l'Austria provvide ai suoi debiti per somministrazioni militari nelle provincie a lei soggette. L'Italia non ancora ha provvisto ai propri.

Il quale confronto alla deputazione provinciale di Udine nella sua petizione al Parlamento nazionale strappa il ricordo che il *regio commissario* nel 15 settembre del 1866 scriveva in *Resiutta*, rioccupata dagli imperiali dopo l'armistizio di Cormons, per lodarne la deputazione comunale del contegno tenuto di fronte al commissariato di Moggio, per avvertirla che i patti dell'armistizio non assicuravano agli Austriaci alcuna ingerenza civile nei paesi temporaneamente occupati da loro, e per infervorarla a continuare a non prestare obbedienza al commissariato distrettuale. Solo alle domande del militare, se *scritte*, ivi s'inculca il rispetto. *Rispetti cotesta deputazione le domande del militare austriaco quando siano scritte.*

Delle lire 336,678 10 della *quinta* partita, la Commissione non ammise domande che per lire 117,196 92, e anche queste da liquidare. Ivi si parla *d'occupazioni temporanee d'immobili.* E se e dove l'occupazione, sebbene temporanea, sia avvenuta in apparecchio di difesa prima del rompere delle ostilità, il danno sarà da risarcire. Come sarà solamente da lamentare il danno di un'occupazione per opere di difesa passeggiera fatte in presenza del nemico, per accampamenti, marcie, e per prendere una posizione.

Dopo la ritirata di Custoza avanti *alla testa di ponte di San Rocco al porto* si atterrarono piante, e improvvisarono alcune opere di difesa, con danno dei proprietari. Con parere del 28 febbraio 1868 il Consiglio di stato si pronunziò per una transazione coi danneggiati. Poichè nel carattere del danno riscontrò mistura di *fatale* e di *volontario ;* di *fatale* nel fatto bellico che aveva determinato l'atterramento delle piante, di *volontario* nelle condizioni nelle quali già era costituita Piacenza, *di punto preordinato di difesa.*

Nell'*ultima* partita di lire 3,929,392 33 siamo in tema di danni veri di guerra o di danni di guerra guerreggiata, *bivacchi, depredazioni, devastazioni, sperperi, taglie.* È il caso non più del § 365, ma tutt'al più del § 1044 del Codice civile austriaco; cioè, non è che l'autorità politica che assegnare possa e ripartire indennità; o siamo nel terreno della equità, della politica convenienza, ed anche della finanziaria, usciti fuori dal campo del diritto.

La Prussia fu ed è larga indennizzatrice di chiunque patí nella guerra e per la guerra del 1870; ma non importa ricordare quanto sia stata nelle sue larghezze incoraggiata dai cinque miliardi imposti da lei sulla Francia debellata, e che la Francia con meraviglia del mondo le ha pagati in sì breve tempo. È piuttosto degno di nota che la stessa Francia, nel momento che scrivo, con la legge del 7 aprile 1873, soccorre con 140 milioni Parigi, e con 120 milioni i dipartimenti invasi daiprussiani.

Non è ancora la *perequazione*, secondo la moderna filosofia del diritto, fra i *soci* del danno per alcuno patito a benefizio o per causa della *società ;* non è ancora il reparto fra tutti i *cittadini* o *nazionali* del danno cagionato a uno o a pochi dalla guerra, intrapresa a nome e per conto della *città* o *nazione ;* ma è qualche cosa che gli somiglia, o che si studia d'assomigliargli.

## IL PROGETTO DI LEGGE DELLA COMMISSIONE.

Signori! La legge *non disponendo che per l'avvenire*, la vostra Giunta, se poteva proporvi una legge *attributiva* di diritti, ha dovuto guardarsi dal proporvene una la quale attentasse al diritto di chi lo ha, o che creda di averlo. Essa non poteva nè volle attentare al diritto di chi lo ha, contro l'articolo 29, pel quale *tutte le proprietà, senz'alcuna eccezione, sono inviolabili*, nè proferire decisioni per le quali potesse alcuno *essere distolto dai suoi giudici naturali*, contro l'articolo 21 dello Statuto.

La Commissione si è studiata di formulare e ha formulato un disegno di legge che stanziasse i fondi per dimettere i debiti che stimava già debiti nazionali; lo stanziamento dei fondi o la iscrizione in bilancio di una partita d'uscita o di una rendita nel Gran Libro, essendo prerogativa del potere legislativo. Essa poteva altresì proporvi e vi propone d'ammettere a pagamento quelle partite sulle quali, se dubbioso il diritto, le appariva imperiosa pel Governo nazionale la ragione politica di provvedere. E tutto ciò combinando le sue proposte con lo spirito di non frastornare il piano dal ministro delle finanze seguito con tanta lodevole costanza per giungere al pareggio. Ma in pari tempo senza pregiudicare ad alcun diritto nè ad alcuna pretesa.

A compiuta soluzione dell'intricato problema, la Commissione ha distribuite le partite dell'*allegato* in tre categorie.

Ha situati nella *prima* i debiti delle amministrazioni permanenti, sostituite dall'italiana nel 1859, 1860, 1866 e 1870, e i quali, secondo gli ordinamenti di allora, si sarebbero pagati o dovuti pagare. E a questi debiti ha destinato tanto consolidato 5 per cento, da conteggiare al cento di capitale per ogni cinque di rendita.

Sotto questa categoria sarebbero, a giudizio della Commissione, da riportare quelle notate nell'*allegato*,

La partita *prima* delle espropriazioni e somministrazioni militari, appropriazioni di stabili del Governo italico;

Le rimanenze del prestito napoletano del 1848, quando se ne trovino;

La partita *settima* del mantenimento delle truppe austriache in Toscana dal 1849 al 1855;

E la *nona* in quanto si riferisce a lavori e prestazioni di opere, a espropriazioni e acquisti di stabili, ad atterramenti di piante e case intorno alle fortezze.

Nella categoria *seconda* ha collocati i debiti lasciati dai Governi provvisorii del 1848, le provviste e requisizioni regolarmente accertate, sia per le truppe nazionali nella guerra del 1848–49, sia fatte dall'Austria nelle guerre del 1848 e 1849 in Italia, fuori del lombardo-veneto, e nelle guerre del 1859 e del 1866 in lombardia, nel veneto e mantovano. E, in pagamento di questi debiti, la Commissione ha destinato tanto consolidato 3 per cento, da conteggiare al cento di capitale per ogni tre di rendita.

Sotto la quale categoria, a suo giudizio, cadrebbero:

La partita *quarta* formati dagli imprestiti dei Governi provvisorii di Roma, della Lombardia, della Venezia, compresi i depositi colpiti dalle restrizioni del 1852, esclusa dal novero la carta ritirata dal corso in Venezia e Roma.

La partita *quinta* delle requisizioni e somministrazioni nelle provincie ex-pontificie, di Lombardia, di Parma e Piacenza, di Modena, della Sicilia, tutte del 1848–49, e della stessa natura o derivazione.

La partita *sesta* dell'incendio delle case del suburbio di Milano nella memorabile notte dal 4 al 5 agosto 1848.

La partita *ottava* delle requisizioni militari del 1859 nelle provincie ex-pontificie, nella Lombardia, in Parma e Piacenza, in Modena e Reggio, e più che tutto nelle provincie di Novara, di Vercelli e della Lomellina;

E la *nona* in quanto si riferisce alle requisizioni del Veneto e Mantovano tanto del 1859 che del 1866, non senza un qualche scrupolo della Commissione. La quale, se nemmeno le requisizioni del 1866 riportò alla categoria prima, fu per aver fatto delle *requisizioni* una sola classe, e anche perchè nel 1866 l'Austria sentiva già mancarle il territorio della Venezia e di Mantova, e lo trattò da nemico più deciso a cederlo che a difenderlo.

Così rimarrebbero per la terza categoria, cioè senza sistemazione o rinviate:

*a*) Le partite *seconda* e *terza* che parvero fuori del tema, la partita *seconda* degli ospizi civili di Borgo San Donnino; la partita *terza* del prestito nazionale napoletano del 1821, di cui non si hanno spiegazioni della rimanenza;

*b*) Le *confische* alle quali sembra che sia da riparare con provvedimenti legislativi speciali;

*c*) Le requisizioni nel Lombardo-Veneto del 1848 e 1849, regolate già dall'Austria col sistema della *perequazione;*

*d*) Gli scapiti nel cambio fatto dai passati Governi di monete patriottiche;

*e*) I veri danni della guerra, che poco più poco meno afflissero pressochè tutte le provincie del regno.

Caduto il primo impero di Francia, l'Austria col mezzo di speciale Commissione liquidò i debiti da esso lasciati nel Lombardo-Veneto, pagando in denaro i depositi giudiziari o fatti con la cassa d'ammortizzazione, e in titoli di rendita *alla pari* con garanzia di un corso più o meno vicino al nominale a seconda della diversa natura dei debiti.[43]

Nel Piemonte si commise a una Giunta provvisoria di classare il debito e il credito dello Stato riferibile all'epoca francese, e si assegnarono termini ai creditori per esibire i titoli, e alla Commissione per compiere il suo lavoro.[44]

La prova più eloquente che l'Italia ha tenuta e tiene la sua amministrazione rispetto ai creditori dello Stato come una *continuazione* delle amministrazioni anteriori, si ha nel fatto che, si sono liquidate per mezzo di Commissioni alcune speci di pendenze, ma per sistema, invece di nominare Commissioni liquidatrici, si è continuato a pagare come se nulla fosse successo.

Dacchè una eccezione si è tuttavia creduto di farla pei debiti, che hanno formato soggetto della relazione, e dacchè si sta per restituire la condizione di *diritto* a partite che l'avevano perduta, spontanea venne l'idea di affidare a una Commissione il liquidare ciò che ancora non sia liquidato, assegnando termini perentorii tanto pei creditori a esibire i propri titoli, che per la Commissione a chiudere le sue liquidazioni.

A esaurimento infine del tema, la Commissione aggiunge un articolo, pel quale si renda palese che vuolsi attribuire un *diritto* ai contemplati nelle nuove disposizioni, e imporre un'*obbligazione* al Governo; non si vuole imporre la obbligazione ai creditori di subire, o attribuire un diritto al Governo d'imporre il disposto trattamento a coloro che non intendessero di accettarlo.

Chi lo rifiutasse non diventerebbe creditore in virtù della nuova legge, e come *avente interesse*, al quale la nuova legge nulla dà e nulla toglie, gli resterebbero le ragioni tali

[43] Notificazioni del 13 dicembre 1814 e del 1° marzo 1816. [44] Regie patenti del 29 ottobre 1816.

quali risultassero protette dalle vigenti leggi e coi modi per farle valere consentiti dalle istituzioni che ci reggono.

È bene a prevedere che ai contemplati dall'articolo 1 del progetto di legge del Ministero, e ad alcuni fra gli altri dell'allegato, alletterà poco un pagamento che li sottopone a scapitare circa un quarto del loro credito. Ed è appunto in vista di ciò che la Commissione e vuol libero il Governo di trattarli come trattò i Piacentini e liberi i creditori d'insistere per essere pagati in contanti.

Per quelli i quali non vorranno accettare il trattamento disposto con la nuova legge, o che per transazione o per sentenza bisognasse invece pagare in contanti, come a contanti si pagarono i danneggiati per le fortificazioni di Piacenza, ci vorrà una nuova legge, o speciale o del bilancio, che stanzi i fondi, dalla legge proposta stanziati fin d'ora in pagamento di quelli i quali consentiranno di essere pagati con titoli di rendita. Questa è la posizione, e non altra, fatta dalla proposta della vostra Commissione, nell'intendimento suo di non turbare alcuna attribuzione e di non offendere alcun diritto.

La Commissione dapprima carezzò l'idea di concepire la riserva con tali parole che garantissero tanto quelli di prima che di seconda e anche di terza categoria, i quali avessero voluto cimentare le loro pretese, che avrebbero trovata sempre la via dei tribunali dischiusa o non intercettata da decreti di conflitto. La incertezza con la quale si è contenuto il Governo che anche per titoli della stessa natura ora oppose, ora no, la declinatoria dei tribunali, e una giurisprudenza non per anche ben ferma, tentavano a raffermare legislativamente una conclusione, quale, del resto, appariva con bastante chiarezza stabilita fin dall'articolo 2 dell'allegato *E* alla legge del 20 marzo 1865.

Considerando pur nonostante che la giurisprudenza nell'ultimo suo stato si è determinata per una via di spiegato progresso, e che la tesi dei conflitti d'attribuzione ha troppa importanza per essere risoluta quasi per incidente in una legge sui danni della guerra, la Commissione ha finito con lasciare nelle sue proposte gli aventi interesse nelle condizioni nelle quali si trovano, tanto rispetto alle leggi sostantive, quanto rispetto alle leggi di competenza e di rito.

Il progetto che si sostituisce al progetto ministeriale viene così a comporsi di quattro articoli.

Col *primo* si offre modo al Governo del Re di pagare con 5 per cento i debiti per causa pubblica, (imprestiti) militare (forniture, somministrazioni) o di guerra (espropriazioni o danni per fortificazioni) delle amministrazioni permanente anteriori.

Col *secondo* si offre modo al Governo del Re di pagare con 3 per cento i debiti d'ugual natura dei Governi provvisorii del 1848, e le requisizioni non regolate o non soddisfatte dall'armata austriaca.

Col *terzo* s'incarica una Commissione dell'accertamento e della liquidazione, con termini perentorii.

E col *quarto* articolo gli aventi interesse non consenzienti vengono lasciati nella posizione che hanno con tutte le azioni, ed esposti a tutte le eccezioni, anche giurisdizionali.

### LA FINE.

Signori! La vostra Commissione accolse unanime i principii esposti nella presente relazione, e unanime combinò le sue proposte. Francamente, essa crede che possa discutersi sopra alcuna delle applicazioni alle quali discese, non dei principii che la guidarono nelle sue conclusioni.

Avverte che potranno aggiungersi ancora altre partite congeneri a quelle dell'allegato; e alcune fra le notate crescere d'importanza; ma che piuttosto è a prevedere che nelle finali liquidazioni l'ultimo resultato sarà per portare una diminuzione vistosa sulla cifra presagita.

Secondo un calcolo, del resto molto approssimativo, con forse due milioni e due o trecento mila lire di rendita, il Tesoro nazionale nel modo proposto si riscatterebbe da ogni debito dipendente dalle fortunose vicende attraverso alle quali l'Italia si è finalmente costituita in libera nazione.

Se pertanto non leggero, il carico che sta per derivarne non può dissestare l'erario nazionale, mentre non vogliono dimenticarsi due cose. La *prima* che il bilancio *passivo* dello Stato si compila per pagare non per disimularne il debito; la *seconda* che nel provvedimento proposto, più del danno erariale diventa apprezzabile la soddisfazione che sta per risentirne la coscienza pubblica.

Poichè, o Signori, è in nome della giustizia, della equità e della politica che la Commissione non esita a raccomandare alla vostra sanzione i quattro articoli del suo disegno di legge.

MANTELLINI, *relatore.*

---

### PROGETTO DEL MINISTERO.

ART. 1. I fondi per ragioni militari dai precedenti Governi espropriati, senza pagamento d'indennità, nelle guerre che prepararono e compierono il nostro nazionale risorgimento, come in quelle onde furono funestate nell'entrare del secolo le provincie del primo regno italico, quando sieno tenuti tuttora dal Governo italiano, saranno da esso restituiti nello stato in cui si trovano attualmente, o ne sarà pagato il prezzo di stima a coloro che, giustificando nei modi legali la proprietà del fondo, dimostreranno insieme il tempo ed il modo del l'espropriazione, e la data della domanda o delle domande d'indennità rimaste insoddisfatte.

ART. 2. Dalla obbligazione di 4,749,000 fiorini nominali, rimessa dal Governo austro-ungarico al Governo italiano ai termini dell'articolo 2 della convenzione *A* del 6 gennaio 1871 approvata con legge del 23 marzo anno medesimo, numero 137 (serie seconda), sarà prelevata una quota parte di fiorini 634,000 del pari nominali, per sovvenire ai cittadini delle provincie lombardo-venete di più ristretta condizione di fortuna, che non fossero stati indennizzati delle requisizioni ed altri danni per essi sofferti a causa delle guerre menzionate nell'articolo precedente, e che fossero d'altronde in grado di fornire la prova del danno e indicare la data dei reclami presentati senza risultato.

ART. 3. Del reparto della somme come sopra stabilita è incaricata una Commissione composta di delegati delle provincie della Lombardia e della Venezia, uno per ciascheduna provincia, nominato dal rispettivo Consiglio provinciale.

La Commissione sarà presieduta dal prefetto della città di Verona, dove avrà la sua sede; e potrà fra i suoi componenti, nominare un Comitato per la esecuzione delle sue deliberazioni.

---

PROGETTO DELLA GIUNTA.

ART. 1. I debiti per causa pubblica, militare o di guerra, che, formati o contratti secondo gli ordinamenti di allora, si lasciarono non regolati o non soddisfatti dalle amministrazioni permanenti dei già Stati italiani, alle quali nel 1859, 1860, 1866 e 1870 si sostituiva l'amministrazione del regno d'Italia, saranno dal Governo del Re pagati con tanto consolidato 5 per cento alla pari: tranne i contemplati dal seguente articolo.

ART. 2. Con tanto consolidato 3 per cento alla pari saranno soddisfatti i debiti di ugual natura lasciati dai Governi provvisorii del 1848, e le requisizioni e provviste regolarmente accertate, sia per le truppe nazionali nelle guerre del 1848 e 1849, sia fatte dall'Austria nelle guerre del 1848, 1849 e 1859 in Italia, fuori del lombardo-veneto, e nelle guerre del 1859 e del 1866 nella Lombardia, nel veneto e mantovano.

ART. 3. Il Governo provvederà col mezzo di apposite Commissioni all'accertamento ed alla liquidazione delle partite di credito contemplate dalla presente legge.

Gli aventi diritto presenteranno alla detta Commissione i loro titoli di credito coi relativi documenti, nel termine perentorio di sei mesi dalla data della nomina della Commissione, che dovra chiudere le sue liquidazioni dentro l'anno successivo alla presentazione dei titoli.

ART. 4. La presente legge non ha effetto per quelli fra gli aventi interesse che non consentano al trattamento disposto coi precedenti articoli 1 e 2.

---

ALLEGATO N°. 1.

*Decreto del Granduca di Toscana del* 3 *novembre* 1850 *sulle spese per le truppe ausiliari.*

NOI LEOPOLDO, ecc.

Visto il decreto nell'assenza nostra ed in nostro nome emanato dal Consiglio dei ministri sotto il dì 13 giugno ultimo passato ed in ordine al quale furono nominati il dottor Girolamo Gargiolli membro, allora, del Consiglio di Stato in servizio ordinario, ed il colonnello in ritiro cavaliere Michele Ceccherelli per liquidare tutte le spese occorse per il corpo di truppe imperiali austriache dal giorno del loro ingresso in Toscana fino a quello del cambio delle ratifiche della convenzione del 22 aprile precedente, a forma di quanto disponeva l'articolo 4 della convenzione surriferita.

Considerando che ad una parte delle spese preindicate hanno supplito le diverse comunità dello Stato, le quali hanno fatto fronte a quello straordinario aggravio, o con i soccorsi ricevuti dalla regia depositeria, o con mezzi loro propri, o con quelli che si sono precariamente procurati a titolo fruttifero da terzi soventori;

Considerando che, per il titolo in ispecie dell'alloggio, le comunità hanno dovuto, anche dopo il primo di luglio ultimo passato, epoca, nella quale il regio trono prese direttamente a provvedere al servizio delle truppe ausiliari, sostenere qualche aggravio per questa dipendenza;

Considerando che anche vari spedali dello Stata sono in sofferenza per spedalità somministrata alle truppe medesime, ed altri aggravi sofferti per questa causa;

E considerando finalmente, che quanto è necessario di dar ordine e regola a tutte le spese occasionate dalla presenza delle truppe ausiliari nel Granducato, altrettanto è impossibile che a tutte simultaneamente, e direttamente provveda subito il regio erario.

Sulle proposizioni del nostro ministro segretario di Stato del dipartimento delle finanze, del commercio e dei lavori pubblici;

E sentito il nostro Consiglio dei ministri;

Abbiamo decretato e decretiamo quanto segue:

ART. 1. I commissari destinati dal decreto del tridici giugno ultimo passato a liquidare le spese occorrenti per il servizio delle truppe imperiali austriache dal momento del loro ingresso nel Granducato a tutto il trenta giugno ridetto, estenderanno pur anco il loro ufficio a liquidare, distintamente, con le comunità, e con gli spedali le spese da essi respettivamente fatte per tal dipendenza, le somme che hanno ricevuto in conto dal regio erario per suppliere alle spese medesime, e quelle di cui rimangono per questo titolo in disborso.

ART. 2. Le subalterne liquidazioni delle quali si tratta nell'articolo precedente saranno frattanto protratte a tutto dicembre prossimo futuro, riserbandoci in seguito a provvedere nei modi che saranno reputati i più giusti, alla distribuzione e reparto delle spese rese necessarie dalla presenza delle truppe austriache in Toscana, ed ai rimborsi di ragione dovuti alle amministrazioni creditrici per tal dipendenza.

ART. 3. Non potranno frattanto però le comunità rivalersi per qualsiasi quota di quei loro crediti sui tributi che per diversi titoli sono, a forma degli ordini, richiamati a versare nelle casse dello Stato nelle epoche consuete, onde queste possan far fronte ai carichi giornalieri, ed alle esigenze del pubblico servizio. Bensì sono autorizzati i commissari liquidatori a tener conto alle singole comunità nelle liquidazioni dei loro crediti, degli interessi passivi che avessero dovuto o dovessero ancora corrispondere sulle somme che sono state nella necessità di procurarsi per supplire a quelli straordinari aggravi, e per un oggetto che interessa l'universalità dello Stato.

I nostri ministri segretari di Stato per i dipartimenti delle finanze, ecc., e dell'interno sono incaricati ciascuno per quanto loro spetta della esecuzione del presente decreto.

Dato il 3 novembre milleottocentocinquanta.

LEOPOLDO.

---

## ALLEGATO N° 2.

*Circolare del ministro dell'interno ai signori governatori provinciali ed intendenti generali pei danni e requisizioni della guerra* 1859: 16 *agosto* 1860.

Dagli atti del Parlamento inserti nel giornale ufficiale del regno, i signori governatori ed intendenti generali avranno veduto che nella tornata della Camera dei deputati del 24 precorso giugno, in seguito a interpellanze mosse dall'onorevole deputato Depretis, il Governo del Re assunse l'impegno di fare vari provvedimenti diretti a recare il maggiore sollievo possibile ai mali cagionati dalla guerra d'indipendenza combattuta nel 1859.

Premendo di tradurre il più presto in atti siffatti propositi, a raggiungere il desiderato scopo, il Governo del Re ha deciso, in Consiglio dei ministri, che gli interessati tutti sarebbero invitati a proporre le loro domande per risarcimento di danni sofferti per causa della guerra entro un discreto termine da stabilirsi mediante apposito avviso da pubblicarsi dai signori governatori ed intendenti generali, e che tali domande raccolte per cura dei signori intendenti di circondario, e corredate di tutti i titoli necessari per accertare la natura, la realtà e l'entità dei danni patiti, non che delle occorrenti informazioni sulle condizioni di fortuna dei ricorrenti, sarebbero poscia riunite per provincie, trasmesse a questo Ministero dai signori governatori ed intendenti generali predetti, accompagnate dalle particolari loro informazioni.

Sebbene le esplicite e precise dichiarazioni da sua eccellenza il presidente del Consiglio dei ministri fatte alla Camera elettiva nella tornata predetta, chiaro dimostrino quali siano le intenzioni del Governo riguardo alle persone ed ai danni che il medesimo, s'incarica di risarcire, si crede tuttavia opportuno di qui riassumerle a scanso d'ogni possibile equivoco ed a più sicura norma tanto degli interessati nel proporre, quanto degli intendenti nel reccogliere le domande di cui si tratta.

A termine adunque delle preaccennate dichiarazioni, conviene ritenere che il Governo si sarebbe proposto:

1° Di provvedere per venire il più sollecitamente possibile in soccorso dei cittadini più poveri stati danneggiati dalla guerra;

2° Di considerare a carico dello Stato il compenso dei danni cagionati:

*a*) Dalle requisizioni regolarmente fatte dagli Austriaci in Lombardia;

*b*) Dalle occupazioni di terreni operate dalle autorità austriache in Lombardia e nei Ducati per opere di fortificazioni stabili o campali prima del cominciamento delle ostilità;

*c*) Dalle occupazioni della stessa natura ordinate dalle autorità nazionali e dai comandanti delle truppe nazionali ed alleate;

*d*) Dalla distruzione di capitali mobili e dalle inondazioni sequite per ordine delle autorità stesse per impedire l'invasione dei nemici;

3° Di dare le necessarie disposizioni perchè la cassa dei depositi e prestiti e quelle di risparmio potessero largamente somministrare dei fondi a quei comuni che più ne avessero di bisogno per sopperire agli oneri contratti per la stessa causa;

4° Infine, di adoperarsi efficacemente presso i Consigli provinciali onde promuovere un'associazione fra tutte le provincie del regno, diretta a sovvenire a quei danni che non saranno o non potranno essere alleviati dal Governo.

Vari e di vario genere essendo i danni ai quali si tratta di riparare nè per tutti potendo essere adottato un solo ed uniforme procedimento, onde pervenire all'esatta e regolare loro constatazione, lo scrivente si limiterà ad accennare che o si tratta di danni cagionati da occupazioni di proprietà per opere di difesa permanente o passeggiera, che non sono ancora state, o non possono più essere restituite al primitivo loro uso, ed in tal caso, ove già non esistano regolari perizie, si dovrà procedere alla loro esecuzione onde far luogo al rimborso del prezzo ed alla refezione dei danni che saranno fissati.

Ovvero si tratta di danni che per la loro natura e per il tempo trascorso non possono più essere determinati per mezzo di periti, ed allora si dovrà ricorrere ad altri idonei mezzi di prova.

Lo stesso dovra praticarsi riguardo allo stato di fortuna dei ricorrenti, avvertendo inoltre, per rispetto a questi, di far conoscere altresì la situazione delle loro famiglie, il numero cioè dei membri di che sono composte, la loro età, ed i mezzi dei quali ciascuno di essi può disporre, per provvedere al proprio ed al comune sostentamento.

Non accade poi di aggiungere che, per quanto sarà possibile, dovrano essere prodotti, od almeno indicati colla maggiore precisione, gli ordini delle autorità in virtù dei quali furono occupate le varie proprietà od arrecati i lamentati danni, come necessaria ugualmente sarà la produzione dei titoli constatanti le requisizioni fatte dalle autorità austriache o nazionali, delle quali si chiederà il rimborso.

A questo fine si trasmettono ai signori governatori ed intendenti generali diversi documenti già prodotti da alcuni danneggiati, onde abbiano a servire di norma alla compilazione di sì importante lavoro.

Il Governo, del resto, fidente nella conosciuta perspicacia ed oculatezza dei signori governatori ed intendenti generali, non crede di poter fare meglio che di rimettersi intieramente al prudente loro arbitrio, persuaso che non tralascieranno cure onde circondarsi di tutti i lumi necessari per porre il Governo in grado di provvedere con piena cognizione di causa, perchè nei limiti del diritto sia concesso ai danneggiati un sollievo senza spreco della pubblica finanza.

Non è poi necessario che lo scrivente qui si estenda in minuti particolari per ciò che concerne i mutui che possono occorrere ai comuni per sopperire agl'impegni da essi contratti per la stessa causa; nel limitarsi pertanto a rinnovare le promesse fatte dal Governo di agevolare, per quanto sta in lui, la concessione, dalla cassa dei depositi e dei prestiti o da quelle di risparmio, delle anticipazioni di fondi dei quali si giustificherà il bisogno, lo scrivente si riferisce quanto al modo di formulare e di istruire le relative domande, alle istruzioni che prima d'ora furono diramate su tale materia, invitando i signori governatori ed intendenti generali ad uniformarvisi esattamente, a scanso di dannosi ritardi che non potrebbero poi essere ascritti a colpa del Governo.

Non rimane quindi più che a parlare del progetto di associazione da attivarsi fra tutte le provincie dello Stato per venire in soccorso di quei danni ai quali il Governo stesso non è chiamato a riparare ed a tale proposito ugualmente lo scrivente pienamente affidato ai caldi sentimenti d'affetto dai quali sa essere le rappresentanze provinciali animate per la causa nazionale, mentre altamente fa plauso al patriotico pensiero che volle tutte le provincie sorelle associate alla pietosa opera di alleviare i mali di una guerra che ha iniziate la liberazione e l'indipendenza della patria comune, nutre ferma fiducia che il medesimo sarà col massimo favore accolto da tutti i Consigli provinciali, e che, grazie al largo e generoso loro concorso, troveranno il maggior possibile riparo i danni cagionati dalla passata guerra sicchè i popoli ne trarranno argomento e conforto a maggiori sacrifizi, quando così il bene della patria richiedesse.

Nel lasciare pertanto ai Consigli stessi tutto il merito della iniziativa, lo scrivente inviterà solo i signori governatori ed intendenti generali a secondarne colla loro autorità le deliberazioni ed a farle poi colla maggiore sollecitudine pervenire a questo Ministero.

Nella persuasione che i signori governatori ed intendenti generali penetrandosi della gravità ed importanza del lavoro che loro è demandato vi apporteranno tutta quella sollecitudine ed impegno che potranno maggiori, sicchè il medesimo concili in modo soddisfacente gli interessi dei privati e dello Stato, lo scrivente starà attendendone il pronto compimento; non senza soggiungere, per maggior chiarezza ed uniformità, che le domande di indennità dovranno essere riepilogate e divise in altrettanti stati quante sono le categorie dei danni ai quali si tratta di riparare, avvertendo inoltre di tener separati i danni e le requisizioni seguite pel fatto dell'Austria, da quelle derivanti dalla autorità e dalle armate nazionale ed alleata, e ne porge loro fin d'ora i più sentiti ringraziamenti.

*Il ministro*

FARINI.

ALLEGATO N° 3.

*Istruzioni 3 agosto 1861 diramate dall'Austria per la liquidazione delle domande di compenso sui danni provenienti dalla guerra del 1859 nelle provincie venete.*

§ 1. Sono ammissibili ad un compenso dall'imperiale e regio erario, dipendentemente dalle vicende della guerra dell'anno 1859, le effettive prestazioni militari ed i danni derivati alla proprietà.

La pertrattazione delle domande di compenso in causa di prestazioni militari, è regolata dall'istruzione abbassata col rescritto 13 maggio 1861, n° 2210 dell'eccelso imperiale e regio Ministero della guerra.

Le norme, a seconda delle quali debbona pertrattarsi le domande di compenso per danni derivanti alla proprietà dalle vicende della guerra (danni della guerra), vengono tracciate colla presente istruzione.

§ 2. La Commissione del Dominio sulla liquidazione delle prestazioni militari effettuate nel regno Lombardo-Veneto, dipendentemente dalla guerra del 1859, e che venne istituita colla sovrana risoluzione 2 marzo 1861, dovrà occuparsi anche della liquidazione delle domande di compenso pei danni della guerra 1859 e dovrà quindi d'ora in poi nominarsi: *Commissione pella liquidazione delle prestazioni militari e delle espropriazioni.*

§ 3. La Commissione del Dominio dovrà prefiggere un congruo termine perentorio pell'insinuazione della domanda.

§ 4. Per poter prender in considerazione tali domande di compenso, non deve constare che chi domanda il compenso abbia durante la guerra del 1859 presse le armi contro l'imperiale e regio Governo e che si abbia reso colpevole d'altra azione ostile contro il medesimo; nascendo il sospetto dovrebbe provarsi il contrario.

§ 5. È massima cardinale nella pertrattazione delle domande di compenso per danni di guerra, che tali danni di regola non sono ammissibili ad un compenso dall'imperiale e reale erario.

§ 6. Eccettuati e quindi ammissibili ad un compenso dall'imperiale e regio erario, sono:

*a*) Le espropriazioni di fondi ad un uso permanente militare, e così pure le servitù speciali addossate ai fondi privati per iscopi di strategia miltare;

*b*) I danni derivati dall'occupazione e dalla distruzione di edifizi o del soprassuolo per iscopi passeggieri di strategia militare.

§ 7. Occupazioni ed usi passeggieri effettuati dal nemico e così pure i danni di ogni sorta dipendenti dalla predisposizione od esecuzione di operazioni militari, da arbitrii e da eccesi sia della mata nemica, sia delle imperiali e regie truppe (danni di guerra propriamente detti), non possono compensarsi dall'imperiale e regio erario.

§ 8. Le domande di compenso, relative ai danni accennati nel § 6, sono da pertrattarsi a norma dell'istruzione, per le stime dei danni recati alla esecuzione di opere pubbliche, del 9 giugno 1826, n° 5315-931. (Collezione di leggi e regolamenti pubblicata dall'imperiale e regio governo delle provincie venete, anno 1826, parte I, n° 62, pagina 114), e devono tenersi dei protocolli separati in tale proposito.

§ 9. Del resto, in quanto trattasi degli amminicoli di prova o della successiva constatazione degli ordini militari relativi alla occupazione, all'uso ed alle servitù in parola, valgono anche qui le norme in proposito tracciato ai §§ 7, 8, 12 dell'istruzione 13 maggio 1861 sulla liquidazione delle prestazioni militari, semprechè tali norme possano trovare applicazione nei casi di espropriazione.

§ 10. Valgono del pari anche pella pertrattazione delle domande di compenso in causa di danni di guerra le norme tracciate ai §§ 2, 3, 4 della detta istruzione, relativamente alla procedura di liquidazione al § 5, relativamente al termine perentorio da fissarsi, ed al § 20, relativo ai rapporti da avanzarsi dalla commissione.

§ 11. Ai rispettivi proprietari competono, a norma del § 995 del Codice civile e della sovrana risoluzione 4 marzo 1837, gli interessi di mora del 4 per cento, decorribili dal momento dell'apprensione e rispettivamente da quelle dell'occupazione passeggiera della proprietà, che, se in tale momento non si lasciasse precisare, gli interessi in parola verranno liquidati decorribilmente dal giorno dell'insinuazione.

§ 12. Nei casi di occupazioni ed usi passeggieri di fondi, dovrà conteggiarsi il compenso senza diffalchi (delle imposte).

§ 13. Sussistendo dei contratti approvati dall'autorità competente, e la di cui approvazione sia già stata notificata, dovrà aversi riguardo ai medesimi nel commissurare il compenso.

§ 14. Le deliberazioni della Commissione liquidatrice dovranno in uno cogli atti di pertrattazione necessari per formarsene un giudizio, assoggettarsi all'eccelso imperiale e regio Ministero della guerra per la decisione dei dicasteri interessati, e tali decisioni finali che verranno abbassati dal prefato Ministero, dovranno subito intimarsi alle parti.

§ 15. È riservata la determinazione sui mezzi coi quali avrà luogo il pagamento dei compensi liquidati ed approvati come sopra.

§ 16. Le parti che non si ritenessero soddisfatte delle decisioni emesse e dei compensi loro assegnati, saranno rimesse alla via civile.

§ 17. Quegli importi di compenso che non fossero prelevati dalle parti entro 14 giorni dall'intimazione della decisione delle autorità centrali, dovranno depositarsi in giudizio.

Ciò avrà luogo anche nel caso di cui al § 16.

Col giorno di tale deposito cessano di decorrere gli interessi di mora del 4 per cento, vale a dire che dal detto giorno in poi non ha più luogo un ulteriore corresponsione d'interessi.

Venezia, 3 agosto 1861.

Dall'I. R. Luogotenenza Lombardo-Veneta.

---

ALLEGATO N° 4.

*Notificazione del governo austriaco sull'approvvigionamento dell'armata mobile del 25 giugno 1866.*

Allo scopo di viemmeglio guarentire i comuni e gli individui che in causa della mobilizzazione dell'imperiale regio esercita nel regno Lombardo-Veneto vengono chiamati a prestare somministrazioni a vantaggio del militare, e per metterli immediatamente in possesso di un titolo legalmente valido e trasmissibile anche a terze persone, trovasi in relazione all'istruzione provvisoria emanata nel 1861 per gli organi, cui incombe l'approvigionamento di un'armata mobile, di disporre quanto segue:

I. Il militare dovrà fare ogni ricerca di somministrazioni soltanto ai comuni e non mai ai singoli abitanti; così pure la consegna degli articoli da somministrarsi non verrà mai effettuata direttamente da parte dei singoli abitanti, ma sempre coll'intervento dei comuni.

Gli oggetti, che saranno chiesti del militare, dovranno essere somministrati dai comuni solo in natura, non mai in danaro. Si ricorda pure in questa occasione il vigente divieto, secondo il quale non si possono comperare oggetti attinenti all'abbigliamento, all'armamento o ad altri scopi militari, nè commestibili, foraggi ad altri articoli di provianda, che fossero venduti dal soldato.

II. Non potrà chiedersi da parte del militare alcuna somministrazione senza rilasciarne quitanza.

Per uniformità i comuni saranno provveduti di appositi bollettari, nei quali la madre formerà la quitanza del militare per gli articoli ricevuti, e la viglia la reversale del comune sulla prestazione medesima.

Tanto la quitanza, quanto la reversale dovranno sempre venir emesse prima della consegna e del rispettivo ricevimento delle prestazioni.

La bolletta madre, cioè la quitanza propriamente detta, rimarrà al comune, e la bolletta figlia staccata, cioè la reversale, sarà rilasciata alla parte militare.

III. Le competenze militari di vitto e d'altro verranno esposte nella quitanza e nella reversale in razioni giornaliere a peso e misura di Vienna.

Le congregazioni provinciali dovranno quindi fornire ai comuni apposite tabelle di ragguaglio dei rispettivi pesi e misure, ed i comuni poi sulle stesse praticare le debite riduzioni per effettuare regolarmente la somministrazione al militare e la ripartizione della medesima sugli abitanti.

Le predette tabelle dovranno presso gli uffici comunali essere sempre ostensibili al militare.

IV. I comuni dovranno riportare le quietanze militari secondo l'ordine cronologico ed eguale a quello in cui furono registrate nel bollettario, in un prospetto, che sarà da chiudersi il 15 e l'ultimo d'ogni mese e da trasmettersi subito dopo siffatti termini in doppio esemplare e col corredo delle quietanze militari costituenti il bollettario della quindicina, all'imperiale regia intendenza dell'esercito, col tramite della congregazione provinciale.

V. L'intendenza dell'esercito procederà alla liquidazione interinale, emetterà dei *Buoni di anticipazione* per due terzi dei prezzi minimi degli oggetti somministrati, prenoterà tale emissione sopra ambedue gli esemplari del prospetto e trasmetterà uno di questi colle relative quitanze all'imperiale regia contabilità centrale militare, perchè trattenga il tutto ne' propri atti, restituendo poi al comune, pel tramite predetto, l'altro esemplare colle eventuali osservazioni, unitivi i relativi Buoni di anticipazione.

VI. I prospetti restituiti ai comuni saranno trattenuti presso i medesimi per essere prodotti a suo tempo alla Commissione liquidatrice del Dominio, mentre i Buoni di anticipazione potrano essere girati dai comuni anche a terze persone, e, senza bisogno di altra liquidazione, saranno a suo tempo pagati nel valore nominale al portatore da quell'imperiale reale cassa, che verrà a ciò autorizzata.

VII. Nella definitiva liquidazione sarà aggiundicata ed assegnata pel pagamento ai comuni l'ultima terza parte, oltre, l'eventuale aumento dei prezzi giusta l'effettivo valore locale, e le indispensabili spese di trasporto sostenute e da comprovarsi mediante regolari documenti.

Venezia, li 25 giugno 1866.

Dall'I. R. Luogotenenza Lombardo-Veneta.

TOGGENBURG.

ALLEGATO N° 5.

*Circolare alle onorevoli Congregazioni provinciali, agli II. RR. commissari distrettuali ed alle Congregazioni municipali e deputazioni comunali.*

Per quanto il Governo siasi dato ognora, e specialmente in occasione della guerra del 1859, tutta la sollecitudine, mediante l'apposita Commissione a ciò istituita, nel definire la liquidazione delle prestazioni fatte al militare, ciò nullostante la natura stessa delle pratiche occorrenti nelle relative operazioni esigeva un lasso di tempo che riusciva lungo ai creditori.

Per ovviare a queste difficoltà, la Luogotenenza, presi gli opportuni concerti coll'I. R. comando dell'esercito in Verona e colla Congregazione centrale lombardo-veneta, ha trovato di pubblicare la qui unita notificazione, che ricorda alcune norme preesistenti e prescrive altre nuove modalità per assicurare l'immediato e pleno riconoscimento dell'intera effettiva prestazione, e perchè, almeno per buona parte del suo valore, sia tosto rilasciato un apposito titolo di credito ai comuni ed individui chiamati a prestare somministrazioni a vantaggio del militare in occasione della mobilizzazione dell'I. R. esercito in questo dominio.

Venezia, 25 giugno 1866.

Dall'I. R. Luogotenenza Lombardo-Veneta.

---

ALLEGATO N° 6.

I. R. LUOGOTENENZA IN TRIESTE.

*Nota all'inclita regia prefettura della provincia di Udine.*

In riscontro al gradito foglio 22 corrente mese, numero 7096, la scrivente ha l'onore di partecipare a cotesta inclita regia prefettura che la notificazione governativa 25 giugno 1866, n° 2852, di cui si unisce una copia, emanata dall'I. R. Luogotenenza lombardo-veneta d'allora, che la medesima non venne pubblicata nella provincia del littorale, e che le dispositive ivi contenute non ebbero vigore per questa provincia.

Per le somministrazioni militari, ed in generale per prestazioni e danni derivati dalla guerra del 1866, si applicarono in Austria le massime stabilite con sovrana risoluzione 10 settembre 1866, le quali si desumono dalla notificazione luogotenenziale 16 ottobre 1866, che pure si allega in copia.

In base a queste massime si procedette anche riguardo alla provincia di Gorizia nella trattazione delle relative domande d'indennizzo, liquidando, a termini della tariffa unita a quella notificazione, quelle prestazioni che risultarono compensabili.

Trieste, 31 marzo 1872.

FERRY.

---

ALLEGATO N° 7.

*Notificazione dell'I. R. Luogotenenza del littorale, concernente il trattamento dei danni derivanti dalla guerra del* 1866.

Sua Maestà I. R. Apostolica, con sovrana risoluzione del 10 settembre anno corrente, si è graziosamente degnata di approvare le seguenti massime fondamentali pel trattamente dei danni che derivano dall'ultima guerra:

§ 1.—*Quali prestazioni e danni vengono dallo Stato compensati per legge.*

Lo Stato compensa:

1° *Le prestazioni militari* per le II. RR. truppe, cioè:

*a*) *L'acquartieramento*, a norma delle vigenti leggi;

*b*) *Le vetture militari* o *carriagi in uso nel paese*, a norma delle vigenti leggi;

*c*) *Le somministrazioni*, *requisizioni*, ed in generale tutte le prestazioni non comprese ad *a* e *b*, per esempio le forniture, le somministrazioni di oggetti in natura, del servizio da tavola, di viveri e di altre occorrenze dell'armata, la prestazione di foraggi, il pascolo di animali da macello appartenenti all'erario militare, i traghetti, i lavori in generale, ecc.;

2° *Le espropriazioni* di terreni per iscopi militari;

3° *I danneggiamenti di beni privati* in causa ad ordini degli II. RR. comandanti di truppe o delle II. RR. autorità per iscopi strategici.

(Danni causati dalle operazioni militari non vengono compensati, se avvenuti in seguito a combattimenti o movimenti di marcia. Così pure i danni fortuiti o causati da disordini non danno diritto a compenso.)

Dei danni commessi per petulanza è responsabile chi ne è l'autore. (Decreto aulico del 16 aprile 1821, n° 10,086.)

Trieste, 16 ottobre 1866.

ALLEGATO N° 8.

MINISTERO DELL'INTERNO.

*Conguaglio delle spese della guerra pel* 1848–1849 *nella Lombardia e Venezia.*

FIRENZE, 1 *aprile* 1869.

*Ai signori prefetti,*

È già noto a cotesta prefettura come, per disposizione del Governo austriaco, tutte le somministrazioni dei generi di sussistenza fornite dal 18 marzo 1848 al 31 dicembre 1849 alle sue truppe accampate nelle provincie lombardo-venete per combattere l'insurrezione e l'armata italiana, più la tassa di guerra che venne imposta e i gravi danni arrecati dal militare in quelle circostanze, furono fatte gravare a totale carico delle provincie stesse in proporzione del loro estimo.

In esecuzione di tale disposizione il Ministero dell'interno di Vienna, con dispaccio 31 dicembre 1851, n° 20,174–194, prescrisse che ciascuna provincia liquidasse i debiti con i rispettivi creditori e quindi presentasse alla contabilità di Stato le proprie liquidazioni per gli effetti della perequazione generale per tutto il territorio del regno Lombardo-Veneto, e successivamente, con istruzioni del 12 luglio 1852, fissò le norme generali per siffatte perequazioni.

Una Commissione in ogni provincia attese quindi alla prima delle liquidazioni accennate dalle istruzioni ministeriali, e le due contabilità di Stato di Milano e Venezia, ciascuna pel rispettivo territorio, attesero alla perequazione generale.

Il prospetto complessivo redatto dalle predette contabilità di Stato venne in seguito sottoposto ad una Commissione centrale di deputati Lombardi e di Veneti radunata in Milano, la quale, e per le predette istruzioni 12 luglio 1852 e pelle posteriori proposte (formulate in base alle risultanze delle esibite giustificazioni ed accolte dal Ministero), modificava in qualche parte quel lavoro, includendo alcune somme che non erano state da dette contabilità ammesse, cioè, per esempio, lire 9439 13 per la provincia di Brescia, lire 1391 54 per quella di Como e lire 5030 per quella di Mantova, ed escludendone altre pur da esse accolte, ma non ritenute abbastanza giustificate, come alcune di Bergamo e di Milano.

I titoli delle spese e danni così ammessi definitivamente riguardavano:

1° Le requisizioni dei generi di sussistenza;

2° Le requisizioni dei mezzi di trasporto;

3° Quelle degli articoli di casermaggio, come lenzuola, coperte, ecc.;

4° Le somministrazioni d'alloggio per parte degli albergatori;

5° I danni cagionati dalla occupazione militare nei locali ad uso dei pubblici stabilimenti;

6° Le somministrazioni d'alloggio in abitazioni date a pigione, quando al proprietario ne fosse causato un danno;

7° Le spese di trasporti, messi od espressi adoperati esclusivamente pel servizio militare;

8° Le spese per i lavori di fortificazione;

9° Quelle per creazione di ospedali militari;

10. Quelle per telegrafi;

11. Quelle per forni di campagna;

12. Quelle per scuole di equitazione;

13. Quelle per bersagli;

14. Quelle per ponti volanti, in quanto avessero carattere di prestazione militare e fosse dimostrato che esse venissero incontrate a favore del militare;

15. La tassa di guerra ordinata in quel tempo;

16. E, pel solo territorio della Lombardia, i crediti (lire 149,468 75) di alcune ditte milanesi per esecuzione di opere o ristauri di fabbricati demaniali militari eseguite durante il periodo del Governo provvisorio (decreto speciale del Ministero dell'interno, in data 16 dicembre, 1857, n° 32,433–1320).

Con tale operazione fu pure regolarizzato il così detto *fondo sociale* cui le provincie, a ciò autorizzate dalla circolare 19 settembre 1848 della intendenza generale dell'armata, avevano ricorso mercè un'imposta speciale nei momenti più gravi, onde raccogliere le somme per corrispondere alle esorbitanti pretese dell'autorità militare.

La perequazione eseguita da questa Commissione centrale colla scorta di tutti i preaccennati criteri veniva definitivamente sancita dal Ministero di Vienna col decreto 17 *novembre* 1858, portato a cognizione delle provincie venete colla circolare 7 dicembre detto anno, e di quelle della Lombardia coll'altra del giorno 13 detto mese ed anno.

Con tale decreto venivano definitivamente ammesse per tutto il Lombardo-Veneto le somme seguenti, cioè:

| | |
|---|---|
| *a*) Per le prestazioni in natura aust. | L. 55,988,741 66 |
| *b*) Per il fondo sociale | 862,863 96 |
| *c*) Per la tassa bellica | 36,045,100 59 |
| In totale austriache | 92,896,706 21 |

Il citato decreto inoltre determinava, nella somma di austriache lire 4,020,017 54, il debito di ragguaglio della Lombardia verso la Venezia, ed assegnando a scarico di questo debito il residuo del *fondo sociale* esistente presso le casse principali del Lombardo-Veneto nella somma di austriache lire 207,204 56, il debito della Lombardia residuavasi così ad austriache lire 3,800,000. Il pagamento di questa residua somma fu stabilito dovesse farsi col prodotto delle imposte da attivarsi negli anni 1859-1860-1861, tanto per questo titolo come per quello della perequazione provinciale in ciascun dominio, e comunale in ciascuna provincia; ed a parziale modificazione di quanto era fissato nelle preliminari istruzioni del Ministero in data 12 luglio 1852, si stabilì che il conguaglio fra i due territori dovesse effettuarsi in base dell'imposta fondiaria dell'anno 1857, con esclusione però dell'imposta sulla rendita dei fabbricati che esisteva nelle provincie lombarde avanti il vecchio censimento. Rispetto poi alle somme concernenti il fondo sociale ed alla tassa bellica, il cui riparto aveva luogo in base al montare degli anni 1848–1849, determinavasi che il conguaglio dovesse effettuarsi secondo le risultanze medie del debito d'imposta del preaccennato biennio. Finalmente fu aperto l'adito ad una *ulteriore* insinuazione (in base sempre ai criteri cui era informata la prima) di quelle pretese che i privati, i comuni e le corporazioni avrebbero creduto di far valere, non ostante l'anteriore recusa delle pretese stesse per ritardata insinuazione, o per difetto di motivazione del titolo, o di regolare giustificazione. In base a tali disposizioni le due contabilità di Stato, procederono alla compilazione del quadro di riparto delle suddette spese per le provincie dei rispettivi territori.

Sottoposto il prospetto di questo riparto delle provincie lombarde (in data 5 marzo 1859) alle deliberazioni della Congregazione centrale in Milano, questa non credette poterne accettare i risultati, in quanto sostenne non doversi prendere per base del riparto stesso l'imposta fondiaria del 1857, regolata da un novissimo censimento che aveva molto variate le condizioni delle proprietà lombarde a tutto vantaggio delle venete, ma bensì (trattandosi di danni e spese verificatesi nel 1848–1849) l'imposta di tale biennio, sulle risultanze del vecchio censo in allora vigente, dal quale diverso calcolo ne resultava che il debito della Lombardia verso la Venezia, anzichè ammontare a lire 4,020,017 54, ascendeva invece a soli 2,638,355 di lire austriache.

Sopraggiunti intanto gli avvenimenti politici del 1859, sia per la impossibilità di prendere concerti col Governo austriaco, per quanto rifletteva la Venezia come per la inutilità di ogni tentativo diretto a modificare il citato decreto ministeriale del 17 novembre 1858, il quale maggiormente favoriva le provincie venete rimaste sotto il suo dominio, questo Ministero non potè dal 1860 al 1866 riattivare le opportune pratiche per quella perequazione, la quale sarebbe rimasta imperfetta, se si fosse limitata al riparto fra le sole provincie lombarde.

D'altronde il Governo italiano aveva potuto conoscere come, malgrado le più vive sollecitazioni della congregazione centrale di Venezia al Ministero di Vienna, onde in via diplomatica ottenesse i pagamenti dovuti dal già dominio lombardo, quel Ministero avesse deciso di sospendere per allora qualunque pratica in proposito, anche pel Veneto.

Cessato finalmente nel 1866 il dominio austriaco anche nella Venezia si fu allora che si avanzarono e si sono ripetute insistenti premure a questo Ministero onde volesse provvedere alla definitiva esecuzione di quel riparto.

Nè questo Ministero era alieno dal secondare a sì giuste domande, e già da qualche anno aveva assunte indagini, e si era dato cura di raccorre tutti i materiali occorrenti in sì complicata vertenza, affidando apposito incarico a funzionari d'ordine superiore, e già versati in quella materia. Raccolti i risultati delle prime insinuazioni dei crediti, il Consiglio provinciale di Milano prendeva a trattarne nella sua tornata del 12 settembre 1862, e promuoveva dal Ministero un invito a tutte le altre provincie lombarde perchè desero mano ad egual lavoro, al che venne adempiuto colla circolare 28 febbraio 1863, nº 22,212. Ma le risposte da queste provocate non esaurirono che in parte le richieste del Ministero, oltredichè rimaneva sempre l'altra questione gravissima posta innanzi dalla già congregazione centrale lombarda, la quale formava il maggiore ostacolo alle operazioni, in quanto ne impugnava le basi fissate col decreto ministeriale austriaco del 17 novembre 1858. Dal canto loro invece le provincie venete appena ricongiunte al regno insisterono per la piena esecuzione del decreto stesso.

In tale stato di cose il Ministero non potè esimersi dallo interpellare in proposito, a termine di legge, il Consiglio di stato, il quale, in data del 17 settembre 1867, emise il parere letteralmente trascritto in fine della presente.

Il Ministero credè dover prendere per base degli ulteriori provvedimenti in proposito quel voto, ed ora intende affrettare la definitiva risoluzione della pendenza con quell'impegno ed urgenza che a buon diritto è reclamata dall'interesse delle provincie della Lombardia e Venezia.

Egli è perciò che richiamando, con questi dettagli che si sono ravisati necessari, l'attenzione del signor prefetto di                    su tutte le fasi subite da tale pendenza, il Ministero intende sia della presente data, a mezzo delle deputazioni provinciali, pronta comunicazione ai rispettivi Consigli provinciali della Lombardia e Venezia, i quali essendo succeduti alle antiche congregarizioni di provincia, ed anche alla centrale hanno le attribuzioni che a quelle erano riservate dalle ordinanze del già Governo austriaco, e possono, ove lo credano, esperimentare le loro ragioni ai termini del citato parere del Consiglio di stato.

Le prelodate deputazioni vorranno raccogliere tutti i materiali che sono richiesti dalla necessità della regolare istruzione dell'affare onde meglio informare di tutto il Consiglio, avvertendo che, oltre agli atti reperibili negli archivi delle antecedenti delegazioni e congregazioni provinciali potranno, quelle delle provincie lombarde ricorrere per maggiori schiarimenti e notizia alla regia prefettura di Milano, ed a quella di Venezia le altre.

Gioverà anzi, per esaurire completamente le informazioni occorrenti, che sia reso noto alle varie autorità provinciali come del citato parere del Consiglio di stato fosse informato il Consiglio provinciale di Milano, il quale, colla, sua deliberazione del 10 settembre prossimo passato, non solo abbandonava ogni opposizione contro il decreto ministeriale austriaco 17 novembre 1858, ma proponeva:

1° Che si attuasse contemporaneamente fra le provincie di Lombardia la perequazione già predisposta dalla contabilità di Milano, onde così raccogliere i mezzi necessari per devenire tanto al conguaglio generale, come alla stessa perequazione interna;

2° Che si curassero le insinuazioni suppletive, e il successivo conguaglio addizionale, facendo però espresso voto che ad ogni modo i lavori inerenti alla prima insinuazione abbiano a procedere separati e indipendenti da quelli della seconda, ciò essendo nello spirito e nella lettera delle disposizioni precitate, e servendo allo scopo di non protrarre più oltre provincie creditrici il rimborso di somme che furono anticipate già da 20 anni, e che dovevano essere rifuse già da 10 anni.

Il signor prefetto di                è pregato di un pronto cenno di ricevimento della presente, come di riferire quando sarà convocato il Consiglio provinciale per la apportuna trattazione di si rilevante affare.

*Pel ministro*

GERRA.

---

ALLEGATO N° 9.

CONSIGLIO DI STATO.

La sezione dell'interno in adunanza del 17 settembre 1867,

Veduta la relazione 26 agosto 1867 del Ministero dell'interno, divisione 5ª, sezione 4ª, n° 67,326-13,700, coi documenti uniti al piano di liquidazione e perequazione fra la Lombardia ed il Veneto delle spese per requisizioni e prestazioni militari durante la guerra 1848 e 1849;

Sentito il relatore,

Ritenuto che, avendo il Governo austriaco ordinato fin dal 1848 e 1851, che le spese della guerra, e particolarmente quelle del mantenimento dell'armata imperiale, dal 18 marzo 1848 al 31 dicembre 1849 fossero a carico delle provincie delle Lombardia e della Venezia, che dovevano contribuire in ragione della rispettiva forza estimale, fu instituita una Commissione, mista di Lombardi e di Veneti, per procedere alla liquidazione dei rispettivi crediti e debiti delle provincie lombarde e venete;

Che concordi in tutti gli altri elementi della liquidazione, i commissari Lombardi dissentirono dai Veneti soltanto in questo che, mentre gli uni assumevano a base del riparto i risultati del nuovo censimento già noti nel 1856 e concedevano soltanto che le contribuzioni del fondo sociale e della tassa bellica fossero ripartite secondo i dati dell'imposta del 1848 e 1849, e Lombardi pretendevano che l'intiero riparto fosse fatto sulle basi di quella imposta;

Che dalla diversità di quelle basi emergeva che secondo i commissari Lombardi il debito delle provincie della Lombardia a favore di quelle della Venezia, in ragione della maggiore spesa sostenuta da esse, sarebbe di lire austriache 2,638,955 30, mentre, secondo i calcoli dei commissari Veneti, risulterebbe di lire austriache 4,020,017 53;

Che, avendo il presidente della Commissione votato coi Veneti, la loro opinione prevalse nella giunta e fu, con relazione del 14 marzo 1858 (in cui si fece larga menzione del voto dei commissari Lombardi) insieme con gli atti verbali delle sedute, sottomessa al Ministero dell'interno in Vienna; il quale approvava la detta liquidazione sulle basi preferite dalla Commissione, con decreto ministeriale del 17 novembre 1858;

Che, communicato il detto decreto dalla luogotenenza di Milano colle norme per darvi esecuzione, la congregazione centrale della Lombardia ne domandava la revisione con sua rappresentanza del 5 maggio, trasmessa in Vienna il 13 maggio 1859, allegando che se per la tassa bellica e per il fondo sociale si era adottata per base di riparto l'imposta del 1848 e 1849, doveva, per parità di ragione, addottarsi anche per le requisizioni militari e per ogni altra causa di debito;

Che avvenuta, poco dopo, l'annessione della Lombardia al regno d'Italia, l'amminii strazione non ebbe più ad occuparsi che del riparto tra le provincie lombarde, per cu-

spediva in Milano un ufficiale del Ministero dell interno, che in data del 15 maggio 1866 elevava nel suo rapporto il dubbio, se alla cessata congregazione centrale della Lombardia competeva ricorso contro una decisione emanata dal Governo imperiale di Vienna;

Che, dovendosi ora procedere all'estinzione del debito sulle istanze della Commissione centrale per l'amministrazione del fondo territoriale Veneto, ed inoltre alla liquidazione delle partite suppletorie (che il decreto ministeriale del 17 novembre 1858 ordinava farsi sulle basi adottate dalla maggioranza della Commissione lombardo-veneta) il Ministero dell'interno avrebbe aggiunto al detto quesito sull'ammissibilità del ricorso, la questione sul merito, se il reclamo della congregazione centrale aveva ragione di essera negli elementi che informarono la repartizione delle spese di cui è parola;

Considerando che, sebbene non possa dubitarische ci la determinazione ministeriale, del 17 novembre 1858 emanata dalla superiore autorità in via gerarchica non era suscettiva di alcun rimedio ordinario in via amministrativa, in modo che nessun reclamo avrebbe potuto sospendere la esecuzione che per effetto della detta determinazione era ordinata dalla luogotenenza tuttavia non potrebbe nemmeno ritenersi che un provvedimento amministrativo di qualsiasi grado non potesse essere riformato in via straordinaria e di revisione, dallo stesso Governo o dal capo dello Stato in una monarchia assoluta, come era quella dell'impero austriaco;

Che anche le leggi del regno d'Italia concedono contro i provvedimenti amministrativi quando non siano più riparabili in via gerarchica, il rimedio del ricorso al Re, udito il Consiglio di stato;

Ma che non è lecito confondere il rimedio straordinario del ricorso al Re, secondo le leggi italiane, col richiamo per revisione al Governo imperiale austriaco nel 1859; dappoichè il primo non potrebbe riuscire che all'esame, se siano state violate le regole date con autorità legislativa dal caduto Governo; ed in tale esame gli atti governativi posteriori alle disposizioni legislative, potrebbero assumere il carattere di atti di interpretazione autentica, e di risoluzioni delle questioni insorte, anche con nuove regole che il potere assoluto era in arbitrio di mutare; nè mai la decisione amministrativa potrebbe, quanto agli effetti, in una questione di riparto di contribuzioni, e dopo esaurita la esecuzione, limitare l'esercizio dei poteri dell'autorità giudiziaria; mentre tutt'altro poteva essere il fine del ricorso per revisione al Governo imperiale austriaco;

Che quindi il richiamo della congregazione centrale lombarda del mese di maggio 1859, omessa ogni altra questione, non potrebbe tener luogo del ricorso al Re secondo la legge sul Consiglio di stato del 20 marzo 1865;

Che d'altronde disciolta la congregazione lombarda non vi sarebbe luogo a discutere l'ammissibilità di un reclamo, non riasunto dalle amministrazioni che le sono succedute;

Che in tale stato della vertenza, sarebbe prematuro il discutere ogni altra questione di merito;

È d'avviso,

Che poteva la congregazione centrale lombarda ricorrere, come fece, al Governo imperiale austriaco per la revisione della determinazione ministeriale del 17 novembre 1858, ma che, non essendovi più luogo all'esercizio dell'autorità a cui essa riferivasi, debba il Governo dare esecuzione alla impugnata determinazione ministeriale, salvi i richiami che potranno sorgere a norma delle leggi vigenti.

Visto: *Il presidente della sezione.*

Firmato:

IANIGRO.

---

ALLEGATO N° 10.

MINISTERO DELL'INTERNO.

*Perequazione delle spese di guerra* 1848–1849 *nella Lombardia e nella Venezia.*

FIRENZE, 1° *settembre* 1870.

*Ai signori prefetti,*

Colla circolare 1° aprile 1869 prossimo passato, numero 1124, questo Ministero, riassumendo tutte le fasi subite dalla vertenza della perequazione delle spese di guerra 1848–1849 per le provincie di Lombardia e Venezia, faceva sentire alla S. V. essere suo intendimento che a sfogo dei reiterati reclami delle provincie stesse, le quali veggono impegnati in tale vertenza importanti interessi, si procurasse o per accordi tra le provincie medesime, o nei modi legali, che le riluttanze fin qui opposte da parecchie rappresentanze venissero rimosse, e fosse data così esecuzione al riparto delle liquidazioni risultanti dalla prima insinuazione già debitamente sanzionate col decreto 17 novembre 1858, n° 22,116–647 del Ministero di Vienna.

Ed ora, poichè i predetti accordi non poterono conchiudersi tra le provincie, comunque si tentassero parecchi convegni delle rispettive rappresentanze, il Ministero intende si attui senza dilazione di sorta il secondo degli accennati propositi, ed invita i signori prefetti a presentare alla deputazione provinciale il riparto predetto perchè ciascuna, per quanto la risguarda, alloghi, nel bilancio della propria provincia, la somma occorrente per soddisfare alla quota di debito che le fa carico in forza del riparto stesso; che se sorgessere nuove opposizioni da parte di taluna provincia, il Governo intende si proceda, senza ulteriore indugio, alle allogazioni di ufficio, salvo il ricorso alle parti interessate come è accennato anche dal parere del Consiglio di stato 17 settembre 1867, letteralmente riportato in fine della precitata circolare 1° aprile 1869.

All'effetto poi che ciascuna prefettura possa avere la copia del riparto delle spese sancite col decreto 17 novembre 1858, i signori prefetti delle provincie lombarde potranno rivolgersi al prefetto di Milano, ed a quello di Venezia gli altri delle venete.

Si prega accusar ricevuta della presente, porgendo a suo tempo solleciti ragguagli sulla esecuzione degli ordini impartiti in essa.

*Pel ministro*

CAVALLINI.

---

ALLEGATO N° 11.

*Parere sugli imprestiti dei Governi provvisori.*

CONSIGLIO DI STATO.

La sezione d'affari interni e finanze in adunanza 3 settembre 1863,

Veduta la nota 30 luglio scorso del Ministero delle finanze colla quale si chiede il parere del Consiglio di stato sulla convenienza di presentare al Parlamento un progetto di legge per il riconoscimento dei debiti contratti sotto forma di debito pubblico dal Governo provvisorio della Lombardia nel 1848:

Vista l'altra nota del 10 agosto 1863;

Sentito il relatore,

Ritenuto, che il governo provvisorio della Lombardia riconoscendo il suo mandato dal fatto della rivoluzione di quell'anno, dopo avere nel proclama 29 marzo interpretato quel fatto come una missione a conquistare l'indipendenza della patria per giungere a costituire l'Italia unita e libera, nel 12 maggio apriva i registri al suffragio universale per l'unione immediata delle provincie lombarde cogli Stati sardi nell'interesse di quelle provincie, e in quello di tutta la nazione, salve le basi e le forme della nuova monarchia costituzionale da stabilirsi colla dinastia di Savoia;

Che, con legge del dì 11 luglio 1848, veduto il risultamento della votazione universale tenutasi nella Lombardia fu accettata la immediata unione di quelle provincie, e fu dichiarato che esse formavano, con gli Stati sardi e cogli altri già uniti, un solo regno;

Che, per effetto dei contrari eventi della guerra dell'indipendenza, col trattato del 6 agosto 1849, reso esecutorio per la legge del 23 gennaio 1850, la felice unione di quegli Stati, venne disciolta, e la monarchia sarda fu costretta a rinunziare i diritti acquistati con la legge dell'11 luglio;

Che, accesa nuova guerra nel 1859, la stessa monarchia rientrò in possesso delle provincie lombarde per i trattati di Zurigo del 10 novembre 1859, resi esecutori con la legge del 1° dicembre di quell'anno, dappoichè l'Austria, avendo rinunziato in favore dell'imperatore dei Francesi ai suoi diritti e titoli sulla Lombardia, questi li trasferì nell'atto stesso in persona di S. M. il Re di Sardegna;

Che, per effetto di detti trattati, la monarchia sarda prese a suo carico tre quinti del debito pubblico del Monte lombardo-veneto, e di quello nascente dal prestito austriaco del 1854, e si costituì successore in tutti i diritti ed obbligazioni risultanti da contratti regolarmente stipulati dall'amministrazione austriaca per causa di pubblico interesse e concernente il paese ceduto. Nulla però fu detto dei prestiti contratti nel 1848 dal Governo provvisorio di Lombardia;

Considerando che i detti prestiti contratti per sostenere la guerra dell'indipendenza e per le spese del Governo provvisorio di Lombardia (al quale succedeva per diritto nazionale il Governo sardo, per effetto della votazione generale di quelle provincie,) obligavano certamente il nuovo regno dell'Alta Italia costituito in quell'anno, essendo giusta e concorde opinione di tutti i pubblicisti che le provincie annesse, in difetto di particolari stipulazioni, se da una parte sottostanno alle leggi dello Stato con cui si annettano, dall'altra portano in esso tutti i diritti inerenti alla sovranità, e le obbligazioni contratte nell' interesse di quelle provincie;

Che però, l'unione del 1848, fu disciolta dagli eventi della guerra che furono causa al diritto stabilito col trattato del 6 agosto 1849;

Che il Governo austriaco, rientrato in possesso delle provincie lombarde, non volle iconoscere i prestiti fatti dal Governo provvisorio, e si ricusò a pagarne gli interesse e sorte

Che in tal modo, il caso di forza maggiore risultante dagli eventi della guerra, se da una parte privò la monarchia subalpina del benefizio dell'annessione delle provincie ombarde, dall'altra la prosciolse dalle obbligazioni correlative ed inerenti all'annessione, e colpi i prestatori nei loro titoli e diritti, senza che da questo fatto possa scaturire alcuna ragione legale d'indennità da una parte verso l'altra, per il noto principio che *res perit domino ;*

Considerando, che per la ragione internazionale dei trattati, il regno di Sardegna succedeva all'impero d'Austria nel dominio delle provincie lombarde, come questo le teneva prima del 1859 e della pace di Villafranca ; e non potrebbe quindi per titolo dei trattati di Zurigo essere tenuto il nuovo regno a maggiori obbligazioni di quelle che scaturiscono dai detti trattati, o dalla natura dell'atto stesso traslativo della sovranità di quelle provincie ;

Considerando per altra parte come importi il rammentare che l'annessione della Lombardia aveva avuta la sua prima origine e salda base dal libero voto dei popoli, sul quale si fonda la formazione del regno italiano ;

Considerando che le mutate condizioni per cui ai primi prestatori sono succeduti i presenti portatori dei titoli dei prestiti lombardi del 1848, da essi acquistati, probabilmente a tenue prezzo, quando caddero in discredito per le infauste vicende degli ultimi mesi di quell'anno, possano plausibilmente essere volutate nello stabilire la misura con la quale dovrebbero essere riconosciuti e soddisfatti i debiti di cui e parola ;

Che se questo criterio fu cagione per cui furono ridotte a minimi termini le ragioni di altri creditori di rivoluzioni, le quali, benchè si avvolgessero in lunghe vicende, come la Francese nel 1792, tuttavia non patirono sconfitte, può meritare maggiore considerazione nel caso dei prestiti lombardi, in cui la forza maggiore troncò le obbligazioni non meno che i diritti del Governo della rivoluzione ;

Considerando che se il Governo italiano adempie ai debiti del Governo provvisorio di Lombardia, nel modo stesso in cui sarebbe tenuto a soddisfarli lo stesso Governo della rivoluzione redivivo dopo la restaurazione austriaca, del 1848, nessuno potrà muovergli rimprovero di avere rinnegata la sua origine popolare nazionale ;

Che lo stesso Governo delle cinque giornate, se fosse tornato in essere nel 1859, non altrimenti sarebbe stato tenuto di soddisfare ai debiti del 1848, che come ad obbligazioni naturali, giuste ed eque, poichè il nesso civile che dava ad esse la sanzione e la forza del diritto positivo era stato distrutto dalla forza maggiore e troncato dalla spada del vincitore ;

Che quindi avrebbe potuto lo stesso Governo della rivoluzione, nello stabilire la misura dei suoi adempimenti, avere riguardo alla picciolezza dei sacrifizi fatti dagli attuali portatori dei titoli di credito, alla trasformazione del diritto acquistato dai creditori, che dopo la pace del 1849 si convertì in semplice speranza; ed anche alle strettezze finanziarie ed al dovere più perfetto che hanno gli Stati, non meno che i privati cittadini di adempiere alle obbligazioni civili prima di soddisfare quelle che hanno il solo sussidio del diritto naturale e della convenienza politica ;

Che un precedente favorevole ai creditori, circoscritto però entro certi limiti, ebbe già luogo in circostanze non molto dissimili per le provincie siciliane ;

Per questi motivi :

È di parere,

Che se per legge positiva non è tenuto il Governo italiano a soddisfare i debiti contratti sotto forma di rendita pubblica dal Governo provvisorio lombardo del 1848, egli deve, per ragioni non meno valide di diritto naturale e per legittima applicazione del diritto nazionale che è fondamento delle istituzioni del regno, proporre al Parlamento una legge che riconosca quei debiti, e restituisca i creditori nel possesso di un'azione civile per chiederne il soddisfacimento ;

Che però il progetto di legge speciale da presentarsi in proposito a norma dell'articolo 2 della 4 legge agosto 1861 debba essere preceduto dalle necessarie verificazione di cui è parola in detta legge, e da una liquidazione da proporsi nello stesso progetto all'approvazione del Parlamento, alla quale darà il Governo regole e norme secondo le considerazioni che precedono, relative alla misura con cui debbono soddisfarsi tali debiti, avuto riguardo agli esempi del Governo della rivoluzione siciliana del 1860 ;

Che, trattandosi di obbligazione naturale a cui si deve restituire il carattere di obbligazione civile, per considerazioni di giustizia, di equità e di convenienza politica, spetti al Governo il giudicare dell'opportunità del tempo in cui debba farsi la proposta di cui è parola.

Visto : *Il presidente della sezione.*

Firmato: SAPPA.

---

## Allegato N° 12.

*Parere sui danni di guerra.*

### CONSIGLIO DI STATO.

La sezione di finanza in adunanza del 27 maggio 1867,

Veduta la relazione del Ministero della guerra (divisione del materiale del genio, n° 10), in data 5 maggio 1867, colla quale si richiede il parere del Consiglio di stato sulli diverse controversie ultimamente insorte per pretese di compenso in conseguenza de danni risentiti dai privati per operazioni militari eseguite durante l'ultima guerra;

Sentito il relatore;

Veduti gli atti che corredano la pratica;

Ha considerato,

Che, giusta la giurisprudenza già adottata dal precedente Consiglio di stato di Torino e applicata in diversi casi anche dal Consiglio di stato del regno d'Italia, i danni della guerra guerreggiata che sono cagionati dall'immediata azione bellica, e che perciò pigliano carattere di un fatto accidentale compiuto sotto l'impero di una istantanea necessità, non possono essere considerati come titolo giuridico per domande di indennità. Questa soluzione è stata accettata dalla maggior parte degli scrittori di diritto pubblico, ed è fondata sul principio della forza maggiore e della mancanza di libertà nello Stato che ha recati i danni solo per necessità e per dovere di difesa, e quindi ad intento di beneficare anzichè di danneggiare.

Il principio giuridico della forza maggiore che scioglie da ogni responsabilità lo Stato, non impedisce però che possa esservi per riguardi di equità e di convenienza politica anche per lo Stato, il caso di soccorrere i danneggiati; ma le due questioni non vogliονsi confondere, e non si deve credere che dove i cittadini sono obbligati a mettere la loro vita per difesa della patria, i possessori che, per ragione della stessa difesa, venissero a subire danni materiali possano costituirsi come veri creditori dello Stato ed avere azione d'indennità.

Il principio che si è indicato porta seco stesso la sua limitazione. Tutti i danni che lo Stato reca deliberatamente, non già sotto la immediata azione dell'attacco, ed in causa dell'urto delle forze belligeranti, dove può dirsi che non vi sia neppure scelta di luogo e di tempo, poichè la determinazione del luogo e del tempo è una necessaria conseguenza del muoversi o dell'appostarsi dei nemici; tutti gli apprestamenti e i preparativi che precedono la guerra o che vengono ordinati lungi dal vero campo d'azione e per sola previsione di successive eventualità belliche, non hanno per se stesse quel carattere d'indispensabile necessità che giustifica la esclusione di ogni compenso dei danneggiati. Perciò i danni recati dalle truppe in marcia, prima che sia effettivamente cominciata la guerra, gli atterramenti di edifici e gli abbattimenti di alberi fatti intorno alle fortezze non attaccate dal nemico, le occupazioni di terreni e l'erezione di fortificazioni passeggere compiute durante gli armistizi e gli altri fatti consimili, di cui è cenno nella relazione ministeriale, non possono recisamente agguagliarsi alle conseguenze della viva e vera azione bellica; e perciò converrà in questi casi procedere con più cauti avvedimenti, e non rifiutare le offerte e le pratiche per venire ad equi componimenti.

Vero è che in alcuni casi anche i lavori di fortificazione, o le occupazioni fatte fuori della presenza e dell'urgenza dell'attacco nemico, possono, per rispetto alla rapidità e la complicazione degli avvenimenti strategici, pigliare carattere d'urgenza o di indeclinabile necessità, ma un giudizio sicuro sulla natura di questi fatti può trarsi solo dall'esame dei singoli casi; ed il Consiglio di stato non crede possibile di porgere alla amministrazione una norma giuridica sicura ed immutabile, che valga per tutti i diversi atteggiamenti di codeste svariate eventualità. Gli è perciò che si è ricordato il principio fondamentale, il quale autorizza, anzi obbliga lo Stato a rifiutare le indennità pei veri danni della guerra guerreggiata, come quello che contiene in se stesso la ragione delle eccezioni.

Il Ministero, per tutti i casi in cui non è evidente la presenza e l'urgenza del fatto bellico, il quale non lascia luogo nè a scelta, nè a libertà nè a responsabilità, e che è in tutto equiparabile ai fatti consimili ed ai disastri naturali, potrà precedentemente raccogliere gli elementi valevoli ad apprezzare l'importanza dei danni; scandagliare l'intenzione dei danneggiati; far valere le incertezze delle questioni di diritto e di fatto; e prima di concordare una transazione, troverà prudente di sentire i suoi consultori legali e lo stesso Consiglio di stato, che, esaminando gli estremi speciali del fatto, potranno valutare le probabilità di una soluzione o di una condanna giuridica, e suggerire per conseguenza i termini più convenienti di una transazione.

A questo scopo s'aggiunge un'avvertenza sul metodo di valutazione dell'entità dei danni. Il Ministero ha già saviamente provveduto che, ove fosse possibile, il genio militare rilevasse sommariamente lo stato dei fatti. La possibilità di constatare quali fossero le condizioni del suolo o dei fabbricati prima che le operazioni militari le trasformassero, e di precisare la natura e l'entità delle opere e delle alterazioni eseguite per gli scopi militari, è già per se stessa un indizio che mancava quell'urgenza e quell'istantaneità la quale trasformava il fatto bellico in caso di forza maggiore.

Nel tempo stesso l'esistenza di queste constatazioni ufficiali dà il modo di sottrarre lo Stato ad esigenze esagerate ed a reclamazioni artificiali.

Oltre ciò, occorre un'altra osservazione sussidiaria. I danni recati dalla bufera bellica o dalle affrettate opere passeggere sono quasi sempre di maggior vista ed apparenza che di sostanza, ed in tutto simili ai guasti di un disastro eventuale, che non toglie al proprietario, nella più parte dei casi, se non se i frutti e le utilità temporanee.

D'altra natura sono invece i danni recati in forza di un disegno preordinato, come, a ragione d'esempio, quelli che sono la conseguenza di fortificazioni stabili, le quali attirano a sè come uno scopo necessario l'azione bellica, ed assoggettano il territorio circostante ad una specie di perpetua servitù. Vero è che la legge sulle servitù militari ha già in parte provveduto a questa materia, ma non è men vero che quando le previsioni generali della guerra, o le speciali della strategia, impongono ai proprietari che stano vicino a questi campi prefissati alle fazioni militari sacrifizi non imposti dalla ordinaria servitù conviene avere maggior riguardo ai loro reclami, essendo la loro situazione deteriore di quella degli altri proprietari dello Stato. Per questo il Consiglio di stato di Torino opinò che si ammettessero le transazioni relative ai danneggiati per gli abbattimenti degli alberi fatti intorno alle fortezze di Casale e di Alessandria, e su questo si potrebbero accogliere come avviamento a ragionevoli transazioni, anche pei reclami dei possessori dei fondi danneggiati lo scorso anno intorno alla fortezza di Piacenza.

Quanto ai danni recati dalle truppe nazionali in marcia, essi non dovrebbero certo riguardarsi come danni di guerra, e, anzi, i compensi relativi dovrebbero ricadere sui corpi e sui comandanti che, allontanandosi dalla rigorosa disciplina, avessero danneggiate le campagne o le abitazioni dei cittadini. Ma anche su ciò il Consiglio di stato si riserva di dare un voto più risoluto quando gli saranno comunicati gli estremi di fatto; imperocchè, se le marcie di cui si è toccato, avessero avuto luogo all'imminenza della dichiarazione di guerra e fossero state fatte sotto l'impero di ordini straordinari, specialmente quanto al tempo da arrivare e alla via da percorrere, ordini che essi stessi si avessero a presumere ragionevolmente motivati dall' attitudine delle forze nemiche, potrebbe darsi che non mancasse qualche elemento di forza maggiore e di necessità, il quale potrebbe essere fatto valere per diminuire la responsibilità di chi ha recati i danni.

Visto: *Il presidente della sezione.*
Firmato: SAPPA.

---

ALLEGATO N° 13.

*Parere sulla obbligazione dell'Italia respetto al debiti dell'ex-pontificio.*

CONSIGLIO DI STATO.

*Adunanza* 6 *febbraio* 1868.

Il Consiglio:

Vista la nota del Ministero degli affari esteri del 14 gennaio prossimo passato, colla quale si chiede il parere del Consiglio di Stato sulla questione: se pel fatto della rioccupazione francese a Roma sia menomata l'efficacia della convenzione stipulata il 7 dicembre 1866 fra l'Italia e la Francia pel riparto del debito pontificio;

Visti gli annessi documenti;

Udito il relatore:

Ritenuto che l'unico motivo di dubitare è nel riguardare la convenzione del 7 dicembre 1866 come intimamente connessa a quella del 15 settembre 1864, della quale sarebbe stata necessaria dipendenza e compimento, e nell'inferirne quindi che la violazione della Convenzione del 15 settembre commessa dalla Francia col recente suo intervento negli Stati pontifici abbia prosciolto l'Italia dall'osservanza degli obblighi assuntisi con essa Convenzione in correspettivo del ritiro delle truppe francesi dagli Stati medesimi;

Considerato che l'obbligo pel Governo italiano di addossarsi una quota del debito pontificio corrispondente a quelle provincie che negli anni 1859 e 1860 si unirono al regno d'Italia, non deriva già dalla Convenzione del 15 settembre 1864, ma sibbene dall'"incontrastibile principio che, quando uno Stato viene a dividersi in pui parti, come ciascuna di esse, od il Governo cui novellamente appartiene, ha diritto ad una parte proporzionale delle attività che allo Stato medesimo spettavano, così reciprocamente non può esimersi da una quota proporzionale delle passività di cui lo stesso si trovava gravato;

Che per tale principio, mentre il regno d'Italia si accollava tutti senza eccezione i debiti degli Stati che si vennero ad esso integralmente annettendo, assumeva a suo carico la quota di debito austriaco corrispondente alla Lombardia e poscia la quota di debito corrispondente alla Venezia, e la Francia la quota di debito italiano corrispondente alla Savoia ed a Nizza;

Che parimenti il Governo italiano non ebbe difficoltà, nel 1859 per le Romagne e nel 1860 per l'Umbria, le Marche e Benevento, di sopperire indi in poi al pagamento di quel milione e mezzo di rendita sul debito pubblico pontificio che stava inscritto in dette provincie;

Che se diversamente avvenne in riguardo alle rendite inscritte sul Gran Libro del debito pubblico pontificio, il pagamento delle quali facevasi nelle capitale o nelle provincie rimaste a quel Governo, ne fu sola cagione l'essere, rispetto a tali rendite, prima di tutto necessaria una liquidazione, alla quale non si poteva procedere nello stato delle relazioni in cui trovavansi i Governi italiano e pontificio;

Che si fu appunto per far cessare una volta gli ostacoli che per ragioni estranee al merito si erano sino allora opposti all'accertamento delle rispettive quote di debito pubblico fra i due Governi interessati, che venne inserto nella Convenzione del 15 settembre l'articolo 4 del tenore seguente: "L'Italie se declare prête à entrer en arrangement pour pendre à sa charge une part proportionelle de la dette des anciens Etats de l'Eglise."

Che questa disposizione non aveva menomamente per oggetto d'imporre all'Italia l'obbligo di prendere a suo carico una parte proporzionale dell'antico debito pontificio, ma soltanto di ottenere dall'Italia la dichiarazione che era pronta ad entrare in trattative ed a fermare un accordo per soddisfare a tale obbligo non mai da essa contestato;

Che, di vero, le parole: *pour prendre à sa charge*, ecc., sono semplicemente enunciative ed altro non indicano che la materia sulla quale dovevansi aggirare le trattative che l'Italia assumeva l'impegno d'intraprendere; giacchè, se quell'articolo, invece di riferirsi ad una obligazione preesistente, avesse importato un nuovo onere, non pur così grave come quello di cui è caso, ma un onere qualunque alla finanze della Stato, la Convenzione del 15 settembre non avrebbe potuto, a termini dell'articolo 5 della Statuto, avere esecuzione senza l'assenso del parlamento, nè sarebbe quindi stata approvata, come fu, per semplice decreto reale;

Che, ciò stante, si fa manifesto che il fatto della rioccupazione di Roma non può avere influenza nello scioglimento della proposta questione, e sarebbe quindi superflua ogni indagine intorno alla violazione della convenzione 15 settembre: imperocchè ad ogni modo, siccome l'obbligo dall'Italia assunto consisteva nell'entrare in trattative e nel devenire ad un accordo, da che quelle furono intraprese e condussero alla convenzione del 7 dicembre 1866, approvata colla legge del 27 maggio 1867, lo scopo della prima convenzione fu raggiunto e si è ora in presenza della seconda, che l'Italia è tenuta a puntualmente eseguire.

Per questi motivi,

Opina:

Che la rioccupazione francese a Roma non abbia in nulla menomata l'efficacia della convenzione 7 dicembre 1866, della quale si tratta.

Per copia conforme:

*Il segretario generale* BRUZZO.

---

### ALLEGATO N° 14.

*Conflitto tra l'autorità amministrativa e l'autorità giudiziaria in causa Faucitano Salvatore contro il prefetto e l'intendente di finanza della provincia di Napoli.*

DECRETO.

Il Consiglio di Stato,

Visto il decreto del prefetto della provincia di Napoli del dì 25 aprile 1872 nella causa vertente avanti il tribunale civile di quella città tra Faucitano Salvatore contro il prefetto della provincia di Napoli e l'intendente di finanza di detta provincia, per controversia concernente il pagamento di oltre lire 400 mila in rivalsa di danni ed interessi per ingiusta condanna del Governo borbonico;

Vista la nota del Ministero di grazia e giustizia e dei culti in data 8 agosta 1872, con cui trasmise al Consiglio di Stato il decreto surriferito del prefetto;

Visto il decreto del presidente del Consiglio di Stato in data 16 agosto 1872 con cui ordinò di fare le intimazioni di rito alle parti interessate nel conflitto, prefiggendo loro il termine di 30 giorni per presentare i documenti e le scritture che stimassero del loro interesse;

Vista la nota del Ministero di grazia e giustizia e dei culti in data 20 settembre 1872 con cui trasmise al Consiglio di Stato le relazioni, che attestano le intimazioni dianzi accennate essere seguite alle parti interessate nel giudicio, addì 9 settembre 1872 in Napoli;

Visti gli atti della causa, non che i memoriali stati presentati dalle parti;

Vista le legge 20 marzo 1865, n° 2248, allegati *D* ed *E;*

Visto il regolamento annesso al regio decreto del 5 giugno 1865, n° 2323;

Sentito il relatore;

Ritenuto in fatto:

Che Salvatore Faucitano, esponendo i gravi danni sofferti per causa politica, con atto di citazione in data 26 ottobre 1871, chiamava il ministro dell'interno a comparire innanzi il tribunale civile di Napoli per sentir condennare l'Erario nazionale a pagargli, per effetto del decreto dittatoriale del 23 ottobre 1860, a titolo di danni ed interessi per ingiusta condanna patita dal Governo borbonico, la somma di lire 400,000 in un con gli interessi al 5 per cento dal di della domanda sino all'effettivo pagamento;

Che in sostegno di tale domanda invocava il decreto del 23 ottobre 1860 del dittatore Garibaldi, il quale aveva ordinato: che dal valore delle rendite iscritte confiscate ai Borboni e poste a beneficio dello Stato con altro decreto precedente, dovevasi distaccare la somma effettiva di 6 milioni di ducati pari a lire 25 milioni, per essere distribuite con equa ripartizione alle vittime politiche delle provincie continentali dell'ex regno delle due Sicilie dal 15 maggio 1848 in poi; che tale distribuzione doveva effettuarsi da una Giunta di cittadini integerrimi, che sarebbe stata a tale scopo nominata;

Che trovandosi il Faucitano nel numero dei condannati politici di quell'epoca, con sentenza della Corte speciale di Napoli del 1° febbraio 1851 che gli aveva inflitta la pena di morte, che gli venne commutata in quella dell'ergastolo e quindi nella deportazione, sosteneva di aver acquistato diritto all'equa ripartizione di quella somma;

Che non avendo potuto ottenere dal Governo italiano giustizia, si revolgeva ai tribunali onde essere accolta la sua domanda;

Che il prefetto della provincia di Napoli, con memoriale ragionato del dì 28 gennaio 1872, chiese, per organo del pubblico Ministero, che il tribunale si dichiarasse incompetente;

Che il tribunale invece, con deliberazione in data 19 aprile 1872, sulle conformi conclusioni del pubblico Ministero, dichiarava di non trovar luogo a deliberare sulla domanda del prefetto per le considerazioni seguenti:

"Stantechè il Faucitano stima fondare la sua azione non meno sul decreto dittatoriale del 23 ottobre 1860 che sulla legge, ed invoca l'articolo 195 del Codice penale che riguarda una fra le molte ipotesi della disposizione comprensiva dell'articolo 1151 del Codice civile;

"Stantechè l'azione per risarcimento di danni è puramente civile, e l'esame se per avventura il Governo nazionale possa rispondere degli atti del cessato Governo, importa una questione di merito;

"Stantechè le ragioni d'inammissibilità e di rigetto enunciate altresì nel memoriale del prefetto concernono appunto il merito e confermano la giurisdizione del tribunale ordinario. Per questi motivi, ecc."

Che il prefetto, venuto a cognizione di questa deliberazione, con decreto in data 25 aprile 1872:

"Dichiarava esistere conflitto di giurisdizione fra l'autorità giudiziaria e l'amministrativa."

Che dietro ciò il tribunale civile, con deliberazione in data 22 maggio 1872, sospendeva il giudizio;

D'onde, dopo essersi eseguite le formalità tutte della legge prescritte, il conflitto attuale;

Tutto ciò ritenuto in fatto.

Considerando in diritto;

Che il decreto dittatoriale del 23 ottobre 1860, invocato dal Faucitano, avendo prescritto che la distribuzione della somma assegnata alle vittime politiche delle provincie continentali dell'ex regno delle due Sicilie, doveva effettuarsi da una Giunta di cittadini che sarebbe stata a tale scopo nominata dal Governo, basta ciò per escludere la competenza dell'autorità giudiziaria;

Che d'altronde l'indole stessa della risoluzione da prendersi, sfuggirebbe da per sè a tale competenza, poichè si tratta di una distribuzione che il decreto voliva esser fatta *con equa estimazione* fra le persone che avevano sofferto, e la Giunta incaricata di procedervi doveva *valutare nella sua prudenza il compenso da attribuirsi* pei danni sofferti, e per conseguenza il decreto ebbe in mira un complesso di criteri non giuridici ma morali e politici;

Che il Faucitano non ha potuto radicare la competenza giudiziaria colla allegazione da lui fatta che venne danneggiato da una sentenza giudiziaria, la quale dice arbitraria e confonde cogli atti arbitrari puniti coll'articolo 195 del Codice penale il caso previsto dall'articolo 1151 del Codice civile, posciachè è evidente che una sentenza passata in giudicato non ha che fare con tali atti;

Dichiara competente il potere amministrativo a risolvere la controversia al cui riguardo venne elevato il presente conflitto.

Dato a Roma, addì 8 aprile 1873.

Firmato:

DES AMBROIS,
*presidente.*

---

### ALLEGATO N° 15.

*Decisioni sui conflitti nelle cause fra Trevisani Vincenzo e i ministri delle finanze e della guerra* (*31 dicembre* 1872).

ESTRATTO DEL DECRETO.

Vincenzo Trevisani, con due separati giudizi, chiedeva in tribunale al Ministero pagamento di tre forni da pane costruiti e di una fogna riparata, in Verona, per ordine del genio militare austriaco, in giugno e settembre del 1866. Con due sentenze separate, ma dello stesso giorno, il tribunale di Verona non accolse la istanza d'incompetenza avanzata dal prefetto nei suoi due memoriali. E non l'accolse, perchè la questione era di mio e di tuo; perchè l'autorità amministrativa non avocandola a sè, e dicendola portata avanti al Parlamento, ora non troverebbe foro avente giurisdizione per definirla; perchè il decidere se e quali obbligazioni contratte dall'Austria obblighino ora civilmente o moralmente l'Italia, se vi sia o no bisogno di un riconoscimento e quale, se di un trattato che all'Italia le imponga, importava una discussione di merito e non di competenza.

Il prefetto invece decretò il conflitto, considerando che il decidere se l'obbligo di pagare le somme richieste dal Trevisani è *questione che va determinata da un trattato internazionale o da un atto del potere legislativo; che in quanto agli obblighi ed ai diritti rispettivi fra i Governi d'Italia e il Governo austro-ungrico, dopo conchiusa la pace, vennero regolati da due speciali convenzioni finanziarie in data del* 6 *gennaio* 1871, *approvate con legge del* 23 *marzo* 1871; *che in occasione della presentazione di quella legge, nella tornata dell'*8 *marzo* 1871, *il Governo, per organo del ministro delle finanze, dichiarò prendere formale impegno di presentare al Parlamento, entro il mese di marzo* 1871, *un progetto di legge speciale atto a definire i diritti che potessero spettare ai terzi in conseguenza dei trattati del* 1814, 1815, 1818 *e delle guerre del* 1848, 1849, 1859 *e* 1866, *progetto che ha presentato alla Camera dei deputati; e che l'autorità giudiziaria non è competente quando è necessario un provvedimento amministrativo, sia che il Governo abbia a statuire da sè, sia che debba invocare, come nella specie, il concorso del potere legislativo.*

Nel 27 novembre in sezione di giustizia, nel 7 dicembre in sezioni riunite, si lesse il progetto di decreto, e si rinviò la decisione all'adunanza del 31 dicembre 1872, nella quale il Consiglio di Stato, riunite le due cause, le dichiarava di competenza dell'autorità giudiziaria.

Richiamato l'articolo 8 del trattato di Vienna del 3 ottobre 1866, considerò il Consiglio che "se le questioni nascenti da trattati pubblici non appartengono ai tribunali ordinari in ciò che riguarda i rapporti internazionali, ove si contenga in essi una disposizione che possa far nascere diritti civili in favore di cittadini di uno Stato verso il proprio Governo, possono questi esperimentarli, come ogni altro diritto civile derivante da legge, innanzi ai rispettivi tribunali; e che l'esaminare e il decidere se le domande del Trevisani si fondino sopra contratti regolarmente stipulati dall'amministrazione austriaca, e per scopo di pubblico interesse, che si riferisca specialmente al territorio ceduto, è discussione essenzialmente di fatto, la quale, allo stato delle cose, non entra nella sfera delle questioni internazionali, e spetta di conseguenza all'autorità giudiziaria."

(Segue la parte deliberativa.)

—

### ALLEGATO N° 16.

*Conflitto tra l'autorità amministrativa e l'autorità giudiziaria in causa Ranucci Ernesto contro il Ministero delle finanze.*

DECRETO.

Il Consiglio di Stato,

Visto il decreto del prefetto della provincia di Roma del 14 novembre 1871 nella causa vertente avanti il tribunale civile di Roma, tra Ernesto Ranucci e il Ministero delle finanze per una controversia relativa alla presentazione di un conto esatto di tutti gli utili, che nel novennio dal 1859 al 1867 devono essere risultati dall'amministrazione dei sali e tabacchi nelle provincie già pontificie;

Vista la nota del Ministero di grazia e giustizia e dei culti in data 27 dicembre 1871 con la quale trasmise al Consiglio di Stato il decreto surriferito del prefetto;

Visto il decreto del presidente del Consiglio di Stato in data 9 novembre 1872 con cui ordinò di fare le intimazioni di rito alle persone interessate nel conflitto prefiggendo loro il termine di 30 giorni per presentare i documenti e le scritture che stimassero del loro interesse;

Vista la nota del Ministero di grazia e giustizia e dei culti in data 18 febbraio 1872 con cui trasmise al Consiglio di Stato le relazioni che attestano le intimazioni dianzi accennate essere seguite, tanto al Ministero delle finanze che al Ranucci in Roma, addì 29 gennaio 1872;

Visti gli atti della causa non che i memoriali stati presentati dalle parti;

Vista la legge del 20 marzo 1865, n° 2248, allegati *D* ed *E*;

Visto il regolamento annesso al regio decreto in data 5 giugno 1865, n° 2323;

Sentito il relatore;

Ritenuto in fatto;

Che Ernesto Ranucci, con citazione in data 19 agosto 1871, sfidava innanzi il tribunale civile di Roma il ministro delle finanze, chiedendo:

Prefiggersi al Ministero delle finanze un unico e breve termine all'effetto di esibire innanzi al tribunale il conto essatto di tutti gli utili che nel novennio dal 1859 al 1867 sono e devono essere risultati dall'amministrazione pontificia dei sali e tabacchi, caricandosi pur anco di aggiungere gli utili corrispondenti alle provincie romane durante il dodicennio;

Liquidare il dividendo, corrispondente a venti centesimi, di tutte le azioni, avendo a base il capitolato notificato addì 3 ottobre 1854 e la osservanza praticata nelle finanze pontificie durante il primo triennio; attribuire la quota proporzinale del comune dividendo a ciascuna azione di quelle che l'istante esibisce; e per la somma cumulativa degli anni nove condannarsi il Ministero stesso al pagamento in favore dell'istante: scorso poi detto termine e non esibito il conto tenersi in sospeso la condanna terminale; ed intanto condannarsi il ministro stesso al pagamento di una multa giornaliera in quella misura e per quel tempo, che il lodato tribunale crederà giusto; nè tornando prossimo siffatto provvedimento, autorizzare l'istante ad esibire esso stesso negli atti una nota giurata degli utili certi e presuntivi, e su quelle basi approvarsi il conto ragionato che esso stesso redigerà o farà redigere onde il risultato sia base alla richiesta definitiva condanna;

Che in sostegno di tale domanda esponeva in fatto;

Che il cessato Governo pontificio con notificazione del 3 ottobre 1854 dichiarava che aveva divisato di assumere per conto proprio l'amministrazione dei sali e tabacchi chiamando a compartecipi degli utili i sovventori della somma di un milione di scudi, onde impiegarli nella restituzione della cauzione all'intraprenditore che andava a cessare, e nell'acquisto di stigli ed attrezzi, nonchè delle provviste necessarie all'andamento dell'amministrazione;

Che a tale oggetto venne istituita un'amministrazione governativa della Regìa dei sali e tabacchi con fissarne a dodici anni la durata, cioè dal 1° gennaio 1856 a tutto l'anno 1867;

Che a tale uopo si fece un prestito per la somma di un milione di scudi romani diviso in 3750 azioni in parte di scudi 200, in parte di scudi 100 per ogni azione, rappresentate da cartelle al portatore; facendosi diritto ai portatori all'interesse del 5 per cento, e ad una compartecipazione degli utili che si avrebbero da ripartirsi fra gli azionisti: dichiarandosi che nel caso di perdita si sarebbe, a titolo di corrispettività, attribuito alle 5000 azioni il riparto della perdita che si potesse verificare, limitata soltanto alla perdita in tutto od in parte dei 20 centesimi degli utili;

Che dalla massa degli introiti si stabiliva il diffalco preventivo a favore del pubblico Tesoro di un milione e seicentomila scudi, più un capitale per soddisfare gli interessi delle azioni, per l'onorario al gestore ed altre provviste;

Che infine, salvo la restituzione del capitale e ciascun azionista tre mesi dopo spirato il dodicennio, il rimanente degli utili netti depurati dai diffalchi, si dovesse ripartire nel modo seguente, cioè:

Per 20 centesimi agli azionisti;

Centesimi 15 al gestore;

Centesimi 65 al Governo;

Che in tal modo costituita la Regìa funcionava regolarmente per alcuni anni con la corresponsione dei relativi interessi sopra le 5000 azioni: che anzi nel 1868 furono rimborsate per intero le azioni dal Governo pontificio stesso;

Che in quanto agli utili, che non vennero più corrisposti dal Governo pontificio dal 1859 in poi epoca in cui vennero annesse alcune provincie dell'ex Stato pontificio al regno italiano, il Ranucci possessore di n° 631 cuponi di quelle azioni, si è fattoea chiedere dinanzi al tribunale civile di Roma che il Governo italiano debba rispondere della domanda surriferita;

Che il prefetto della provincia di Roma venuto a cognizione di un tale giudizio, con suo memoriale ragionato, in data 11 settembre 1871 diretto al procuratore del Re, chiese: che il tribunale dichiarasse la propria incompetenza a senso dell'articolo 13 della legge sui conflitti del 20 novembre 1859, n° 3780, pubblicata in Roma col decreto reale 18 ottobre 1870, n° 5957;

Che il procuratore del Re con sua requisitoria del 27 settembre 1871 conchiuse, che il tribunale, sul conflitto sollevato dal prefetto di Roma, dichiarasse la propria competenza a conoscere e giudicare le causa promossa dal Ranucci contro il Ministero delle finanze con l'atto di citazione del 19 agosto 1871, per le considerazioni seguenti, adottate dal tribunale civile di Roma nella sua deliberazione in data 3 settembre 1871 dichiarando la propria competenza.

Ritenuto, che l'azione dedotta in giudizio dal Ranucci, giusta i termini della domanda, si fonda sulla convenzione del 3 ottobre 1854 stipulata fra l'attore ed altri azionisti con il cessato Governo pontificio; non meno che sui decreti 9 ottobre 1870 mercè i quali il Principe ha accettato il plebiscito romano, pubblicando nella provincia di Roma e Comarca lo Statuto imperante nelle altre parti del regno,

Che per effetto dell'unione di Roma alle altre provincie del regno si deve intendere effettuato il completo trapasso dello stato giuridico dei diritti e doveri pertinenti al Governo che cessò al Governo che gli succedette; e ciò non solo per principio di assoluta giustizia e di morale, ma ancora perchè il fatto complesso implica trattato e convenzione d'interno pubblico diritto nei molteplici rapporti del Principe coi cittadini dello Stato, e presuppone necessariamente consultate le ragioni di Stato ed ogni altra convenienza;

Che se pure non voglia ammettersi che veramente fra il Principe ed i cittadini sia intervenuto un trattato ed una convenzione, la quale senz'altro partorisca diritti perfetti nel rapporto del Governo di fatto, come molti pubblicisti insegnano, cessa ogni ragione di dubitare, dacchè dopo il plebiscito romano venne pubblicato lo Statuto, il quale con l'articolo 31 guarontisce il debito pubblico, e dichiara inviolabile ogni impegno dello Stato verso i suoi creditori;

Che come corollario dei summentovati principii, ne discende che Ranucci con l'affermarsi creditore dello Stato nell'atto di citazione abbia dedotta avanti il tribunale una materia civile, un diritto perfetto alla base della convenzione e della legge.

Che per tanto il còmpito dell'autorità giudiziaria nel caso di cui si tratta, non si estende sino al punto di sottoporre ad esame un atto dell'autorità amministrativa per revocarlo o modificarlo; e neanche si limita ad un semplice interesse insussistente sul pratico terreno del jure civile; ma ha per obLietto un punto certo di diritto, scritto nella legge civile e diretto allo esclusivo scopo di regolare e guarentiee gli interessi dei singoli cittadini;

Che sono devolute alla giurisdizione ordinaria tutte le materie nelle quali si faccia questione di un diritto civile, comunque possa esservi interessata la pubblica amministrazione; articolo 2 della legge 20 marzo 1865, allegato *E*;

Ritenuto che dalla sapiente sentenza pronunziata dalla Corte d'appello di Firenze il 14 maggio 1870, alle cui giuste considerazioni si appoggia il prefetto di Roma, per sostenere la incompetenza del tribunale adito dal Ranucci, non si possano oggidì trarre norme incontrastabili, atteso il mutamento del diritto pubblico interno di Roma dopo la prolazione di detta sentenza: dappoichè quel magistrato giudicò bensì sopra una domanda consimile a quella proposta dal Ranucci, ma al cospetto di terre riscattate col valore delle armi italiane, ad annesse allo Stato d'Italia, pur rimanendo in vita, sebbene in più angusto territorio quel Governo di cui le terre anzidette furono emancipate, e col quale i soci capitalisti trattarono nel 1854 intorno ad un'operazione, che spaziava tra i confini dello Stato romano di quell'epoca; appariva quindi chiaro, che trovandosi allora due eserciti belligeranti e due Principi l'uno vinto e l'altro vittorioso, quest'ultimo in rapporto alle provincie annesse assumesse il morale dovere di far fronte agli impegni quantitativi corrispondenti alle medesime, e che gli impegni stessi potessero di poi, in virtù di trattati internazionali, addivenire attuabili ed esperibili in giudizio come doveri perfetti.

Era a dedursi pertanto, siccome acconciamente è stato ritenuto nella sovraccennata sentenza, che infino a quando non avesse termine il lavoro tracciato nella convenzione internazionale del 27 maggio 1867, n° 3745 e relativo protocollo in data 15 agosto 1868, le istanze tendenti ad ottenere il pagamento dei ratizzi pertinenti a' creditori delle città annesse sfugisse al sindacato dell'autorità giudiziaria;

Che non vi ha chi non vegga quanto le condizioni e le leggi di quei tempi siano in oggi disformi.

Nè si dica che la domanda del Ranucci, afferente alla convenzione del 3 ottobre 1854, implica simultaneamente interessi di cittadini romani, nonchè delle Marche e dell'Umbria, e come almeno per quest'ultima parte trovi ostacolo nel trattato internazionale del 27 maggio 1867 tra il Re d'Italia ed il Pontefice ammesso pure che per l'altra l'unione recente di Roma, abbia recato gli effetti superiormente accennati; od in altri termini, non si dica, che se il plebiscito romano trasferì nell'attuale gli oneri del caduto Governo: non si possano avere per trasferiti se non in quanto essi stavano per gli antichi domini del Pontefice a norma delle condizioni segnate nella convenzione del 1867 vigente all'istante in cui ebbe luogo il plebiscito anzidetto; imperochè, essendo nel concreto caso avvenuto, che provincie dello stesso regno nella successione del tempo e sotto condizioni e modi diversi, si sono annesse ed unite ad altro regno; la risultanza che ne consegue si concreta e si compenetra nello stesso ente e rende di per sè inattuabile ed inefficace la esecuzione di trattati che siansi antecedentemente stipulati. D'altronde, anche sotto quest'ordine d'idee, la domanda del Ranucci, che è cosa individua, riferendosi almeno per una parte ad un diritto perfetto, è evidente in obbedienza alle leggi imperanti, che non si possa sottrarre al potere giudiziario;

Che le altre ragioni addotte dal prefetto, comechè si attengano al merito della causa promossa dal Ranucci, non possono in oggi essere valutate ed apprezzate; versandosi unicamente il giudizio sulla competenza del magistrato, udito, ecc.

Che il prefetto, vista la deliberazione surriferita, con decreto in data 14 novembre 1871 eccitava il conflitto di giurisdizione per le considerazioni seguenti:

Considerato, che non può ammettersi in via assoluta il principio proclamato dal pubblico Ministero nelle sue conclusioni adottate dal tribunale giudicante, che essendosi il Ranucci affermato creditore dello Stato ha con ciò dedotto avanti il tribunale una materia civile, un diritto perfetto; e che siano devolute, alla giurisdizione ordinaria tutte le materie nelle quali si faccia questione di un diritto civile, poichè fra le altre disposizioni avvi pur quella, che per l'articolo 10 della legge 20 marzo 1865, n° 2248 pubblicata in questa provincia col regio decreto 18 ottobre 1870, numero 6957, è riservata alla giurisdizione propria del Consiglio di Stato ogni controversia fra lo Stato ed i suoi creditori risguardante l'interpretazione dei contratti di prestito pubblico, delle leggi relative a tali prestiti e delle altre sul debito pubblico.

Considerato, che non può trattarsi nel caso concreto di un diritto perfetto, perchè non venne finora riconosciuto dal potere legislativo dello Stato, che solo ha veste legislativa per disporre che un debito diventi obbligo civile dello Stato.

Considerato, che se alcune delle considerazioni già svolte dalla Corte d'appello di Firenze nell'identica materia con la sentenza 14 maggio 1870 cessarono di essere applicabili all'odierna lite pel fatto dell'unione di Roma e' sua provincia al regno d'Italia, non cessano però d'essere sempre applicabili i principii di diritto pei quali fu sottratta alla competenza giudiziaria la identica causa promossa da Forini Emilio.

Considerato in fatto, che le questioni, che si fondano suatti del Governo aventi il ca rattere essenzialmente politico sono di competenza esclusiva della pubblica amministrazione, perchè dominate dalla suprema ragione di Stato; e che nel caso concreto devonsi per l'appunto ritenere di tale natura quelle che si devono svolgere per la decisione della promossa vertenza; in quanto è necessario far risalire le indagini alle conseguenze legali derivate da atti e fatti di natura esclusivamente politica, siccome la prima occupazione della provincie, che furono staccate dallo Stato pontificio negli anni 1859 e 1860, e dall'ultimo fatto che soppresse interamente ed annullò lo Stato pontificio.

Considerato, che fu generalmente ammesso in tutti gli Stati, che la presa di possesso di un nuovo territorio è un fatto tale le cui conseguenze non possono essere apprezzate dall'autorità giudiziaria, e che nel caso speciale l'apprezzamento di tutte queste conseguenze di fatti politici è complicato anche dall'esame degli effetti e della validità della convenzione internazionale 7 dicembre 1866 posta in rapporto ed in armonia coi fatti politici posteriormente avvenuti.

Ritenute le altre considerazioni svolte nella succitata domanda in data 11 settembre 1871.

Per queste considerazioni, ecc.,

Che in seguito a ciò il tribunale civile di Roma con deliberazione in data 24 novembre 1871 ordinò la sospensione del giudizio; d'onde, dopo essersi eseguite regolarmente le formalità tutte prescritte dalla legge il conflitto attuale.

Tuttociò ritenuto in fatto:

Considerando, che la sostanza della controversia sta nell'apprezzere le conseguenze di un contratto stipulato dal Governo pontificio;

Che se alcune parti dell'antico Stato pontificio, ora fuso nel regno d'Italia, furono anteriormente staccate dallo Stato stesso, le domande od eccezioni che possano nascere da questo fatto e dalle circostanze che lo accompagnarono o lo seguirono in ordine all'oggetto della controversia anzidetta, non potrebbero nello stato attuale delle cose considerarsi altrimenti che come accessorie e connesse alla medesima;

Che ormai si tratta unicamente di questioni di diritto interno in materia civile;

Che non è il caso d'interpretazione di un vero imprestito di Stato, cui possa essere applicabile la competenza giurisdizionale del Consiglio di Stato;

Dichiara competente l'autorità giudiziaria a risolvere la controversia nella quale fu elevato il presente conflitto.

Dato in Roma, addì 28 marzo 1873.

*Il presidente*
Firmato: DES AMBROIS.

---

ALLEGATO N° 17.

*Catalogo delle Petizioni intorno ai danni di guerra.*

1916. Il Parrcco di Olengo e vari possidenti di quel comune rinnovano le loro istanze perchè si ripari ai danni cagionati dall'invasione Austriaca.

1947. Il Sindaco e gli abitanti del comune de Nibbiola chiedono riparazione dei danni cagionati dall'invasione Austriaca.

2091. Il Consiglio delegato del comune di Candia (Lomellina) fa vive istanze perchè siano rimborsate le requisizioni e risarciti i danni che ebbero luogo in occasione della guerra.

2157. N° 19 abitanti del mandamento e comune di Momo, provincia di Novara, supplicano per il compenso dei danni della guerra.

2247. Alcuni abitanti di Novara chiedono che siano sollecitamente fissati i soccorsi da darsi ai danneggiati dalla guerra.

2253. I Sindaci e molti proprietari della provincia di Novara ricorrono onde ottenere un sollecito risarcimento dei danni derivati dall'invasione Austriaca.

2290. Albini avvocato Pietro chiede si provvedá pel risarcimento dei danni sofferti da alcuni abitanti di Vigevano durante la guerra, già liquidati dall'azienda generale di guerra fino dall'agosto 1848.

2293. Vari sindaci, proprietari ed affittajoli della provincia di Lomellina chiedono il risarcimento dei danni sofferti dall'occupazione Austriaca.

2378. Sinforiani Antonio, di professione domestico, domiciliato in San Fedele (Lomellina), lagnasi di essere stato inscritto nelle liste dei danneggiati dalla guerra per un compenso di sole lire 50, mentre i danni ricevuti ammontano a lire 415, e chiede che la Commissione lo compensi proporzionatamente.

6642. Brigatti Luigi, da Suno, provincia di Novara, chiede di essere indennizzato almeno in parte dei danni da lui sufferti nella ritirata delle truppe in seguito alla battaglia di Novara, siccome risulta da giudiziale perizia annessa alla petizione.

6853. N° 75 cittadini di Messina chedono sia posto in esecuzione il decreto emanato nel 1848 dal Parlamento Siciliano, relativo all'obbligo del Governo di indennizzare gli abitanti di quella città dei danni sofferti dall'incendio, dal bombardamento e dal saccheggio delle truppe Borboniche.

6889. N° 27 cittadini di Caserta rappresentano i guasti sofferti nei loro poderi per lo stanziamento delle truppe volontarie e regolari durante l'assedio di Gaeta, e chiedono di essere indennizzati.

7639. Il Sindaco di Borgo Vercelli trasmette una deliberazione del Consiglio municipale per ottenere dal Governo l'integrale rimborso dell'ammontare delle requisizioni e dei danni a cui soggiacque quel comune par la guerra del 1859.

8247. I fratelli Mastroddi, di Tagliacozzo, promuovono istanza per ottenera il rimborso dei danni sofferti dal combattimento delle truppe contro lo spagnuolo Borjes, seguito in una casa rurale di loro proprietà, stata incendiata.

8446. Tosti conte Raffaele rappresenta i danni sofferti in conseguenza dell'assedio di Gaeta, e ne chiede indennizzazione.

8800. Sartori Lucia vedova contessa Tracagni ed i di lei figli Fabio ed Emilio, di Salò, proprietari dello stabile detto di San Martino, sul quale si decisero nel 1859 le sorti dell'Italiana indipendenza, domandano che sulla indennità che loro può spettare pei danni di guerra, gli sia intanto accordata una anticipazione in quella misura che meglio si crederà dal Parlamento.

9065. La Giunta municipale di Basiglio, circondario di Milano, sollecita il pagamento delle somme dovute al comune per requisizioni forzate fatte dall'armata austriaca, durante la guerra del 1859.

9858. Gli orfani Camillo ed Angiolina Licenziati, di Gaeta, ricorrono al Parlamento perchè sia loro concesso un sussidio mensile come indennizzazione della loro casa, la quale, crollando intieramente durante l'assedio di quella piazza, li lasciò privi di ogni mezzo di sussistenza.

11,326. Le rappresentanze civica e commerciale di Venezia domandano al Parlamento il riconoscimento dei debiti contratti dal Governo provvisorio di Venezia negli anni 1848–49 per la causa della nazionale indipendenza.

11,579. Il sindaco di Bormio, provincia di Sondrio, rassegna alla Camera i conti delle spese incontrate dai comuni di quel mandamento pei fatti d'armi degli anni 1848, 1859 e 1866, affinchè vengano presi in considerazione e soddisfatti.

11,677. Il sindaco del comune di Bormio, provincia di Sondrio, aggiunge alle petizione presentata per risarcimento di spese incontrate durante le guerre dal 1848 in poi, un nuovo prospetto di altre spese occorse per sgombro di frane.

12,067. La Giunta municipale di Adria, provincia di Ravigo, rivolge alla Camera una petizione per ottenere a carico dello Stato la rifusione della forzosa contribuzione di fiorini 10,000 imposta nel luglio 1866 dal comando dell armata Austriaca su quel comune in punizione della parte presa da quegli abitanti in favore delle truppe Italiane.

12,500. Il municipio de Montechiaro sul Chiese, provincia di Brescia, ricorre alla Camera per ottenere il rimborso delle spese sopportate per somministrazioni fatte alla truppe Nazionali ed Austriache nel 1848, 1859 e 1866.

12,507. Muratori Giovanni, di Modena, ed altri 17 barocciari e carrettieri dei paesi finitimi di detta provincia, presentano alcuni documenti onde essere compensati pei servizi di trasporto forzato, prestato d'ordine municipale alle truppe Estensi ed Austriache fino dalli 7, 11 e 12 giugno 1859.

12,528. Vari proprietari di mulini natanti sull'Adige nel comune di anguillara, invocano il pagamento dei compensi pei danni loro cagionati dalle truppe Austriache nel 1866.

12,885. Il sindaco e parecchi abitanti del comune di Castelfranco veneto invocano dal Parlamento una disposizione legislativa per cui dal Governo s'addivenga tosto all'indennizzo dei comuni e dei privati che nell'anno 1866 soggiacquero alle requisizioni forzati e subirono depredazioni dall'esercito Austriaco in ritirata.

13,463. Danieli Ciovanni Battista, di Borgo Santa Lucia in Vicenza, dopo avere ricorso inutilmente onde ottenere di essere indenizzato dei danni sofferti in signeto al ritorno degli Austriaci, nel 1848, in quella città i quali gli incendiarono case e sostanze, invoca dal Parlamento un sollecito provvedimento.

13,479. Murer Pietro, di San Donà di Piave, nella provincia di Venezia, si rivolge alla Camera per ottenere il refacimento di danni patiti a causa delle fazioni militari del 1848 e 1849.

13,485. I danneggiati dagli incendi del 4 e 5 agosto 1848, nel comune dei Corpi Santi di Milano, chiedono che, ove siano approvate le convenzioni finanziarie conchiuse coll'Austria in esecuzione del trattato di pace 3 ottobre 1866, vengano con apposita riserva dichiarati impregiudicati ed illesi tutti e singoli i diritti e le ragioni ed azioni anche reali ed ipotecarie ad essi competenti.

13,488. La Giunta municipale di Ostiglia, provincia di Mantova, rivolge istanza perchè, nell'ammettere la convenzione finanziaria stipulata coll'Austria, siano dichiarate salva le ragioni creditorie dei terzi pei danni di guerra degli anni 1813, 1814, 1848, 1849, 1859 e 1866.

13,491. Il Consiglio provinciale de Novara rinnova al Parlamento le sue istanze perchè provveda, in quella misura che stimerà più equa, al compenso delle requisizioni Austriache praticatesi nel 1859 in quelle terre.

13,493. Alcuni cittadini di Mantova, espropriati dall'Austria per opere di fortificazione, domandano il pagamento dei loro crediti già liquidati dall'Austria stessa, ai quali furono fino al presente opposte le trattative che pendevano a Vienna.

13,504. La Giunta municipale de San Benedetto-Po, provincia di Mantova, chiede il rimborso a quel comune di lire 21,178 72 per danni di guerra e requisizioni fatte dall'armata Piemontese, Toscana, Modenese, Lombarda e Corpi volontari nell'anno 1848.

13,509. Damiani-Galvani Lucia, Marcon Angelo, Brusadia Marco ed altri 5 cittadini possidenti di Pordenone, nel Friuli, chiedono il pagamento dei danni che alle rispettive loro proprietà arrecò l'armata Austriaca ritirandosi dal Veneto nel luglio 1866.

13,563. Gli eredi del barone Gaetano Testa, di Parma, si rivolgono alla Camera per ottenere il risarcimento di danni da questi sofferti pella distrusione ordinata dall'autorità locale nel 1849 degli edifizi e macchine costituenti lo stabilimento di brondolo dal medesimo eretto per la bonificazione dei terreni adiacenti.

13,606. Giovanni ed Antonio David e Molduzzi Gaetano, di Ravenna, si rivolgono alla Camera con distinte petizioni per ottenere il risarcimento di danni sofferti per fatto d'un corpo d'armata Austriaca, mentre abbandonava la città d'Ancona per ritirarsi nel Veneto.

13,620. Sette cittadini rappresentanti i creditori dello Stato della provincia di Verona per espropriazioni di suolo e soprassuolo durante la dominiazione Austriaca, fanno istanza perchè dalla Camera venga respinto il progetto di legge presentato dal ministro delle finanze per le indennità dei danni di guerra.

13,638. Guaita Cristoforo e Croce Paolo, di Milano, si rivolgono alla Camera per ottenere l'integrale pagamento delle diverse odere eseguite e delle sommistrazioni fatte di materiali a stabilimenti militari nell'anno 1848 durante il Governo provvisorio di Lombardia.

516. La deputazione provinciale di Milano sottopone al Parlamento una petizione diretta ad ottenere che nella discussione del progetto di legge per l'indennità dei danni di guerra sia dichiarato che il fondo della guardia nobile Lombardo-Veneta nella prima cifra assegnata all'Italia dal Governo austriaco, debba ritenersi di ragione della fondiaria delle provincie lombardo-venete ed assegnarsi alla provincia di Milano, sulla base dell'estimo censuario del 1859, la somma proporzionale di lire 163,069 11.

543. La deputazione provinciale di Udine si rivolge alla rappresentanza nazionale perchè voglia invitare il Governo a provvedere al pagamento dei crediti che i comuni di quella provincia professano per le somministrazioni fatte all'esercito Austriaco in base alla notificazione luogotenenziale 25 giugno 1866.

550. La Camera di commercio ed arti della provincia di Venezia aggiunge schiarimenti e dimostrazioni per constatare la giustizia della domanda inoltrata al Parlamento colla petizione 11,326 da quella rappresentanza civica e commerciale onde ottenere il riconoscimento ed il rimborso dei prestiti dal Governo provvisorio di Venezia incontrati negli anni 1848—49.

574. La deputazione provinciale di Padova, associandosi alle considerazioni esposte nella petizione inoltrata da quella di Udine, domanda che sia invitato il Ministero a provvedere al pagamento dei crediti che i comuni della provincia di Padova professano verso il Governo per le somministrazioni fatte all'esercito Austriaco nel 1866.

586. La deputazione provinciale di Belluno si associa alla petizione presentata da quella di Udine per ottenere che sia provveduto al pagamento dei crediti che professano i comuni contro il Governo per le somministrazioni fatte all'esercito Austriaco nel 1866.

648. La Giunta municipale della città di Como domanda il pagamento del residuo suo credito per somministrazioni fatte ai Cacciatori delle Alpi nell'anno 1859.

654. La rappresentanza municipale del comune di San Giovanni Incarico, provincia di Terra di Lavorro, ricorre al Parlamento perchè voglia provvedere che dal Governo siano rimborsate le spese incontrate da quel comune per somministrazioni militari fatte alle truppe Borboniche negli anni 1859 e 1860, ed alle truppe nazionali nel 1861.

667. La Commissione municipale di Gaeta rivolge istanza perchè quei cittadini vengano risarciti dei danni di guerra sofferti nell'assedio 1860—61.

Una Commissione delegata dai danneggiati di Brescia pei fatti del 1848 e 1849 fa istanza onde sia decretata l'indennizzazione dei danni di guerra sostenuti dalle provincie Lombarde, e specialmente dalla città di Brescia, in dette epoche, avendo anzi uno speciale riguardo all'anteriorità di tale debito della Nazione in confronto dei danni causati nelle guerre successive.

Queste petizioni si riferiscono a danni di guerra e requisizioni, a espropriazioni per opere di fortificazioni, a forniture militari e imprestiti. Quelle di esse petizioni, e sono le più, che porsero tema all'*Allegato* ministeriale, trovano espresso il loro trattamento nella relazione della Commissione, la quale, una dopo l'altra, ha preso ad esaminare tutte le partite dell'*Allegato*. Per le petizioni ivi non tradotte, basta la sola evvertenza che la Commissione ha, nella sua relazione, esposti principii e, nel suo disegno di legge, fatte proposte con formule generali, e però applicabili caso per caso, secondo la diversa natura e i termini della fattispecie di ciascuna petizione.

MANTELLINI, *relatore.*

---

## *General Schenck to Mr. Fish.*

No. 624.] LEGATION OF THE UNITED STATES,
*London, October* 17, 1874. (Received October 30.)

SIR: Immediately after receiving your circular of the 23d of June, instructing me to obtain trustworthy information in regard to the course pursued by the government of Great Britain in relation to the adjustment of claims against it by its own subjects or by aliens, and the mode of procedure adopted in the investigation and determination of such claims, I addressed a note to Lord Derby, asking to be supplied with the information desired, and inclosing a copy of the schedule of inquiries which accompanied your circular.

On the 10th instant I received from his lordship a note in reply, inclosing what purports to be a legal memorandum and opinion on the subject, forwarded to him from the home department for my information.

The opinion thus given in answer to my request is not exactly of the character, nor in the form, which I think you desired, and which I expected to obtain. But it seems to be all that there is a disposition now to furnish. This memorandum appears to me not so much to explain the forms of procedure, and to indicate the tribunals to be appealed to, in order to establish a claim against Her Majesty's government, as it notes the doubts and difficulties in the way of the prosecution of any such claim.

I inclose herewith copies of my note to Lord Derby; his answer; the paper communicated from the law-office of the home department; and my acknowledgment of his note and its inclosure.

I have, &c.,

ROBT. C. SCHENCK.

[Inclosures.]

1. General Schenck to Lord Derby, August 19, 1874.
2. Lord Derby to General Schenck, October 8, 1874.
3. Legal opinion of the home department, September 26, 1874.
4. General Schenck to Lord Derby, October 15, 1874.

---

[Inclosure No. 1 in No. 624.]

### *General Schenck to Lord Derby.*

LEGATION OF THE UNITED STATES,
*London, August* 19, 1874.

MY LORD: For the purpose of facilitating the adjustment and determination of claims presented against the Government of the United States, whether held by its own citizens or by the subjects or citizens of foreign governments, and with a view to establishing as far as may be practicable a general and uniform system and mode of procedure for the investigation and determination of these classes of claims, my Government is desirous of obtaining exact and trustworthy information in regard to the course pursued by Her Majesty's government in relation to the adjustment of claims of a similar character against her government, and the mode of procedure adopted in the investigation and determination of such claims.

I have the honor to inclose herewith a list of inquiries, numbered from 1 to 7, inclusive, pointing more directly to the particular information sought and the specific points upon which it is most desired; and I will thank your lordship to cause me to be favored with replies to these questions, and, when the information is based upon legislative enactments or public and general regulations by the executive department of Her Majesty's government, with copies of such laws and published regulations, so far as you may be pleased to supply them.

I have the honor to be, my lord, your lordship's most obedient, humble servant,

ROBT. C. SCHENCK.

The Right Honorable the EARL OF DERBY.

---

[Inclosure No. 2 in No. 624.]

*Lord Derby to General Schenck.*

FOREIGN OFFICE,
*October* 8, 1874. (Received October 10.)

SIR: I referred to Her Majesty's secretary of state for the home department your note of the 19th of August, in which you asked, on behalf of your Government, to be furnished with information as to the course pursued by Her Majesty's government in regard to claims prosecuted against it by its own subjects or by aliens, and I have now the honor to transmit to you a legal opinion on the subject, which has been forwarded to me from the home department, for your information.

I have the honor to be, with the highest consideration sir, your most obedient, humble servant,

DERBY.

---

[Inclosure No. 3 in No. 624.]

## LEGAL OPINION OF THE HOME DEPARTMENT.

### OPINION.

In his letter of August 19, 1874, General Schenck asks for exact and trustworthy information in regard to the course pursued by Her Majesty's government in relation to the adjustment of claims prosecuted against it, whether by its own subjects or by the subjects or citizens of foreign governments, and the mode of procedure adopted in the investigation and determination of such claims; and he supplements each request by a series of questions of the most minute character, having reference not only to the subject-matter of his more general question, but also to the status of aliens in respect of proceedings before British tribunals, as well as regards aliens residing in Great Britain as those resident elsewhere.

To answer these questions with a sufficient amount of detail to be of any practical utility to the United States minister, would involve the compilation of a treatise of considerable bulk, which, when compiled, would only contain information to be found in the text-books of greater or less authority.

We propose to indicate presently some of the chief sources of information upon these subjects. With respect to claims made against the Crown, the common-law method of obtaining possession or restitution of real or personal estate has, for the most part, been by petition of right, a form of proceeding dating from the time of Edward the First; but in 1860 an act of Parliament was passed, (23 and 24 Vic., C. 34,) by which provision was made for assimilating, as nearly as may be, the proceedings on petitions of right to the course of practice and procedure in actions and suits between subject and subject; but inasmuch as it is provided by the seventh section that nothing in the act shall be construed as giving to the subject any remedy against the Crown in any case in which he would not have been entitled to such remedy before the passing of the act, recourse must still be had to the state of the law as it existed before the passing of the act, for the purpose of determining the class of cases in which the remedy exists.

A few years since a very able treatise on the subject, in the form of a letter addressed to Chief-Justice Bovill, was compiled by the present Mr. Justice Archibald. It was printed for private circulation, but it is to be found in most law libraries. It contains the most valuable information, within a narrow compass, to be found upon the subject, and has references to all the older leading authorities, among which we may mention Ryley's Placita Parliamentaria; Stamford's Prerogative, title Petition; The Bankers Case, 14 Howard's State Trials, with Lord Lomer's celebrated judgment; Skinner's Reports, page 613, containing Lord Holt's judgment in the Bankers Case; Manning's Practice in the Exchequer, vol. 1, pages 84–88. As regards this latter authority, it should be stated that the soundness of the views expressed in it has been questioned in several recent cases.

Among the more important of the recent decisions upon the subject of the petition of right, we may refer to Viscount Canterbury *vs.* Attorney-General, 1 Phil., 306; Re Carl Von Frantzius, 2 De Gex & Jones, 126; the case of Baron de Bode, 8 Q. B., 271; Tobin *vs.* The Queen, 16 C. B., (N. S.,) 353; Feather *vs.* The Queen, 6 Best & Smith, 294; Churchward *vs.* The Queen, 1 L. R., (Q. B.,) 173.

We think, however, right to add that in some respects the law upon the subject of claims against the Crown must be considered as still unsettled, inasmuch as a case (Thomas *vs.* The Queen) was argued, at considerable length, before the Court of Queen's Bench, in the month of June last, in which a variety of questions of great importance were raised, and, among others, whether a petition of right would lie for breach of contract or to recover money claimed by way of debt or damages, or, indeed, for any other object than specific chattels or land. The court reserved its judgment, which has not yet been delivered. Whatever may be the ultimate decision of the Court of Queen's Bench in this case, it is to be hoped that a clear exposition of the present state of the law will be obtained.

As regards the inquiries of the United States minister which have reference to the "status of aliens," we may state, in general terms, that an alien, whether resident or not in this country, may sue and be sued before the ordinary tribunals, and will be bound by, and have the benefit of, the same forms of procedure and rules of evidence as a native; but an alien enemy cannot, during the continuance of war, unless under license from the Crown, bring an action or continue an action commenced before the war began.

As regards the inquiries which have reference to the course adopted by the various departments of the executive government with respect to claims made upon or against them, we are not in a position to afford any information or to express any opinion.

——— ———.

SEPTEMBER 26, 1874.

---

[Inclosure No. 4 in No. 624.]

*General Schenck to Lord Derby.*

LEGATION OF THE UNITED STATES,
*London, October* 16, 1874.

MY LORD: I have the honor to acknowledge the receipt of your lordship's note of the 8th instant, inclosing for my information, in reply to my letter to you of the 19th of August, a legal opinion from the home department on the course pursued by Her Majesty's government in regard to claims prosecuted against it by its own subjects or by aliens, and I have much pleasure in expressing to your lordship, and through you to Her Majesty's home department, my thanks for the opinions in question.

I am, with the highest consideration, my lord, your lordship's most obedient servant,

ROBT. C. SCHENCK.

The Right Honorable the EARL OF DERBY, *&c.*

---

DEPARTMENT OF STATE,
*Washington, December* 23, 1874.

SIR: Referring to previous correspondence, I have the honor to inclose herewith, for your further information, a copy of a dispatch of the

29th of October last, No. 90, and of its accompaniment, from Mr. Lewis, the minister of the United States to Portugal, relative to the presentation of claims against that government.

I have the honor to be, sir, your obedient servant,

HAMILTON FISH.

Hon. WM. LAWRENCE,
*Chairman of the Committee on War-Claims,*
*House of Representatives.*

[Inclosure.]

Mr. Lewis to Mr. Fish, October 29, 1874, No. 90, with an accompaniment.

---

*Mr. Lewis to Mr. Fish.*

No. 90.] LEGATION OF THE UNITED STATES,
*Lisbon, October* 29, 1874. (Received December 4.)

SIR: I herewith have the honor to inclose the several replies to the "schedule of inquiries," inclosed in circular dated June 20, from the Department of State, relative to the course pursued by the government of Portugal in the adjustment of claims against that government, and the mode of procedure adopted in the investigation and determination of such claims.

I have the honor to be, sir, your obedient servant,

CH. H. LEWIS.

Hon. HAMILTON FISH,
*Secretary of State, Washington.*

[Inclosure.]

1. Replies to schedule of inquiries.

---

[Inclosure No. 1 with dispatch No. 90.]

*Answers to "schedule of inquiries" contained in circular (June 23) from Department of State.*

1. The claim is investigated by the government, and if considered valid, they may pay it, provided it may be included under any of the appropriations; otherwise it is necessary for the government to propose a bill to the Cortes asking an appropriation.

2. A bill proposed by the government to pay a claim is referred to the usual committees of the two houses, and follows the same course as any other measure. The Cortes may ask for the necessary evidence from the executive branch of the government, but there is no special law regulating the means for obtaining such information.

3. The case is investigated by the "procurador geral," (attorney-general.) There is no special mode of procedure designated by law. The usual means for obtaining evidence are employed. There are no privileges enjoyed by subjects over foreigners in this respect; either may on equal terms sue the government in the courts.

5. Foreigners have the same rights as subjects. They may maintain whatever action against a subject, and resident and non-resident aliens have same privileges in this respect.

6. There are neither classes nor distinctions in the systems of adjudication. The government has no privileges in questions of proof.

7. The government in a case with an individual has no privileges. The appropriation by the Cortes is always necessary when the amount to be paid is not included in the annual and regular appropriations.

DEPARTMENT OF STATE,
*Washington, January* 2, 1875.

SIR: Referring to previous correspondence, I have the honor to inclose herewith, for your further information, a copy of a dispatch of the 12th of November last, No. 28, from Mr. Osborn, minister resident of the United States to the Argentine Republic, relative to the presentation of claims against that government.

I have the honor to be, sir, your obedient servant,

HAMILTON FISH.

Hon. WILLIAM LAWRENCE,
*Chairman of the Committee on War-Claims,*
*House of Representatives.*

[Inclosure.]

Mr. Osborn to Mr. Fish, November 12, 1874, No. 28.

---

UNITED STATES LEGATION,
*Buenos Ayres, November* 12, 1874.

Sir: In my dispatch No. 9, dated September 10, I had the honor to acknowledge the receipt of dispatch from the Department of State, dated June 23, 1874, with schedule of inquiries inclosed, relative to information in regard to the course pursued by the government of the Argentine Republic in relation to the adjustment of claims against the government, and the mode of procedure adopted in the investigation and determination of such claims.

I now have the honor to reply that, on account of the breaking out of the rebellion in this country, and the consequent excitement here, I have been delayed in my investigation, and it has not been perhaps as thorough and complete as it might have been under other circumstances.

In my examination I found that previous to the last administration (President Sarmiento's) there was no settled mode of procedure in the presentation and adjustment of claims, but their rejection or acceptance seemed to depend upon favor and influence.

Dr. Tejidore accepting the position of minister of foreign affairs, some three years ago, under President Sarmiento, adopted at once, and for the first time in the history of this country, American precedents, refusing to foreigners all indemnity in cases of revolt or rebellion, other than that granted by the law of nations, and referring them to the courts, under the constitution, rejecting the intervention of ministers, but recognizing the claim to be just in the initiative, when based upon alleged injustice of the courts.

The course pursued by the government in the adjustment and final determination of claims, when based upon the alleged injustice of the courts, and presented to the executive, will be answered in my reply to the inquiries presented from 1 to 7 inclusive.

*Schedule of inquiries and answers.*

Question 1. "Are claims against the government investigated, determined, and, if allowed, then payment directed and provided for by the legislative branch of the government?"

Answer. Every claim is presented to the executive and proper department, according to its nature. It must be substantiated by the report of that department which may be acquainted with its antecedents, and with the opinion of the attorney of the treasury or the attorney-general of the nation.

The executive can also ask for all the data, reports, or testimony that may be considered necessary to establish the truth of the alleged facts. In this respect there is no law whatever establishing a fixed form of procedure. If the executive finds the claim admissible, and there exists in the general budget of the administration or in special laws authority to make payments of the nature of the claim, he then orders its payment by the finance department, charging it to the budget or the special law, as the case may require.

If there should be no authority in law to make such payments, then the case is passed to Congress, accompanied with a bill to vote the necessary funds to meet the payment.

Congress studies the claim anew, and if found admissible, accepts the bill submitted by the executive. If the executive finds the claim inadmissible, he rejects it.

In this latter case the interested party sometimes presents himself direct to Congress, complaining of the decision of the executive, and asking that by a special law the payment be ordered for the amount claimed.

Congress has admitted this kind of claims, and has acted on them, deciding, after due examination, in favor or against them. During the last administration the executive rejected this custom, upon the ground that, in administrative affairs, as he considered these claims, Congress cannot assume the power of a chamber of appeal from the resolutions of the executive, and that these questions ought to be finally closed with the decision of the executive, unless he should allow the party interested to carry the case before the national Congress. Upon this controversy no definitive jurisprudence is as yet established.

Question 2. "If the legislative authority does entertain such claims, what is the mode of procedure, by the committee or otherwise; and what means, if any, are provided for procuring evidence on behalf of the government?"

Answer. Even though the claim has been passed by the executive, asking funds to meet its payment, or even presented direct to Congress by the interested party, the chambers to which the claim has been sent refers it to one of the committees, according to its nature.

The committees of the chambers are six, denominated, on "Constitutional Affairs," on "Legislation," on "Finance," on the "Budget," "Military," and on "Petitions." They are composed of five members in the Chambers of Deputies, and three in the Chamber of Senators.

The claim being passed to the competent committee, it can obtain all the particulars, and make all the investigations that may be considered necessary, without any limitation whatever, or without any certain form of proceeding to establish the truth of the facts.

When this committee requires information, details, or antecedents of any other authority, or dependency of another department, it then demands authorization of the chambers, which, once granted, it asks for such detailed information or antecedents through the president of the respective chambers.

After the case has been only considered, the committee presents to the chamber, in the form of a project of law or bill, its decision, accepting, rejecting, or modifying the claim.

Afterward, both chambers observe the forms of procedure established in the constitution, for the framing and sanction of laws, until the affair is definitely ended.

Question 3. "What provision, if any, is made for the examination and determination of claims by the executive department? What is the mode of procedure in the investigation of claims by or before executive officers; and what means are provided for procuring evidence on behalf of the government?"

Answer. The principal part is already found in the reply to the first question.

There is no fixed form of procedure determined by law in contentious administrative affairs, as these claims generally are.

The established procedure is the one I have indicated in answering the first question. It can be, and has been, varied in certain cases.

There have been cases in which claims have been submitted to the decision of arbitrators appointed by the party and the executive.

There is also a certain kind of claims that are governed by special laws, in which regular forms of proceedings have been established. At the conclusion of this report I will speak of these laws.

The means of proof in favor of the government, as well as in favor of the party interested, have no limitation or special form; all the means of legal proof are admitted on the basis of good faith.

Question 4. "Is there any provision of law allowing a citizen or subject to sue the government in the regularly-established courts, or in any special tribunal, and the privilege of maintaining an action against the Government (if it exists) extends to aliens."

Answer. The federal supreme court has declared that the executive cannot be sued To establish an action against him it is necessary, first, that he should previously.

permit it by a special resolution in each case. This permission has been granted by both branches of the government, executive and legislative; by a simple resolution when granted by the executive, or by a formal law when given by the legislative power.

This is the jurisprudence established in order to prevent all arbitrary proceedings, which might ensue should Congress refuse such application. A bill has been presented to Congress to create a tribunal of claims, and to determine the proceedings which should be followed before it.

Although this is only a project as yet, there is no doubt that it will be converted into law, with more or less modifications. Public opinion is already settled in its favor.

Foreigners may bring suit in all respects as the citizens. See the following question for the explanation of this assertion.

Question 5. "What is the status of aliens before the regularly-established courts of the country? Can they maintain an action in such courts against a citizen or subject; and, if so, does the privilege extend to all aliens, or is it confined to resident aliens only?"

Answer. The statute on aliens is fixed by the following article of the constitution:

"ART. 20. Aliens enjoy in the territory of the republic all the civil rights that citizens do. They can follow their occupation or profession, possess, buy, or sell real estate, navigate the rivers and coasts, exercise freely their religion, testate and marry according to its laws. They are not obliged to become citizens, or pay extraordinary or forced contributions."

From these primordial rights given by the constitution to foreigners spring all the rights that are correlative to them, and, among others, the right of suing or being sued by any individual, native or foreign, before the courts or the government, in the cases and conditions before mentioned, or in any civil or criminal suit that originates from the exercise of the rights above mentioned, or for the violations of said rights. Furthermore, when a question arises between a foreigner and a native, they are not obliged to submit to the local tribunals, but either of them can oblige the other to appear before the federal tribunals of the nation. This right does not exist when the question is between two foreigners or two natives, in which case they are obliged to submit to the decision of the province in which they reside.

The resident foreigner and the temporary sojourner have equal rights in law. The only difference, therefore, between a citizen and an alien in the republic is, that the latter cannot be an elector for members of any of the three highest positions in the nation, nor can he, on the other hand, be obliged to perform military service, or pay extraordinary obligatory contributions.

The foreigner can nevertheless, in some provinces of the republic, be elector and elected for municipal posts, without incurring any obligation in consequence. The alien who resides two years in the republic can obtain citizenship, or sooner, if he has rendered important services to the country. The certificate of citizenship permits him to exercise the political rights of the native-born without being obliged to give military services, and it can only be issued by the supreme federal court.

From the above it can be affirmed, without exaggeration, that in no other country of the world has the foreigner fuller privileges than in the Argentine Republic.

Question 6. "If different systems of adjudication exist, as regards different classes of claims, what is the system with reference to each class; and what the mode of procedure, and the privilege of the Government in relation to evidence in its behalf, and the means of procuring such evidence?"

Answer. The only laws that establish formalities for certain claims, and special forms of payments, are those to which I referred in answering the first question, and which I now proceed to give in detail.

The damages suffered by individuals during the civil wars, the assistance given to the armies which fought against the tyranny of Rosas, that ended in 1852, and the debt which was left unpaid by the old government of the confederation, which ceased the year 1860 by the incorporation of the province of Buenos Ayres, have been recognized by laws of Congress as public debts of the nation, and ordered to be paid in public funds, at 6 per cent. interest and 1 per cent. annual amortization.

Those laws have fixed the forms of procedure that are to be followed in prosecuting private claims.

All of them decide that the executive shall appoint an especial commission to examine the claims.

This commission, after the proper study of the case, for which it had full powers for taking all the evidence it may judge necessary, passes the claim to the executive, with the draught of the resolution prescribed by its judgment.

In view of it, the executive, according to the case, acknowledges the debt, and orders the corresponding payment in public funds, or rejects the claim.

In the law upon assistance rendered to the armies that fought against the tyranny of Rosas, it has ordered that the written documents originally given by the chiefs of the armies, by the commissions officially named to procure means, or by the government of provinces that helped said armies, should be admitted as proof.

In all the other cases there was no limitation as to the means or burden of proof, this always belonging to the part of the plaintiff.

These laws fixed the time in which the claimants ought to present themselves, and that term having expired, no more claims were allowed; on the other hand, there were very few who did not present themselves.

Treaties, also, have been made with various nations as to the form of proceeding and payments of the same kind of damages done to aliens, besides those caused during the war of independence, that have not been paid yet to the citizens. The amount of those damages has been generally fixed by commissioners of arbitrators appointed by the executive and foreign ministers, and paid in public funds or treasury bonds.

Nearly all these claims are already decided, there being very few that are as yet unsettled.

The government has no privilege whatever respecting proofs, but simply those belonging to its condition as defendant.

It is incumbent in the claimant, who is called the creditor, to produce sufficient proof of the truth of his demand, and not on the executive, who only judges the merits of the proof without in any wise preventing the presentation of documents or declarations to the contrary, whenever they can be obtained, as would happen with any other party sued.

I have the honor to be, your obedient servant,

THOS. O. OSBORN.

Hon. HAMILTON FISH,
*Secretary of State, Washington, D. C.*

---

DEPARTMENT OF STATE,
*Washington, February* 12, 1875.

SIR: Referring to previous correspondence upon the subject, I have now the honor to inclose, for the information of the committee over which you preside, a copy of a dispatch of the 8th of January ultimo, No. 303, from the minister of the United States at Copenhagen, and of its inclosure, in relation to the course pursued by the government of Denmark in the adjustment of claims presented by its own subjects, or by the subjects or citizens of foreign governments.

I have the honor to be, sir, your obedient servant,

HAMILTON FISH.

Hon. WILLIAM LAWRENCE,
*Chairman of the Committee on War-Claims,*
*House of Representatives.*

[Inclosure.]

Mr. Cramer to Mr. Fish, January 8, 1875, No. 303, with accompaniments.

---

*Mr. Cramer to Mr. Fish.*

No. 303.] LEGATION OF THE UNITED STATES,
*Copenhagen, January* 8, 1875.

SIR: Referring to the Department's communication of June 23, 1874, requesting exact and trustworthy information in regard to the course pursued by the government of Denmark in relation to the adjustment of claims presented against that government, either by its own subjects or by the subjects or citizens of foreign governments, as well as in regard to the mode of procedure adopted in the investigation and determination of such claims, I have the honor to inform you that on the 30th of July, 1874, I addressed a note to the Danish minister for foreign affairs, requesting him to furnish me with the desired information for transmission to the Government of the United States. For the purpose of showing him more precisely the nature of the information desired, I inclosed in my note a copy of the "Schedule of Inquiries" that had been inclosed in the Department's communication. A copy of my note I herewith inclose, marked No. 1.

The reasons for addressing the said note to the minister for foreign affairs were: 1. The belief that, as the Department desired *exact* and *trustworthy* information, none would be better able to furnish it than the government itself. 2. That, had I requested an able lawyer to furnish me with the same, he would have, in all probability, asked a large fee for it, for the payment of which I had no authority.

After having waited five months—though, during that time, I have twice alluded to the subject in my conversations with the minister for foreign affairs—I received, on the 2d instant, a note from him, dated December 31, 1874, in which he answers *seriatim* the questions contained in the schedule of inquiries referred to. A copy of this note is herewith inclosed, marked No. 2.

I have the honor to be, sir, very respectfully, your obedient servant,

M. J. CRAMER.

Hon. HAMILTON FISH,
*Secretary of State, Washington, D. C.*

*List of inclosures.*

1. Copy of a note addressed by Mr. Cramer to the minister for foreign affairs, marked No. 1.
2. Copy of a note addressed by the Danish minister for foreign affairs to Mr. Cramer, marked No. 2.
3. A printed copy (in French) of the constitution of the Kingdom of Denmark, referred to in the minister's note, marked No. 3.

---

[Inclosures.]

No. 1.

LEGATION OF THE UNITED STATES OF AMERICA,
*Copenhagen, July* 30, 1874.

EXCELLENCY: My government desires me to procure exact and trustworthy information in regard to the course pursued by the government of His Majesty the King of Denmark, in relation to the adjustment of claims presented against the said government, whether by its own subjects or by citizens or subjects of foreign governments.

The reason why my Government wishes to possess such information is the desire to establish, as far as may be practicable, a general and uniform system and mode of procedure for the investigation and determination of claims presented against the Government of the United States, whether by its own citizens or by citizens or subjects of other governments.

I therefore take the liberty to request your excellency to have the goodness, so far as may be consistent with the rules and regulations of His Majesty's government in such cases, to furnish me with the desired information; and also, where such information is based upon legislative enactments, or public and general regulations by the executive departments, to send me copies of such laws and published regulations, for transmission to my Government.

For the purpose of showing more precisely the nature of the information desired I take the liberty to inclose herewith a list of inquiries numbered from 1 to 7, inclusive, pointing more directly to the particular points upon which information is most desired.

Be pleased, your excellency, to accept renewed assurances of my most distinguished consideration.

M. J. CRAMER.

His Excellency BARON O. D. ROSENÖRN-LEHN,
*Royal Danish Minister for Foreign Affairs, &c.*

No. 2.

[Translation.]

COPENHAGEN, *December* 31, 1874.

SIR: In the note which you were pleased to address me, under date of the 30th of July last, you expressed a desire to be furnished with information as to the rules established in Denmark relative to claims presented against the government of the King, either by its own subjects or by foreigners, and especially in regard to the manner in which claimants are required to furnish evidence of the validity of their claims.

In order to comply with this request I have requested the competent departments to answer the various questions propounded by you, and I am now enabled, by the communications which have been received by me from these departments, to furnish you with the desired information, which, for the sake of greater clearness, I shall have the honor to submit to you in such a way that each question will be answered separately.

1. "Are claims against the government investigated, determined, and, if allowed, their payment directed and provided for, by the legislative branch of the government?"

1. According to the laws of Denmark it is the province of the executive department of the government, properly so called, to examine all claims presented against the treasury, to decide to what extent they can be allowed, and finally to cause to be paid to the claimants the sums to which they are entitled according to the decision. Although, therefore, the legislative branch does not interfere directly in matters of this nature, the competency of the executive branch is essentially limited in matters of this nature by section 49 of the constitution of the Kingdom of Denmark of June 5, 1849, revised and promulgated July 28, 1866, according to which "no expenditure can be made which is not authorized by the said law, or by a supplementary appropriation."

The executive branch of the Danish government cannot, therefore, allow such claims, unless the Rigsdag has previously appropriated the money deemed necessary for this purpose; and it is only in urgent cases that it can, on its own responsibility, allow any claims without having been authorized to do so by the Rigsdag, to which it must then apply in order to obtain, by means of a supplementary appropriation, the sanction of the expenditure made by it. For the sake of greater control over the acts of the executive department, it is prescribed by section 50 of the constitution that each of the chambers of the Rigsdag, namely, the folkething and the landsthing, are to appoint two paid examiners, whose duty it is "to examine the accounts of the fiscal year, and to see whether all moneys received by the state have been properly entered, and whether any expenditures, other than those allowed by the budget, have been made." When this examination, which is very different from the examination made in the bureaus of the various ministries, has been made, the annual accounts of the state, together with the remarks of the examiners, are to be laid before the Rigsdag, which, according to section 14 of the constitution, has the right to impeach the ministers of the King for any disbursements made by them without authority from the legislative branch.

It appears from the foregoing that the general rule is that any person having claims against the Danish treasury must address the executive department, whose duty it is, within the limits above stated, to examine them, and to allow them if they are found to be just.

2. "If the legislative authority does entertain such claims, what is the mode of procedure, by committee or otherwise, and what means, if any, are provided for procuring evidence on behalf of the government?"

2. This rule, however, does not prevent a claimant, if he prefers doing so, from presenting his claim to the Rigsdag, provided he observe the provision of section 63 of the constitution, which is "that no proposal shall be submitted to the chambers except through one of their members." If the claim has not been presented to the executive department before it is laid before the Rigsdag, that body confines itself to transmitting it, without comment, to the competent minister, who then treats it as if it had been submitted to him directly. On the other hand, if the claim has been rejected by the executive department, and if, in consequence, the fact of its presentation to the Rigsdag implies dissatisfaction with the executive decision, the Rigsdag may, according to section 64 of the constitution, return it to the competent minister with or without recommendation. In acting thus, the Rigsdag indicates that, in its opinion, the claim deserves to be taken into consideration by the executive department, although its return to the minister can give the claim no legal value other than that which it intrinsically possesses.

3. "What provision, if any, is made for the examination and determination of claims by the executive department; what is the mode of procedure in the investigation of claims by or before executive officers; and what means are provided for procuring evidence on behalf of the government?"

3. As regards proofs of the validity of claims against the Danish treasury, the executive department demands none stricter than those which, according to the ordinary laws of procedure, are admissible before the courts in private cases. Save the exception which will be mentioned under number four, the claimant may, even if he con-

siders himself aggrieved by the attitude taken by the executive department in regard to his claim, bring suit against the competent minister in the manner prescribed for civil cases between private citizens.

4. "Is there any provision of law allowing a subject to sue the government in the regularly-established courts or in any special tribunal; and does the privilege of maintaining an action against the government (if it exists) extend to aliens?"

4. According to the laws of Denmark, both the subjects of the kingdom and the subjects of another state have a right to bring suit before the courts against the executive department as well as against a private citizen. To this rule there is but one exception, employés appointed since April 1, 1870, not being allowed, according to section 12 of a law of March 26, 1870, to cause such disputes as may arise between them and the ministers with regard to their salaries to be submitted to the decision of the courts. Disputes of this nature are settled by the minister of finance conjointly with the minister under whom the functionary interested is employed.

5. "What is the status of aliens before the regularly-established courts of the country? Can they maintain an action in such courts against a subject; and, if so, does the privilege extend to all aliens, or is it confined to resident aliens only?"

5. As regards the status of aliens in the courts of Denmark, they are placed upon the same footing as the subjects of the kingdom. They may, therefore, although not domiciled in Denmark, bring suit against the subjects of the country before these courts.

6. "If different systems of adjudication exist as regards different classes of claims, what is the system with reference to each class, and what the mode of procedure and the privilege of the government in relation to evidence in its behalf, and the means of procuring such evidence?"

6. As has already been observed under number 3, the laws of Denmark prescribe no different rules of procedure, whether the suit be brought against the government of the King or against a private individual.

* * * * * * *

I inclose to you a copy of the constitution of the kingdom of Denmark; and I avail myself of this occasion to beg you, sir, to accept the assurances of my most distinguished consideration.

O. D. ROSENÖRN-LEHN.

Mr. CRAMER,
*Minister Resident of the United States of America.*

# THE LAW OF CLAIMS

IN

# THE UNITED STATES.

THE MODE OF ADJUSTING CLAIMS AGAINST THE GOVERNMENT,

AND

THE PROCEDURE ADOPTED IN THEIR INVESTIGATION.

# INTRODUCTORY.

---

## THE OFFICERS AND TRIBUNALS HAVING JURISDICTION TO INVESTIGATE CLAIMS.

Claims against the United States are examined either by officers in the Departments of the Government, by the Court of Claims, the Commissioners of Claims, by committees of Congress, or by mixed commissions, under treaties.

Claims may be presented in either House of Congress, by petition or by bills introduced by members. These are generally referred to appropriate committees, and by these examined, and then a report is made to the House in which the claim was presented, and if in favor of the claim with a bill or joint resolution for an appropriation to make payment, which is considered and passed or rejected as other private bills. Sometimes the bill refers the examination of the claim to the Court of Claims or to the Commissioners of Claims.

The Court of Claims renders judgments subject to an appeal to the Supreme Court of the United States, in which final judgment is entered, and these judgments are regarded as conclusive and paid without examination by appropriations made by Congress.

The Commissioners of Claims examine certain classes of claims, and report their conclusions to the House of Representatives, where they are open to examination, and, subject to such supervision, are rejected or paid by appropriations.

The officers of the several Departments of the Government examine the ordinary claims for salaries and other expenses of the Government, when they are reported to the proper officers of the Treasury Department and paid out of appropriations made from time to time by Congress.

An examination of the statutes will show the jurisdiction exercised by the officers of the Departments, the Court of Claims, and the Commissioners of Claims, in the examination of claims, and the mode of procedure authorized by law.

It is not practicable to give all these in this connection, but sufficient will be presented as to each to show the general course of proceeding, with some of the acts of Congress relative to the Departments, and all relating to the Court of Claims and the Commissioners of Claims.

Mixed commissions, under treaties, exercise such jurisdiction and in such mode as the treaties provide, aided by such legislation of Congress as may be necessary, and their awards are paid by appropriations made by Congress.

# THE LAW OF CLAIMS.

---

## CHAPTER I.

### OF WAR—REBELLION—THE CLASSES OF WAR-CLAIMS—GENERAL PRINCIPLES.

During the progress of the wars in which the United States have been engaged, many claims[45] have been from time to time made against the Government, by citizens, corporations under national, or State, or foreign authority, and by aliens.[46] Some of these may be properly arranged into *classes*, with a view to consider the questions of law which arise as to the liability of the Government to make compensation either under the Constitution, the laws of nations, common or statutory law. The expediency of providing compensation where no legal liability exists, involves questions which a powerful and just nation should be ever ready to consider.

[45] For claims see American State Papers, class IX, vol. 1, "Claims."

Also Senate Mis. Doc. 43, 3d sess. 40th Cong., list of private claims brought before Senate from commencement of 14th to close of 39th Congress.

House list of private claims, vols. 1, 2, and 3, from 1st to 31st Congress, entitled "Digested Summary and Alphabetical List of Private Claims," &c. House Mis. Doc. 109, 42d Cong., 3d sess., digested summary private claims, presented to House of Reps. from 32d to 41st Congress inclusive. See an article on "Government Claims," 1 American (Boston) Law Review, 653, (July, 1867.)

[46] Claims of aliens have frequently been made the subject of diplomatic arrangements. See report of Hon. R. S. Hale, November 30, 1873, to Secretary of State, of proceedings of commission under 12th article treaty of 8th May, 1871, between United States and Great Britain.

See "opinions of heads of Executive Departments and other papers relating to expatriation, naturalization, and change of allegiance," in House Ex. Doc. 1, part 1, 1st sess. 43d Congress, Report of Secretary of State on Foreign Relations, p. 1177, part 1, vol. 2.

The act of July 27, 1868, (15 Stat., 243, sec. 2,) gave aliens a right to sue in the Court of Claims, when the government of such aliens gave a similar right to our citizens.

In Fichera *v.* U. S., 9 Court Claims R., decided in 1873, Nott, J., said:

"The only question presented by this case is whether, under the Italian law, an American citizen may maintain an action against the government of Italy. As we have before found, the perfected justice of the civil law made the government, in matters of ordinary obligation, subject to the suit of the citizen, in the ordinary tribunals of the country. We have found this right to be preserved under modern codes in Prussia, Hanover, and Bavaria, (*Brown's Case*, 5 C. Cls. R., p. 571;) in the republic of Switzerland, (*Lobsiger's Case*, id., p. 687;) in Holland, the Netherlands, the Hanseatic Provinces, and the Free City of Hamburg, (*Brown's Case*, 6 C. Cls. R., p. 193;) in France, (*Dauphin's Case*, id., p. 221;) in Spain, (*Molina's Case*, id., p. 269;) and in Belgium, (*De Gives's Case*, 7 C. Cls. R., p. 517.)

It was also shown in *Brown's Case*, (5 C. Cls. R., p. 571,) by a distinguished historical writer who was examined as a witness, Mr. Frederick Kapp, that this liability of a government under the civil law is not a device of modern civilization, but has been deemed inherent in the system, and has been so long established that, to use the phrase of the common law, the memory of man runneth not to the contrary. Therefore, it is to be expected that in Italy, the seat and fountain of the civil law, this same liability of government is to be found existing. The "Civil Code of the Kingdom of Italy" of 1866 recognizes, rather than establishes, the fundamental principle of liability; but it expressly provides (article 10) that, "in suits pending before the judicial authority between private persons and the public administration, the proceedings shall always take place formally at the regular session.

During the late rebellion, or civil war, property of immense value, of every kind, was taken, used, or destroyed, on sea and land, by rebel and Union civil authorities and military forces, without any compensation rendered. It is, of course, a duty of the Government to patiently and attentively hear every claimant for compensation or damages, and pass upon the merits of the claim in the light of reason and law.

Perhaps no classification can be made which would comprehend every

---

It is also provided, by the third article of the same code, that "the alien is admitted to enjoy all the civil rights granted to citizens." These provisions establish the right of an Italian citizen to maintain his action in this court, within the meaning of the *Act July* 27, 1868, (15 Stat., p. 243, § 2,) which prohibits the subject of a foreign government from maintaining a suit for captured property, unless "the right to prosecute claims against such government in its courts" is reciprocal and extends to citizens of the United States.

In England aliens have a remedy by "petition of right," regulated by act 23 and 24 Victoria, July 3, 1860. U. S. *v.* O'Keefe, 11 Wallace, 179; Carlisle *v.* U. S., 16 Wallace, 148. See Whiting's War Powers of the President, 51; The Venus, 8 Cranch; The Hoop, 1 Robinson, 196; The Amy Warwick, Sprague, J.

See Whiting's "War Claims," affixed to 43d ed. of "War Powers," p. 333, ed. of 1871; Perrin *v.* U. S., 4 Court Claims, 547.

The claims of aliens cannot properly be examined by a committee of Congress.

This was so held in Report No. 498 of the Committee on War-Claims, first session Forty-third Congress, May 2, 1874. That case was as follows:

Charles Bombonnel represents, in a memorial referred to the committee, that he is and always has been a citizen of France, and resides in Dijon; that prior to the rebellion, and ever since, he owned certain real estate, with buildings thereon, at Carrollton, in the parish of Jefferson, Louisiana; that the military authorities of the United States took possession of these August 23, 1862, and that the said premises were thereafter used by the Union military authorities as a hospital, and for other purposes, to September 1, 1865; that the premises were damaged $1,600 by the occupancy, and that the use and occupation was worth $55 per month. He asks payment of $3,580 and interest. He alleges that he, by his agent, had leased the premises, and they were in the occupancy of his lessee when the military authorities required the tenant to vacate them in August, 1862. He also alleges that he has made repeated efforts to obtain justice through the military authorities, through the French legation at Washington, and through the Quartermaster-General, and has uniformly received the reply that there is no authority to settle the claim but Congress.

The *right of a citizen of the United States* to petition Congress is recognized in the first article of amendments of the Constitution, and it is declared this right shall not be abridged. The language of this amendment is that it shall be "the right of *the people* * * to petition," &c.

In Paschal's annotated Constitution, it is said the expression, "*the people*," here is used in the broad sense of the preamble, and a broader sense than "electors." (See Story, Const., sec. 1994–1995; discussions on 21st Rule of the House of Representatives in 1838 and 1846.) The preamble to the Constitution recites that "We, the people of the United States, * * do ordain this Constitution," &c.

The "people" who did ordain the Constitution, and to whom the right of petition is secured so that it cannot be abridged, were, and are, *citizens of the United States*. When such *right* is secured, it carries with it the *duty* of Congress to hear and consider the petition, for otherwise the right would be *vox et prœterea nihil*.

But such right of petition is not thus secured to aliens. It is not a *legislative duty* to hear their petitions.

There is a department of government in which most questions of an international character may be considered, that which has charge of foreign affairs.

A foreign government may, on behalf of its citizens or subjects, treat with the Government of the United States in relation to claims of such citizens or subjects, but when this is done the United States can arrange to secure the claims of their citizens, or such other rights as international justice may require.

Congress cannot safely, and by piecemeal, surrender the advantages which may result from diplomatic arrangements.

This has been the general policy of the Government. Congress has not generally entertained the claims of aliens, and certainly should not unless on the request of the Secretary of State representing our foreign interests.

In support of this the following is submitted:

"DEPARTMENT OF STATE, *Washington, April* 22, 1874.

"SIR: In reply to your telegram stating that claims are presented by French citizens and other aliens through Congress, to the Committee on War-Claims, I have to remark

claim that has been or could be made. The liability of the Government for any class of claims growing out of the war of the rebellion depends somewhat upon the status of the so-called rebel States and the people thereof, their relations to the National Government, and the place where the right to demand compensation arose.

It is now determined, by the highest court, that the civil war *began* at least for some purposes and at some localities, as early as April, 1861.[46a] By the President's proclamations of April 15 and 19, 1861, an insurrection was declared to exist in certain States. Under, and it may be correct to say by virtue of, the act of Congress of July 13, 1861, the

---

that such presentation is entirely inconsistent with usage, which requires that aliens must address this Government only through the diplomatic representatives of their own governments.

"This Department refuses to entertain applications or to receive claims from aliens, except through a responsible presentation by the regularly accredited representative of their government.

"I have also been under the impression that Congress refused to receive petitions or claims from aliens. Such I am advised was at one time the rule of the House of Representatives, and such is the rule at present in the Senate as I am informed. The propriety of the refusal to allow an alien to intrude his claims upon Congress cannot be questioned.

"I have the honor to be, sir, your obedient servant,

"HAMILTON FISH.

"Hon. WM. LAWRENCE, *House of Representatives*."

But there are very many claims of French citizens growing out of the war of the rebellion, and it would be utterly impracticable for Congress to become a claims commission to pass on all these. Similar claims of subjects of Great Britain were submitted to a commission under the 12th article of the treaty of 8th May, 1871, and the report of its proceedings will be found in House Ex. Doc. 1, part 1, first session Forty-third Congress, with the papers relating to foreign relations.

For the acts relating to debts due by or to the United States see act of 3 March, 1797, chapter 20, volume 1, page 512; act of June 6, 1798, chapter 49, sections 1, 3, volume 1, pages 561, 562; act of 3 March, 1817, chapter 114, volume 3, page 399; *act of 19 February, 1833, chapter 33, volume 4, page 613; *act of 30 June, 1834, chapter 153, volume 4, page 726; *act of 18 January, 1837, chapter 5, volume 5, page 142; act of 14 October, 1837, chapter 5, volume 5, page 204; act of 7 July, 1838, chapter 177, volume 5, page 288; resolution of 31 May, 1838, number 4, volume 5, page 310; act of 3 March, 1839, chapter 93, section 1, volume 5, pages 537, 538; act of 27 February, 1841, chapter 13, volume 5, page 414; act of 23 August, 1842, chapter 185, volume 5, page 511; act of 3 March, 1843, chapter 103, volume 5, page 648; act of 15 June, 1844, chapter 73, section 2, volume 5, page 673; act of 29 July, 1846, chapter 66, volume 9, page 41; act of 6 August, 1846, chapter 90, section 19, volume 9, page 64; *act of 2 March, 1847, chapter 39, volume 9, page 154; act of 3 March, 1849, chapter 129, volume 9, page 414; act of 31 August, 1852, chapter 108, section 2, volume 10, pages 97, 98; act of 26 February, 1853, chapter 81, sections 1, 7, volume 10, pages 170, 171; act of 1 March, 1862, chapter 35, volume 12, page 352; act of 17 March, 1862, chapter 45, section 1, volume 12, page 370; act of 17 July, 1862, chapter 205, volume 12, page 610; act of 3 March, 1863, chapter 76, section 10, volume 12, page 740; act of 3 March, 1863, chapter 78, section 5, volume 12, page 743; act of 25 June, 1864, chapter 150, volume 13, page 182; act of 4 July, 1864, chapter 240, sections 2, 3, volume 13, page 381; act of 28 July, 1866, chapter 297, section 8, volume 14, page 327; resolution of 18 June, 1866, number 50, volume 14, page 360; resolution of 28 July, 1866, number 99, volume 14, page 370; act of 21 February, 1867, chapter 57, volume 14, page 397; resolution of 2 March, 1867, number 46, volume 14, page 571; act of 20 April, 1871, chapter 21, section 27, volume 17, page 12.

[46a] The Prize Cases, (2 Black, p. 636.) The court held that war commenced with the President's proclamation of blockade, April 27, 1861. The dissenting judges held that it commenced with the act of Congress of July 13, 1861. (12 Stat., p. 257.) See proclamations of April 15, April 19, and April 27, 1861, (12 Stat., pp. 1258–1260;) Lawrence's Wheaton, second annotated ed., sup., 44; proclamation of July 1, 1862; act June 7, 1862. The treaty of Washington fixes the commencement April 13, 1861. (17 Stat., p. 867, sec. 12.) See the diplomatic correspondence with Great Britain, April and July, 1865, pp. 362, 365, 367, 388, 394, 397, 407, 421, 422, 423; proclamations May 10, 1865, (13 Stat., p. 757,) May 22, 1865, (13 Stat., p. 758.) See schedule of proclamations in appendix B to this report.

---

* Acts distinguished by a * have been heretofore repealed.

proclamation of insurrection was extended so as to declare eleven States, with unimportant exceptions, in rebellion.[47]

War was continued in those States until the President's proclamation of August 20, 1866,[48] proclaimed the "insurrection at an end." A "state

[47] The Venice, 2 Wallace, 277. See proclamation of August 16, 1861, &c., and July 1, 1862, 12 Stat., 1260-1266. Proclamation September 22, 1862, and January 1, 1863, 12 Stat., 1267-1269. See letter of Quartermaster-General M. C. Meigs, in appendix to this report, February 26, 1874.

[48] McPherson's History Reconstruction, 194; 13 Stat., 763. Tennessee, June 13, 1866; 14 Stat., 812, 816. Sundry States, April 2, 1866. Texas, August 20, 1866. Fleming *v.* Page, 9 Howard, 615. Cross *v.* Harrison, 16 Howard, 189. United States *v.* Anderson, 9 Wallace, 56. Grossmeyer *v.* United States, 9 Wallace, 72. Lawrence's Wheaton, 513, note. 7 Court of Claims, Protector *v.* United States, 9 Wallace, 687. Treaty of Washington of May 8, 1871, art. 12; 17 Stat., 867. Act March 2, 1867, sec. 2; 14 Stat., 428. Grossmeyer *v.* United States, 4 Court of Claims. Martin *v.* Mott, 12 Wheaton. 29 Law Reporter, July, 1861, p. 148.

*Schedule of proclamations of Presidents Lincoln and Johnson respecting the condition of the insurrectionary States.*

*April* 15, 1861.—Militia (75,000) called out, the laws of the United States having been opposed, and the execution thereof obstructed in the following States: South Carolina, Georgia, Alabama, Florida, Mississippi, Louisiana, and Texas.

*April* 19, 1861.—Whereas an insurrection has broken out in the following States, a blockade of the ports within the States is hereby declared: South Carolina, Georgia, Alabama, Florida, Mississippi, Louisiana, and Texas.

*April* 27, 1861.—Whereas, for reasons assigned in the proclamation of April 19, a blockade was established in States therein named; and whereas, since that date, the collection of revenue has been obstructed in North Carolina and Virginia, a blockade of the ports of these States is proclaimed.

*May* 19, 1861.—Whereas an insurrection exists in the State of Florida, the commander of the United States forces is allowed to suspend the writ of habeas corpus if necessary.

*August* 16, 1861, (issued in compliance with an act of Congress prohibiting commercial intercourse.)—Whereas on the 15th of April, 1861, the militia were called out, in view of an insurrection which had broken out in the following States: South Carolina, Georgia, Alabama, Florida, Mississippi, Louisiana, and Texas;

And whereas such insurrection has since broken out, and yet exists, within the following-named States: Virginia, North Carolina, Tennessee, and Arkansas:

Now, therefore, I, Abraham Lincoln, in pursuance of act of Congress, July 15, 1861, do hereby declare the inhabitants of the following States to be in insurrection: South Carolina, Georgia, Alabama, Florida, Mississippi, Louisiana, Texas, Virginia, (except the part of Virginia lying west of the Alleghany Mountains,) North Carolina, Tennessee, and Arkansas. And except the inhabitants of such parts of the States herein before named as may maintain a loyal adhesion to the Union and the Constitution, or may be, from time to time, occupied or controlled by forces of the United States engaged in the dispersion of said insurgents.

*May* 12, 1862.—Relaxes the blockade of the following-named ports: Port Royal, S. C., New Orleans, La., Beaufort, N. C.

*July* 1, 1862.—Whereas, by the act of Congress approved June 7, 1862, entitled "An act for the collection of direct taxes in insurrectionary districts," it is made the duty of the President to declare the following States in insurrection: South Carolina, Georgia, Alabama, Florida, Mississippi, Louisiana, Texas, [a] Virginia, North Carolina, Tennessee, and Arkansas.

*January* 1, 1863.—Emancipation proclamation declares the following States and parts of States to be in rebellion this day; the excepted parts to remain precisely the same as if this proclamation had not been issued: South Carolina, Georgia, Alabama, Florida, Mississippi, [b] Louisiana, Texas, [c] Virginia, North Carolina, and Arkansas.

[a] Except the following counties: Hancock, Brooke, Ohio, Marshall, Wetzel, Marion, Monongalia, Preston, Taylor, Pleasants, Tyler, Ritchie, Doddridge, Harrison, Wood, Jackson, Wirt, Roane, Calhoun, Gilmore, Barbour, Tucker, Lewis, Braxton, Upshur, Randolph, Mason, Putnam, Kanawha, Clay, Nicholas, Cabell, Wayne, Boone, Logan, Wyoming, Webster, Fayette, and Raleigh; 39 counties.

[b] Except the parishes of Saint Bernard, Plaquemines, Jefferson, Saint John, Saint Charles, Saint James, Ascension, Assumption, Terre Bonne, La Fourche, Saint Mary, Saint Martin, and Orleans, including the city of New Orleans.

[c] Except forty-eight counties of West Virginia, as follows: Hancock, Brooke, Ohio, Marshall, Wetzel, Marion, Monongalia, Preston, Taylor, Tyler, Pleasants, Ritchie, Doddridge, Harrison, Wood, Jackson, Wirt, Roane, Calhoun, Gilmore, Barbour, Tucker, Lewis, Braxton, Upshur, Randolph, Mason, Putnam, Kanawha, Clay, Nicholas, Cabell, Wayne, Boone, Logan, Wyoming, Mercer, McDowell, Webster, Pocahontas, Fayette, Raleigh, Greenbrier, Monroe, Pendleton, Hardy, Hampshire, and Morgan; and also the counties of Berkely, Accomac, Northampton, Elizabeth City, York, Princess Anne, and Norfolk, including the cities of Norfolk and Portsmouth.

of war" continued beyond this time, more or less extensive in its theater—"non flagrante bello sed nondum cessante bello."[49]

This condition of war is recognized by the law of nations.[50]

The existence of what is called "*a state of war*" after flagrant war had ceased is recognized on the same principle as the personal right of self-defense. This is not limited to the right *to repel an attack;* but so long as the *purpose of renewing it* remains—the *animus revertendi*—so long as the danger is imminent or probable, the party assailed may employ reasonable force against his adversary to disarm and disable him until the danger is past, and in doing this and judging of its necessity precise accuracy as to the means and time is not required, but only the exercise of reasonable judgment in view of the circumstances.[51]

If after the forces under the command of Lee surrendered in April, 1865, the United States forces had been immediately withdrawn, the rebellion would possibly have resumed its hostile purposes.

It was upon this theory, coupled with the Constitutional duty of Congress to "guarantee to each State a republican form of government,"[52] that the reconstruction[53] acts of Congress were passed, and military as well as civil measures adopted in pursuance of them. During some portions of the period of rebellion flagrant war existed, not only in the

*April* 2, 1863.—Whereas certain States, by proclamation of August 16, 1861, were declared in insurrection; and whereas experience has shown that the exceptions made embarrass the enforcement of the act of July 13, 1861, the exceptions are revoked, and the following States declared in rebellion: South Carolina, (except Port Royal,) Georgia, Alabama, Florida, (except port of Key West,) Mississippi, Louisiana, (except port of New Orleans,) Texas, Virginia, (except forty-eight counties of West Virginia,) North Carolina, (except port of Beaufort,) Tennessee, and Arkansas.

*September* 24, 1863.—Releases blockade of Alexandria, Va.

*February* 18, 1864.—Releases blockade of Brownsville, Tex.

*November* 19, 1864.—Releases blockade of Fernandina and Pensacola, Fla., and Norfolk, Va.

*June* 13, 1865.—The President declares the insurrection in the State of Tennessee to have been suppressed, and the authority of the United States therein to be undisturbed.

*April* 5, 1866.—After reciting the various proclamations, the President states that whereas no armed resistance to the authority of the United States exists in the following States, it is declared that the insurrection which heretofore existed in those States is at an end, and is henceforth to be so regarded:[a] South Carolina, Georgia, Alabama, Florida, Mississippi, Louisiana, Virginia, North Carolina, Tennessee, and Arkansas.

[49] Mrs. Alexander's Cotton, 2 Wallace, 419.

[50] Cross *v.* Harrison, 16 Howard, 164; Whiting, War Powers, 55; Article 2 of Francis Leiber, rules for government of the armies, Scott's Digest Military Laws, p. 442, sec. 1142; Elphinstone *v.* Bedreechund, 1 Knapp's P. C. R., 300, cited in Coolidge *v.* Guthrie, by Swayne, J., U. S. circuit court southern district Ohio, October, 1868. Appendix to 43d edition Whiting's War Powers, 591, edition 1871. Letter of Hon. Hamilton Fish, Appendix C to this report.

For sundry cases relating to the rebellion, see The Prize Cases, 2 Black, 635; Mrs. Alexander's Cotton, 2 Wallace, 404; The Venice, 2 Wallace, 258; The Baigorn, 2 Wallace, 474; Mansan *v.* Insurance Company, 6 Wallace, 1; The Ouachita Cotton, 6 Wallace, 52; Hanger *v.* Abbott, 6 Wallace, 532; Coppell *v.* Hall, 7 Wallace, 542; McKee *v.* United States, 8 Wallace, 153; United States *v.* Grossmayer, 6 Wallace, 72; Vallandigham's case, Appendix to Whiting's War Powers, (43 ed. of 1871,) 524; The Circassian, 2 Wallace, 150; Cummings *v.* Missouri, 4 Wallace, 316; Ex-parte Garland, 4 Wallace, 374; Mississippi *v.* Johnson, 4 Wallace, 497.

[51] 1 Bishop, Crim. Law, (5th ed.,) secs. 301, 305, 838, and numerous authorities cited. Stewart *v.* State, 1 Ohio State R., 66-71.

[52] Constitution, art. 4, sec. 4.

[53] See McPherson's Hist. of Rebellion, 317, &c., and McPherson's Hist. Reconstruction, *passim.*

Act of March 2, 1867, 14, Stat., 428. Act of March 23, 1867, 15 Stat., 2.

[a] August 20, 1866, all the States declared as out of insurrection.

NOTE.—Joint resolution of June 18, 1866, extends act of July 4, 1864, (chap. 240,) to counties of Berkely and Jefferson, W. Va.

States proclaimed as in rebellion, but, as we all know as a matter of history, in Missouri, Kentucky, Maryland, West Virginia, and temporarily in parts of Indiana, Ohio, and Pennsylvania. The war in the three former States partook of the character of civil war, and of an invasion from the rebel States, while in Indiana, Ohio, and Pennsylvania, it was purely of the character of invasion.[54] The war in Missouri, Kentucky, Maryland, and West Virginia, so far as resident insurrectionists organized or engaged in rebellion, was none the less civil war, because these States were not proclaimed as in rebellion.[55]

The lawful State governments were not subverted in these States as they were in the eleven rebel States, but the fact of flagrant war without any proclamation or declaration by Congress is a matter of history, and is judicially recognized by the courts.[56]

War, either foreign or civil, may exist where no battle has been or is being fought.[57]

The rights, duties, and liabilities of governments in cases of foreign war or invasion are generally well defined by the laws of nations. But before stating these as they are established by the usage of nations and laid down by writers, it is important to see how far they apply in cases of a civil war.

It may be stated, then, in comprehensive terms, that the usages and laws of nations, applicable in cases of war between independent nations, apply generally to civil wars, including the recent war of the rebellion, and especially when, as in the States proclaimed in insurrection, the lawful State governments were entirely overthrown, and the courts and civil authority of the National Government equally disregarded and powerless.

The Supreme Court of United States decided in December, 1862, while the war was in progress, that—

> The present civil war between the United States and the so-called Confederate States has such character and magnitude as to *give the United States* the same rights and powers which they might exercise in case of a national or foreign war." [58]

The court determined also that citizens in the rebel States owed "supreme allegiance to the" National Government, and that "in organizing this rebellion they have *acted as States.*"

In the prize cases it was insisted by counsel "that the President in his proclamation admits that great numbers of persons residing" in the rebel States "are loyal," and the court were asked to hold "that they * have a right to claim the protection of the Government for their persons and property, and to be treated as loyal citizens."

But the court answered this by declaring that—

> *All persons* residing within this territory whose property may be used to increase the

---

[54] "Ex parte Milligan, 4 Wallace, 140.
See report of the Judge-Advocate-General to the Secretary of War, on the "Order of the American Knights," or "Sons of Liberty," a western conspiracy in aid of the southern rebellion. Washington, Government Printing Office, 1864.

[55] Prize Cases, 2 Black, 636.

[56] Prize Cases, 2 Black, 636; Ex parte Milligan, 4 Wallace, 140; Whiting's War-Power of the President, 140; President Grant's veto message, June 1, 1872; id., June 7, 1872; id., January 31, 1873; id., February 12, 1873; Lawrence's Wheaton, 513, note.

[57] Const., art. 3., sec. 3, clause 3; Ex parte Milligan, 4 Wallace, 127, 140, 142. *Luther* v *Borden; Grant* v. *United States*, 1 Nott & Hopkins, Court Claims, 41; S. C., 2; id., 551; Whiting's War-Powers, 43; Ex parte Milligan, 127: The court say to justify martial law "the necessity must be actual and present;" Paschal, Annotated Const., 212, note 215; Ex parte Bollman, 4 Cranch, 126; *United States* v. *Burr*, 4 Cranch, 469–508; Sergeant, Const., ch. 30, [32;] *People* v. *Lynch*, 1 Johns., 553.

[58] The Prize Cases, 2 Black, 636; Vattel, 425, § 294.

revenues of the hostile power are in this contest liable to be treated as *enemies* though not foreigners.[59]

The inhabitants of the invaded States of Indiana, Ohio, and Pennsylvania, never having rebelled, are all to be deemed loyal except on proof to the contrary.

Having thus marked out the boundaries of the theater of the war of the rebellion, and ascertained the *status* of all within the States proclaimed in rebellion, or where actual rebellion existed, and in the invaded but not rebellious States, it becomes proper to ascertain the rights of the National Government over these, and its liability to the inhabitants for injuries to person or property of whatever kind. It may be proper to say first, however, that the power of a nation over its own rebel citizens is greater in a civil war than over alien enemies, because over the former it "may exercise both belligerent and sovereign rights"[60] —that is, the belligerent rights of war, and the sovereign right to confiscate and punish for treason—while over alien enemies it can only exercise belligerent rights.

The inquiry also arises, within what boundaries are citizens to be regarded as enemies? Certainly not in Indiana, Ohio, or Pennsylvania, for there was no insurrection in those States.[61] There was only invasion. In some portions of Kentucky, Missouri, and Maryland, and for limited times, there was insurrection, but these States were not proclaimed as in insurrection, and, as States, they never were so in fact. These States are therefore to be deemed loyal, and the citizens thereof as having all the rights of loyal citizens, except so far as they were in fact disloyal, and subject only to the sovereign and belligerent rights of the Government.[62]

In the prize cases, Nelson, J., said, "This act of Congress, [July 13, 1861,] we think, recognized a state of civil war between the Government and the Confederate States, and made it territorial." The Government was at war with all the rebel States, just as much so as it was in other wars with England or Mexico. In the Venice, 2 Wallace, 274, Chief-Justice Chase said: "Either belligerent may modify or limit its operation as to persons or territory of the other, but in the absence of such modification or restriction judicial tribunals cannot discriminate in its application." The District of Columbia was never declared in insurrection, but martial law was proclaimed, and it was subjected to the laws of war. It was a fortified military stronghold, and all civil authority was superseded so far as deemed necessary, and the civil safeguards of the Constitution withdrawn from the inhabitants.[63]

---

[59] Prize Cases, 2 Black, 674, 678, 693; Halleck's Laws of War, 425, 446; Mrs. Alexander Cotton, 2 Wallace, 419; Whiting's War-Power of the President, 58; Vattel, 425, § 293; Bynkershoek, Laws of War, 25; United States *vs.* Anderson, 9 Wallace, 64; Whiting's "War-Claims" affixed to "War-Powers" (43d ed.) of 1871, p. 335; Marcy's Letter to Jackson, January 10, 1854, House Ex. Doc. 41, 1st sess. 33d Cong.; Huberus, tom. ii, l. i, tit. 3, De Conflict Lex., § 2; Jecker *vs.* Montgomery, 18 Howard, 112; The Peterhoff, 5 Wallace, 60.

[60] Prize Cases, 2 Black, 673; 4 Cranch, 272; Whiting, War-Powers, 44–47. But see Lawrence's Wheaton, 2d anotated ed., sup., 33. Whiting, in his War-Powers, says: "*Rebels in civil war*, if allowed the rights of belligerents, are not entitled to all the privileges usually accorded to *foreign* enemies," 43d ed. of 1871, p. 331.

[61] Ex parte Milligan, 4 Wallace 3, 127.

[62] Prize Cases, 2 Black, 274; Ex parte Milligan, 4 Wallace, 127; President Grant's veto messages of June 1 and June 7, 1872, and February 12, 1873; Debates on Sue Murphy, claim 71, Globe, 299, 386, 86, 161, 278.

[63] DEPARTMENT OF STATE, *Washington, February* 6, 1874.

SIR: By direction of the Secretary of State, I have to acknowledge the receipt of your letter of the 3d instant, in which you request to be informed as to the date of the

The obligation of a government after a civil war is terminated to those whom the severe rules of the laws of war denominate "enemies," is on the strict principle of such laws as stated by writers on the subject no greater than to alien enemies whose territory is invaded in an international war. But a humane government may always in such a case discriminate between alien enemies in fact, and its own citizens who are not so in fact, but only by legal construction. It is also conceded that the rule of law which stamps as "enemies" in a rebel State men who are in fact loyal to the flag, sometimes operates harshly. But the highest court has declared them enemies at given times and under certain circumstances, and this has been done upon principles recognized among civilized nations which antedate our Constitution.

Harsh as the rule sometimes is in its application, there are reasons of State policy on which it rests, or it would not exist as law. It may be proper to refer to some of them. It is a matter of history that secession was carried in the rebel States, with one or two exceptions, against the real wishes of a decided majority of the voters and people.[64] They

---

proclamation declaring martial law in the District of Columbia, and, second, the period of continuance of martial law within the same.

The date of the President's proclamation declaring martial law in the District of Columbia is September 15, 1863, (13 Stat. at Large, p. 734,) and the continuance thereof in the language of the proclamation was "throughout the duration of the said rebellion."

There might and probably would be a difference of opinion as to the date at which martial law ceased to exist in the District. The President's proclamation of the 2d of April, 1866, (14 Stat. at Large, p. 811,) may without impropriety be taken to fix the limitation referred to, but the Department does not wish to be understood as expressing an opinion on that point, as it would seem more properly to present a question for the opinion of the Attorney-General.

I am, very respectfully, your obedient servant,

SEVELLON A. BROWN, *Chief Clerk.*

HENRY H. SMITH, Esq., *Clerk of the Committee on War-Claims, House of Representatives.*

See the trial of the conspirators, May, 1865; Attorney-General's opinion, July, 1865; 11 Opinions, 297.

In Ex parte Milligan, 4 Wallace, 137, Chase, C. J., said:

"The Constitution itself provides for military government as well as for civil government. And we do not understand it to be claimed that the civil safeguards of the Constitution have application in cases within the proper sphere of the former.

* * * * * * *

"We think, therefore, that the power of Congress, in the government of the land and naval forces, and of the militia, is not at all affected by the fifth or any other amendment. It is not necessary to attempt any precise definition of the boundaries of this power. * * * * * *

"There are under the Constitution three kinds of military jurisdiction: one to be exercised both in peace and war; another to be exercised in time of foreign war, without the boundaries of the United States, or in time of rebellion and civil war, within States or districts occupied by rebels treated as belligerents; and a third, to be exercised in time of invasion or insurrection within the limits of the United States, or, during rebellion, within the limits of States maintaining adhesion to the National Government, when the public danger requires its exercise. The first of these may be called jurisdiction under military law, and is found in acts of Congress prescribing rules and articles of war, or otherwise providing for the government of the national forces; the second may be distinguished as military government, superseding, as far as may be deemed expedient, the local law, and exercised by the military commander under the direction of the President, with the express or implied sanction of Congress; while the third may be denominated martial law proper, and is called into action by Congress, or temporarily, when the action of Congress cannot be invited, and in the case of justifying or excusing peril, by the President, in times of insurrection or invasion, or of civil or foreign war, within districts or localities where ordinary law no longer adequately secures public safety and private rights." * * * *

[64] *Alabama.*—Delegates to convention elected December 24, 1860. Popular majority claimed at 50,000. Ordinance of secession passed by a vote of 61 to 39, January 11, 1861, the minority being from counties where the free population predominated. (Greeley's American Conflict, vol. 1, p. 347.)

*Arkansas.*—Legislature voted a call for convention, which met November 16, 1860.

had power to avert it. If they had reflected that secession and rebellion would stamp them all as *enemies* of the lawful National Government, subject to have their property taken or destroyed, by or in aid of its military operations, or to weaken the power in revolt, without any compensation, it might have induced a vigilance which would have averted the calamity of civil war. Their inaction or want of energy in resisting secession brought death and all the woes of war. Even loyal men were not everywhere or in all cases guiltless. Their moral guilt was an omission of duty. In the transgression of active secessionists all in legal contemplation transgressed. If now, all loyal citizens should be compensated for all property taken or destroyed by the Union Armies, the rebellion might be to some of them, with the opportunity which always exists to fabricate fraudulent claims, rather a profitable pastime,

---

The popular vote showed a majority for Union. Subsequently another convention was called for March 1, 1861, and after listening to a message from Jeff. Davis, that convention voted 39 to 35 *not* to secede from the Union. This last convention decided to provide for a vote of the people on August 1, 1861, and adjourned to meet August 17. On receiving the news of the firing on Fort Sumter the convention was reconvened at the instance of the governor, and May 6, 1861, passed an ordnance of secession by a vote of 69 to 1. (Ibid., vol. 1, pp. 348–486.)

*Florida.*—Legislature voted December 1, 1860, to call a convention for January 3, 1861, and January 10 passed an ordinance of secession by yeas 62, nays 7, many delegates expressly elected as Unionists voting for secession. (Ibid., vol. 1, p. 347.)

*Georgia.*—Was the first State to follow South Carolina. Legislature passed an act November 13, 1860, appropriating $1.000 000 to arm and equip the State, and called a convention for January 9, 1861. On the 18th it passed ordinance of secession by a vote of 208 to 89, A. H. Stephens and Herschel V. Johnson voting no, though the day previous a resolution declaring it to be the right and duty of Georgia to secede, was adopted by a vote of 165 to 130, and on March 16 following it ratified the confederate constitution by a vote of 96 to 5. (Ibid., vol, 1, p. 347.)

*Louisiana.*—Legislature met December 10, 1860, and called a convention for December 17. On the 26th of January, 1861, it passed an ordinance of secession by a vote of 103 to 17. The convention voted 84 to 45 to submit the ordinance of secession to a vote of the people. The popular vote stood 20,448 for secession to 17,296 against, only two-fifths of the vote cast for President just before. (Ibid., vol. 1, 348.)

*Mississippi.*—Legislature assembled November 26, 1860, and fixed upon December 20 as date of election of delegates to a convention; the same to meet January 7, 1861. On January 9 it passed an ordinance of secession by a vote of 84 to 15. The slave population of Mississippi was at that time next to that of South Carolina. (Ibid., vol. 1, pp. 347, 348.)

*North Carolina.*—Legislature called a convention in November, 1860. This convention was strongly for the Union, and December 22, 1860, adjourned, having provided that it should not again meet. A State's-right convention was called for March 22, 1861, but no action was taken. After the firing on Fort Sumter, the governor called an extra session of the legislature for May 1, which called a convention for May 20, 1861, the delegates to be elected May 13. On that day an ordinance of secession was passed by a unanimous vote, inspired largely by a resolution reciting grossly false statements. (Ibid., vol. 1, pp. 347, 485.)

*South Carolina.*—Legislature called for November 5, 1860, and a convention was called for December 17, delegates to be elected on the 6th of December. On the 20th of December an ordinance of secession was reported from a committee of seven, and immediately passed without dissent, the yeas being 169. (Ibid., vol. 1, p. 347.)

*Tennessee.*—Legislature met January 7, 1861. On the 19th it decided to call a convention, subject to a vote of the people. That vote was taken early in March, and on the 10th the result was officially proclaimed as follows: for the Union, 91,803; for disunion, 24,749; a Union majority of 67,054, many counties not rendering any returns.

After the firing on Fort Sumter, the legislature, on May 1, 1861, secretly adopted a resolution authorizing the appointment of "three commissioners on the part of Tennessee, to enter into a military league with the authorities of the Confederate States, and with the authorities of such other slave-holding States as may wish to enter into it; having in view the protection and defense of the entire South against the war which is now being carried on against it." These commissioners framed a convention "between the State of Tennessee and the Confederate States of America," which practically placed the military force of the State under the control and direction of the Confederate States, and turned over to said Confederate States all the public property,

and future attempts at revolt would stimulate them to no earnest resistance to prevent it.

Grotius, referring to foreign invasion and the liability of an invaded city to make compensation, assigns as a reason why "no action [that is,

naval stores, and munitions of war belonging to the State of Tennessee, which had been acquired from the United States.

This convention was submitted to the legislature, in secret session, and was ratified in the senate by yeas 14, nays 6, absent or not voting 5; in the house by yeas 43, nays 15, absent or not voting 18. On the preceding day the legislature had passed an ordinance of secession, to be submitted to the people June 8, 1861. The State was covered with confederate soldiers, so that freedom of opinion and expression on the side of the Union was completely crushed out, as is illustrated by the following article from the Louisville *Journal* of May 13, 1861.

The Louisville *Journal* of May 13 said:

"The spirit of secession appears to have reached its culminating point in Tennessee. Certainly the fell spirit has as yet reached no higher point of outrageous tyranny. The whole of the late proceeding in Tennessee has been as gross an outrage as ever was perpetrated by the worst tyrant of all the earth. The whole secession movement, on the part of the legislature of that State, has been lawless, violent, and tumultuous. The pretense of submitting the ordinance of secession to the vote of the people of the State, after placing her military power and resources at the disposal and under the command of the Confederate States, without any authority from the people, is as bitter and insolent a mockery of popular rights as the human mind could invent."

On the 24th of June, Governor Harris issued his proclamation, declaring that the vote of the 8th had resulted as follows:

| | Separation. | No separation. |
|---|---|---|
| East Tennessee | 14,780 | 32,923 |
| Middle Tennessee | 58,265 | 8,198 |
| West Tennessee | 29,127 | 6,117 |
| Military camps | 2,741 | none. |
| Total | 104,913 | 47,238 |

A convention was held at Greenville, in East Tennessee, in which thirty-one counties were represented. This convention adopted a resolution which declared the result of the election as in no sense "expressive of the will of a majority of the freemen of Tennessee." (Ibid., vol. 1, pp. 481, 482, 483, 484.)

*Texas.*—Convention assembled January 28, 1861, and passed ordinance of secession, yeas 166, nays 7, February 1, 1861, which was submitted to popular vote snd ratified by a considerable majority, in many districts it being safer to vote secession than not vote at all, and not to vote at all rather than vote Union. (Ibid., vol. 1, page 348.)

*Virginia.*—Legislature met January 7, 1861, on call of Governor Fletcher; and, on the 13th, passed a bill calling a convention, a Union majority being returned. April 4 the convention decided, by a vote of 89 to 45, *not* to pass an ordinance of secession. Subsequently, April 17, three days after the firing on Fort Sumter, the convention passed an ordinance of secession by a vote of 88 to 55, the convention being largely influenced by an act of the confederate congress forbidding the importation of slaves from States out of the confederacy, a blow at Virginia's most important and productive branch of her industry. (Ibid., vol. 1, pp. 348, 452.)

The Louisville *Journal* of June 1 said:

"The vote of Virginia last week on the question of secession was a perfect mockery. The State was full of troops from other States of the confederacy, while all the Virginia secessionists, banded in military companies, were scattered in various places to overawe the friends of Union or drive them from the polls. The Richmond convention, in addition to other acts of usurpation, provided that polls should be opened in all the military encampments, besides the ordinary voting-places. * * * No man voted against secession on Thursday last but at the peril of being lynched or arrested as an incendiary, dangerous to the State."

*West Virginia.*—The people of West Virginia hostile to the confederacy met at Kingwood May 4, 1861. A similar meeting was held at Wheeling May 5, and another May 13, 1861; on the 13th, a convention of delegates, representing thirty-five counties of West Virginia, and, after calling a provisional convention for June 11, adjourned on the 15th. June 20 a unanimous vote in favor of ultimate separation was cast, the

no claim] may be brought against a city for damages by war," that it is "in order to make every man more careful to defend his own."[65]

Vattel assigns as reasons that the damages would be so great that "the public finances would soon be exhausted. * * * Besides, these indemnifications would be liable to a thousand abuses, and there would be no end of the particulars. It is therefore to be presumed no such thing was ever intended."[66]

There is a maxim, too, the force of which cannot be overlooked: *Salus populi suprema lex.*

It is a principle of law, applicable alike to nations and individuals, that there is no wrong without a remedy. A nation has its rights—its remedies.

Citizens have their rights and remedies as well when a right of person or property is invaded by the nation as by individuals. The Constitution recognizes all these, leaving details to common or statutory or international law.

The fifth article of amendments to the Constitution provides that—

No person shall be * * deprived of life, liberty, or property without due process of law; nor shall private property be taken for public use without just compensation. Article V, amendment.

The phrase "due process of law," in this connection means that—

The right of the citizen to his property as well as life or liberty could only be taken away upon an open, public, and fair trial before a judicial tribunal according to the forms prescribed by the laws of the land.[67]

If there were no other provision in the Constitution on the subject of life or property, the life of a rebel citizen could never be lawfully taken by command of the Government, even in battle, and property for army supplies, hospitals, and other military purposes, could never be taken for the public use against the owner's will, except by the tedious process of a judicial proceeding in court, in the exercise of the civil right of eminent domain.

In a foreign war the Government, of course, does not organize an army for the purpose of taking the lives of our citizens, and it may be said that the constitutional provision referred to may in such case be operative, and is not violated. But in a civil war the very object of organizing an army is to take the lives of rebel citizens without any "process of law," and the fifth article of amendments has no application to such case.

---

convention having voted two days previous that the separation of Western from Eastern Virginia was one of its paramount objects. Congress ratified the action taken, and January 6, 1862, admitted the State of West Virginia into the Union. (Ibid., vol. 1, pp. 519, 520.)

The following table exhibits the population of the States declared in insurrection in 1860, with the vote cast in each at the presidential election of that year:

| | Population. | Vote cast. |
|---|---|---|
| Alabama | 964, 201 | 90, 357 |
| Arkansas | 435, 450 | 54, 053 |
| Florida | 140, 424 | 14, 347 |
| Georgia | 1, 057, 286 | 106, 365 |
| Louisiana | 708, 002 | 50, 510 |
| Mississippi | 791, 305 | 69, 020 |
| North Carolina | 992, 622 | 96, 230 |
| South Carolina[a] | 703, 708 | |
| Tennessee | 1, 109, 801 | 145, 333 |
| Texas | 604, 215 | 62, 657 |
| Virginia | 1, 596, 318 | 167, 123 |

[65] Book 3, ch. XX, sec. 8, p. 290.

[66] Vattel, ch. XV, p. 403.

[67] Paschal, Annotated Constitution, 260, note 257; Whiting's War-Powers, 60.

---

[a] Elects by legislature.

But if it be said that on some principle recognized among nations, justified by reason and necessity, rebels forfeit all constitutional rights, yet some of the provisions of the fifth amendment still cannot apply to a state of war, because a citizen who is conscripted against his will, arrested, and carried into the army, is deprived of his "liberty" without any "process of law." The war-power in such case is operating, and the fifth amendment so far yields to it and is not applicable to such case.[68]

In what has been said no reference is intended to be made to the last clause of the fifth amendment, which requires compensation for private property taken for public use. That presents a separate inquiry as to what is a "public use," and whether compensation is to be made by force of that clause or on general principles of international law.

Since war could not be carried on if all the provisions of the fifth amendment applied in time and on the theater of war, the Constitution, in view of the fact that war would or might exist, gives to Congress the power—

"to define and punish "offenses against the *law of nations;*"
"to declare war, grant letters of marque and reprisal, and make rules concerning captures on land and water;"
"to raise and support armies;"
"to provide for the common defense and general welfare of the United States,"

and makes other equally emphatic provisions relative to a state of war.[69]

The Constitution recognizes, and, *for their appropriate uses, adopts* "the laws of nations," and these include the *laws of war.*

The *laws of war*, equally with the amendments to the Constitution, determine certain rights of person and property. Here, then, *in the Constitution* are two systems of law, each having a purpose. By well-known legal rules of construction they are to be construed *in pari materia;* effect is to be given to each, so that neither shall fail of having an object or be defeated in its application to that object exclusively, when necessary to accomplish it.

Both systems of law cannot have full or exclusive force, effect, and operation at the same time and place or over the same rights of person and property.[70]

The laws of peace, and the amendments to the Constitution for the security of life and property, apply in time of peace and in time of war where no war or state of war exists.[71]

But where war is actually flagrant, or a state of war and the exercise of military authority exist, the laws of war prevail; and, so far as clearly necessary for all purposes of the war, they are so far exclusive that no antagonistic law or exercise of jurisdiction can be allowed.[72]

It is not to be inferred from this that there is no protection for life or property. The laws of peace, the ordinary tribunals, may be allowed,

---

[68] In ex-parte Milligan, 4 Wallace, 137, Chief-Justice Chase said: "The Constitution itself provides for military government as well as civil government. And we do not understand it to be claimed that the civil safeguards of the Constitution have application *in cases within the proper sphere of the former.*" P. 137. (See 11 Opinions, 297.)

[69] Whiting's War Powers, 27.

[70] Whiting's War Powers, 51.

[71] Ex-parte Milligan, 4 Wallace, 127.
This view is taken in Grant *vs.* U. S., 1 N. & H. Court Claims, 44; but that case cannot be sustained in some other respects.

[72] In ex parte Milligan, 4 Wallace, 127, the test applied as to whether the laws of war were in force *quo ad rights of person,* was whether the civil courts were open, and it was held that the court was the judge of this. And see Coke, Com. Lit., lib. 3, ch. 6, sec. 412, p. [249 *b.*]

even on the theater of war, to be operative, so far as practicable. And in all cases the laws[73] of nations, including the laws of war, promise protection to life and property, as clearly and as sacred as if written in plain terms in the Constitution. The *laws of war* are, therefore, *constitutional laws*, as obligatory for their purposes as any other.

Loyal men residing in loyal States during the rebellion but having property, real or personal, in States proclaimed in rebellion, held it not as enemies, but nevertheless subject to the laws of war as affecting loyal citizens in a theater of war.[74]

From what has been said it will be seen that the laws of war prevailed—

1. Generally in the eleven States proclaimed in rebellion, subject to some limitations, from the commencement to the close of the state of war.
2. In large portions of Missouri, Kentucky, Maryland, and West Virginia, during a less period, including only the actual state of war.
3. In the District of Columbia, while under martial law.
4. In a small portion of Ohio and Indiana, for a few days, during the actual existence of the "Morgan raid."
5. In a small portion of Pennsylvania, during the actual existence of Lee's invasion and the battle of Gettysburgh.

The citizens of the eleven seceded States, for the period of war and by strict law, can only claim those rights of property accorded by the law of nations under the principles of the Constitution.

Elsewhere where actual war existed, and during its legal continuance, the rights of person and of property, so far as they were interrupted by warlike operations, are, in considering the liability of the Government, to be determined by the laws of war.

The laws of war affecting rights of person and property exist independent of legislative sanction back of the Constitution itself. It does not make but recognizes them as existing and known laws. This common law of war is liable to change by treaty stipulations, by circumstances, and for all internal purposes Congress may, and during the rebellion did, materially change it,[75] and has since wisely ameliorated[76]

---

Lawrence's Wheaton 526, (2 Am. ed.) Lawrence says this is the English rule, and applies to the seizure of real estate, "so as the courts were shut up, *et silent inter leges arma.*" See U. S. *vs.* Russell, 13 Wallace, 627. As to this see note 113 post.

Grant *vs.* U. S., 1 N. & H. Court Claims, 41.

But the *mere fact* that under the protection of military power civil courts aided the administration of justice could not exclude rightful military authority. The civil courts were open more or less in the District of Columbia and some of the States during a portion of the period of the rebellion.

Upon the same principle as in the text either branch of Congress has power to punish for contempts, and the 5th amendment of the Constitution has no application to it. See proceedings in House of Representatives, January, 1875, in relation to Richard B. Irwin.

[73] There is a summary of these by Francis Lieber, p. 441 et seq., in Scott's Digest of Military Laws United States, and in the appendix to report of trial assassination of President Lincoln.

[74] Lawrence's Wheaton, 565-576; The Gray Jacket, 5 Wallace, 342-364; Whiting's War Powers, (43d ed., 1872,) p. 582; Attorney-General's opinion, November 24, 1865; 11 Opinions, 405; Elliott's claim, September 7, 1868; 12 Opinions, 488; Prize cases, 2 Black, 674; Senator Carpenter, in Cong. Record of March 20, 1874, p. 22.

[75] U. S. *vs.* Klein, 13 Wallace, 128.

[76] Act March 12, 1863—12 Stat., 591; Mrs. Alexander's Cotton, 2 Wallace, 404; act May 18, 1872—17 Stat., 134; act March 3, 1871—16 Stat., 524; act May 11, 1872—17 Stat., 97; act March 3, 1873—17 Stat., 577; House Mis. Doc. 16—2d sess. 42 Cong.; Mis. Doc. 21, Mis. Doc. 213, Mis. Doc. 218, all, 2 sess. 42 Cong.; Mis. Doc. 12, 3 sess. 42 Cong.; Joint Res. No. 50—1 sess. 39 Cong., June 18, 1866; Joint Res. No. 99—1 sess. 39 Cong., July 28, 1866; act July 4, 1864, ch. 240, 1 sess. 38 Cong. U. S. *vs.* Klein, 13 Wallace, 128.

its rules or made concessions gratuitously in the interest of justice, humanity, or benevolence.

But the right of military authorities to seize, use, or destroy property by the laws of war, is not abridged merely because Congress has provided other modes of seizing and disposing of property. A statute which does not by negative words necessarily abolish a common-law rule leaves the latter in force.[77]

As during and since the war rights of property were and are affected by the laws of war and by statutes independent of them, it becomes necessary to consider rights of property as affected by both classes.

Questions may arise in several classes of cases relating to compensation for property, *real* or *personal*, taken, used, destroyed, or damaged on land or sea:

1. By the enemy.
2. By the Government military forces in battle, or wantonly or unauthorized by troops.
3. By the temporary occupation of, injuries to, and destruction of property caused by actual and necessary Government military operations in flagrant war.
4. And as to property useful to the enemy, seized and destroyed, or damaged, to prevent it from falling into their hands.

Questions arise as to these in wars with foreign nations, in the late civil war as to States proclaimed in rebellion, in other States and Territories and the District of Columbia, during the period of flagrant war, and the succeeding state of war, in behalf of resident and non-resident crtizens, aliens, and corporations.

Upon ordinary claims the Government is not liable for interest unless by contract so providing.[78]

---

[77] Mrs. Alexander's Cotton, 2 Wallace, 404, held "cotton in the southern rebel districts was a proper subject of capture by the Government during the rebellion *on general principles of law relating to war*, though private property; and the legislation of Congress authorized such captures."

See Planters' Bank *vs.* Union Bank, 16 Wallace, 496. Sedgwick on Construction of Statutes.

Congress has power to make rules concerning captures on land. But this does not exclude the exercise of the military right of capture by the common law of war: Brown *vs.* U. S., 8 Cranch, 110, 228, 229.

[78] In an able article in the Boston Law Review, it is said:

"A few leading principles affecting the responsibility of the United States, which have now received the sanction of judicial approval, may be briefly noticed.

"First, the United States is not liable for interest unless upon special agreement, as in the public loans. Such was the uniform rule, from the earliest times, in accordance with the advice of the Attorneys-General. The question was fully discussed in *Todd's case*, and the principle sustained by the court. It was held that the right of individuals to interest is merely conventional in its origin, depending upon law and usage, and that neither law nor usage can be found to render government liable. As this decis'on has been re-affirmed, and an act of Congress, recently passed, forbids the payment of interest on Government claims, the principle is finally settled. It was also held, in *Keith's case*, that a resolution of Congress, directing the settlement of an account 'upon principles of equity and justice,' does not imply the payment of interest.'' (American Law Review, Boston, July, 1867, vol. 1, p. 657; Court of Claims Reports, &c.)

In an argument by John A. Andrew and Albert G. Browne, jr., it is said:

"Interest has always been paid upon the advances of the *States* for war purposes.

"*The Revolutionary war.*—By the acts of Congress of 5th August, 1790, and May 31, 1794, providing for the settlement of their advances during the revolutionary war, interest was allowed and paid.

"*The war of* 1812–'15.—The whole subject of interest upon advances of States, during the war of 1812–'15, was discussed in 1824–'25, in a message of President Monroe, and accompanying papers, upon the case of Virginia. (See Senate Documents, 18th Congress, 1st session, 3d volume, document 64.)

"The act of March 3, 1825, (United States Laws, vol. 4, page 132,) was the result, and settled the principle upon which interest has been allowed for advances in 1812–'15,

The fourth article of the treaty of peace of September 3, 1783, between the United States and Great Britain (8 Stat., 80) provides that—

Creditors on either side shall meet with no lawful impediment to the recovery of the full value in sterling money of all *bona-fide* debts heretofore contracted.

The subject of interest under this article is discussed in a volume entitled:

"Secret journals of the acts and proceedings of Congress, from the first meeting thereof to the dissolution of the confederation by the adoption of the Constitution of the United States. Published under the direction of the President of the United States, conformably to resolution of Congress of March 27, 1818, and April 21, 1820. vol. 4. Boston: Printed and published by Thomas B. Wait, 1821."

In a report to Congress therein found, it is said:

In short, your secretary does not know of any act of Congress whereby debts due from Americans to Britons were either extinguished, remitted, or confiscated, and therefore concludes, that the fourth article of the treaty must be understood not as reviving or restoring those debts, but as considering them to be and remain exactly and precisely in their pristine and original state, both with respect to extent and obligation. If this conclusion be just, your secretary can perceive no ground for the singular reasons and questions that have prevailed respecting the payment of interest claimed by British creditors in virtue of express contracts between them and their American debtors. However harsh and severe the exaction of this interest, considering the war and its effects, may be and appear, yet the treaty must be taken and fulfilled with its bitter as well as its sweets; and although we were not obliged to accept peace on those terms, yet having so accepted it, we cannot now invalidate those terms or stipulations, nor with honor or justice refuse to comply with them. Much better would it be for the United States, either severally or jointly, by their bounty to relieve those suffering and deserving individuals on whom the performance of this article may press too hard, than by reasonings and comments which neither posterity or impartial contemporaries can think just, to permit our national reputation for probity, candor, and good faith, to be tarnished.

Your secretary will conclude what he has to say on the subject of interest with a few short remarks.

It appears to him that there are only three cases in which interest can with justice

---

and since. Virginia was allowed interest, but not 'on any sum on which she has not paid interest.' Interest, upon this rule, has been allowed to every State, except Massachusetts, which made advances in the war of 1812–'15.

"See the following cases:

"Maryland, United States Laws, vol. 4, page 161. Delaware, United States Laws, vol. 4, page 175. New York, United States Laws, vol. 4, page 192. Pennsylvania, United States Laws, vol. 4, page 241. South Carolina, United States Laws, vol. 4, page 499.

"The same principle was applied to the case of the advances of the city of Baltimore. (See act of April 2, 1830.)

"*Indian and other wars.*—See the following cases of the allowance of interest: Alabama, United States Laws, vol. 9, page 344. Georgia, United States Laws, vol. 9, page 626. Washington Territory, United States Laws, vol. 17, page 429. New Hampshire, United States Laws, vol. 10, page 1.

"*The Mexican war.*—The rule of allowing interest has been applied not only to States, but to corporations and individuals. See (U. S. Laws, vol. 9, p. 236) third section of the act to refund advances, &c., for the Mexican war, as follows:

"'That, in refunding moneys under this act, and the resolution which it amends, it shall be lawful to pay interest at the rate of six per centum per annum on all sums advanced by States, corporations, or individuals, in all cases where the State, corporation, or individual paid or lost the interest, or is liable to pay it.' (See H. Rep. No. 119, 38th Cong., 1st sess.)"

The interest on the Massachusetts advances was paid by act of July 8, 1870, (16 Stat., 197. See Sumner's Sen. Rep. No. 4, 1st sess. 41st Cong., April 1, 1869; Ela's H. Rep. No. 76, 2d sess. 41st Cong.)

Senate Mis. Doc. No. 121, 1st sess. 43d Cong., memorial of P. P. Pitchlynn.

In Hale's Rep. of November 30, 1873, to the Secretary of State, of claims before the American British Mixed Commission under Article 12 of the treaty of 8th May, 1871, he says: "The commission ordinarily allowed interest at the rate of six per cent. per annum from the date of the injury to the anticipated date of the final award." (See Ex. Doc., part 1, 1st sess. 43d Cong. Part 2, Foreign Affairs, p. 21, Hale's Report. And see the British and American arguments as to interest, delivered to the Tribunal of

be demanded, and that in the first of the three the courts of justice are not and ought not to be at liberty to refuse it, viz:

1. In all cases where interest is fairly and expressly contracted and agreed to be

---

Arbitration at Geneva, June 15, 1872, vol. 3, Geneva Arbitration, being Foreign Relations of United States, part 2, 3d sess. 42d Cong., pp. 550–578.)

The following is from House Report No. 391, Forty-third Congress, first session, submitted by Mr. I. C. Parker, from the Committee on Appropriations, (to accompany bill H. R. 2189:)

*The Committee on Appropriations, to whom was referred the bill (H. R. 2189) "to provide for the payment of the award made by the Senate of the United Statates in favor of the Choctaw Nation of Indians, on the 9th day of March, 1859," respectfully submit the following report:*

The object and purpose of this bill is to provide for the satisfaction of an award made by the Senate of the United States in favor of the Choctaw Nation of Indians, on the 9th day of March, 1859. This award was made in pursuance of treaty stipulations, and was to carry into effect obligations assumed by the United States to the Choctaw Nation, under the treaty with the said nation concluded June 22, 1855. So much of the said treaty as relates to the manner in which the indebtedness of the United States to the said nation should be ascertained and determined is as follows:

"ARTICLE XI. The Government of the United States not being prepared to assent to the claim set up under the treaty of September 27, 1830, and so earnestly contended for by the Choctaws as a rule of settlement, but justly appreciating the sacrifices, faithful services, and general good conduct of the Choctaw people, and being desirous that their rights and claims against the United States shall receive a just, fair, and liberal consideration, it is therefore stipulated that the following questions be submitted for adjudication to the Senate of the United States:

"'First. Whether the Choctaws are entitled to, or shall be allowed, the proceeds of the sale of the land ceded by them to the United States by the treaty of September 27, 1830, deducting therefrom the costs of their survey and sale, and all just and proper expenditures and payments under the provisions of said treaty; and, if so, what price per acre shall be allowed to the Choctaws for the lands remaining unsold, in order that a final settlement with them may be promptly effected; or,

"'Second. Whether the Choctaws shall be allowed a gross sum in further and full satisfaction of all their claims, national and individual, against the United States; and, if so, how much.'"

"ARTICLE XII. In case the Senate shall award to the Choctaws the net proceeds of the lands ceded as aforesaid, the same shall be received by them in full satisfaction of all their claims against the United States, whether national or individual, arising under any former treaty; and the Choctaws shall thereupon become liable and bound to pay all such individual claims as may be adjudged by the proper authorities of the tribe to be equitable and just; the settlement and payment to be made with the advice and under the direction of the United States agent for the tribe; and so much of the fund awarded by the Senate to the Choctaws as the proper authorities thereof shall ascertain and determine to be necessary for the payment of the just liabilities of the tribe shall, on their requisition, be paid over to them by the United States. But should the Senate allow a gross sum in further and full satisfaction of all their claims, whether national or individual, against the United States, the same shall be accepted by the Choctaws, and they shall thereupon become liable for and bound to pay all the individual claims as aforesaid; it being expressly understood that the adjudication and decision of the Senate shall be final."

(11 Stat. at Large, page 611.)

In pursuance of this agreement between the two contracting parties, the Senate of the United States, acting in the character of arbitrator, or as commissioners under a treaty, proceeded to an adjudication of the questions submitted to it under the eleventh article of said treaty; and on the 9th day of March, 1859, the matter having been previously considered and investigated by the Senate, the following award was made and declared in favor of the Choctaw Nation:

"Whereas the eleventh article of the treaty of June 22, 1855, with the Choctaw and Chickasaw Indians, provides that the following questions be submitted for decision to the Senate of the United States:

"'First. Whether the Choctaws are entitled to or shall be allowed the proceeds of the sale of the lands ceded by them to the United States by the treaty of September 27, 1830, deducting therefrom the costs of their survey and sale, and all just and proper expenditures and payments under the provisions of said treaty; and, if so, what price per acre shall be allowed to the Choctaws for the lands remaining unsold, in order that a final settlement with them may be promptly effected; or,

"'Secondly. Whether the Choctaws shall be allowed a gross sum in *further* and full

paid. In such cases the debtor is unquestionably bound to pay it, and ought not to be absolved or excused from it by any act of legislature. In the opinion of your secretary every legislature deviates from the reason and limits of their institution, when

---

satisfaction of *all* their claims, national and individual, against the United States; and, if so, how much?'

"*Resolved*, That the Choctaws be allowed the proceeds of the sale of such lands as have been sold by the United States on the 1st day of January last, deducting therefrom the costs of their survey and sale, and all proper expenditures and payments under said treaty, excluding the reservations allowed and secured, and estimating the scrip issued in lieu of reservations at the rate of $1.25 per acre; and, further, that they be also allowed twelve and a half cents per acre for the residue of said lands.

"*Resolved*, That the Secretary of the Interior cause an account to be stated with the Choctaws, showing what amount is due them according to the above-prescribed principles of settlement, and report the same to Congress."

(Senate Journal, 2d session 35th Congress, page 493.)

In pursuance of this award, the Secretary of the Interior, as directed by the second of the above resolutions, proceeded to state an account between the United States and the Choctaw Nation, upon the principles decided by the Senate as the basis of such account, as declared in the first resolution; and the result of such accounting, as shown in the report of the Secretary of the Interior, was an indebtedness on the part of the United States to the Choctaw Nation amounting to *two million nine hundred and eighty-one thousand two hundred and forty-seven dollars and thirty cents*.

The Committee on Indian Affairs of the House of Representatives, in its report made at the last session of Congress, speaking of this award, used the following language:

"By every principle of law, equity, and business transaction, the United States is bound by the accounting of the Secretary of the Interior, showing $2,981,247.30 due to the Choctaws at the date of the Secretary's report.

"First. The Senate was the umpire, and, in the language of the treaty of 1855, which made it such, its decision was to be final.

"Secondly. The Senate, in the exercise of its power under the treaty of 1855, chose to allow the net proceeds of the land as the better of the two modes of settlement proposed by that treaty, and not to allow a sum in gross.

"Thirdly. The Senate directed the Secretary of the Interior to make the accounting, which he did, May 28, 1860, as shown above.

"Fourthly. The Senate did not, as umpire, or otherwise, reject this accounting; but, on March 2, 1861, Congress made an appropriation of $500,000 on it, and the Senate has not, since the Secretary's report, rejected any part of it, though near fourteen years have elapsed."

(House Report No. 80, Forty-second Congress, third session.)

The Senate Committee on Indian Affairs having had this subject under consideration, at the last session of Congress, speaking of this award and of the obligation of the United States to pay it, said:

"If the case were re-opened and adjudicated as an original question by an impartial umpire, a much larger sum would be found due to the said Indians, which they would undoubtedly recover were they in a condition to compel justice."

Your committee, from a most careful examination of the whole subject, concur in these conclusions, and refer to them only for the purpose of showing that the honesty, the fairness, or the integrity of the award thus made in favor of the Choctaw Nation cannot successfully be called in question or denied. It was a final settlement and award, conclusive alike upon the Choctaw Nation and the United States. Neither party to the treaty could rightfully disavow it or refuse to be bound by it.

The United States has recognized the conclusiveness of this award by legislative enactment; for in the Indian appropriation bill, approved March 2, 1861, it was provided that the sum of $500,000 should be paid to the said nation *on account of this award*. (12 Stat. at Large, p. 238.)

In pursuance of this act the sum of $250,000 in money was paid to the said nation; but the bonds for a like amount, which the Secretary of the Treasury was directed to issue, were not delivered on account of the interruption of intercourse with the said nation caused by the war of the rebellion. These bonds have never been issued or delivered to the said nation, and all that has ever been paid to the said nation on account of the said award, therefore, is the sum of $250,000, paid (under the said act of March 2, 1861,) on the 12th day of April, 1861. The balance remaining unpaid on the said award since the 12th day of April, 1861, therefore, is $2,731,247.30.

THE OBLIGATION TO PAY INTEREST ON THE AMOUNT AWARDED THE CHOCTAW NATION.

Your committee have given this question a most careful examination, and are obliged to admit and declare that the United States cannot, in equity and justice, nor without

they assume and exercise the power of annulling or altering *bona-fide* contracts between individuals.

2. Interest may be claimed in certain cases by custom, viz, in cases where it has long been usual for merchants to expect and to allow interest on debts, after the stipulated

---

national dishonor, refuse to pay interest upon the money so long withheld from the Choctaw Nation. Some of the reasons which force us to this conclusion are as follows:

1. The United States acquired the lands of the Choctaw Nation, on account of which the said award was made, on the 27th day of September, 1830, and it has held them for the benefit of its citizens ever since.

2. The United States had in its Treasury, many years prior to the 1st day of January, 1859, the proceeds resulting from the sale of the said lands, and have enjoyed the use of such moneys from that time until now.

3. The award in favor of the Choctaw Nation was an award under a treaty, and made by a tribunal whose adjudication was final and conclusive. (Comegys *vs.* Vasse, 1 Peters, 193.)

4. The obligations of the United States, under its treaties with Indian nations, have been declared to be equally sacred with those made by treaties with foreign nations. (Worcester *vs.* The State of Georgia, 6 Peters, 582.) And such treaties, Mr. Justice Miller declares, are to be construed liberally. (The Kansas Indians, 5 Wall., 737–760.)

5. The engagements and obligations of a treaty are to be interpreted in accordance with the principles of the public law, and not in accordance with any municipal code or executive regulation. No statement of this proposition can equal the clearness or force with which Mr. Webster declares it in his opinion on the Florida claims, attached to the report in the case of Letitia Humphreys. (Senate report No. 93, 1st session Thirty-sixth Congress, page 16.) Speaking of the obligation of a treaty, he said:

"A treaty is the supreme law of the land. It can neither be limited, nor restrained, nor modified, nor altered. *It stands on the ground of national contract, and is declared by the Constitution to be the supreme law of the land*, and this gives it a character higher than any act of ordinary legislation. It enjoys an immunity from the operation and effect of all such legislation.

"A second general proposition, equally certain and well established, is that the terms and the language used in a treaty are *always* to be interpreted according to the law of nations, and not according to any municipal code. This rule is of universal application. When two nations speak to each other, they use the language of nations. Their intercourse is regulated, *and their mutual agreements and obligations* are to be interpreted, by that code only which we usually denominate the public law of the world. This public law is not one thing at Rome, another at London, and a third at Washington. It is the same in all civilized states, everywhere speaking with the same voice and the same authority."

Again, in the same opinion, Mr. Webster used the following language:

"We are construing a treaty, a solemn compact between nations. This compact between nations, this treaty, is to be construed and interpreted throughout its whole length and breadth, in its general provisions, and in all its details, in every phrase, sentence, word, and syllable in it, by the settled rules of the law of nations. No municipal code can touch it, no local municipal law affect it, no practice of an administrative department come near it. Over all its terms, over all its doubts, over all its ambiguities, if it have any, the law of nations 'sits arbitress.'"

6. By the principles of the public law, interest is always allowed as indemnity for the delay of payment of an ascertained and fixed demand. There is no conflict of authority upon this question among the writers on public law.

This rule is laid down by Rutherford in these terms:

"In estimating the damages which any one has sustained, when such things as he has a perfect right to are unjustly taken from him, or WITHHOLDEN, or intercepted, we are to consider not only the value of the thing itself, but the value likewise of the fruits or profits that might have arisen from it. He who is the owner of the thing is likewise the owner of the fruits or profits. So that it is as properly a damage to be deprived of them, as it is to be deprived of the thing itself." (Rutherford's Institutes, Book I, chap. 17, sec. 5.)

In laying down the rule for the satisfaction of injuries in the case of reprisals, in making which the strictest caution is enjoined not to transcend the clearest rules of justice, Mr. Wheaton, in his work on the law of nations, says:

"If a nation has taken possession of that which belongs to another, IF IT REFUSES TO PAY A DEBT, to repair an injury, or to give adequate satisfaction for it, the latter may seize something of the former and apply it to [his] its advantage, till it obtains payment of what is due, together with INTEREST and damages." (Wheaton on International Law, p. 341.)

A great writer, Domat, thus states the law of reason and justice on this point:

"It is a natural consequence of the general engagement to do wrong to no one, that they who cause any damages, by failing in the performance of that engagement, are

term and time of credit and payment has expired. This custom, in the ordinary course of things, is reasonable; for equity demands that he who does not pay at the appointed day should thereafter pay interest to his creditor, as well by way of compensation for the disappointment as for the use of the money. Whether the reason of this custom

---

obliged to repair the damage which they have done. Of what nature soever the damage may be, and from what cause soever it may proceed, he who is answerable for it ought to repair it by an *amende* proportionable either to his fault or to his offense, or other cause on his part, and to the loss which has happened thereby." (Domat, Part I, Book III, Tit. V, 1900, 1903.)

"Interest" is in reality, in justice, in reason, and in law, too, a part of the debt due. It includes, in Pothier's words, the loss which one has suffered, and the gain which he has failed to make. The Roman law defines it as "quantum mea interfruit; id est, quantum mihi abest, quantumque lucraci potui." The two elements of it were termed "lucrum cessans et damnum emergens." The payment of both is necessary to a complete indemnity.

Interest, Domat says, is the reparation or satisfaction which he who owes a sum of money is bound to make to his creditor for the damage which he does him by not paying him the money he owes him.

It is because of the universal recognition of the justice of paying, for the retention of moneys indisputably due and payable immediately, a rate of interest considered to be a fair equivalent for the loss of its use, that judgments for money everywhere bear interest. The creditor is deprived of this profit, and the debtor has it. What greater wrong could the law permit than that the debtor should be at liberty indefinitely to delay payment, and, during the delay, have the use of the creditor's moneys for nothing? They are none the less the creditor's moneys because the debtor wrongfully withholds them. *He holds them, in reality and essentially, in trust; and a trustee is always bound to pay interest upon moneys so held.*

In closing these citations from the public law, the language of Chancellor Kent seems eminently appropriate. He says: "In cases where the principal jurists agree, the presumption will be very great in favor of the solidity of their maxims, *and no civilized nation that does not arrogantly set all ordinary law and justice at defiance will venture to disregard the uniform sense of established writers on international law.*"

7th. The *practice* of the United States in discharging obligations resulting from treaty-stipulations has always been in accord with these well-established principles. It has exacted the payment of *interest* from other nations in all cases where the obligation to make payment resulted from treaty-stipulations, and it has acknowledged that obligation in all cases where a like liability was imposed upon it.

The most important and leading cases which have occurred are those which arose between this country and Great Britain: the first under the treaty of 1794, and the other under the first article of the treaty of Ghent. In the latter case the United States, under the first article of the treaty, claimed compensation for slaves and other property taken away from the country by the British forces at the close of the war in 1815. A difference arose between the two governments, which was submitted to the arbitrament of the Emperor of Russia, who decided that "the United States of America are entitled to a just indemnification from Great Britain for all private property carried away by the British forces." A joint commission was appointed for the purpose of hearing the claims of individuals under this decision. At an early stage of the proceedings the question arose as to whether *interest* was a part of that "*just indemnification*" which the decision of the Emperor of Russia contemplated. The British commissioner denied the obligation to pay interest. The American commissioner, Langdon Cheves, insisted upon its allowance, and, in the course of his argument upon this question, said:

"Indemnification means a re-imbursement of a loss sustained. If the property taken away on the 17th of February, 1815, were returned now uninjured it would not re-imburse the loss sustained by the taking away and consequent detention; it would not be an indemnification. The claimant would still be unindemnified for the loss of the use of his property for ten years, which, considered as money, is nearly equivalent to the original value of the principal thing."

Again he says:

"If interest be an incident usually attendant on the delay of payment of debts, damages are equally an incident attendant on the withholding an article of property."

In consequence of this disagreement, the commission was broken up, but the claims were subsequently compromised by the payment of $1,204,960, instead of $1,250,000, as claimed by Mr. Cheves; and of the sum paid by Great Britain, $418,000 was expressly for interest.

An earlier case, in which this principle of interest was involved, arose under the treaty of 1794 between the United States and Great Britain, in which there was a stipulation on the part of the British government in relation to certain losses and damages sustained by American merchants and other citizens, by reason of the illegal or irregu-

can apply in time of war, or whether the equity of the demand of interest in virtue of the custom is, or is not, overbalanced by the equity of refusing it by reason of the effects of the war, are questions proper for the consideration of the jury; and your secretary sees nothing in the treaty to prevent their deciding as to them shall appear just and right.

---

lar capture of their vessels, or other property, by British cruisers; and the seventh article provided in substance that "full and complete compensation for the same will be made by the British government to the said claimants."

A joint commission was instituted under this treaty, which sat in London, and by which these claims were adjudicated. Mr. Pinckney and Mr. Gore were commissioners on the part of the United States, and Dr. Nicholl and Dr. Swabey on the part of Great Britain; and it is believed that in all instances this commission allowed interest as a part of the damage. In the case of The Betsey, one of the cases which came before the board, Dr. Nicholl stated the rule of compensation as follows:

"To re-imburse the claimants the original cost of their property, and all the expenses they have actually incurred, together with interest on the whole amount, would, I think, be a just and adequate compensation. This, I believe, is the measure of compensation usually made by all belligerent nations, and accepted by all neutral nations, for losses, costs, and damages occasioned by illegal captures." (*Vide* Wheaton's Life of Pinckney, p. 198; also p. 265, note; and p. 371.)

By a reference to the American State Papers, Foreign Relations, vol. 2, pages 119, 120, it will be seen by a report of the Secretary of State of the 16th February, 1798, laid before the House of Representatives, that interest was awarded and paid on such of these claims as had been submitted to the award of Sir William Scott and Sir John Nicholl, as it was in all cases by the board of commissioners. In consequence of some difference of opinion between the members of this commission, their proceedings were suspended until 1802, when a convention was concluded between the two governments, and the commission re-assembled, and then a question arose as to the allowance of interest on the claims during the suspension. This the American commissioner claimed, and though it was at first resisted by the British commissioners, yet it was finally yielded, and interest was allowed and paid. (See Mr. King's three letters to the Secretary of State, of 25th March, 1803, 23d April, 1803, and 30th April, 1803, American State Papers, Foreign Relations, vol. 2, pp. 387, 388.)

Another case in which this principle was involved arose under the treaty of the 27th October, 1795, with Spain; by the twenty-first article of which, "in order to terminate all differences on account of the losses sustained by citizens of the United States in consequence of their vessels and cargoes having been taken by the subjects of His Catholic Majesty during the late war between Spain and France, it is agreed that all such cases shall be referred to the final decision of commissioners, to be appointed in the following manner," &c.; the commissioners were to be chosen, one by the United States, one by Spain, and the two were to choose a third, and the award of the commissioners, or any two of them, was to be final, and the Spanish government to pay the amount in specie. This commission awarded interest as part of the damages. (See American State Papers, vol. 2, Foreign Relations, p. 283.) So in the case of claims of American citizens against Brazil, settled by Mr. Tudor, United States minister, interest was claimed and allowed. (See Ex. Doc. No. 32, first session Twenty-fifth Congress, House of Representatives, p. 249.)

Again, in the convention with Mexico of the 11th of April, 1839, by which provision was made by Mexico for the payment of claims of American citizens for injuries to persons and property by the Mexican authorities, a mixed commission was provided for, and this commission allowed interest in all cases. (House Ex. Doc. No. 291, Twenty-seventh Congress, second session.)

So also under the treaty with Mexico of February 2, 1848, the board of commissioners for the adjustment of claims under that treaty allowed interest in all cases from the origin of the claim until the day when the commission expired.

So, also, under the convention with Colombia, concluded February 10, 1864, the commission for the adjudication of claims under that treaty allowed interest in all cases as a part of the indemnity.

So under the recent convention with Venezuela, the United States exacted interest upon the awards of the commission, from the date of the adjournment of the commission until the payment of the awards.

The Mixed American and Mexican Commission, now in session here, allows interest in all cases from the origin of the claim, and the awards are payable with interest.

Other cases might be shown, in which the United States, or their authorized diplomatic agents, have claimed interest in such cases, or where it has been paid in whole or in part. (See Mr. Russell's letters to the Count de Engstein, of October 5, 1818, American State Papers, vol. 4, p. 639, and Proceedings under the Convention with the Two Sicilies of October, 1832, Elliot's Diplomatic Code, p. 625.)

It can hardly be necessary to pursue these precedents further. They sufficiently and

3. Interest may be demanded, and is often given, under the idea of damages for wrongful and vexatious delays of payment. Every case of this kind must stand on its own merits; and the treaty leaves the jury at liberty to give such a verdict as their opinion of those merits may dictate.

Your secretary will not proceed to examine the acts complained of as infractions of

---

clearly show the practice of this Government with foreign nations, or with claimants under treaties.

8th. The practice of the United States in its dealings with the various Indian tribes or nations has been in harmony with these principles.

In all cases where money belonging to Indian nations has been retained by the United States, it has been so invested as to produce *interest*, for the benefit of the nation to which it belongs; and such interest is *annually* paid to the nation who may be entitled to receive it.

9th. The United States, in adjusting the claim of the Cherokee Nation for a balance due as purchase-money upon lands ceded by that nation to the United States, in 1835, allowed interest upon the balance due them, being $189,422.76, until the same was paid.

The question was submitted to the Senate of the United States as to whether interest should be allowed them. The Senate Committee on Indian Affairs, in their report upon this subject, used the following language:

"By the treaty of August, 1846, it was referred to the Senate to decide, and that decision to be final, whether the Cherokees shall receive interest on the sums found due them from a misapplication of their funds to purposes with which they were not chargeable, and on account of which improper charges the money has been withheld from them. It has been the uniform practice of this Government to pay and demand interest in all transactions with foreign governments, which the Indian tribes have always been said to be both by the Supreme Court and all other branches of our Government, in all matters of treaty or contract. The Indians, relying upon the prompt payment of their dues, have, in many cases, contracted debts upon the faith of it, upon which they have paid, or are liable to pay, interest. If, therefore, they do not now receive interest on their money so long withheld from them, they will, in effect, have received nothing." (Senate Report No. 176, first session Thirty-first Congress, p. 78.)

10th. That upon an examination of the precedents where Congress has passed acts for the relief of private citizens, it will be found that, in almost every case, Congress has directed the payment of interest, where the United States had withheld a sum of money which had been decided by competent authority to be due, or where the amount due was ascertained, fixed, and certain.

The following precedents illustrate and enforce the correctness of this assertion, and sustain this proposition:

1. An act approved January 14, 1793, provided that lawful interest from the 16th of May, 1776, shall be allowed on the sum of $200 ordered to be paid to Return J. Meigs, and the legal representatives of Christopher Greene, deceased, by a resolve of the United States, in Congress assembled, on the 28th of September, 1785. (6 Stat. at L., p. 11.)

2. An act approved May 31, 1794, provided for a settlement with Arthur St. Clair, for expenses while going from New York to Fort Pitt and till his return, and for services in the business of Indian treaties, and "allowed interest on the balance found to be due him." (6 Stat. at L., p. 16.)

3. An act approved February 27, 1795, authorized the officers of the Treasury to issue and deliver to Angus McLean, or his duly-authorized attorney, certificates for the amount of $254.43, bearing interest at six per cent. from the 1st of July, 1783, being for his services in the Corps of Sappers and Miners during the late war. (6 Stat. at L., p. 20.)

4. An act approved January 23, 1798, directed the Secretary of the Treasury to pay to General Kosciusko an interest at the rate of six per cent. per annum on the sum of $11,289.54, the amount of a certificate due to him from the United States, from the 1st of January, 1793, to the 31st of December, 1797. (6 Stat. at L., p. 32.)

5. An act approved May 3, 1802, provided that there be paid Fulwar Skipwith the sum of $4,550, advanced by him for the use of the United States, with interest at the rate of six per cent. per annum from the 1st of November, 1795, at which time the advance was made. (6 Stat. at L., p. 48.)

6. An act for the relief of John Coles, approved January 14, 1804, authorized the proper accounting officers of the Treasury to liquidate the claim of John Coles, owner of the ship Grand Turk, heretofore employed in the service of the United States, for the detention of said ship at Gibraltar from the 10th of May to the 4th of July, 1801, inclusive, and that he be allowed demurrage at the rate stipulated in the charter-party, together with the interest thereon. (6 Stat. at L., p. 50.)

7. An act approved March 3, 1807, provided for a settlement of the accounts of Oliver Pollock, formerly commercial agent for the United States at New Orleans, allowing him certain sums and commissions, with interest until paid. (6 Stat. at L., p. 65.)

8. An act for the relief of Stephen Sayre, approved March 3, 1807, provided that the

this article. The first on the list is called an act of Massachusetts, passed the 9th November, 1784; but it was a resolution of the legislature rather than a formal act. As the abridgment of it in the list of grievances may not be so satisfactory to Congress as a recital of it at large, your secretary thinks it best to report it.

"COMMONWEALTH OF MASSACHUSETTS,
"*In Senate, November* 9, 1784.

"Whereas the payment of interest which might have accrued during the late war upon debts due from the citizens of this or any of the United States prior to the commence-

---

accounting officers of the Treasury be authorized to settle the account of Stephen Sayre, as secretary of legation at the court of Berlin, in the year 1777, with interest on the whole sum until paid. (6 Stat. at L., p. 65.)

9. An act approved April 25, 1810, directed the accounting officers of the Treasury to settle the account of Moses Young, as secretary of legation to Holland in 1780, and providing that after the deduction of certain moneys paid to him, the balance, with interest thereon, should be paid. (6 Stat. at L., p. 89.)

10. An act approved May 1, 1810, for the relief of P. C. L'Enfant, directed the Secretary of the Treasury to pay to him the sum of $666, with legal interest thereon from March 1, 1792, as a compensation for his services in laying out the plan of the city of Washington. (6 Stat. at L., p. 92.)

11. An act approved January 10, 1812, provided that there be paid to John Burnham the sum of $126.72, and the interest on the same since the 30th of May, 1796, which, in addition to the sum allowed him by the act of that date, is to be considered a re-imbursement of the money advanced by him for his ransom from captivity in Algiers. (6 Stat. at L., p. 101.)

12. An act approved July 1, 1812, for the relief of Anna Young, required the War Department to settle the account of Col. John Durkee, deceased, and to allow said Anna Young, his sole heiress and representative, said seven years' half-pay, and interest thereon. (6 Stat. at L., p. 110.)

13. An act approved February 25, 1813, provided that there be paid to John Dixon the sum of $329.84, with six per cent. per annum interest thereon from the 1st of January, 1785, "being the amount of a final-settlement certificate, No. 596, issued by Andrew Dunscomb, late commissioner of accounts for the State of Virginia, on the 23d of December, 1786, to Lucy Dixon, who transferred the same to John Dixon." (6 Stat. at L., p. 117.)

14. An act approved February 25, 1813, required the accounting-officers of the Treasury to settle the account of John Murray, representative of Dr. Henry Murray, and that he be allowed the amount of three loan-certificates for $1,000, with interest from the 29th of March, 1782, issued in the name of said Murray, signed Francis Hopkinson, treasurer of loans. (6 Stat. at L., p. 117.)

15. An act approved March 3, 1813, directed the accounting-officers of the Treasury to settle the accounts of Samuel Lapsley, deceased, and that they be allowed the amount of two final-settlement certificates, No. 78,446, for $1,000, and No. 78,447, for $1,300, and interest from the 23d day of March, 1783, issued in the name of Samuel Lapsley, by the commissioner of Army accounts for the United States on the 1st day of July, 1784. (6 Stat. at L., p. 119.)

16. An act approved April 13, 1814, directed the officers of the Treasury to settle the account of Joseph Brevard, and that he be allowed the amount of a final-settlement certificate for $183.23, dated February 1, 1785, and bearing interest from the 1st of January, 1783, issued to said Brevard by John Pierce, commissioner for settling Army accounts. (6 Stat. at L., p. 134.)

17. An act approved April 18, 1814, directed the receiver of public moneys at Cincinnati to pay the full amount of moneys, with interest, paid by Dennis Clark, in discharge of the purchase-money for a certain fractional section of land purchased by said Clark. (6 Stat. at L., p. 141.)

18. An act for the relief of William Arnold, approved February 2, 1815, allowed interest on the sum of $600 due him from January 1, 1873. (6 Stat. at L., p. 146.)

19. An act approved April 26, 1816, directed the accounting-officers of the Treasury to pay to Joseph Wheaton the sum of $836.42, on account of interest due him from the United States upon $1,600.84, from April 1, 1807, to December 21, 1815, pursuant to the award of George Youngs and Elias B. Caldwell, in a controversy between the United States and the said Joseph Wheaton. (6 Stat. at L., p. 166.)

20. An act approved April 26, 1816, authorized the liquidation and settlement of the claim of the heirs of Alexander Roxburgh, arising on a final-settlement certificate issued on the 18th of August, 1784, for $480.87, by John Pierce, commissioner for settling Army accounts, bearing interest from the first of January, 1782. (6 Stat. at L., p. 167.)

21. An act approved April 14, 1818, authorized the accounting-officers of the Treasury Department "to review the settlement of the account of John Thompson," made

ment of the same, the real British subjects and others commonly called absentees, would be not only inequitable and unjust, but the legislature of this Commonwealth conceive repugnant to the spirit and intendment of the fourth article in the treaty of peace, which provides only for the payment of *bona-fide* debts; and as the legislature have taken measures to obtain the sense of Congress upon the said article, so far as the same respects the payment of interest which might have accrued as aforesaid, and in the mean time judgment may be obtained in some of the courts of law within this Commonwealth for interest accruing as aforesaid, contrary to the true design of the said treaty: Therefore,

---

under the authority of an act approved the 11th of May, 1812, and "to allow the said John Thompson interest at six per cent. per annum from the 4th of March, 1787, to the 20th of May, 1812, on the sum which was found due to him, and paid under the act aforesaid." (6 Stat. at L., p. 208.)

22. An act approved May 11, 1820, directed the proper officers of the Treasury to pay to Samuel B. Beall the amount of two final-settlement certificates issued to him on the 1st of February, 1785, for his services as a lieutenant in the Army of the United States during the revolutionary war, together with interest on the said certificates, at the rate of six per cent. per annum from the time they bore interest, respectively, which said certificates were lost by the said Beall, and remain yet outstanding and unpaid. (6 Laws of U. S., 510; 6 Stat. at L., p. 249.)

23. An act approved May 15, 1820, required that there be paid to Thomas Leiper the specie value of four loan-office certificates, issued to him by the commissioner of loans for the State of Pennsylvania, on the 27th of February, 1779, for $1,000 each; and also the specie value of two loan-certificates, issued to him by the said commissioner on the 2d day of March, 1779, for $1,000 each, with interest at six per cent. annually. (6 Stat. at L., p. 252.)

24. An act approved May 7, 1822, provided that there be paid to the legal representatives of John Guthry, deceased, the sum of $123.30, being the amount of a final-settlement certificate, with interest at the rate of six per cent. per annum, from the first day of January, 1783. (6 Stat. at L., p. 269.)

25. An act for the relief of the legal representatives of James McClung, approved March 3, 1823, allowed interest on the amount due at the rate of six per cent. per annum, from January 1, 1788. (6 Stat. at L., 284.)

26. An act approved March 3, 1823, for the relief of Daniel Seward, allowed interest to him for money paid to the United States for land to which the title failed, at the rate of six per cent. per annum from January 29, 1814. (6 Stat. at L., p. 286.)

27. An act approved May 5, 1824, directed the Secretary of the Treasury to pay to Amasa Stetson the sum of $6,215, "being for interest on moneys advanced by him for the use of the United States, and on warrants issued in his favor, in the years 1814 and 1815, for his services in the Ordnance and Quartermaster's Department, for superintending the making of Army clothing and for issuing the public supplies." (6 Stat. at L., p. 298.)

28. An act approved March 3, 1824, directed the proper accounting-officers of the Treasury to settle and adjust the claim of Stephen Arnold, David and George Jenks, for the manufacture of three thousand nine hundred and twenty-five muskets, with interest thereon from the 26th day of October, 1813. (6 Stat. at L., p. 331.)

29. An act approved May 20, 1826, directed the proper accounting-officers of the Treasury to settle and adjust the claim of John Stemman and others for the manufacture of four thousand one hundred stand of arms, and to allow interest on the amount due from October 26, 1813. (6 Stat. at L., p. 345.)

30. An act approved May 20, 1826, for the relief of Ann D. Taylor, directed the payment to her of the sum of $354.15, with interest thereon at the rate of six per cent. per annum from December 30, 1786, until paid. (6 Stat. at L., p. 351.)

31. An act approved March 3, 1827, provided that the proper accounting-officers of the Treasury were authorized to pay to B. J. V. Valkenburg the sum of $597.24, "being the amount of fourteen indents of interest, with interest thereon from the 1st of January, 1791, to the 31st of December, 1826." (6 Stat. at L., p. 365.)

In this case the United States paid interest on interest.

32. An act approved May 19, 1828, provided that there be paid to the legal representatives of Patience Gordon the specie value of a certificate issued in the name of Patience Gordon by the commissioner of loans for the State of Pennsylvania, on the 7th of April, 1778, with interest at the rate of 6 per cent. per annum from the 1st day of January, 1788. (7 Stat. at L., p. 378.)

33. An act approved May 29, 1830, required the Treasury Department "to settle the accounts of Benjamin Wells, as deputy commissary of issues at the magazine at Monster Mills, in Pennsylvania, under John Irvin, deputy commissary-general of the Army of the United States, in said State, in the revolutionary war;" and that "they credit him with the sum of $574.04, as payable February 9, 1779, and $326.67, payable July 20, 1780, in the same manner, and with such interest, as if these sums, with their inter-

"*Resolved*, That in all actions or suits which are or may be instituted or brought to any of the judicial courts within this Commonwealth, wherein any real British subject or absentee is plaintiff or defendant, and which actions or suits by the laws thereof are sustainable therein, the justices of the same courts are hereby severally directed to

---

est from the times respectively as aforesaid, had been subscribed to the loan of the United States." (6 Stat. at L., p. 447.)

34. An act approved May 19, 1832, for the relief of Richard G. Morris, provided for the payment to him of two certificates issued to him by Timothy Pickering, Quartermaster-General, with interest thereon from the 1st of September, 1781. (6 Stat. at L., p. 486.)

35. An act approved July 4, 1832, for the relief of Aaron Snow, a revolutionary soldier, provided for the payment to him of two certificates issued by John Pierce, late commissioner of Army accounts, and dated in 1784, with interest thereon. (6 Stat. at L., p. 503.)

36. An act approved July 4, 1832, provided for the payment to W. P. Gibbs of a final-settlement certificate dated January 30, 1784, with interest at 6 per cent. from the 1st of January, 1783, up to the passage of the act. This act went behind the final certificate and provided for the payment of interest anterior to its date. (6 Stat. at L., p. 504.)

37. An act approved July 14, 1832, directed the payment to the heirs of Ebenezer L. Warren of certain sums of money illegally demanded and received by the United States from the said Warren as one of the sureties of Daniel Evans, formerly collector of direct taxes, with interest thereon at the rate of 6 per cent. per annum from September 9, 1820. (6 Stat. at L., p. 373.)

38. An act for the relief of Hartwell Vick, approved July 14, 1832, directed the accounting-officers of the Treasury to refund to the said Vick the money paid by him to the United States for a certain tract of land which was found not to be the property of the United States, with interest thereon at the rate of 6 per centum per annum, from the 23d day of May, 1818. (6 Stat. at L., p. 523.)

39. An act approved June 18, 1834, for the relief of Martha Bailey and others, directed the Secretary of the Treasury to pay to the parties therein named the sum of $4,837.61, being the amount of interest upon the sum of $200,000, part of a balance due from the United States to Elbert Anderson on the 26th day of October, 1814; also the further sum of $9,595.36, being the amount of interest accruing from the deferred payment of warrants issued for balances due from the United States to the said Anderson from the date of such warrants until the payment thereof; also the further sum of $2,018.50 admitted to be due from the United States to the said Anderson by a decision of the Second Comptroller, with interest on the sum last mentioned from the period of such decision until paid. (6 Stat. at L., p. 562.)

40. An act approved June 30, 1834, directed the Secretary of the Treasury to pay balance of damages recovered against William C. H. Waddell, United States marshal for the southern district of New York, for the illegal seizure of a certain importation of brandy, on behalf of the United States, with legal interest on the amount of said judgment from the time the same was paid by the said Waddell. (6 Stat. at L , p. 594.)

41. An act approved February 17, 1836, directed the payment of the sum therein named to Marinus W. Gilbert, being the interest on money advanced by him to pay off troops in the service of the United States, and not repaid when demanded. (6 Stat. at L., p. 622.)

42. An act approved February 17, 1836, for the relief of the executor of Charles Wilkins, directed the Secretary of the Treasury to settle the claim of the said executor, for interest on a liquidated demand in favor of Jonathan Taylor, James Morrison, and Charles Wilkins, who were lessees of the United States of the salt-works in the State of Illinois. (6 Stat. at L., p. 626.)

43. An act approved July 2, 1836, for the relief of the legal representatives of David Caldwell, directed the proper accounting-officers of the Treasury to settle the claim of the said David Caldwell for fees and allowances, certified by the circuit court of the United States for the eastern district of Pennsylvania, for official services to the United States, and to pay on that account the sum of $496.38, with interest thereon at the rate of six per centum from the 25th day of November, 1830, till paid. (6 Stat. at L., p. 664.)

44. An act approved July 2, 1836, provided that there be paid Don Carlos Delossus, interest at the rate of six per centum per annum on $333, being the amount allowed him under the act of July 14, 1832, for his relief, on account of moneys taken from him at the capture of Baton Rouge, La., on the 23d day of September, 1810, being the interest to be allowed from the said 23d day of September, 1810, to the 14th day of July, 1832. (6 Stat. at L., p. 672.)

In this case the interest was directed to be paid four years after the principal had been satisfied and discharged.

suspend rendering judgment for any interest that may have accrued upon the demand contained in such actions or suits between the 19th day of April, 1775, and the 20th day of January, 1783, until the third Wednesday of the next sitting of the general court: *Provided, always*, That if in any such actions or suits the plaintiff shall move for,

---

45. An act approved July 7, 1838, provided that the proper officers of the Treasury be directed to settle the accounts of Richard Harrison, formerly consular agent of the United States at Cadiz, in Spain, and to allow him, among other items, the interest on the money advanced, under agreement with the minister of the United States in Spain, for the relief of destitute and distressed seamen, and for their passages to the United States from the time the advances respectively were made, to the time at which the said advances were re-imbursed. (6 Stat. at L., p. 734.)

46. An act approved August 11, 1842, directed the Secretary of the Treasury to pay to John Johnson the sum of $756.82, being the amount received from the said Johnson upon a judgment against him in favor of the United States, together with the interest thereon from the time of such payment. (6 Stat. at L., p. 856.)

47. An act approved August 3, 1846, authorized the Secretary of the Treasury to pay to Abraham Horbach the sum of $5,000, with lawful interest from the 1st of January, 1836, being the amount of a draft drawn by James Reeside on the Post-Office Department, dated April 18, 1835, payable on the 1st of January, 1836, and accepted by the treasurer of the Post-Office Department, which said draft was indorsed by said Abraham Horbach at the instance of the said Reeside, and the amount drawn from the Bank of Philadelphia, and, at maturity, said draft was protested for non-payment, and said Horbach became liable to pay, and, in consequence of his indorsement, did pay the full amount of said draft. (9 Stat. at L., p. 677.)

48. An act approved February 5, 1859, authorized the Secretary of War to pay to Thomas Laurent, as surviving partner, the sum of $15,000, with interest at the rate of 6 per cent. yearly, from the 11th of November, 1847, it being the amount paid by the firm on that day to Maj. Gen. Winfield Scott, in the city of Mexico, for the purchase of a house in said city, out of the possession of which they were since ousted by the Mexican authorities. (11 Stat. at L., p. 558.)

49. An act approved March 2, 1847, directed the Secretary of the Treasury to pay the balance due to the Bank of Metropolis for moneys due upon the settlement of the account of the bank with the United States, with interest thereon from the 6th day of March, 1838. (9 Stat. at L., p. 689.)

50. An act approved July 20, 1852, directed the payment to the legal representatives of James C. Watson, late of the State of Georgia, the sum of $14,600, with interest at the rate of 6 per cent. per annum, from the 8th day of May, 1838, till paid, being the amount paid by him under the sanction of the Indian agent, to certain Creek warriors, for slaves captured by said warriors while they were in the service of the United States against the Seminole Indians, in Florida. (10 Stat. at L., p. 734.)

51. An act approved July 29, 1854, directed the Secretary of the Treasury to pay to John C. Frémont $183,825, with interest thereon from the 1st day of June, 1851, at the rate of 10 per cent. per annum, in full for his account for beef delivered to Commissioner Barbour, for the use of the Indians in California, in 1851 and 1852. (10 Stat. at L., p. 804.)

52. An act approved July 8, 1870, directed the Secretary of the Treasury to make proper payments to carry into effect the decree of the district court of the United States for the district of Louisiana, bearing date the *fourth* of June, 1867, in the case of the British brig Volant, and her cargo; and also another decree of the same court, bearing date the *eleventh* of June, in the same year, in the case of the British bark Science, and cargo, vessels illegally seized by a cruiser of the United States; such payments to be made as follows, viz: To the several persons named in such decrees, or their legal representatives, the several sums awarded to them respectively, *with interest to each person from the date of the decree under which he receives payment*. (16 Stat. at L., p. 650.)

53. An act approved July 8, 1870, directed the Secretary to make the proper payments to carry into effect the decree of the district court of the United States for the district of Louisiana, bearing date July 13, 1867, in the case of the British brig Dashing Wave, and her cargo, illegally seized by a cruiser of the United States, which decree was made in pursuance of the decision of the Supreme Court, *such payments to be made with interest from the date of the decree*. (16 Stat. at L., p. 651.)

An examination of these cases will show that, subsequent to the seizure of these several vessels, they were each sold by the United States marshal for the district of Louisiana as prize, and the proceeds of such sales deposited by him in the First National Bank of New Orleans. The bank, while the proceeds of these sales were deposited there, became insolvent. The seizures were held illegal, and the vessels not subject to capture as prize. But the proceeds of the sales of these vessels and their cargoes could not be restored to the owners in accordance with the decrees of the district court, because the funds had been lost by the insolvency of the bank. In these cases, there-

or by default have right to judgment, then, and in such case, the justices aforesaid shall cause judgment to be entered for the principal sum, which, by the laws of this Commonwealth such plaintiff shall be entitled to recover, and all such interest as accrued thereon before the said 19th day of April, and subsequent to said 20th day of

---

fore, Congress provided indemnity for losses resulting from the acts of its agents, and made the indemnity complete by providing for the payment of interest.

Your committee have directed attention to these numerous precedents for the purpose of exposing the utter want of foundation of the often-repeated assumption that "the Government never pays interest." It will readily be admitted that there is no statute-law to sustain this position. The idea has grown up from the custom and usage of the accounting officers and departments refusing to allow interest generally in their accounts with disbursing officers, and in the settlement of unliquidated domestic claims arising out of dealings with the Government. It will hardly be pretended, however, that this custom or usage is so "reasonable," well known, and "certain," as to give it the force and effect of law, and to override and trample under foot the law of nations and also the well-settled practice of the Government itself in its intercourse with other nations.

11th. Interest was allowed and paid to the State of Massachusetts, because the United States delayed the payment of the principal for twenty-two years after the amount due had been ascertained and determined. The amount appropriated to pay this interest was $678,362.41, more than the original principal. (16 Stat. at L., 198.)

Mr. Sumner, in his report upon the memorial introduced for that purpose, discussing this question of interest, said:

"It is urged that the payment of this interest would establish a bad precedent. If the claim is just, the precedent of paying it is one which our Government should wish to establish. Honesty and justice are not precedents of which either Government or individuals should be afraid." (Senate Report, 441st Cong., 1st sess., p. 10.)

12th. Interest has always been allowed to the several States for advances made to the United States for military purposes.

The claims of the several States for advances during the revolutionary war were adjusted and settled under the provision of the acts of Congress of August 5, 1790, and of May 31, 1794. By these acts interest was allowed to the States, whether they had advanced money on hand in their treasuries or obtained by loans.

In respect to the advances of States during the war of 1812–'15, a more restricted rule was adopted, viz: That States should be allowed interest only so far as they had themselves paid it by borrowing, or had lost it by the sale of interest-bearing funds.

Interest, according to this rule, has been paid to all the States which made advances during the war of 1812–'15, with the exception of Massachusetts. Here are the cases: Virginia, Stats. at L., vol. 4, p. 161; Delaware, Stats. at L., vol. 4, p. 175; New York, Stats. at L., vol. 4, p. 192; Pennsylvania, Stats. at L., vol. 4, p. 241; South Carolina, Stats. at L., vol. 4, p. 499.

In Indian and other wars the same rule had been observed as in the following cases: Alabama, Stats. at L., vol. 9, p. 344; Georgia, Stats. at L., vol. 9, p. 626; Washington Territory. Stats. at L., vol. 11, p. 429; New Hampshire, Stats. at L., vol. 10, p. 1.

13th. The Senate Committee on Indian Affairs, in the report to which reference has heretofore been made, speaking of this award and of the obligation of the United States to pay interest upon the balance remaining due and unpaid thereon, used the following language:

"Your committee are of opinion that this sum should be paid them with accrued interest from the date of said award, deducting therefrom $250,000, paid to them in money, as directed by the act of March 2, 1861; and, therefore, find no sufficient reason for further delay in carrying into effect that provision of the aforenamed act, and the act of March 3, 1871, by the delivery of the bonds therein described, with accrued interest from the date of the act of March 8, 1861."

Your committee have discussed this question with an anxious desire to come to such a conclusion in regard to it as would do no injustice to that Indian nation whose rights are involved here, nor establish such a precedent as would be inconsistent with the practice or duty of the United States in such cases. Therefore your committee have considered it not only by the light of those principles of the public law—always in harmony with the highest demands of the most perfect justice—but also in the light of those numerous precedents which this Government, in its action in like cases, has furnished for our guidance. Your committee cannot believe that the payment of interest on the moneys awarded by the Senate to the Choctaw Nation would either violate any principle of law or establish any precedent which the United States would not wish to follow in any similar case; and your committee cannot believe that the United States are prepared to repudiate these principles, or to admit that, because their obligation is held by a weak and powerless Indian nation, it is any the less sacred or binding than if held by a nation able to enforce its payment and secure complete indemnity under it. Could the United States escape the payment of *interest* to Great

January; and execution shall issue accordingly. And if Congress shall hereafter determine that the interest, which might have accrued on any *bona-fide* debt aforesaid during the war, ought by the treaty aforesaid to be considered as part of such debt, then the said courts, respectively, shall proceed to enter a further judgment for the

---

Britain, if it should refuse or neglect, after the same became due, to pay the amount awarded in favor of British subjects by the recent joint commission which sat here? Could we delay payment of the amount awarded by that commission for fifteen years, and then escape by merely paying the principal? The Choctaw Nation asks the same measure of justice which we *must* accord to Great Britain; and your committee cannot deny that demand unless they shall ignore and set aside those principles of the public law which it is of the utmost importance to the United States to always maintain inviolate.

Your committee are not unmindful that the amount due the Choctaw Nation under the award of the Senate is large. They are not unmindful, either, that the discredit of refusing payment is increased in proportion to the amount withheld and the time during which such refusal has been continued. That the amount to be paid is large is no fault of the Choctaw Nation. The whole amount was due when, on the 2d day of March, 1861, Congress authorized the payment, on account of the award, of the sum of $250,000; and if, at that time, the bonds of the United States had been issued in satisfaction of the award, the Choctaw Nation would have received interest on them from that time, and thus derived such advantage as would have resulted, from time to time, from the payment of semi-annual interest and the sale of the gold which they would have received in the payment of interest. The bill under consideration provides that the amount due upon the award of the Senate shall be satisfied and paid (both principal and interest) in the bonds of the United States of like character and description as those authorized to be issued under the act of Congress, entitled "An act authorizing a loan," approved February 8, 1861. They were bonds of this issue that the Secretary of the Treasury was required to deliver in part payment of the amount authorized to be paid on account of the said award, under the provisions of the act of March 2, 1861. If this award had then been wholly satisfied and discharged, it would have been in bonds of this description. The act of February 8, 1861, authorized the issue of bonds to the amount of $25,000,000, of which there have been issued $18,485,000. There is, therefore, to the credit of this act bonds to the amount of $6,515,000, which may be issued for any purpose which Congress shall direct. Your committee, bearing in mind that the moneys so long withheld from the Choctaw Nation are in the nature of trust-funds, and that the United States had the use of these moneys for so many years before the making of the award in favor of the Choctaw Nation by the United States Senate, and that the Choctaw Nation is in a certain sense a ward of the United States, cannot recommend any other payment to them, except such as will do them perfect justice and provide for them complete indemnity. This result will be most nearly accomplished by the issue and delivery to the Choctaw Nation of those bonds which would have been issued to them had the whole award been paid at the time provision was made for its part payment, as provided in the act of March 26, 1861; and interest on the said award should be added from the time the same was made by the United States Senate; and that for these, both principal and interest, bonds of the United States, of the character and description of other bonds issued under the act of February 8, 1861, should be issued for the use and benefit of the Choctaw Nation.

Your committee believe that this course, and nothing less, will satisfy the demands of justice, and relieve the United States from the imputation of bad faith and an inexcusable disregard of treaty obligations.

The Senate report No. 209, 1st session 43d Congress, March 26, 1874, embodies all the reports on "the claim of the officers of the [revolutionary] army to the half-pay promised them by the act of October 21, 1780."

In the House report of March 5, 1858, it is said that the claim to this pay became a *vested* right, and the report then makes this statement upon the subject of interest:

"Your committee are of opinion that the contract of half-pay has not been fulfilled on the part of the Government, nor have the claimants been guilty of laches or neglect, for they have again and again presented and urged upon Congress the payment of their just demands. The claimants had no way in which to enforce their rights, and could only sue for them in the language of solicitation. Their rights may, in fact, be said to have been suspended by the judiciary act of 1789, and were never restored until the act of February 24, 1855, organizing the Court of Claims. Since the establishment of that court the cause of Dr. Baird *vs.* The United States has been decided, in which he claimed half-pay for life, under the act of October, 1780, his commutation of five years' full pay having been paid by special act of Congress. The court, per Gilchrist, chief-justice, decided that the petitioner was entitled to the half-pay for life, and that the acceptance of a less sum than the half-pay by way of commutation was no discharge of the original contract, the payment of a sum of money not being of itself a discharge of a debt for a larger amount, and adds: 'A plea of payment of a small sum in satis-

amount of all such last-mentioned interest, without any new process, and issue execution for such further sum accordingly; and all attachments made or bail given upon any action instituted as aforesaid, shall be holden to respond the final judgment that may be given for the amount of such last-mentioned interest.

"Sent down for concurrence.

"SAMUEL ADAMS, *President.*

"In the house of representatives, November 10, 1784. Read and concurred.

"SAMUEL A. OTIS, *Speaker.*

"Approved.

"JOHN HANCOCK.

"A true copy. Attest:

"JOHN AVERY, JUN.,
"*Secretary.*"

However this resolution may deviate from the treaty, and perhaps from the proper jurisdiction of the legislature, yet it bears strong marks of fairness and regard to equal justice. It states their doubts on the construction of the article. It does not assume the power of deciding those doubts. It refers that question to Congress; and although it suspends judgment for interest, yet it does it impartially, and not only in cases where British creditors are plaintiffs, but also where they are defendants. It also provides, that if Congress should decide in favor of interest, then judgment and execution shall be given accordingly.

Your secretary is nevertheless of opinion that this resolution was an infraction of the said fourth article:

Because, State legislatures have no cognizance of questions respecting the construction of treaties, can with no propriety suspend their operation on account of any fears or apprehensions which they may entertain of and concerning such questions.

Because, as it appertained to the courts of judicature to decide such questions, the legislature ought not to have restrained those courts from rendering such judgments as to them appeared consistent with the treaty and the law. For by restraining the courts from giving judgment for interest in cases where they would have given such judgment, unless so restrained, the legislature did certainly interpose a lawful impediment to the plaintiff's recovering what the courts were ready to adjudge to be his right under that article of the treaty, and their so doing was, therefore, a violation of it.

---

## CHAPTER II.

### OF PROPERTY TAKEN, USED, DAMAGED, OR DESTROYED IN THE STATES PROCLAIMED IN REBELLION.

As to the eleven States proclaimed in rebellion during the period of flagrant war, it may be said in general terms that the United States, by the strict rules of international law, incurred no liability whatever for property taken, used, damaged, or destroyed therein by Government authority, so far as dictated by the necessary operations of the war, nor by the operations of the enemy. This is well settled by every writer on the laws of war.

Halleck says:

War * * makes legal enemies of all the individual members of the hostile states;

---

faction of a larger is bad even after verdict,' (2 Parsons on Contracts, 130, and notes.) The case was conceded not to be within any of the acts of limitation. The court allowed the demand *with interest*, and their decision was approved by both Houses of Congress, and the money paid at the Treasury. The high character of the Court of Claims, and action of Congress in carrying their decision into effect, is a judicial and legislative construction and declaration of the rights of other claimants founded upon the same contract and governed by the same rules of evidence. Considering, then, the commutation certificates as not amounting to an accord and satisfaction, the claim of Dr. Baird and those embraced in the bill are governed by the same principles."

* * *it also extends to property, and gives to one belligerent the right to deprive the other of everything which might add to his strength and enable him to carry on hostilities.*[79]

A firm possession is sufficient to establish the captor's title to personal or movable property on land, but a different rule applies to immovables or real property. A belligerent who makes himself master of the provinces, towns, public lands, buildings, &c., of an enemy, *has* a perfect right to their possession and use. * * The possession * * gives a right to its *use* and its *products*.[80]

By modern usage there are, and ought to be, humane limitations on the ancient right of seizure, which restrict it to what is useful in the prosecution of the war or necessary to disable the enemy.[81]

By General Order No. 100, approved by the President April 24, 1863, "instructions for the government of the armies" were issued, which were prepared by the eminent jurist, Francis Lieber, LL. D., embodying the laws of war as recognized among civilized and Christian nations, in which it is declared that—

Churches, hospitals, or other establishments of an exclusively charitable character, establishments of education, museums, &c., * * may be taxed or *used* when the public service may require it.[82]

The Supreme Court has determined that during the rebellion—

Cotton in the southern rebel districts—constituting, as it did, the chief reliance of the rebels for means to purchase munitions of war, an element of strength to the rebellion—was a proper subject of capture by the Government during the rebellion *on general principles of public law relating to war, though private property*; and the legislation of Congress during the rebellion authorized such captures.

And the court said, as to cotton:

Being enemy's property, the cotton was liable to capture and confiscation by the adverse party. It is true that this rule, as to property on land, has received very important qualifications from usage, from the reasonings of enlightened publicists, and from judicial decisions. It may now be regarded as substantially restricted "to special cases, dictated by the necessary operation of the war," and as excluding, in general, the seizure of the private property of pacific persons for the sake of gain. The commanding general may determine in what special cases its *more stringent application is required by military emergencies*; while considerations of public policy, and positive provisions of law, and the general spirit of legislation, must indicate the cases in which its application may be properly denied to the property of non-combatant enemies.

In the case before us, the capture seems to have been justified by the peculiar character of the property and by legislation. It is well known that cotton has constituted the chief reliance of the rebels for means to purchase the munitions of war in Europe. It is matter of history that, rather than permit it to come into the possession of the national troops, the rebel government has everywhere devoted it, however owned, to destruction. The value of that destroyed at New Orleans, just before its capture, has

---

[79] International Law, 446; id., 457–460; 71 vol. Globe, 300, Sumner's Speech, January 12, 1869; Prize Cases, 2 Black, 671–674; Lawrence's Wheaton, 596. This includes cotton. The rebels destroyed $80,000,000 in value to prevent it from being captured by Union forces. (Mrs. Alexander's Cotton, 2 Wallace, 420.)

[80] Halleck, 447; Wheaton, Int. Law, pt. 4. ch. 2, §§ 5–11; 1 Kent, 110; Heffert, Droit International, § 130; Martens, Précis du Droit des Gens, § 280; Requelme, Derecho Pub. Int., lib. 1, tit. 1, cap. 12.

[81] United States *v.* Klein, 13 Wallace, 138; Whiting's War Powers, 48, 52, 53; Lawrence's Wheaton, 630; Dana's Wheaton, section 256, note 171; Halleck, 448-451; Vattel, Law Nat., 365, book 3, chapter 9; Bynkershoek's Laws of War; Brown *v.* United States, 8 Cranch, 122, 228; 71 Globe, 383; 1 Kent, 92, 93, 120; Alexander *v.* Duke of Wellington, 2 Russell and Mylne, 35; 1 Kent's Com., 357. In United States *v.* Paddleford, 9 Wallace, 531, the court said: "The rights in private property are not disturbed by the capture of a district of country or a city or town until the captor signifies by some declaration or *act, and generally by actual seizure*, his determination to regard a particular description of property as not entitled to the immunity usually conceded in conformity with the humane maxims of the public laws."

Cooledge *v.* Guthrie, United States circuit court, southern district Ohio, October, 1868, Appendix 591 to (43d ed., 1871) Whiting's War Powers.

Mrs. Alexander's Cotton, 2 Wallace, 419; 1 Kent, 92, 93; United States *v.* Klein, 13 Wallace, 137.

[82] Scott's Digest Military Laws, 446. See McPherson's chapter "The Church and the Rebellion," History of Rebellion, 460, &c.

been estimated at eighty millions of dollars. The rebels regard it as one of their main sinews of war; and no principle of equity or just policy required, when the national occupation was itself precarious, that it should be spared from capture and allowed to remain, in case of the withdrawal of the Union troops, an element of strength to the rebellion. And the capture was justified by legislation as well as by public policy.[83]

Tobacco and other property was also an element of strength, and by the laws of war might equally with cotton, and upon the same principles, be destroyed.[84]

---

[83] Mrs. Alexander's Cotton, 2 Wallace, 419.

[84] The commissioners of claims, under the act of March 3, 1871, in their third annual report of December 8, 1873, House Mis. Doc. No. 23, 1st sess. 41st Cong., p. 3, say:

"As we now, for the first time, present reports allowing for tobacco taken for Army use, we desire to state the reasons for such allowances.

"Tobacco was by law never made an Army supply till the act of March 3, 1865, provided that it might be furnished at cost to those who desired it, and at their expense. All the claims for tobacco which have been examined by us are for tobacco taken before that date.

"After the capture of Atlanta, in September, 1864, General Sherman found that he was short of rations for his army, and that the soldiers were subject to many privations. To make his army contented, and, as far as possible, to make up to them for their usual rations, of which they were for the time deprived, he issued an order on the 8th of September, 1864, authorizing the chief commissary of subsistence to take possession of and issue to the troops all the tobacco in Atlanta, and give certificates thereof to the owners, to be accounted for in accordance with existing orders.

"Pursuant to this order, tobacco belonging to George J. Stubblefield was taken, and upon his making claim for payment the Commissary Department recommended, 'As this tobacco was taken *by order of General Sherman* and issued to the troops *in lieu of other rations*, and as the loyalty of the claimant is clearly established,' that payment should be made. This was approved by the Secretary of War, Mr. Stanton, and the claim was paid.

"The payment stands upon the ground that when an army is deprived of its usual rations the commanding general can, in his judgment, authorize an article not a supply to be taken and used for the time being as a supply, and *in lieu of other rations*; and in such case the Government is bound to pay for it. We have strictly followed this precedent, and have not allowed for tobacco except when taken under this order."—(3d Genl. Rep. Com. of Claims, art. 6, p. 3.)

The commission of claims, under 12th article of treaty of 8th May, 1871, between the United States and Great Britain, adopted the same principle; Hale's report to the Secretary of State, November 30, 1873, page 45, showing an award only when it was "allowed as an Army ration."

In Senate Report No. 338, 1st ses. 43d Cong., on a claim for tobacco, General Sherman said in a letter to the Committee on Claims:

"HEADQUARTERS ARMY OF THE UNITED STATES,
"*Washington, D. C., April* 18, 1874.

"SIR: I have the honor to acknowledge receipt of your communication of the 16th instant, inclosing the brief for claimant in the 'claim of N. P. Harben, of Georgia,' for tobacco seized at Covington and Oxford, on or about the 22d day of July, 1864.

* * * * * * *

"As a rule I endeavored, as far as circumstances permitted, to check the tendency to 'cause wanton waste,' which is the natural impulse of invading armies, but always authorized the appropriation of such things as soldiers needed to keep them strong and contented; and tobacco is one of those things which, whether authorized or not, soldiers will have by fair means or foul. I do not wish, however, to be construed as advocating Mr. Harben's claim, for, whatever his sentiments may have been, he was in bad company; his property was lost to him, and our army recovered possession of it, and were entitled to salvage at the rate of about a hundred per cent.

"W. T. SHERMAN,
"*General.*"

This claim was before the commissioners of claims, and they disposed of it as follows:

"No. 329. *The claim of N. P. Harben, of Whitfield County, in the State of Georgia.*

"This claim is for 342 boxes of tobacco valued at $51,438. Claim rejected.

"This claim is for tobacco taken in July, 1864, by a party of Union soldiers at Covington and Oxford, Ga. It was carried off by the soldiers on horseback and in large quantities in wagons. It was taken to a camp of the Army in the vicinity of Atlanta. What was then done with it does not appear, but probably most of it, perhaps all, was

Bynkershoek says:

It is a question whether our friends are to be considered as enemies, when they live among the latter, say in a town which they occupy. *Petrinus Bellus de R. Milit.*, part 2, tit. 11, note 5, thinks they are not. *Zauch, de Jure Fec.*, part 2, § 8, q. 4, gives no opinion. For my part, I think that they must also be considered as enemies. * * * They say that our friends, although they are among our enemies, yet are not hostilely inclined against us; for if they are there, it is not from choice, and the *quo animo* only is to be considered. But the thing does not depend only on the *quo animo;* for, even among the subjects of our enemy there are some, however few they may be, who are not hostilely inclined against us; but the matter depends upon the law, because those goods are with the enemy, and because they are of use to them for our destruction.[85]

---

used by the Army. Tobacco was not an Army supply. The Government has never paid for tobacco, except in the one single and exceptional case of tobacco taken at Atlanta under the general order issued by General Sherman on the 8th September, 1864, where it has been paid for as taken in an emergency by an order of the commanding general of the army in lieu of other rations. Claim must be rejected.

"A. O. ALDIS,

"*Commissioner of Claims.*"

[85] Laws of War, 25; Manning's Law of Nations, ch. iv, p. 122; Thomas Jefferson vindicated the confiscation of property of colonists who adhered to Great Britain during the Revolution on this principle. Jefferson's Works, vol. 3, p. 369. Sumner's speech, 71 Globe, 380.

On the 30th January, 1866, the House of Representatives passed the following:

"*Resolved*, That, until otherwise ordered, the Committee of Claims be instructed to reject all claims referred to them for examination by citizens of any of the States lately in rebellion, growing out of the destruction or appropriation of or damage to property by the Army or Navy while engaged in suppressing the rebellion."

(See debates in Globe, vol. 56, pp. 509–512.)

This resolution was reported from the Committee of Claims by Hon. C. Delano, now Secretary of the Interior. (See House Rep. No. 10, 1st sess. 39th Cong., January 18, 1866.)

In the debate, Mr. Delano said:

"I do not deem it necessary to go into an argument to show that *there is no responsibility resting on Congress* to pay those damages that are the result of the necessary ravages of war."

As to claims for "damages resulting from the appropriation of property by our Army for subsistence," he said that "an effort to discriminate between the loyal and disloyal would be an impracticability."

As a question of law, he said, "I am not furnished with any authorities that would enable me to draw a distinction" between loyal and disloyal claimants.

The nation has power to make a rule, however, and reason and justice, the bases of all law, would draw a line when necessary or practicable.

Mr. Delano, in the report of the committee unanimously made in favor of that resolution, said:

"The committee are therefore of the opinion that, in view of the magnitude of these losses, as well as the magnitude of the public debt, and the thousand abuses necessarily resulting from an attempt to satisfy these claims, in the words of Vattel, 'the thing is utterly impracticable,' and ought not to be encouraged.

"It may be suggested that a distinction should be made between losses arising out of the destruction of property incident to the ravages of war and damages growing out of the appropriation of property for the uses of the Army. Without controverting the propriety of this distinction, so far as citizens of the loyal States are concerned, it is suggested that it will be dangerous and inexpedient to apply it to claims coming from States lately in rebellion. It will be difficult to determine with a sufficient degree of certainty the question of individual loyalty; and, if it be established as a rule that property taken from loyal citizens in rebellious States for military supplies shall be paid for, it may be conceded that every claimant will find *some* proof to present of his devotion and suffering in the cause of the Government."

The report also says that in our former history some claims had been allowed "in cases of doubtful propriety;" but the cases were not such as to impose great burdens on the nation. And the report says:

"Appeals to our sympathy, humanity, and benevolence are not easily resisted, and it is a credit to human nature that we are so constituted as to be accessible to such appeals. It is to be remembered, however, that such appeals ought *not to induce* and *cannot authorize* us to levy extraordinary taxation upon our constituents in order to gratify our charitable impulses. We are not *almoners* merely *for the nation*, and *have no just right to impose increased taxation in order to gratify our feelings of benevolence*, nor to establish principles of abstract justice and equity, *when there is no rule or law requiring it*, and particularly when the attempt is to be attended with great uncertainty, and be subjected to *innumerable impositions and frauds*."

While these are the rights which the Government *might* lawfully enforce against all the inhabitants of the seceded States during actual insurrection, yet in practice they were wisely and humanely modified by acts of Congress, and the military authorities in virtue of their general power in special cases advised departures from strict rules.[86]

Congress has also, as a gratuity, provided for the payment—

To those citizens who remained loyal adherents to the cause and the Government of the United States during the war, for stores or supplies taken or furnished during the rebellion for the Army and Navy of the United States in States proclaimed as in insurrection, including the use and loss of vessels or boats while employed in the military service of the United States.[87]

The right to take property in the insurgent States, *by the common laws of war*, remained generally in force, but Congress also provided modes of taking property *in statutory modes.*[88]

---

[86] General Halleck, in his instructions of March 5, 1863, to the commanding officers in Tennessee, said:

"The people of the country in which you are likely to operate may be divided into three classes: "First. The truly loyal, who neither aid nor assist the rebels, except under compulsion, but who favor or assist the Union forces. Where it can possibly be avoided, this class of persons should not be subjected to military requisitions, but should receive the protection of our armies. It may, however, sometimes be necessary to take their property, either for our own use or to prevent its falling into the hands of the enemy. They will be paid at the time the value of such property; or, if that be impracticable, they will hereafter be fully indemnified. Receipts should be given for all property so taken without being paid for."

(Lawrence's Wheaton, supplement, p. 40.) This related only to Tennessee, and after March 5, 1863, the general rule was prescribed, by an order of the War Department, July 22, 1862, as follows:

"Ordered, that the military commanders within the States of Virginia, Georgia, Florida, Alabama, Mississippi, Louisiana, Texas, and Arkansas, in an orderly manner, seize and use any property, real or personal, which may be necessary or convenient for their several commands as supplies or for other military purposes, and while property may be destroyed for military objects, none shall be destroyed in wantonness or malice."

(Lawrence's Wheaton, note, page 625.)

Halleck's International Law and Laws of War, p. 460, § 17, cites Mr. Marcy, Secretary of War, as giving directions to our commanding generals, during the war with Mexico, that they might obtain supplies from the enemy:

1. "By buying them in open market at such prices as the enemy might exact;" (this, of course, they could do if they saw fit.)

2. They might take the supplies and pay the owners *a fair price, without regard to what they might themselves demand on account of the enhanced value resulting from the presence of a foreign army.*

3. They might require contributions without paying or engaging to pay.

Halleck says:

"There can be no doubt of the correctness of the rules of war as here announced by the American Secretary."

He cites many authorities, and the letters from Marcy to Scott and Taylor, &c. (See Ex. Doc. 60, House Reps., 1 sess. 30 Cong., p. 963.)

As to cotton, &c., act March 12, 1863, 12 Stat., 591; act May 18, 1872, 17 Stat., 134; House Ex. Doc. 97, 39 Cong., 2 sess.; Senate Ex. Doc. 37, 2 sess. 39 Cong.; House Ex. Doc. No. 114, 2 sess. 39 Cong.; Senate Ex. Doc. No. 22, 2 sess. 40 Cong.; House Rep. No. 7, 1 sess. 40 Cong.; Senate Ex. Doc. 56, 2 sess. 40 Cong.; House Ex. Doc. 82, 3 sess. 40 Cong.; House Ex. Doc. 113, 3 sess. 41 Cong; House Ex. Doc. , 1 sess. 43 Cong.

[87] Act March 3, 1871, 16 Stat., 524; May 11, 1872, 17 Stat., 97; March 3, 1873, 17 Stat., 577. See the peports of Commissioners of Claims, House Mis. Doc. 16, 2 sess. 42 Cong.; Mis. Doc. 21, Mis. Doc. 213, Mis. Doc. 218, 2 sess. 42 Cong, ; Mis. Doc. 12, 3 sess. 42 Cong. Joint Res. No. 50, 1 sess. 39 Cong., June 18, 1866; Joint Res. No. 99, 1 sess. 39 Cong., July 28, 1866; act July 4, 1864, ch. 240, 1 sess. 38 Cong.

[88] In United States *vs.* Klein, (13 Wallace, p. 128,) the court said:

It may be said, in general terms, that property in the insurgent States may be distributed into four classes: [1.] That which belonged to the hostile organizations, or was employed in actual hostilities on land; [2.] That which at sea became lawful subject of capture and prize; [3.] That which became the subject of confiscation; [4.] A peculiar description, known only in the recent war, called captured and abandoned property.

The statutes in relation to captured and abandoned property authorized the Secretary of the Treasury to appoint special agents to receive all abandoned or captured property in the States proclaimed as in insurrection, and required the military and naval authorities who took or received any such abandoned property, or cotton, sugar, rice, or tobacco, to turn the same over to the Treasury agents, who were required to sell the same and pay the proceeds into the Treasury. These acts provide, also, that any person claiming to have been the owner of any such property might, at any time within two years after the suppression of the rebellion, prefer his claim to the proceeds thereof in the Court of Claims, and, on proof of ownership and loyalty, he shall receive the proceeds, less costs and expenses.[89]

The act of May, 1872, required the Secretary of the Treasury to pay

---

1. The first of these descriptions of property, like property of other like kind in ordinary international wars, became, wherever taken, *ipso facto* the property of the United States. (Halleck's Int. Law.)

2. The second of these descriptions comprehends ships and vessels, with their cargoes, belonging to the insurgents, or employed in aid of them; but property in these was not changed by capture alone, but by regular judicial proceeding and sentence.

Accordingly it was provided, in the abandoned and captured property act of March 12, 1863, (12 Stat., p. 820,) that the property to be collected under it "shall not include any kind or description used, or intended to be used, for carrying on war against the United States, such as arms, ordnance, ships, steamboats and their furniture, forage, military supplies, or munitions of war."

3. Almost all the property of the people in the insurgent States was included in the third description, for after sixty days from the date of the President's proclamation of July 25, 1862, (12 Stat., p. 1266,) all the estates and property of those who did not cease to aid, countenance, and abet the rebellion became liable to seizure and confiscation, and it was made the duty of the President to cause the same to be seized and applied, either specifically or in the proceeds thereof, to the support of the Army. (12 Stat., p. 590.) But it is to be observed that tribunals and proceedings were provided, by which alone such property could be condemned, and without which it remained unaffected in the possession of the proprietors.

It is thus seen that, except to property used in actual hostilities, as mentioned in the first section of the act of March 12, 1863, no titles were divested in the insurgent States unless in pursuance of a judgment rendered after due legal proceedings. The Government recognized to the fullest extent the humane maxims of the modern laws of nations, which exempt private property of non-combatant enemies from capture as booty of war. Even the law of confiscation was sparingly employed. The cases were few indeed in which the property of any not engaged in actual hostilities was subjected to seizure and sale.

The spirit which animated the Government received special illustration from the act under which the present case arose. We have called the property taken into the custody of public officers under that act a peculiar species, and it was so. There is, so far as we are aware, no similar legislation mentioned in history.

As to captured and abandoned property, see—

39th Congress, 2d session, House of Representatives. Ex. Doc. No. 97. Captured and forfeited cotton.

39th Congress, 2d session, Senate. Ex. Doc. No. 37. Relative to proceeds of sale of cotton, &c.

39th Congress, 2d session, House of Representatives. Ex. Doc. No. 114. Relative to cotton claims.

House Report, No. 7. 1st session 40th Congress. November 25, 1867.

40th Congress, 2d session, Senate. Ex. Doc. No. 22. Letter from the Secretary of the Treasury relative to captured and abandoned property.

40th Congress, 2d session, Senate. Ex. Doc. No. 56. Relative to sales of captured and abandoned property.

40th Congress, 3d session, House of Representatives. Ex. Doc. No. 82. Letter from Secretary of Treasury relative to proceeds of captured and abandoned property.

41st Congress, 3d session, House of Representatives. Ex. Doc. No. 113. Sale of captured vessels, cotton, &c.

Alexander's Cotton, 2 Wallace, 421.

89 See acts of March 12, 1863, and July 2, 1864. See a compilation of acts of Congress and rules and regulations prescribed by the Secretary of the Treasury, concerning commercial intercourse with the States declared in insurrection, and as to captured, abandoned, and confiscable property, reprint, 1872.

to the lawful owners who filed claims within six months the net proceeds of sales of cotton seized after June 30, 1865, and actually paid into the Treasury by agents of the Government unlawfully and in violation of their instructions.

No proof of loyalty was required under this act, and under the prior acts it was held that a pardon restored loyalty so as to give a right to recover.[90]

The time has expired within which claims can be made for proceeds of cotton and other captured and abandoned property, and many claimants are now asking that they be permitted to make proof either before the Court of Claims or the proper committees of Congress, with a view to receive the proceeds of property which they allege to have been sold by the Treasury agents.

There are claims also for pay for cotton and other property seized by the military authorities and used in military operations as breast-works for defense and otherwise.[91]

---

[90] It was also held that the Government became a trustee for the benefit of those whom it should thereafter recognize as entitled. United States *vs.* Klien, 13 Wallace, 128, the court say:

"That it was not the intention of Congress that the title to these proceeds should be divested absolutely out of the original owners of the property seems clear upon a comparison of different parts of the act.

"We have already seen that those articles which became by the simple fact of capture the property of the captor, as ordnance, munitions of war, and the like, or in which third parties acquired rights which might be made absolute by decree, as ships and other vessels captured as prize, were expressly excepted from the operation of the act; and it is reasonable to infer that it was the purpose of Congress that the proceeds of the property for which the special provision of the act was made should go into the Treasury without change of ownership. Certainly such was the intention in respect to the property of loyal men. That the same intention prevailed in regard to the property of owners who, though then hostile, might subsequently become loyal, appears probable from the circumstance that no provision is anywhere made for confiscation of it; while there is no trace in the statute-book of intention to divest ownership of private property not excepted from the effect of this act, otherwise than by proceedings for confiscation.

"In the case of Padelford we held that the right to the possession of private property was not changed until actual seizure by proper military authority, and that actual seizure by such authority did not divest the title under the provisions of the captured and abandoned property act. The reasons assigned seem fully to warrant the conclusion. (The Government constituted itself the trustee for those who were by that act declared entitled to the proceeds of captured and abandoned property, and for those whom it should thereafter recognize as entitled.) By the act itself it was provided that any person claiming to have been the owner of such property might prefer his claim to the proceeds thereof, and, on proof that he had never given aid or comfort to the rebellion, receive the amount after deducting expenses.

"This language makes the right to the remedy dependent upon proof of loyalty, but implies that there may be proof of ownership without proof of loyalty. The property of the original owner is in no case absolutely divested. There is, as we have already observed, no confiscation, but the proceeds of the property have passed into the possession of the Government, and restoration of the property is pledged to none except to those who have continually adhered to the Government. Whether restoration will be made to others, or confiscation will be enforced, is left to be determined by considerations of public policy subsequently to be developed."

Carlisle *vs.* United States, 16 Wallace, 147.

United States *vs.* Padelford, 9 Wallace, 531.

Planters' Bank *vs.* Union Bank, 16 Wallace, 496.

For the circular-letter of the Secretary of the Treasury of June 27, 1865, being instructions to officers relative to captured and abandoned property, see the reprint pamphlet copy of 1872, of acts, rules, and regulations as to such property. The act of May 18, 1872, was based on the letter of June 27, 1865.

[91] The Judge-Advocate-General decided that cotton taken to strengthen fortifications and so destroyed has been regarded as a "loss by casualty of war." (Digest of Opinions Judge-Advocate, 97, 98.) (See Opinions, vol. 26, p. 247; Parham *v.* The Justices, 9 Georgia, 341.) The act of February 9, 1867, 14 Stat., 397, indicated the sense of Con-

On the 12th July, 1862, before the date (March 12, 1863) of this "captured and abandoned property act," the Union general, Curtis, seized cotton owned by private citizens at Helena, Ark. This was sold by the military authorities July 26, 1862. The proceeds were in part applied to support the starving negro population, and a portion otherwise appropriated.

This seizure was determined to be lawful.

Since the act of March 12, 1863, cotton has been seized by Union forces in the insurrectionary States and used in fortifications, and otherwise disposed of, by virtue of general military authority.

But this was a lawful exercise of power, and created no liability on the part of the Government.[92]

---

gress by declaring that no payment should be made for property destroyed in the insurrectionary States.

The act of June 1, 1870, 16 Stat., 640, authorized payment to Cutler for cotton seized by General Grant for military purposes, 78 Globe, 3085, April 29, 1870. But Cutler had raised the cotton by contract with the Government, made under the captured and abandoned property act.

The commissioners of claims allowed for cotton used for beds in hospitals; see first report, Mis. Doc. 16, 2 sess. 42d Cong., p. 7.

[92] Coolidge *v.* Guthrie, Swayne, J., October term, 1868, southern district Ohio, United States circuit court, Appendix, p. 591 to (43d ed., 1871) Whiting's War-Powers.

The right to seize and destroy cotton, to impair the power of the enemy to carry on war, and in the "enemy's country," has been much discussed. It was considered before the commission under twelfth article, treaty of May 8, 1871, between the United States and Great Britain. (See Hale's report to Secretary of State, November 30, 1873.) Authorities were cited: Vattel, book 3, c. 9, §§ 161, 163, 164; Twiss, v. 2, (war,) pp. 122 to 124; Rutherford, book 2, c. 9, § 16; Mrs. Alexander's cotton, 2 Wall., 404; The United States *vs.* Padelford, 9 *id.*, 531; The United States *vs.* O'Keeffe, 11 *id.*, 178; 1 Kent's Com., pp. 92, 93.

Commissioner Frazer in his opinion said:

The capture or destruction of property on land belonging to individual enemies is justified by the modern law of nations, if there be military reasons for it; in the absence of good military reasons such captures are generally without the support of the public law. When such reasons do exist, such capture or destruction is, in the nature of things, quite as proper as the capture or destruction of such property on the high seas.

The latter is maintained because an enemy's commerce and navigation are "the sinews of his naval power," to take or destroy which is, therefore, a legitimate act of war. (Wheat. Int. Law; Lawrence, 626.)

"The sinews" of his *military* power on land must, in view of the natural law, be equally the subject of capture or destruction by an invading army. Cotton was held to be such by the Supreme Court, in the case of Mrs. Alexander's cotton, (2 Wall., 404.) The reasoning of the opinion of the Chief-Justice in that case is, I think, unanswerable.

The war of the American rebellion was a civil war—an immense one, too, and the Government had all the rights of war which it would have had if its enemy had been an independent nation. Even the rebel organization was recognized by Her Majesty's government as a belligerent, *i. e.*, having the rights of war; and certainly that government is thereby estopped from denying, and, indeed, never has denied, that belligerent rights also belonged to the Government of the United States. Every act of war recognized as lawful by the public law between independent states at war was, therefore, lawful on the part of the United States, and involved no cause for reclamation on the part of neutrals. On this ground only, as a lawful belligerent act, could a blockade be maintained. The subject is discussed very fully by the Supreme Court in the prize cases, 2 Black; and I think the reasoning of that court is conclusive.

* * * * * * *

But are we to be told that the Government of the United States is compelled by its Constitution to pay its rebellious citizens for their property destroyed as a lawful, *belligerent* act? Has its Constitution thus tied its hands as against a rebellion? Might the rebels, without liability, exercise all recognized belligerent rights against it, including the capture of the property of British subjects found in the loyal States, and yet it do the like only subject to the duty of making compensation?

From all this absurdity there is no escape if the belligerent right of capture and destruction shall be confounded with the sovereign right of eminent domain. And, indeed, captures on the high seas must then go into the same general category.

The question now arises, whether provision should be made in any mode, and, if so, what, in behalf of these classes of claimants, or any of them.

---

In fine, a constitution provision—the condition of compensation for property taken for public use—intended only to restrain civil administration, would be held to so trammel belligerent rights in time of civil war that effective hostilities against rebels might sometimes be practically impossible.

The commission held that property in the rebel States might lawfully be destroyed "as a means of weakening the enemy."

The report, p. 49, says:

"Also claims for property available to the enemy for military purposes, or for the prosecution of the war, and purposely destroyed in the enemy's country as a means of weakening the enemy, as in the cases of Samuel H. Haddon, No. 107, and John Murphy, No. 326. Also, for property incidentally involved in the destruction of public stores, works, and means of transportation of the enemy, as in the cases of John K. Byrne, No. 200; Charles Black, No. 128, and A. K. McMillan, No. 250. In these claims for the destruction of property * * * no awards were made against the United States."

The claim of Henry E. and Alfred Cox, No. 229, was for a saw-mill and its motive-power, machinery, &c., destroyed by raiding parties from General Sherman's army, near Meridian, Miss., in February, 1864. The expedition by which the mill was destroyed was sent out by General Sherman for the express purpose of destroying the confederate mills, supplies, railroads, and means of transportation.

The proofs showed that the saw-mill in question had been actually employed in the sawing of railroad-ties for the confederate government, and was available for this and similar purposes.

On the part of the defense it was claimed that the destruction was a lawful act of war.

The claim was unanimously disallowed.

The case of William Smythe, No. 333, was a claim for an iron and brass foundery, machine-shop, and machinery, fixtures, supplies, &c., for same, destroyed by General Sherman in Atlanta, after the capture of that city, and before his advance upon Savannah. The establishment had been employed in the manufacture of shot, shell, and other military supplies for the confederate government.

The claim was unanimously disallowed.

In Mr. Hale's report it is also said, "A large number of claims was brought for cotton destroyed by the United States forces at various points in the insurrectionary States."

In several of these cases the proof was clear and undisputed that the cotton was destroyed under express orders from the commanding officers, and for the purpose of preventing it from falling into the hands of the enemy, and of weakening the resources of the enemy.

On the part of the United States it was maintained that a belligerent might lawfully, in the enemy's country, destroy any property, public or private, the possession or control of which might in any degree contribute to sustain the enemy and increase his ability to carry on the war. That the occasion for such destruction and its extent must always be left solely to the discretion of the invading belligerent, who is of necessity the sole judge as to the requirements of his military position, and of the necessity or propriety of the destruction of property, and of the extent to which such destruction shall be carried.

The counsel for the United States, in his arguments, cited the letter from Earl Russell to Lord Lyons of 31st May, 1862, from the British Blue-Book, relating to the United States, 1863, vol. 2, p. 33, in which his lordship said:

"Mr. Seward, in his conversation with your lordship, reported in your dispatch of the 16th instant, appeared to attribute blame to the confederates for destroying cotton and tobacco in places which they evacuate on the approach of the Federal forces. But it appears to be unreasonable to make this a matter of blame to them, for they could not be expected to leave such articles in warehouses to become prize of war, and to be sold for the profit of the Federal Government, which would apply the proceeds to the purchase of arms to be used against the South.".

He cited also Vattel, (Am. ed. of 1861,) pp. 364 to 370, §§ 161 to 173; the case of Mrs. Alexander's cotton in the Supreme Court of the United States, (2 Wall., 404, 420;) and the opinion of Sir Hugh Cairns and Mr. Reilly, given in March, 1865, on the application of the Canadian government, and published in the "Saint Albans Raid," compiled by L. N. Benjamin, Montreal, 1865, page 479, as follows:

"Though in the conduct of war on land the capture by the officers and soldiers of one belligerent of the private property of subjects of the other belligerent is not often in ordinary crisis avowedly practiced, it is yet legitimate."

Her Majesty's counsel cited the case of the United States *vs.* Klein, in the Supreme

There is no longer any claim resting on any law. The acts of Congress referred to fixed a limit of time, and said, in effect, that no claim should be made beyond it.

---

Court of the United States, (13 Wall., 128;) also the case of Mitchell *vs.* Harmony, in the same court, (13 How., 115;) also, the case of W. S. Grant *vs* United States, (1 C. Cls., 41;) also, Brown *vs.* The United States, (8 Cranch, 110;) also, Lawrence's Wheaton, Part IV, c. 2, pp. 586 to 626, 635*n*, 640*n*; Halleck, p. 546, § 12; Calvo, § 434, 436, 443, 444, 550; Vattel, pp. 368–9, § 173.

All the claims for cotton destroyed in the enemy's country, with a single exception, (that of A. R. McDonald, No. 42,) were disallowed by the unanimous voice of the commissioners.

In the argument of this case it was said that, by the United States and Mexican Claims Commission "it has been decided at the date of the 23d of February, 1871, in the test case of Fayette Anderson and William Thompson *vs.* Mexico, (No. 333,) that governments are entitled, in time of war, and owing to the necessities of war, to take the property of private citizens, or destroy it, &c., but that this is always done with the understanding that the government which has taken or destroyed said property is bound to pay for it. Such is the view held by the American commissioner. This rule of law has been constantly applied by said commission to claims of American citizens against Mexico, and *vice versa.*

Furthermore, the United States have recognized the solemn obligation to compensate for the destruction of property through positive treaty stipulations. Thus, in the ninth article of the treaty of 1819, between the United States and Spain, it was agreed between the high contracting parties that they "respectively renounced all claims to indemnity for any of the recent events or transactions of their respective commanders and officers in the Floridas," thus releasing both parties from their respective international obligations.

But at the same time, inasmuch as extensive destruction of private property had been the result of the invasion of Florida by the United States forces, the following provision was inserted in the same article:

"The United States will cause satisfaction to be made for injuries, if any, which by process of law shall be established to have been suffered by Spanish officers and individual Spanish inhabitants by the late operations of the American Army in Florida." (See treaties and conventions concluded between the United States of America and other powers, Forty-first Congress, 3d sess., Senate Ex. Doc. No. 36, pp. 791, 792.)

In accordance with this treaty provision, Congress passed an act conferring jurisdiction upon the United States courts in Florida, and appropriated money to pay its decrees.

But the practice of this Government is shown to be against this in the case of Perrin *vs.* United States, 4 Court of Claims, 545, and Seward's letter, therein referred to.

In the case of A. R. McDonald, Nos. 42 and 334, the commission made an award in favor of the claimant, Mr. Commissioner Frazer dissenting. In that case the cotton was alleged to have been purchased by the claimant principally in Ashley County, Arkansas, under permits issued by the proper officers of the United States Treasury, under the statutes regulating trade in the insurrectionary States, and the regulations of the Secretary of the Treasury, made pursuant to said statutes, and to have been destroyed in the same region by United States forces under the command of General Osband, in February, 1865. These statutes and regulations only authorized trade in the insurrectionary States within the lines of military occupancy of the United States forces; and it was contended on the part of the claimants that the issuing of such permits by the Treasury officers was controlling evidence that the region covered by the permits, and within which the cotton was alleged to have been purchased and destroyed, was actually within the military lines of the United States.

The entire claim of this claimant amounted, including interest, to over $3,000,000. The award was for the sum of $197,190, including interest. I am advised that, in the making of this award, the majority of the commission did not intend to depart from the principle held by them in the other claims for cotton destroyed; but that they regarded the permits as controlling evidence that the region where the cotton was situated was within the lines of Federal occupancy.

After the capture of Knoxville, Tenn., the cotton of Cowan & Dickinson in a warehouse was taken by Union military forces for fortifications, to repel the rebel attack of Longstreet, whose forces beleaguered the city November 17, 1863, and made an assault upon the defenses November 28. (See Senate Claims Committee report, No. 85, 2d sess. 42d Cong., March 27, 1872.)

As to claim of Cowan & Dickinson, of Knoxville, Tenn., see 93 Globe for January and February, 1873; House proceedings, 93 Globe, 697, 1022, 1088, 1196, 1200, 1401, 1468, 1492; Senate, 1039, 1061, 1214, 1360, 1434, 1474, 1477. A bill passed Congress February 19, 1873, to pay for this cotton, but Congress adjourned in less than ten days from the time the President received it, and it failed for want of his approval.

By the common law of war, as has been shown, no claim can be made.

The questions therefore arise, Is it *practicable*, at this late day, to do justice alike to the Government and claimants, and are there reasons for now admitting claims to be made?

Congress doubtless prescribed the period of two years after the suppression of the rebellion within which claims should be filed in order that some end should exist to demands of this class on the Treasury. And the act of March 30, 1868, required all money arising from captured and abandoned property to be covered into the Treasury, (15 Stat., 251.) This was intended to put an end to payments from the Treasury, except on judgments in pursuance of prior statutes. This policy so settled should not be changed unless for urgent reasons.

The policy of the law was not to allow claims in favor of those who had organized or aided rebellion. They had no legal claims on the Government. Nearly ten years have passed since much of this cotton was seized, and if the time is extended for making claims, very many, if not most of those who were really disloyal, will be able to assert and prove loyalty. The evidence of disloyalty will be almost entirely lost. The Commissioners of Claims, in their first annual report, in December, 1871, say:

> It is easier and more profitable to be loyal now than it was during the war, and much of the proof of disloyalty has perished or been forgotten in the lapse of time.

In their second annual report, December 9, 1872, they say:

> We find by experience that, to form a correct opinion as to whether a claimant was or was not loyal during the war, *we cannot safely rely upon* the *mere* opinion of witnesses as to his loyalty, and upon statements at this late day of alleged conversations.[93]

The immense number of claims rejected for disloyalty, yet supported by much of apparent proof of loyalty, shows how unreliable the evidence is at this late day.

Mr. Delano, with his experience as chairman of the Committee on Claims in the Thirty-ninth Congress, said in the House of Representatives as to claimants from the States proclaimed in rebellion:

> If we go into an inquiry as to the loyalty of these individuals, my word for it every one of them will give us some evidence of loyalty. You will find that they will be able to procure *ex-parte* affidavits or evidence of some sort apparently sufficient for the establishment of their loyalty. These, and like considerations, have brought the committee to the conclusion—and that conclusion was unanimous—that an effort to discriminate between the loyal and the disloyal would be an impracticability, and that the result of it would be to bring this House to the payment of all this class of claims.[94]

The net proceeds of captured and abandoned property remaining in the Treasury February 27, 1874, was $14,410,429. The awards made by the Court of Claims, and not yet paid, out of this fund are $1,834,011, and the claims still pending in that court aggregate over $20,000,000. To this are to be added claims now pending before Congress, reaching some millions.

The cotton captured after June 1, 1865, approximates $5,500,000, representing about fifty thousand bales, nearly all seized as owned by the so-called confederate government, which had purchased it of citizens in exchange for confederate bonds delivered them. Yet, on this fund, most of it confessedly arising from cotton of this character, claims are filed before the Secretary of the Treasury by individual claimants, under

[93] See Lawrence's House Rep. No. 91, 1 sess. 43 Cong., Feb. 9, 1874, p. 7.
[94] 56 Globe, 509, January 30, 1866.

the act of May 18, 1872, covering 136,000 bales, nearly three times the amount seized, and aggregating nearly $18,000,000.[95]

From all this it is apparent that no committee of Congress could with any degree of justice either to the Government or claimants, investigate separate claims. This could only be done by a body clothed with power to visit southern localities and ascertain facts by a searching scrutiny and personal conferences with witnesses. If any provision should be made in this class of claims it should be in a mode very different than

[95] *Memorandum.*

TREASURY DEPARTMENT, *February* 27, 1874.

| | | |
|---|---|---|
| Gross proceeds of captured and abandoned cotton, (including premium on coin proceeds) | $21,500,000 00 | |
| Expenses of collection, sale, &c | 3,000,000 00 | |
| Net proceeds | | $18,500,000 00 |
| Gross proceeds of miscellaneous property | 1,375,000 00 | |
| Expenses of collection, sale, &c | 86,000 00 | |
| Net proceeds | | 1,289,000 00 |
| Miscellaneous receipts, rents of abandoned houses, &c | | 1,121,656 44 |
| Total amount covered in from above sources | | 20,910,656 44 |
| Refunded to claimants upon awards of the Court of Claims under section 3, act of March 12, 1863 | 6,300,463 80 | |
| Refunded to claimants upon awards of the Secretary of the Treasury under section 5, act of May 18, 1872 | 97,734 10 | |
| Paid for expenses, &c., under section 3, joint resolution of March 30, 1868 | 75,000 00 | |
| Upon judgments of United States circuit court, New York, under act of July 27, 1868 | 27,029 37 | |
| Amounting in the aggregate to | | 6,500,227 27 |
| The balance of said fund still remaining in the Treasury is | | 14,410,429 17 |

*Additional amount awarded by the Court of Claims, and claims still pending for captured and abandoned lands.*

| | |
|---|---|
| Awards made by the Court of Claims not yet paid, amount to | $1,834,011 00 |
| The claims still pending in the Court of Claims under the captured and abandoned property acts aggregate over | 20,000,000 00 |
| The claims filed before the Secretary of the Treasury, under the act of May 18, 1872, cover 136,000 bales of cotton; estimated value about | 18,000,000 00 |

The proceeds of cotton collected after June 1, 1865, and paid into the Treasury, approximate $5,500,000, representing about 50,000 bales, of which over 40,000 bales, it is estimated, had been sold to the confederate government.

*Moneys covered into the Treasury to credit of captured and abandoned property fund.*

| | |
|---|---|
| Proceeds of captured and abandoned property, including premium on coin proceeds | $20,910,656 44 |
| Profits to Government arising from purchase and resale of products under section 8, act of July 2, 1864 | 3,441,548 09 |
| Amount expended from proceeds of captured and abandoned property and returned | 2,465,833 69 |
| Total | 26,818,038 22 |
| Deduct premium on coin proceeds of Savannah, Charleston, and Mobile cotton | 2,566,768 29 |
| Amount covered in as proceeds of captured and abandoned property | 24,251,269 93 |

M. L. NOERR, *In charge of captured and abandoned property.*

*List of executive documents relating to captured and abandoned property, &c.*

39th Congress, 2d session, House of Representatives, Ex. Doc. No. 97: Captured and forfeited cotton.

39th Congress, 2d session, Senate, Ex. Doc. No. 37: Letter from the Secretary of the Treasury, relative to the proceeds of sale of cotton, &c.

that of an examination of claims in detail on *ex-parte* evidence by a committee of Congress.

Loyal citizens residing in the loyal States during the rebellion, but having property, real or personal, in the States proclaimed in insurrection, can by the strict rules of international law claim for it no immunity. Its local *situs* imparts to it the character and status of enemy's property. It may be lawfully used for military purposes, or destroyed if it will be useful to the enemy.[96]

The property situated in the enemy's country owned by corporations existing by virtue of charters granted by foreign governments, or loyal States, or rebel States, before or since secession, can claim no protection beyond that accorded to other enemy's property. A large part of the property in the insurrectionary States might be held by corporations, and thus be a means of strength to the rebellion.[97]

---

39th Congress. 2d session, House of Representatives, Ex. Doc. No. 114: Letter of the Secretary of the Treasury, relative to cotton-claims.

40th Congress, 2d session, Senate, Ex. Doc. No. 22: Letter from the Secretary of the Treasury, relative to captured and abandoned property.

40th Congress, 2d session, Senate, Ex. Doc. No. 56: Letter of the Secretary of the Treasury, relative to the sale of captured and abandoned cotton.

40th Congress, 3d session, House of Representatives, Ex. Doc. No. 82: Letter from the Secretary of the Treasury, relative to the proceeds of captured and abandoned property.

41st Congress, 3d session, House of Representatives, Ex. Doc. No. 113: Letter from the Secretary of the Treasury, relative to the sale of captured vessels, cotton, &c.

43d Congress, 2d session, Ex. Doc. No. 23: Report of Acting Secretary of the Treasury, February 1, 1875.

[96] Lawrence's Wheaton, 565-576; The Gray Jacket, 5 Wallace, 342-364; Whiting War Powers, (43d ed., 1872, p. 582;) Attorney-General's opinion, November 24, 1865, 11 Opinions, 405; Elliott's Claim, September 7, 1868, 12 Opinions, 488; Perrin *vs.* United States, 4 Court Claims, 543. See note 31, *ante.*

[97] This rule is not changed by the fact that the confiscation acts do not apply to corporate property. Planters' Bank *vs.* Union Bank, 16 Wallace, 483.

House Rep. 777, 1st sess. 43d Cong., June 22, 1874—Book-agents M. E. Church South, p. 12, &c.

As to southern railroad companies, see House Report 34, 39th Congress, 2d session, March 2, 1867; House Rep. No. 3, 2d sess. 40th Cong., Dec. 11, 1867; Ex. Doc. No. 73, 2d sess. 40th Cong., Jan. 7, 1868; House Rep. No. 15, 2d sess. 40th Cong., Feb. 7, 1868; House Rep. No. 78, 2d sess. 41st Cong., June 9, 1870; see opinion of Stanton in House Rep. No. 7, 1st sess. 40th Cong., Nov. 25, 1867.

It must be apparent that a rebellion cannot shield itself behind one or many corporations, and thus use property for its purposes and deny the right of seizure for loyal purposes.

And it is the *right* and *duty* of military officers to select such property as best suits the purposes of military operations, and their decision is final—necessarily so.

The Supreme Court, in *Mrs. Alexander's Cotton* case, asserted the *power* and *duty* of military officers to seize property, and said:

"It is true that this rule, as to property on land, has received very important qualifications from usage, from the reasonings of enlightened publicists, and from judicial decisions. It may now be regarded as substantially restricted 'to special cases, dictated by the necessary operations of war,' and as excluding, in general, the seizure of private property of pacific persons for the sake of gain. *The commanding general may determine in what special cases its more stringent application is required by military emergencies;* while considerations of public policy, and positive provisions of law, and the general spirit of legislation must indicate the cases in which its application may be properly denied to the property of non-combatant enemies."

The *right* and *duty* of the Government to seize and occupy the property of corporations to aid in suppressing the rebellion and in preserving the territorial integrity of the nation and the unity of its people, are not based on the disloyalty of the owner. Disloyalty gives strength to the right, and additional ground for refusing to make compensation. The *right* and *duty* rest on the imperative necessity to seize it—an "overruling necessity" which admits of no choice or discretion, but compels it, under penalty of imperiling the cause of the Union, or which renders it reasonably certain that such seizure is proper. It does not depend on the *animus* of the person whose property is seized—his loyalty or disloyalty.

Loyal citizens residing in the loyal States, or in the States proclaimed in rebellion, can, as a general rule, by the strict rules of law, make no claim to compensation for use and occupation of real property in the States proclaimed in insurrection, of buildings or lands, by military authorities during the rebellion.

As by the laws of war the lawful military authorities might destroy houses in these States to prevent them from being a means of aid and comfort to the rebellion, or to hasten its speedy overthrow, so they may much the more be used without liability to make compensation.[98]

---

Thus Bynkershoek says:

"But the thing does not depend only on the *quo animo;* for, even among the subjects of our enemy, there are some, however few they may be, who are not hostilely inclined against us; but the matter depends upon the law, *because those goods are with the enemy, and because they are of use to them for our destruction.*"

To which may be added, *because they are essential to our success.*

It is certainly true that the members of a corporation, as such, are incapable of disloyalty, but it is not true in every respect. Both the corporation and its members may be guilty of disloyal acts, and so disloyal.

A corporation, like a tree, is known by its fruits. A corporation which encourages men to make war—to convert pruning-hooks into spears, and plowshares into swords—is by no means loyal.

There was a time when it was held that a corporation could not commit a trespass. But that doctrine has long since been exploded. A corporation acts by its agents. Their authorized acts within the scope of the corporate authority are the acts of the corporation. The maxim applies, *qui facit per alium facit per se.* [a]A corporation may be guilty of disloyalty.

[98] See letter of Quartermaster-General M. C. Meigs, of February 26, 1874, in appendix to this report.

No claim was made for use and occupation in the insurrectionary States before the commission held under twelfth article of the treaty between the United States and Great Britain of May 8, 1871, except "within the *loyal* portions of the United States, or within those portions of the insurrectionary States permanently reclaimed by the United States, and for damages resulting from such use and occupation."

It was conceded that use and occupation should be paid for in loyal States, and the only objection made to the consideration of such claims was, that the Court of Claims had jurisdiction.

In Mr. Hale's report, it is said:

"The counsel cited the letter of Earl Granville to Mr. Stewart, (No. 23 of parliamentary papers, No. 4, on the Franco-German war, 1871, British State Papers;) Professor Bernard's "Neutrality of Great Britain," &c., pp. 440, 454; also the note of Mr. Abbot (Lord Tenterden) relating to this identical claim of Mr. Crutchett, id., 456; also, the case of William Cook before the commissioners under the convention of 1853 between the United States and Great Britain, (United States Senate Documents, first and second

---

[a] Angel and Ames on Corporations, 9th ed., sections 311, 382, 384.

*Union Bank* v. *McDonough*, 5 La., 63; and see *Ware* v. *Barrataria Canal Company*, 15 La., 168; *Beers* v. *Housatonic Railroad Co.*, 19 Conn., 566; *Bradley* v. *Boston R.*, 2 Cush., 539; *Baltimore R. Co.* v. *Woodruff*, 4 Md., 242; *Sharrod* v. *London R. Co.*, 4 Exch., 585, 586; *Gillenwater* v. *Madison R. Co.*, 5 Ind., 939.

*Marlatt* v. *Levee Steam Cotton Press Co.*, 10 La., 583; and see *Memphis* v. *Lasser*, 9 Humph., 757; *Duncan* v. *Surry Canal*, 3 Starke, 50; *Smith* v. *Birmingham Gas Co.*, 1 A. and E., 526, 3 Nev. and M., 771; *Rex* v. *Medley*, 6 C. and P., 292, per Denman, C. J.; *Maund* v *Monmouthshire Canal Co.*, 1 Car. and M., 606, 4 Man. and G., 452, 455; *Regina* v. *Birmingham R. Co.*, 2 Gale and D., 236, 9 C. and P., 469; *Eastern Counties R.* v. *Broom*, 6 Exch., 314, 2 Eng. L. and Eq., 406; *Hawkins* v. *Dutchess Steamboat Co.*, 2 Wend., 452; *Beach* v. *Fulton Bank*, 7 Cowen, 485; *New York* v. *Bailey*, 2 Denio, 433; *Hay* v. *Cohoes Co.*, 3 Barb., 42; *Watson* v. *Bennett*, 12 Barb., 196; *Kneass* v. *Schuylkill Bank*, 4 Wash. C. C., 106; *Lyman* v. *White River Bridge Co.*, 2 Aik., 255; *Rabassa* v. *Orleans Nav. Co.*, 3 La., 461; *Goodloe* v. *City of Cincinnati*, 4 Ohio, 513; *Smith* v. *same, id.*, 414; *McCready* v. *Guardians of the Poor.* 9 S. and R., 94; *McKim* v. *Odum*, 3 Bland, ch. 421; *Humes* v. *Knoxville*, 1 Humph., 403; *Edwards* v. *Union Bank of Fla.*, 1 Fla., 136; *Bank of Kentucky* v. *Schuylkill Bank*, 1 Parsons's Sel. Cas., 251; *Whiteman* v. *Wilmington R. Co.*, 2 Harring., Del., 514; *Ten Eyck* v. *Delaware Canal Co.*, 3 Harrison, 200; *Underwood* v. *Newport Lyceum*, 5 B. Mon., 130; *Hamilton County* v. *Cincinnati T. Co.*, Wright, 603; *Town of Akron* v. *McComb*, 18 Ohio, 229; *Riddle* v. *Proprietors, &c.*, 7 Mass., 187; *Thayer* v. *Boston*, 19 Pict., 516, 517; *Carman* v. *Steubenville R. Co.*, 4 Ohio State, 399; *Moore* v. *Fitchburgh R. Corp.*, 4 Gray, 465; *McDougald* v. *Bellamy*, 18 Ga., 411.

Chitty on Plead., 68; *Fowle* v. *Common Council of Alexandria*, 3 Pet., 409; *Bushel* v. *Commonwealth Ins. Co.*, 15 S. and R., 173.

*Chestnut Hill T. Co.*, in error, v. *Rutter*, 4 S. and R., 6. In this case much learning will be found on the subject and many references to the Year-Books, and other ancient as well as modern authorities. *First Baptist Church* v. *Schenectady R. Co.*, 5 Barb., 79; see, also, *N. Y. T. Co.* v. *Dryburg*, 35 Penn. State, 298, (c.)

*Yarborough* v. *Bank of England*, 16 East, 6; *Smith* v. *Birmingham Gas-Light Co.*, 1 A. and E., 526; *Mayor of Lynn* v. *Turner*, Cowp., 86; *Denton* v. *Great Northern R. Co.*, 5 Ellis and B., 860; 34 Eng. L. and Eq., 154; see, also, *Conger* v. *Chicago R. Co.*, 15 Ill., 366; *Keegan* v. *Western R. Co.*, 4 Seld., 175.

*Lee* v. *Village of Sandy Hill*, 40 N. Y., 422; *Beach* v. *Fulton Bank*, 7 Cowen, 485; *Brown* v. *South Kennebec Ag. Soc.*, 47 Maine, 275; *N. Y. R. Co.* v. *Schuyler*, 38 Barb., 534; 34 N. Y., 30.

The policy determined on by Congress is clearly expressed in the act of February 21, 1867, which prohibits "the settlement of any claim for

---

sessions Thirty-fourth Congress, vol. 15, No. 103, pp. 169, 463;) also the case of the United States *vs.* O'Keeffe, in the Supreme Court of the United States, (11 Wall., 178;) and the cases of Waters, (4 C. Cls. Rep., 390;) Russell, (5 id., 120;) Filor *vs.* United States, (9 Wall., 45;) also Campbell's case, (5 C. Cls. Rep., 252,) and Provine's case, (id., 455.)

On the part of the claimant it was contended that, while the claimant was entitled to compensation for the use of his property under the Constitution of the United States, the jurisdiction of the Court of Claims in the case was taken away by the act of Congress of July 4, 1864, (13 Stat., 381,) citing Filor *vs.* United States, (9 Wall., 45.)

An award was made in favor of the claimant for the value of the use and occupation, in which all the commissioners joined.

The cases decided by the commission under art. 12, treaty 8th May, 1871, between United States and Great Britain, hold the same principle. Compensation was only demanded by British subjects owning real estate "within the *loyal portions of the United States*, or within those portions of the insurrectionary States *permanently reclaimed by the United States*, and for damages resulting from such use and occupation." See Hale's report to Secretary of State, November 30, 1873, p 46. The Government has always paid for any substantial use and occupation of real property in the loyal States when voluntarily taken by contract or impressment, and not as a military necessity by reason of hostile military operations.

This will be seen from the following:

"WAR DEPARTMENT, QUARTERMASTER-GENERAL'S OFFICE,
*Washington, D. C., February 19, 1874.*

"SIR: I have to acknowledge receipt of your letter of February 16, 1874, asking information in regard to the laws under which this Office recommends payment 'for occupation of real estate during the war,' and 'what has been the usage of the Government in such cases,' &c.

"The fifth amendment to the Constitution of the United States provides that private property shall not be taken for public uses without just compensation.

"The law of March 3, 1813, chapter 513, section 5, authorizes the Secretary of War to 'fix and make reasonable allowances for the store-rent, storage, &c., for the safe keeping of all military stores and supplies.'

"By the 42d Article of Revised Regulations (Authorized and effect. See House Rep. No. 6, Committee War-Claims, 2d sess. 43d Congress, p. 4) of the Army, August 10, 1861, approved by the President, and published for the information and government of the military service, it is made the duty of the Quartermaster's Department to provide quarters, store-houses, offices, and lands for encampments for the Army. When public buildings, &c., are not sufficient to quarter troops, authority to hire private property for such uses is given by said regulations to the commanding officer of the department, who reports the case, and his orders therein, to the Quartermaster-General.

"Claims for such rents due and not already paid, arising in loyal States during the war, when presented for payment, are investigated by the officer of this Department in the district wherein the claim originated, and reported to this Office. If they are found, on examination here, to be correct and just, the claims are forwarded with all the facts to the Secretary of War with report, and recommendation that authority be given to transmit the same to the Third Auditor of the Treasury, with recommendation for settlement.

"(The act of March 3, 1817, chapter 218, section 2, for the 'prompt settlement of accounts,' &c., provides that all claims against the United States shall be settled and adjusted in the Treasury Department.)

"If the accounts before referred to are approved by the Third Auditor and Second Comptroller, they issue a Treasury certificate showing the sum which those officers consider to be legally due to the claimants, and the appropriation to the credit of the War Department applicable to the payment of their award.

"The Treasury settlement is returned to this Office for entry, when the Secretary of War is asked to make a requisition on the Treasury for payment for the amount.

"These are in brief the law and the usage governing the disposition of rent-claims, arising in loyal States, filed in this Office.

"It has been decided that the law of July 4, 1864, providing for settlement of claims for quartermaster stores taken during the war, does not apply to claims for rent.

"Very respectfully, your obedient servant,

"M. C. MEIGS,
"*Quartermaster-General, Brevet Major-General, U. S. A.*

"Hon. WILLIAM LAWRENCE, M. C.,
"*House of Representatives, the Capitol, D. C.*"

the occupation of or injury to real estate when such claim originated during the war for the suppression of the southern rebellion in a State or part of a State declared in insurrection."[99]

"WAR DEPARTMENT,
BUREAU OF MILITARY JUSTICE,
"*Washington, D. C., January* 4, 1875.

"SIR: I have the honor to acknowledge the receipt from you of two communications of the 29th ultimo: one relating to a claim for the use and occupation of a building taken and used by the military authorities in New Orleans in March, 1863; and the other referring to the matter of the settlement of claims of a similar character arising, however, in a State not in insurrection. To these communications I have to reply as follows:

"2. *As to the claim for rent of building taken and used (without contract) for officers' quarters, in Saint Joseph, Mo.* In your communication in reference to this claim, while you recognize the general liability of the United States to pay a claim of this character, you at the same time inquire as to the point of the practice of the War Department in the disposition of such claims. You say: 'What I want to know is, whether the naked power to examine and recommend for payment still exists in the War Department.'

"In my judgment claims of this character are strictly excluded from examination by the War Department. Rent cannot, in my opinion, as heretofore frequently expressed, be held to be embraced within the term 'quartermaster's stores' as employed in the act of July 4, 1864, (see Digest, p. 99, sec. 3,) and I know of no other general statute empowering the Secretary of War, or any military official, to adjust and settle claims for the rent of land or buildings used or occupied by military authority, in the absence of any authorized contract for the purpose.

"It is understood, however, that claims of this character have sometimes been considered and reported upon as to their merits at the War Department, on the theory that they came within the fifth amendment of the Constitution, providing compensation for property taken for public use; but that even this practice has now been discontinued, because the funds which were supposed to be applicable to the payment of the cost of investigating the claims (which was customarily done through an officer of the Quartermaster's Department) have all been turned into the Treasury under recent statutes.

"In my own opinion, the general declaration of the fifth amendment can, *per se*, confer no authority whatever upon an Executive Department or officer to adjudicate a claim of this character. It clearly confers no authority upon such Department or officer to *pay* such a claim; and if the authority to pay does not exist, to assume (in the absence of any specific direction by Congress) to investigate and pass upon the merits of the claim, would certainly appear to be as extra-official, and uncalled for in fact, as it would be futile in law.

"Very respectfully, your obedient servant,

"J. HOLT,
"*Judge-Advocate-General.*

"Hon. WM. LAWRENCE,
"*Chairman Committee on War-Claims,*
"*House of Representatives.*"

99 14 Stat., 397; 11 Opinions, Nov. 24, 1865, p. 405; 12 Opinions, 486, Sept. 7, 1868, declares that "a claim for use and occupation of real estate in Tennessee by the Army in January, 1863, cannot be settled by the Executive Department of the Government, under act July 4, 1864, and February 21, 1867." Filor *vs.* United States, 9 Wallace, 45; Provine's Case, 5 Court of Claims, 455; Kimball's Case, *id.*, 252.

For some time after the passage of the act of July 4, 1864, the Quartermaster-General's Department paid for rents in certain parts of the rebel States under regulations of that Department, as follows:

"Proofs required in support of the above classes of claims, (claims for supplies furnished for use of the Army.)

"That the claimant is a citizen of a State not in rebellion. Claims of citizens of the following States and parts of States, declared by the President of the United States, by his proclamation of 1st January, 1863, to be in rebellion, will not be considered, viz: Arkansas, Texas, Louisiana, (except the parishes of Saint Bernard, Plaquemines, Jefferson, Saint John, Saint Charles, Saint James, Ascension, Assumption, Terre Bonne, La Fourche, Saint Mary, Saint Martin, and Orleans, including the city of New Orleans,) Mississippi, Alabama, Florida, Georgia, South Carolina, North Carolina, and Virginia, (except the forty-eight counties designated as West Virginia, and also the counties of Berkeley, Accomack, Northampton, Elizabeth City, York, Princess Anne, and Norfolk, including the cities of Norfolk and Portsmouth.")

See letter of Quartermaster-General M. C. Meigs of February 26, 1874, in appendix to this report.

A question has been made as to the right of the Government in war to seize the private houses of citizens. It seems clear that on the prin-

---

But after the act of February 21, 1867, the regulations were altered as follows:

I. CLAIMS TO BE SUBMITTED TO AND EXAMINED BY THE QUARTERMASTER-GENERAL.

All claims of loyal citizens, in States not in rebellion, for "quartermaster's stores" actually furnished to the Army of the United States, and receipted for by the proper officer receiving the same, or which may have been taken by such officers without giving such receipts.

II. CLAIMS TO BE SUBMITTED TO AND EXAMINED BY THE COMMISSARY-GENERAL OF SUBSISTENCE.

All claims of loyal citizens, in States not in rebellion, for "subsistence" actually furnished to said Army, and receipted for by the proper officer receiving the same, or which may have been taken by such officers without giving such receipts.

III. PROOFS REQUIRED IN SUPPORT OF THE ABOVE CLASSES OF CLAIMS.

1st. That the claimant is a loyal citizen of a State not in rebellion. (Claims of citizens of the following States, declared by the President of the United States, by his proclamation of the first day of July, 1862, to be in insurrection, will not be considered, viz: Arkansas, Texas, Louisiana, Mississippi, Alabama, Florida, Georgia, South Carolina, North Carolina, and Virginia.)

2d. Citizenship.—The claimant will be required to show by his own affidavit, supported by the certificate of the clerk or recorder of the town or county of which he claims to be a citizen, that said claimant is a citizen of said town or county.

3d. Loyalty.—The claimant will be required to file with his claim the oath of allegiance," &c.

*Claim of Joseph Segar.*—Claim for compensation for use and occupation of his farm near Fortress Monroe in Virginia, during the late war, by the United States military forces. For Senate proceedings and debates, see Globe, vol. 89, second session Forty-second Congress, pages 2261, 2262, 2674, 2675; see Senate Report No. 95, second session Forty-second Congress. For House proceedings and debates, see Globe, vol. 91, page 3844. See Stat., vol. 17, page 670.

The act of June 10, 1872, 17 Stat., 699, paid for damages done to leased premises.

But the general rule of public law is, that the Government is not liable for such unauthorized damages during the rebellion.

In the report of the Committee on War-Claims, No. 740, 1 sess. 43 Cong., on a claim for use and occupation of, and damages to, a building used by the Government in Alexandria, Va., in 1862 and 1864, it was said:

"It is proper to consider first the claim for damages done to the premises by rebel soldiers confined therein August 31, 1862.

"On the 13th of February, 1863, the Committee on Military Affairs of the House reported in favor of paying $5,044 for these damages. From that time to this Congress has never made any compensation. (House Report No. 38, 3d session, 37th Congress, February 13, 1863.) This claim for *damages* is very different from a claim for *use and occupation*. The Government is not liable by any principle of public law to make compensation for wanton damage or depredations committed by rebel soldiers, even when imprisoned.

"The Government only performed *a duty* when its forces captured the rebels, and having them in custody it had *a right* to imprison them and to seize the necessary buildings for that purpose. And, as a general rule, a government can incur no liability for performing a duty or exercising a right in flagrant war. An *unlawful* act by *government authority* might bring liability. All this is shown in the House Report No. 262, made by the Committee on War-Claims, March 26, 1874.

"In a report made by Alexander Hamilton, Secretary of the Treasury, to the House of Representatives, November 19, 1792, he stated the rule of law to be—

"That, according to the laws and usages of nations, a state is not obliged to make compensation for damages done to its citizens by an enemy, or wantonly or unauthorized by its own troops.

"'This is a rule adopted in a resolve of the Continental Congress June 3, 1784; Journals, vol. 4, p. 443. It was re-iterated and approved by a committee of House of Representatives March 29, 1822. American State Papers, Claims, 858.'

"The rule, as thus stated, applies to all damages, whether in battle, or by the seizure of army supplies, or the wanton destruction of private property on a raid or march, or otherwise. Undoubtedly it was a duty of the Government officers in charge of the rebel prisoners to use proper care that they should commit no waste. But it is not shown that they failed in their duty. It is presumed that they did their duty, and exercised proper care. This presumption rests on a well-known maxim.

ciples of the laws of war—the generally accepted law of nations—the Government has a right in an insurrectionary district, or in "enemy's

---

"But if this were not so, the Government is not liable to make compensation for injuries resulting from the torts, misfeasances, or omissions of duty of its officers. (See House Rep. No. 262, 1st ses. 43d Cong., p. 46, note 91; Gibbons *vs.* U. S., 8 Wallace, 269.)

"The Government, therefore, is not liable for any part of this claim.

"This is the rule as against even loyal claimants, and in a loyal State."

This subject has been still more fully discussed in other reports of the committee. The following is given for information on the same subject:

War Department, *Washington City, February* 24, 1874.

Sir: In reply to your letter of the 16th instant, requesting information concerning the practice of the Government in regard to the payment of war-claims, the Secretary of War has the honor to inform you that there is nothing in the records of the War Department illustrating the practice of the Government in that regard during the revolutionary war, or that of 1812.

It may be remarked, however, that those were wars with foreign powers, when no portion of the inhabitants of the United States occupied the relation of enemies to the other portion, and no distinction prevailed between loyal and disloyal territory. At such periods, therefore, there could have arisen none of that class of claims which, during the late rebellion, grew out of such relation or distinction.

With reference to the three classes of claims originating in loyal States, specified in your letter, the following remarks are presented, not as exhausting the subject, but as affording you, without delay, a general statement of the present usage and opinion of this Department. You say: "I wish to know what has been the practice of the War and Treasury Departments and of the Government during the war of 1812, and the rebellion, and revolutionary war, in the following cases:

"1. For damage to crops, fences, &c., by an army in its march, (in loyal States.)

"2. For temporary occupancy of houses and lands necessary (A) on a march, (B) preparatory to a battle, (C) after battle. These will be required for officers, hospitals, stores, &c.

"3. For cotton-bales, timber, and materials to build a fort or breast-work in war, to meet or repel an enemy—this in a loyal State. This is different from the erection of a fort in time of peace. * * * Now, I want the usage of all our wars. I also want the law and reference to cases, authorities, &c. * * * To save time, I respectfully ask you to send answer direct to me, for if sent to Speaker of House the delay may be considerable."

In regard to claims of the third class mentioned, it is believed to have been the uniform practice of the War Department to abide by the well-established legal principle which precludes the executive branch of the Government from allowing claims for damages to property destroyed or injured in the common defense or due prosecution of war against a public enemy. This principle is clearly laid down in Parham *vs.* Justices of Decatur County, 9 Georgia, 348, 349, cited in Digest of Opinions of the Judge-Advocate-General, p. 97, and is very fully set forth in "Whiting's War-Powers under the Constitution," (Boston, 1871,) pp. 331–341, a work, indeed, which may throughout be found to throw much light upon the questions propounded in your letter.

The same general principle of law is believed to have been uniformly observed in practice in regard to claims of the *first* class mentioned in your letter, for damages to crops, fences, &c. Cases, indeed, may have occurred where growing crops, fence-timber, &c., may have been seized for the use of the Army in loyal States, and claims for the same may have been legally adjustable by the Quartermaster-General and Commissary-General of Subsistence, under the act of July 4, 1864, as claims for supplies taken under an implied contract. But claims of this sort for damages are wholly excluded from the jurisdiction of the Executive Departments of the Government. (See Whiting, p. 340.)

As to claims of the *second* class mentioned, (for rent for houses or lands seized and occupied by the military authorities in loyal States during the rebellion,) where such occupation is an intrinsic part of active maneuvers, and the damage is clearly incidental to the critical operations of war, it may be unnecessary to say that such a claim, if presented, could not be allowed by this Department. In other cases of private lands and buildings, taken for military purposes, the practice is as follows: Claims for rent due, and not already paid, arising in loyal States during the war, when presented for payment, are investigated by the officer of the Quartermaster's Department in the district wherein the claim originated, and reported to the office of the Quartermaster-General. If they are found on examination there to be correct and just, the claims are forwarded, with all the facts, to the Secretary of War, with report, and recommendation that authority be given to transmit the same to the Third Auditor of the

country," to take and use whatever may be necessary for the convenience or support of the Army.

---

Treasury. If approved, they are then transmitted with recommendation for settlement.

This is done by virtue of an implied contract, under the fifth amendment of the Constitution. An act of March 3, 1813, ch. 513, sec. 5, authorizes the Secretary of War to "fix and make reasonable allowance for the store-rent, storage, &c., for the safe-keeping of all military stores and supplies. By the forty-second article of Revised Regulations of the Army, August 11, 1861, approved by the President, and published for the information and government of the military service, it is made the duty of the Quartermaster's Department to provide quarters, store-houses, offices, and lands for encampments for the Army. When public buildings are not sufficient to quarter troops, authority to hire private property for such uses is given by said regulations to the commanding officer of the department, who reports the case, and his orders therein, to the Quartermaster-General.

It must be admitted that the regular mode of providing lands and buildings for the temporary occupation of the Army is by express contract, and that there is no specific statutory authority for the allowance of rent-claims on the ground of an implied contract, as there is in the case of quartermaster's stores and subsistence; but it is believed that the practice of the War Department in this regard is well known to Congress, and thus far it has met with no mark of disapproval.

Respectfully,

WM. W. BELKNAP, *Secretary of War.*

Hon. WILLIAM LAWRENCE,
*Chairman Committee on War-Claims, House of Representatives.*

WAR DEPARTMENT, QUARTERMASTER-GENERAL'S OFFICE,
*Washington, D. C., February* 26, 1874.

SIR: I have the honor to acknowledge the receipt of your letter of the 24th instant, on the subject of this Department paying for rent of property in certain parts of the rebel States, subsequent to the act of July 4, 1864; and to invite your attention to the inclosed printed schedule of proclamations of Presidents Lincoln and Johnson, respecting the condition of the insurrectionary States.

By reference thereto, it will be seen that the proclamation of July 1, 1862, declares, among other States, Louisiana in rebellion. The proclamation of January 1, 1863, declares Louisiana in rebellion, except certain parishes. The proclamation of April 2, 1863, declares the whole State in rebellion, *except the port of New Orleans.*

The proclamation of January 1, 1863, shows what States and parts of States were, at that time, in rebellion.

The act of July 4, 1864, to restrict the jurisdiction of the Court of Claims, was made applicable to all States and parts of States, except such as were excluded by proclamation of January 1, 1863.

On June 18, 1866, Congress extended the benefit of the act (4th July, 1864) to the counties of Berkeley and Jefferson, West Virginia.

On July 28, 1866, the same benefits were extended to loyal citizens of Tennessee.

The Judge-Advocate-General having held, February 16, 1866, that a claim for subsistence-stores, taken for Army use during the war, in one of the parishes in Louisiana excepted by the President from the operations of his proclamation of January 1, 1863, was not within the provisions of the act of July 4, 1864, authorizing the settlement of such claims, no claim for quartermaster's stores arising in this State was favorably entertained after that date. This decision was also made applicable to the counties of Berkeley and Jefferson, in West Virginia, until the passage of the act of July 18, 1866.

New Orleans having been excepted in proclamation of April 2, 1863, claims for rent in that city were paid, based on certified accounts, and authority of accounting officers of the Treasury, up to close of war, August 20, 1866.

Since the passage of the act of February 21, 1867, which made it unlawful for the Executive Departments to favorably entertain any claim arising in any States declared in rebellion in proclamation of July 1, 1862, none have been recommended by the Quartermaster-General for payment.

*Rents*, arising in Tennessee during the war, were favorably considered up to *June* 12, 1865, when the Secretary of War made what is known as the "Murfreesborough" decision, (copy inclosed.) Between that date and peace proclamation of August 20, 1866, none have been recommended by this Office.

Rent-claims arising in counties of West Virginia during the war, including Berkeley and Jefferson, have been and are now being favorably considered, as no law or orders have been found adverse thereto.

Under an opinion of the honorable the Attorney-General,[a] that contracts are not

---

[a] Opinion, September 2, 1870, vol. 13, p. 314, Opinions Attorneys-General.

These laws are recognized as existing laws, and sanctioned as such by the Constitution, art. 1, sec. 8, clause iii; Opinions of Attorneys-

affected by the law of February 21, 1867, it is understood that claims for rent, in which contracts have been proved to the satisfaction of the accounting-officers, have been settled by them without regard to locality.

I am, very respectfully, your obedient servant,

M. C. MEIGS,
*Quartermaster-General, Bvt. Maj. Gen., U. S. A*

Hon. WILLIAM LAWRENCE,
*Chairman Committee on War-Claims, House of Representatives,*
*Washington, D. C.*

*Memorandum for government of officers charged with the consideration of claims from hostile districts.*

QUARTERMASTER-GENERAL'S OFFICE,
*Washington, D. C., June 12*, 1865.

Murfreesborough hospital.—Claim of Mrs. S. D. Willard.

Murfreesborough was a hostile town captured by our troops from an enemy who did not surrender on terms, but was driven out by force of arms. Everything in it was prize of war, as at Savannah and Atlanta. Buildings were occupied for shelter of troops, and for sick and wounded soldiers of the capturing enemy.

It does not appear that the military department should order payment of any rents, under such circumstances. When active operations of war are over, and peace is restored to the district, the Government will doubtless give up the property which it does not confiscate as rebel property, or as used against it, or will pay rent from the time of restoration of peace and re-establishment of civil authority.

Claims for destruction of property, fences, crops, &c., in hostile districts, by the march or occupation of troops, are on the same footing as claims for rent of buildings in captured towns.

All these should be left for the consideration of Congress, to be finally disposed of under such general legislation as may be enacted.

The appropriations for the Quartermaster's Department are not sufficient to provide for such claims which will be presented.

The claims for fences burned and crops destroyed by the presence, on the march or in encampments, of the troops, would amount to many millions of dollars.

M. C. MEIGS, *Quartermaster-General, Bvt. Maj.-Gen., U. S. A.*

August 14, 1865, approved by Secretary of War.

True copy of decision.

M. I. LUDINGTON, *Quartermaster, U. S. A.*

Q. M. G. O., Feb. 26, 1874.

BARRACK AND QUARTERS BRANCH,
*Quartermaster-General's Office, December* 16, 1874.

Case of ———.

Request of Hon. William Lawrence for an opinion as to whether the Government is liable to pay rent, "even under General Buell's proclamation," for property used by military authorities at Nashville, Tenn., and for information as to whether "if rent was paid, was it under contract?" The claim under consideration being the Southern Methodist Publishing-House of Nashville, Tenn., stated at $457,150.

In a letter to the Secretary of War, 10th December, 1874, Hon. Mr. Lawrence says:

"In my report from Committee on War-Claims, No. 777, June 22, 1874, (Report No. 777, H. of R., 43d Congress, 1st session, herewith,) I said in substance, that during all the time of our (military) occupancy of Nashville, the military authorities did seize and occupy whatever buildings were necessary for military purposes, and the Government has never recognized a liability to pay for them. (See p. 22 of report.)

"This is controverted, and it is alleged that the Army uniformly paid for the use of all property occupied by them in Nashville.

"Now, I wish you would inform me if this be true, that the Army uniformly paid &c. What was the usage?

"You, of course, know the act of February 21, 1867, prohibits the payment of rent.

"Also, in my Report No. 262, of March 26, 1874, which I inclose herewith, you will see on pages 75 and 76 the 'Murfreesborough Decision' against paying rent.

"I wish *especially* to be advised: 1st. What was the usage? 2d. If rent was paid at Nashville, was it under contract? 3d. On page 20 of Report 777, you will see a reference to General Buell's proclamation. Now, I want to know if my construction of that proclamation in that report is the one adopted by the War Department and the Judge Advocate-General?

"I insist the proclamation imposed no duty to pay rent, independent of the act of

General, vol. 11, p. 299; Speed's opinion, July, 1865; 1 Opinions, p. 27.

And the Constitution recognizes, and to some extent limits, the right of military authorities to occupy the houses of private citizens. The third article of amendments declares that—

> No soldier shall, in time of peace, be quartered in any house without the consent of the owner, nor in time of war but in a manner to be prescribed by law.[100]

---

February 21, 1867. By public law, as decided in the Murfreesborough decision, the Government is not liable to pay rent *even under Buell's* proclamation.

"These are very important questions, and I hope to have an early and well-considered reply.

"If necessary, please let me have your opinion, and, if proper, that of Judge Holt."

The letter being referred by the Secretary of War to the assistant judge-advocate-general, it was, December 12, 1874, referred to the Quartermaster-General, "with request for early report."

1st. "As to the usage."

On examination of the returns of the various quartermasters stationed at Nashville during 1862, 1863, 1864, and 1865, it is found that they take up a large quantity of property, namely, store-houses, hospitals, stables, shops, quarters, and various lots, as having been rented by the Quartermaster's Department and rent paid therefor, including the full year of 1865; some of the returns indicating a yearly rental of over $36,000.

2d. "If rent was paid at Nashville, was it under contract?"

Under the head of "date of agreement, contract, or entry into service," various dates are given in the reports; but after a very careful examination of the records, no *written* agreements or contracts covering said rents in Nashville are found on the files of this Office or at the Treasury. It is reasonable to infer that the agreement was a verbal one between the officer who certifies the report "No. 2" as a "true report of all the persons and articles employed and hired" by him during the month, and the owner of the building.

While the Government is not bound by the unauthorized promise of an officer of the Department, as decided in the "Filor" case, in December, 1869, the question arises whether the Government (the accounting officers) had not, previous to that decision, approved the contract or agreement of the quartermaster by the settlement of his accounts covering the disbursement of public money under said "contract," "agreement," or "entry into service."

On page 28 (Report No. 262) it is shown that "a contract is an agreement between competent parties, upon a sufficient consideration, to do or omit some lawful act. Where the assent of both parties is not given there is no contract."

Is not the assent of the Government given by the action of the accounting officers, as above stated? And the assent of the property-owner given when he received the rent? The act of renting was "lawful" under Revised Army Regulations of 1861 and 1863, par. 1071, doubtless.

Does not this bring the payment of rents already made in Nashville within the exceptional cases marked on page 27 of Report No. 262, for which "the Government, in honor and in law, is bound to make compensation?"

The attention of the Quartermaster-General is invited to his letters of February 19, 1874, (notes of page 25, Rep. No. 262,) and of February 26, 1874, (p. 74 *ibid.*) In the last it is shown that rents arising in Tennessee during the war were favorably considered up to June 12, 1865, when the Secretary of War made what is known as the Murfreesborough decision, (on p. 76.) Between that date and peace proclamation of August 20, 1866, none has been recommended by this Office.

No unbound copy of General Order No. 100, Adjutant-General's Office, April 24, 1863, ("instructions for the government of armies of the United States in the field,") is found in the inspection branch. The library copy, however, is at hand, and attention is respectfully invited to paragraph 34, p. 7, a portion of which only appears to be quoted on page 14 of Report No. 777, with reference to the claim being considered.

Referring to Mr. Lawrence's inquiry, whether his construction of General Buell's proclamation (given on pp. 20, 21 of Report No. 777) is the one adopted by the War Department and Judge-Advocate General, attention is also invited to section 8, page 22, of said General Order No. 100, of 1863, relating to "armistice capitulation."

Respectfully submitted to the Quartermaster-General.

M. I. LUDINGTON,
*Quartermaster United States Army.*

---

[100] It has been said that "no [express] provision has ever been made by statute for billeting troops upon the citizens of the United States; but in time of war, rebellion, &c., troops have thus been quartered, under the authority of the 'customs of war in like cases.'" (Scott's Digest Military Laws, p. 24, note 14, edition of 1873.)

Here is a limitation on the exercise of the right of eminent domain, in time of peace, to quarter soldiers in the houses of private citizens, even by virtue of an act of Congress, and with just compensation, "without the consent of the owners." Here, also, is a recognition or concession of the prior existing military common-law right, in cases of

---

QUARTERMASTER-GENERAL'S OFFICE,
*December* 22, 1874.

Respectfully returned to the honorable the Secretary of War.

The intention and rule of the Government in regard to rents in captured towns and places was first formally declared, I think, in the "Murfreesborough decision," as printed in Report H. R. No. 262, Forty-third Congress, first session, page 76.

The Quartermaster-General considered, when his attention was brought to this subject, that errors had obtained in the practice of disbursing quartermasters, acting generally under orders or instructions of commanding officers occupying the country, in paying rent in towns held by troops, Nashville and Murfreesborough being among them. A considerable claim having been preferred for rent of premises occupied as a hospital in Murfreesborough, he drew up the memorandum of his views, (page 76 of the report,) which, having been duly considered at the War Department, was approved by the Secretary of War and published as a guide for the future.

In cases in which, under a wrong impression of their duties, officers had ordered payment or had paid rents in Nashville or other towns, the accounting officers of the Treasury, it is believed, allowed and passed their accounts for such disbursements.

But the Murfreesborough decision was an authoritative decision of the question, and instructions were given to conform thereto thereafter.

The records of the Quartermaster-General's Office contain much correspondence on this subject, and the inclosed memoranda, prepared by officer in charge of the claims branch of this Office, give some information upon the history of the question.

It is not to be doubted that considerable money was paid for rent in Nashville and in some other towns, before the practice was corrected by the promulgation of the Murfreesborough decision.

Whether binding contracts were made is a question to be decided by the written documents in each case.

The mere fact of issue of a voucher certified by an officer, does not constitute or prove a contract. A voucher is merely a bill of prices and quantities, with certificate of the officer who issued it, of his opinion that it is justly due.

Such a voucher, if transmitted to the Quartermaster-General's Office, or finally to the accounting officers, for settlement, is liable to correction in price, in time, and in every particular in which it may be shown to be wrong, or in conflict with superior orders of the central authority of the Executive, through the head of the War Department.

The principles which govern such cases have been sufficiently laid down by the tribunal of last resort, the Supreme Court, in the "Filor" case.

As regards the alleged "proclamation" of General Buell, and "capitulation" of Nashville, I find no such proclamation, and no such capitulation. If they ever existed, they should be of record, and be produced.

The proclamation of the disloyal mayor of a disloyal town is not the evidence to prove, against the Government of the United States, the existence of such important historical acts or documents.

Respectfully,

M. C. MEIGS,
*Quartermaster-General, Brt. Maj. Gen., U. S. A.*

WAR DEPARTMENT, BUREAU OF MILITARY JUSTICE,
*December* 30, 1874.

Respectfully returned to the Secretary of War.

The within inquiries of Hon. William Lawrence relate mainly to matters of fact and usage, of which the evidence is principally contained in the records of the Quartermaster Department, and the same have accordingly been answered from that Department.

As to the action of General Buell, referred to by Mr. Lawrence as a "proclamation," but which appears to have been simply a general assurance given prior to the occupation of Nashville, in February, 1862, that ample protection would be extended to the persons and property of peaceable citizens by the Army—this, it is clear, is of no significance whatever in connection with the subject of war-claims. Even if General Buell had issued a proclamation or made an order, by which claims of this character were recognized or their recognition was guaranteed in the future, such action would have been wholly futile, in the absence of authority or sanction from the Government.

As to the further point, of the effect of a contract, in excepting war-claims from the operation of the acts of 1864 and 1867, prohibiting their settlement, it is only necessary to refer to Filor's case in 9 Wallace, which settles the law that no agreement nor promise

military necessity in time of war, to quarter soldiers in the houses of citizens within the theater of military operations.

And this military common-law right is limited by the third article of amendments, so that in the conditions stated the right can only be exercised "in a manner to be prescribed by law."

But this limitation only extends to the dwelling-houses, with their proper appendages, of loyal citizens.

Story says of this provision:

Its plain object is to secure the perfect enjoyment of that great right of the common law, that a man's house shall be his own castle, privileged against all civil and mili-

---

for compensation given by an officer of the Army, upon the taking or occupation of property for public uses during the war, can amount to a *contract*, unless the same is authorized or sanctioned by the Government, acting through the Secretary of War, the head of a staff-department, or other properly-accredited superior, immediately representing the Executive. In the absence of such authority the pretended contract is, as the court indicates, no more than an agreement of an unauthorized agent and a stranger. Moreover, it is a contract prohibited by the laws of war, which, in making every inhabitant of the rebel States *prima facie* a public enemy, interdicted all intercourse and commercial relations between such enemies and our own citizens.

J. HOLT,
*Judge-Advocate-General.*

WAR DEPARTMENT, *January* 4, 1875.

The Secretary of War has the honor to transmit to the House of Representatives, in reply to a communication from the chairman of the Committee on War-Claims, dated December 10, 1874, inclosing copies of Report No. 777, of June 22, 1874, and No. 262, of March 26, 1874, from the Committee on War-Claims, and requesting to be advised as to the usage of the Government in regard to the payment of rent for property occupied for public uses during the war, at Nashville, Tenn., the inclosed copy of a report from the Quartermaster-General of the Army on the subject, together with the memoranda referred to therein, prepared by the officer in charge of the claims branch of the Quartermaster-General's Office.

Regarding the "proclamation" of General Buell, referred to by the chairman of the Committee on War-Claims, and his (the chairman's) request to be informed if his construction of that proclamation (pages 20 and 21 of Report No. 777, 43d Congress 1st session) is the one adopted by the War Department and the Judge-Advocate-General, the Secretary of War respectfully invites attention to the inclosed copy of the opinion of the Judge-Advocate-General, dated December 30, 1874, relative thereto.

WM. W. BELKNAP,
*Secretary of War.*

WAR DEPARTMENT,
BUREAU OF MILITARY JUSTICE,
*Washington, D. C., January* 6, 1875.

SIR: In reply to your communication of the 5th instant, I have to advise you that I am unable to recall any case in which rent was, within my knowledge, paid by the United States for the use of real estate seized and occupied by the military authorities in the State of Tennessee during the war, and while that State remained in the attitude of a State in insurrection. Nor am I aware of any general liability to pay such rent ever having been recognized by the Government. I have always supposed, on the contrary, that the well-established rule of public law, (indicated or had in view by me, in opinions cited in Digest, p. 96, § 33, and p. 99, §§ 2, 3,) that a government was empowered to seize and use the property of an enemy during a war without becoming liable to render compensation therefor, had been an axiom with our Government during the rebellion, and that the usage had uniformly been in accordance with this principle. If any exceptions occurred they are not known to me; but if such were actually, by inadvertence, will probably be found in the Quartermaster-General's Office, or in the "claims branch" of the War Department; and to these I would respectfully refer you.

I would add, specifically, that no information in regard to the cases noted on pages 3 and 4 of the statement of the "Church claim" is to be found in the files of this Bureau.

Very respectfully, your obedient servant,

J. HOLT,
*Judge-Advocate-General.*

Hon. WM. LAWRENCE,
*House of Representatives, Washington, D. C.*

tary intrusion. The billeting of soldiers in time of peace upon the people has been a common resort of arbitrary princes, and is full of inconvenience and peril. In the petition of right (Charles I) it was declared by Parliament to be a great grievance. (2 Story Const., 4 ed., § 1900; 2 Cobbett's Parl. Hist., 375; Rawle on Const., ch. 10, pp. 126, 127; 1 Tuck. Blackst. Comm., Appx. 300, 301; 2 Lloyd's Debates, 223.)

From all this it is apparent the limitation, in time of war only, extends to dwellings, as stated, and not to other buildings or lands; and it cannot extend to States proclaimed in rebellion by the President, in pursuance of an act of Congress.

This is so on general principles. The usage of our Government during the rebellion, the acts of Congress, and the authority of the courts, all unite in declaring that, in military parlance, the States proclaimed in insurrection thereby became "enemy's country," and the inhabitants subject to the laws of war. The rebellion itself operated to forfeit the protection to which the inhabitants and property of the insurrectionary States would otherwise, under the Constitution, be entitled. (House Rep. No. 262, Com. War-Claims, 1st sess. 43d Congress, March 26, 1874, pp. 5, 10, 11, 14; The Prize Cases, 2 Black, 636; Mrs. Alexander's Cotton Case, 2 Wallace, 419.)

This article of the Constitution is to be construed with reference to its evident purpose. The reason of law is the life of the law. The object of the article was to give protection to the homes of citizens entitled to protection. It could not have been designed to protect citizens in rebellion. It is absurd to suppose provision would be made to protect those on whom the Government was making war—enemies.

It cannot apply, then, to rebels, nor can it apply to loyal citizens in an insurrectionary district in time of rebellion. It would be impossible to execute such an exception. The inquiry in time of war could not be made. The attempt to do so, or to execute it, might defeat the object of carrying on a war to suppress rebellion, or render it impracticable. This must be so for the same reason which induced the Supreme Court to declare that "all" the inhabitants of an insurrectionary district are to be "treated as enemies." (2 Black, 636.)

The term "war," then, in this article of the Constitution, must be understood to refer to war with a foreign power, that war which Congress has "power to declare." In case of rebellion, Congress does not "declare war," but executes the laws, and carries on war for national existence and defense.

This amendment of the Constitution applies to the quartering or billeting of soldiers in houses. This was the evil aimed at. A practice had existed of sending soldiers to the private houses of citizens for shelter and support. This is a very different affair from taking a house for use as a hospital or for other military purposes.

The seizure and occupancy of houses for military use may become an imperative military necessity in a rebellious district. It may be necessary as a means of disabling the enemy as well as providing shelter for loyal troops.

In case of war with a foreign power this right of impressment may exist even with no statute to prescribe the mode of its exercise on the theater of war and among our own citizens.

But soldiers could not be quartered in houses or billeted on citizens for support, except in pursuance of regulations prescribed by law.

But, in addition to this, the seizure of houses in the insurrectionary States was authorized "in a manner prescribed by law."

The President was authorized to proclaim States in insurrection, and he did so. (Act July 13, 1861, § 5, ch. 3; act July 31, 1861, ch. 32; H.

Rep. No. 262, Committee on War-Claims, 1st sess. 43d Congress, March 26, 1874, p. 3.)

This by necessary intendment and in effect carried with it all military common-law rights. The acts of Congress of April 24, 1816, section 9, (ch. 69, § 9, 3 Stat. at L., 298,) and of May 7, 1822, (3 Stat. at L., 689,) authorize the President to prescribe "Army regulations" having the force of law. (Scott's Digest Military Laws, p. 134, § 182; U. S. *vs.* Eliason, 16 Peters, 291; U. S. *vs.* Freeman, 3 How., 566; Gratiot *vs.* U. S., 4 How., 80; Opinions Attorney-General, January 1, 1857, and May 19, 1821; Harney *vs.* U. S., 3 Nott & H., 42.)

The regulations so prescribed declare that—

> The laws of the United States and the general laws of war authorize, in certain cases, the seizure and conversion of private property for the subsistence, transportation, and other uses of the Army. * * * All property lawfully taken from the enemy, or from the inhabitants of an enemy's country, instantly becomes public property, and must be used and accounted for as such. (Regulations of 1861; Appendix to 1863, p. 512, § 21.)

The "instructions for the government of the armies of the United States in the field," approved by the President and published in General Orders No. 100, Adjutant-General's Office, April 24, 1863, only reiterate what had been done under previous orders. These declare that—

> The United States acknowledge and protect, in hostile countries occupied by them, strictly private property. * * * This rule does not interfere with the right of the victorious invaders to tax the people or their property, to levy forced loans, to *billet soldiers*, or to appropriate property, *especially houses*, land, boats or ships, and churches, for temporary and military uses. (Scott's Digest Military Laws, pp. 447 and 1177; House Rep. No. 262, Committee on War-Claims, 1st session 43d Congress, March 26, 1874, p. 14.)

Here, then, is a regulation *by law* applicable to the States proclaimed in insurrection.[101]

In House report No. 44, 2d session 43d Congress, January 8, 1875, a question was decided on of an analogous character. During the rebellion, on the 8th March, 1864, William P. Mellen, supervising special agent of the Treasury Department, leased to Hiram W. Love, of Iowa, from that date to 1st January, 1865, about 88 acres of "abandoned" lands in Desha County, Arkansas, and Love agreed to pay, as rent, one cent per pound on all cotton, and a proportionate sum upon all other products raised by him, to employ freedmen, &c. The land was cultivated by Love in cotton, which promised a productive crop, but before it was picked, Brig. Gen. E. S. Dennis, of the United States forces, commanding some 15,000 troops, arrived at the mouth of White River, in carrying on military operations against the enemy, and, after examining the vicinity to select a proper place of encampment for his forces, issued an order reciting that—

> There being no ground in this vicinity suitable for an encampment excepting this field of growing cotton, claimed as private property by Major Hiram W. Love, the troops of this command will at once disembark and go into camp on this field aforesaid, the same being necessary for military purposes.

The forces did so encamp on the land leased to Love, and most of the crop of cotton was destroyed.

This was discussed May 15, 1874, and, without disposing of the bill,

---

[101] It has been said "that the Executive Departments must necessarily do many things essential to the proper action of the Government, for which there is no [express] statutory provision; and it is necessary that *they* should construe such laws as they are required to execute. Their construction of a statute when not affecting private rights *is held to be binding in the courts*." (Scott's Digest Military Laws, p. 134, § 182, note *a*, citing United States *v.* MacDaniel, 7 Peters, 2; United States *v.* Lytle, 5 McLean, 9.)

the Senate went into executive session, the effect of which was to recommit it. (Congressional Record, vol. 2, part 4, 1st session 43d Congress, vol. 5, pp. 3922, 3935.)

The proper inquiry for this committee now is as to the duty or liability of the Government to make compensation in any form for the damage which the claimant sustained.

The State of Arkansas was one of those declared by authorized proclamation of the President in insurrection.

At the time of the damage complained of the State was in insurrection—war was flagrant.

The encampment which resulted in the damage was an unavoidable military necessity. The Government, and its military officers, in making the encampment, *performed an indispensable duty*, and the injury complained of was, therefore, the result of acts entirely lawful and proper.

The claimant insists that his crop would have amounted to 154 bales of cotton, of 500 pounds each, so that the Government would have received at this estimate $770 as rent; but little more probably than the cost of leasing and managing the abandoned lands, with all the losses, expenses and risks of collecting.

Yet it is assumed that for this, and the general purposes stated, Congress consented to incur in this case a liability ranging from $5,000 to $128,170.

It is assumed that Congress ingrafted an exception on public law, without saying so in any words, which may involve a liability for many millions.

It is certainly a misfortune that this claimant should suffer; but it is equally certain that he and all others having leases would have lost all but for the marching and encamping and battles of our armies.

On the principles already stated, if the Government had *sold* and *patented* this land to the claimant, either prior to or during the war, he would have had no claim for the injury he sustained.

In all the insurrectionary States there were very many loyal men who suffered as much and more than this claimant.

Their land-titles were as sacred as his. This claimant went into an enterprise, expecting, if successful, to make immemse profits. He took the risks of war—of the march of armies. His chances were better than those in a lottery, but he knew in advance the hazards, and chose to incur them.

It was forcibly said, in the Senate debate on this claim, that "the *reason* that the Government is not responsible for property destroyed in the crash of battle" is, "that the Government is about *its lawful business*, and that this destruction of property is a necessary consequence of a lawful act on the part of the Government in defense of itself and in defense of its citizens." And it was well insisted that "all the *incidents* of a campaign are covered by the same principle as the battle-fields."

We "cannot have battle-fields without having previously had camps, and marches, and all the conveniences and incidents which enable an army to reach the battle-field."

This cotton-field in question was occupied during a campaign.

By the general principles of public law, by the usage of nations, this claimant is entitled to no relief, *unless he is for some reason excepted out of the general doctrines stated.*

It has been supposed that he is so excepted because the grounds on which our military forces encamped *were at the time under lease to the claimant from the Government for the purpose of being cultivated in cotton.*

No such *exception* is provided in the act of Congress under which the lease was made, (act July 2, 1864, 13 Stat. at Large, 375.)

None is found in the lease.

None is implied from the *purpose* Congress had in view in providing for leases. This was to give loyal men opportunity to grow cotton if they chose to incur the risks of war. It was to secure employment for freedmen and furnish the country with cotton.

But these were objects which Congress could not by any rule of construction or reason have designed to carry out *at the peril of impairing the efficiency of the military service.*

It is unjust to attribute to Congress a purpose to agree to anything by mere inference that would seriously interfere with the highest of all duties to suppress the rebellion by marches of armies, by battle, and by all the means requisite to success.

The claim was disallowed.

By the strict rules of law literary institutions are equally subject to use by the lawful military authorities. But on grounds of public policy nothing but urgent necessity could justify such use. The proper military authorities must, as a general rule, be allowed to judge of the necessity, or military operations could not be successfully carried on. And certainly when such institutions are a source of strength to the enemy, or are engaged in actually inculcating the sentiment of rebellion, it may be a necessity to withdraw them from a work so dangerous and destructive of public interests.[102]

---

[102] In the Senate, January 12, 1869, Mr. Sumner said: "From the beginning of our national life Congress has been called to deal with claims for losses by war. Though new in form, the present case belongs to a long list whose beginning is hidden in revolutionary history. The folio volume of State Papers now before me, entitled 'Claims,' attests the number and variety. Even amid the struggles of the war, as early as 1779, the Reverend Dr. Witherspoon was allowed $19,040 for repairs of the college at Princeton damaged by the troops. [Claims, pp. 197, 198, 6 Stat., 40.] There was afterward a similar allowance to the academy at Wilmington, in Delaware, [Claims p. —, 6 Stat., 8,] and also to the college in Rhode Island. These latter were recommended by Mr. Hamilton while Secretary of the Treasury, as 'affecting the interests of literature.' On this account they were treated as exceptional. It will also be observed that *they concerned claimants within our own jurisdiction.*"

See Globe, vol. 71, third session Fortieth Congress, page 301, January 12, 1869.

It might be added, *they were loyal to the Government.* Congress has considered the subject since the close of the rebellion.

See claim of William and Mary College. Claim for indemnity for destruction of buildings and property by "disorderly soldiers of the United States during the late rebellion."

For House proceedings and debates see Globe, vol. 87, 2d sess. 42d Congress, pages 784, 785, (February 2, 1872,) and vol. 88, pages 934, 940, 941, 942, 943, 1190, 1191, 1192, 1193, 1194, 1195.

The bill was defeated.

See House Report No. 9, 2d sess. 42d Congress, January 29, 1872.

*East Tennessee University.*—Claims for damages by reason of use and occupation of buildings by United States troops.

For Senate proceedings in 42d Congress, see Globe, vol. 89, page 2288, 2d sess. 42d Congress, (April 9, 1872.) For House proceedings, see Globe, vol. 93, page 697, (January 18, 1873.) See Senate Report No. 17, 2d sess. 42d Congress.

No debate in either House.

Vetoed, January 30, 1873.

See Senate Ex. Doc. 33, 3d sess. 42d Congress.

See Globe, vol. 93, page 991, January 31, 1873.

*Kentucky University.*—Claim for damages by reason of use and occupation of buildings by United States troops.

For Senate proceedings, 41st Congress, see vol. 78, p. 3145, (May 2, 1870,) vol. 80, p. 5538, (July 13, 1870.)

For House proceedings, see Globe, vol. 82, page 480, (January 13, 1871.)

Approved January 17, 1871. See Statutes at Large, vol. 16, p. 678.

In the application of the general principles stated there are some recognized exceptions.

The Government, in honor and in law, is bound to make compensation for property of citizens used, damaged, or destroyed, when—

1. The commander of an army, under proper authority, or other officer duly authorized, in advance or at the time of the use, damage, or destruction, distinctly *agrees* with the owner of the property that the Government shall make compensation, and when, *upon the faith of this*, the *promise is accepted* and the property voluntarily surrendered.[103]

But a *contract* is not necessarily created by the mere fact that the highest military authority gives instructions to subordinate officers, or issues orders *to them*, advising them that enemies "will be paid at the time," or that "they will hereafter be fully indemnified." A contract is an agreement between competent parties, upon a sufficient consideration, to do or omit some lawful act. Where the assent of both parties is not given there is no contract.

---

[103] Steven *vs.* United States, 2 Court Claims 95; Elliott's Claim, 12 Opinions Attorneys-General, 485; Provene *vs.* United States, 5 Court Claims, 456; Kimball *vs.* United States, id., 253; Waters *vs.* United States, 4 Court Claims, 390; Filor *vs.* United States, 9 Wallace, 45; Ayres *vs.* United States, 3 Court Claims.

As to unauthorized contracts see act March 2, 1861, ch. 84, sec. 10, vol. 12, Stat., 220; joint res. No. 8, January 31, 1868, 15 Stat., 246; act June 2, 1862, 12 Stat., 411; 4 Court Claims, 75, 359, 549; 5 Court Claims, 65; 1 Opinions Attorneys-General, 320; 7 Wallace, 666; 4 Court Claims, 176, 401, 495; 5 Court Claims, 302; 8 Wallace, 7.

The act of February 21, 1867, prohibits payment for occupancy, &c., in the insurrectionary States, but this did not divest the right to pay for rent arising on an *authorized contract;* this was decided by the Attorney-General, September 2, 1870, vol. 13, Opinions, p. 314; House Report, No. 262, Committee on War-Claims, 1st session 43d Congress, p. 75.

The acts in relation to public contracts are:

[Acts distinguished by a * have been heretofore repealed.]

Act of 8 May, 1792, chapter 37, section 5, volume 1, page 280; act of 16 July, 1798 chapter 85, sections 3, 6, volume 1, page 610; act of 21 April, 1808, chapter 48, volume 2, page 484; act of 3 March, 1809, chapter 28, sections 3, 5, volume 2, page 536; act of 14 April, 1818, chapter 61, section 7, volume 3, page 427; act of 1 May, 1820, chapter 52, sections 6, 7, volume 3, page 568; resolution of 10 February, 1832, number 1, volume 4, page 605; act of 3 March, 1835, chapter 49, section 1, volume 4, page 780; act of 23 August, 1842, chapter 186, section 5, volume 5, page 513; act of 3 March, 1843, chapter 83, volume 5, page 617; resolution of 18 February, 1843, number 2, volume 5, page 648; act of 17 June, 1844, chapter 107, section 2, volume 5, page 703; act of 17 June, 1844, chapter 107, sections 5, 6, volume 5, p. 703; act of 3 March, 1845, chapter 77, sections 3, 12, volume 5, pages 794, 795; act of 10 August, 1846, chapter 176, section 6, volume 9, page 101; act of 3 August, 1848, chapter 121, section 11, volume 9, page 272; resolution of 9 May, 1848, number 6, volume 9, page 334; act of 28 September, 1850, chapter 80, section 1, volume 9, page 513; act of 28 September, 1850, chapter 80, section 1, volume 9, pages 513, 515; act of 3 March, 1851, chapter 34, section 1, volume 9, page 621; act of 5 August, 1854, chapter 268, section 1, volume 10, pages 583, 585; resolution of 27 March, 1854, number 8, volume 10, page 592; act of 4 May, 1858, chapter 25, section 4, volume 11, page 269; *act of 23 June, 1860, chapter 205, section 3, volume 12, page 103; act of 21 February, 1861, chapter 49, section 5, volume 12, page 150; act of 2 March, 1861, chapter 84, section 10, volume 12, page 220; act of 2 June, 1862, chapter 93, sections 1, 2, 3, 5, volume 12, page 411; act of 14 June, 1862, chapter 164, section 1, volume 12, page 561; act of 17 July, 1862, chapter 200, sections 13, 14, 15, volume 12, page 596; act of 17 July, 1862, chapter 203, volume 12, page 600; resolution of 12 July, 1862, number 53, volume 12, page 624; resolution of 3 March, 1863, number 32, section 2, volume 12, page 828; act of 4 July, 1864, chapter 252, section 7, volume 13, page 394; act of 2 March, 1865, chapter 74, section 7, volume 13, page 467; act of 23 June, 1866, chapter 138, section 3, volume 14, page 73; act of 13 July, 1866, chapter 176, section 4, volume 14, page 92; act of 28 June, 1868, chapter 72, volume 15, page 77; act of 25 July, 1868, chapter 233, section 3, volume 15, page 177; resolution of 31 January, 1868, number 8, volume 15, page 246; act of 11 July, 1870, chapter 243, volume 16, page 229; act of July 15, 1870, chapter 292, volume 16, pages 291–296; act of 3 March, 1871, chapter 117, section 3, volume 16, page 535.

See letter of Quartermaster-General M. C. Meigs, February 26, 1874, in Appendix to this report.

The Government is not bound, either, by the unauthorized promise of an officer.[104]

The mere fact that a voucher or receipt is given for property taken in enemy's country by a military officer does not make the Government liable to pay for it.[105]

Military officers frequently organize a "board of survey" or commission to assess the value of property taken in the enemy's country, or destroyed on loyal territory. This is done to preserve the history of military operations, to enable superior officers to hold subordinates to a proper responsibility in the conduct of war, and in cases where, from special causes, Congress may deem it advisable to make some compensation, it may furnish a means of judging of the proper amount.[106]

But such assessment is for the benefit of the Government, and imposes no liability on it. The liability is determined by the laws of war.

2. When, by the terms of the capitulation of a hostile city or army, there is a distinct stipulation by the proper officer commanding the Union Army that rights of person and property shall be respected, this pledge is to be respected, and a violation of it by military officers clothed with authority to act in the name of the Government would create a liability to repair any damages. This, however, requires some explanation. The "Instructions for the government of the armies in the field," prepared by Francis Lieber, LL. D., promulgated under General Orders No. 100, April 24, 1863, embody the well-recognized laws of civilized[107] warfare as universally understood and in force. These rules declare (No. 37) that—

The United States acknowledge *and protect* in hostile countries occupied by them strictly private property. *This rule* does not interfere with the right of the victorious invader to tax the people, or their property, to levy forced loans, to billet soldiers, or

---

[104] In Filor *vs.* United States, 9 Wallace 45, the court refer to a case, at Key West, of contract for the use of the Quartermaster's Department, and say it was not "binding upon the Government until approved by the Quartermaster-General."

Ayres *vs.* United States, 3 Court Claims, 1; Gibbons *vs.* United States, 8 Wallace, 269. See letter of Meigs in note 53, *ante*.

See the acts relating to the Court of Claims; act March 3, 1863, 12 Stat., 767, section 12, and other acts cited in the volumes of reports of that court.

"The law of agency, as applicable to the United States, is far more strict than to individuals, for the agent must have *actual authority* in order to bind the Government." 1 Boston American Law Review, section 58.

[105] The Revised Army Regulations of 1861, as corrected to June 25, 1863, edition of 1867, p. 512, section 22, provides that "all property, public or private, taken from alleged enemies, must be inventoried and duly accounted for. If the property be claimed as private, receipts must be given to such claimants or their agents." But this does *not change the laws of war*, and give a liability which does not exist by such law. The laws of war are prescribed by another power, and cannot be abrogated by Army regulations.

In the report of November 30, 1873, of Hon. R. S. Hale to the Secretary of State, of claims allowed by the commission under the 12th article of the treaty of 8th May, 1871, between the United States and Great Britain, it is said:

"In the case of John Kater, No. 19, claimant was allowed for two horses taken by Sheridan's army on its raid through the valley of Virginia, in August, 1864, all the commissioners joining in this award, General Sheridan's order of August 16, 1864, directing the seizure of mules, horses, and cattle for the use of the Army, having in effect promised compensation for such property to loyal citizens."

[106] Such valuation was made by order of General Jackson, after the battle of New Orleans, of certain damages to real estate. American State Papers, class ix, claim 752. Such boards were frequently organized during the rebellion.

[107] These regulations are authorized and have the force of law.

House Rep. Com. War-Claims, No. 6, 2d sess. 43d Congress, p. 4.

The acts of Congress of April 24, 1816, section 9, (ch 69, § 9, 3 Stat. at L., 298,) and of May 7, 1822, (3 Stat. at L., 689,) authorized the President to prescribe "Army regulations" having the force of law. (Scott's Digest Military Laws, p. 134, § 182; U. S. *vs.* Eliason, 16 Peters, 291; U. S. *vs.* Freeman, 3 How., 566; Gratiot *vs.* U. S., 4 How., 80;

*to appropriate property, especially houses, land, boats,* or ships and churches, for temporary and military purposes.

And this is the effect of a proclamation promising "protection of persons and property." "*Protection*" implies, that there shall be no *destruction* unless imperatively required by military emergencies. It does *not* imply that military officers shall refrain from using the means necessary for their own shelter or protection, or that of the Army, or those necessary for military operations.

And this is all the more certain, because during all the time of our occupancy of the States in insurrection the military authorities did seize and occupy whatever buildings were necessary for military purposes and operations, and the Government has never recognized a liability to pay for them. In the early part of the war this rule was not strictly adhered to, but the settled doctrine and practice of the Government afterward became as stated. It is not to be presumed that military officers violated pledges, and their conduct is evidence then of what was understood. It is a *contemporaneous construction*, and the highest evidence of the understanding.

In *Planters' Bank* vs. *Union Bank*, 16 Wallace, 496, the court held that such proclamation prohibited the seizure of private property "*as booty of war.*"

But "booty of war" is very different from necessary military seizure for use. And the protection afforded by a promise of protection of persons and property only extends to such enemies as strictly observe neutrality and the terms of the capitulation, and to property the nature of which does not take it out of the condition of neutrality [108]

Opinions Attorney-General, January 1, 1857, and May 19, 1821; Harney *vs.* U. S., 3 Nott & H., 42.)

The regulations so prescribed declare that—

"The laws of the United States and the general laws of war authorize, in certain cases, the seizure and conversion of private property for the subsistence, transportation, and other uses of the Army. * * * All property lawfully taken from the enemy, or from the inhabitants of an enemy's country, instantly becomes public property, and must be used and accounted for as such." (Regulations of 1861; Appendix to 1863, p. 512, § 21.)

The "instructions for the government of the armies of the United States in the field," approved by the President, and published in General Orders No. 100, Adjutant-General's Office, April 24, 1863, only reiterate what had been done under previous orders.

[108] Case of Thorshaven, Edwards, 107; Alexander's Cotton, 2 Wallace, 421; Vattel book 3, ch. 18. sec. 294, p. 425. The Venice, 2 Wallace, 258; Winthrop's Digest Opinions of Judge-Advocate-General, 1862 to 1868, p. 86, (ed. of 1868,) vol. xviii, p. 511, Records of Bureau of Military Justice; House Rep. 777, 1st sess. 43d Cong., p. 20.

Planters' Bank *vs.* Union Bank, 16 Wallace, 468.

The commission under the 12th article of the treaty of 8th May, 1871, between the United States and Great Britain, held substantially thus: The report of Hon. R. S. Hale shows that where aliens claimed compensation for property used by the United States troops, taken by proper authority, the commission were unanimous in the allowance of claims for property coming under this head when taken within the loyal States or within those portions of the insurrectionary States permanently occupied by the Federal forces, except when something in the nature of the property or in the conduct of the claimant took him out of the condition of neutrality. Thus, for instance, in the case of Robert Davidson, No. 66, the claim was for gun-carriages and other artillery apparatus, manufactured by the claimant for the use of the confederate government, and remaining in his possession at the surrender of New Orleans, together with material for use in the same manufacture, which was taken and appropriated by the Federal forces, under the orders of General Banks, some months after the capture of New Orleans. The claim was unanimously disallowed.

In the case of Samuel Brook, No. 99, the claim was for certain tarpaulins taken by an authorized officer for the use of the United States, at Memphis, Tenn., in June, 1862, shortly after the capture of that city by the Federal forces.

An award was made in favor of the claimant, Mr. Commissioner Frazer dissenting upon the question of the sufficiency of proof, but the commissioners all agreeing as to the principle involved.

And it cannot be an absolute guarantee against unauthorized pillage or other damages incident to surrounding circumstances.

3. The same rule of protection is extended to persons and property where there is no capitulation, but an authorized military proclamation promising it, when a city or district of the enemy is subdued and occupied.[109] This principle will apply generally to duly authorized safeguards.[110]

A passport may be given which does not amount to a safeguard, and which will impose less of liability and no absolute guarantee of safety. But a safeguard for the purpose of protection under a flag of truce may amount to a guarantee of the safety of persons, and of such property as may be named, or may reasonably accompany the person, excluding unnecessary valuables.[111]

---

[109] And while the conditions of the proclamation are observed by the enemy, and hostilities are not renewed by them, the pledge of protection cannot be revoked by military authority. Planters' Bank *vs.* Union Bank, 16 Wallace, 496. See also act July 13, 1861, sec. 5, (12 Stat., 257,) and President's proclamation, August 16, 1861, (12 Stat., 1262.)

[110] See act February 13, 1862, sec. 5; Army Regulations of 1861, revised to June 25, 1863, (ed. of 1867,) pp. 112, 113.

The following is a copy of one issued by General Grant:

HEADQUARTERS DEPARTMENT OF THE TENNESSEE,
*Vicksburgh, Miss., September* 18, 1863.

By authority of Maj. Gen. U. S. Grant:

A safeguard is hereby granted to Mrs. Eugenie Bass, her plantations, houses, horses, cattle, sheep, hogs, poultry, and all other property, real or personal, situated near Princeton, in the county of Washington, and State of Mississippi.

All officers and soldiers belonging to the armies of the United States are therefore commanded to respect this safeguard, and to afford, if necessary, protection to the said Mrs. Eugenie Bass and property.

"Whoever, belonging to the armies of the United States in foreign parts, or at any place within the United States or their Territories during rebellion against supreme authority of the United States, shall force a safeguard, shall suffer death." (55 Art. of War.)

By order of Maj. Gen. U. S. Grant:

JOHN A. RAWLINS,
*Brig. Gen. and A. A. A. Gen.*

Under this the question has been made whether the award of a military board of survey for property taken by Union military authorities should be paid, or a less sum awarded by the Commissioners of Claims. By submitting a claim to the latter there is an implied agreement to accept their award, subject to revision by Congress. But without this the Government can determine by law how valuations shall be made. The loyalty of this claimant was proved to the satisfaction of the commissioners.

[111] Chancellor Kent defines the general rule with regard to flags of truce:

"He who promises security by a passport is morally bound to defend it against any of his subjects or forces, and make good any damages the party might sustain by violation of the passport. The privilege being so far a dispensation from the legal effects of war, it is always to be taken strictly, and must be confined to the purpose and place and time for which it was granted. A safe-conduct generally includes the *necessary* baggage and servants of the person to whom it is granted." (1 Kent's Com., 161.)

Also as to the inviolability secured under a flag of truce, Vattel, ch. xvii, p. 416: "A safe-conduct given to a traveler naturally includes his baggage or his clothes and other things *necessary* for his journey." (Id., 417, § 270; Woolsey's International Law, p. 250.)

"The sovereign can revoke the passport even before the fulfillment of its terms, by giving to the bearer the liberty of return." (Bello, p. 265.)

"Passports should not be granted for the purpose of attracting persons or effects with the object of confiscating them afterward by means of revocation, because to act thus would be a perfidy contrary to the laws." (1 Bello, p. 265.)

"The violation of the good faith pledged by passports and documents of that character draws after it the most condign punishment. If it is committed on the part of the authorities or agents of the government which gives it, its bearer will be amply indemnified for the consequences that result from the violation; and the person who commits the violation will be punished in accordance with the laws of his country." (Calvo, 2 v., p. 87, edition of 1868.) On the same page, Calvo confirms the principles

4. During the rebellion the ordinary laws of war as to enemy's country were by the general policy of the Government, sanctioned by Congress and the President's proclamation of August 16, 1861, so far modified that in such parts of the rebel States as were permanently occupied and controlled by the Union military forces, and where rebellion had ceased and was no longer probable, the Government assumed to interfere no further with the rights of person and property of the enemy than should be required by necessary subjection to military government.[112]

But this immunity would only extend to those who were loyal, or who ceased to engage in or aid or encourage rebellion.

---

stated by a citation of the most distinguished writers on the laws of nations of all civilized countries from the time of Grotius to the present.

In 1863, while General Banks was in command at New Orleans, Mrs. Flora A. Darling, intending to go north, was received through the enemy's lines from Mobile, on a flag of truce boat at New Orleans, with baggage, including a trunk containing, as alleged, confederate bonds. She claimed to have a passport, or safe-conduct, and alleged that while on the boat she was arrested, her baggage taken, including money and confederate bonds, and never returned to her. Several years after this she applied to the War Department for redress for money taken. The War Department found it impossible to ascertain the facts as to the alleged loss. The Judge-Advocate-General, as to this case, among other things, said:

"In regard to the merits of such claim, it need only be said that as far as the rebel securities are concerned the seizure was clearly authorized.

"No flag of truce could protect such bonds—which have invariably heretofore been held as illegal and disloyal publications, intended to give aid and comfort to the enemy—from confiscation and destruction. On the contrary, a party availing himself of a flag of truce to bring such securities within our lines would be guilty of a violation of the truce, and become amenable to trial and punishment.

"It was probably the discovery of these bonds in Mrs. Darling's baggage which led to her subsequent detention by the military authorities."

[112] The Venice, 2 Wallace, 259; Planters' Bank *vs.* Union Bank, 16 Wallace, 483; Mrs. Alexander's Cotton, 2 Wallace, 419; Prize Cases, 2 Black, 674; Senator Carpenter in Cong. Record, March 20, 1874, p. 22. See letter of February 26, 1874, of Quartermaster-General M. C. Meigs, in appendix to this report; Senate Claims Committee's Report, No. 85, 2d sess. 42d Cong., March 27, 1872. In the claim of Cowan & Dickinson, referred to in this report, it was insisted that Knoxville, Tenn., was not "enemy's country." Early in September, 1863, General Burnside occupied Knoxville with Union forces. The city was beleaguered by the rebel General Longstreet on the 17th November, and his forces made an assault upon the defenses on the 28th. In this assault three brigades of assailants lost about 800 men, and the Union forces about 100. The cotton of Cowan & Dickinson was seized on the nights of the 17th and 18th November, by order of General Burnside, for fortifications. The siege of the city was raised on the 5th of December, and the enemy left that part of Tennessee. This report asserts that Knoxville was not "enemy's country" at the time the cotton was seized. The authority relied on is the case of The Venice, 2 Wallace, 259. The report was made March 27, 1872. But afterward, in December, 1872, the Supreme Court decided the case of Planters' Bank *vs.* Union Bank, 16 Wallace, 495. That case will give some idea as to what is such "permanent occupancy and control by Union forces" as will show that a district is no longer enemy's country. In that case the court, referring to the exercise of military authority ordering a seizure on the 17th of August, 1863, say: "Then the city of New Orleans was *in quiet possession of the United States*. It had been captured more than fifteen months before that time, and *undisturbed possession* was maintained *ever after its capture*. *Hence* the order was no attempt to seize property '*flagrante bello*.'"

But this described a very different condition of affairs than existed at Knoxville. There was *no* "undisturbed possession." There the seizure was *flagrante bello*. In this case the Judge-Advocate-General, in an opinion to the War Department, December 4, 1867, said: "The cotton was seized in the enemy's country, and on the theater of the war, and was appropriated to the strengthening of one of our forts, then threatened with an attack by an advancing column of rebel forces. For this act of legitimate warfare the Government incurred no responsibility."

The following letter from Hon. B. F. Butler, late major-general, is appended for information:

HOUSE OF REPRESENTATIVES, *Washington, D. C., December* 22, 1874.

SIR: I have the honor to reply to your letter of December 16, asking certain opinions in matters of law.

The proposition you state to me is, "that I occupied the buildings sometimes of

And this is true so long as the proclamation continued in force and as to the places covered by its exceptions.

The President's proclamation of August 16, 1861, declared the inhabitants of Tennessee and other States "in a state of insurrection against the United States." (12 Stat. at L., 1262.) But *it excepted* "such parts of States as may maintain a loyal adhesion to the Union and the Constitution, or may be, from time to time, occupied and controlled by forces of the United States engaged in the dispersion of said insurgents."

The proclamation of July 1, 1862, (12 Stat., 1266,) declared eleven States in insurrection, and excepted only certain counties of Virginia.

---

loyal citizens for the use of the officers of the Army." That I never did. All the buildings that I occupied while in New Orleans were buildings belonging to the Government, or were those of officers in the confederate army who had deserted New Orleans. By the proclamation made at or about the first day of May, all private property was to be held "inviolate." Of course that referred to the property of those who were present in the city, and who should remain under the authority of the United States, and conduct themselves in a quiet and peaceable manner, obedient to the laws of the United States; and no such man's property was occupied by me. In Algiers, opposite New Orleans, certain buildings, the property of those who, whether loyal or not, were absent from the city and left their property unprotected, were taken down by the negroes for the purpose of making themselves shanties. That was not done by the order of the military authorities, nor was there permission—but it would have been permitted if it had been asked—and under no circumstances could the United States be held liable for that unauthorized act of trespass. There was no authorization of or contracts under which by the negroes or by others any buildings were occupied.

The law governing all this matter seems to be simply this—I speak, of course, without examination of authorities: that where an army occupies and garrisons a town in time of actual war, the occupation of such buildings as are necessary to the use of the army and those depending upon them, with all the costs and damages, is an incident of war, for which the government is in no sense responsible, and ought not to be so held or considered. An army cannot hold a city without occupying some portion of it; and if they do do so, that is one of the incidents of war, and gives no contract, explicit or implied, against the government of the occupying army.

This is the law, and fully understood in Europe, where the capture and occupation of a city or capital of one nation by the army of another is frequently the case, and no reclamation would ever be made under those circumstances against the government of the conquering army, and none can be made here.

I have the honor to be, very respectfully, your friend and servant,

BENJ. F. BUTLER.

Hon. WM. LAWRENCE, *Chairman Committee on War-Claims,*
*House of Representatives, Washington, D. C.*

The law-officer of the War Department holds that the proclamation of April 2, 1863, did not give even loyal citizens in New Orleans during the rebellion a right to demand compensation for rent of buildings used as a military necessity. This is shown in the following:

WAR DEPARTMENT, BUREAU OF MILITARY JUSTICE,
*Washington, D. C., January* 4, 1875.

SIR: I have the honor to acknowledge the receipt from you of two communications of the 29th ultimo: one relating to a claim for the use and occupation of a building taken and used by the military authorities in New Orleans in March, 1863; and the other referring to the matter of the settlement of claims of a similar character, arising, however, in a State not in insurrection. To these communications I have to reply as follows:

1. *As to claim for rent of building taken in New Orleans.* In your note in regard to this claim, while recognizing the general principle that the United States cannot be held liable for the use of property taken and used in rebel territory pending the late war, you, however, suggest that "the President's proclamation of April 2, 1863, seems to put New Orleans on the footing of loyal territory, just as Ohio or Pennsylvania would be;" and you conclude with the inquiry, "whether a loyal owner of property in New Orleans is entitled to pay for use and occupation after April 2, 1863," (the date of the proclamation,) "where the occupancy was a military necessity, during 1863 and 1864. Or was there such a state of war that the Government was excused from paying?"

The very question raised by you, viz, that of the proper construction of the term

And it may well be maintained that this latter proclamation *withdrew the exceptions contained in the former.*

The exceptions made in the proclamation of August 16, 1861, interfered with the enforcement of the act of July 13, 1861, regulating trade and intercourse, (12 Stat., 257,) and the President issued a proclamation, April 2, 1863, (13 Stat., 731,) *revoking the exceptions contained in the former proclamation,* but again making or continuing certain local exceptions, but Nashville was not one of them.

Culver *vs.* United States, N. and H., Court Claims R., 418; S. C. on appeal in Supreme Court; *The Venice,* 2 Wallace, 258; *Planters' Bank* vs. *Union Bank,* 16 Wallace, 493; *Ouachita Cotton,* 6 Wallace, 531.

But where there has been no hostile military operations, it must be remembered that by the laws of nations *war,* either foreign or civil, may exist where no battle has been or is being fought.[113]

No nation in the world's history ever failed to seize any property and occupy it where its armies were surrounded with great perils.

---

"port of New Orleans," as employed in the proclamation referred to, was fully considered by me in a report addressed to the Secretary of War in 1866. The substance of this report is very fully presented in the following abstract, published in the Digest of Opinions of the Judge-Advocates-General, p. 95, section 29:

"*Held,* That the President's proclamation of April 2, 1863, by which the '*port* of New Orleans' was excepted from the declaration of places in insurrection and the operation of the prohibition of commercial intercourse, did not alter the *status* of real estate occupied by our military forces during the war, or authorize the payment of rent therefor, for the period of occupation subsequent to the date of such proclamation; that the object of this proclamation, which revoked the exceptions of that of August 16, 1861, as too general, and substituted others which were precise and definite, was more effectually to prevent an illegal commercial intercourse with insurrectionary districts by restricting such intercourse to certain few localities specified; that it was the Executive intent to exempt from the *status* and penalties of rebellion the port of New Orleans as a *harbor,* to remove the ban of non-intercourse from it, *as such,* and not to relieve the people of the city from the legal condition of insurrection in which they had been formerly declared to be, nor to modify in any manner their *political* relations; that, had it been the design of the Executive to rehabilitate the citizens of New Orleans by this proclamation in all those rights of which they had been restrained by an antecedent solemn decree, it would have been easy so to decree, and clear and positive language would have been employed for the purpose; and that, in view of the general rule of interpretation, that a law, whether statutory or otherwise, which repeals or restricts the scope of a previously existing provision, is to be strictly construed, the use of the specific word '*port,*' in connection with New Orleans, must be regarded as limiting the operation of the exception to the port alone as such."

This opinion (which is still entertained) appears to me to cover your inquiry.

In view of the decision of the Supreme Court in the prize-cases, that all the inhabitants of the States in rebellion became public enemies upon the inauguration of the civil war, I scarcely need add that the personal loyalty of the claimant in the instance mentioned by you, (however much it might commend his claim to Congress as proper to be excepted from the general rule of exclusion,) cannot, of course, affect the *legal* aspect of the case.

J. HOLT, *Judge-Advocate-General.*

Hon. WILLIAM LAWRENCE, *Chairman Committee on War-Claims, House of Representatives.*

(See House Report 740, p. 5, and No. 748, p. 2, and No. 777, p. 24, all at 1st session 43d Congress. Cutner *vs.* U. S., 6 Court Claims R., 418.)

[113] Const., art. 3, sec. 3, clause 3; Ex parte Milligan, 4 Wallace, 121, 140, 142; *Luther* v. *Borden; Grant* v. *United States,* 1 Nott & Hopkins, Court Claims, 41; S. C., 2 id, 551; Whiting's War-Powers, 43; Ex parte Milligan, 127. The court say to justify martial law "the necessity must be actual and present;" Paschal, Annotated Const., 212, note 215; Ex parte Bollman, 4 Cranch, 126; *United States* v. *Burr,* 4 Cranch, 469–508; Sergeant, Const., ch. 30, [32;] *People* v. *Lynch,* 1 Johns., 553.

## CHAPTER III.

### OF DAMAGES DONE BY THE ENEMY.

When private property is destroyed by the unlawful acts of individuals, governments seek to give redress by civil action, or to punish for acts which are criminal. But they do not indemnify the parties who may lose by such depredations.

If a loss is sustained by arson, burglary, theft, robbery, or by an act which constitutes only a trespass, governments do not make good the loss. And this is so whether the illegal acts are done by one or many persons.

Nations apply the same rule when their citizens suffer losses by a foreign or domestic enemy. They are no more bound to repair the losses of citizens by the ravages of war than to indemnify them against losses by arson, or other individual crimes, or the destruction of flocks by wolves.

In a report made by Alexander Hamilton, Secretary of the Treasury, to the House of Representatives, November 19, 1792, he stated the rule of law to be—

> That according to the laws and usages of nations, a state is not obliged to make compensation for damages done to its citizens by an enemy, or wantonly or unauthorized, by its own troops.[114]

The rule, as thus stated, applies to all damages, whether in battle, or by the seizure of army supplies, or the wanton destruction of private property on a raid or march.

This was declared to be the law as to property destroyed in battle, and not controverted, in the Senate of the United States on the 4th of January, 1871, in these words:

"I admit that it is the law of nations, it is a principle of universal law, that property destroyed in the course of a fight, in the progress of a fight as it is going on, is not to be paid for by even the United States where it is a party to such conflict. I admit that the Constitution of the United States does not bear the interpretation that property destroyed under such circumstances should be paid for by the United States."[115]

Vattel says:

> There are damages caused by inevitable necessity; as, for instance, the destruction caused by the artillery in retaking a town from the enemy. These are merely accidents. They are misfortunes, which chance deals out to the proprietors on whom they happen to fall.
>
> The sovereign, indeed, ought to show an equitable regard for the sufferers, if the situation of his affairs will admit of it; but no action lies against the state for misfortunes of this nature—for losses which she has occasioned, not willfully, but through necessity and by mere accident, in the exertion of her rights. The same may be said of damages caused by the enemy. All the subjects are exposed to such damages; and woe to him on whom they fall! The members of a society may well encounter such risk of property, since they encounter a similar risk of life itself. Were the state strictly to indemnify all those whose property is injured in this manner, the public

---

[114] American State Papers, class ix, vol. 1 of Claims, p. 55; Pitcher *vs.* United States, 1 Court Claims R., 9; Mitchell *vs.* Harmory, 13 Howard, p. 115.

This is the rule adopted in a resolve of the Continental Congress June 3, 1784, Journals, vol. 4, p. 443. It was re-iterated and approved by a committee of House of Representatives March 29, 1822, American State Papers, Claims, 858.

[115] Senator Davis, January 4, 1871, 82 Globe, p. 297. His State of Kentucky was largely interested in insisting on the liability of the United States wherever the laws of nations, or the Constitution, would admit.

finances would soon be exhausted; and every individual in the state would be obliged to contribute his share in due proportion—a thing utterly impracticable. Besides, these indemnifications would be liable to a thousand abuses, and there would be no end of the particulars. It is therefore to be presumed that no such thing was ever intended by those who united to form a society.[116]

The same rule of law was adopted in England when, during the American Revolution, the property of British loyalists in the colonies was destroyed.

Mr. Pitt said in Parliament:

The American loyalists could not call upon the House to make compensation for their losses as a matter of strict justice; but they most undoubtedly have strong claims on their generosity and compassion.[117]

---

[116] Vattel, book 3, chap. xv, § 232, p. 403.

[117] Hansard's Parliamentary History, vol. 27, p. 610–618, June 3, 1788; Sumner's speech January 12, 1869, 71 Globe, 301. He shows that the British loyalists at the close of the war appealed to Parliament. The number of their claims was 5,072; the amount claimed £8,026,045, of which commissioners appointed allowed not quite half.

This subject was discussed before the American-British Claims Commission, under the twelfth article of the treaty of May 8, 1871, between the United States and Great Britain.

Mr. Hale, in his report, says:

AMERICAN-BRITISH CLAIMS COMMISSION.

3.—*Claims for property alleged to have been destroyed by the rebels.*

In the case of John H. Hanna, No. 2, the memorial alleged in effect that the claimant was the owner of 819 bales of cotton, situated within the rebel States of Louisiana and Mississippi, and that "without fault of petitioner, against his consent, and by force and arms, said cotton was destroyed by rebels in arms against the Government of the United States prior to the year 1863." By the schedules annexed to his memorial, and made a part of the same, it appeared that the cotton in question was destroyed by order of the authorities of the Confederate States and of the rebel State of Louisiana, for the purpose of preventing the same from falling into the hands of the Federal forces.

A demurrer to the memorial was interposed on behalf of the United States.

On the argument of the demurrer it was contended by Her Majesty's counsel, on behalf of the claimant, that the acts of destruction alleged in the memorial appearing to have been deliberately committed under the orders of the commander of the forces of the Confederate States, and with the concurrent authority of the governor of the State of Louisiana and commander of the troops of that State, reclamation must lie on behalf of the British government, in the interest of the claimant as a subject of that government, against the United States as representing and including the State of Louisiana, as well as all the other States forming the so-called Confederate States; that the persons engaged in these acts of destruction were not liable, either civilly or criminally, either for reparation or punishment in respect of those acts, they having been committed in the course of military operations under the authority of the existing government, whether lawful or usurped.

That for the wrongful acts of the several States in respect to foreign nations or their subjects, reclamation could be made only against the United States, to the Government of which, by its Constitution, was reserved the power of making treaties, declaring war, and making peace, and all international powers generally, the same being denied to the individual States; that no foreign nation could negotiate with or make demand upon individual States in respect of such acts, but could deal only with the Government of the United States; that in case of wrongs committed by any State upon foreign nations, in regard to which that State, if wholly independent and not a member of the Federal Union, would be liable to reclamation, and to be called to account in the mode practiced between nations—by treaty or by war—these remedies against such State being denied to foreign powers by the Constitution of the United States, the liability for reparation devolved upon the United States, and the Federal Government must be held to answer as well for the acts of the authorities of its several constituent States as for those of the Federal Government.

That the so-called secession of the State of Louisiana and the other States forming the so-called Confederate States did not extinguish or suspend the liability of the United States for wrongful acts committed by said States.

That by the treaties of 1794, 1815, and 1827, the United States had stipulated with Great Britain for the protection of her subjects in the State of Louisiana as well as in all other territory of the United States; that the United States not having allowed the claim of Louisiana to be released from her constitutional obligations and restric-

Nations sometimes do grant relief even for ravages of war, not as a

---

tions, but having held her to her constitutional obligations, and having insisted that their political relations with foreign powers were in no wise affected by the insurrection in the Southern States, and that the Government of the United States was rightfully supreme in Louisiana and the other States in rebellion, and having finally maintained its authority over those States, its liability to Great Britain for violation of these treaties by those respective States remained precisely as if there had been no insurrection or civil war.

Her Majesty's counsel further contended that, as a principle of international law, if the rightful government of a country be displaced and the usurping government becomes liable for wrongs done, such liability remains, and devolves on the rightful government when restored; that this principle equally applied when the usupation was only partial; that the restored and loyal government of Louisiana was liable for wrongs done by the insurrectionary government of the same State; and that it was only by the provisions of the Constitution of the United States that the State of Louisiana was prevented from being compelled to discharge that liability toward foreign governments, and that on this ground the Government of the United States must be held responsible for the acts of the State of Louisiana.

He cited in support of these propositions the treaties of 1815 and 1827 between the United States and Great Britain, (8 Stat., p. 228, art. 1; id., 361, art. 1;) Phillimore, vol. 1, pp. 86, 94, 139; Wheaton, p. 77; Constitution of the United States, art, 1, sec. 10; Works of Daniel Webster, vol. 3, p. 321; id., vol. 6, pp. 209, 253, 265; U. S. Att. Gen. Op., vol. 1, p. 392; The United States *vs.* Palmer, 3 Wheat. Sup. Ct. R., 210; The Collector *vs.* Day, 11 id., 113, 124 to 126; The Prize Cases, 2 Black, 636; the treaty between the United States and Great Britain of August 9, 1842, (8 Stat., 575, art. 5;) and the acts of Congress of December 22, 1869, (16 Stat., 59, 60,) and of April 20, 1871, (17 id., 13 to 15.)

The argument on behalf of the United States was summed up as follows:

"First. That whatever may be the relations of the separate States of the Union to the Government of the United States, it is manifest that no responsibility can attach to the United States for the destruction of the claimant's property under color of the authority of the State of Louisiana, because its destruction was not authorized by any officials representing or authorized to represent or act for the State of Louisiana under the Constitution and laws of the United States. There can be no legitimate officers of a State to constitute its government, except such as have taken an oath to support the Constitution of the United States. All others are usurpers and pretenders. But, further, a State of the Union has no political existence which can be or has been recognized by Great Britain, except as a part of the United States, in subordination to the National Government. The rebels, who, by usurpation, undertook to act for the State of Louisiana, declared their action to be in behalf of the State, which they claimed as a component part of another and hostile nation

"Secondly. The destruction of the claimant's cotton was done under the order of the commander of a military force engaged in hostilities against the United States, and whose acts Great Britain had recognized as those of a lawful belligerent, having all the rights of war against the United States that any foreign invader could have had. The men professing to act as the local authorities, in concurring in the order of destruction, acted as the assistants and allies of the hostile and belligerent power, and subject to its control. It is as absurd to hold the United States responsible in the case of Hanna, as it would be to hold France responsible for the destruction of the property of a British subject in the part of France held by the German armies in the late war, on the ground that a French official, at the head of some *arrondissement* or *commune*, might have joined in the order of the German forces for its being done, he having been put in office or retained there by the German forces for the very purpose, and having first renounced his allegiance to France and taken an oath of allegiance to Germany."

The commission unanimously sustained the demurrer in the following award:

"The claim is made for the loss sustained by the destruction of cotton belonging to the claiment by men who are described by the claimant as rebels in arms against the Government of the United States.

"The commissioners are of opinion that the United States cannot be held liable for injuries caused by the acts of rebels over whom they could exercise no control, and which acts they had no power to prevent.

"Upon this ground, and without giving any opinion upon the other points raised in the case, which will be considered hereafter in other cases, the claim of John Holmes Hanna is, therefore, disallowed."

Mr. Commissioner Frazer read an opinion, which will be found in the appendix H.

This was among the earliest of the decisions of the commission, and it is understood that in consequence of it a large number of claims of similar character awaiting presentation were never presented to the commission.

matter of strict right by principles of international law, but as a gratuitous act of benignity.[118]

*Opinion of Mr. Commissioner Frazer, in the case of John H. Hanna vs. The United States No. 2,* (*See p. 58, ante.*)

This is a claim for the destruction of 819 bales of cotton belonging to the claimant by rebels in arms against the United States. The property was destroyed in Louisiana and Mississippi in 1862 by the confederate forces, with the concurrence of the rebel authorities of Louisiana, one of the Confederate States so called. Her Britannic Majesty had recognized the co-called Confederate States as a belligerent, and the contest of arms then prevailing as a public war. After such recognition by the sovereign, the subject of such sovereign cannot, in his character as such subject, aver that the fact was not so. The act of his government in that regard is conclusive upon him.

Aside from this recognition by Her Majesty, it is public history, of which this commission will take notice without averment or proof, that the confederate forces were engaged at the time in a formidable rebellion against the Government of the United States. It may not be important to the question in hand, therefore, that Her Majesty had taken the action already stated.

It should be further observed that the particular "State of Louisiana" which concurred and participated in the destruction of the claimant's property was a rebel organization, existing and acting as much in hostility to the Government of the United States as was the Confederate States so called. It was in form and fact a creature unknown to the Constitution of the United States, and acting in hostility to it. It was an instrumentality of the rebellion. Its agency, therefore, in the spoliation of this cotton cannot be likened to the act of a State of the American Union claiming to exist under the Constitution; and any argument tending to show that under international law the National Government is liable to answer for wrongs committed by such a State upon the subjects of a foreign power, can have no application to the matter now under consideration. The question presented is simply whether the Government of the United States is liable to answer to a neutral for the acts of those in rebellion against it, under the circumstances stated, who never succeeded in establishing a government. It is not deemed necessary in this case to inquire whether the claimant, having a commercial domicile in Louisiana at the time, is to be deemed a British "subject of Her Britannic Majesty" in the sense of Article XII of the treaty which creates this commission. That question is argued by counsel, but it is thought better to meet the question above stated for the reason that the case will thereby be determined more distinctly upon its merits.

The statement of the question would seem to render it unnecessary to discuss it. It is not the case of a government established *de facto* displacing the government *de jure;* but it is the case merely of an unsuccessful effort in that direction, which, for the time being, interrupted the course of lawful government without the fault of the latter.

Its acts were lawless and criminal, and could result in no liability on the part of the Government of the United States.

[118] Senator Howe, in Senate Report No. 412, third session Forty-second Congress, February 7, 1873, said:

"In September, 1871, immediately upon the close of the Franco-German war, France, although defeated and subjected to the payment of a fine of 3,000,000,000 of francs to her conquerors, did not ask to avoid the obligation of making compensation to her despoiled subjects. Accordingly, the national assembly provided not only for the payment of all private damages inflicted by the French authorities, but also provided for the repayment of all exactions made upon French subjects in the name of taxes by the German authorities. The same decree appropriated 100,000,000 of francs, to be placed at once in the hands of the ministers of the interior and of finance, to be apportioned between the most necessitous victims of the war, and appropriated a further sum of 6,000,000 of francs to be distributed by the same ministers 'among those who suffered the most in the operations attending the attack made by the French army to gain entrance into Paris.' A translation of the whole decree is appended to this report."

[Official journal of the French republic, Versailles, September 11, 1871.]

*The National Assembly has adopted—the President of the French Republic promulgates the law, the tenor of which is as follows:*

Considering that, during the late war, the portion of the territory invaded by the enemy bore exactions and suffered devastations without number; that the sense of patriotism which animates the heart of the French people enjoins upon the government the duty of indemnifying those who have, in the common conflict, undergone these exceptional privations, the National Assembly, without intending to depart from the principles laid down in the law of July 10, 1791, and the decree of August 10, 1853, decree:

In the discussions which preceded the "Provisional Articles" of November 30, 1782, (8 Stat., 54,) and the "definitive treaty of peace,"

---

ARTICLE 1. An indemnification will be allowed to all those who have borne, during the invasion, the contributions of war-requisitions, either in money or in kind, fines, and material damages.

ART. 2. These contributions, requisitions, fines, and damages will be verified and estimated by the cantonal commissions who act for the time being under the direction of the minister of the interior. A departmental commission will revise the labor of the cantonal commissions and fix the definite sum-total of the losses proven. This commission will be composed of the *préfét*, president, four counsellors-general, designated by the council-general, and of four representatives of the ministers of the interior and finances.

ART. 3. When the extent of the losses shall have been thus verified, a law will fix the sum the state of the public treasury will permit to be appropriated for their indemnification, and determine the distribution of the same.

A sum of one hundred millions will be immediately placed at the disposition of the minister of the interior and of the minister of finances, and apportioned between the departments *pro rata*, according to the losses respectively proven, to be distributed by the *préfét*, assisted by a commission appointed by the council-general and taken from its number, between the most necessitous victims of the war, and the *communes* the most involved in debt. This first allowance will be part of the sum-total assigned to each department to be distributed among all the claimants.

ART. 4. A sum of six million francs is placed equally at the disposition of the ministers of the finances and of the interior, to be, without further legislative enactment, distributed among those who suffered the most in the operations attending the attack made by the French army to gain re-entrance into Paris.

ART. 5. Independently of the preceding provisions the contributions in money collected under the title of taxes by the German authorities will be settled as follows:

SECTION 1. The *communes* that have paid any sums under the title of taxes will be re-imbursed their advances by the treasury.

SEC. 2. The tax-payers who will prove payment of any sum under the same title, either into the hands of the Germans or to the French municipal authorities, will be permitted to apply the whole sum on account of their contributions for 1870 and 1871. They will be required to produce their vouchers within the period of a month.

SEC. 3. The settlement specified above will comprise:

1. The whole sum of the French direct tax.

2. The double of that tax, as showing the indirect taxes levied by the Prussians. All that which in the payments will exceed the direct tax doubled will be considered as simple contribution of war, and governed by the principles laid down in the preceding article.

Deliberated in public sessions, at Versailles, July 3, August 8, and September 6, 1871.

*President:*

JULES GRÉVY.

*Secretaries:*

PAUL BETHMONT.
VISCOMPTE DE MEAUX.
PAUL DE RÉMUSAT.
BARON DE BARANTE.
MARQUIS DE CASTELLANA.
N. JOHNSTON.

*President of the republic:*

A. THIERS.

*Minister of the interior:*

F. LAMBRECHT.

By the act of March 30, 1862, 2 Stat., 143, the United States, subject to certain limitations, "guarantee to the party injured an eventual indemnification in respect to" certain property "taken, stolen, or destroyed" by Indians, under certain circumstances. The act of June 30, 1834, 4 Stat., 731, does the same. But these look to reclamation from Indian tribes. (S. Rep. of Committee of Claims, No. 12, 1st session 43d Cong., January 19, 1874.

And see act February 28, 1859, sec. 8, 11 Stat., 401; joint resolution June 25, 1860, 12 Stat., 120; act July 15, 1870, sec. 4, 16 Stat., 360; act May 29, 1872, sec. 7, 17 Stat., 190; and see as to Indians H. Rep. No. 780, 1st session 43d Cong., Committee on Indian Affairs on claim of Fletcher.

Certain other statutes secure compensation for damage done by the enemy: Act April 9, 1816, 3 Stat., 263, sec. 9. (See as to this American State Papers, Claims, 486, Report December 17, 1816.) Act March 3, 1817, 3 Stat., 397, sec. 1, injury to military de-

of September 3, 1783, (8 Stat., 80,) between Great Britain and the United States, the subject of indemnity for war-damages was considered.

posits. Act March 3, 1849, ch. 129, sec. 2, 9 Stat., 414, loss or destruction of property in service by contract or impressment.

The argument on behalf of Frederick City, in H. Rep., Committee on War-Claims, 1st session 43d Cong., June 22, 1874, says:

"Among other instances in which compensation for injuries inflicted by the public enemy has been granted by Congress, without specially distinguishing the particular case in exercising its bounty, we would mention the following acts, the body of which we quote, and which, it will be seen, suggest no reasons for affording the relief but the bare statement of the loss sustained. Possibly, the evidence on which these acts were based may have disclosed some grounds of discrimination; but as these are omitted in the laws themselves, while in other acts of a kindred character they have been expressed, it would seem that, in the cases in question, Congress did not consider itself bound to confine its generosity within limitations suggestive of legal responsibility, and thus indicated the policy of extending relief whenever a citizen had been subjected to a greatly disproportionate share of loss in a common struggle, even at the hands of those with whom we are at war."

The precedents indicated are as follows: Act of 1822, chap. 65: William Henderson compensated "for value of his property destroyed by the enemy during the late war, at Monday's Point, Virginia;" act of 1832, chap. 271: John Brunson, "for house and store in the village of Buffalo, N. Y., destroyed by the enemy;" act of 1832, chap. 292: Augustine Taney, "for destruction by fire of buildings on Soller's Point, near Baltimore, by the enemy during the late war;" act of 1836, chap. 33: Legal representatives of Thomas Beacham, "for the value of a barn in Northumberland County, Virginia, burned by the British in the late war;" act of 1836, chap. 241: Heirs of William Forbes, "for certain houses which were destroyed at Kinsella, Virginia, by the enemy in the late war with Great Britain;" act of 1836, chap. 307: Charles Cattell, "for tobacco destroyed by *British or American* troops in Maryland;" act of 1838, chap. 43: James Pattison, "for his house and property on the Patuxent, destroyed by British troops:" act of 1838, chap. 49: William Eadres, "for his house burned by the British at Sodus, New York;" act of 1842, chap. 212: John King, "for dwelling-house burned by the British in Richmond County, Virginia, during the late war."

This list might be extended, but is probably sufficient for illustration. These cases, with many similar ones, may be found in United States Statutes at Large, vol. 6, Private Laws, to which reference is made.

Act June 25, 1864, 13 Stat., 182, horses of military persons surrendered by order of superior officers. See Senate Rep. 137, 1st sess. 34th Cong., April 18, 1856, in favor of paying for personal property destroyed by the enemy in the war of 1812. The committee held that where property was used by the Government, and the enemy destroyed it in consequence of that use, it should be paid for. Congress did not pass the bill recommended by the committee.

The legislature of Ohio, by act of March 30, 1864, (61 Ohio Laws, 85,) provided for a commission "to examine claims of citizens of this State for property taken, destroyed, or injured by rebels or Union forces within this State during the Morgan raid in 1863."

This act makes three classes of claims:

1. For property taken, destroyed, or injured by rebels.
2. By Union forces under command of United States officers.
3. By Union forces not under command of United States officers.

On the 15th December, 1864, the commissioners made their report to the governor, showing claims made, $678,915.03, on which was allowed $576,225. This consisted of "damages by the rebels," $428,168; "damages by Union forces under command of United States officers," $141,855; and "damages by Union forces not under command of United States officers," $6,202. The report does not distinguish between property taken and that damaged or destroyed.

The act of April 27, 1872, (69 Laws, 176,) authorized a re-examination of these claims.

The act of May 5, 1873, appropriates $11,539.56 to pay claims under class three, as classified under the act of April 27, 1872, (70 Laws, 260.) The same act (p. 265) requires the governor to appoint a commissioner to proceed to Washington to urge upon the proper officers of the Government or Congress the payment of all just claims of the people of Ohio growing out of the Morgan raid.

The legislature of Pennsylvania also made provision for indemnifying citizens of Chambersburgh for property destroyed by the rebel invasion.

See act approved April 9, 1868, No. 39, laws of 1868, p. 74. This act provides for the appointment of commissioners to investigate claims of citizens in counties invaded by rebel forces "for the amount of their losses in the late war."

The preamble to this act recites that "during the late war to suppress the rebellion several of the southern counties of this State were several times invaded by the rebels in great force," and that "there was occasioned great destruction, devastation, and

There is a brief account of these in "The works of John Adams, second President of the United States, with a life of the author, notes and illustrations by his grandson, Charles Francis Adams. Vol. 1. Boston: Little, Brown & Co., 1856;" The writer says, (page 387, &c.:)

One other obstacle had been in the way, the more difficult to remove, that it rested on a point of honor in the British heart. Those individuals who had taken the side of the mother country in the colonies, and who, for doing so, had been subjected to the mortification, disasters, and personal losses consequent upon a failure to re-establish her authority, naturally looked to her to protect their rights, in any and every attempt that might be made at accommodation. And this was a valid claim on her, in spite of the fact of the difficulties into which the mother country had fallen were mainly owing to the interested misrepresentations made by leading persons of this class in America. On this point, the instructions to obtain an acknowledgment of their claims to indemnity had been most positive. But the American commissioners, on their side well knowing the impossibility of reconciling their countrymen to the acknowledgment of such odious pretensions, and little disposed themselves to recognize their validity, manifested no inclination to concede anything beyond what the strict rule of justice would demand. Here Dr. Franklin took the lead; finding that the British were about to urge their views on this subject and the fisheries together, he prepared an article, making, by way of set-off, a counter-claim of compensation for the severe and not unfrequently wanton injuries inflicted upon the patriots by the British troops. Neither did this lose force by its reference to the voluntary acts of those very adherents to the British cause, whose pretensions were set up for consideration. The fact that this contest had, in many of its parts, been marked with the most painful characteristics of civil convulsion, in the course of which the parties had suffered shocking outrages from each other, was too well known to be denied; and the wounds were too fresh to permit the supposition that the victorious side would be prepared at once to replace in their former position those of their brethren who had not only forfeited their confidence by joining the oppressor, but had been guilty of the greatest barbarities in conducting the struggle. The earnest and strenuous resistance of Dr. Franklin, re-inforced by the representations of the other commissioners, at last produced an effect in convincing the British envoys that further urgency in their behalf was useless. To prolong the war a single day only for their sakes, without prospect of a better result, was obviously a waste of means, which might be better employed in supplying the very remuneration which was now in agitation. The good sense of Mr. Fitzherbert, confirming that of Mr. Oswald, prevailed, and this troublesome discussion was finally terminated by the preparation of two articles to which all agreed, providing that further hostilities to the tories should cease, and that Congress should earnestly recommend to the States the restitution of their estates to such persons as could be proved to be real British subjects, and such Americans as had not borne arms against the United States.

---

loss of property of citizens," and "these losses were sustained in the common cause, and for the general welfare of the whole people of this Commonwealth, and it is *reasonable and proper* that citizens who have thus suffered should receive *generous consideration* and active relief from this great Commonwealth," &c.

The governor of Pennsylvania has furnished the following:

EXECUTIVE CHAMBER, *Harrisburgh, Pa., March* —, 1874.

*Statement of war-claims.*

| | |
|---|---|
| Adams County | $489,438 99 |
| Fulton County | 56,544 98 |
| Franklin County, burning of Chambersburgh | 1,625,435 55 |
| Franklin County, other claims | 846,053 30 |
| Cumberland County | 211,778 95½ |
| York County | 214,720 05 |
| Bedford County | 6,818 03 |
| Somerset County | 120 00 |
| | 3,450,909 85½ |

*Amounts paid.*

| | |
|---|---|
| Under act of August 20, 1864 | $100,000 |
| Under act of February 15, 1866 | 500,000 |
| Under act of May 27, 1871 | 300,000 |

Commission to re-examine and re-adjudicate was raised under act of May 22, 1871. (P. L. 1871, p. 272.)

It will be seen that this act does not put the claims upon the ground of a *legal right* to demand compensation, but on the *ground of generosity.*

There is a work entitled the Diplomatic Correspondence of the American Revolution, being the letters of Benjamin Franklin, Silas Deane, John Adams, John Jay, Arthur Lee, Wm. Lee, Ralph Izard, Francis Dana, Wm. Carmichael, Henry Laurens, M. De Lafayette, M. Dumas, and others, concerning the foreign relations of the United States during the whole Revolution, together with the letters in reply from the Secret Committee of Congress and the secretary of foreign affairs; also the entire correspondence of the French ministers, Gerard and Luzerne, with Congress. Published under the direction of the President of the United States from the original manuscripts in the Department of State, conformably to a resolution of Congress of March 27, 1818. Edited by Jared Sparks. Volume X. Boston: Nathan Hale and Gray & Brown; 1830.

The proposed article will be found in this work (p. 106, &c.,) as follows:

*Article proposed and read to the commissioners before signing the preliminary articles.*

It is agreed that His Britannic Majesty will earnestly recommend it to his Parliament to provide for and make a compensation to the merchants and shop-keepers of Boston, whose goods and merchandise were seized and taken out of their stores, warehouses, and shops, by order of General Gage and others of his commanders, and officers there, and also to the inhabitants of Philadelphia, for the goods taken away by his army there, and to make compensation also for the tobacco, rice, indigo, and negroes, &c., seized and carried off by his armies under Generals Arnold, Cornwallis, and others, from the States of Virginia, North and South Carolina, and Georgia, and also for all vessels and cargoes belonging to the inhabitants of the said United States, which were stopped, seized, or taken, either in the ports, or on the seas, by his governors, or by his ships of war, before the declaration of war against the said States.

FACTS.

There existed a free commerce, upon mutual faith between Great Britain and America. The merchants of the former credited the merchants and planters of the latter with great quantities of goods, on the common expectation that the merchants having sold the goods, would make the accustomed remittance; that the planters would do the same by the labor of their negroes, and the produce of that labor, tobacco, rice, indigo, &c.

England, before the goods were sold in America, sends an armed force, seizes those goods in the stores—some even in the ships that brought them—and carries them off; seizes, also, and carries off the tobacco, rice, and indigo provided by the planters to make returns, and even the negroes, from whose labor they might hope to raise other produce for that purpose.

Britain now demands that the debts shall, nevertheless, be paid.

Will she, can she, justly refuse making compensation for such seizures?

If a draper, who had sold a piece of linen to a neighbor on credit, should follow him, take the linen from him by force, and then send a bailiff to arrest him for the debt, would any court of equity award the payment of the debt without ordering a restitution of the cloth?

Will not the debtors in America cry out that, if this compensation be not made, they were betrayed by the pretended credit, and are now doubly ruined; first by the enemy, and then by the negotiators at Paris, the goods and negroes sold them being taken from them, with all they had besides, and they are now to be obliged to pay for what they have been robbed off?

But the article was not agreed on.

There is in the fourth volume of the secret journals of the Congress of the Confederation, prior to the treaty of peace, much information on this subject. The result of all is that, on principles of international law, nations do not recognize a liability to indemnify citizens who suffer osses from acts of the public enemy in war.

There is a class of cases which may be said in some sense to form an exception to this rule.

A receiver of public money is not accountable for funds in his hands which were *forcibly* seized by the rebel authorities during the rebellion, against his will and without fault or negligence on his part. (United States *v.* Thomas, 15 Wallace, 337.)

But in such case he is not protected if he has neglected to promptly disburse or pay money into the Treasury as his duty requires. (Bevans *v.* United States, 13 Wallace, 56; Halliburton *v.* United States, 13 Wallace, 63. See, also, the report of the Committee on War-Claims in House of Representatives, second session Forty-third Congress, as to the so-called Saint Albans raid, and report of Senate Committee on Claims as to the claim of the First National Bank of Saint Albans to be indemnified for loss of Government bonds in the bank seized and carried away by the rebel raiders.)

There is another class of cases in which compensation is sometimes provided for damages inflicted by the enemy. During the rebellion in the United States the rebels frequently made raids on loyal citizens in the insurrectionary States and carried away and destroyed their property. In such cases the Union military authorities sometimes made and collected assessments on disloyal citizens in the vicinity of the raids, and with it indemnified the parties suffering loss. One object of this was to give indemnity and protection to loyal citizens, and another was to discourage such raids and to make disloyal citizens earnest in opposing them. The indemnity-money in such cases was generally paid by the military authorities directly to the parties injured. If for any cause they were absent or could not be found, the money was used by the Army or paid into the Treasury. When so used or paid the Government has deemed it just to pay, on proper application and proof, by special act of Congress.[119]

---

## CHAPTER IV.

### PROPERTY DESTROYED OR DAMAGED IN BATTLE BY THE GOVERNMENT FORCES, OR WANTONLY, OR UNAUTHORIZED BY ITS OWN TROOPS.

The American rule of international law was early adopted, that the Government was under no obligation to compensate its citizens for property destroyed or damages done in battle or by necessary military operations in repelling an invading enemy.[120]

To this rule Alexander Hamilton added that—

> According to the laws and usages of nations a state is not obliged to make compensation for damages done to its citizens * * wantonly or unauthorized by its own troops.[121]

This is the general rule which is recognized now.[122]

---

[119] This subject is discussed in the debate in the House of Representatives February 12, 1875, on a bill for the relief of John Aldridge.

[120] American State Papers, Claims, 199, February 15, 1797: A committee of the House of Representatives made a report on a claim for "compensation for a dwelling-house burned in Massachusetts, in March, 1776, by order of General Sullivan, commanding the American troops. The house was in possession of British troops, and for the purpose of dislodging them General Sullivan sent troops with orders to set fire to the building, which was done."

The committee say: "The loss of houses, and other sufferings by the general ravages of war, have never been compensated by this or any other government. In the history of our Revolution sundry decisions of Congress against claims of this nature may be found. Government has not adopted a general rule to compensate individuals who have suffered in a similar manner."

[121] Report to Congress, November 19, 1792; American State Papers, Claims, 55.

[122] In the report made November 30, 1873, by Hon. Robert S. Hale, counsel of the United States before the commission of claims under the 12th article of treaty of 8th May, 1871, between the United States and Great Britain, is a statement of claims made by citizens of Great Britain against the United States, and the decision thereon as follows:

"In the case of Thomas Stirling, No. 12, were included as well claims for property

It has been said, again, that—

No government, but for a special favor, has ever paid for property even of its own citizens, destroyed in its own country, on attacking or defending itself against a common public enemy, much less is any government obliged to pay for property belonging to neutrals domiciled in the country of its enemy which may possibly be destroyed by its forces in their operations against such enemy.[123]

Mr. Seward, Secretary of State, said, in relation to a claim made upon the United States by a French subject for property destroyed by the bombardment of Greytown, in July, 1854, that—

The British government, upon the advice of the law-officers of the Crown, declared to Parliament its inability to prosecute similar claims. In 1857 Lord Palmerston applied the decision in the case of Greytown as a precedent for refusing compensation to British merchants whose property in a Russian port had been destroyed by a British squadron during the Crimean war. (See note in Lawrence's Wheaton, p. 145.)

The governments of Austria and Russia have applied the doctrine involved in the Greytown case to the claims of British subjects injured by belligerent operations in Italy in 1849 and 1850. (See note p. 49, vol. 2, of Vattel, Guilaumin & Co.'s edition, 1863.)

We have applied the same principle in declining to make reclamations for citizens of the United States whose property was destroyed in the bombardment of Valparaiso by a Spanish fleet, and in resisting the claims of subjects of neutral powers who sustained injury from our military operations in the Southern States during the recent rebellion. It will probably be found a sufficient answer to the reclamations of many of our citizens who have sustained losses from belligerent operations on both sides during the recent occupation of Mexico by French troops.[124]

---

destroyed by the United States Army in its marches and encampments in the State of Virginia, as for horses, carriages, cattle, hogs, flour, corn, and bacon alleged to have been taken and carried off by the soldiers. The proofs showed nothing beyond the disappearance of the property in the presence of the United States Army. The decision of the commission, in which all the commissioners joined, was made in the following words:

"The acts done upon which this claim is based seem to have been the ordinary results incident to the march of an invading army in a hostile territory, with possibly some unauthorized acts of destruction and pillage by the soldiery, with no proof of appropriation by the United States. Under such circumstances there is ground for a valid claim against the United States. The claim is, therefore, disallowed."

"In the case of the Misses Hayes, No. 100, milliners, at Jackson, Miss., a claim was made for a stock of millinery goods and like property, alleged to have been taken by soldiers of the United States Army on the first capture of Jackson, in May, 1863. The acts complained of appeared, if committed by United States soldiers, to have been acts of pillage merely, and the claim was unanimously disallowed."

"In the cases of Michael Grace, No. 132, Elizabeth Bostock, No. 133, Thomas McMahon, No. 136, and others, at Savannah, being claims for property alleged to have been taken and appropriated by United States soldiers, the same appeared to have been by acts of unauthorized pillage, and were rejected."

And Mr. Hale says, again, as to property taken, "where the property was in its nature not a proper subject of military use, or, being such, was not applied to military use, or where the taking appeared to be mere acts of unauthorized pillage or marauding, the claims were disallowed."

And again, page 50:

"In several cases there were allegations of the wanton destruction of property by United States troops, and in some cases satisfactory proof was made of the fact of such destruction by soldiers without command or authority of their commanding officers and in defiance of orders.

"In the case of Anthony Barclay, No. 5, allegations were made of wanton destruction of property, including valuable furniture, china, pictures, and other works of art, books, &c. The proof was conflicting as to whether the injuries alleged were committed by soldiers or not; but if committed by soldiers, it was plainly not only without authority, but in direct violation of the orders of General Sherman. In the award made in favor of Mr. Barclay, I am advised that nothing was included for property alleged to have been destroyed.

"For property alleged to have been wantonly and without provocation or military necessity destroyed or injured in the enemy's country, as in the cases of Anthony Barclay, No. 5; Godfrey Barnsley, No. 162, and in the Columia cases."

The claims were not allowed.

[123] Perrin *vs.* U. S., 4 Court Claims, 547.

[124] Letter to Hon. Charles Sumner, February 26, 1868, 4 Court Claims R., 548.

This is the rule recognized by Vattel, who says: "But there are other damages caused by inevitable necessity; as, for instance, the destruction caused by the artillery in retaking a town from the enemy. These are merely accidents. They are misfortunes, which chance deals out to the proprietors on whom they happen to fall. * * No action lies against the state for misfortunes of this nature; for losses which she has occasioned, not willfully, but through necessity and by mere accident in the exertion of her rights."[125]

These principles are generally recognized, and any departure from them rests on mere gratuity or other exceptional reasons.[126]

---

## CHAPTER V.

### TEMPORARY OCCUPATION OF, INJURIES TO, AND DESTRUCTION OF PROPERTY CAUSED BY ACTUAL AND NECESSARY GOVERNMENT MILITARY OPERATIONS TO REPEL A THREATENED ATTACK OF, OR IN ADVANCING TO MEET, AN ENEMY IN FLAGRANT WAR.[127]

By the principles of universal law recognized anterior to the Constitution, in force when it was adopted, and never abrogated, every civilized nation is in duty bound to pay for army supplies taken from its loyal citizens, and for all property voluntarily taken for or devoted to "public use."

But there is a class of cases in which property, real or personal, of loyal citizens may be temporarily occupied or injured, or even destroyed, on the theater of and by military operations, either in a loyal State or in enemy's country, in time of war, as a military necessity. The advance or retreat of an army may necessarily destroy roads, bridges, fences, and growing crops.

In self-defense an army may, of necessity, erect forts, construct embankments, and seize cotton-bales, timber, or stone, to make barricades.

In battle or immediately after, and when it may be impossible to procure property in any regular mode by contract or impressment, self-preservation and humanity may require the temporary occupancy of houses for hospitals for wounded soldiers, or for the shelter of troops, and for necessary military operations which admit of neither choice nor delay.

In these and similar cases the question arises whether there is a deliberate voluntary taking of property for public use requiring compensation, or whether these acts arise from and are governed by the law of overruling military necessity—mere accidents of war inevitably and unavoidably incidental to its operations—and which by international law impose no obligation to make recompense. It seems quite clear that they are of this latter class.

This is so upon reason, authority, and the usage of nations.

---

[125] Vattel, book 3, ch. xv, § 232, p. 403.

[126] In report of Hon. R. S. Hale to Secretary of State, Nov. 30, 1873, of the proceedings of the commission under 12 art., treaty of 8 May, 1871, between United States and Great Britain, it is said, "In the case of Watkins and Donnelly, administrators, No. 329, an award was made against the United States, in which all the commissioners joined, for property pillaged by United States soldiers in the night from a country store in Missouri, a State not in insurrection, upon proof showing great neglect of discipline on the part of Colonel Jennison, the commanding officer, and his neglect and refusal to take any steps for the surrender of the stolen property or the punishment of the offenders when notified of the facts, and that a part, at least, of *the stolen property was then in possession of his troops.*"

[127] See this subject discussed somewhat in notes 53–64.

Most of the considerations applicable to the destruction of property in battle, or to prevent it from falling into the hands of the enemy, are equally appropriate here. Some of these have been and others will hereafter be more fully stated. And if property may be so destroyed without incurring liability, why may not property temporarily occupied or even damaged, when the purpose is the same, to prevent it from being useful to the enemy? The greater includes the less. These cases rest on principles entirely distinct from those which relate to and govern ordinary army supplies. There is no reason why one citizen should furnish quartermaster's or commissary supplies rather than another. The Government can, as to these, exercise a discretion; it can buy from any who may have to sell, or select those from whom it will impress. Here is a deliberate voluntary taking for public use.

But an army advancing to meet an enemy has no discretion in selecting its route. The public safety compels it to pursue that which is most practicable.

If crops stand in the way, their destruction by the march may be inevitable and unavoidable, a mere accident and incident of military operations, as much so as the destruction caused by battle.

On principle, the Government cannot be liable to make restitution for the damage, unless it has assumed to do so by an implied contract or has been guilty of a wrong.

There is in such case no contract, for this implies consent, deliberation, choice. It implies that what is done is not done as of right or by lawful authority, but by consent of all parties in interest. "If a man is assaulted, he may (lawfully) fly through another's close," and he does not thereby become a party to a contract to pay any damage he does,[128] because his act is lawful. It is the exercise of a legal right.

So a nation, on the same principle, makes no implied promise to pay when its army retreats from a pursuing enemy or advances to prevent his blow.

Nor is a nation in such case liable as a trespasser or wrong-doer. "A trespass * * from the very nature of the term *transgressio* imports to go beyond what is right."[129] An army in its march performs an imperative duty—justified by the law of nations—required by the public safety.

The rule has been thus stated by the late solicitor of the War Department:

> If one of our armies marches across a corn-field, and so destroys a growing crop, or fires a building which conceals or protects the enemy, or cuts down timber to open a passage for troops through a forest, the owner of such property, citizen or alien, has no legal claim to have his losses made up to him by the United States. Misfortunes like these must be borne wherever they fall. If any government is obliged to guarantee its subjects against losses by casualties of public war, such obligations must be founded upon some constitutional or statute law. Thus far no such obligations have been recognized in our system of congressional legislation. (Whiting's War-Powers, 43d ed., 1871, p. 340.)

Damages done by the erection of forts, the seizure of timber or materials for barricades, under pressure of military necessity, give no legal right to compensation.

"In time of war," said the supreme court of Pennsylvania, "bulwarks

---

[128] 5 Bacon, Abr., 183; Respublica *v.* Sparhawk, 1 Dallas, Pa., 362.

[129] 5 Bacon, Abr., 150; Respublica *v.* Sparhawk, 1 Dallas, 362.

In Perrin *v.* United States, 4 C. of Cls. R., 547, where a French subject made a claim against the Government for property destroyed by the bombardment of Greytown, the court said:

"The claimant's case must necessarily rest upon the assumption that the bombardment and destruction of Greytown was illegal, and not justified by the law of nations."

may be built on private ground, and the reason assigned is * * because it is for the public safety."[130]

It is a lawful act, imposing no liability on the Government, which is guilty of no wrong, and which makes no promise by the act.

In principle it can make no difference whether a forest or cotton-bales are destroyed by cannonading in battle, in case an army seeks shelter behind them, or seizes them in advance to throw up breastworks for safety.[131] Yet all writers agree that a nation is not bound to make compensation in such cases as these.

The same position has been judicially assumed. The supreme court of Georgia has said:

It is not to be doubted but that there are cases in which private property may be taken for a public use without the consent of the owner, and without compensation, and without any provision of law for making compensation. There are cases of urgent public necessity, which no law has anticipated, and which cannot await the action of the legislature. In such cases the injured individual has no redress at law—those who seize the property are not trespassers—and there is no relief for him but by petition to the legislature: for example, the pulling down of houses and raising bulwarks for the defense of the State against an enemy, seizing corn and other provisions for the sustenance of an army in time of war, or taking cotton-bags, as General Jackson did at New Orleans, to build ramparts against an invading foe.[132]

---

[130] Respublica *v.* Sparhawk, 1 Dallas, 362; Dyer, 8; Brook's Trespass, 213; 5 Bacon, Abr., 175; 20 Viner, Abr., (Trespass,) B, a, sec. 4, fo. 476.

[131] The report of Hon. R. S. Hale to the Secretary of State, November 30, 1873, as to claims of British subjects before the American-British claims commission, under article 12, treaty of May 8, 1871, shows that claims of this character were unanimously rejected. The report says, p. 49:

"2.—*Claims for property alleged to have been wrongfully injured or destroyed by the forces of the United States.*

"These claims were also numerous, and involved a large variety of questions. They included claims for property injured or destroyed by the bombardment of towns of the enemy, as in the case of Charles Cleworth, No. 48; and in other ordinary operations of war, such as the passage of armies, the erection of fortifications, as in the case of Trook, administrator, No. 58, &c.

"Also, for timber felled in front of forts and batteries to give clear range for the guns and deprive the enemy of cover, as in the cases of Trook, administrator, No. 58, and of William B. Booth, No. 143.

"In these claims for destruction of property, it may be stated generally that, with very few exceptions, and those mostly insignificant, no awards were made against the United States.

"The claims for injuries by bombardment, the passage of armies, the cutting of timber to clear away obstructions, the erection of fortifications, &c., in the enemy's country, were all disallowed by the unanimous voice of the commissioners.

"The same may be said of the incidental destruction of innocent property involved in the destruction of public stores and works of the enemy." These were in the States proclaimed in insurrection and they asked compensation for property damaged or destroyed in battle.

[132] 1. Parham *vs.* The Justices, &c., 9 Georgia R., 341. See report, November 30, 1873, of Hon. R. S. Hale to Secretary of State, of claims decided by commission under 12th article of treaty of May 8, 1871, between United States and Great Britain, pages 44–235. Commissioner Frazer said, as to cotton seized by the United States military forces under orders of General Banks, in Louisiana, and used for fortifications, "No citizen of the United States could, under like circumstances, claim compensation." He adds:

"2. The cotton was the property of an enemy of the United States, so recognized by every writer upon international law and so held by all tribunals, both American and British, as well as continental, in every reported case involving the question. The mixed commission, constituted under the convention of 1853, between the two countries, so held in Laurent's case. Indeed, it went further, and held that an unnaturalized Englishman voluntatily domiciled in a country at war with the United States was not even to be regarded as a British subject; thus going a little too far, as I think.

"The property of Henderson was as liable to capture as the property of Jeff. Davis himself, or any rebel in arms. I believe this is not questioned. That the property itself was a proper subject of capture on land under the modern rules by which civil ized nations govern themselves in war, seems to me to be quite as clear.

"The legislation and the known practice of the rebel authorities made it so. They

The same principle was stated in a report made by the Committee on Claims to the House of Representatives December 11, 1820. From this report it appeared that a claimant alleged that—

She was possessed of a plantation, with sundry buildings, situated below New Orleans, and that during the invasion by the enemy in December, 1814, and subsequently, her dwelling-house was occupied as quarters for some of the officers and a hospital for the sick and wounded, and, while so occupied, her house, outhouses, fences, &c., were damaged.

She claimed compensation for use and occupation and for damages.

The committee in their report say, in effect, that compensation cannot be claimed by virtue of the constitutional provision as to taking "private property for public use," because this provision—

Seems to imply a *voluntary act* on the part of the Government, which in the present case could hardly be alleged, particularly as it respects a large portion of it. * * * There are no *known rules* or established usage of the Government which would seem to authorize an allowance in a case thus involved in obscurity.[133]

The Government has always paid loyal citizens for the use and occupation of buildings and grounds in loyal States when used for officers' quarters, regular recruiting camps, and in cases where the occupation was voluntary and the result of choice, superinduced by no overruling military necessity, and for this the law provides.[134]

---

made cotton the basis of their public credit by a policy which aimed to deal largely in it on Government account, to purchase it even before it was grown, and hypothecate it as security for the payment of loans, with the proceeds of which they did, to a large extent, supply themselves with arms and munitions of war, and with a fleet of armed vessels to infest the ocean and destroy American commerce. They committed it to the flames, whether owned by friend or foe, rather than permit it to reach the markets of the world otherwise than through their own ports; thus endeavoring by warlike operations to secure to themselves a monopoly in supplying the foreign demand, that they might thereby constrain nations abroad to aid them in their struggle. In short, cotton was a special and formidable foundation of the rebel military power. It was more important than arms or ships of war, for it supplied these and all else beside. It was more potent than gold, for it not only commanded gold, but it largely enlisted in behalf of the rebels the interests of foreigners whose manufacturing industry was in a measure paralyzed because this staple was needed to keep it in motion. The necessities and purposes of war, therefore, required its capture at every opportunity more imperatively than the capture of munitions and implements of war; indeed, that necessity was quite as pressing and certainly as humane as the killing of men in battle; for it was no less efficient as a means of accomplishing the subjugation of the rebel armies, and re-establishing the national authority. It is to me astonishing if there is a difference of opinion upon this subject.

"The Supreme Court of the United States, recognizing to the fullest extent all the limitations which the practice of nations has lately engrafted upon the right of capture upon land, so held in the case of a loyal American widow. (See the case of Mrs. Alexander's cotton, 2 Black.) This is high authority, especially when it is remembered that that august tribunal has certainly exhibited no tendency whatever to give undue license to military authority or warlike operations. Complaint, if any, has been altogether in the other direction. But I would be quite content, in the absence of any authority, to trust the question with the common sense of all civilized nations so long as war in any form shall be recognized as a lawful method of deciding differences. If the capture was rightful by laws of war, it would be a novelty in international law that its exercise involves an obligation to make compensation."

The commission allowed the claim, *a voucher having been given by military officer*, "by order of Col. S. B. Holabird, for the United States Government."

133 But the report concludes that "in a case of such extreme apparent hardship, it would best comport with the dictates of sound policy that in the exercise of the *discretion* of Congress *some* relief should be granted." (American State Papers, Claims, class ix, p. 753. Here the relief is put on the ground of a discretion, not *law*.) (See act March 2, 1821, 6 Stat., 258.)

134 House Ex. Doc. No. 124, 1st sess. 43d Congress; see letter of Quartermaster-General M. C. Meigs, February 19, 1874, in part 2 of this report, and letter February 26, 1874, in appendix to this report; act July 16, 1798, sec. 3, ch. 85; act May 8, 1792, sec. 5; act March 3, 1799, sec. 24, ch. 48; United States *vs.* Speed, 8 Wallace, 83; Stevens *vs.* United States, 2 N. & H. Court Claims, 101; Crowell's case, id., 501; McKenney *vs.* United States, 4 N. & H. Court Claims, 540; Wentworth *vs.* United States, 5 Court Claims, 309; Scott's Digest Military Laws, 1873, p. 102, sec. 96, &c.

But a temporary occupancy of real estate imposed by overruling necessity—an occupancy continued during the actual existence of such impending necessity—or the application of materials to purposes of defense in an emergency, has not, by the usage of the Government, been regarded as giving any claim for compensation.

This has been the uniform usage of the War Department, founded on the opinion not only of the Solicitor, but also of the Judge-Advocate-General.[135]

The Executive Department of the Government has laid down certain rules of law in relation to some questions growing out of the war of the rebellion.

The President, in his message of June 1, 1873, said:

It is a general principle of both international and municipal law that all property is held subject not only to be taken by the Government for public uses, in which case, under the Constitution of the United States, the owner is entitled to just compensation, *but also subject to be temporarily occupied*, or even actually destroyed, in times of great public danger and *when the public safety demands it;* and in this latter case governments do not admit a legal obligation on their part to compensate the owner. The

[135] See opinions of Judge-Advocates-General, vol. 20, pp. 598–525; vol. 26, pp. 52, 242, 247; id., 27, p. 304; Digest of Opinions of Judge-Advocates, 1868, pp. 97, 98. As an example, the following is presented:

WAR DEPARTMENT, BUREAU OF MILITARY JUSTICE,
*August* 4, 1866.

To the SECRETARY OF WAR:

Dr. W. P. Jones claims $35,000 for damages sustained by the erection by the United States of a fort upon his land near Nashville.

Major-General Thomas reports that he is thoroughly loyal, and recommends allowance of the claim.

In the case of N. Vignie, this Bureau, under date of May 7, 1863, submitted the following remarks:

"A clear distinction has always been recognized between the taking of real estate or personal property for such purposes, and the taking of the same for the ordinary uses of peace."

(Here follows a reference to Whiting's War-Powers, 340, and to 9 Georgia R., 341.)

Entertaining the conclusions pointed to by the two foregoing citations, this Bureau is of opinion that the claim under consideration, and others of like description, for compensation for the use of land taken and occupied by the forces of the United States for the sites of forts or other works of defense against the public enemy, must be rejected by the War Department, and all parties making such claims must be referred to Congress for relief, if they shall be deemed entitled to any under the general principles of the law of war.

If the above views are approved by the Department, this case, notwithstanding the loyalty of the claimant, must be referred to Congress.

W. WINTHROP,
*Brevet Colonel and Judge-Advocate, in the absence of the Judge-Advocate-General.*

Official copy, for the Hon. William Lawrence, M. C.

J. HOLT, *Judge-Advocate-General.*

The same principles have been reiterated since, (Digest of Opinions of Judge-Advocates-General, 97,) as follows:

"So held in the case of a claim arising in Tennessee during the war, for alleged damages sustained by the claimant in the erection by the military authorities of a fort upon his land. XXII, 304. So held in the case of the claim of an alleged Spanish subject for indemnity for the destruction of buildings and other property in Louisiana, in the course of the erection of fortifications by our forces. XX, 525. So held in the case of a claim for the value of certain buildings (with their contents) burned by our troops in West Virginia, in January, 1863, by way of a ruse to deceive and divert the enemy—a legitimate act of ordinary warfare—the loss incurred being one of those casualties for which the Government does not become liable to the individual injured. XXVI, 242. And see XXVI, 247, for a case of a claim (preferred subsequently to the passage of the act of February 19, 1867, and so expressly precluded from settlement) for the value of cotton seized at Knoxville, Tenn., in the enemy's country and on the theater of war, and used for strengthening a fort threatened with attack by the rebel forces. XXVI, 247."

temporary occupation of, injuries to, and destruction of property caused by actual and necessary military operations are generally considered to fall within the last-mentioned principle. If a government makes compensation under such circumstances, it is a matter of bounty rather than of strict legal right.[136]

## CHAPTER VI.

### PROPERTY WHICH MAY BE USEFUL TO THE ENEMY SEIZED AND DESTROYED OR DAMAGED TO PREVENT IT FROM FALLING INTO THEIR HANDS.

The question now to be considered is, whether the Government is liable to make compensation for the property of a loyal citizen in a loyal State seized and destroyed or damaged by competent military authority—*flagrante bello*—to prevent it from falling into the hands of the enemy, as an element of strength where warlike operations are in progress, or where the approach of the enemy is prospectively imminent.

The same law prevails when our territory is invaded by a foreign enemy or a loyal State by a rebel invading force.

It has been asserted with great emphasis that the duty to make compensation in such cases as have frequently arisen in each House of Congress—

> Is a principle not recognized by public law, by the law of nations, or any other code of law or morals known to the civilized world. It has never been applied by our own Government, by the government of Great Britain, or any other civilized government in the world.[137]

It has been said, on the contrary, with equal earnestness, that there has never been—

> One single instance in the whole history of this Government since the Constitution was adopted where a claimant of this kind has been turned from the doors of Congress unsatisfied.[138]

---

[136] Senate Ex. Doc. 85, 2 sess. 42 Cong., veto bill for relief of J. Milton Best.

In Senate Rep. 412, 3 sess. 42 Cong., it is said of this statement of the law by the President:

"The committee has not found any such general principle affirmed either in international or municipal law, but has found the very reverse of that to be affirmed by all law, international and municipal."

Among the text-writers, Vattel discusses the very question, "Is the state bound to indemnify individuals for the damage they have sustained in war?" But the report *omits to quote the next sentence* in Vattel, in which he says:

"We may learn from Grotius *that authors are divided on this question.*" Vattel then says:

"The damages under consideration are to be distinguished into two kinds—those done by the state itself or the sovereign, and those done by the enemy. Of the first kind some are done deliberately and by way of precaution, as when a field, a house, a garden, belonging to a private person, is taken for the purpose of erecting on the spot a town-rampart, or any other piece of fortification, or when his standing corn or his store-houses are destroyed to prevent their being of use to the enemy. *Such damages are to be made good to the individual, who should bear only his quota of the loss.*" But there are other damages caused by inevitable necessity; as, for instance, the destruction caused by the artillery in retaking a town from the enemy. These are merely accidents. They are misfortunes, which chance deals out to the proprietors on whom they happen to fall. (Vattel, 6th Am. ed., 402.)

The rule stated by Vattel is elsewhere hereafter referred to, and it is shown that its correctness has been denied in a note to the American edition of 1872, referring to 4th Term R., 382, and by Grotius and many other authorities.

[137] Roscoe Conkling in Senate, December 14, 1870, 82 Globe, 98, on claim of J. Milton Best; see President's veto-message, June 1, 1872.

[138] Senator Howe, January 4, 1871, 82 Globe, 302, referring to the claim of J. Milton Best.

In this conflict of opinion it becomes necessary to consider the question somewhat elaborately.

There are five modes in which the Government has a right to take or use private property:

1. By taxation.[139]

2. As punishment for crime under judicial sentence, or by sentence of a court-martial.[140]

3. In virtue of the right of *eminent domain* for public use, with just compensation.[141]

4. By the law of "*overruling necessity*," which Lord Hale calls the *lex temporis et loci*, and which is both a war and peace power.[142]

5. By the war-power on the theater of military operations, *flagrante bello*, for military purposes.[143]

The power to take in these several modes must have for each an appropriate sphere of operation; they all stand *in pari materia*, and the right in no one can be so omnipresent or exclusive as to enroach upon or destroy the other. These are axiomatic principles, universally admitted.

The right to take property in the first, second, and fourth class of cases named exists without any duty to make "just compensation" in money.

The question of the liability of the Government to make compensation for property taken and damaged, or destroyed to prevent it from falling into the hands of an enemy, must be determined by a consideration of the character of the power exercised, and the purpose or reason of the seizure.

This question, as was very well said by the supreme court of Pennsylvania in September, 1788, in the case of *Respublica* v. *Sparhawk*, 1 Dallas, 362, is to be governed—

By reason, by the law of nations, and by precedents analogous to the subject before us.

First, then, on principles of reason, should the Government be liable to make compensation? This may be considered with reference to the reason as applied to citizens, and as applied to the Government. Upon the plainest principles of right and propriety, a military officer, even in flagrant war, would not be justified in seizing and destroying the property of a private citizen to prevent it from falling into the hands of the enemy, unless the "danger be immediate and impending," or be reasonably certain to happen during hostile military operations; for if this be not so, the officer acting without necessity or excuse would become a trespasser, and his act would be one of lawless violence, for which he would, and the nation would not, be liable in damages.[144]

---

[139] Constitution, art. 1, sec. 8, clause 1, (*ante*,) Clark *v.* Mayor, 13 Barb., N. Y. S. C. R., 35. This is not an exercise of the right of eminent domain, Gilman v. Sherloygan, 2 Black R., 510; see Steubenville and Ind. R. R. Co. *v.* Tascarance Co., 6 Pittsburgh Legal Journal, 68, cited in Brightley's Federal Digest, 158, sec. 4, O. C.; Hallenback *v.* Hahn, 2 Nebraska, 400; People *v.* Mayor, 4 Comst., N. Y., 424; Hanson *v.* Vernon, 27 Iowa, 28; Booth *v.* Woodbury, 5 Am. Law. Regr., N. S., 212; Commissioners *v.* Miller, 7 Kansas; McCullough *v.* Maryland, 4 Wheat., 425.

[140] Constitution, art. 3, sec. 1, clause 3, &c.; amendments, art. v, vi, viii. Grotius, b. 2, ch. 14, sec. 7.

[141] Constitution, art. v, amendments. "*Eminent domain* is a *civil* right." Grant *v.* U. S., 1 Court Claims, 45; American Print-Works *v.* Lawrence, 1 Zabriskie, 258. Grotius, b. 2, ch. 14, sec. 7; id., b. 3, ch. 20, sec. 7; 2 Nebraska, 400, note 113 *post.*

[142] *Hale* v. *Lawrence*, 3 Zabriskie, 728–'9; Grant *v.* U. S., 1 Court Claims, 45; Respublica *v.* Sparhawk, 1 Dallas, p. 362.

[143] 13 Howard, 140; Whiting's War-Powers, 26.

[144] Mitchell *v.* Harmony, 13 Howard, 115; Grant *v.* U. S., 1 Nott & H., Court of Claims, 45, 47, 48; American State Papers, part ix, Claims, vol. 1, p. 55; Pitcher *v.* U. S., 1 Court of Claims, 9; Gibbons *v.* U. S., 8 Wallace, 269.

It has been determined, also, that under certain circumstances the officer is not the sole judge of the necessity of seizing and destroying.[145]

Now, as a matter of common sense and reason, the owner of property is no more injured if it is destroyed by our own Government than if by the enemy. The loss to him is the same in either case.

Yet no statesman or writer on the laws of nations ever claimed that a Government is bound by any principle or rule of law to make compensation for property taken or destroyed by the enemy in time of war,[146] nor by its own military forces in actual battle.[147]

It has been said, with a force of reason which has not yet been answered, that where property is taken to prevent it from falling into the hands of the enemy, the *position* of property so situated is the owner's misfortune.

> He is not to be relieved of it at the cost of the United States, for they are not responsible to him for the circumstances that created it.[148]

To require the Government to pay where it is guilty of no wrong, no omission of duty, in the exercise of both a right recognized by the civilized world and enjoined by the highest duty and for the common good, would be the harshest rule that could be recognized. If the property of a citizen is in a position where it is reasonably certain he will lose it by the seizure of an enemy, he cannot be said to be in any worse position because it is seized by his own government.

All writers agree that the government incurs no liability by destroying it in battle, or for destroying it in an attempt to recapture it from an enemy. Bynkershoek says of the property of loyal citizens:

> Those goods may be properly taken by us, by the laws of war, if they have been before taken by our enemies.[149]

What difference can it make to the owner whether his property is destroyed immediately in advance of a battle, or in the conflict, or in an effort to recapture? To say that a nation is not liable if it applies the match and blows up a house a moment after the enemy gets in it, but is liable for doing the same thing a moment before, would seem a very *reductio ad absurdum*.[150]

---

[145] Mitchell *v.* Harmony, 13 Howard, 115, perhaps does not necessarily so decide. In that case, property was taken, not from "*necessity*," but "for the purpose of insuring the success of a distant expedition," thereafter to be prosecuted. The property was not *destroyed*. See Ex parte Milligan, 4 Wallace, 2; Martin *v.* Mott, 12 Wheat., 19; Whiting's War Powers, 67; Luther *v.* Borden, 7 Howard, 45; American Print-Works *v.* Lawrence, 1 Zabriskie, 260, and cases cited. A ratification by the Government of an act done by military authority relieves the officer from liability; Baron *v.* Denman, 2 Exchequer, 189. This modifies a case found in vol. ix, p. 404, of Niles Register, March, 1816, in which it is said martial law cannot be declared but subsequent to an act of the legislature authorizing it, and that a British farmer in Upper Canada recovered damages from a commissary for taking 100 bushels of wheat under martial law. See Milligan *v.* Hovey, 3 Bissell, U. S. Circuit Court R., 13 American Law Register, N. S., 122; Stevens *v.* U. S., 2 Court Claims, 95. See Linds *v.* Rodney, 2 Douglass, 613; Elphintone *v.* Bedreechund, 1 Knapp's P. C. R., 300; Coolidge *v.* Guthrie, Swayne, J., U. S. circuit court, S. district Ohio, Oct., 1868, in appendix to (43d ed., 1871) Whiting's War Powers, 591. In Report No. 600, House Reps., 1 sess. 36 Congress, May 26, 1860, Mr. Stanton, of the Committee on Military Affairs, in a case similar to that of Mitchell *v.* Harmony, said the officer "was the proper judge." See Ex parte Milligan, 4 Wallace, 2; Martin *v.* Mott, 12 Wheaton, 19; Whiting's War Powers, 67; Luther *v.* Borden, 7 Howard, 45.

[146] Senator Davis, January 4, 1871, 82 Globe, 297; Alexander Hamilton, Nov. 19, 1792, American State Papers, part ix, vol. 1, Claims, p. 55.

[147] Vattel, ch. xv, p. 402, and authorities heretofore cited.

[148] Loring, J., dissentiente, Grant's case, 2 Court Claims, 552; 1 Id., 41.

[149] 1 Laws of War, ch. v.

[150] See President Grant's veto-message, February 12, 1872, Senate Ex. Doc. 42, 3d sess. 42d Cong., as to Manchester, Ky., salt-works.

It may be said the Government should be liable for destroying a house when its seizure by the enemy might be only for the purpose of temporary occupancy, but not with a purpose to destroy it.

But if the enemy occupy a house the Government may in battle destroy it to dislodge him, and in such case incur no liability. It can make no difference to the owner whether it be destroyed a moment before or a moment after the enemy enter it. The destruction is an accident of war growing out of the situation of the house with reference to the conflict.

In such case, too, the reason of the rule mentioned by Grotius, which exempts a nation from liability for damage done by the enemy, may well apply, "in order to make every man more careful to defend his own."

To hold the Government liable under such circumstances would furnish an inducement to owners of property in times of danger to magnify it in order to induce the Government to destroy it and so become an insurer against peril; it would remove the inducement of citizens to throw obstacles in the way of the enemy's approach; it might encourage citizens rather to invite or aid it; it would diminish the motive to furnish supplies and aid to our Army in advancing to anticipate or defeat the approach of the enemy, and in all these modes disregard the maxim *salus populi suprema lex*. This overpowering and relentless rule of the supreme law of public safety is one which the stern necessities of war can neither safely omit nor mitigate.

A rule which would hold the Government liable might sometimes furnish an excuse for treacherous officers to omit necessary destruction of property, or induce a nation financially embarrassed to desist from the only means of preserving its existence. These considerations, so immeasurably important, should never be left to turn the hesitating scale in a moment of peril.

A nation should not be liable for property taken to prevent it from falling into the hands of an enemy, because it is impossible to establish any just measure of damages. What is the value of property liable to the imminent impending danger of being taken or destroyed by rebels? Why should the Government pay when the markets of the world could not supply another purchaser?

There are other considerations of public policy connected with this subject which cannot be overlooked.

Vattel, in assigning reasons why an invaded nation is not liable to its citizens for the ravages of war, says, "the public finances would be exhausted," and "these indemnifications would be liable to a thousand abuses."

Now, all these reasons apply with very great if not equal force to the damages now under consideration.[151]

[151]See 2 Greeley's American Conflict, 611; Sumner's Speech, January 12, 1869, 71 Globe, 301; Alexander's Cotton, 2 Wallace, 420; Senator Conkling, December 14, 1870, 82 Globe, 98; Senator Chandler, December 14, 1870, 82 Globe, 100; Senator Howe, January 4, 1871, 82 Globe, 303; Whiting's Opinion, January 15, 1864, in Globe, May 20, 1864, vol. 52, p. 2390.

The President, in his annual message, December, 1873, says to Congress:

"Your careful attention is invited to the subject of claims against the Government, and to the facilities afforded by existing laws for their prosecution. Each of the Departments of State, Treasury, and War have demands for many millions of dollars upon their files, and they are rapidly accumulating. To these may be added those now pending before Congress, the Court of Claims, and the southern claims commission, making, in the aggregate, an immense sum. Most of these grow out of the rebellion, and are intended to indemnify persons on both sides for their losses during the war; and not a few of them are fabricated and supported by false testimony. Projects are

This question involves to some extent the theory and nature of government.

The preamble to the Constitution declares that it was ordained—

To form a more perfect Union, establish justice, insure domestic tranquillity, provide for the common defense, promote the general welfare, and secure the blessings of liberty.

A government organized to insure domestic tranquillity and the common defense is *ex necessitate* clothed with the power to employ the necessary means to secure the end. But it is not necessary to invoke the aid of this well-known rule. The Constitution, in recognizing the laws of nations and the war-power, gives the Government a right to employ the means which it may declare necessary, or which nations usually employ, to make the common defense. These laws give the *power* and *create* the *duty* to seize property in time of war to prevent it from falling into the hands of an enemy. Where a nation exercises a lawful power in a lawful mode in the performance of an absolute duty, it would reverse every precept of reason, justice, and the whole logic of the common law, to hold it liable and guilty as a trespasser or a *tort feasor*. Nor is there any principle on which to rest an express or implied contract to pay in the class of cases under consideration. No act of Congress has created any such liability.

It cannot grow out of any obligation of the Government, for no principle of law, no writer, has ever declared it an *insurer* of the safety of its citizens from the perils which exist in all wars. On the contrary, the Constitution, by recognizing and conferring war-powers, admonishes all who share the privileges of Government of the dangers and perils of war.

There is no constitutional obligation to make compensation in this class of cases, unless it be found in the last clause of the fifth amendment to the Constitution, which, after reciting certain principles, most of which relate to rights of person and property *in a state of peace* and by *civil administration*, concludes by saying:

Nor shall private property be taken for *public use* without just compensation.

This can have no reference to the war seizure and destruction o property, unless—

1. This clause relates to war-measures and the exercise of military powers; nor unless—

2. The destruction indicated is a "public use."

This constitutional provision does relate to property in time of peace. It does relate to property not in the "enemy's country," and not in the

on foot, it is believed, to induce Congress to provide for new classes of claims, and to revive old ones through the repeal or modification of the statute of limitations, by which they are now barred. I presume these schemes, if proposed, will be received with little favor by Congress, and I recommend that persons having claims against the United States cognizable by any tribunal or department thereof, be required to present them at an early day, and that legislation be directed as far as practicable to the defeat of unfounded and unjust demands upon the Government; and I would suggest, as a means of preventing fraud, that witnesses be called upon to appear in person to testify before those tribunals having said claims before them for adjudication. Probably the largest saving to the national Treasury can be secured by timely legislation on these subjects of any of the economic measures that will be proposed."

On the 11th March, 1818, a report was made to the House of Representatives as to war-claims, under the act of April 9, 1816, in which it is said the documents from the commissioners of claims "develop the fact that on the frontiers of New York a system of fraud, forgery, and perhaps perjury, has been in operation, which the committee believe has never been witnessed in this country. It may well be questioned whether, in a national point of view, it would not have been better that the law of April, 1816,

immediate theater where armies are operating or war is flagrant, and battle in progress or imminent, in loyal territory. In such cases the laws of peace prevail. By its very terms, and upon the maxim, *noscitur a sociis*, this provision applies wherever the laws of peace prevail. That a provision confessedly so applicable can be ubiquitous or operative in a double capacity in peace, and concurrently with the laws of war, operating differently at the same time, in different places, may be more difficult to conceive.

That it does admit the right of *eminent domain* is clear, but that it does not extend *such right* to the cases of property seized by *military* authority and destroyed in war, upon principles of *overruling military*

---

had never been passed. It is the duty of a good government to attend to the morals of the people as an affair of primary concern."

There are now pending before the commissioners of claims, under the act of March 3, 1871, 17,048 claims, amounting to $50,000,000.

In a speech in the House of Representatives, February 7, 1874, Mr. Lowndes said:

"By reference to the Quartermaster-General's report for 1871, we find that from 1864 to 1871 there were filed in his department 28,039 claims. Out of that number 4,950 were approved, and claims allowed amounting to the sum of $2,078,083.05. There were 12,923 claims rejected, which amounted to $8,308,254.07; and 6,231 were suspended, amounting to $2,663,036.35; and only 3,935 claims remained to be acted upon, representing the sum of $3,884,094.45.

"A great many of the claims marked suspended are virtually rejected, as they have been laid aside on account of insufficiency of proof; which insufficiency or deficiency can never be given or supplied.

"Since the report of 1871 there has been filed in the Department 3,087 claims, representing $3,508,039.34; and during the same time 1,905 claims, representing $2,232,340.59 have been acted upon, leaving about 5,116 claims, amounting to $5,159,793.20, still pending, requiring action by the Department."

See also House Executive Document No. 121, first session Forty-third Congress; report Quartermaster-General, page 225, of Executive Document No. 1, part 2, House of Representatives, Forty-second Congress, second session.

The following statement of the amount of claims, as made and as allowed by the commissioners of claims under the act of March 3, 1871, in their first three annual reports, will illustrate this subject also:

| | Claimed. | Allowed. |
|---|---|---|
| Alabama | $533, 803 91 | $143, 529 30 |
| Arkansas | 696, 539 31 | 154, 566 48 |
| Florida | 48, 313 19 | 21, 168 00 |
| Georgia | 1, 057, 204 66 | 84, 142 29 |
| Louisiana | 1, 478, 326 85 | 274, 659 51 |
| Mississippi | 1, 306, 469 48 | 208, 715 46 |
| North Carolina | 576, 332 17 | 99, 853 76 |
| South Carolina | 592, 901 30 | 30, 173 43 |
| Tennessee | 1, 253, 988 55 | 257, 635 19 |
| Texas | 77, 460 19 | 46, 926 11 |
| Virginia | 2, 834, 728 63 | 524, 885 47 |
| West Virginia | 29, 054 60 | 6, 632 00 |
| | 10, 485, 122 84 | 1, 852, 887 00 |

See remarks of Mr. Delano (now Secretary of the Interior) in the House of Representatives, January 30, 1866, 56 Globe, 509–512; and in the report he made from the Committee of Claims, January, 1866, House of Representatives, No. 10, first session Thirty-ninth Congress. In the debate he said that the magnitude of the ravages of war were such that it would be an act of injustice to the people to heap upon the Government the liability resulting from their assumption. He added: "It would result, I think, in shaking the credit of the nation. It would place us in a condition of liability, I imagine, *vastly beyond our capacity of endurance.*"

As to criminal liability for making fraudulent claims on the Government, see act 2 March, 1863, ch. 67, 12 Stat., 696, secs. 1–3; act 2 March, 1867, ch. 169, 14 Stat., 484, sec. 30; Scott's Analytical Digest Military Laws, sec. 78.

See Garfield's speech in Congressional Record of June 29, 1874. Senator Davis's speech in Senate, May 13, 1874, estimates claims $88,527,121 before Congress—Commissioners of Claims, Commissary, and Quartermaster-General.

*necessity* analogous to the "belligerent right of capture and destruction of enemy's property in enemy's country,"[152] has been often affirmed.

But there is a law of "OVERRULING NECESSITY," entirely distinct from the right of *eminent domain*. Clark *v.* Mayor, 13 Barbour, N. Y. S. C. R., 35.

The Constitution, as originally made, contained no provision requiring just compensation for private property taken for public use. It was silent as to that. But the principle that such compensation should be made, as Story says,

Is founded on natural equity, and is laid down by jurists as a principle of universal law.[153]

This principle antedates the Constitution, existed when it was adopted, is not abrogated by it, and was therefore in force without the fifth amendment, which only affirms it, but makes no new law in this respect. So the law of overruling necessity antedated the Constitution, existed when it was adopted, is not abrogated by it, therefore admits it, and has through our whole history been recognized in courts, both under national and State authority.

It is a law, too, for peace and war, and may be exercised by civil and military authorities.

And, unlike the right of *eminent domain*, whatever power is exercised in virtue of the law of overruling necessity, does not generally create a claim for compensation or damages on the citizens or Government

---

[152] Senator Carpenter, January 4, 1871, 82 Globe, 300. Senator Edmunds, January 5, 1871, 82 Globe, 311. Grant *vs.* United States, 1 Court of Claims, 45.

Vattel says: "No action lies against the state for losses which she has occasioned, *not willfully* but *through necessity*." (Ch. xv, p. 403.)

On the 11th December, 1820, the Committee on Claims of the House of Representatives made a report on a claim for *use and occupation* of houses, and damages thereto, by General Jackson's officers, and for hospitals, during the invasion of the British at New Orleans in 1814, in which it is said, referring to the demand as based on the fifth amendment to the Constitution, that "the taking of 'private property for public use' would seem to imply a *voluntary act* on the part of the Government, which in the present case could hardly be alleged." (American State Papers, Class ix, Claims, vol. 1, p. 753.)

This is possibly more doubtful than the question whether property *destroyed* as a military necessity is taken for a *use*. Such property is not *used*. *All writers* agree that the *destruction* of property *in a battle* is not a taking for *public use* within the meaning of the Constitution. Then how is a *destruction* for war purposes just before a battle a *use* of the property? It cannot be so. The Government does not *use*, but *destroys*, to prevent the enemy from using. A *destruction* of property is very different from an ordinary *taking for the public use*. This belligerent right of destruction is distinct from and should not be confounded with the right of eminent domain. It is agreed by writers that this clause of the fifth amendment recognizes and affirms the right of *eminent domain*, and that is a peace power—"a *civil right*."[a]

Undoubtedly even in time of war Congress may, by law, authorize the exercise of the right of *eminent domain* in aid of military operations. But this is a *peace power*. It operates by or in pursuance of a statute. It employs judicial process.

But the *war power* may act without statute, and in flagrant war may seize supplies where needed. But in time of peace, or in time of war, but away from the theater of war, the war power is as powerless as is the peace power in the conflict of battle.

It was in reference to this supremacy of the laws of peace over military power in time of peace that enabled Lord Chatham to illustrate the celebrated maxim of the English law, that "every man's house is his castle," by a brilliant eulogy, in which he said of it:

"The poorest man may in his cottage bid defiance to all the forces of the Crown. It may be frail, its roof may shake, the wind may blow through it, the storm may enter, the rain may enter, but the King of England cannot enter; all his forces dare not cross the threshold of the ruined tenement."

[153] 2 Story Const., (4th ed.,) sec. 1790; 2 Kent Com., Lect. 24, pp. 275, 276, (2d ed., 339, 340;) 3 Wils. Law Lec., 203; Ware *vs.* Hylton, 3 Dallas, 194, 235; 1 Blackst. Com., 138–140; Parham *vs.* The Justices, 9 Georgia, 348.

---

[a] Grant *vs.* United States, 1 Court Claims, 45; "is a civil right;" Halleck, Int. Law, 124; 6 Cranch, 145.

rightfully using it in a case proper for its exercise. It is law as sacred, valid, and operative as a statute or the Constitution itself.

The exercise of the right of eminent domain admits of a discretion—the choice to condemn in pursuance of a statute one or another location for a post-office, "for the erection of forts, magazines, arsenals, dock-yards, and other needful buildings," roads and other works for "public use." The law of necessity, the "*lex instantis*," on the contrary, admits of neither delay nor choice.

The existence of these two independent rights, and the distinction between them, is fully recognized by the authorities.

Vattel recognizes the law of necessity *in time of war* thus:

> But there are other damages caused by *inevitable necessity;* as, for instance, the destruction caused by the artillery in retaking a town from the enemy. These are merely accidents. They are misfortunes, which chance deals out to the proprietors on whom they happen to fall.[154]

The supreme court of Pennsylvania recognized this law of necessity in time of war, as distinct from the civil right of *eminent domain*, by saying:

> Many things are lawful in that season (*flagrante bello*) which would not be permitted in time of peace. * * * The *rights of necessity* form a part of our law.[155]

The supreme court of Georgia recognizes this same law of necessity both in peace and *war:*

> There are cases of *urgent public necessity*, which no law has anticipated, and which cannot await the action of the legislature; those who seize the property are not trespassers, and there is no relief but by petition to the legislature. * * * For example, the pulling down houses and raising bulwarks for the defense of the state against an enemy; seizing corn and other provisions, for the sustenance of an army, in time of war; or taking cotton-bags, as General Jackson did at New Orleans, to build ramparts against an invading foe.

These cases illustrate the maxim, *Salus populi suprema lex.* Plate-Glass Co. *vs.* Meredith, 4 T. R., 797; Noys' Maxims, 9 ed., 36; Dyer, 60 b; Broom's Maxims, 1; 2 Bulst., 61; 12 Coke, 13, *the Prerogative case;* id., 63; 2 Kent, 338; 1 Blackst. Com., 101, note 18, by Chitty. Extreme necessity alone can justify these cases.[156]

The supreme court of New Jersey recognize the distinction:

> It is true that by many writers of high authority, the grounds of justification of an act done for the public good and of an act committed *through necessity* are not accurately distinguished. They are both spoken of as grounded on necessity, and they doubtless are so. But the one is a *State* the other an *individual* necessity, though oftentimes resulting in a public or general good. The one is a *civil* the other a *natural* right. The one is founded on property, and is an exercise of sovereignty; the other has no connection with the one or the other.[157]

And again, contrasting the right of *eminent domain* with the *law of necessity*, the court say:

> They are both spoken of sometimes as grounded on necessity, and they doubtless are so. But the latter stands strongly distinguished from that urgent necessity which, for immediate preservation, imperatively demands immediate action. His case who should throw up trenches upon his neighbors' land for the protection of a town from immediate hostile attack, as regards his justification, would certainly stand on a very differ-

---

[154] Ch. xv, p. 403. In Russell *vs.* Mayor, 2 Denio, 486, it was said: "The first case on the subject was the celebrated saltpeter case. The Government asserted the arbitrary right to provide munitions of war from private property, under pretext of overruling necessity, and all the justices sustained it. 12 Co., 12."

[155] Respublica *vs.* Sparhawk, 1 Dallas, 362, Sept., 1788.

[156] Parham *vs.* The Justices, &c., 9 Georgia, 348, the court fall into the error of referring the seizure to a *public use*, but in effect correct it so as to show it is not a "public use" within the meaning of the fifth amendment, by declaring that the taking is "without compensation, and without any provision of law for making compensation."

[157] *American Print-Works* vs. *Lawrence*, 1 Zabriskie, 258.

ent footing from one who, under the *authority of law*, should do the same act in order to guard the town from prospective and merely possible future harm.[158]

Again it has been said:

The right arising out of *extreme necessity* is a *natural right* older than States. * * It is the right of self-defense, of self-preservation, and has no connection whatever with the super-eminent right (*eminent domain*) of the State. The one [eminent domain] may be fettered by constitutional limitations; the other is beyond the reach of constitutions.[159]

There are many cases where the law of *overruling necessity* has been applied in time of peace for individual benefit.[160]

One reason for bearing in mind the clear distinction between the right of *eminent domain* and the *law of necessity* is, that where property is taken by virtue of the former, "just compensation" is to be made, while under the latter, neither individuals on common-law principles nor the Government on principles of public law incur any such liability.

The cases of individuals are numerous.

No well-considered case has determined that where a building is destroyed to arrest the progress of a fire that any liability to make compensation is thereby incurred.

The Government is not liable if by its command property is destroyed to arrest the hostile march of an enemy. This has already been shown from *reason* as applied to the Government, and to those whose property may be taken.

The courts, elementary writers, and usage of Government lead to the same result.[161]

During the revolutionary war, in April, 1777, the Pennsylvania board of war, acting by authority of the legislature, took possession of certain provisions owned by private individuals, in Philadelphia, to prevent them falling into the hands of the enemy, then approaching that city, but with a pledge to the owners that this was not designed to divest the property in the articles, but "that the same should be liable to the order

---

158 *Hale* vs. *Lawrence*, 3 Zabriskie, 605.

159 *Grant* vs. *United States*, 1 Court Claims, 45.

160 *American Print-Works* vs. *Lawrence*, 1 Zabriskie, 248, 3 Zabriskie, 591, 615; *Hale* vs. *Lawrence*, 1 Zabriskie, 728; *Russell* vs. *Mayor New York*, 2 Denio, 473; 82 vol. Globe, 300; *Respublica* vs. *Sparhawk*, 1 Dallas, Pa., 362.

All these cases conceded that *at common* law this law of "overruling necessity" is separate and distinct from the right of *eminent domain*, and that the exercise of the right conferred by the former creates no liability. In New York it is held, also, that a *statute* which regulates the law of overruling necessity is not an exercise of *eminent domain*, but only a regulation of the *law of necessity*. In New Jersey it was at first held that when a *statute* authorizes the destruction of property to arrest a fire, that is an exercise of the right of *eminent domain*. But this was overruled, and the doctrine of the New York court adopted. That which is not a "public use" at common law does not become so because a statutory regulation is made as to it.

161 Respublica *vs.* Sparhawk. 1 Dallas, p. 372, Sept.. 1788; 9 Georgia, 341; Wiggins *vs.* U. S., 1 Nott & H. Court Claims, 182; 2 id., 345. The doctrine of non-liability is approved in 2 Story Const., (4th ed.,) sec. 1790, note 6, saying:

"There may be cases of extreme necessity, as the pulling down of houses and raising bulwarks for the public defense, seizing private provisions for the army in time of war, when the owner has no redress. (See 9 Georgia R., 341; Mitchell *vs.* Harmony, 13 Howard S. C. R., 115, E. H. B.) (Whether the Government is liable for the destruction of property by a naval officer in the course of hostilities, may depend upon the time and circumstances and the necessity of the act; it will generally be a question of fact. Wiggins *vs.* United States, 1 Court of Claims Report, 182.) 2 id., 345."

Whiting says:

"If one of our armies marches across a corn-field, and so destroys a growing crop, or fires a building which conceals or protects the enemy, or cuts down timber to open a passage for troops through a forest, the owner of such property has no legal claim against the Government for his losses." War-Powers, 43 ed., p. 340.

No record has been found to show that the Russian government compensated the owners of the buildings burned in Moscow to defeat the object of the invasion by Napoleon.

of the owners, provided they were not exposed to be taken by the enemy." They were captured by the enemy. The statute provided for payment by the State "for services performed, moneys advanced, or *articles furnished.*" The proper accounting-officer refusing to pay, the owner of the property brought suit. The supreme court of Pennsylvania held that these were *not* "articles furnished;" in other words, that the taking was *not* for "*public use;*" that the articles were taken by the law of "overruling necessity."

The syllabus of the case is:

During the war of the Revolution, Congress had a right to direct the removal of any articles that were necessary to the Continental Army, or useful to the enemy, and in danger of falling into their hands; and one whose property, so removed, was afterward captured by the enemy, was held not to be entitled to compensation from the commonwealth.[162]

The proclamation of emancipation was declared to be "warranted by the Constitution upon military necessity." (12 Stat., 1267–1269.) It concludes thus: "And upon this act, sincerely believed to be an act of justice, warranted by the Constitution upon military necessity, I invoke the considerate judgment of mankind and the gracious favor of Almighty God."

See the subject fully discussed in Whiting's War-Powers and the authorities quoted. Unless the theory of the Constitution is correct, and but for the XIII and XIV Amendments, the Government would be bound to make compensation for slaves. But their liberation was not a taking for *public use;* it was the destruction of a private right, if so it can be called, to prevent it from giving aid and comfort to the enemy.

Chief-Justice McKean, in delivering the unanimous opinion of the court, said:

The transaction, it must be remembered, happened *flagrante bello;* and many things are lawful in that season which would not be permitted in time of peace. The seizure of the property in question, can, indeed, only be justified under this distinction; for otherwise it would clearly have been a *trespass;* which, from the very nature of the term, *transgressio,* imports to go beyond what is right. (5 *Bac. Abr.*, 150.) It is a rule, however, that it is better to suffer a private mischief than a public inconvenience; and the *rights of necessity* form a part of our law.

Of this principle, there are many striking illustrations. If a road be out of repair, a passenger may lawfully go through a private inclosure. (2 *Black. Com.*, 36.) So, if a man is assaulted, he may fly through another's close. (5 *Bac. Abr.*, 173.) In time of war, bulwarks may be built on private ground. (*Dyer & Brook. Trespass*, 213; 5 *Bac. Abr.*, 175.) And the reason assigned is particularly applicable to the present case, because it is for the public safety. (20 *Vin. Abr.*, trespass, B'a sec. 4, fo. 476.) Thus, also, every man may, of common right, justify the going of his servants or horses, upon the banks of navigable rivers, for towing barges, &c., to whomsoever the right of the soil belongs, (1 *Ld. Raymond*, 725.) The pursuit of foxes through another's ground is allowed, because the destruction of such animals is for the public good. (2 *Buls.* 62; *Cro.* 1 *I*, 321.) And as the safety of the people is a law above all others, it is lawful to part affrayers in the house of another man. (*Keyl.*, 46; 5 *Bac. Abr.*, 177; 20 *Vin. Abr.*, fo. 407, sec. 14.) Houses may be razed to prevent the spreading of fire, because for the public good. (Dyer, 36; Reed, L. and E., 312; see Puff., lib. 2, c. sec. 8; Hutch Mor. Philos., lib. 2, c. 16.) We find, indeed, a memorable instance of folly recorded in the third volume of Clarendon's History, where it is mentioned that the lord mayor of London, in 1666, when that city was on fire, would not give directions for, or consent to, the pulling down forty wooden houses, or to the removing of the furniture, &c., belonging to the lawyers of the temple, then on the circuit, for fear he should be answerable for a trespass; and in consequence of this conduct half that great city was burned. We are clearly of opinion that Congress might lawfully direct the removal of any articles that were necessary to the maintenance of the Continental Army or useful to the enemy and in danger of falling into their hands, for they were vested with the powers of peace and war, to which this was a natural and necessary incident. And having done it lawfully, there is nothing in the circumstances of the case which we think entitles the appellant to a compensation for the consequent loss.

This case is especially valuable. It was decided by one of the ablest courts of that period. It gives construction to what is a *public use.*

---

[162] Respublica *vs.* Sparhawk, 1 Dallas, 362.

It shows when a taking is referable to the *law of necessity* and when by the law of *public use.* It draws the line between these two laws. In view of that construction, the fifth amendment to the Constitution was afterward adopted, and with a knowledge that the *destruction* of private property for the purpose indicated was *not* a taking for public use, the Constitution made no provision for such case.

It was made in view of the known rule of international law on the subject, and of the impossibility of making payment, and of the fact that no nation had ever done so.[163]

---

[163]In Senate Rep. 412, 3d sess. 42d Cong., it is said:

"The war of the Revolution was fought before we had any constitutional prohibition against taking private property for public use without compensation. The troops for that war were furnished by the several States. Congress did not assume the obligation of making compensation for property taken by the military authority; but it clearly recognized the principle that compensation should be made. Accordingly, in 1784, a resolution was adopted from which the following is an extract:

"'That it be referred to the several States, at their own expense, to grant such relief to their citizens, who may have been injured as aforesaid, as they may think requisite, and if it shall hereafter appear reasonable that the United States should make any allowance to any particular State, which may be burdened much beyond others, that the allowance ought to be determined by Congress.'

"In accordance with that resolution, when, in 1818, Mary Brower and others petitioned for compensation to be made to them for property burned and destroyed on Long Island by the American Army on the advance of the British forces in August, 1776, the Committee on Revolutionary Claims of the House denied the prayer, not upon the ground that compensation should not be made, but upon the express ground that the sufferers ought to have appealed to the State of New York for such compensation." (American State Papers, Claims, 608.)

It is proper to notice this and to say:

1. There was of course no national constitutional prohibition against taking private property. But the principles of *Magna Charta* were in force here as fully as if adopted in the Constitution.

In Perham *vs.* The Justices, 9 Georgia R., 349, the court, referring to the provision of *Magna Charta*, that no person should be deprived of property "but by the law of the land and by judgment of his peers," said:

"This great rule of right and liberty was the law of this State at the adoption of the Constitution. It is not therefore necessary to go to the Federal Constitution for it. It came to us with the common law; it is part and parcel of our social polity; it is inherent in ours as well as every other free government. At common law the legislature can compel the use of private property, but not arbitrarily. It treats with the citizen as owner for the purchase, and while he cannot withhold it upon offer of compensation, they cannot seize it without such tender."

The authorities are collected on page 350.

And see 2 Story, Constitution, (fourth edition,) sections 1784, 1790. Story says the fifth amendment of our Constitution "is an affirmance of a great doctrine established by the common law."

2. The Senate report 412, above referred to, treats of the claim of J. Milton Best. This was for compensation for his house, destroyed at Paducah, Ky., March, 1864, by Union military authorities, "in anticipation of another attack" from the rebels—"destroyed by order of a commanding officer to save his imperiled army." It was destroyed to prevent it from falling into the hands of the enemy to be used by them. (Senate report No. 69, Forty-first Congress, second session.)

The Senate report No. 134, above referred to, asserts that the Continental Congress by resolution of [June 3] 1784, "clearly recognized the principle that compensation should be made for property taken by the military authority." That is, for property taken as was that of J. Milton Best, and under similar circumstances. It is said this "principle" is found in the resolution of 1784.

But it is clear the resolution asserts no such "principle" as *law*.

The journals of the Continental Congress show the following proceedings:

In Continental Congress June 3, 1784, the following proceedings were had:

"On the report of a committee consisting of Mr. Spaight, Mr. Gerry, Mr. Lee, Mr. Beatty, and Mr. Sherman, to whom was referred a report of a committee, on a report of the superintendent of finance, dated the 5th of November, 1783, in answer to questions proposed by the commissioner for settling the accounts of the State of Pennsylvania with the United States," it was

"*Resolved,* That the commissioners make reasonable allowance for the use of stores, and

Another case will illustrate this law of "overruling necessity" where property had been destroyed to arrest the progress of a fire, and it was claimed to be a taking for "the public use," within the meaning of the constitution of New York.[164]

The court says:

But I apprehend that the assumption of the plaintiff, that this was a case of the exercise of the right of *eminent domain*, will prove a fallacy. I have arrived at this conclusion after a patient examination of all the authorities, and after adverting to the usual *indicia* that distinguish such a grant from the powers that are frequently granted to municipal corporations. The destruction of this property was authorized by the law of overruling necessity; it was the exercise of a natural right belonging to every individual; not conferred by law, but tacitly excepted from all human codes. The best elementary writers lay down the principle, and adjudications upon adjudications have for centuries sustained, sanctioned, and upheld it, that in a case of actual necessity, to prevent the spreading of a fire, the ravages of a pestilence, or any other great public calamity, the private property of any individual may be lawfully destroyed for the relief, protection, or safety of the many without subjecting the actors to personal responsibility for the damages which the owner has sustained. (See 2 Kent's Com., 4th ed., 338; 15 Vin., tit. Necessity, p. 8; Malevener *vs.* Spink, 1 Dyer, 36, b; 17 Wendell, 297; 18 id., 129; 20 id., 144; 25 id., 162, 163, 174; Respublica *vs.* Sparhawk, 1 Dallas, 357.) The latter case goes very fully into the discussion of the nature and extent of the natural right arising from pressing and inevitable necessity; and the great fire which occurred in London in 1666 is referred to, when the lord mayor of London refused to destroy about forty wooden houses, and also certain tenements occupied by lawyers, in consequence of which the fire spread and threatened the destruction of the whole city.

---

other buildings hired for the use of the United States by persons having authority to contract for the same; but that rent be not allowed for buildings which, being abandoned by the owners, were occupied by the troops of the United States. That such compensation as the commissioner may think reasonable be made for wood, forage, or other property of individuals taken by order of any proper officer, or applied to, or used for the benefit of the Army of the United States, upon producing to him satisfactory evidence thereof, by the testimony of one or more disinterested witnesses.

"That, according to the laws and usages of nations, a State is not obliged to make compensation for damages done to its citizens by an enemy, or wantonly and unauthorized by its own troops; yet humanity requires that some relief should be granted to persons who, by such losses, are reduced to indigence and want; and, as the circumstances of such sufferers are best known to the State to which they belong, it is the opinion of the committee that it be referred to the several States (at their own expense) to grant such relief to their citizens, who have been injured as aforesaid, as they may think requisite; and if it shall hereafter appear reasonable that the United States should make any allowance to any particular States who may be burdened much beyond others, that the allowance ought to be determined by Congress; but that no allowance be made by the commissioners for settling accounts for any charges of that kind against the United States." (See Journals of Congress, vol. 4, from 1782 to 1788, page 443.)

Now, from these proceedings of Congress it will be seen that the *only* principle of law asserted is that "a State is not obliged to make compensation for damage done to its citizens by an enemy, or wantonly and unauthorized by its own troops."

3. The Senate report asserts that "in *accordance* with that resolution" (of the Congress of 1784,) the Congress of 1818 denied the claim of Mary Brower, (similar to that of J. Milton Best,) "not upon the ground that compensation should not be made, but upon the express ground that the sufferers ought to have appealed to the State of New York for such compensation."

The report of the committee of the House on the case of Mary Brower is in American State Papers, Claims, 608, November 30, 1818. It asserts that "Congress have not made any general provision assuming to compensate and pay for claims of this description which may have originated in the revolutionary war." It refers to the resolution of the Congress of 1784, and says the claimants "ought, if they did not, to have made application to the State of New York."

But the resolution of 1784 expressly *refers to no such* case as Mary Brower's. And if it did, it only suggested that the States make compensation not as a *legal* duty, but because "humanity requires *some* relief should be granted *to persons who, by such losses, are reduced to indigence and want.*"

The States never did make such compensation. Their usage settled the *law* against such claims.

[164] Russell *vs.* The Mayor, &c., of New York, 2 Denio, 473.

There are some unauthoritative dicta, and perhaps a single decided case, apparently in conflict with these views.[165]

The Judge-Advocate-General held, in the case of a claim for the value of certain buildings, with their contents, burned by Union troops in West Virginia, a loyal State, in January, 1863, by way of a *ruse* to de-

[165] House Rep. No. 43, 42d Cong., 3d sess.; 13 Wend., 372; Vattel, ch. xv, p. 403; Whiting, War-Powers, 15. In Grant *vs.* United States, 1 N. & H., Court., Claims, 41, it was held that "the taking of private property for destruction by a military officer [in a state of war, to prevent it from falling into the hands of the enemy] is an exercise of the right of *eminent domain*." That "there is no discrimination to be made between property taken to be *used* and property taken to be *destroyed*," and that a right of action against the Government as upon an implied contract, arises in favor of the party whose property is destroyed.

So far as this holds that military officers by right of common military law exercised a power of *eminent domain*, it is contradicted in the same case, which declares that "*eminent domain* is a *civil* right," and it is contradicted by many reliable authorities.

If the seizure was in fact a military necessity in a state of war, the officer was not liable. Buron *vs.* Denman, 2 Exchequer, 189; Mitchell *vs.* Harmony, 13 Howard, 134.

If it was not a necessity, the act was unauthorized and the Government is not liable. (Am. State Papers, Claims, 55; 13 Howard, 115; Res. Cont. Cong., June 3, 1784, Journal, vol. 4, p. 443; Gibbons *vs.* U. S., 8 Wallace, 269)

So far as it holds the Government liable it is contradicted by the authorities already cited. It is practically overruled in the same court by the learned Chief-Justice Casey, and the court in Wiggins *vs.* United States, 1 Court Claims, 182. The case of Grant *vs.* United States goes the extreme length of declaring that a seizure for *destruction* is a taking for "public *use*." If this be so, why is not property *destroyed in a battle* taken for the *public use?* Where is the difference in principle? Yet *no writer* can be found to declare that destruction by battle is a taking for public use.

Senator Davis, of Kentucky, a conceded strict constructionist, declared that property so destroyed, even by the Union military forces, was *not taken for public use.* (In Senate, January 4, 1871; Globe, vol. 82, p. 297.)

The case of Grant *vs.* United States is in principle overruled by the able opinion of the learned Chief-Justice of the Court of Claims, who, in Perrin *vs.* United States, 4 Court of Claims, 546, said of a claim for compensation for property destroyed in the bombardment of Greytown: "The claimant's case must necessarily rest upon the assumption that the bombardment and destruction of Greytown was illegal, and not justified by the law of nations." (Gibbons *vs.* U. S., 8 Wallace, 269, overrules Grant's case.)

If the destruction was legal, the act was not wrong; and if not wrong, no action would lie for it. An action is only given to redress a *wrong.* No action lies for doing what is right. And it is remarkable that no lawyer has ever since brought a suit in that court on any one of the many cases since of a similar character.

Congress by act of July 4, 1864, prohibited the Court of Claims from taking jurisdiction of "any claim against the United States growing out of the destruction, or appropriation of, or damage to property by the Army or Navy engaged in the suppression of the rebellion, from the commencement to the close thereof."

It is to be presumed Congress would not deny any claim justified by the laws of nations.

In Mitchell *vs.* Harmony, 13 Howard, 134, the court said, not as authority, but on a mere *obiter dictum*, that—

"There are, without doubt, occasions in which private property may lawfully be taken possession of or destroyed to prevent it from falling into the hands of the public enemy; and also, where a military officer charged with a particular duty may impress private property into the public service or take it for public use. Unquestionably in such cases the Government is bound to make full compensation to the owner." (13 How., 134; and see numerous authorities cited *infra.*) United States *v.* Russell, 13 Wallace, 627. In this case there was a military impressment, and the court cited, with approval, the case of Mitchell *v.* Harmony. But this was a seizure *not on the theater of war*, and where the laws of peace were prevailing.

Unquestionably, by the law of nations, where the private property of citizens is by common international military authority impressed into the public service, it is, by *virtue of the same law*, generally to be paid for independently of any constitutional provision; but this is not at all so when property is lawfully taken to prevent it from falling into the hands of an enemy. That is an exercise of the law of overruling necessity, as has been shown.

In Russell *v.* The Mayor, &c., 2 Denio, 484, it was said by one of the judges that—

"A vessel may in time of war be taken from the owner, when the interests of the public demand it, or it may be destroyed to prevent its falling into the hands of an enemy, and thereby increase its power of aggression or resistance, and the owner

ceive and divert the enemy, a legitimate act of ordinary warfare, that the loss incurred was one of those accidents of war for which the Government does not become liable to individuals.[166]

The opinions of elementary writers have not been entirely uniform.

Grotius seems to assert that the government is not liable to make compensation, by saying:

> This also may be constituted by the civil law, that no action may be brought against such a city for damages by war, in order to make every man more careful to defend his own.[167]

Vattel admits the law of overruling necessity by saying:

> But there are other damages caused by inevitable necessity; as, for instance, the destruction caused by the artillery in retaking a town from the enemy. These are merely accidents. They are misfortunes, which chance deals out to the proprietors on whom they happen to fall.[168]

But he differs with Grotius, by saying:

> Of the damages done by the state or the sovereign, some are done deliberately and by way of precaution, as when a field, a house, or a garden belonging to a private person is taken for the purpose of erecting on the spot a town, a rampart, or any other piece of fortification, or when his standing corn or store-houses are destroyed to prevent their being of use to the enemy. Such damages are to be made good to the individual, who should bear only his quota of the loss.

In the edition of 1872 there is a note to this, as follows:

> It is legal to take possession of these for the benefit of the community, and no action lies, that is, no claim for compensation, nor is any recoverable, unless given by act of Parliament. (4 Term. R., 382.)

And he says:

> No action—claim for damages—lies against the state for misfortunes of this nature for losses which she has occasioned, not *willfully, but through necessity*, and by mere accident, in the exertion of her rights.

The principle here stated applies to the *necessary destruction* of property to prevent it from falling into an enemy's hands, when his approach is imminent.

Notwithstanding anything elsewhere said, the right to compensation finds no sanction by the usage of the Government.

During the revolutionary war property was often destroyed to prevent it from falling into the hands of the enemy.

It was determined by the courts in Pennsylvania that in such cases there was no claim for redress.

Congress never made provision for paying any such claims.[169]

The States made no such compensation.

During the war of 1812 with Great Britain property was destroyed by the military authorities of the United States to prevent it from falling into the hands of the enemy. But no general provision was made by act of Congress for paying for such loss.

Congress did, by act of April 9, 1816, provide for paying for horses killed while in service, and for paying—

> Any person who * * sustained damage by the destruction of his or her house or building by the enemy while the same was occupied as a military *deposite* under the authority of an officer or agent of the United States.[170]

---

would be entitled upon this principle of the Constitution to be paid a just compensation. In these cases private property is taken for public use. The right of *eminent domain* is here asserted."

This is merely *obiter*, and the same remarks apply as to the cases above noticed. (See note 88, ante; see Clark *v.* Mayor, 13 Barbour, N. Y. S. C. R., 35.)

[166] See Opinions of Judge-Advocate-General, vol. 26, p. 242. See Digest of Opinions of Judge-Advocate-General from September, 1862, to July, 1868, (3d ed.,) p. 93.

[167] Book 3, ch. xx, sec. 8.

[168] Ch. xv, p. 402.

[169] See American State Papers, class ix, vol. 1, Claims, *passim.*

[170] 3 Stat. at L., p. 263, sec. 9; 3 Stat. at L., p. 397, sec. 1.

So the act of 3 March, 1849, (ch. 129, sec. 2,) and March 3, 1863, (ch. 78, sec. 5,) provided compensation for the loss or destruction of property in the service by impressment or contract. (Scott's Digest Military Laws, 1874, p. 112, sec. 115, 116.) And the act of June 25, 1864, (13 Stat. at L., p. 182,) secures compensation to any officer, non-commissioned officer, or private, during the rebellion, who surrendered horses to the enemy by order of superior officer.

But this was, by act of March 8, 1817, limited to—

Houses or buildings occupied as a place of deposit for military or naval stores, or as barracks for military forces of the United States.[171]

But it was said by a committee of Congress that, so far as this related to houses destroyed by the enemy, it was enacted by Congress as—

A law originating in *its benignity* and aimed gratuitously for the benefit of a suffering portion of the community.[172]

They declared it—

A law originating in the benign and charitable disposition of the Government.

The original act barred all claims not exhibited within two years from its date, and Congress refused to extend the time.

But claims for compensation for property destroyed to prevent it from falling into the hands of the enemy are so rare as to show them entirely exceptional.[173]

---

171 See Reports of Court of Claims to Congress, vol. 1, 1857–'58; Rep. No. 96, 1st. sess. 35th Cong., sec. 15, 1857; House Rep. 746, 1st sess. 43d Cong., June 22, 1874, p. 2; note Frederick City Claim.

In the case of Joseph Loranger *vs.* The United States, Judge Blackford, delivering the opinion of the Court of Claims, used the following language:

"We consider the law to be that, if the Government, by its authorized agents, takes possession of a private building and make use of it as a military depot or as barracks, and the enemy, in consequence of such possession and use, destroy the building while it is so used, the Government would be liable to the owner for the value of the building. There would be reason for saying in such case that the Government had given a character to the property which, by the usage of civilized warfare, would justify the enemy in destroying it." (See Report No. 96, 1st session 35th Congress, December 15, 1857, Reports Court of Claims, vol. 1, 1857–'58. See, also, sec. 9 of the act of April 9, 1816, 3 Stats. at Large, 263; also, act of March 3, 1817, 3 Stats. at Large, 397.)

172 American State Papers, class ix, vol. 1, Claims, 590. See letter No. 150 of Secretary of War to House of Representatives, February 20, 1818, in Ex. Doc. vol. 4, for 1817–'18, 1st sess. 15th Congress.

173 William H. Washington was paid for a house blown up in August, 1814, by order of our military officers. (6 Stat. at L., 151; American State Papers, Claims, 446.) But this was a case which came within the principle of the act of April 9, 1816. The Government placed stores in the house and blew up the house to destroy the stores, to prevent them from falling into the hands of the enemy.

On February 5, 1817, a report was made to the House of Representatives recommending the payment of a precisely similar claim for damages done at Valley Forge, in 1777, but Congress did not give the relief. (Claims, vol. 1, p. 522.)

So a rope-walk, destroyed September, 1814, at Baltimore, to prevent it from falling into the hands of the enemy, was paid for, but this is clearly exceptional. (Am. St. Papers, Claims, 444; 6 Stat. at L., p. 150.)

A report made February 14, 1816, states a liberal view, by saying "that indemnity is due to all those whose losses have arisen from the acts of our own Government, or those acting under its authority, while losses produced by the conduct of the enemy are to be classed among the unavoidable calamities of war, and do not entitle the sufferers to indemnification by the Government." (Claims, vol. 1, 462; Sumner's speech, 71 Globe, 301, January 12, 1869.)

But a very different *rule of law* was subsequently stated by a committee, December 11, 1820, (Claims, vol. —, 752,) as to property taken at New Orleans. The report says:

"There have been thousands of instances during the late war * * * where the loss to the owners can be traced, directly or indirectly, to the acts of the Government. * * * There are no *known rules* or established usages of the Government which would seem to authorize an allowance in a case thus involved in obscurity."

Mr. Sumner, in an elaborate and masterly speech in the Senate, January 12, 1869, (71 Globe, 300,) gives a summary, thus:

"After the battle of New Orleans, the question was presented repeatedly. In one

The usage of the Government during and since the rebellion is a clear denial of all liability in this class of cases.

No general provision has been made for paying them. This undoubtedly would have been done if there had been any admitted liability.

On the contrary, Congress, while providing for the payment of quartermaster's and commissary supplies taken *in the loyal States*, by the act of July 4, 1864, has made a provision *applicable everywhere:*

That the jurisdiction of the Court of Claims shall not extend to or include any claim against the United States growing out of the destruction or appropriation of or damage to property by the Army or Navy, or any part of the Army or Navy engaged in the suppression of the rebellion, from the commencement to the close thereof.

Even where provision has been made for special reasons in exceptional cases, the policy of this has generally been denied by the executive branch of the Government, and the broad rule of international law contained in the act of 1864 has been re-asserted by the President.[174]

Where compensation has been made it has been for exceptional reasons.[175]

The rule of law as stated is that recognized by the executive branch of the Government. The President, in his message of February 12,

case a claim for 'a quantity of fencing,' used as fuel by troops of General Jackson, was paid by Congress; so also was a claim for damages to a plantation 'upon which public works for the defense of the country were erected;' also a claim for 'an elegant and well-furnished house,' which afforded shelter to the British army, and was, therefore, fired on with hot shot; also a claim for damage to a house and plantation on which a battery was erected by our troops." (American State Papers, Claims, p. 521.)

"There was also another case where Congress seems to have acted on a different principle. On the landing of the enemy near New Orleans, the levee was cut, in order to annoy him. As a consequence the plantation of the claimant was inundated, and suffered damages estimated at $19,250. But the claim was rejected on the ground that 'the injury was done in the necessary operations of war.'" (Ibid., p. 835.)

[174] See veto messages of June 1, 1872; Senate Ex. Doc. 8, 2d sess. 42d Cong., act for relief of J. Milton Best; June 7, 1872, Senate Ex. Doc. 86, 2d sess. 42d Cong., act for relief of Thomas B. Wallace; January 31, 1873, Senate Ex. Doc. 33, 3d sess. 42d Cong., act for relief of East Tennessee University; February 12, 1873, Senate Ex. Doc. 42, 3d sess. 42d Cong., bill for relief for destruction of Manchester, Ky., Salt-Works.

On the 27th November, 1864, General Sheridan issued an order, which was executed, to destroy all "forage and subsistence, burn all barns, mills, and their contents, and drive off all stock in Loudoun County, Va." (See Senate Report No. 80, second session Forty-second Congress, Court of Claims.) The stock was used by the Army, in part, and the residue driven into Pennsylvania and sold, and the proceeds paid into the Treasury. Much of the property so used or destroyed belonged to men whose loyalty had never been questioned, many of them members of the Society of Friends. The Senate committee reported in favor of paying not only for property of loyal citizens so destroyed, but for cattle and supplies so used and sold. Congress, by act of January 23, 1873, authorized payment to "loyal citizens of Loudoun County, Va., for their live-stock partly slaughtered and used and partly sold, and the proceeds paid into the Treasury." (17 Stat., 713.) The House refused to pass any bill to pay for property destroyed.

[175] *Claim of Josiah O. Armes.*—Act of January 31, 1867, provides for paying $9,500 "in consequence of the burning of his buildings at Annandale, Fairfax County, Va., by United States troops." (See 14 Stat., page 617; see, also, Senate Report No. 112, second session Thirty-ninth Congress; also, vol. 62, pages 758, 759, second session Thirty-ninth Congress.) The report shows that the house was burned "to prevent its being used by the enemy as a stronghold." For House proceedings and debates in Thirty-eighth Congress, see Globe, vol. 50, pages 313, 758, 759; vol. 51, pages 1286, 2388. For Senate proceedings and debates, see Globe, vol. 54, page 547; vol. 55, pages 1273, 1274, 1275, 1388. For Senate proceedings and debates in Thirty-ninth Congress, see vol. 56, pages 7, 134, 147, 162; vol. 60, page 3873. For House proceedings and debates, see Globe, vol. 56, page 148; vol. 60, page 3907; vol. 61, pages 414, 755, 758, 759, 760, 761.

But this case is exceptional, and seems to have been a reward made in consideration that "Armes was of service to our troops in giving information of the movement and situation of the rebels," and that his wife "came in one dark night *at the risk of her life*" to give information to the Union military authorities.

1873, says, in relation to the Kentucky salt-works destroyed by order of General Craft, commanding Union military forces:

I understand him to say, in effect, that the salt-works were captured from the rebels, that it was impracticable to hold them, and that they were demolished so as to be of no further use to the enemy.

I cannot agree that the owners of property destroyed under such circumstances are entitled to compensation therefor from the United States. Whatever other view may be taken of the subject, it is incontrovertible that these salt-works were destroyed by the Union Army while engaged in regular military operations, and that the sole object of their destruction was to weaken, cripple, or defeat the armies of the so-called southern confederacy.

I am greatly apprehensive that the allowance of this claim could and would be construed into the recognition of a principle binding the United States to pay for all property which their military forces destroyed in the late war for the Union. No liability by the Government to pay for property destroyed by the Union forces in conducting a battle or siege has yet been claimed; but the precedent proposed by this bill leads directly and strongly in that direction; for it is difficult upon any ground of reason or justice to distinguish between a case of that kind and the one under consideration. Had General Craft and his command destroyed the salt-works by shelling out the enemy found in their actual occupancy, the case would not have been different in principle from the one presented in this bill. What possible difference can it make in the rights of owners or the obligations of the Government, whether the destruction was in driving the enemy out, or in keeping them out, of the possession of the salt-works?

This bill does not present a case where private property is taken for public use, in any sense of the Constitution. It was not taken from the owners, but from the enemy; and it was not then used by the Government, but destroyed. Its destruction was one of the casualties of war; and though not happening in actual conflict, was perhaps as disastrous to the rebels as would have been a victory in battle.

Owners of property destroyed to prevent the spread of a conflagration, as a general rule, are not entitled to compensation therefor, and, for reasons equally strong, the necessary destruction of property found in the hands of the public enemy, and constituting a part of their military supplies, does not entitle the owner to indemnity from the Government for damages to him in that way.[176]

---

# CHAPTER VII.

## CLAIMS IN THE DEPARTMENTS OF THE GOVERNMENT.

Upon this subject the following information has been transmitted to the House of Representatives:

WAR DEPARTMENT,
*February* 6, 1874.

The Secretary of War has the honor to transmit to the House of Representatives, for the information of the Committee on War-Claims,

---

176 Veto message February 12, 1873, Senate Ex. Doc. 42, 3d sess. 42d Congress.

Claim of Dr. J. Milton Best, of Paducah, Ky. Claim for compensation of his dwelling-house, taken by United States military authority, and destroyed by order of United States officer as a military necessity, March 26, 1862.

Forty-first Congress, Senate proceedings and debates, for which see Globe, vol. 82, pp. 97, 98, 99, 100, 101, 165, 166, 167, 168, 169, 295, 296, 297, 298, 299, 300, 301, 302, 303, 304, 311, 312, 313, 314, 315, 316, 317, 318, 319.

See Senate Rep. No. 69, 2d sess. 41st Cong. For House proceedings and debates see vol. 84, p. 1934.

Senate proceedings and debates for 42d Cong. See Globe, vol. 89, pp. 2252, 2253, (April 8, 1872;) vol. 91, pp. 4156, 4157, (June 1, 1872.) See, also, Senate Rep. No. 9, 2d sess. 42d Cong.

For House proceedings and debates see Globe, vol. 91, pp. 3621, 3622, 3623, 3624. See veto message, June 1, 1872, Senate Ex. Doc. 85, 2d sess. 42d Cong.

Kentucky salt-works. Claim for indemnity be reason of destruction of salt-works near Manchester, Ky., by order of Major-General Buell as a military necessity.

reports of the Quartermaster-General and Commissary-General of Subsistence, giving their views upon certain classes of claims growing out of the late war.

These reports to accompany letter of the 24th ultimo, transmitting to the House a copy of General Orders No. 100, dated April 24, 1863, publishing "instructions for the government of armies of the United States in the field."

WM. W. BELKNAP,
*Secretary of War.*

---

WAR DEPARTMENT,
QUARTERMASTER-GENERAL'S OFFICE,
*Washington, D. C., January* 30, 1874.

SIR: I have the honor to return herewith the communication of the Committee on War-Claims, House of Representatives, (by its clerk,) requesting "a copy of the report or rules prepared by Dr. Francis Lieber in regard to, or regulating intercourse with, rebel States," which was referred to the Quartermaster-General for any suggestions he may desire to make thereon in connection with the subject of claims for quartermaster's stores which originated during the war.

---

For Senate proceedings and debates see Globe, vol. 89, pp. 2258, 2259, 2d sess. 42d Cong., (April 8, 1872;) also Globe, vol 93, p. 1288, (February 12, 1873;) Senate Rep. 50, 2d sess. 42d Cong.

For House proceedings and debates see Globe, vol. 93, pp. 694, 695, 696, 697, (January 18, 1873.)

See veto message, Senate Ex. Doc. 42, 3d sess. 42d Cong.

The Committee on War-Claims was organized at the opening of the 43d Congress.

There were before the Committee on War-Claims of the House of Representatives fourteen hundred and twenty claims up to date of February 22, 1875. Some of these claims, however, propose relief to numerous persons. The clerk of the committee has made an estimate of claims, as follows:

Amount (estimated) of claims of the following classes pending before committees of the House of Representatives of the 43d Congress, March 1, 1874:

| | |
|---|---|
| Quartermaster's and commissary stores | $4,600,000 |
| Tobacco | 450,000 |
| Cotton | 1,850,000 |
| Steamboats, barges, &c., use of and damages | 650,000 |
| Use of railroads and damages to same | 2,000,000 |
| Rents and use of, and damage to, real estate (rebel States) | 3,000,000 |
| Rents and use of, and damage to, real estate (loyal States) | 700,000 |
| Property taken, occupied, and destroyed by the United States as a military necessity in the rebel States | 6,000,000 |
| Property taken, occupied, and destroyed by the United States as a military necessity in the loyal States | 3,000,000 |
| Property destroyed by enemy on account of military occupation by the United States | 5,800,000 |
| Property captured by enemy while in possession or employ of the United States | 500,000 |
| Claims of officers, soldiers, &c., for additional pay, bounty, &c | 400,000 |
| | 28,950,000 |

Many of these are doubtless test claims; that is, they are presented, and, if successful, others of like character will follow when once Congress shall be committed to the payment of any particular class.

The claim of J. Milton Best has been before Congress some years. Its success would

Claims for quartermaster's stores taken and used during the war in certain States and districts are investigated by the Quartermaster-General, under the law of July 4, 1864. The law makes it his duty to report each case, when certain conditions are satisfied, to the Third Auditor, with a recommendation for settlement.

The Quartermaster-General has done this so far as the clerical and other force at his command has permitted. He has always himself held that his action is confined to a report with recommendation, and that if any error appears in his conclusion, his report and recommendation are properly, like all other matters of account or settlement of which he takes official cognizance, subject to revision and correction by the accounting-officers, viz, the Third Auditor and Second Comptroller of the Treasury.

Payment is made, finally, only upon a statement and settlement of the account, approved by these officers.

Over 30,000 of these claims have been filed in the Quartermaster-General's Office. About 12,000 are still on file, which may be considered as not definitely settled or disposed of. It is not possible for the Quartermaster-General to definitely and absolutely reject a claim. Under the law, it is his duty to examine it, and, when convinced that it is just

---

secure, on the same principle, the payment of other claims arising at the same place, called "the Paducah claims," only recently presented, to the amount of $300,000. And claims of like character would arise from very many localities, amounting to very many millions. And the same may be said of other classes of claims.

If the ordinary rules of law on these subjects are not adhered to, the war-claims growing out of the rebellion will probably reach $500,000,000, without including pay for emancipated slaves or debts contracted in aid of rebellion, which are excluded from payment by the fourteenth amendment to the Constitution.

In addition to these, there are before the Committee on War-Claims the allowed and rejected claims reported to the House by the commissioners of claims, and referred to the committee, and the claims reported to the House under section 2 of the act of June 16, 1874.

But it will be seen the claims from Pennsylvania and Ohio alone for damages done by the enemy largely exceed the estimate for all the loyal Sates. The real damages done in all the loyal States by the enemy during the rebellion could not be compensated, probably, by $50,000,000, or possibly $100,000,000. There are also before the Senate Committees on Claims and Military Affairs over one thousand war-claims, involing over $20,000,000, and also claims of religious and educational institutions in Southern States, not before the House of Representatives.

There were before the Committee on War-Claims of the House of Representatives of the Forty-third Congress 1,420 claims up to date of February 22, 1875.

Of this number 216 have been reported upon to the House, of which number 148 were reported adversely and 68 favorably.

The cases reported favorably covered appropriations specifically of $300,000, most of the cases being referred to the Court of Claims or Commissioners of Claims, where the amount cannot be determined.

Of the number reported favorably, 33 were claims of officers and soldiers of Union Army; the cases reported adversely covering over $4,000,000.

Of the number reported favorably, 21 became laws, of which 11 were for relief of officers and soldiers of Union Army during late war; the amount appropriated being $75,000. At this date (February 25, 1875) Congress has not acted on all the reports of the committee.

The committee also examined and considered the third and fourth annual reports of the Commissioners of Claims. The third report of the commissioners embraced 2,465 cases, of which 1,092 were allowed and 1,373 disallowed.

The amount allowed was $643,713.04, and amount disallowed $4,074,174.25.

The amount appropriated in the bill reported by the committee was $676,274.03. The fourth report of the commissioners embraced 2,407 cases, of which 1,163 were allowed and 1,244 disallowed.

The amount allowed was $740,409.72, and amount disallowed over $4,400,000.

The amount appropriated by the bill reported by the committee was $748,296.39, five cases being added by the committee of cases reported allowed in former reports, but suspended for further examination.

The bill now pending making appropriations for claims allowed and reported, as required by section 2 of the act of June 16, 1874, proposes to pay $112,729.56.

and right, to report it with recommendation. Hence, if at any time not so convinced, he can only lay it aside and decline to make a report and recommendation, and the claimant is able and has a right to call it up again upon the production of additional evidence, or upon new argument addressed to the merits of the case.

Certain claims, apparently fraudulent, have been reported to the Auditor, with suggestion that the parties be prosecuted under the law relative to attempts to collect fraudulent claims against the United States. The Quartermaster-General, himself, has no authority to institute criminal proceedings. Such proceedings are for the Department of Justice, upon request of the Treasury.

The Quartermaster-General has several times advised members of

---

The committee reported adversely four claims, involving nearly $2,500,000, viz: Publishing House, Methodist Episcopal Church South, $457,000; invasion of Pennsylvania by Lee's army, $553,000; J. and T. Green, $982,201.75; Marie P. Evans, $495,355.

There are sundry claims before committees of both Houses of Congress for use and occupation of church, college, and school buildings, for injuries to them, or for destruction thereof. If Congress shall provide for their payment in whole or in part, either in detail or by some general scheme as a gratuity, there will of course be very many more which will doubtless be presented.

The claims of this character now before the House Committee on War-Claims are as follows:

METHODIST CHURCHES.

| | |
|---|---|
| Methodist Episcopal Church, Alexandria, Va | $11,000 |
| Methodist Episcopal Church, Charlestown, W. Va | 10,000 |
| Methodist Episcopal Church, Decatur, Ala | 12,000 |
| Methodist Episcopal Church, Huntsville, Ala | 13,354 |
| Methodist Episcopal Church, Harper's Ferry, W. Wa | 3,000 |
| Methodist Episcopal Church, Martinsburgh, W. Wa | 1,886 |
| Methodist Episcopal Church, Old Town, W. Va | 1,200 |
| Book-Agents' Publishing-House, Methodist Episcopal Church South | 457,150 |
| Methodist Episcopal Church Parsonage, Newtown, Va | 5,000 |

EPISCOPAL CHURCHES.

| | |
|---|---|
| Saint Paul's Episcopal Church, Selma, Ala | 12,000 |
| Saint Paul's Episcopal Church, Sharpsburgh, Md | 3,500 |
| Saint George's Episcopal Church, Accomac, Va | 5,000 |
| Saint Philip's Episcopal Church, Atlanta, Ga | 5,000 |
| Saint Mary's Episcopal Church, Fredericksburgh, Va | 725 |

CHRISTIAN CHURCHES.

| | |
|---|---|
| Christian Church, Woodsville, Ky<br>Christian Church, Danville, Ky | } 2,500 |

UNIVERSITIES AND COLLEGES, &c.

| | |
|---|---|
| Alabama University | 250,000 |
| East Tennessee University | 18,500 |
| Jackson College, Tennessee | 11,092 |
| Alleghany College, West Virginia | 8,000 |
| Madison Female Academy, Richmond, Va | 10,300 |
| Male Academy, Athens, Ga | 5,000 |
| Strawberry Plains High School, Tennessee | 8,650 |
| Seaman's Friend Society, Charleston, S. C | 2,500 |
| Cypress Lodge F. and A. M., Florence. Ala | 15,000 |
| Columbia Lodge F. and A. M., No. 31, Tennessee | 11,000 |

The following papers are now before the committee:

OFFICE POST-QUARTERMASTER,
*Atlanta, Georgia, July* 14, 1865.

GENERAL: I have the honor to state that, in compliance with instructions contained in your communication of the 7th instant, herewith inclosed, I instituted a careful investigation into the amount of damage done to Saint Luke's Church, in this city, its parsonage and fencing, and caused an estimate to be made by Mr. Frank Day, an architect of this city, of the necessary expense of repairing the same. I found that the

Congress calling upon him on business of their constituents in relation to these claims, that, in his opinion, the preferable method of disposing of them would be to institute commissions to visit the various districts of country, give public notice that they would receive claims between certain dates, and then at proper times hear and examine witnesses, and thus close up and determine the claims before the lapse of time makes it impossible to ascertain the facts for or against the justice of the

---

church, parsonage, and fencing had been entirely destroyed by our forces at the evacuation of this place by General Sherman, and that the probable cost of rebuilding the same, as estimated by the mechanic above named, is as follows:

| | |
|---|---|
| Saint Luke's Church | $2,500 |
| Parsonage and out-buildings | 2,250 |
| Fencing | 150 |

And that the earthworks on the lot belonging to Saint Philip's Church could be leveled at a cost of $150.

I am, general, very respectfully, your obedient servant,

ALONZO CLARK,
*Captain Fourth Iowa Cavalry, and A. A. Q. M.*

Bvt. Brig. Gen. J. L. DONALDSON,
*Chief Quartermaster Military Division of the Tennessee.*

[Copy of indorsement.]

HEADQUARTERS OF THE ARMY,
*Washington, D. C., January* 21, 1873.

I have not the least doubt this paper contains a fair and truthful account of the loss to this church in Atlanta. But instead of appealing to the Congress of the United States for indemnification, I advise the pastor of the church to appeal to the charitable members of the Episcopal Church for aid to rebuild their church and parsonage.

W. T. SHERMAN, *General.*

The following is extracted from speech of Hon. Henry G. Davis, of West Virginia, in United States Senate May 13, 1874, on the subject of war-claims. This table is subject to corrections elsewhere noted:

| | No. of claims presented. | Amount. | Number allowed. | Amount. |
|---|---|---|---|---|
| Commissary-General | 6,096 | $3,312,757 68 | 1,406 | $317,448 54 |
| Quartermaster-General, (up to close of fiscal year of 1874) | 31 126 | 21,319,180 02 | 6,257 | 2,741,961 67 |
| Quartermaster-General, (since beginning of above fiscal year) | 1,000 | 700,000 00 | ........ | ........ |
| Commissioners of Claims | 22,298 | 60,258,150 44 | 5,254 | 1,794,580 55 |
| Senate of United States | 104 | 3,500,000 00 | ........ | ........ |
| House of Representatives | 500 | 16,300,000 00 | ........ | ........ |
| Yet to be presented | ........ | 10,0..0,000 00 | ........ | ........ |
| Total | 61,124 | 115,390,088 14 | 12,917 | 4,853,990 76 |

| | Number rejected. | Amount. | Number pending. | Amount. |
|---|---|---|---|---|
| Commissary-General | 4,443 | $2,682,644 18 | 247 | $190,527 44 |
| Quartermaster-General, (up to close of fiscal year of 1874) | 13,522 | 9,048,044 57 | 11,347 | 7,822,829 55 |
| Quartermaster-General, (since beginning of above fiscal year) | ........ | ........ | 1,000 | 700,000 00 |
| Commissioners of Claims | ........ | ........ | 17,044 | 50,033,764 12 |
| Senate of United States | ........ | ........ | 104 | 3,500,000 00 |
| House of Representatives | ........ | ........ | 500 | 16,300,600 00 |
| Yet to be presented | ........ | ........ | ........ | 10,000,000 00 |
| Total | 17,965 | 11,730,688 75 | 30,242 | 88,547,121 11 |

But the claims are largely more than stated by Mr. Davis.

claim made. This, in his opinion, would secure a speedier settlement than he is able to afford, and would enable the United States to fix a time after which no claim should be entertained by any other authority than that of Congress itself.

Other claims against the Quartermaster's Department arise out of the occupation of real estate, lands, and buildings, by the Army. Others are for services not paid for when rendered. In fact, a claim may arise out of any unpaid obligation of the military service through the Quartermaster's Department. Excepting the claims to which the law of July 4, 1864, applies, all claims presented to this Office are examined, and, if believed to be just, settled; under the general authority and duty of the Executive to pay the debts of the Government for the War Department, by reference to the Secretary of War with report and recommendation, and then by payment either by a disbursing-officer, subject to subsequent revision and settlement by the accounting-officers of the Treasury, or, if the claim be for a liability of some standing, generally by reference to the Third Auditor, who examines all the evidence, and the report and action of the Quartermaster-General, and of the Secretary of War, and submits his report thereon to the Second Comptroller. If that officer approve, a settlement is made, which is transmitted to the War Department for request and requisition, and with these returned to the Treasury, when warrants and drafts are issued, and the debt is finally paid.

All these claims for old debts are settled out of the balance of appropriations made during and since the war, which have not yet been carried to the surplus fund. As there are many claims, (see Report of Quartermaster-General, page 225 of Ex. Doc. 1, part 2, House of Representatives, 42d Congress, 2d session,) they are in constant course of settlement, and many drafts are thus made every day upon these appropriations, which are by law to go to the surplus-fund only when no drafts have been made upon them for two years. If these balances are now, as proposed by House bill 1009, carried to the surplus-fund, the War Department will have no fund out of which to pay any old debt, however just and meritorious, and some provision should be made to do justice in cases which are not the less just because the debts were not paid when first due.

The labor of examining these claims, whether under the law of 1864 or under general laws, is very great, and it occupies a large part of the time of the Quartermaster-General and other officers of the War Department; and also costs a considerable sum in hire of clerks and agents to make the necessary investigation, and prepare the papers so as to enable the Quartermaster-General and the Secretary of War to act understandingly.

If any other tribunal, or means of settling all just claims can be devised, the Quartermaster-General will feel personally relieved from a heavy responsibility and laborious duty, but this is not a reason which would justify him in making any recommendation on the subject. Whatever the law imposes upon him, he is ready to perform to the best of his ability.

A copy of General Orders No. 59, Quartermaster-General's Office, series of 1867, publishing the act of July 4, 1864, and the regulations thereunder, is inclosed.

Very respectfully, your obedient servant,

M. C. MEIGS,
*Quartermaster-General United States Army.*

The Hon. SECRETARY OF WAR,
*Washington, D. C.*

OFFICE COMMISSARY-GENERAL OF SUBSISTENCE,
*Washington City, February 3, 1874.*

SIR: I have the honor to return herewith the letter of the 30th of January last, by its clerk, of the House of Representatives Committee on War-Claims, asking for a copy of certain rules and regulations concerning intercourse with rebel States during the war of the rebellion, &c., which was referred to the Commissary-General of Subsistence for such suggestions as he may wish to make concerning the general bill referred to in the letter as being considered covering the various classes of claims growing out of the war, and would respectfully suggest simply that, if practicable, in any future bill for the adjustment of claims for provisions or subsistence stores furnished, received, or taken for public use by the United States Army during the war of the rebellion, provision be made for the receipt and examination of such claims from all parts of the country alike, without regard to the place of their origin, whether in a loyal or an insurrectionary State, and that a reasonably early day be fixed, prior to which every such claim must be filed, complete in detail of items and evidence, to entitle it to examination, and any claim not so filed prior to that date to be barred, and, if presented thereafter, returned without examination; and, in any case, claims once examined and decided not to be re-opened.

Now, under the 3d section of the act of July 4, 1864, claims of loyal citizens of non-insurrectionary States come before this Office "for subsistence actually furnished to said [United States] Army, and receipted for by the proper officer receiving the same, or which may have been taken by such officer without giving such receipt," while claims "for stores or supplies taken or furnished during the rebellion for the use of the Army of the United States in States proclaimed as in insurrection," come before the commissioners of claims for examination, and by special statutes like claims for subsistence from the State of Tennessee, and from the counties of Jefferson and Berkeley, West Virginia, came before this Office prior to March 3, 1871, the date of the act establishing the commission of claims, and before that commission since, so that claimants from Tennessee, and the two West Virginia counties named, have had the benefit of both these acts; while claimants from the insurrectionary States in general, by the more liberal or less restricted terms of the act under which the commission is authorized than the section governing the action of this Office, may perhaps be considered to have somewhat the advantage over claimants in the loyal States. It is known, too, that the same claimants in not a few instances have presented claims to this Office, and also to the commission of claims, and it is believed for about the same stores. The propriety of the law being general and uniform is therefore suggested. And that justice may be done uniformly to claimants and the Government alike, it is deemed highly desirable, if practicable, that all claims of the character under consideration be submitted to and examined by one jurisdiction or authority.

Very respectfully, your obedient servant,

A. B. EATON,
*Commissary-General.*

HON. W. W. BELKNAP,
*Secretary of War.*

So far as any citizen furnished quartermaster's stores or commissary supplies during the rebellion, or so far as these were taken for the Union military forces, ample provision is made by law for their adjudication by application to the War Department.[177]

The laws and regulations as to claims are as follows:

[General Orders No. 59.]

QUARTERMASTER-GENERAL'S OFFICE,
*Washington, D. C., October* 11, 1867.

The following joint resolutions and acts of Congress, with rules and regulations established thereon to govern in the submission and examination of claims to be presented to the Quartermaster-General and to the Commissary-General of Subsistence, respectively, are published for the information and guidance of officers and agents of the Qurtermaster's Department.

D. H. RUCKER,
*Acting Quartermaster-General, Brevet Major-General, U. S. A.*

## CHAPTER 240, FIRST SESSION 38TH CONGRESS.

AN ACT to restrict the jurisdiction of the Court of Claims, and to provide for the payment of certain demands for quartermaster's stores and subsistence supplies furnished to the Army of the United States.

*Be it enacted by the Senate and House of Representatives of the United States of America in Congress assembled*, That the jurisdiction of the Court of Claims shall not extend to or include any claim against the United States growing out of the destruction or appropriation of or damage to property by the Army or Navy, or any part of the Army or Navy, engaged in the suppression of the rebellion, from the commencement to the close thereof.

SEC. 2. *And be it further enacted*, That all claims of loyal citizens in States not in rebellion for quartermaster's stores actually furnished to the Army of the United States, and receipted for by the proper officer receiving the same, or which may have been taken by such officers without giving such receipt, may be submitted to the Quartermaster-General of the United States, accompanied with such proofs as each claimant can present of the facts in his case; and it shall be the duty of the Quartermaster-General to cause such claim to be examined, and if convinced that it is just, and of the loyalty of the claimant, and that the stores have been actually received or taken for the use of and used by said Army, then to report each case to the Third Auditor of the Treasury, with a recommendation for settlement.

SEC. 3. *And be it further enacted*, That all claims of loyal citizens in States not in rebellion for subsistence actually furnished to said Army, and receipted for by the proper officer receiving the same, or which may

[177] See House Report No. 262, of Committee on War Claims, 1st session 43d Congress, March 26, 1874, pp. 25–74; also, report No. 754, June 22, 1854; act of March 3, 1813, ch. 513, sec. 5; art. 42, Revised Army Regulations, August 11, 1861, authorized by act of April 24, 1816, sec. 9, (ch. 69, 3 Stat. at L., 298,) and act May 7, 1822, (3 Stat. at L., 689;) Scott's Digest Military Laws, p. 134, sec. 182; United States *vs.* Eliason, 16 Peters, 291; United States *vs.* Freeman, 3 How., 566; Gratiot *vs.* United States, 4 Howard, 80; Harney *vs.* United States, 3 Nott & H., 42; Opinions Attorneys-General, May 19, 1821, and January 1, 1857; House Ex. Doc. No. 121, 1st session 43d Congress; act July 4, 1864, ch. 240.

have been taken by such officer without giving such receipt, may be submitted to the Commissary-General of Subsistence, accompanied with such proofs as each claimant may have to offer; and it shall be the duty of the Commissary-General of Subsistence to cause each claim to be examined, and if convinced that it is just, and of the loyalty of the claimant, and that the stores have been received or taken actually for the use of and used by said Army, then to report each case for payment to the Third Auditor of the Treasury, with a recommendation for settlement.

Approved July 4, 1864.

To extend to the counties of Berkeley and Jefferson, of West Virginia, the provisions of the preceding act, as follows:

### JOINT RESOLUTION NO. 50, FIRST SESSION 39TH CONGRESS.

*Be it resolved by the Senate and House of Representatives of the United States of America in Congress assembled*, That the provisions of the act of Congress of July 4, 1864, entitled "An act to restrict the jurisdiction of the Court of Claims, and for other purposes," be, and the same are hereby, construed to extend to the counties of Berkeley and Jefferson, of the State of West Virginia.

Approved June 18, 1866.

To extend the provisions of the act of July 4, 1864, limiting the jurisdiction of the Court of Claims, to the loyal citizens of Tennessee, as follows:

### JOINT RESOLUTION NO. 99, FIRST SESSION 39TH CONGRESS.

*Be it resolved by the Senate and House of Representatives of the United States of America in Congress assembled*, That the provisions of the act of the 4th of July, 1864, entitled "An act to limit the jurisdiction of the Court of Claims," is hereby extended to the loyal citizens of the State of Tennessee.

Approved July 28, 1866.

### CHAPTER 57, SECOND SESSION 39TH CONGRESS.

AN ACT to declare the sense of an act entitled "An act to restrict the jurisdiction of the Court of Claims, and to provide for the payment of certain demands for quartermaster's stores and subsistence supplies furnished to the Army of the United States," as follows:

*Be it enacted by the Senate and House of Representatives of the United States of America in Congress assembled*, That the provisions of chapter 240 of the acts of the Thirty-eighth Congress, first session, approved July 4, 1864, shall not be construed to authorize the settlement of any claim for supplies or stores taken or furnished for the use of or used by the armies of the United States, nor for the occupation of or injury to real estate, nor for the consumption, appropriation, or destruction of or damage to personal property by the military authorities or troops of the United States, when such claim originated during the war for the suppression of the southern rebellion, in a State, or part of a State, declared in insurrection by the proclamation of the President of the United States, dated July first, 1862, or in a State which, by an ordinance of secession, attempted to withdraw from the United States Government: *Provided*, That nothing herein contained shall repeal or modify the effects of any act or joint resolution extending the provisions of the said act of July 4, 1864, to the loyal citizens of the State of Tennessee, or to the State of West Virginia, or any county thereof.

Indorsed by the President: "Received February 9, 1867."

[Note by the State Department: The foregoing act having been presented to the President of the United States for his approval, and not having been returned by him to the House of Congress in which it originated within the time prescribed by the Constitution of the United States, has become a law without his approval.]

To extend the provision of section two of the act of July 4, 1864, limiting the jurisdiction of the Court of Claims to cases of quartermaster's stores furnished to the forces of Major-General Lewis Wallace during the Morgan raid through the States of Indiana and Ohio in the summer of 1863, as follows:

## JOINT RESOLUTION NO. 50, SECOND SESSION 39TH CONGRESS.

*Be it resolved by the Senate and House of Representatives of the United States of America in Congress assembled*, That the provisions of section two of the above-entitled act be, and they are hereby, extended to cover all cases where quartermaster's stores were actually furnished to the forces under the command of Major-General Lewis Wallace, and duly receipted for by persons acting under his authority, and whose authority shall be proven to the satisfaction of the accounting-officers, during the Morgan raid through the States of Indiana and Ohio, in the summer of eighteen hundred and sixty-three, and for the purpose of giving such receipts for property so applied the said persons shall be held to be proper officers of the Government.

Approved March 2, 1867.

The following rules and regulations, to govern in the submission and examination of claims to be presented to the Quartermaster-General and to the Commissary-General of Subsistence, respectively, under the act of July 4, 1864, (and the several acts and joint resolutions amendatory and explanatory thereof, as herein published,) entitled "An act to restrict the jurisdiction of the Court of Claims, and to provide for the payment of certain demands for quartermaster's stores and subsistence supplies furnished to the Army of the United States," and the evidence of proofs which must accompany them, are hereby established:

### I—.CLAIMS TO BE SUBMITTED TO AND EXAMINED BY THE QUARTERMASTER-GENERAL.

All claims of loyal citizens in States not in rebellion for "quartermaster's stores" actually furnished to the Army of the United States, and receipted for by the proper officer receiving the same, or which may have been taken by such officers without giving such receipts.

### II.—CLAIMS TO BE SUBMITTED TO AND EXAMINED BY THE COMMISSARY-GENERAL OF SUBSISTENCE.

All claims of loyal citizens in States not in rebellion for "subsistence, actually furnished to said Army, and receipted for by the proper officer receiving the same, or which may have been taken by such officers without giving such receipts.

## III.—PROOFS REQUIRED IN SUPPORT OF THE ABOVE CLASSES OF CLAIMS.

1st. That the claimant is a loyal citizen of a State not in rebellion. (Claims of citizens of the following States, declared by the President of the United States, by his proclamation of the 1st day of July, 1862, to be in insurrection, will not be considered, viz: Arkansas, Texas, Louisiana, Mississippi, Alabama, Florida, Georgia, South Carolina, North Carolina, and Virginia.)

2d. Citizenship.—The claimant will be required to show, by his own affidavit, supported by the certificate of the clerk or recorder of the town or county of which he claims to be a citizen, that said claimant is a citizen of said town or county.

3d. Loyalty.—The claimant will be required to file with his claim the oath of allegiance to the Government of the United States, as prescribed by the President's proclamation of the 8th of December, 1863, supported by the certificate of a United States officer, civil or military, that the said claimant was, at the date his claim originated, and has been ever since, loyal to the United States, or the sworn statement of the same facts of at least two witnesses, whose loyalty and credibility shall be vouched for by the certificate of the officers before mentioned.

4th. Claims arising under this act must be presented by the claimant or his authorized attorney; and, in the latter case, it must be shown by the certificate of the assessor or collector of his district that he has been duly licensed and authorized to act as a claim-agent.

## IV.—VALIDITY OF CLAIMS.

1st. When quartermaster's stores or subsistence supplies have been taken by officers and receipted for, all of such receipts or vouchers must be filed; or their absence, in any case, must be fully and satisfactorily explained by proper evidence.[178]

2d. When such stores or supplies have been taken by officers without giving such receipts, the claim must set forth the kinds and quantity of stores or supplies, when, where, and by what officer taken, the price or value thereof, and must be supported by the affidavit of the claimant as to the correctness of the claim; that the articles named in the claim were actually delivered to or taken by said officer for the use of the Army; that no receipt or voucher has been received therefor; that no payment has been made or compensation received, in any way or from any source whatever, for the whole or any part of said claim; that it has not been transferred to any person or persons whomsoever; and that the rates or prices charged are reasonable and just, and do not exceed the market-rate or price of the article at the time and place stated.

3d. In all cases, whether or not receipts have been given for the stores or supplies, the affidavit required by the next preceding paragraph must be supported by such additional affidavits, or other proofs, in relation to the facts stated, as may be attainable. The credibility of the claimant and of the witnesses must be vouched for by the certificate of an officer of the United States, civil or military. If receipts have been given, the affidavit above referred to will be modified, so far as it

[178] By "receipts or vouchers" is meant each and every copy of any and all documents—in whatever form, *whether in ink or pencil*—given by or bearing the signature of any officer in the service of the United States (or by any enlisted man in such service, acting under proper authority) for or relating to the whole or any portion of the stores for which payment is claimed. The attention of *agents* and *attorneys* is particularly called to a strict compliance with this requirement in presenting claims.

relates to receipts or vouchers, substantially as follows: That all of the receipts or vouchers given for such stores or supplies are hereto annexed.

4th. Proof must be furnished, as far as attainable, that the quartermaster's stores or subsistence supplies mentioned have been actually used by the Army of the United States. This proof should, whenever practicable, consist of the certificate or affidavit of the officer who took the stores, or who ordered them taken, or who, after such taking, took them in charge, setting forth the fact of such taking, to what use the stores were applied, and whether or not they have been accounted for as required by the Regulations of the Army; and if accounted for, upon what returns, or, if not, the reason for failing to account for the same; or, in case the above proof is not attainable, the certificates of other officers, or the affidavit of a soldier, or some other credible witnesses, knowing the facts, setting forth by whom and for what purpose the property was taken, and to what use it was applied.

5th. Claims for damages or for losses sustained by thefts or depredations committed by troops, or so much of a charge for stores or supplies as is an element of damages, will not be considered under these acts and joint resolutions.

6th. Powers of attorney, legally executed by claimants to agents, (bearing properly affixed and canceled internal-revenue stamps,) must accompany claims presented by agents.

7th. The general allegation that stores, for which payment is claimed, were taken by the officer in command of a large body of troops, for whose subsistence or use the property was applied, or by his order, is not sufficient to establish a claim under this act. Such officers seldom, if ever, personally receive stores, (that duty devolving upon subordinate officers,) and though issuing orders authorizing the taking of the property as a military necessity, seldom have any knowledge whatever of the particular cases affected by the execution of such orders on the part of their subordinates, except, perhaps, in some few cases arising under peculiar circumstances. Therefore, to facilitate the examination of claims, and to enable the officers deciding them to comply with that clause of the law requiring them, before recommending claims for payment, to be "convinced" that the property was taken in the manner and for the purpose therein set forth, (as distinguished from thefts and depredations, by whomsoever committed,) claimants are required to furnish the following information (or so much of it as they reasonably may) as a part of their sworn declaration in each case, viz:

1. The name, rank, regiment, and, when known, the post-office address of each officer who took any portion of the stores.

2. Immediately after each officer's name and designation, state the articles and quantities (with their prices) taken by him, together with the exact date when, and locality where, taken.

3. Name the brigade, division, and corps with which, or the station or post at which, each officer was serving; the name and official designation of the commissary or acting commissary of subsistence of that brigade, station, or post, and that of the officer in immediate command thereof at the time; and add thereto such attendant facts and circumstances as transpired at the time in any way bearing upon the case.

4. State the exact locality of claimant's present residence; if in a city, give street and number; if in the country, the nearest post-office.

5. The claims must be legibly written; and particular care should be taken in the "declarations" of claimants, and in the affidavits of witnesses, to correctly state the month and year in which the transaction occurred.

8th. Claimants will be required to prove the genuineness of the signatures to the receipts filed in support of claims submitted under joint resolution No. 50, of March 2, 1867, and to furnish evidence that the persons executing such receipts were acting under the authority of Major-General Wallace.

D. H. RUCKER,
*Brevet Major-General and Acting Quartermaster-General.*
A. B. EATON,
*Brevet Major-General and Commissary-General of Subsistence.*

Approved October 10, 1867.
U. S. GRANT,
*Secretary of War ad int.*

The following forms also have been prescribed:

CLAIM, FORM L.

WAR DEPARTMENT,
QUARTERMASTER-GENERAL'S OFFICE,
*Washington, D. C.*, ——, 187–.

To —— ——:

SIR: In the claim of —— ——, a citizen of ——, it is alleged that —— were taken from him, on or about ——, by ——.

The evidence presented is not sufficient to enable the Quartermaster-General to certify that he is convinced that the claim is just, and that the stores were actually received or taken for the use of, and used by, the United States Army, as required by the act of July 4, 1864, before recommending it to the Third Auditor for settlement.

*In the absence of receipts, or other official evidence given at the time the stores are alleged to have been taken, there is required the testimony of some officer, soldier, or person employed by the Government, personally cognizant of the alleged appropriation, detailing in full the circumstances attendant thereon, and setting forth, of his own knowledge, the details of the seizure, the quantities and values, and the use to which the property was applied, and the regiment, company, detachment, or other military body, to the use of which the stores were appropriated.*

Very respectfully, your obedient servant,
By order of the Quartermaster-General,
—— ——.

FORM No. 13.—(Voucher to Abstract B.)

THE UNITED STATES,
To —— ——, DR.

| Place and date. | | Dolls. | Cts. |
|---|---|---|---|
| | | | |

I certify that the above account is correct and just; that the services were rendered as stated; that they were necessary for the public service, and are borne on my report of persons, &c., for the month of ———, 18—.

——— ———,
——— ———.

Received, at ———, the ——— day of ———, 18—, of ——— ———, quartermaster ——— United States Army, the sum of ——— dollars and ——— cents, in full of the above account.

——— ———,
——— ———.

(Signed in duplicate.)

Indorsed as follows:

Form No. 13. Voucher No. —, Abstract B. ———, 18—. ——— ———. Dollars, ——— $\frac{}{100}$. Paid ———, 18—. Check: No. —. Date, ———. Amount, $———. Depository, ———. [To be in duplicate; one copy to be retained by the officer, the other to be forwarded to the Quartermaster-General with Abstract B. This form is used for payment of services not entered on the receipt-rolls, for rent of buildings, and for other miscellaneous disbursements. When a man is discharged without being paid, his account will be stated on this form, certified, and given to him. It may sometimes be used as a voucher to Abstract C.]

FORM No. 9.—(Voucher to Abstract A.)

THE UNITED STATES,

To ——— ———, Dr.

| Place and date of purchase. | | Dolls. | Cts. |
|---|---|---|---|
| | | | |

I certify that the above account is correct and just, and that the articles have been accounted for on my property-return for the quarter ending on the ——— of ———, 187–.

——— ———,
——— *Quartermaster* ———.

Received, at ———, the ——— of ———, 187–, of ——— ———, quartermaster ——— U. S. Army, the sum of ——— dollars and ——— cents, in full of the above account.

——— ———.

(Signed in duplicate.)

Indorsed as follows:

Form No. 9. Voucher No. —, Abstract A. ———, 187–. ——— ———. Dollars, ——— $\frac{}{100}$. Paid ———, 187–. Check: No. —. Date:———. Amount, $———. Depository, ———. To be made in duplicate; one copy to be retained by the officer, one to be forwarded to the Quartermaster-General with Abstract A. The authority for making a purchase and a statement of the object and necessity for the same must accompany the voucher. If such authority has already been filed, it should be referred to in all subsequent vouchers for purchases under it. If the purchase is made under a contract, the name of the contractor, and its object, should be given, as per example: Under contract of John Smith, for forage, Nov. 17, 18—. No reference should be made to any agreement not in writing, and not transmitted to the Quartermaster-General's Office for file.

The act of July 4, 1864, only applied to "quartermaster's *stores*" and "*subsistence*."

This did not cover *rent*, or *use and occupation*. But these were authorized to be paid by *prior acts*.

The acts of July 4, 1864, and February 21, 1867, prohibited the executive officers of the Government from paying for *stores, supplies, use and occupation*, or *rent*, in the States proclaimed in insurrection.

But the act of February 21, 1867, did not exclude payment where the claim arose on *contract*.

This was decided by the Attorney-General September 2, 1870; vol. 13, Opinions, p. 314. (See House Report No. 262, Committee on War-Claims, 1st session 43d Congress, p. 75.)

This opinion of the Attorney-General has a valuable review of the *legislation* on the subject.

Since then the mode of providing for the payment of claims arising under the act of July 4, 1864, and the amendatory acts, has been changed, as will be seen from the following:

[General Orders No. 58.]

"WAR DEPARTMENT, ADJUTANT-GENERAL'S OFFICE,
"*Washington, June* 18, 1874.

The following act of Congress is published for the information and government of all concerned:

AN ACT making appropriations for the support of the Army for the fiscal year ending June thirtieth, eighteen hundred and seventy-five, and for other purposes.

*Be it enacted by the Senate and House of Representatives of the United States of America in Congress assembled*, That the following sums be, and the same are hereby, appropriated, out of any moneys in the Treasury not otherwise appropriated, for the support of the Army for the year ending June thirtieth, eighteen hundred and seventy-five, as follows:

Then the appropriations follow.

SEC. 2. That all balances of appropriations, for whatever account, made for the service of the Department of the Quartermaster-General *and of the Commissary-General of Subsistence prior to July first, eighteen hundred and seventy-two*, which, *on the thirtieth day of June, eighteen hundred and seventy-four*, shall remain *on* the books of the Treasury, *shall be carried to the surplus fund*, except such as the Auditor of the Treasury, whose duty it is to settle accounts against such appropriations, shall certify to the Secretary of the Treasury to be necessary in the settlement of such accounts as have been reported to him for payment by the Quartermaster's and Commissary Departments pending in his office. *And the Quartermaster-General, Commissary-General, and Third Auditor of the Treasury shall continue to receive, examine, and consider the justice and validity of such claims as shall be brought before them under the act of July fourth, eighteen hundred and sixty-four, and the acts amendatory thereof; and the Secretary of the Treasury shall make report of each claim allowed by them, at the commencement of each session of Congress, to the Speaker of the House of Representatives, who shall lay the same before Congress for consideration.*

*Approved June* 17, 1874.

By order of the Secretary of War:

E. D. TOWNSEND,
*Adjutant-General.*

Official:

——— ———,
*Assistant Adjutant-General.*

The annual report of the Quartermaster-General, dated October 10, 1874, page 26, contains the following:

## CLAIMS AND ACCOUNTS.

By section 2 of the act making appropriations for the support of the Army for the year ending 30th June, 1875, the Quartermaster-General is directed to continue to receive and investigate claims for quartermaster's stores under the act of July 4, 1864, and the acts amendatory thereof, and to report them as heretofore, in order that the Secretary of the Treasury may report those recommended for allowance to the Speaker of the House of Representatives at the commencement of each session of Congress.

The legislative, executive, and judicial appropriation act of June 20, 1874, (Laws, p. 110,) directed all unexpended balances of appropriations, which have remained on the books of the Treasury for more than two fiscal years, to be carried to the surplus fund and covered into the Treasury. The operation of this law concluded the payment by the Treasury of claims and debts of the United States incurred more than two years before the time of proof and acknowledgment.

There were in this Office, unsettled, on 1st July, 1873, 11,347 claims under the act of 4th July, 1864, amounting, as claimed, to $7,822,829.55. There were filed during the year 2,606, for $3,144,572.34. Total, 13,953, for $10,967,401.89. Of these, 881, claiming $1,032,484.88, have been reported, recommending allowance of $495,234.38, a reduction of $537,280.47; 528, claiming the sum of $694,152.19, have been reported unfavorably. Thus 1,409 claims have been disposed of, amounting, as presented, to $1,726,637.04, and there remained at the end of the year 12,544 claims, for $9,240,764.85.

## CLAIMS AND ACCOUNTS CONNECTED WITH THE SERVICE OF TRANSPORTATION OF THE ARMY.

Two hundred and twelve accounts for transportation, amounting to $613,395.72, were on file on 1st July, 1873. Eight hundred and eighty-five accounts, for $767,876.32, and 448 claims, for $897,008.80, were filed during the year. Total, 1,545, for $2,278,278.84. Of these 1,310 have been disposed of; their amount is $1,664,952.75. Ninety-five, amounting to $400,016.19, were rejected. Seventy-five, amounting to $117,935.41, were suspended. The remainder were either reported for settlement or transferred to other Departments to which they properly pertained. There remained on 30th June, 1874, 235 accounts and claims for transportation, amounting to $613,326.11.

## MISCELLANEOUS CLAIMS AND ACCOUNTS.

Fourteen thousand and forty-six claims, amounting to $7,475,120.87, were on file at beginning of fiscal year; 12,246 were received during the year, amounting to $1,745,024.29. Total, 26,292 claims and accounts, for $9,220,145.16.

Five thousand and forty claims were approved, for $738,950.73, being a reduction in the amount as presented of $269,916.37; 540, amounting to $271,992.79, were rejected; 53, amounting to $5,703.25, were referred to other Departments to which they pertained; 6,180 accounts were approved, for $442,956.93, being a reduction in the accounts as presented of $4,682.01; 35 accounts were rejected, amounting to $7,935.42; total disposed of, 11,848 accounts and claims, amounting, as presented, to $1,742,147.50. Thirteen thousand five hundred and ninety-seven miscellaneous claims and 847 accounts remain on file, amounting to $7,477,997.66.

The annual report of the Commissary-General of Subsistence, dated October 10, 1874, p. 4, says:

Under the third section of the act of July 4, 1864, 310 claims, amounting to $235,956.85, for subsistence supplies alleged to have been used by the Army or taken by officers for the use of the Army, in the late war, in States not in rebellion, were filed in this office for examination; 73 claims, amounting to $66,712.93, were examined and recommended to the Third Auditor of the Treasury for payment; and 109 claims, amounting to $129,327.49, were examined and rejected.

Under the joint resolution of Congress of July 25, 1866, and section 3 of the act of March 2, 1867, 175 certificates for commutation of rations to Union soldiers while prisoners of war were received and paid to the claimants or their legal heirs. These payments amounted to $5,739.75.

And see report of Third Auditor.

---

# CHAPTER VIII.

## THE COURT OF CLAIMS.

The law of Congress organizing the Court of Claims and defining its jurisdiction is, as found in the Revised Statutes of the United States, as follows:

### ORGANIZATION AND SESSIONS.



SEC. 1049. The Court of Claims, established by the act of February twenty-four, eighteen hundred and fifty-five, shall be continued. It shall consist of a chief-justice and four judges, who shall be appointed by the President, by and with the advice and consent of the Senate, and hold their offices during good behavior. Each of them shall take an oath to support the Constitution of the United States, and to discharge faithfully the duties of his office, and shall be entitled to receive an annual salary of four thousand five hundred dollars, payable quarterly from the Treasury.

Judges.

24 Feb., 1855, c. 122, s. 1, v. 10, p. 612.
3 Mar., 1863, c. 92, s. 1, v. 12, p. 765.
8 May, 1872, c. 140, s. 13, v. 17, p. 85.

SEC. 1050. The Court of Claims shall have a seal, with such device as it may order.

Seal.

3 Mar., 1863, c. 92, s. 4, v. 12, p. 766.

SEC. 1051. It shall be the duty of the Speaker of the House of Representatives to appropriate such rooms in the Capitol, at Washington, for the use of the Court of Claims, as may be necessary for their accommodation, unless it appears to him that such rooms cannot be so appropriated without interfering with the business of Congress. In that

Court-rooms, &c., how provided.

24 Feb. 1855, c. 122, s. 10, v. 10, p. 614.

case, the court shall procure, at the city of Washington, such rooms as may be necessary for the transaction of their business.

Sessions, quorum.

24 Feb., 1855, c. 122, s. 10, v. 10, p. 614.
6 Aug., 1856, c. 81, s. 1, v. 11, p. 30.
17 Mar., 1866, c. 19, s. 2, v. 14, p. 9.
3 Mar., 1863, c. 92, s. 13, v. 12, p. 768.

SEC. 1052. The Court of Claims shall hold one annual session, at the city of Washington, beginning on the first Monday in December, and continuing as long as may be necessary for the prompt disposition of the business of the court. And any two of the judges of said court shall constitute a quorum, and may hold a court for the transaction of business.

Officers of the court.

24 Feb., 1855, c. 122, s. 11, v. 10, p. 614.
3 Mar., 1863, c. 92, s. 4, v. 12, p. 765.

SEC. 1053. The said court shall appoint a chief clerk, an assistant clerk, if deemed necessary, a bailiff, and a messenger. The clerks shall take an oath for the faithful discharge of their duties, and shall be under the direction of the court in the performance thereof; and for misconduct or incapacity they may be removed by it from office; but the court shall report such removals, with the cause thereof, to Congress, if in session, or, if not, at the next session. The bailiff shall hold his office for a term of four years, unless sooner removed by the court for cause.

Salaries of clerks, bailiff, and messenger.

24 Feb., 1855, c. 122, s. 11, v. 10, p. 614.
3 Mar., 1863, c. 92, s. 4, v. 12, p. 765.
7 June, 1870, c. 124, v. 16, p. 148.
12 July, 1870, c. 251, s. 3, v. 16, p. 250.
8 May, 1872, c. 140, s. 1, v. 17, p. 82.

SEC. 1054. The salary of the chief clerk shall be three thousand dollars a year, of the assistant clerk two thousand dollars a year, of the bailiff fifteen hundred dollars a year, and of the messenger eight hundred and forty dollars a year, payable quarterly from the Treasury.

Clerk's bond.

6 Aug., 1856, c. 81, s. 3, v. 11 p. 30.

SEC. 1055. The chief clerk shall give bond to the United States in such amount, in such form, and with such security as shall be approved by the Secretary of the Treasury.

Contingent fund.

6 Aug., 1856, c. 81, s. 3, v. 11, p. 30

SEC. 1056. The said clerk shall have authority, when he has given bond as provided in the preceding section, to disburse, under the direction of the court, the contingent fund which may from time to time be appropriated for its use; and his accounts shall be settled by the proper accounting officers of the Treasury in the same way as the accounts of other disbursing agents of the Government are settled.

Report to Congress, copies for Departments, &c.

25 June, 1868, c. 71, s. 9, v. 15, p. 77.
17 Mar., 1866, c. 19, s. 3, v. 14, p. 9.

SEC. 1057. On the first day of every December session of Congress, the clerk of the Court of Claims shall transmit to Congress a full and complete statement of all the judgments rendered by the court during the previous year, stating the amounts thereof and the parties in whose favor they were rendered, together with a brief synopsis of the nature of the claims upon which they were rendered. And at the end of every term of the court he shall transmit a copy of its decisions to the heads of Departments; to the Solicitor, the Comptrollers, and the Auditors of the Treasury; to the Commissioners of the General Land-Office and of Indian

Affairs; to the chiefs of Bureaus, and to other officers charged with the adjustment of claims against the United States.

SEC. 1058. Members of either House of Congress shall not practice in the Court of Claims.

Members of Congress not to practice in the court.

3 Mar., 1863, c. 92. s. 4, v. 12, p. 765.

---

## JURISDICTION, POWERS, AND PROCEDURE.



SEC. 1059. The Court of Claims shall have jurisdiction to hear and determine the following matters:

Jurisdiction.

First. All claims founded upon any law of Congress, or upon any regulation of an Executive Department, or upon any contract, expressed or implied, with the Government of the United States, and all claims which may be referred to it by either House of Congress.

Claims founded on statutes or contracts, or referred by Congress.

24 Feb., 1855, c. 122, s. 1, v. 10, p. 612.—Nichols *vs.* U. S., 7 Wall., 129; Dorsheimer *vs.* U. S. 7 Wall., 166; Bonner *vs.* U. S., 9 Wall., 156.

Second. All set-offs, counter-claims, claims for damages, whether liquidated or unliquidated, or other demands whatsoever, on the part of the Government of the United States against any person making claim against the Government in said court.

Set-offs and counter-claims of United States.

3 Mar., 1863, c. 92, s. 3, v. 12, p. 765.—Clyde *vs.* U. S., 13 Wall., 38; U. S., *vs.* Russell, 13 Wall., 623.

Third. The claim of any paymaster, quartermaster, commissary of subsistence, or other disbursing officer of the United States, or of his administrators or executors, for relief from responsibility on account of capture or otherwise,

Disbursing officers.

9 May, 1866, c. 75, s. 1, v. 14, p. 44.

while in the line of his duty, of Government funds, vouchers, records, or papers in his charge, and for which such officer was and is held responsible.

Claims for captured and abandoned property.

12 Mar., 1863, c. 120, s. 3, v. 12, p. 820.
2 July, 1864, c. 225, ss. 2, 3, v. 13, pp. 375, 376.
27 July, 1868, c. 276 s. 3, v. 15, p. 243.

U. S. *vs.* Anderson, 9 Wall., 56; Pugh *vs.* U. S., 13 Wall, 633; U. S. *vs.* Kimball, 13 Wall., 636; U. S. *vs.* Crussell, 14 Wall., 1; Slawson *vs.* U. S., 16 Wall., 310.

Fourth. Of all claims for the proceeds of captured or abandoned property, as provided by the act of March 12, eighteen hundred and sixty-three, chapter one hundred and twenty, entitled "An act to provide for the collection of abandoned property and for the prevention of frauds in insurrectionary districts within the United States," or by the act of July two, eighteen hundred and sixty-four, chapter two hundred and twenty-five, being an act in addition thereto: *Provided*, That the remedy given in cases of seizure under the said acts, by preferring claim in the Court of Claims, shall be exclusive, precluding the owner of any property taken by agents of the Treasury Department as abandoned or captured property in virtue or under color of said acts from suit at common law, or any other mode of redress whatever, before any court other than said Court of Claims.

Private claims in Congress, when transmitted to Court of Claims.

3 Mar., 1863, c. 92, s. 2, v. 12, p. 765.

SEC. 1060. All petitions and bills praying or providing for the satisfaction of private claims against the Government, founded upon any law of Congress, or upon any regulation of an Executive Department, or upon any contract, expressed or implied, with the Government of the United States, shall, unless otherwise ordered by resolution of the House in which they are introduced, be transmitted by the Secretary of the Senate or the Clerk of the House of Representatives, with all the accompanying documents, to the Court of Claims.

Judgments for set-off or counter-claim, how enforced.

3 Mar., 1863, c. 92, s. 3, v. 12, p. 765.

Allen *vs.* U. S., 17 Wall., 207.

SEC. 1061. Upon the trial of any cause in which any set-off, counter-claim, claim for damages, or other demand is set up on the part of the Government against any person making claim against the Government in said court, the court shall hear and determine such claim or demand both for and against the Government and claimant; and if upon the whole case it finds that the claimant is indebted to the Government, it shall render judgment to that effect, and such judgment shall be final, with the right of appeal, as in other cases provided for by law. Any transcript of such judgment, filed in the clerk's office of any district or circuit court, shall be entered upon the records thereof, and shall thereby become and be a judgment of such court and be enforced as other judgments in such courts are enforced.

Decree on accounts of paymasters, &c.

9 May, 1866, c. 75, s. 2, v. 14, p. 44.

SEC. 1062. Whenever the Court of Claims ascertains the facts of any loss by any paymaster, quartermaster, commissary of subsistence, or other disbursing officer, in the cases hereinbefore provided, to have been without fault or negligence on the part of such officer, it shall make a decree setting forth the amount thereof, and upon such decree the proper accounting officers of the Treasury shall allow to such officer the amount so decreed, as a credit in the settlement of his accounts.

Claims referred by Departments.

25 June, 1868, c. 71, s. 7, v. 15, p. 76.

SEC. 1063. Whenever any claim is made against any Executive Department, involving disputed facts or controverted questions of law, where the amount in controversy exceeds three thousand dollars, or where the decision will affect a class of cases, or furnish a precedent for the future action of any Executive Department in the adjustment of a class of cases, without regard to the amount involved in the particular case, or where any authority, right, privilege, or exemption is claimed or denied under the Constitution of the United States, the head of such Department may cause such claim, with all the vouchers, papers, proofs, and documents pertaining thereto, to be transmitted to the Court of Claims, and the same shall be there proceeded in as if originally commenced by the voluntary action of the claimant; and the Secretary of the Treasury may, upon the certificate of any Auditor or Comptroller of the Treasury, direct any account, matter, or claim of the character, amount, or class described in this section, to be transmitted, with all the vouchers, papers, documents, and proofs pertaining thereto, to the said court, for trial and adjudication: *Provided*, That no case shall be referred by any head of a Department unless it belongs to one of the several classes of cases which, by reason of the subject-matter and character, the said court might, under existing laws, take jurisdiction of on such voluntary action of the claimant.

Procedure in cases transmitted by Departments.

25 June, 1868, c. 71, s. 7, v. 15, p. 76.

Clyde *vs.* U. S., 13 Wall., 38.

SEC. 1064. All cases transmitted by the head of any Department, or upon the certificate of any Auditor or Comptroller, according to the provisions of the preceding section, shall be proceeded in as other cases pending in the Court of Claims, and shall, in all respects, be subject to the same rules and regulations.

Judgments in cases transmitted by Departments, how paid.

25 June, 1868, c. 71, s. 7, v. 15, p. 76.

SEC. 1065. The amount of any final judgment or decree rendered in favor of the claimant, in any case transmitted to the Court of Claims under the two preceding sections, shall be paid out of any specific appropriation applicable to the case, if any such there be; and where no such appropriation exists, the judgment or decree shall be paid in the same manner as other judgments of the said court.

Claims growing out of treaties not cognizable therein.

3 Mar., 1863, c. 92, s. 9, v. 12, p. 767.

*Ex parte* Atocha, 17 Wall., 439.

SEC. 1066. The jurisdiction of the said court shall not extend to any claim against the Government not pending therein on December one, eighteen hundred and sixty-two, growing out of or dependent on any treaty stipulation entered into with foreign nations or with the Indian tribes.

Claims pending in other courts not to be prosecuted in Court of Claims.

25 June, 1868, c. 71, s. 8, v. 15, p. 77.

SEC. 1067. No person shall file or prosecute in the Court of Claims, or in the Supreme Court on appeal therefrom, any claim for or in respect to which he or any assignee of his has pending in any other court any suit or process against any person who, at the time when the cause of action alleged in such suit or process arose, was, in respect thereto, acting or professing to act, mediately or immediately, under the authority of the United States.

Aliens.

27 July, 1868, c. 276, s. 2, v. 15, p. 243.

U.S. *vs.* O'Keefe, 11 Wall., 178; Carlisle *vs.* U. S., 16 Wall., 147.

SEC. 1068. Aliens, who are citizens or subjects of any government which accords to citizens of the United States the right to prosecute claims against such government in its courts, shall have the privilege of prosecuting claims against the United States in the Court of Claims, whereof such court, by reason of their subject-matter and character, might take jurisdiction.

Limitation.

3 Mar., 1863, c. 92, s. 10, v. 12, p. 767.

SEC. 1069. Every claim against the United States, cognizable by the Court of Claims, shall be forever barred unless the petition setting forth a statement thereof is filed in the court, or transmitted to it by the Secretary of the Senate or the Clerk of the House of Representatives as provided by law, within six years after the claim first accrues: *Provided*, That the claims of married women first accrued during marriage, of persons under the age of twenty-one years first accrued during minority, and of idiots, lunatics, insane persons, and persons beyond the seas at the time the claim accrued, entitled to the claim, shall not be barred if the petition be filed in the court or transmitted, as aforesaid, within three years after the disability has ceased; but no other disability than those enumerated shall prevent any claim from being barred, nor shall any of the said disabilities operate cumulatively.

Rules of practice; contempts.

24 Feb., 1855, c. 122, s. 3, v. 10, p. 613.
3 Mar., 1863, c. 92, s. 4, v. 12, p. 765.

SEC. 1070. The said court shall have power to establish rules for its government and for the regulation of practice therein, and it may punish for contempt in the manner prescribed by the common law, may appoint commissioners, and may exercise such powers as are necessary to carry into effect the powers granted to it by law.

Oaths and acknowledgments.

3 Mar., 1863, c. 92, s. 4, v. 12, p. 765.

SEC. 1071. The judges and clerks of said court may administer oaths and affirmations, take acknowledgments of instruments in writing, and give certificates of the same.

Petition.

24 Feb., 1855, c. 122, s. 1, v. 10, p. 612.
3 Mar., 1863, c. 92, s. 12, v. 12, p. 767.

SEC. 1072. The claimant shall, in all cases, fully set forth in his petition the claim, the action thereon in Congress, or by any of the Departments, if such action has been had; what persons are owners thereof or interested therein, when and upon what consideration such persons became so interested; that no assignment or transfer of said claim, or of any part thereof or interest therein, has been made, except as stated in the petition; that said claimant is justly entitled to the amount therein claimed from the United States, after allowing all just credits and offsets; that the claimant, and, where the claim has been assigned, the original and every prior owner thereof, if a citizen, has at all times borne true allegiance to the Government of the United States, and, whether a citizen or not, has not in any way voluntarily aided, abetted, or given encouragement to rebellion against the said Government, and that he believes the facts as stated in said petition to be true. And the said petition shall be verified by the affidavit of the claimant, his agent, or attorney.

Petition dismissed, if issue found against claimant as to allegiance, &c.

3 Mar., 1863, c. 92, s. 12, v. 12, p. 767.

SEC. 1073. The said allegations as to true allegiance and voluntary aiding, abetting, or giving encouragement to rebellion against the Government may be traversed by the Government, and if on the trial such issues shall be decided against the claimant, his petition shall be dismissed.

Burden of proof and evidence as to loyalty.

25 June, 1868, c. 71, s. 3, v. 15, p. 75.

SEC. 1074. Whenever it is material in any claim to ascertain whether any person did or did not give any aid or comfort to the late rebellion, the claimant asserting the loyalty of any such person to the United States during such rebellion shall be required to prove affirmatively that such person did, during said rebellion, consistently adhere to the

United States, and did give no aid or comfort to persons engaged in such rebellion; and the voluntary residence of any such person in any place where, at any time during such residence, the rebel force or organization held sway, shall be prima-facie evidence that such person did give aid and comfort to said rebellion and to the persons engaged therein.

SEC. 1075. The Court of Claims shall have power to appoint commissioners to take testimony to be used in the investigation of claims which come before it; to prescribe the fees which they shall receive for their services, and to issue commissions for the taking of such testimony, whether taken at the instance of the claimant or of the United States.

Commissioners to take testimony.

24 Feb., 1855, c. 122, s. 3, v. 10, p. 613.
3 Mar., 1863, c. 92, s. 4, v. 12, p. 765.

SEC. 1076. The said court shall have power to call upon any of the Departments for any information or papers it may deem necessary, and shall have the use of all recorded and printed reports made by the committees of each House of Congress, when deemed necessary in the prosecution of its business. But the head of any Department may refuse and omit to comply with any call for information or papers when, in his opinion, such compliance would be injurious to the public interest.

Power to call upon Departments for information.

24 Feb., 1855, c. 122, s. 11, v. 10, p. 614.

SEC. 1077. When it appears to the court in any case that the facts set forth in the petition of the claimant do not furnish any ground for relief, it shall not be the duty of the court to authorize the taking of any testimony therein.

When testimony not to be taken.

24 Feb., 1855, c. 122, s. 4, v. 10, p. 613.

SEC. 1078. No witness shall be excluded in any suit in the Court of Claims on account of color.

Witnesses not excluded on account of color.

2 July, 1864, c. 210, s. 3, v. 13, p. 351.
2 Mar., 1867, c. 166, s. 2, v. 14, p. 457.
25 June, 1868, c. 71, s. 4, v. 15, p. 75.

SEC. 1079. No claimant, nor any person from or through whom any such claimant derives his alleged title, claim, or right against the United States, nor any person interested in any such title, claim, or right, shall be a competent witness in the Court of Claims in supporting the same; and no testimony given by such claimant or person shall be used except as provided in the next section.

Parties and persons interested excluded as witnesses.

25 June, 1868, c. 71, s. 4, v. 15, p. 75.
3 Mar., 1863, c. 92, s. 8, v. 12, p. 766.

SEC. 1080. The court may, at the instance of the attorney or solicitor appearing in behalf of the United States, make an order in any case pending therein, directing any claimant in such case to appear, upon reasonable notice, before any commissioner of the court, and be examined on oath touching any or all matters pertaining to said claim. Such examination shall be reduced to writing by the said commissioner, and be returned to and filed in the court, and may, at the discretion of the attorney or solicitor of the United States appearing in the case, be read and used as evidence on the trial thereof. And if any claimant, after such order is made, and due and reasonable notice thereof is given to him, fails to appear, or refuses to testify or answer fully as to all matters within his knowledge material to the issue, the court may, in its discretion, order that the said cause shall not be

Examination of claimant.

3 Mar., 1863, c. 92, s. 8, v. 12, p. 766.
25 June, 1868, c. 71, s. 4, v. 15, p. 75.

brought forward for trial until he shall have fully complied with the order of the court in the premises.

Testimony taken where deponent resides.

24 Feb., 1855, c. 122, s. 3, v. 10, p. 613.

SEC. 1081. The testimony in cases pending before the Court of Claims shall be taken in the county where the witness resides, when the same can be conveniently done.

Witnesses, how compelled to attend before commissioners.

24 Feb., 1855, c. 122, s. 3, v. 10, p. 613.

SEC. 1082. The Court of Claims may issue subpœnas to require the attendance of witnesses in order to be examined before any person commissioned to take testimony therein, and such subpœnas shall have the same force as if issued from a district court, and compliance therewith shall be compelled under such rules and orders as the court shall establish.

Cross examination.

24 Feb., 1855, c. 122, s. 5, v. 10, p. 613.

SEC. 1083. In taking testimony to be used in support of any claim, opportunity shall be given to the United States to file interrogatories, or by attorney to examine witnesses, under such regulations as said court shall prescribe; and like opportunity shall be afforded the claimant, in cases where testimony is taken on behalf of the United States, under like regulations.

Witnesses, how sworn.

24 Feb., 1855, c, 122, s. 3, v. 10, p. 613.

SEC. 1084. The commissioner taking testimony to be used in the Court of Claims shall administer an oath or affirmation to the witnesses brought before him for examination.

Fees of commissioner, by whom paid.

24 Feb., 1855, c. 122, s. 3, v. 10, p. 613.

SEC. 1085. When testimony is taken for the claimant, the fees of the commissioner before whom it is taken, and the cost of the commission and notice, shall be paid by such claimant; and when it is taken at the instance of the Government, such fees, together with all postage incurred by the Assistant Attorney-General, shall be paid out of the contingent fund provided for the Court of Claims, or other appropriation made by Congress for that purpose.

Claims forfeited for fraud.

3 Mar., 1863, c. 92, s. 11, v. 12, p. 767.

SEC. 1086. Any person who corruptly practices or attempts to practice any fraud against the United States in the proof, statement, establishment, or allowance of any claim, or of any part of any claim against the United States, shall ipso facto forfeit the same to the Government; and it shall be the duty of the Court of Claims, in such cases, to find specifically that such fraud was practiced or attempted to be practiced, and thereupon to give judgment that such claim is forfeited to the Government, and that the claimant be forever barred from prosecuting the same.

New trial on motion of claimant.

24 Feb., 1855, c. 122, s. 9, v. 10, p. 614.

SEC. 1087. When judgment is rendered against any claimant, the court may grant a new trial for any reason which, by the rules of common law or chancery in suits between individuals, would furnish sufficient ground for granting a new trial.

New trial on motion of United States.

25 June, 1868, c. 71, s. 2, v. 15, p. 75.

*Ex parte* Russell, 13 Wall., 664 *ex parte*, in matter of United States, 16 Wall., 699.

SEC. 1088. The Court of Claims, at any time while any claim is pending before it, or on appeal from it, or within two years next after the final disposition of such claim, may, on motion on behalf of the United States, grant a new trial and stay the payment of any judgment therein, upon such evidence, cumulative or otherwise, as shall satisfy the court that any fraud, wrong, or injustice in the premises has been done to the United States; but until an order is made staying the payment of a judgment, the same shall be payable and paid as now provided by law.

SEC. 1089. In all cases of final judgments by the Court of Claims, or, on appeal, by the Supreme Court, where the same are affirmed in favor of the claimant, the sum due thereby shall be paid out of any general appropriation made by law for the payment and satisfaction of private claims, on presentation to the Secretary of the Treasury of a copy of said judgment, certified by the clerk of the Court of Claims, and signed by the chief-justice, or, in his absence, by the presiding judge of said court.

Payment of judgments.

3 Mar., 1863, c. 92, s. 7, v. 12, p. 766.

SEC. 1090. In cases where the judgment appealed from is in favor of the claimant, and the same is affirmed by the Supreme Court, interest thereon at the rate of five per centum shall be allowed from the date of its presentation to the Secretary of the Treasury for payment as aforesaid, but no interest shall be allowed subsequent to the affirmance, unless presented for payment to the Secretary of the Treasury as aforesaid.

Interest.

3 Mar., 1863, c. 92, s. 7, v. 12, p. 766.

SEC. 1091. No interest shall be allowed on any claim up to the time of the rendition of judgment thereon by the Court of Claims, unless upon a contract expressly stipulating for the payment of interest.

Interest on claims.

3 Mar., 1863, c. 92, s. 7, v. 12, p. 706.

SEC. 1092. The payment of the amount due by any judgment of the Court of Claims and of any interest thereon allowed by law, as hereinbefore provided, shall be a full discharge to the United States of all claim and demand touching any of the matters involved in the controversy.

Payment of judgment a full discharge, &c.

3 Mar., 1863, c. 92, s. 7, v. 12, p. 766.

SEC. 1093. Any final judgment against the claimant on any claim prosecuted as provided in this chapter shall forever bar any further claim or demand against the United States arising out of the matters involved in the controversy.

Final judgments a bar.

3 Mar, 1863, c. 92, s. 7, v. 12, p. 766.

---

## CHAPTER IX.

### THE COMMISSIONERS OF CLAIMS.

The following are the acts of Congress under which the commissioners of claims are organized and their jurisdiction defined. This tribunal is popularly, but erroneously, called the "Southern Claims Commission."

AN ACT making appropriations for the support of the Army for the year ending June thirty, eighteen hundred and seventy-two, and for other purposes.

* * * * * * * *

SEC. 2. That the President of the United States shall be, and he is hereby, authorized to nominate, and, by and with the advice and consent of the Senate, appoint a board of commissioners, to be designated as commissioners of claims, to consist of three commissioners, who shall be commissioned for two years, and whose duty it shall be to receive, examine, and consider the justice and validity of such claims as shall be brought before them, of those citizens who remained loyal adherents to the cause and the Government of the United States during the war, for stores or supplies taken or furnished during the rebellion for the use of the Army of the United States, in States proclaimed as in insurrection against the United States, including the use and loss of vessels or boats while employed in the military service of the United States. And the said commissioners in considering said claim shall be satisfied from the testimony of witnesses under oath, or from other sufficient evidence, which shall accompany each claim, taken under such rules and regulations as the commissioners may adopt, of the loyalty and adherence of the claimant to the cause and the Government of the United States before and at the time of the taking or furnishing of the property for which any claim shall be made, and of the quantity, quality, and value of the property alleged to have been taking or furnished, and the time, place, and material circumstances of the taking or furnishing of the same. And upon satisfactory evidence of the justice and validity of any claim, the commissioners shall report their opinion in writing in each case, and shall certify the nature, amount, and value of the property taken, furnished, or used as aforesaid. And each claim which shall be considered, and rejected as unjust and invalid, shall likewise be reported, with the reasons therefor; and no claimant shall withdraw any material evidence submitted in support of any claim.

SEC. 3. That said commissioners shall each take the oath of office provided by law to be taken by all officers of the United States, and shall proceed without delay to discharge their duties under this act. The President of the United States shall designate in his appointment one of said commissioners to be president of the board, and shall be authorized to fill any vacancy which may occur, by reason of death or resignation, in said board; and each commissioner shall have authority to administer oaths and affirmations, and to take the depositions of witnesses in all matters pertaining to their duties. The said commissioners shall meet and organize said board and hold their sessions at Washington. Two members of the board shall constitute a quorum for the transaction of business, and the agreement of two shall decide all questions in controversy. The said commissioners shall have authority to make and publish rules for their procedure, not inconsistent with this act, and shall publish notice of their sessions. They shall keep a journal of their proceedings, to be signed by the president of the board, and a register of all claims brought before the board, showing the date of presentation, number, name, and residence of claimant, subject-matter and amount of claim, and the amount, if any allowed; which records shall be open to the inspection of the President and Attorney-General of the United States, or of such officer as the President may designate.

SEC. 4. That said commissioners shall make report of their proceedings, and of each claim considered by them, at the commencement of each session of Congress, to the Speaker of the House of Representatives, who shall lay the same before Congress for consideration; and all claims within this act and not presented to said board shall be barred, and shall not be entertained by any department of the Government without further authority of Congress.

SCE. 5. That the commissioners of claims shall be paid quarterly under this act, at the rate of five thousand dollars per annum each, and they shall have authority to appoint one clerk and one short-hand reporter, to be paid quarterly at the rate of two thousand five hundred dollars per annum each, and one messenger, to be paid at the rate of one thousand two hundred dollars per annum, who shall perform the services required of them respectively, and said board shall be further allowed the necessary actual expenses of office-rent, furniture, fuel, stationery, and printing, to be certified by the president of the board, and to be audited on vouchers, and paid as other judicial expenses are.

SEC. 6. That a sufficient appropriation to carry this act into effect is hereby made out of any money in the Treasury not otherwise appropriated.

Approved March 3, 1871.

(See Statutes at Large, vol. 16, page 524.)

---

AN ACT to authorize the commissioners of claims to appoint special commissioners to take testimony, and for other purposes.

SECTION 1. *Be it enacted, &c.*, That the commissioners of claims shall have authority to appoint special commissioners to take testimony, to be used in cases pending before them, who shall have authority to administer oaths and affirmations, and to take the depositions of witnesses: *Provided*, The claimants shall pay the fees of such special commissioners for taking the depositions of witnesses called by them; but such fees shall in no case exceed ten cents per folio if the claim is less than one thousand dollars.

SEC. 2. That any person who shall knowingly and willfully swear falsely before the said commissioners of claims, or either of them, or before any special commissioner appointed by virtue of this act, in any matter or claim pending before said commissioners, shall be deemed guilty of perjury, and on conviction thereof, shall be punished in the same manner prescribed by law in cases of willful and corrupt perjury.

SEC. 3. That the commissioners of claims may appoint and employ agents, but not more than three at any time, whose duty it shall be, under the direction and authority of said commissioners, to investigate claims pending before them, to procure evidence, to secure the attendance of witnesses on behalf of the Government, and to examine the same, and to cross-examine the witnesses produced by claimants, and to perform such other duties as may be required of them by said commissioners, who may discharge them at any time. The said agents shall be allowed their actual and necessary traveling expenses, the expenses paid out in investigating claims, procuring witnesses, and taking testimony, and six dollars a day while employed in the discharge of their duties; of all which, at the end of each month, they shall make a statement in detail, specifying the amounts by them paid out, to whom paid, when and where and for what purpose, and the number of days employed in their duties, and shall transmit the same, duly certified, to the commissioners. But no claim where the amount exceeds ten thousand dollars shall be examined, decided, and reported by the commissioners to Congress, except the testimony on behalf of the claimant in such case shall have been taken orally before the commissioners or some one of them personally, or shall have been taken previous to the third day March, eighteen hundred and seventy-one, to be used in the Court of Claims, or before some Department of the Government.

SEC. 4. That the commissioners may employ three additional clerks at a salary of one thousand two hundred dollars per year; and may employ, at the usual rates, such assistance for the short-hand reporter as may be necessary, from time to time, in reporting, copying, and preparing for Congress the oral testimony taken in cases before the said commissioners.

SEC. 5. That all the expenses incurred under the provisions of this act shall be allowed and paid in the same manner, and out of the same appropriation provided for in the act organizing the said commissioners of claims, being an act entitled "An act making appropriations for the support of the Army for the year ending June thirtieth, eighteen hundred and seventy-two, and for other purposes," approved March third, eighteen hundred and seventy-one.

SEC. 6. That it shall be the duty of the said commissioners of claims to receive, examine, and consider the justice and validity of such claims as shall be brought before them of those citizens who remained loyal adherents to the cause and Government of the United States during the war, for stores or supplies taken or furnished during the rebellion for the use of the Navy of the United States, in the same manner and with the like effect as they are now required by law to do in the case of stores or supplies taken or furnished for the use of the Army.

Approved May 11, 1872.

(See Statutes at Large, vol. 17, page 97.)

---

AN ACT to extend for four years the act establishing the board of commissioners of claims, and the acts relating thereto.

*Be it enacted by the Senate and House of Representatives of the United States in Congress assembled*, That the second, third, fourth, fifth, and sixth sections of the act entitled "An act making appropriations for the support of the Army for the year ending June thirtieth, eighteen hundred and seventy-two, and for other purposes," approved March third, eighteen hundred and seventy-one; and the act entitled "An act to authorize the commissioners of claims to appoint special commissioners to take testimony, and for other purposes," approved May eleventh, eighteen hundred and seventy-two, be and the same are hereby extended and continued in force for four years from the tenth day of March, anno Domini eighteen hundred and seventy-three.

SEC. 2. That the commissioners of claims shall not receive any petition for the allowance of any claim or claims, unless such petition shall be presented to and filed with them on or before the third day of March, eighteen hundred and seventy-three; and all claims not so presented shall be deemed to be barred forever thereafter.

Approved March 3, 1873.

(See Statutes at Large, vol. 17, page 577.)

These commissioners have made four annual reports, which are given as follows:

FIRST GENERAL REPORT OF THE COMMISSIONERS OF CLAIMS.

*To the honorable the Speaker of the House of Representatives:*

SIR: The undersigned, commissioners of claims under the act of Congress of March 3, 1871, respectfully report:

Upon receiving our commissions we took the oath of office and appointed Charles F. Benjamin clerk, James L. Andam short-hand reporter, and Thomas Phipps messenger.

On the 20th of March we published a notice that our sessions for examining claims and hearing the testimony of witnesses would begin on the 10th April, 1871, at our office in Washington.

We adopted rules prescribing the form of petitions for the allowance of claims, the necessary averments, and the oath of verification. These and subsequent rules and regulations are annexed to this report.

## EXTENT OF JURISDICTION.

Questions at once arose as to the extent of the jurisdiction conferred by the act of Congress. The words of the act conferring jurisdiction are as follows:

"SEC. 2. That the President of the United States shall be, and he is hereby, authorized to nominate and, by and with the advice and consent of the Senate, appoint a board of commissioners, to be designated as commissioners of claims, to consist of three commissioners, who shall be commissioned for two years, and whose duty it shall be to receive, examine, and consider the justice and validity of such claims as shall be brought before them, of those citizens who remained loyal adherents to the cause and the Government of the United States during the war, for stores or supplies taken or furnished during the rebellion for the use of the Army of the United States in States proclaimed as in insurrection against the United States, including the use and loss of vessels or boats while employed in the military service of the United States."

I. *Who are "citizens" within the meaning of the act?*

Claims were presented by foreigners not naturalized, but domiciled in this country, and who had resided here during the rebellion. The case of Peter Klaine, a French subject, was of this kind; and we refer to the brief of his counsel, Mr. Durant, to show the grounds upon which such claims were urged.

As this commission is created by act of Congress, and its jurisdiction limited by the statute, as it is only to examine and report to Congress, and has not the authority or functions of a court, its jurisdiction must be kept within the very terms of the statute.

The word "citizen," when used to express the relation of the individual to the Government, *ordinarily* means "one owing paramount allegiance to the state." It is so used in distinction from the word "inhabitant," which is employed to denote a foreigner domiciled in the country and owing a minor and qualified allegiance. This ordinary meaning should be given to it as used in the statute. Deeming the act intended to apply to matters of municipal legislation, and not to affect rights standing upon international law, we do not follow the decisions cited from the prize courts, which seem in some cases to extend its meaning. The context, "citizens who remained loyal adherents to the cause and Government of the United States," indicates that those persons are meant of whom "loyalty" could be *required* "during the war." Loyalty during the war cannot reasonably be interpreted as meaning less than that relation from which the Government might have required military service. But the Government uniformly directed that foreigners should be discharged from military service whenever they claimed exemption on that ground. Loyalty was not required of a foreigner. He was deemed to do his whole duty if he kept strictly neutral. But neutrality during the war in a citizen of the United States was not loyalty.

It is urged that foreigners domiciled and remaining here during the war have no right to require their own governments to interfere in their behalf to obtain compensation for losses sustained from military operations, and therefore ought to have the same rights and remedies as citizens. But in their cases other considerations arise, such as the law of domicile, the right, though only neutral and not loyal, to demand compensation, and other questions growing out of their relations as foreigners. We think Congress intended to reserve exclusively to itself the consideration of the rights of foreigners to compensation.

We have, therefore, held that foreigners domiciled here are not "citizens" within the meaning of the act.

We have also held that where the claimant was an alien when the claim accrued, his naturalization since the war does not remove his disability.

II. *Loyalty and the proof of it.*

Many questions have arisen as to wh at was loyalty, and how it may be proved. We have held—

1. That the party claiming to be loyal must *prove* his loyalty. It is a fact to be established by proof, and is not to be presumed.

2. Voluntary residence in an insurrectionary State during the war is *prima-facie* evidence of disloyalty, and must be rebutted by satisfactory evidence.

3. Claims have come before us of persons who have served in the rebel army. They claim that they were really loyal at heart, but acted under duress—"moral duress;" that they could not get away, and would have been taken by force if they had not gone without force, and therefore they yielded and went into the rebel service, apparently but not really of their free will. We have held that such personal service in the rebel army is proof of disloyalty, and that the duress to excuse it must be actual force used against the claimant, or *imminent* danger of *immediate, forcible*, and *serious* injury. The claimant must prove fully and in detail the facts which he claims to have constituted the duress; and opinions and general statements of danger will not suffice. Furnishing a substitute to the rebel army stands upon the same ground as personal service.

4. Voting for the ordinance of secession, holding civil or military office under the confederacy, furnishing aid or supplies to the rebel service, or to persons about to enter it, giving information to aid the rebels in their military operations, and engaging in a business whose object was to supply munitions of war or army supplies to the confederate government, we regard as acts of disloyalty.

5. Neutrality of one residing in an insurrectionary State is not sufficient to establish "loyal *adherence* to the cause and Government of the United States."

Beyond these we have not had occasion to lay down any general tests of loyalty. The cases vary so greatly that it is difficult to apply any general and absolute rule. Truly loyal persons in the rebellious States, except when within the lines of the Union Army, or in special localities, were obliged to be silent, to say nothing and do nothing for the Union cause. Expulsion from their homes, confiscation of property, imprisonment and death by law or lawless violence, were the penalties that hung over the heads of active and outspoken friends of the Union. Hence the difficulty of proving overt acts of loyalty. On the other hand, we must bear in mind that it is easier and more profitable to be loyal now than it was during the war, and that much of the proof of disloyalty has perished, or been forgotten in the lapse of time. Hence false evidence of loyalty is more readily manufactured and more easily escapes detection.

An examination of the interrogatories to be put to claimants, as to their loyalty, (a copy of which is annexed to this report,) will show the general tenor of our inquiries.

Where there has been a doubt or difference of opinion as to the loyalty of the claimant, we have suspended the case for further inquiry.

III. *Stores and supplies.*

What is the extent of the term "stores or supplies," as used in the act?

1. The act of July 4, 1864, by which the Quartermaster-General and the Commissary General of Subsistence were authorized to examine the claims of loyal citizens, *in States not in rebellion*, uses the terms "claims for quartermaster's stores," and "claims for subsistence."

The act of March 3, 1871, uses the words "stores or supplies," without any words of restriction. We think it was the intent of Congress not to confine the act to quartermasters' and commissary stores, but to extend it to *all* stores and supplies for the use of the Army, and thus to include medical and hospital stores, and supplies for the Engineer Department.

2. But stores and supplies taken for the use of the Navy are not included, and a claim of that kind has been rejected for that reason.

3. Claims for *rent* and the use of real estate have been urged for allowance as quartermasters' supplies.

If rent be included in quartermasters' supplies, then claims for rent by loyal citizens in the States *not in rebellion* should have been allowed under the act of July 4, 1864; but the uniform usage of the Department under that act has been to reject them as not being quartermasters' supplies. The opinions of the Judge-Advocate-General to this effect are abundant and decisive. (See Decisions of the Judge-Advocate-General, in his Bureau; case of Thomas C. Elliott, vol. 16, p. 51; also vol. 18, p. 506. See Digest of his Opinions, p. 99.)

We think this usage must have been well known to Congress, and that the terms were used in the sense of their settled construction. However just claims for rent and the occupation of land may be, if it had been intended to submit them to this board, they would have been named in express words in the act. Claims of loyal citizens at the North and the South must stand on the same basis, and be governed by the same rules of construction.

4. The *destruction* of or *damage* to buildings, growing crops, and personal property is not embraced within stores and supplies. Military necessity sometimes requires the destruction of buildings, because they shelter the enemy or obstruct the range of guns; but the buildings do not thereby become supplies. Armies, in marching through a country, cannot be kept within the lines of the highways, but necessarily pass through fields of grass and growing crops, and are often obliged to encamp upon them. The grass and crops are thus trampled down and destroyed; but they are not supplies taken for the use of the Army.

When buildings are torn down, if the materials are taken to erect other buildings for the use of the Army, such *materials* thereby become supplies, and their value, *as materials for the purpose for which they are used*, is paid to the owner. It is a very inadequate compensation to him. But this rule, which allows only for the materials as supplies, and nothing for damage to the building from which they are obtained, has been acted upon uniformly for many years, and is regarded as an established usage not to be departed from. So where fields of grass or growing crops are partly trampled down and destroyed, and partly used for forage or pasturage, the latter is paid for, but the former is not. In such cases we have found great difficulty in determining how much is destroyed and how much taken for Army use. It would have been difficult at the time; how much more so after the lapse of many years.

Nothing in the act of March 3, 1871, authorizes us to allow claims for the damage or destruction of property; and in allowing for supplies we follow the long-settled rules of the Quartermaster's Department. By adopting this rule, the claims of loyal citizens North and South are treated alike.

In some cases boards of survey, appointed by military commanders according to the usages of war, have allowed for such damage and destruction as well as for forage and other Army use. When their awards have been brought before us as evidence, we have felt restricted by the act from following their allowances in this particular, and have deducted from them what we have believed to be mere damage.

5. Articles taken by the soldiers, without lawful authority or real necessity, we have not allowed. The strictest discipline could not prevent acts of lawless depredation. Whatever was deemed better than their regular rations, pigs, poultry, &c., would be seized and used by the soldiers. The ready excuse was that their supplies had not come up, and they had orders to get their subsistence where they could find it; when, in fact, they were supplied with their regular rations.

But where a real necessity existed for the taking of subsistence, and it was used in lieu of regular rations, there compensation should be given. In military operations where rapidity of movement is necessary and the troops unable to carry their supplies with them, they must get their subsistence where they can; in hasty retreats, where disorder exists and provisions are not at hand; in times of difficult transportation, when supply-trains fall behind; in such and similar cases the seizure of subsistence is necessary, and we have allowed claims for property so taken.

6. Articles not on the list of commissary supplies we reject, unless furnished to the hospitals for the refreshment and cure of the sick, when we allow for them.

IV. *The act provides that the commissioners "shall be satisfied from the testimony of witnesses under oath, or from other sufficient evidence, taken under such rules and regulations as the commissioners may adopt," of the loyalty of the claimant and the validity of the claim.*

1. We have deemed it our duty to examine witnesses orally in all cases where it was practicable. The advantage, by oral examination, of hearing the witness, of observing his appearance on the stand, of judging of his intelligence, fairness, and honesty, and by cross-examination, of ascertaining his means of knowledge and testing his credibility is very great. Where the witnesses were so near Washington that it was reasonable for them to come before us and testify, we have required them to do so. Most of such claims have come from Virginia. In some cases of larger amount, the claimants and their witnesses have come from North Carolina, South Carolina, Georgia, Tennessee, and Louisiana.

2. Where the claims are small, the claimants poor, and they and their witnesses live remote from Washington, it would amount to a denial of justice to require them to come here. In aid of such claimants, and under the authority given to the commissioners to adopt rules and regulations for the taking of evidence, we decided to allow claimants, whose claims did not exceed $3,000, to have the depositions of themselves and their witnesses taken by special commissioners, to be designated by us. We limited this right to claims not exceeding $3,000 because most of the claims are under that amount, and we believed that attempts to defraud the Government would generally be aimed at larger sums. With this limitation the cases have been numerous enough to employ all the time of the special commissioners, and to furnish us with more cases than we have had time to examine and decide.

A list of the special commissioners, the instructions we have given them, and the questions we have directed them to put, are annexed to this report. We have sought to make the examination something better than an *ex-parte* proceeding. But questions prepared beforehand, and necessarily for *all* witnesses, and without any knowledge of what the particular witness will swear to, cannot be expected to elicit facts as a personal examination on the spot would do. Much, of course, depends on the skill and thoroughness of the special commissioners. They have generally shown a disposition to be thorough and faithful in their examinations; yet, after all, on reading the depositions, one cannot but feel that the results would have been far more satisfactory if some competent person on behalf of the Government had investigated the claims and been present to examine the witnesses. Under the existing law we do not see what more can be done than we have done to avoid the evil of *ex-parte* depositions. We have been strongly urged to allow depositions to be taken in the larger cases; but have decided to retain the limitation as it is, at $3,000, until Congress should have the opportunity to prescribe some more thorough mode of inquiry and examination as to the larger claims. In the larger cases which are yet to come before us, in some of which hundreds of thousands of dollars are demanded, the temptation and opportunity to procure the allowance of unjust claims exist; and high ability, ingenuity, and skill in procuring and presenting evidence to sustain them may be expected. In such cases, if persons could be designated by proper authority to investigate the claims on the spot where they arose, and to inquire in regard to them of those officers or other persons who must at the time have known about them, it would greatly aid in guarding against disloyal and fictitious claims.

In designating special commissioners to take testimony, we have been confined to persons already appointed as United States commissioners, or to notaries and magistrates authorized to administer oaths and take depositions under State laws, as the act of Congress does not authorize this board to confer such powers. A list of the special commissioners so designated is appended to this report.

3. Where claims have heretofore been brought before the Court of Claims or any other tribunal or Department of the Government, and evidence has been filed and used either for or against them, we have treated all such evidence as admissible, when the same claims have been brought before us. We require that all the papers pertaining to a claim should be furnished us, and have often found evidence in the papers thus sent to us from the Departments of great use in the examination of claims.

4. Letters and papers from the archive office have also been furnished us, very useful and often decisive upon the question of loyalty.

V. *When claims have been heretofore presented to any Department of the Government having jurisdiction of them, and have been fully considered and decided upon their merits, we do not open them for examination, if brought before us, unless new and material evidence has been found, and such as would induce the former tribunal to hear them again.*

When a claim is presented which is also pending before some other tribunal or Department, we decline to examine it, unless the Department before which it is pending signify to us that it is withdrawn by consent in order to have it come before us.

VI. *Value of property.*

In estimating the value of property we have been guided not only by the evidence on behalf of the particular claimant, but by the knowledge of prices which we obtain in examining the numerous cases before us, and by the tables of prices furnished by the Commissary and Quartermaster's Departments. The report of the Commissary-General, showing the prices paid by the Department for all the leading articles of subsistence for each month during the war at all the principal markets of the Union, has been of great service. By adding to the price at the nearest market the cost of transportation to the place where the claim accrued, we get a fair measure of the value of the property claimed.

Similar tables of prices have been furnished by the Quartermaster-General. They have been of much use in reducing the inflated and exaggerated estimates which claimants generally put upon their property. The natural tendency of men to overestimate the value of their property (especially when compensation is expected from the Government) is well illustrated by the compensation asked for the "superior and elegant" horses, the "best" mules, the "remarkably fine and fat" cattle, and the "new" rails which the Army seems always to have found wherever it went. We have endeavored to ascertain the fair market-price, and not to allow for an enhanced value occasioned by the temporary presence of the Army.

There are some articles of which particular notice should be taken.

*Fence-rails.*—These were usually taken for fuel. We have allowed for them as *wood*, at the rate of 100 rails per cord, (the rule adopted by the Quartermaster's Department, and which is believed to be just for the average of farm fences,) and at the price usually of $2 per cord, the average common price of wood when taken upon the farms to be hauled to the camp or the market. The damage to the owner is more than this, for rails are worth more than wood, and without fences the farmer loses to a great extent the use of his land; and the country being denuded of wood, he has to pay an increased price to replace them. But we are precluded from estimating the damage, and, in conformity to the usage as to supplies, can only allow for the rails as fuel.

*Cotton.*—This seems to have been taken in some instances to strengthen fortifications, but probably only in cases of emergency. It has never been paid for by the Government when so used, but has been regarded as "loss by the casualty of war." (See Digest of the Opinions of the Judge-Advocate-General, pp. 97 and 98, and cases there cited.) When taken for beds in hospitals it has been paid for as hospital stores.

*Tobacco.*—Until the act of March 3, 1865, tobacco was not furnished to the Army. Under that act it has been issued to those who use it, and charged to them on the pay-rolls.

In the claims that have come before us, tobacco has not usually been regarded as a supply, and therefore has been disallowed.

Claims for tobacco alleged to have been taken and issued to the troops at Atlanta, Ga., under the order of General Sherman, of September 8, 1864, are pending before us. The examination of them is still going on, and they will be reported upon hereafter.

VII. *The whole number of claims presented for allowance up to the end of November*, 1871, *is ten thousand and ninety-nine.*

The whole amount claimed is $26,509,123.91.

The monthly receipts of claims have been as follows:

|  |  |
|---|---|
| March, (last few days) | 17 |
| April | 550 |
| May | 1,221 |
| June | 1,562 |
| July | 1,539 |
| August | 1,261 |
| September | 1,762 |
| October | 1,206 |
| November | 981 |
| Total | 10,099 |

The number not exceeding in amount $3,000 is 8,800; number that exceeds $3,000 is 1,299. The 8,800 claims (averaging about $1,350 each) amount to about $11,880,000. The 1,299 larger claims amount to about $14,629,000.

We transmit herewith our reports in five hundred and eighty-eight cases, which we have examined and decided. They are accompanied by the testimony taken orally before us, and all the papers and evidence pertaining to such cases which we have received from any Department of the Government. Congress thus becomes the custodian of all the evidence, vouchers, and papers pertaining to these claims.

It may be noted that the act of March 3, 1871, provides that "no claimant shall withdraw any material evidence submitted in support of any claim."

Annexed to this report is a list of the cases so decided and reported, with the number of the claim, the name of the claimant, and the amounts claimed, allowed, and disallowed.

The number disallowed for want of satisfactory proof of "loyal adherence to the cause and the Government of the United States" is about two hundred and thirty. Some have been rejected for want of jurisdiction, and some for insufficient proof upon other material points. The whole number rejected is two hundred and fifty-six.

The claims examined by us in the months of April, May, and June, were chiefly from the counties in Virginia near Washington. The witnesses came before us and were examined orally. These claimants mostly resided within the Union lines. Many of them were originally from New Jersey, Pennsylvania, and the North. They were generally loyal, and could prove their loyalty by overt acts, or by the testimony of Federal officers and well-known loyal men.

In the cases more recently examined by us, which come from regions more decidedly hostile to the Government, and to which the Union forces did not penetrate till toward the close of the war, we have found the proportion of claims in which loyalty is not satisfactorily proved to be considerably larger.

Of the claimants found loyal, many (about forty) have actually served in the Union Army, many have aided our military operations as scouts and guides, and in other ways. Some have been arrested, imprisoned, and cruelly treated by the rebels. The evidence on behalf of some of these claimants in Virginia, the mountain-regions of Tennessee, Georgia, and Alabama, and other portions of the South, furnishes instances of peril, hardship, sacrifice, and suffering, of steadfast courage and patriotic devotion to the Union, which do them honor and entitle them to the grateful consideration of the Government.

Among those whose claims have been disallowed, about forty have served in the rebel army, and some as guards at Andersonville; others have held civil office under the confederacy, or furnished supplies to the rebel army, or voted for the ordinance of secession, or sworn allegiance to the confederate government, or have otherwise given aid and comfort to the rebellion.

In the cases decided and herewith reported the amount claimed is $1,656,357.98; the amount allowed is $344,168.20; the amount disallowed is $1,312,189.78.

We have not considered the "Loudoun County claims," so called. They are numerous; are chiefly for property taken by military necessity under the order to General Sheridan of November 27, 1864. The claims for property taken for the use of the Army are so intermingled with those in which the property was sold and the proceeds put into the

Treasury that it is almost impossible to separate them. As large herds of horses, cattle, and sheep were driven off together, the claimants cannot trace their separate property to Army use. We have therefore declined examining them, thinking Congress may make some special provision in regard to their examination and settlement.

Lists of the cases presented to us for allowance have been published and distributed through the country, that public attention might be called to the loyalty of the claimants and the justice of their claims. The publication of these lists and of the questions as to the loyalty of claimants has had the effect, it is believed, of deterring many from pressing disloyal and unjust claims.

The large number of claims presented, the extensive correspondence to be kept up, and other necessary official business, have thrown a great burden of duty upon the clerk, and one which could not have been performed but for the aid of the clerks kindly furnished to us from the Departments of War and the Treasury. Four clerks have been spared from those Departments for the time being to help this commission; but, as they can be spared no longer, and must soon be withdrawn, it is obvious that a considerable addition ought soon to be made to the clerical force of this commission.

The stenographer has taken the testimony of nearly one thousand witnesses. The transcription of his minutes for the use of this board and of Congress imposes upon him a great labor, in which he ought to have some aid. Without it the important work of the commission in examining claimants and witnesses orally will be hindered. A month's labor is now required to enable him to transcribe the minutes of testimony taken in the months of October and November.

About forty cases have been examined by us which we have suspended for further inquiry and examination. It has been suggested that loyal persons have sometimes been used to cover with their names the claims of the disloyal, sometimes persons formerly slaves endeavoring, from friendship, to help their former masters, and we have felt it our duty to carefully investigate claims in which such suspicions might be justly entertained.

Respectfully submitted.

ASA OWEN ALDIS,
J. B. HOWELL,
ORANGE FERRISS,
*Commissioners of Claims.*

WASHINGTON, D. C., *December* 11, 1871.

---

## SECOND GENERAL REPORT OF THE COMMISSIONERS OF CLAIMS.

WASHINGTON, D. C., *December* 6, 1872.

*To the honorable the Speaker of the House of Representatives:*

SIR: The commissioners of claims herewith respectfully present their second general report.

Our views as to the jurisdiction conferred by the act establishing this commission, as to loyalty, and the proof of it; as to the meaning of the terms "stores and supplies;" as to the rules and regulations for taking evidence, and as to the nature of the claims which we could and could not allow, were so fully set forth in our first general report, made December 11, 1871, that we do not deem it necessary here to repeat them. A few new questions have arisen to which we shall refer; and on some points, where our views do not seem to have been regarded by claimants, and further elucidation seems desirable, we may make some further suggestions.

## I.—NUMBER AND AMOUNT OF CLAIMS.

By referring to our first general report, made December 11, 1871, it will be seen that the number of claims presented for allowance up to the end of November, 1871, was .......... 10,099
The number presented since, up to the end of November, 1872, is .......... 7,601

Whole number presented .......... 17,700

The monthly receipts of claims during the past year have been as follows:

|  |  |  |  |
|---|---|---|---|
| December, 1871 | 693 | July | 540 |
| January, 1872 | 665 | August | 694 |
| February | 507 | September | 649 |
| March | 741 | October | 563 |
| April | 858 | November | 413 |
| May | 742 | | |
| June | 536 | Total | 7,601 |

| | |
|---|---|
| The amount of claims presented, up to the end of November, 1871, was | $26,509,123 91 |
| The amount of claims presented since, to the end of November, 1872, is | 18,494,980 57 |
| Total amount of claims presented | 45,004,104 48 |

With our first general report we presented to Congress special reports in 580 cases, which we had examined and decided.

We herewith transmit to Congress special reports in 2,209 cases, which we have examined and decided during the past year.

Whole number reported to Congress, 2,789.

Of the claims herewith reported there are from—

| State | Claims | State | Claims |
|---|---|---|---|
| Alabama | 345 | South Carolina | 41 |
| Arkansas | 184 | Tennessee | 397 |
| Florida | 3 | Texas | 8 |
| Georgia | 174 | Virginia | 545 |
| Louisiana | 27 | | |
| Mississippi | 213 | Total | 2,209 |
| North Carolina | 272 | | |

Of these cases we have allowed, in whole or in part, 1,061; we have wholly rejected 1,148.

Of those allowed, 122 were the claims of persons who had served as soldiers in the Union Army, or had been otherwise employed in the military service of the United States. A still greater number is of persons who had sons in the Union Army.

Of those rejected—

| | |
|---|---|
| There had been in the military service of the confederacy, or had furnished substitutes | 227 |
| Voted for secession, or taken oath of allegiance to the confederacy | 154 |
| Total | 381 |

Of the 2,209 claims herewith reported—

| | |
|---|---|
| The whole amount claimed is ........................... | $3,850,141 05 |
| The amount allowed is .................................. | 806,699 31 |
| The amount disallowed is ............................... | 3,043,541 74 |

Our reports are accompanied with all the evidence and papers belonging to the reported cases.

Annexed to this report is a list of the cases decided during the year, with the number of the claim, name of the claimant, and the amounts claimed, allowed, and disallowed.

Besides the 2,209 cases which we have thus examined and decided during the year, and herewith report, we have thus examined about 700 more cases which, for various reasons, we have been obliged to suspend for further investigation; although, in many of them, reports have been drawn, and in all the chief part of the work has been done. Of this last class many appear so meritorious that we are not willing to reject them, and yet, from lack of proof, or other cause, require further investigation. It has been impossible for us, with only three agents, to fully investigate all the large cases already heard.

Many of the largest claims are in this list of suspended cases, the whole amounting to about $2,500,000. They have taken much time in hearing and examining the evidence. They ought not to be decided till our agents have thoroughly investigated them.

We regret that our agent has not been able to make a final report upon many important cases in Georgia, and especially upon the tobacco cases of Atlanta, to which we referred in our last report.

The time for presenting claims expires on the 3d of March, 1873. The number, by that time, will probably be about 19,000, and the probable amount about $50,000,000. This estimate is made upon the supposition that the claims will continue to be presented at the rate at which they are now coming in.

## II.—JURISDICTION.

Since our last report a question has arisen as to the construction of the words used in the act of March 3, 1871, "the claims of those citizens who remained loyal adherents to the cause and Government of the United States during the war."

The original owner of the property for which compensation is now asked was loyal and living when it was taken. He has since died. If he were living *his* claim would be allowed. His heirs now present the claim. They were disloyal during the war. The act authorizes us to consider only "the claims of those citizens who remained loyal adherents to the cause and Government of the United States during the war."

We construe the act to mean that the claimants who present the claim before us, that is, the heirs, must prove their loyalty—that it is not enough that the ancestor was loyal.

When the claim is presented by one who is a mere representative of others, and who has no beneficial interest, such as an executor or an administrator, we do not require him to prove his loyalty, but he must prove the loyalty of those he represents—that is, the legatees or heirs.

When it appears that the heirs are the real owners of the claim, and that some or all of them were disloyal during the war, we reject so much as would go to the disloyal and allow what should go to the loyal ones.

III.

The act of Congress of May 11, 1872, authorized us to employ three agents to investigate claims. We immediately appointed three agents, and directed them, in the first instance, to proceed to Virginia, where the number and urgency of the claims seemed especially to require their employment. Since then they have also been to Tennessee, Georgia, and Alabama. We have been urgently requested to send them to other States to speed the examination of claims there. As yet we have not been able to comply with these requests, but recently have sent one to Mississippi.

The employment of these agents has, so far, proved very useful. We have directed them to inquire and report alike whether claims are just or unjust, and whether the claimants were loyal or disloyal, and to inquire as to *all* claims, so far as time, expense, and opportunity make investigation reasonable. Their attention is, of course, more especially directed to the large and doubtful cases, and they cannot reasonably be expected to investigate the multitude of little claims.

Now that we can examine cases through these agents, whenever we have reason to doubt as to their allowance we have authorized the special commissioners to take depositions in all cases not exceeding $5,000.

We have directed the agents to examine all claims between $5,000 and $10,000, to correspond with the special commissioners to whom such cases are assigned, and with the claimants as to the time and place of taking the evidence, and to be present and cross-examine the witnesses whenever they think it expedient, or to advise the special commissioner as to questions which he should put on behalf of the Government.

In investigating claims we have directed them to pursue the course which the agents of the Departments have been accustomed to pursue; to inquire in the vicinity of the claimants, of respectable and credible witnesses, and ascertain the truth as to the loyalty of the claimant and the justice and validity of the claim, and to report to us the evidence, the names of witnesses, and all facts that may throw light upon the case. We do not require them to take the depositions of witnesses, or to confine themselves to strict legal evidence; but as this commission allows the same latitude of inquiry in its oral hearings that the committees of the Senate and House allow, and admit any evidence that they think will reasonably aid their inquiries, we require these agents to do the same.

In all cases the claimants are allowed to see the reports of the agents filed in the case, and, if they wish, to rebut the evidence contained in them.

IV.—LOYALTY, AND THE PROOF OF IT.

In our first general report we stated very fully our views as to "loyalty, and the proof of it." Some further suggestions on this topic may not be amiss.

Loyalty is a fact to be proved. Claims are not unfrequently disallowed not because there is positive proof of disloyalty, but because the proof of loyalty is not satisfactory. Where the evidence leads us to think that the party may have been really loyal, and that the want of proof can be supplied, we suspend the case for further inquiry.

We find, by experience, that to form a correct opinion as to whether a claimant was or was not loyal during the war, we cannot safely rely upon the mere *opinion* of witnesses as to his loyalty, and upon statements, at this late day, of alleged conversations. We must rather look to his surroundings—to the vicinity where he lived; the pressure that bore upon him; the opportunity he had to show his loyalty by aiding the Union cause; his acts and his omissions to act; whether he was threatened, molested, or injured in person, family, or property; whether he rendered any aid to the confederate cause; whether he had sons in the confederate service; in short, to all the circumstances of the case. It is not difficult for a claimant to select witnesses from his acquaintances who will testify in general terms, "I knew the claimant; he was a Union man; I so regarded him. I think he was so regarded by his Union neighbors. I have often heard him express Union sentiments. He was bitterly opposed to secession." These are common phrases, and constantly repeated.

How little such testimony is worth appears from the fact that such or similar phrases are constantly used in support of the loyalty of the claimants, who have served, sometimes, for three years in the rebel army, or who are otherwise clearly shown to be disloyal. We deem such evidence much weaker than the proof derived from surrounding circumstances.

We have been led, by our experience in examining the proofs in these cases, to another opinion, not fully appreciated by us at first. It is this: that the proof to excuse disloyal acts, such as voting for secession, holding civil office under the confederacy, furnishing a substitute, &c., is rarely of actual force, or of danger from the action of the constituted authorities. These existed and are sometimes proved. But the real, imminent danger of injury was from another quarter: There was, in certain districts, so much of terrorism and intimidation that loyal men felt a constant and oppressive apprehension of lawless violence. There was real danger to life, family, and property from the lawless violence of individuals and from the fury of the mob. To escape these perils, men who were at heart true friends of the Union felt compelled to appear friendly to the confederate cause and to do disloyal acts. Where such facts are satisfactorily proved, and *the whole tenor of the claimant's conduct before and after* shows him to have been really loyal, where, perhaps, the suffering and losses he was afterward subjected to by the rebels show that they regarded him as an enemy, we think it our duty to regard the disloyal act as springing from duress, and find the claimant loyal. In weighing such evidence we do not forget that many pretend to have acted under duress where none existed.

## V.—STORES AND SUPPLIES.

In our first general report we stated that *all* stores and supplies for the use of the Army might be included in the claims presented to us for allowance. Since then the act of May 11, 1872, has extended our jurisdiction to stores and supplies taken for the use of the Navy.

We also stated that rent, damage, and destruction of property, losses by lawless depredations, property taken by soldiers without authority or real necessity, and articles of luxury, wines, liquors, tobacco, and cotton, (unless used in hospitals,) were not included in the term "stores and supplies" for the use of the Army, and would not be allowed. We regret to see that such items still continue to be embraced in claims, and that the sum-total of the claims is thereby increased to a great amount.

## VI.—VALUE OF PROPERTY; PRICES; THE PROOF OF TAKING; DEPREDATIONS.

In our first report we said:

"In estimating the value of property, we have been guided not only by the evidence on behalf of the particular claimant, but by the knowledge of prices which we obtain in examining the numerous cases before us, and by the table of prices furnished by the Commissary and Quartermaster's Departments. The report of the Commissary-General, showing the prices paid by the Department for all the leading articles of subsistence for each month during the war, at all the principal markets of the Union, has been of great service. By adding to the price at the nearest market the cost of transportation to the place where the claim accrued, we get a fair measure of the value of the property claimed.

"Similar tables of prices have been furnished by the Quartermaster-General. They have been of much use in reducing the inflated and exaggerated estimates which claimants generally put upon their property."

We deem it proper to add, in reference to the report of the Commissary-General above referred to, that it was made not long after the close of the war, with great care, for the use of the Government, from bills, vouchers, and data of actual purchases made by the Government during each month of the war; was published with the report of the Commissary-General, and may be regarded as the highest authority for the price of commissary supplies during the war.

So the prices from the Quartermaster-General stand upon similar data, and are equally reliable. We refer to these authorities (which differ so widely from the prices set forth in the petitions of claimants) because claimants and their counsel sometimes seem to think that the evidence they present in each particular case should be the rule of the case.

We not only find the prices claimed in the petitions are generally greatly exaggerated, but that sometimes both prices and amounts increase with the lapse of time. Some claims presented to the Departments soon after the close of the war now appear before us much increased in amount and price.

Horses and mules appear to be of very uncertain value, ranging in the claims from $50 to $6,000. We allow for them as animals of average value, for Army use, according to the quartermaster's prices at the time, unless the evidence clearly shows a higher value. There was no kind of property so much the object of theft and depredation, so frequently and so lawlessly taken for private gain, under the pretense of Army use, as horses and mules.

### PROOF OF TAKING.

Claimants seem to think that if soldiers took property, pretending to have authority, and promising it should be paid for, that the Government is thereby bound to pay for it. But such pretenses were frequently used by the lawless, and for private gain, as well as by those really having authority. Such artifices must not be allowed to prevail. We must look beyond them, at all the circumstances connected with the taking, in order to discriminate between lawful taking and lawless depredation. The Government is not bound to pay for theft or pillage. Hence it is not enough for witnesses to say, "The property was taken by soldiers." All the facts connected with the taking should be stated, and, if possible, in the natural order of narrative.

If not so narrated, questions should be put as to the number of soldiers, whether only one or two, whether officers were with them, and ordered or knew of the taking, the hour of the day, the distance from the main body or the camp; what and all that was said and done; whether threats of violence were used; whether there was other property taken, and especially household articles or valuables; whether application was made for the restoration of the property to officers, and what was said and done in reply, and all the attending circumstances.

Our instructions to the special commissioners are positive that the questions on all these points must be put and answers insisted upon. It is their duty to enforce these directions, to have them obeyed, or the refusal noted in the body of the depositions. If claimants or their counsel allow witnesses to omit answering, or to evade the questions, the result must be that the claim is not proved, or is seriously discredited.

### VII.—AS TO QUANTITIES TAKEN.

Where a receipt or voucher was given at the time, we follow it, and have no difficulty in ascertaining the quantity taken. But where the testimony depends on the testimony of witnesses testifying eight or ten years after the property was taken, the quantity becomes uncertain. Witnesses rarely furnish any certain data. Their attention was not called, at the time, to the amount taken. They swear in round numbers, or to the "property claimed in the petition," but rarely show any means of knowledge. In perhaps a majority of cases, proof of the amount depends on the evidence of the claimant, or his wife or minor children, or of some colored dependent once his slave. When we reflect upon the lapse of time since the claims accrued, and the facilities with which the memories of such interested or easily influenced witnesses may be manufactured, it is obvious that we must receive such evidence with caution.

Still, in most of these cases, there was some property taken, and it would be unjust to wholly reject the claim. No other evidence than such as the claimant offers can usually be had, and that is subject to the serious objections above alluded to. Hence, in such cases, it is extremely difficult to make any satisfactory decision.

### VIII.—REBEL ARCHIVES.

The rebel archives in the possession of the Secretary of the Treasury and of the Secretary of War have been most obligingly opened for our use. They contain written contemporary evidence of the position of thousands of persons in the service of, or having dealings with, the confederacy. They are thus evidence of the highest value. Already they have furnished proof for the rejection of claims to a large amount. The knowledge that such papers are in the hands of the Government doubtless deters others from being presented.

The Secretary of the Treasury has occasionally, when it was needful and convenient, allowed us the aid of agents in investigating claims.

The Secretary of War has also, when the duties of the service will permit, very kindly directed officers of the Army to examine claims in the vicinity where they were stationed. This has been of great utility. In one case satisfactory proof was obtained for the rejection of a claim of about $100,000.

### IX.—OF THE UNFINISHED WORK.

As this commission, by the limitation of the act of Congress which created it, will expire in March next, we deem it our duty to report upon the amount of unfinished work before it, and the time required to finish it.

The whole number of claims presented for allowance by March 3, 1873, will probably be about 19,000.

We reported at the last session of Congress 580 cases; herewith we send reports in 2,209 cases. We have examined about 700 other cases, which we have suspended for further investigation, but in which the work is chiefly done. By the 3d of March next we shall probably have examined and disposed of at least 500 more. There will remain, therefore, on the 3d of March next, about 15,000 cases to be examined and decided.

Perplexing questions having been settled, the labors of the commission systematized, and all employed having become familiar with their duties, and having acquired facility in the dispatch of business, it is reasonable to conclude that the work will hereafter progress with more rapidity. From the rate of progress now being made, we think the remaining work can be finished in four years. When it is considered that the evidence in all cases over $10,000 must be taken orally before the commissioners, or some one of them, and that the depositions taken by the special commissioners are in some cases quite voluminous, and require long and laborious examination, it is plain that it will require diligence and industry to do the work in that time.

ASA OWEN ALDIS,
J. B. HOWELL,
ORANGE FERRISS,
*Commissioners of Claims.*

The Hon. the SPEAKER
*Of the House of Representatives.*

---

THIRD GENERAL REPORT OF THE COMMISSIONERS OF CLAIMS.

*To the honorable the Speaker of the House of Representatives:*

SIR: The commissioners of claims respectfully present their third general report.

The first and second general reports, presented in December, 1871 and 1872, contain a full statement of the rules as to presenting and proving claims, and of the principles upon which we allow or reject them. We deem it sufficient to refer to those reports.

I. The time for presenting claims to this commission expired on the 3d of March, 1873. By referring to our last general report it will be seen that the whole number of claims presented up to the end of November, 1872, was 17,700, and the aggregate amount claimed $45,004,104.48.

The monthly receipts of claims since, up to the 3d March, 1873, have been as follows:

| | |
|---|---|
| December, 1872 | 658 |
| January, 1873 | 804 |
| February, 1873 | 1,621 |
| March, (the first three days) | 1,515 |
| Total | 4,598 |

The amount of the above claims was $15,254,045.96.

The whole number of claims presented to the commissioners is 22,298.

The gross amount of all the claims filed is $60,258,150.44.

The number disposed of in our—

| | |
|---|---|
| First report was | 580 |
| Second report was | 2,209 |
| (This) third report is | 2,465 |
| Total | 5,254 |

The aggregate amount of the claims so passed upon is $10,224,386.32.

There remain, therefore, 17,044 claims, amounting to $50,033,764.12, yet to be disposed of.

II. The act of Congress of May 11, 1872, requires that in all cases exceeding $10,000 the witnesses for the claimant must be examined orally before us. This obliges the claimant to bring his witnesses to Washington, for there is no provision in the law authorizing us to take the testimony of claimants elsewhere than at Washington, and providing for the expense thereby incurred.

Annexed is a table of the claims, showing the amounts by tens of thousands. From this it appears that 949 claims exceeding $10,000 each have been presented; of this number 50 claims exceed $100,000, and 145 exceed $50,000. Some of these have been reduced below $10,000 by the voluntary act of the claimants. About 138 have been disposed of in this and former reports.

III. We present herewith special reports in 2,465 cases. Of this number there are—

| | |
|---|---|
| Wholly disallowed | 1,373 |
| Allowed in whole or in part | 1,092 |
| Total | 2,465 |

Of the number *disallowed*, 249 are claimants who have served in the confederate army or furnished a substitute; and 56 are of persons who were in the civil service of the confederacy, or who took the oath of allegiance to the confederacy.

Of the number *allowed*, 164 are persons who served in the United States Army.

The aggregate amount claimed in these 2,465 cases is $4,717,887.29.

| | |
|---|---|
| Amount allowed | $643,713 04 |
| Amount disallowed | 4,074,174 25 |
| Total | 4,717,887 29 |

Many cases, especially from Alabama, Mississippi, and Louisiana, remain in our hands, heard, partly examined, but not finished, because our special agents have not been able to find time to examine them and report to us. This has been owing partially to their necessary investigation of claims in other States, and in part (in Mississippi and Louisiana) to the prevailing sickness which interrupted their work.

It is but justice to the special agents to say that they have worked industriously, and that their services have been of great value.

IV. The numerous disallowances of claims in which the testimony offered did not satisfy us of the loyalty of the claimant, or of the justice and validity of the claim, have been followed by efforts on the part of claimants to get their cases reconsidered. Our only action upon the matter so far has been to receive petitions for the rehearing of claims, whenever the claimant sets forth specifically, over his own signature, and upon oath or affirmation, what new and material facts he relies upon to prove the disallowance to be erroneous, what witnesses are to prove the alleged facts, and why the proposed new evidence was not produced on the original examination. We also require the affidavits of the intended witnesses to be filed, embracing all the matters upon which they will testify. Until somewhat relieved from the pressure of unreported cases, it will be impracticable to take up any disallowed claims for reconsideration.

V. In consequence of frequent applications from volunteer officers and other adherents of the Union cause who had served or resided, or now live in the insurrectionary States, for information concerning the claims brought before the commissioners, measures were taken, as soon as all the claims had been filed, to prepare a printed list, giving the name of each claimant, the State and county in which he resides, or in which his property was taken, and the number and amount of his claim. In the preface to the list explanation is made of the facts that the names were those of professed adherents to the cause and Government of the United States during the rebellion, the amounts charged, and the value of the personal property taken for the necessary and proper use of the Union Army. This list, containing the recorded particulars of nearly 23,000 claims, has been extensively circulated and distributed wherever it has been thought probable that information serviceable to the just determination of claims might be obtained, and it is intended to continue the distribution as long as such a measure is deemed advisable.

VI. TOBACCO.—As we now, for the first time, present reports allowing for tobacco taken for Army use, we desire to state the reasons for such allowances.

Tobacco was never by law made an Army supply till the act of March 3, 1865, provided that it might be furnished at cost to those who desired it, and at their expense. All the claims for tobacco which have been examined by us are for tobacco taken before that date.

After the capture of Atlanta, in September, 1864, General Sherman found that he was short of rations for his army, and that the soldiers were subject to many privations. To make his army contented, and, as far as possible, to make up to them for their usual rations, of which they were for the time deprived, he issued an order on the 8th of September, 1864, authorizing the chief commissary of subsistence to take possession of and issue to the troops all the tobacco in Atlanta, and give certificates thereof to the owners, to be accounted for in accordance with existing orders.

Pursuant to this order, tobacco belonging to George J. Stubblefield was taken, and upon his making claim for payment, the Commissary Department recommended, "as this tobacco was taken *by order of General Sherman* and issued to the troops *in lieu of other rations*, and as the loyalty of the claimant is clearly established," that payment should be made. This was approved by the Secretary of War, Mr. Stanton, and the claim was paid.

The payment stands upon the ground that, when an army is deprived of its usual rations, the commanding general can, in his judgment, authorize an article not a supply to be taken and used for the time being as a supply and *in lieu of other rations;* and in such case the Government is bound to pay for it. We have strictly followed this precedent, and have not allowed for tobacco except when taken under this order.

VII. We have heretofore set forth the necessity that exists for more clerks in order to dispatch with reasonable speed the business of the commission. We again respectfully request attention to this subject.

It is a great hardship for a loyal and honest claimant to be delayed year after year in the examination and payment of his just claim. But it would be unjust to the Government to allow claims without thoroughly and carefully examining all reasonable sources of information, in order to determine whether the claimant is loyal and the claim just.

A thorough examination of the rebel archives, and of the papers purchased, as furnishing evidence in claims against the Government, is very essential. In this we have been greatly aided by the Secretary of the Treasury, the Secretary of War, and the Adjutant-General, and the subordinate officers of these Departments and Bureaus having the custody of these papers. But there is much in the examination of these papers that we cannot reasonably ask them to do, and for which we have no clerks to spare.

So, too, in preparing summaries of the evidence taken by special commissioners, of papers, often long and bulky, received from the Departments, and heretofore used on behalf of claimants, in examining papers received from the Treasury and War Departments, and making copies of them for Congress, and in giving directions to agents in examining claims, there is a great amount of work to be done which might well be done by clerks under the instruction of the commissioners.

A moderate increase in the number of clerks would greatly relieve the commissioners, and enable them to devote more time to the decision of cases, and thus aid in the work of the commission.

ASA OWEN ALDIS,
J. B. HOWELL,
ORANGE FERRISS,
*Commissioners of Claims.*

WASHINGTON, D. C., *December* 6, 1873.

---

## FOURTH GENERAL REPORT OF THE COMMISSIONERS OF CLAIMS.

WASHINGTON, D. C., *December* 14, 1874.

*To the honorable the Speaker of the House of Representatives:*

SIR: The commissioners of claims respectfully present their fourth general report.

I. The time for presenting claims to this commission expired on the 3d of March, 1873. A bill for extending the time for presenting claims was passed by the House of Representatives at the last session, but was not acted upon by the Senate. No claims have, therefore, been received by us during the last year.

The whole number of claims presented for allowance is 22,298.

| | |
|---|---|
| The number disposed of in our first report was | 580 |
| Second report was | 2,209 |
| Third report was | 2,465 |
| Fourth (this) report is | 2,407 |
| Whole number disposed of is | 7,661 |
| Remaining not disposed of | 14,637 |
| Total | 22,298 |

II. *Of the unfinished business.*—Of this number of 14,637 cases yet in our hands, a large number have been examined, and have been suspended for further investigation by our special agents.

About fifteen hundred doubtful cases are thus awaiting examination. It is proper to add that the work done during the year is not to be measured by the number of reported cases. These suspended cases, difficult and doubtful, and frequently involving large sums, consume a great portion of our time.

In twelve of the larger cases so being investigated, the claims amount to $3,035,000. In many of the large cases our agents have made reports. These are shown to the claimants, or their attorneys, that they may, if they see fit, produce rebutting testimony. This leads to delay; for in almost every case so suspended and reported upon by our agents, the claimants have requested further time to put in their rebutting evidence.

The number of agents which we are authorized to employ for the investigation of cases in all the Southern States is limited by law to three. We would again respectfully suggest that this number is wholly inadequate for doing, with reasonable dispatch, the work that is to be done. The claims we refer to the agents are numerous, large, and difficult of investigation. Reluctance of witnesses to give testimony against their neighbors, opposition in various and unexpected forms, and other unavoidable causes of delay constantly meet them, and hinder their work.

The employment of such agents is of great utility and advantage to honest claimants, and to the Government. They often report favorably in cases which, upon the evidence filed in their favor, appear doubtful, or deserving of rejection. In other cases, often involving large amounts, they find facts establishing disloyalty, fraud, or other sufficient cause for rejection, and thus save large sums to the Government.

The case of Whitty M. Sasser for $100,498, which was referred back to us by Congress at its last session for further examination, is now in the hands of an agent for investigation. We have not been able to include it in this report.

In the case of Sarah Polk, for $2,040, the papers having been sent to the House of Representatives, at its request, we have not felt at liberty to further examine and report upon the claim until the pleasure of the House should be manifested, either by taking jurisdiction of and acting upon the claim, or by returning it to us for examination.

A large portion of our time has heretofore been taken up with the oral examination of witnesses. We think that the number of cases in which witnesses will be thus brought before us is diminishing, and that we shall soon have more time for the examination of the other cases, in which the evidence is taken by the special commissioners. This will materially aid us in disposing of the unfinished business.

III. We present herewith special reports in 2,407 cases. They are distributed among the States, as follows:

| | |
|---|---|
| Alabama | 299 |
| Arkansas | 277 |
| Florida | 7 |
| Georgia | 210 |
| Louisiana | 59 |
| Mississippi | 180 |
| North Carolina | 273 |
| South Carolina | 34 |
| Tennessee | 554 |

| | |
|---|---|
| Texas | 7 |
| Virginia | 475 |
| West Virginia | 32 |
| | 2,407 |

| | |
|---|---|
| Of this number, there are wholly disallowed | 1,244 |
| Allowed in whole or in part | 1,163 |

Of the number disallowed, 150 are claimants who served in the confederate army or sent a substitute, and 89 are persons who were in the civil service of the confederacy or voluntarily voted for secession.

Of the number allowed, 120 are persons who served in the Army of the United States.

| | |
|---|---|
| The whole amount claimed in the 2,407 cases included in this report is | $5,242,706 40 |
| Amount allowed | 770,911 37 |
| Amount disallowed | 4,471,995 09 |
| Total | 5,242,706 46 |

The number and amount of disallowed cases is somewhat increased by claims not within the jurisdiction of the commission, and therefore reported as disallowed without reference to their merits.

IV. In many cases where we had disallowed claims, the claimants filed petitions to us for new hearings. Our action in receiving these petitions was fully set forth in our last report. Doubts having been expressed whether we had any jurisdiction of cases to grant rehearings and hear them anew after having reported them to Congress, we addressed notes to the Committees on Claims of the Senate and War-Claims of the House, asking for their judgment upon the question. They replied that, in their judgment, we had no jurisdiction of cases reported to Congress, and therefore that we could not grant rehearings in such cases. Being fully satisfied of the correctness of this decision of the committees, we have since refused to receive such petitions.

V. *Of citizenship.*—We have held that aliens who had only declared their intention of becoming citizens, but who were not actually admitted to American citizenship, and had not renounced their foreign allegiance, were not citizens within the meaning of the act of Congress establishing this commission.

This, we believe, is in consonance with the practice of the Government during the war, and with the recent decision of the mixed commission on British and American claims.

VI. Some misapprehension still seems to exist as to what in our judgment constitutes the proof of loyalty and disloyalty. It is thought that we hold that service in the rebel army, furnishing a substitute, holding civil office under the confederacy, furnishing munitions of war, supplies, cotton, or money, to aid the confederacy, are disloyal acts on the part of the claimant, which necessarily and in all cases require us to reject the claim. This is a mistake. They are *prima-facie* disloyal acts which require the rejection of the claim unless explained and shown to be not the voluntary acts of the claimants, but done under duress, from necessity, or through personal fear of danger to life, family, or property. The proof that they were not voluntary acts is always received and considered. In our present report there are many cases of claimants *who have served in the confederate army* whose claims have been allowed; but the proof that such service was involuntary has been ample, as, for instance, that they were loyal, were conscripted, served for a short time, deserted at the first opportunity, enlisted in the Union Army, served one, two, or three years, and were honorable discharged. Such proof—and it is found in quite a number of cases—must satisfy every fair mind that the service in the confederate army was not voluntary, and that the party was really loyal to the Union cause.

The *principle* applies to all cases where the disloyal act appears. But no two cases are alike. It is impossible to lay down a general rule as to the weight of evidence, and what is and what is not satisfactory proof that the disloyal act was done voluntarily or not. The circumstances are *all* to be weighed; the *whole* evidence is to be considered; and it is only by so doing that a reasonable judgment can be formed.

VII. *Bankruptcy.*—After the war numerous claimants availed themselves of the benefit of the bankrupt law. In every such case the claim passed to the assignee in bankruptcy. Counsel have strenuously urged that, as there was no liability on the part of the Government to make payment to any one, and no tribunal before which claims could be adjudicated or enforced, they were mere naked, intangible rights, invested with no attributes of property, and not the subject of assignment or transfer. If this is true, we have erred in recommending payment to heirs and legatees. We have never doubted that these claims were the subject of inheritance and bequest. If they pass by will, then assuredly they pass in bankruptcy. The fourteenth section of the bankrupt law defines the property that goes to the assignee, and includes not only all real and personal property and choses in action, but in terms "all rights in equity."

The act of March 3, 1871, does not create claims. It recognizes their existence, and provides a tribunal for their adjudication and settlement. At the beginning of the war they were paid through the proper accounting officers, and it required affirmative legislation to suspend payment. If a regular voucher was given for stores or supplies, no matter where taken, the proper officers of the Government always have been authorized to make payment. They refuse it because the highest evidence is not produced. Yet the character of the evidence to establish it neither creates, enlarges, nor diminishes the claim.

ASA OWEN ALDIS,
J. B. HOWELL,
ORANGE FERRISS,
*Commissioners of Claims.*

---

The following are the regulations for taking testimony in support of claims pending before the commissioners of claims at Washington. (Revised and re-issued July 1, 1874.)

### ADMISSIBLE EVIDENCE.

1. Admissible evidence consists only of oral testimony given before the commissioners of claims or one of them, personally; or of testimony taken previous to March 3, 1871, to be used in the Court of Claims, or before some Department of the Government; or of depositions taken under the rules and authority of the commissioners of claims in cases not exceeding $10,000 in amount; or of papers used in evidence before any Department of the Government prior to March 3, 1871, in the consideration of any claim not now exceeding $10,000 in amount.

### AUTHORITY OF SPECIAL COMMISSIONERS.

2. Special commissioners appointed by the commissioners of claims are authorized to administer oaths and affirmations; to take the depositions of witnesses in any case not exceeding $5,000 in amount, upon application of the claimant or attorney, and to take the depositions of witnesses in any case not exceeding $10,000 in amount when so ordered by the commissioners.

### DELEGATION OF AUTHORITY PROHIBITED.

3. Special commissioners must themselves administer all oaths and affirmations, examine all witnesses, write down all testimony, and fill up and sign all certificates. No part of their authority or duty can be delegated.

### MODE OF TAKING DEPOSITIONS.

4. Depositions must be written in presence of the witnesses and while they are testifying, and the record must be as closely as possible in the words spoken by the witnesses, who must sign their depositions after hearing them read.

The testimony must be written on legal-cap paper, and on both sides of the sheets. Testimony concerning loyalty should be separately recorded from testimony concerning property, so that all the depositions affecting loyalty may be brought together before the several pages are fastened and the certificate appended.

### CERTIFYING AND INDORSING DEPOSITIONS.

5. All depositions taken at one time and in the same case should be securely fastened together and covered by a certificate of the form furnished by the commissioners; each signature being also attested by the special commissioner. The depositions should be then folded, and so indorsed as to exhibit, without unfolding, the number of the case, the name and residence of the claimant, the amount of the claim, the names of the deponents, the name of the special commissioner, the amount of fees and expenses actually charged, and the name and address of the attorney at Washington, if there be any such attorney.

### SWEARING OF WITNESSES.

6. Every deponent, before testifying, must be duly and properly sworn or affirmed to tell the truth, the whole truth, and nothing but the truth, concerning the matters under examination, and each deponent so swearing should be informed that false testimony, knowingly given before any special commissioner, is punishable as in cases of willful and corrupt perjury.

### EXAMINATION OF WITESSES BY SPECIAL COMMISSIONERS.

7. Claimants, or the heirs or legatees of deceased claimants, are to be first examined when present; the other witnesses in any order that may be arranged. When a claimant, or a witness, is testifying, the other witnesses must not be present; but a claimant, or other beneficiary, or a claimant's counsel, is entitled to be present during the examination of all the witnesses.

The special commissioner will begin the examination of each deponent by putting, one after another, the printed questions prescribed for such a witness, reading each question deliberately, and repeating and explaining it, if necessary, and being careful to obtain and to write down a direct and explicit answer to every part of it. Printed questions are neither to be written down as questions, nor their contents repeated in the answers, but they will be mentioned only by numbers according to the following form: "To question numbered , the witness answers:"

After putting each printed question, or after putting all the printed questions, if he so prefers, the special commissioner will put such questions of his own as will draw out all the facts, whether they be favorable or unfavorable to the claim; also, such as will disclose the means of knowledge possessed by the witness, distinguish between what he actually knows and what he only believes, or thinks, or has heard, clear up what is obscure and indefinite, and test the bias, the accuracy, the memory, and the honesty of the witness.

A witness under examination should be reminded, by frequent questions, of the necessity of giving times, places, names, and particular circumstances connected with the more important facts to which he testifies, and, if careless or reluctant, should be informed that omissions to answer questions or parts of questions, or evasive answers, or uncertainties in the testimony, throw injurious doubts upon the merits of the claim and jeopardize its success.

A witness should be permitted to tell all that he desires, and induced by searching questions to tell all that he knows; yet the special commissioner must not permit a witness to ramble in his statements, but cause him to fully answer one question, or testify on one topic, before passing to another.

### EXAMINATION BY CLAIMANTS OR COUNSEL.

8. When the special commissioner has completed his examination of a witness, the claimant or counsel can put such questions as may tend to draw out additional facts, but must not be allowed, either ignorantly or through design, to put "leading questions," or questions liable to induce the witness to state as facts what he does not positively know or remember; and if any such question is insisted upon by claimant or counsel, the special commissioner will write it down as part of the record.

### RE-EXAMINATION BY SPECIAL COMMISSIONERS.

9. After a witness has been examined by the claimant or counsel, the special commissioner should put any further questions suggested by the questions and answers that have just passed between claimant or counsel and the witness, using, as before, his best efforts to bring out both sides of the case and free it from doubt and obscurity.

### QUESTIONS NOT TO BE RECORDED.

10. None of the questions put to witnesses by special commissioners, claimants, or counsel, need be written in the depositions, unless they be "leading questions," as already mentioned, or their appearance in the record is necessary to a proper understanding of the answers.

### SPECIAL TESTIMONY CONCERNING DECEASED CLAIMANTS.

11. Where the original claimant is dead, the questions that would be put to such claimant, if living, should be answered by the nearest or

most intimate relative, but the answers must contain only actual personal knowledge, and not mere belief, hearsay, or supposition; and the means of knowledge must be stated in every answer where knowledge is professed.

REFRESHMENT OF THE MEMORY OF WITNESSES.

12. Witnesses are not to be permitted to refresh their memory during their examination by referring for information to either persons or papers, excepting to memoranda made by themselves on the spot and at the time of the transactions to which they relate; and any such memoranda, used to refresh the memory, must be put into the record as evidence. In other respects, they are to testify from their own recollection, especially when testifying to number or quantity in connection with the items of a claim.

TESTIMONY TO BE TAKEN ON FORMAL APPLICATIONS.

13. Before proceeding to take testimony, a special commissioner must have before him a formal application containing the record number, title, and amount of the claim, and the list of items corresponding with the items in the petition filed at Washington.

The application on which testimony is taken should be attached firmly to the deposition as part of the record, and should be inserted just before the depositions relating to the property.

MODE AND TIME OF FORWARDING TESTIMONY.

14. Depositions must be forwarded direct to the commissioners at Washington by the special commissioner, by mail or express, with postage or expressage prepaid, and as soon as possible after the proper costs are paid or secured.

FEES AND EXPENSES.

15. The fees of a special commissioner for taking, certifying, and forwarding depositions in support of a claim not exceeding one thousand dollars in amount, are limited by law to ten cents per folio; a folio being construed to be one hundred words, and the words to be counted being those in the certificate, head-lines, testimony, and indorsement.

In cases above one thousand dollars in amount, the authorized fees are twenty cents per folio, with an attendance-fee of three dollars for each day of actual service, divided among all the claimants served in one day, but not more than one day's attendance-fee to be collected in any one case.

Copies of depositions may be furnished to claimants who desire them, at the rate of ten cents per folio.

By special agreement, previously made, a special commissioner may receive from claimants or their agents the amount of his actual traveling expenses, including the necessary cost of board and lodging, for the actual distance traveled and the actual time consumed in their service.

Any agreement for fixing the cost of taking testimony in any other way than herein provided, must, if made, be made in writing and signed by the claimant or his attorney, and the writing forwarded to the commissioners, to be filed and preserved, subject to the uses of either party, but the agreement must not be in excess of the legal fees.

The actual or estimated amount of postage may be collected by a special commissioner on each set of depositions, and used to pay the cost of forwarding such depositions.

Claimants are not entitled to have their depositions forwarded or considered till the authorized costs are paid or secured, but a special commissioner must accept no promise or security that would give him a pecuniary interest in the success of a claim.

### STANDING INTERROGATORIES.

The following questions will be put to every person who gives testimony:

1. What is your name, your age, your residence, and how long has it been such, and your occupation?

2. If you are not the claimant, in what manner, if any, are you related to the claimant or interested in the success of the claim?

The following questions will be put to every claimant, except claimants who were slaves at the beginning of the war:

[NOTE.—If the original claimant be dead, these questions are to be answered by each of the heirs or legatees who were not less than sixteen years of age when the war closed.]

3. Where were you born? If not born in the United States, when and where were you naturalized? Produce your naturalization-papers, if you can.

4. Where were you residing and what was your business for six months before the outbreak of the rebellion, and where did you reside and what was your business from the beginning to the end of the war? And if you changed your residence or business, state how many times, and why such changes were made.

5. On which side were your sympathies during the war, and were they on the same side from beginning to end?

6. Did you ever do anything or say anything against the Union cause; and if so, what did you do and say, and why?

7. Were you at all times during the war willing and ready to do whatever you could in aid of the Union cause?

8. Did you ever do anything for the Union cause or its advocates or defenders? If so, state what you did, giving times, places, names of persons aided, and particulars. Were the persons aided your relations?

9. Had you any near relatives in the Union Army or Navy; if so, in what company and regiment, or on what vessel, when and where did each one enter service, and when and how did he leave service? If he was a son, produce his discharge-paper, in order that its contents may be noted in this deposition, or state why it cannot be produced.

10. Were you in the service or employment of the United States Government at any time during the war; if so, in what service, when, where, or how long, under what officers, and when and how did you leave such service or employment?

11. Did you ever voluntarily contribute money, property, or services to the Union cause; and if so, when, where, to whom, and what did you contribute?

12. Which side did you take while the insurgent States were seceding from the Union in 1860 and 1861, and what did you do to show on which side you stood?

13. Did you adhere to the Union cause after the States had passed into rebellion, or did you go with your State?

14. What were your feelings concerning the battle of Bull Run or Manassas, the capture of New Orleans, the fall of Vicksburgh, and the final surrender of the confederate forces?

15. What favors, privileges, or protections were ever granted you in recognition of your loyalty during the war, and when and by whom granted?

16. Have you ever taken the so-called "iron-clad oath" since the war, and when and on what occasions?

17. Who were the leading and best-known Unionists of your vicinity during the war? Are any of them called to testify to your loyalty; and if not, why not?

18. Were you ever threatened with damage or injury to your person, family, or property on account of your Union sentiments, or were you actually molested or injured on account of your Union sentiments? If so, when, where, by whom, and in what particular way were you injured or threatened with injury?

19. Were you ever arrested by any confederate officer, soldier, sailor, or other person professing to act for the confederate government, or for any State in rebellion? If so, when, where, by whom, for what cause; how long were you kept under arrest; how did you obtain your release; did you take any oath or give any bond to effect your release; and if so, what was the nature of the oath or bond?

20. Was any of your property taken by confederate officers or soldiers, or any rebel authority? If so, what property, when, where, by whom; were you ever paid therefor, and did you ever present an account therefor to the confederate government, or any rebel officer?

21. Was any of your property ever confiscated by rebel authority, on the ground that you were an enemy to the rebel cause? If so, give all the particulars, and state if the property was subsequently released or compensation made therefor.

22. Did you ever do anything for the confederate cause, or render any aid or comfort to the rebellion? If so, give the times, places, persons, and other particulars connected with each transaction.

23. What force, compulsion, or influence was used to make you do anything against the Union cause? If any, give all the particulars demanded in the last question.

24. Were you in any service, business, or employment, for the confederacy, or for any rebel authority? If so, give the same particulars as before required.

25. Were you in the civil, military, or naval service of the confederacy, or any rebel State, in any capacity whatsoever? If so, state fully in respect to each occasion and service.

26. Did you ever take any oath to the so-called Confederate States while in any rebel service or employment?

27. Did you ever have charge of any stores, or other property, for the confederacy, or did you ever sell or furnish any supplies to the so-called Confederate States, or any State in rebellion; or did you have any share or interest in contracts or manufactures in aid of the rebellion?

28. Were you engaged in blockade-running, or running through the lines, or interested in the risks or profits of such ventures?

29. Were you in any way interested in any vessel navigating the waters of the confederacy, or entering or leaving any confederate port? If so, what vessel, when and where employed, in what business, and had any rebel authority any direct or indirect interest in vessel or cargo?

30. Did you ever subscribe to any loan of the so-called Confederate States, or of any rebel State; or own confederate bonds or securities, or

the bonds or securities of any rebel State issued between 1861 and 1865? Did you sell, or agree to sell, cotton or produce to the confederate government, or to any rebel State, or to any rebel officer or agent; and if so, did you receive or agree to receive confederate or State bonds or securities in payment; and if so, to what amount, and for what kind and amount of property?

31. Did you contribute to the raising, equipment, or support of tooops, or the building of gunboats in aid of the rebellion; or to military hospitals or invalids, or to relief-funds or subscriptions for the families of persons serving against the United States?

32. Did you ever give information to any person in aid of military or naval operations against the United States?

33. Were you at any time a member of any society or organization for equipping volunteers or conscripts, or for aiding the rebellion in any other manner?

34. Did you ever take an oath of allegiance to the so-called Confederate States? If so, state how often, when, where, for what purpose, and the nature of the oath or affirmation.

35. Did you ever receive a pass from rebel authority? If so, state when, where, for what purpose, on what conditions, and how the pass was used.

36. Had you any near relatives in the confederate army, or in any military or naval service hostile to the United States? If so, give names, ages on entering service, present residence, if living, what influence you exerted, if any, against their entering the service, and in what way you contributed to their outfit and support.

37. Have you been under the disabilities imposed by the fourteenth amendment to the Constitution? Have your disabilities been removed by Congress?

38. Have you been specially pardoned by the President for participation in the rebellion?

39. Did you take any amnesty oath during the war, or after its close? If so, when, where, and why did you take it?

40. Were you ever a prisoner to the United States authorities, or on parole, or under bonds to do nothing against the Union cause? If so, state all the particulars.

41. Were you ever arrested by the authorities of the United States during the war? If so, when, where, by whom, on what grounds, and when and how did you obtain your release?

42. Were there any fines or assessments levied upon you by the authorities of the United States because of your supposed sympathy for the rebellion? If so, state all the facts.

43. Was any of your property taken into possession or sold by the United States under the laws relating to confiscation, or to captured and abandoned property?

The following questions will be put to all male claimants or beneficiaries who were not less than sixteen years of age when the war closed:

44. After the presidential election of 1860, if of age, did you vote for any candidate or on any questions, during the war, and how did you vote? Did you vote for or against candidates favoring secession? Did you vote for or against the ratification of the ordinance of secession, or for or against separation in your State?

45. Did you belong to any vigilance committee, or committee of safety, home-guard, or any other form of organization or combination designed to suppress Union sentiment in your vicinity?

46. Were you in the confederate army, State militia, or any military

or naval organization hostile to the United States? If so, state when, where, in what organizations, how and why you entered, how long you remained each time, and when and how you left. If you claim that you were conscripted, when and where was it, how did you receive notice, and from whom, and what was the precise manner in which the conscription was enforced against you? If you were never in the rebel army or other hostile organization, explain how you escaped service. If you furnished a substitute, when and why did you furnish one, and what is his name, and his present address, if living?

47. Were you in any way connected with or employed in the confederate quartermaster, commissary, ordinance, engineer, or medical department, or any other department, or employed on any railroad transporting troops or supplies for the confederacy, or otherwise engaged in transportation of men and supplies for the confederacy? If so, state how employed, when, where, for how long, under whose direction, and why such employment was not giving "aid and comfort" to the rebellion.

48. Did you at any time have charge of trains, teams, wagons, vessels, boats, or military supplies or property of any kind for the confederate government? If so, give all the facts as in previous questions.

49. Were you employed in saltpeter-works, in tanning or milling for the confederate goverment, or making clothing, boots, shoes, saddles, harness, arms, ammunition, accouterments, or any other kind of munitions of war for the confederacy? If so, give all the particulars of time, place, and nature of service or supplies.

50. Were you ever engaged in holding in custody, directly or indirectly, any persons taken by the rebel government as prisoners of war, or any person imprisoned or confined by the confederate government, or the authorities of any rebel State, for political causes? If so, when, where, under what circumstances, in what capacity were you engaged, and what was the name and rank of your principal?

51. Were you ever in the Union Army or Navy, or in any service connected therewith? If so, when, where, in what capacity, under whose command or authority, for what period of time, and when and how did you leave service? Produce your discharge-papers, so that their contents may be noted herein.

The following questions will be put to every person testifying to the loyalty of claimants or beneficiaries:

52. In whose favor are you here to testify?

53. How long have you known that person altogether, and what part of that time have you intimately known him?

54. Did you live near him during the war, and how far away?

55. Did you meet him often, and about how often, during the war?

56. Did you converse with the claimant about the war, its causes, its progress, and its results? If so, try to remember the more important occasions on which you so conversed, beginning with the first occasion, and state with respect to each, when it was, where it was, who were present, what caused the conversation, and what the claimant said, in substance, if you cannot remember his words.

57. Do you know of anything done by the claimant that showed him to be loyal to the Union cause during the war? If you do, state what he did, when, where, and what was the particular cause or occasion of his doing it. Give the same information about each thing he did that showed him to be loyal.

58. Do you know of anything said or done by the claimant that was against the Union cause? If so, please state, with respect to each

thing said or done, what it was, when it was, where it was, and what particular compulsion or influence caused him to say or do it.

59. If you have heard of anything said or done by the claimant, either for the Union cause or against it, state from whom you heard it, when you heard it, and what you heard.

60. What was the public reputation of the claimant for loyalty or disloyalty to the United States during the war? If you profess to know his public reputation, explain fully how you know it, whom you heard speak of it, and give the names of other persons who were neighbors during the war that could testify to his public reputation.

61. Who were the known and prominent Union people of the neighborhood during the war, and do you know that such persons could testify to the claimant's loyalty?

62. Were you, yourself, an adherent of the Union cause during the war? If so, did the claimant know you to be such, and how did he know it?

63. Do you know of any threats, molestations, or injury inflicted upon the claimant or his family, or his property, on account of his adherence to the Union cause? If so, give all the particulars.

64. Do you know of any act done or language used by the claimant that would have prevented him from establishing his loyalty to the confederacy? If so, what act or what language?

65. Can you state any other facts within your own knowledge in proof of the claimant's loyalty during the war? If so, state all the facts and give all the particulars.

The following questions concerning the ownership of property charged in claims will be put to all claimants, or the representatives of deceased claimants:

66. Who was the owner of the property charged in this claim when it was taken, and how did such person become owner?

67. If any of the property was taken from a farm or plantation, where was such farm or plantation situated, what was its size, how much was cultivated, how much was woodland, and how much was waste-land?

68. Has the person who owned the property when taken since filed a petition in bankruptcy, or been declared a bankrupt?

The following questions will be put to female claimants:

69. Are you married or single? If married, when were you married? Was your husband loyal to the cause and Government of the United States throughout the war? Where does he now reside, and why is he not joined with you in the petition? How many children have you? Give their names and ages. Were any of them in the confederate service during the war? If you claim that the property named in your petition is your sole and separate property, state how you came to own it separately from your husband; how your title was derived; when your ownership of it began. Did it ever belong to your husband? If the property for which you ask pay is wood, timber, rails, or the products of a farm, how did you get title to the farm? If by deed, can you file copies of the deeds? If single, have you been married? If a widow, when did your husband die? Was he in the confederate army? Was he in the civil service of the confederacy? Was he loyal to the United States Government throughout the war? Did he leave any children? How many? Are any now living? Give their names and ages. Are they not interested in this claim? If they are not joined in this petition, why not? State fully how your title to the property specified in the petition was obtained. Did you ever belong to any

sewing-society organized to make clothing for confederate soldiers or their families, or did you assist in making any such clothing, or making flags or other military equipments, or preparing or furnishing delicacies or supplies for the confederate hospitals or soldiers?

The following questions will be put to colored claimants:

70. Were you a slave or free at the beginning of the war? If ever a slave, when did you become free? What business did you follow after obtaining your freedom? Did you own this property before or after you became free? When did you get it? How did you become owner, and from whom did you obtain it? Where did you get the means to pay for it? What was the name and residence of your master, and is he still living? Is he a witness for you; and if not, why not? Are you in his employ now, or do you live on his land or on land bought from him? Are you in his debt? What other person beside yourself has any interest in this claim?

The following questions will be put to all colored witnesses in behalf of white claimants:

71. Were you formerly the slave of the claimant? Are you now in his service or employment? Do you live on his land? Are you in his debt? Are you in any way to share in this claim, if allowed?

The following questions will be put to claimants and witnesses who testify to the taking of property, omitting in the case of each claimant or witness any questions that are clearly unnecessary:

72. Were you present when any of the property charged in this claim was taken? Did you actually see any taken? If so, specify what you saw taken.

73. Was any of the property taken in the night-time, or was any taken secretly, so that you did not know of it at the time?

74. Was any complaint made to any officer of the taking of any of the property? If so, give the name, rank, and regiment of the officer, and state who made the complaint to him; what he said and did in consequence; and what was the result of the complaint.

75. Were any vouchers or receipts asked for or given? If given, where are the vouchers or receipts? If lost, state fully how lost. If asked and not given, by whom were they asked; who was asked to give them, and why were they refused or not given? State very fully in regard to the failure to ask or obtain receipts.

76. Has any payment ever been made for any property charged in this claim? Has any payment been made for any property taken at the same times as the property charged in this claim? Has any payment been made for any property taken from the same claimant during the war; and if so, when, by whom, for what property and to what amount? Has this property, or any part of it, been included in any claim heretofore presented to Congress, or any court, Department, or officer of the United States, or to any board of survey, military commission, State commission or officer, or any other authority? If so, when and to what tribunal or officers was the claim presented? Was it larger or smaller in amount than this claim; and how is the difference explained; and what was the decision, if any, of the tribunal to which it was presented?

77. Was the property charged in this claim taken by troops encamped in the vicinity, or were they on the march; or were they on a raid or expedition; or had there been any recent battle or skirmish?

78. You will please listen attentively while the list of items, but not the quantities, is read to you, and as each kind of property is called off, say whether you saw any such property taken.

79. Begin now with the first item of property you have just said you

saw taken, and give the following information about it: First. Describe its exact condition—as, for instance, if corn, whether green or ripe, standing or harvested, in shuck or husked or shelled; if lumber, whether new or old, in buildings or piled; if grain, whether growing or cut, &c. Second. State where it was. Third. What was the quantity? Explain fully how you know the quantity; and if estimated, describe your method of making the estimate. Fourth. Describe the quality, to your best judgment. Fifth. State as nearly as you can the market-value of such property at the time in United States money. Sixth. Say when the property was taken. Seventh. Give the name of the detachment, regiment, brigade, division, corps, or army taking the property, and the names of any officers belonging to the command. Eighth. Describe the precise manner in which the property was taken into possession by the troops, and the manner in which it was removed. Ninth. State as closely as you can how many men, animals, wagons, or other means of transport, were engaged in the removal; how long they were occupied, and to what place they removed the property. Tenth. State if any officers were present; how you knew them to be officers; what they said or did in relation to the property, and give the names of any, if you can. Eleventh. Give any reasons that you may have for believing that the taking of the property was authorized by the proper officers, or that it was for the necessary use of the Army.

80. Now take the next item of property you saw taken, and give the same information, and so proceed to the end of the list of items.

---

## CHAPTER X.

### MIXED COMMISSIONS UNDER TREATIES.

Since the organization of the Government there have been many mixed commissions under treaties for the adjustment of claims between this and foreign powers.

It would be impracticable to give a history of these now. The join commission of the United States and Mexico under the convention of July 4, 1868, is now in session in Washington. The treaty which provided for this and the rules and orders thereof are as follows:

*By the President of the United States of America.*

A PROCLAMATION.

Whereas a convention between the United States of America and the republic of Mexico, providing for the adjustment of the claims of citizens of either country against the other, was concluded and signed by their respective plenipotentiaries, at the city of Washington, on the fourth day of July, in the year of our Lord one thousand eight hundred and sixty-eight, which convention, being in the English and Spanish languages, is word for word as follows:

Whereas it is desirable to maintain and increase the friendly feelings between the United States and

Considerando que es conveniente mantener y ensanchar los sentimientos amistosos entre la repú-

the Mexican republic, and so to strengthen the system and principles of republican government on the American continent; and whereas since the signature of the treaty of Guadalupe Hidalgo, of the 2d of February, 1848, claims and complaints have been made by citizens of the United States, on account of injuries to their persons and their property by authorities of that republic, and similar claims and complaints have been made on account of injuries to the persons and property of Mexican citizens by authorities of the United States; the President of the United States of America and the President of the Mexican republic have resolved to conclude a convention for the adjustment of the said claims and complaints, and have named as their plenipotentiaries—the President of the United States, William H. Seward, Secretary of State; and the President of the Mexican republic, Matias Romero, accredited as envoy extraordinary and minister plenipotentiary of the Mexican republic to the United States; who, after having communicated to each other their respective full powers, found in good and due form, have agreed to the following articles:

blica Mexicana y los Estados Unidos, y afianzar así el sistema y principios de gobierno republicano en el continente Americano; y considerando que con posterioridad á la celebracion del tratado de Guadalupe Hidalgo, de 2 de Febrero de 1848, ciudadanos de la república Mexicana han hecho reclamaciones y presentado quejas con motivo de perjuicios sufridos en sus personas ó sus propiedades, por autoridades de los Estados Unidos, y reclamaciones y quejas semejantes se han hecho y presentado con motivo de perjuicios sufridos por ciudadanos de los Estados Unidos, en sus personas ó sus propiedades, por autoridades de la república Mexicana; el Presidente de la república Mexicana y el Presidente de los Estados Unidos de América han determinado concluir una convencion para el arreglo de dichas reclamaciones y quejas, y han nombrado sus plenipotenciarios; el Presidente de la república Mexicana, á Matias Romero, acreditado como enviado extraordinario y ministro plenipotenciario de la república Mexicana en los Estados Unidos; y el Presidente de los Estados Unidos, á William H. Seward, Secretario de Estado, quienes despues de haberse mostrado sus respectivos plenos poderes y encontrádolos en buena y debida forma, han convenido en los artículos siguientes:

### ARTICLE I.

All claims on the part of corporations, companies, or private individuals, citizens of the United States, upon the government of the Mexican republic arising from injuries to their persons or property by authorities of the Mexican republic, and all claims on the part of corporations, companies, or private individuals, citizens of the Mexican republic, upon the Government of the United States, arising from injuries to their persons or property by authorities of the United States, which may have been presented to either

### ARTÍCULO I.

Todas las reclamaciones hechas por corporaciones, compañías ó individuos particulares, ciudadanos de la república Mexicana, procedentes de perjuicios sufridos en sus personas ó en sus propiedades, por autoridades de los Estados Unidos, y todas las reclamaciones hechas por corporaciones, compañías ó individuos particulares, ciudadanos de los Estados Unidos, procedentes de perjuicios sufridos en sus personas ó en sus propiedades, por autoridades de la república Mexicana, que hayan sido pre-

government for its interposition with the other since the signature of the treaty of Guadalupe Hidalgo between the United States and the Mexican republic of the 2d of February 1848, and which yet remain unsettled, as well as any other such claims which may be presented within the time hereinafter specified, shall be referred to two commissioners, one to be appointed by the President of the United States, by and with the advice and consent of the Senate, and one by the President of the Mexican republic. In case of the death, absence, or incapacity of either commissioner, or in the event of either commissioner omitting or ceasing to act as such, the President of the United States or the President of the Mexican republic, respectively, shall forthwith name another person to act as commissioner in the place or stead of the commissioner originally named.

sentadas á cualquiera de los dos gobiernos, solicitando la interposicion para con el otro, con posterioridad á la celebracion del tratado de Guadalupe Hidalgo entre la República Mexicana y los Estados Unidos, de 2 de Febrero de 1848, y que aún permanecen pendientes, de la misma manera que cualesquiera otras reclamaciones que se presentaren dentro del tiempo que mas adelante se especificará, se referirán á dos comisionados, uno de los cuales será nombrado por el Presidente de la república Mexicana y el otro por el Presidente de los Estados Unidos, con el consejo y aprobacion del Senado. En caso de muerte, ausencia ó incapacidad de alguno de los comisionados, ó en caso de que alguno de los comisionados cese de funcionar como tal, ó suspenda el ejercicio de sus funciones, el Presidente de la república Mexicana ó el Presidente de los Estados Unidos, respectivamente, nombrarán desde luego otra persona que haga de comisionado en lugar del que originalmente fué nombrado.

The commissioners so named shall meet at Washington within six months after the exchange of the ratifications of this convention, and shall, before proceeding to business, make and subscribe a solemn declaration that they will impartially and carefully examine and decide, to the best of their judgment, and according to public law, justice, and equity, without fear, favor, or affection to their own country, upon all such claims above specified as shall be laid before them on the part of the governments of the United States and of the Mexican Republic, respectively; and such declaration shall be entered on the record of their proceedings.

Los comisionados nombrados de esta manera, se reunirán en Washington dentro de seis meses, despues de cangeadas las ratificaciones de esta convencion, y ántes de desempeñar sus funciones, harán y suscribirán una declaracion solemne de que examinarán y decidirán imparcial y cuidadosamente, segun su mejor saber, y conforme con el derecho público, la justicia y equidad, y sin temor ó afeccion á su respectivo país, sobre todas las reclamaciones ántes especificadas, que se les sometan por los gobiernos de la república Mexicana y de los Estados Unidos, respectivamente, y dicha declaracion se asentará en la acta de sus procedimientos.

The commissioners shall then name some third person to act as an umpire in any case or cases on which they may themselves differ in opinion. If they should not be able to agree upon the name of such third person, they shall each name a per-

Los comisionados procederán entonces á nombrar una tercera persona que hará de árbitro en el caso ó casos en que difieran de opinion. Si no pudieren convenir en el nombre de esta tercera persona, cada uno de ellos nombrará una

son, and in each and every case in which the commissioners may differ in opinion as to the decision which they ought to give, it shall be determined by lot which of the two persons so named shall be umpire in that particular case. The person or persons so to be chosen to be umpire shall, before proceeding to act as such in any case, make and subscribe a solemn declaration in a form similar to that which shall already have been made and subscribed by the commissioners, which shall be entered on the record of their proceedings. In the event of the death, absence, or incapacity of such person or persons, or of his or their omitting, or declining, or ceasing to act as such umpire, another and different person shall be named, as aforesaid, to act as such umpire, in the place of the person so originally named, as aforesaid, and shall make and subscribe such declaration as aforesaid.

persona, y en todos y cada uno de los casos en que los comisionados difieran de opinion respecto de la decision que deban dar, se determinará por suerte quien de las dos personas así nombradas hará de árbitro en ese caso particular. La persona ó personas que se eligieren de esa manera, para ser árbitros, harán y suscribirán ántes de obrar como tales, en cualquier caso, una declaracion solemne en una forma, semejante á la que deberá haber sido ya hecha y suscrita por los comisionados, lo cual se asentará tambien en la acta de los procedimientos. En caso de muerte, ausencia ó incapacidad de la persona ó personas nombrados árbitros, ó en caso de que suspendan el ejercicio de sus funciones, se rehusen á desempeñarlas ó cesen en ellas, otra persona será nombrado árbitro de la manera que queda dicha, en lugar de la persona originalmente nombrada, y hará y suscribirá la declaracion ántes mencionada.

## ARTICLE II.

The commissioners shall then conjointly proceed to the investigation and decision of the claims which shall be presented to their notice, in such order and in such manner as they may conjointly think proper, but upon such evidence or information only as shall be furnished by or on behalf of their respective governments. They shall be bound to receive and peruse all written documents or statements which may be presented to them by or on behalf of their respective governments in support of or in answer to any claim, and to hear, if required, one person on each side on behalf of each government on each and every separate claim. Should they fail to agree in opinion upon any individual claim, they shall call to their assistance the umpire whom they may have agreed to name, or who may be determined by lot, as the case may be; and such umpire, after having examined the evidence adduced for

## ARTÍCULO II.

En seguida procederán juntamente los comisionadas á la investigacion y decision de las reclamaciones que se les presenten, en el órden y de la manera que de comun acuerdo creyeren conveniente, pero recibiendo solamente las pruebas ó informes que se les ministren por los respectivos gobiernos ó en su nombre. Tendrán obligacion de recibir y leer todas las manifestaciones ó documentos escritos que se le presenten por sus gobiernos respectivos, ó en su nombre, en apoyo ó respuesta á cualquiera reclamacion, y de oir, si se les pidiere, á una persona por cada lado, en nombre de cada gobierno, en todas y cada una de las reclamaciones separadamente. Si dejaren de convenir sobre alguna reclamacion particular, llamarán en su ausilio al árbitro que hayan nombrado de comun acuerdo, ó á quien la suerte haya designado, segun fuere el caso, y el árbitro, despues de

and against the claim, and after having heard, if required, one person on each side as aforesaid, and consulted with the commissioners, shall decide thereupon finally and without appeal. The decision of the commissioners and of the umpire shall be given upon each claim in writing, shall designate whether any sum which may be allowed shall be payable in gold or in the currency of the United States, and shall be signed by them respectively. It shall be competent for each government to name one person to attend the commissioners as agent on its behalf, to present and support claims on its behalf, and to answer claims made upon it, and to represent it generally in all matters connected with the investigation and decision thereof.

haber examinado las pruebas producidas en favor y en contra de la reclamacion y despues de haber oido, si se le pidiere, á una persona por cada lado, como queda dicho, y consultado con los comisionados, decidirá sobre ella finalmente y sin apelacion. La decision de los comisionados y del árbitro se dará en cada reclamacion por escrito, especificará si la suma que se concediere se pagará en oro ó en moneda corriente de los Estados Unidos, y será firmada por ellos respectivamente. Cada gobierno podrá nombrar una persona que concurra á la comision en nombre del gobierno respectivo, como agente; que presenta ó defienda las reclamaciones en nombre del mismo gobierno, y que responda á las reclamaciones hechas contra él, y que le represente en general en todos los negocios que tengan relacion con la investigacion y decision de reclamaciones.

The President of the United States of America and the President of the Mexican Republic hereby solemnly and sincerely engage to consider the decision of the commissioners conjointly or of the umpire, as the case may be, as absolutely final and conclusive upon each claim decided upon by them or him respectively, and to give full effect to such decisions without any objection, evasion, or delay whatsoever. It is agreed that no claim arising out of a transaction of a date prior to the 2d of February, 1848, shall be admissible under this convention.

El Presidente de la república Mexicana y el Presidente de los Estados Unidos de América se comprometen solemne y sinceramente en esta convencion, á considerar la decision de los comisionados de acuerdo, ú del árbitro, segun fuere el caso, como absolutamente final y definitiva, respecto de cada una de las reclamaciones falladas por los comisionados ó el árbitro respectivamente, y á dar entero cumplimiento á tales decisiones sin objecion, evasion ni dilacion ninguna. Si conviene que ninguna reclamacion que emane de acontecimientos de fecha anterior al 2 de Febrero de 1848, se admitirá con arreglo á esta convencion.

## ARTICLE III.

Every claim shall be presented to the commissioners within eight months from the day of their first meeting, unless in any case where reasons for delay shall be established to the satisfaction of the commissioners, or of the umpire in the event of the commissioners differing

## ARTÍCULO III.

Todas las reclamaciones se presentaran á los comisionados dentro de ocho meses contados desde el dia de su primera reunion, á no ser en las casos en que se manifieste que haya habido razones para dilatarlas, siendo éstas satisfactorias para los comisionados ó para el

in opinion thereupon, and then and in any such case the period for presenting the claim may be extended to any time not exceeding three months longer.

The commissioners shall be bound to examine and decide upon every claim within two years and six months from the day of their first meeting. It shall be competent for the commissioners conjointly, or for the umpire if they differ, to decide in each case whether any claim has or has not been duly made, preferred, and laid before them, either wholly or to any and what extent, according to the true intent and meaning of this convention.

árbitro, si los comisionados no se convinieren, y en ese y otros casos semejantes, el período para la presentacion de las reclamaciones podrá estenderse por un plazo que no exceda de tres meses.

Los comisionados tendrán la obligacion de examinar y decidir todas las reclamaciones dentro de dos años y seis meses, contados desde el dia de su primera reunion. Los comisionados de comun acuerdo ó el árbitro, si ellos difirieren, podrán decidir en cada caso, si una reclamacion ha sido ó no debidamente hecha, comunicada y sometida á la comision, ya sea en su totalidad ó en parte y cual sea esta, con arreglo al verdadero espíritu y á letra de esta convencion.

ARTICLE IV.

When decisions shall have been made by the commissioners and the arbiter in every case which shall have been laid before them, the total amount awarded in all the cases decided in favor of the citizens of the one party shall be deducted from the total amount awarded to the citizens of the other party, and the balance, to the amount of three hundred thousand dollars, shall be paid at the city of Mexico, or at the city of Washington, in gold or its equivalent, within twelve months from the close of the commission, to the government in favor of whose citizens the greater amount may have been awarded, without interest or any other deduction than that specified in Article VI of this convention. The residue of the said balance shall be paid in annual installments to an amount not exceeding three hundred thousand dollars, in gold or its equivalent, in any one year until the whole shall have been paid.

ARTÍCULO IV.

Cuando los comisionados y el árbitro hayan decidido todos los casos que les hayan sido debidamente sometidos, la suma total fallada en todos los casos decididos en favor de los ciudadanos de una parte, se deducirá de la suma total fallada en favor de los ciudadanos de la otra parte, y la diferencia hasta la cantidad de trescientos mil pesos en oro, ó su equivalente, se pagará en la ciudad de Mexico ó en la ciudad de Washington, al gobierno en favor de cuyos ciudadanos se haya fallado la mayor cantidad, sin interes, ni otra deduccion que la especificada en el Articulo VI de esta convencion. El resto de dicha diferencia se pagará en abonos anuales que no excedan de trescientos mil pesos en oro, ó su equivalente, hasta que se haya pagado el total de la diferencia.

ARTICLE V.

The high contracting parties agree to consider the result of the proceedings of this commission as

ARTÍCULO V.

Las altas partes contratantes convienen en considerar el resultado de los procedimientos de esta

a full, perfect, and final settlement of every claim upon either government arising out of any transaction of a date prior to the exchange of the ratifiations of the present convention; and further engage that every such claim, whether or not the same may have been presented to the notice of, made, preferred, or laid before the said commission, shall, from and after the conclusion of the proceedings of the said commission, be considered and treated as finally settled, barred, and thenceforth inadmissible.

comision, como arreglo completo, perfecto y final, de toda reclamacion contra cualquiera gobierno, que proceda de acontecimientos de fecha anterior al canje de las ratificaciones de la presente convencion; y se comprometen además á que toda reclamacion, ya sea que se haya presentado ó no á la referida comision, sera considerada y tratada, concluidos los procedimientos de dicha comision, como finalmente arreglada, desechada y para siempre inadmisible.

### Article VI.

The commissioners and the umpire shall keep an accurate record and correct minutes of their proceedings, with the dates. For that purpose they shall appoint two secretaries versed in the language of both countries to assist them in the transaction of the business of the commission. Each government shall pay to its commissioner an amount of salary not exceeding forty-five hundred dollars a year in the currency of the United States, which amount shall be the same for both governments. The amount of compensation to be paid to the umpire shall be determined by mutual consent at the close of the commission, but necessary and reasonable advances may be made by each government upon the joint recommendation of the commission. The salary of the secretaries shall not exceed the sum of twenty-five hundred dollars a year in the currency of the United States. The whole expenses of the commission, including contingent expenses, shall be defrayed by a ratable deduction on the amount of the sums awarded by the commission, provided always that such deduction shall not exceed five per cent. on the sums so awarded. The deficiency, if any, shall be defrayed in moieties by the two governments.

### Artículo VI.

Los comisionados y el árbitro llevarán una relacion fiel y actas esactas de sus procedimientos con especificacion de las fechas; con este objeto nombrarán dos secretarios versados en las lenguas de ámbos países, para que les ayuden en el arreglo de los asuntos de la comision. Cada gobierno pagará a su comisionado un sueldo que no exceda de cuatro mil quinientos pesos al año, en moneda corriente de los Estados Unidos, cuya cantidad será la misma para ámbos gobiernos. La compensacion que haya de pagarse al árbitro se determinará por consentimiento mútuo, al terminarse la comision; pero podrán hacerse por cada gobierno adelantos necesarios y razonables en virtud de la recommendacion de los dos comisionados. El sueldo de los secretarios no excederá de la suma de dos mil quinientos pesos al año, en moneda corriente de los Estados Unidos. Los gastos todos de la comision, incluyendo los contingentes, se pagarán con una reduccion proporcional de la cantidad total fallada por los comisionados, siempre que tal deduccion no exceda del cinco por ciento de las cantidades falladas. Si hubiere algun deficiente, lo cubrirán ámbos gobiernos por mitad.

ARTICLE VII.

The present convention shall be ratified by the President of the United States, by and with the advice and consent of the Senate thereof, and by the President of the Mexican Republic, with the approbation of the Congress of that republic, and the ratifications shall be exchanged at Washington within nine months from the date hereof, or sooner, if possible.

In witness whereof the respective plenipotentiaries have signed the same and have affixed thereto the seals of their arms.

Done at Washington, the fourth day of July, in the year of our Lord one thousand eight hundred and sixty-eight.

WILLIAM H. SEWARD. [L. S.]
M. ROMERO. [L. S.]

ARTÍCULO VII.

La presente convencion será ratificada por el Presidente de la república Mexicana, con aprobacion del Congreso de la misma, y por el Presidente de los Estados Unidos, con el consejo y aprobacion del Senado de los mismos, y las ratificaciones se caugearán en Washington dentro de nueve meses contados desde la fecha de la convencion, ó ántes, si fuere posible.

En fé de lo cual, los respectivos plenipotenciarios la hémos firmado y sellado con nuestros sellos respectivos.

Hecho en Washington el dia cuatro de Julio del año del Señor mil ochocientos sesenta y ocho.

M. ROMERO. [L. S.]
WILLIAM H. SEWARD. [L. S.]

And whereas the said convention has been duly ratified on both parts, and the respective ratifications of the same have this day been exchanged:

Now, therefore, be it known that I, Andrew Johnson, President of the United States of America, have caused the said convention to be made public, to the end that the same, and every clause and article thereof, may be observed and fulfilled with good faith by the United States and the citizens thereof.

In testimony whereof, I have hereunto set my hand, and caused the seal of the United States to be affixed.

Done at the city of Washington this first day of February, in the year of our Lord one thousand eight hundred and sixty-nine, and of the independence of the United States of America the ninety-third.

[SEAL.] ANDREW JOHNSON.

By the President:

WILLIAM H. SEWARD, *Secretary of State.*

---

CONVENTION BETWEEN THE UNITED STATES OF AMERICA AND THE MEXICAN REPUBLIC FOR THE FURTHER EXTENSION OF THE DURATION OF THE JOINT COMMISSION RESPECTING CLAIMS, ORIGINALLY FIXED BY THE CONVENTION OF JULY 4, 1868. CONCLUDED NOVEMBER 20, 1874; RATIFICATION ADVISED BY SENATE JANUARY 20, 1875; RATIFIED BY PRESIDENT JANUARY 22, 1875; RATIFIED BY PRESIDENT OF MEXICO DECEMBER 21, 1874; RATIFICATIONS EXCHANGED AT WASHINGTON JANUARY 28, 1875; PROCLAIMED JANUARY 29, 1875.

*By the President of the United States of America.*

A PROCLAMATION.

Whereas a convention between the United States of America and the Mexican Republic for further extending the time originally fixed by the convention between the same parties of the 4th of July, 1868,

and extended by those of the 19th of April, 1871, and of the 27th of November, 1872, for the duration of the joint commission on the subject of claims, was concluded and signed by their respective plenipotentiaries at Washington on the 20th day of November, 1874, the original of which convention, being in the English and Spanish languages, is word for word as follows:

*Convention between the United States of America and the Mexican Republic.*

Whereas, pursuant to the convention between the United States and the Mexican Republic of the 19th day of April, 1871, the functions of the joint commission under the convention between the same parties of the 4th of July, 1868, were extended for a term not exceeding one year from the day on which they were to terminate according to the convention last named;

And whereas, pursuant to the first article of the convention between the same parties, of the twenty-seventh day of November, one thousand eight hundred and seventy-two, the joint commission above referred to was revived and again extended for a term not exceeding two years from the day on which the functions of the said commission would terminate pursuant to the said convention of the nineteenth day of April, 1871; but whereas the said extensions have not proved sufficient for the disposal of the business before the said commission, the said parties being equally animated by a desire that all that business should be closed, as originally contemplated, the President of the United States has for this purpose conferred full powers on Hamilton Fish, Secretary of State, and the President of the Mexican Republic has conferred like powers on Don Ignacio Mariscal, Envoy Extraordinary and Minister Plenipotentiary of that republic to the United States; and the said Plenipotentiaries having exchanged their full powers, which were found to be in due form, have agreed upon the following articles:

*Convencion entre la República Mexicana y los Estados Unidos de América.*

Considerando: Que, conforme á la convencion celebrada entre la República Mexicana y los Estados Unidos el 19 de Abril de 1871, las funciones de la comision mista establecida por la convencion entre las mismas partes, del 4 de Julio de 1868, fueron prorogadas por un término que no excediera de un año contado desde el dia en que debian terminar con arreglo á la convencion últimamente citada:

Y que, si bien conforme al artículo primero de la convencion entre las mismas partes, del veintisiete de Noviembre de mil ochocientos setenta y dos, la referida comision mista fué revivida y de nuevo prorogada por un término que no excediese de dos años contados desde el dia en que las funciones de dicha comision habian de terminar segun la citada convencion del diez y nueve de Abril de 1871, dichas prorogas no han sido suficientes para el despacho de los negocios pendientes ánte dicha comision, hallándose las referidas partes igualmente animadas del deseo de que todos esos negocios queden concluidos como se estipuló originalmente, el Presidente de la República Mexicana ha conferido con este fin plenos poderes á Don Ignacio Mariscal, Enviado Extraordinario y Ministro Plenipotenciario de dicha República en los Estados Unidos, y el Presidente de los Estados Unidos ha conferido iguales poderes á Hamilton Fish, Secretario de Estado. Y estos Plenipotenciarios, habiendo cangeado sus poderes plenos, que se encontráron en debida forma, han convenido en los artículos siguientes:

### Article I.

The high contracting parties agree that the said commission shall again be extended, and that the time now fixed for its duration shall be prolonged for one year from the time when it would have expired pursuant to the convention of the twenty-seventh of November, 1872; that is to say, until the thirty-first day of January, in the year one thousand eight hundred and seventy-six.

It is, however, agreed that nothing contained in this article shall in any wise alter or extend the time originally fixed by the convention of the 4th July, 1868, aforesaid, for the presentation of claims to the commission.

### Artículo I.

Las altas partes contratantes convienen en que el término ahora fijado para la duracion de la comision mencionada se extienda de nuevo, prorogándose por un año contado desde el tiempo en que espiraría con arreglo á la convencion del veintisiete de Noviembre de mil ochocientos setenta y dos: es decir, hasta el treinta y uno de Enero de mil ochocientos setenta y seis.

Queda sin embargo convenido que nada de lo que contiene este artículo alterará ó extenderá de modo alguno el término originalmente fijado por la convencion del cuatro de Julio de mil ochocientos sesenta y ocho, ya referida, para presentar reclamaciones ánte la comision.

### Article II.

It is further agreed that, if at the expiration of the time when, pursuant to the first article of this convention, the functions of the commissioners will terminate, the umpire under the convention should not have decided all the cases which may then have been referred to him, he shall be allowed a further period of not more than six months for that purpose.

### Artículo II.

Se conviene además en que, si al espirar el tiempo en que conforme al artículo primero de la presente convencion terminen las funciones de los comisionados, el árbitro establecido por la convencion no hubiese decidido todos los casos que se le hubieren sometido hasta entónces, quedará facultado para hacerlo en un nuevo período que no exceda de seis meses.

### Article III.

All cases which have been decided by the commissioners or by the umpire heretofore, or which shall be decided prior to the exchange of the ratifications of this convention, shall from the date of such exchange be regarded as definitively disposed of, and shall be considered and treated as finally settled, barred, and thenceforth inadmissible. And, pursuant to the stipulation contained in the fourth article of the convention of the fourth day of July, one thousand eight hundred and sixty-eight, the total amount awarded in cases

### Artículo III.

Todas las reclamaciones que han sido sentenciadas por los comisionados ó por el árbitro hasta la presente fecha, ó que sean sentenciadas ántes del cange de las ratificaciones de esta convencion, serán consideradas desde la fecha de ese cange como definitivamente resueltas, y se considerarán y tratarán como finalmente arregladas y en lo futuro inadmisibles. Y, conforme á la estipulacion contenida en el artículo cuarto de la convencion del cuatro de Julio de 1868, la suma total fallada en casos ya decididos, y que se decidan ántes del cange

already decided, and which may be decided before the exchange of ratifications of this convention, and in all cases which shall be decided within the times in this convention respectively named for that purpose, either by the commissioners or by the umpire, in favor of citizens of the one party, shall be deducted from the total amount awarded to the citizens of the other party, and the balance, to the amount of three hundred thousand dollars, shall be paid at the city of Mexico, or at the city of Washington, in gold or its equivalent, within twelve months from the 31st day of January, one thousand eight hundred and seventy-six, to the government in favor of whose citizens the greater amount may have been awarded, without interest or any other deduction than that specified in article VI of that convention. The residue of the said balance shall be paid in annual installments, to an amount not exceeding three hundred thousand dollars, in gold or its equivalent, in any one year, until the whole shall have been paid.

de ratificaciones de esta convencion, y en todos los casos que estuvieren decididos dentro de los plazos respectivamente fijados con tal fin en la convencion presente, ya sea por los comisionados ó por el árbitro, en favor de ciudadanos de una de las partes, será deducida de la suma total fallada en favor de los ciudadanos de la otra parte, y la diferencia hasta la cantidad de trescientos mil pesos, se pagará en la ciudad de México ó en la de Washington, en oro ó su equivalente, dentro de doce meses contados desde el 31 de Enero de mil ochocientos setenta y seis, al gobierno en favor de cuyos ciudadanos se hubiere fallado la mayor cantidad, sin interes, ni otra deduccion que la especificada en el artículo VI de aquella convencion. El resto de dicha diferencia se pagará en abonos anuales que no excedan de trescientos mil pesos en oro, ó su equivalente, hasta que se haya pagado el total de la diferencia.

ARTICLE IV.

The present convention shall be ratified, and the ratifications shall be exchanged at Washington, as soon as possible.

In witness whereof the above-named Plenipotentiaries have signed the same and affixed thereto their respective seals.

Done in Washington the twentieth day of November, in the year one thousand eight hundred and seventy-four.

[SEAL.] HAMILTON FISH.
[SEAL.] IGNO. MARISCAL.

ARTÍCULO IV.

La presente convencion será ratificada y las ratificaciones se cangearán en Washington á la brevedad posible.

En testimonio de lo cual, los Plenipotenciarios ántes mencionados firmáron la presente y le pusiéron sus respectivos sellos.

Hecho en Washington el dia veinte de Noviembre del año mil ochocientos setenta y cuatro.

[SELLO.] IGNO. MARISCAL.
[SELLO.] HAMILTON FISH.

And whereas the said convention has been duly ratified on both parts, and the respective ratifications were exchanged in this city on the 28th instant:

Now, therefore, be it known that I, ULYSSES S. GRANT, President of the United States of America, have caused the said convention to be made public, to the end that the same, and every clause and article thereof, may be observed and fulfilled with good faith by the United States and the citizens thereof.

In witness whereof I have hereunto set my hand, and caused the seal of the United States to be affixed.

Done at the city of Washington, this twenty-ninth day of January, in the year of our Lord one thousand eight hundred and seventy-five, and of the Independence of the United States the ninety-ninth.

[SEAL.]

U. S. GRANT.

By the President:

HAMILTON FISH,
*Secretary of State.*

---

RULES AND ORDERS OF THE UNITED STATES AND MEXICAN JOINT COMMISSION.

JOINT COMMISSION OF THE UNITED STATES OF AMERICA AND THE UNITED STATES OF MEXICO.

*Ordered*, That the commission adopts and prescribes the following rules for the regulation of the business of the commission, namely:

*Rules and regulations of the commissioners appointed under the convention between the United States of America and the United States of Mexico, of July* 4, 1868, *as adopted August the* 10*th*, 1869, *and amended by order of the* 23*d of December*, 1869.

1. All claims filed with the commission by the respective governments shall be entered in duplicate dockets, one kept by each of the two secretaries, in his respective language, in the order in which they are referred.

Separate dockets shall be kept for the claims, respectively, of citizens of the United States and for those of citizens of the Mexican Republic.

Duplicate records shall be kept in like manner of all the proceedings of the commissioners.

2. All claims provided for by the convention shall be presented through the respective governments on or before the 31st day of March, 1870, unless at a later day, for special cause shown to the satisfaction of the commissioners.

3. All persons having claims shall file memorials of the same with the respective secretaries.

Every memorial shall be signed and verified by the claimant, or, in his absence from the District of Columbia, by his attorney in fact, such absence being averred by such attorney, and it shall be subscribed by his solicitor or counsel.

It shall set forth particularly the origin, nature, and amount of the claim, with other circumstances, as follows:

(*a*.) The amount of the claim; the time when and place where it arose; the kind or kinds and amount of property lost or injured; the facts and circumstances attending the loss or injury out of which the claim arises; and all the facts upon which the claim is founded.

(*b*.) For and on behalf of whom the claim is preferred.

(*c*.) Whether the claimant is now a citizen of the United States or of the Mexican Republic, as the case may require; and, if so, whether he is a native or naturalized citizen, and where is now his domicile; and if he claims in his own right, then whether he was a citizen when the claim had its origin, and where was then his domicile; and if he claims in the right of another, then whether such other was a citizen when the claim had its origin, and where was then, and where is now, his domicile; and if in either case the domicile of the claimant, at the time the claim had its origin, was in any foreign country, then whether such claimant was then a subject of the government of such country, or had taken any oath of allegiance thereto.

(*d.*) Whether the entire amount of the claim does now, and did at the time when it had its origin, belong solely and absolutely to the claimant, and if any other person is or has been interested therein or in any part thereof, then who is such other person, and what is or was the nature and extent of his interest; and how, when, and by what means, and for what consideration, the transfer of rights or interests, if any such was made, took place between the parties.

(*e.*) Whether the claimant, or any other who may at any time have been entitled to the amount claimed, or any part thereof, had ever received any, and, if any, what sum of money, or other equivalent or indemnification for the whole or any part of the loss or injury upon which the claim is founded; and, if so, when and from whom the same was received.

(*f.*) Whether the claim was presented prior to the 1st of February, 1869, to the department of state of either government, or to the minister of the United States at Mexico, or that of the Mexican Republic at Washington, and to which and at what time.

4. All motions and arguments addressed to the commissioners shall be made in writing and filed with the secretaries, who shall note thereon the time when they are received.

Brief verbal explanations may be made after the opening of each day's session, by or in behalf of the agents of the respective governments.

5. Of all memorials, twenty printed copies in quarto form in English, and twenty in Spanish, shall be filed with the respective secretaries.

Citizens of the United States may file their documents and proofs in English, and citizens of the Mexican Republic may file theirs in Spanish, and in both cases in manuscript, subject to the further order of the commissioners in this respect.

6. When a claimant shall have filed his proofs in chief and argument in support thereof, the adverse proofs and argument on the part of the United States, or of the Mexican Republic, shall be filed within the term of four months; but, upon good cause shown on either side, this period may be extended in particular cases.

By order of the commissioners:

GEORGE G. GAITHER,
J. CARLOS MEXIA,
*Secretaries.*

---

### ADDITIONAL ORDERS.

On the 12th of August, 1869, the commission adopted the following

#### ORDER.

That the secretaries of this commission take charge of all the papers belonging to the commission, and not allow them to be withdrawn from the office, but furnish parties interested or their counsel all convenient opportunities, in the office and in presence of either of the secretaries, of examining and making extracts from the same.

On the 29th of December, 1869, the commission adopted the following

ORDER.

That the secretaries keep a book, to be called the "notice docket."

(*a.*) A claim is prepared in chief whenever a memorial, with the proofs and argument relied on in support thereof, shall be filed. Such claim shall be entered, by direction of the agent representing it, on the notice docket, the secretaries noting the date of the entry on the docket.

(*b.*) Such entry shall be notice, under the rules, to the government against whom such claim is preferred, that the claimant is ready; thereupon proofs and arguments in answer thereto (if any are insisted on) must be filed in four months from the date of such entry, unless, for cause shown, further time is allowed.

(*c.*) Rebutting proofs and argument in support of the claim may be afterwards filed or waived, and in either case the claim shall be entered "heard" by the commissioners.

On the 21st of January, 1870, the commission adopted the following

ORDER.

Every claimant purporting to be a citizen of either country, party to this convention, shall disclose the facts upon which he bases his citizenship, either in his memorial or by affidavit. If a native, he shall, so far as in his power, disclose the time and place of his birth; if naturalized, he shall file a copy of his naturalization papers, in all cases where it is in his power, and if not in his power to do so, he shall show why: *Provided*, The affidavit above required may be put in at any time before a hearing, on such terms as may be deemed proper.

On the 20th of June, 1870, the commission adopted the following

ORDERS.

1. That all claims presented to the commission since the adjournment[179] be received and entered upon the dockets for preparation, investigation, and decision, as in other cases.
2. That the time for filing claims before this commission be extended from the 31st day of March last to the 30th of June, instant, and including the latter day, after which time no further claims will be received.
3. That further time be granted to all claimants whose cases are or may hereafter be entered on the dockets of this commission, to file memorials of the same until the 1st day of January, 1871.

On the 13th of July, 1870, the commission adopted the following

ORDER.

All claimants who have heretofore filed memorials, as required by the rules, and have not prepared their claims for hearing, must make preparation on or before the 1st of November next, at which date the secre-

[179] The adjournment referred to was from January 31, 1870, to June 1, 1870.

taries of this Commission are directed to enter such claims upon the notice-docket; and all other claims not now ready must be prepared by claimants on or before the 1st of January next, at which period the secretaries are directed to place them, also, upon the said docket; and claims thus placed will be disposed of under the rules applicable to other cases on that docket.

The foregoing orders are truly copied from the originals of record.

RANDOLPH COYLE,
J. CARLOS MEXIA,
*Secretaries.*

---

IN THE JOINT COMMISSION OF THE UNITED STATES AND MEXICO, UNDER THE CONVENTION OF JULY 4, 1868.

SATURDAY, *January* 20, 1872.

The Commissioners now give notice that all claims by the United States *vs.* Mexico, and all claims by the latter government *vs.* the former, not disposed of before that date, will, on the first day of April next, be entered "heard;" whereupon the Commission will proceed immediately to dispose of them, in obedience to the requirements of the convention.

True copy from the record.

RANDOLPH COYLE,
J. CARLOS MEXIA,
*Secretaries.*

# ADDENDA.

The following is inserted because the books are referred to in the matter furnished by foreign governments:

LIBRARY OF CONGRESS,
*Washington, February* 23, 1875.

In behalf of the Joint Committee of both Houses of Congress on the Library, the undersigned has the honor to acknowledge the reception of Oesterreich Gesetze, 4 vols., 12mo; Turkey, Législation ottomane, 2 vols.; Italy, Codice civile, 2 vols.; Italy, Legge per l'unificazioni del Regno, 1 vol.; Danemark, Constitution du Royaume, 1 vol.; France, Bulletin des Lois, and Journal officiel, 3 pamphlets, presented by yourself to the Library of Congress.

Very respectfully, your obedient servant,

A. R. SPOFFORD,
*Librarian of Congress.*

To Hon. WM. LAWRENCE,
*Chairman Committee on War-Claims.*

P. S.—The above works are placed in the law department of the Library, in the chapter of national codes and statute law.

## THE ASSIGNMENT OF CLAIMS AGAINST THE UNITED STATES.

The act of Congress of February 26, 1853, (10 Statutes, 170,) which seems to be an enlargement of the act of July 29, 1846, (9 Statutes, 41,) prohibits the assignment of claims against the United States. See Revised Statutes, § 3477. On this subject see Painter *vs.* Drum, 40 Penn. R., 467; Child *vs.* Trist, 1 Washington Law Reporter, 1; Sines *vs.* The United States, 1 Nott & H., 12; Peirce *vs.* United States, 1 N. & H., 270.

## OF CONTRACTS TO PROCURE LEGISLATION FOR THE PAYMENT OF CLAIMS.

This subject was discussed before the Supreme Court of the United States in February, 1875, in the case of Nicholas P. Trist *vs.* Linus M. Child. The report of that case will doubtless show much learning on the subject.

Among the questions discussed were these:

Is a contract to secure the passage of a bill through Congress to pay a claim void as against public policy?

If not, can the claimant be enjoined from collecting the money from the Treasury appropriated by such act without paying for such services?

Can a lien be created on the money so appropriated?

If the lien can exist, is the holder of it entitled to interest on the amount?

On these questions see—

*As to public policy*—Marshall *vs.* Baltimore R. R., 16 Howard, 314; Tool Company *vs.* Norris, 2 Wallace, 54; Harris *vs.* Roof, 10 Barbour, 489; Hunt *vs.* Test, 8 Alabama, 713; Paschal's Case, 10 Wallace, 483; Mills *vs.* Mills, 36 Barbour, 474.

*As to lien*—Vice-Chancellor Malins, Bank of Hindustan, L. R., ch. 7, p. 126, note I; Mercer *vs.* Greaves, L. R., 7 Queen's B., 503; Brunsdon *vs.* Allard, 2 E. and E., 19 vol., 105 C. L. R; Jenkins *vs.* Hooker, 19 Barbour, 435.

*As to the practice in England*—A statement of the English parliamentary practice will be found in Riddell's Railway Parliamentary Practice, London, 1846.

See, also, Standing Orders of the House of Commons, 1859; List of Charges for Parliamentary Agents, Attorneys, Solicitors, and others, prepared by the Clerk of Parliament, 1867.

For interesting statistics of private bills, see Parliamentary Acts and Papers, 1862, vol. 44: Returns relating to private bills.

A large mass of valuable testimony concerning the method, cost, &c., of prosecuting private bills in Parliament will be found in the Parliamentary Reports from Committees, vol. 14, 1857–8.

In this last will be found the testimony of Mr. T. Coates, who is the parliamentary agent referred to in the brief.

## OTHER QUESTIONS.

Various other questions as to claims will be found referred to in Brightley's Federal Digest, title "Public Accounts," 714, and in the supplement, p. 308.

---

## CONSTRUCTION OF THE ACT OF JULY 4, 1864, &C.

The following opinion of the Attorney-General is given for information:

DEPARTMENT OF JUSTICE,
*April* 6, 1871.

Hon. GEORGE S. BOUTWELL,
*Secretary of the Treasury:*

SIR: I have received your letter of the 21st ultimo, requesting my opinion upon certain questions arising under the act making appropriations for the support of the Army for the year ending June 30, 1872, and for other purposes, approved March 3, 1871.

The second section of that act provides for the appointment of a board of commissioners, "whose duty it shall be to receive, examine, and consider the justice and validity of such claims as shall be brought before them of those citizens who remained loyal adherents to the cause and the Government of the United States during the war, for stores or supplies taken or furnished during the rebellion for the use of the Army of the United States in States proclaimed as in insurrection against the United States, including the use or loss of vessels or boats while employed in the military service of the United States. * * * *. And upon satisfactory evidence of the justice and validity of any claim, the commissioners shall report their opinion, in writing, in each case, and shall certify the nature, amount, and value of the property taken, furnished, or used, as aforesaid."

The fourth section is in these words: "That said commissioners shall make report of their proceedings, and of each claim considered by them, at the commencement of each session of Congress to the Speaker of the House of Representatives, who shall lay the same before Congress for consideration; and all claims within this act, and not presented to said board, shall be barred, and shall not be entertained by any Department of the Government, without further authority of Congress."

On the 16th day of August, in the year 1861, President Lincoln issued a proclamation declaring the inhabitants of the States of Georgia, South Carolina, Virginia, North Carolina, Tennessee, Alabama, Louisiana, Texas, Arkansas, Mississippi, and Florida, ("except the inhabitants of that part of the State of Virginia lying west of the Alleghany Mountains, and of such other parts of that State and the other States hereinbefore named, as may maintain a loyal adhesion to the Union and the Constitution, or may be from time to time occupied and controlled by forces of the United States engaged in the dispersion of said insurgents,") to be in a state of insurrection against he United States. (12 U. S. Stats., p. 1262.)

The act of June 7, 1862, section 2, directs, "That, on or before the 1st day of July next, the President, by his proclamation, shall declare in what States and parts of States said insurrection exists." In accordance with this act, President Lincoln, on the 1st day of July, 1862, issued his proclamation declaring that the States of South Carolina, Florida, Georgia, Alabama, Louisiana, Texas, Mississippi, Arkansas, Tennessee, North Carolina, and the State of Virginia, except thirty-nine named counties, all in what was then the western part of that State, were in insurrection and rebellion. (12 U. S. Stats., p. 1266.) The counties of Berkeley and Jefferson are not among the counties named.

The act of July 4, 1864, provided that all claims of loyal citizens in States not in rebellion, for quartermaster's stores and subsistence actually furnished to the Army of the United States, and receipted for by the proper officers receiving the same, or which might have been taken by such officers without giving such receipt, should be submitted to the Quartermaster-General of the United States, or the Commissary-General of Subsistence, (as the case may be,) accompanied with the proofs presented by the claimant; and these officers were required to cause each claim to be examined, and, if convinced that it was just, and of the loyalty of the claimant, and that the stores had been actually received or taken for the use of, and used by, the Army, then to report each case to the Third Auditor of the Treasury, with a recommendation for settlement. (13 U. S. Stats.; pp. 381, 382.)

The joint resolution of June 18, 1866, extends the provisions of this act to the counties of Berkeley and Jefferson, which had become part of the State of West Virginia. (14 U. S. Statutes, 360.) The joint resolution of July 28, 1866, extends the provisions of the same act to loyal citizens of the State of Tennessee. (14 U. S. Statutes, 370.)

The act of February 21, 1867, declares that the act above cited, of July 4, 1864, "shall not be construed to authorize the settlement of any claim for supplies or stores taken or furnished for the use of, or used by, the armies of the United States, nor for the occupation of or injury to real estate, nor for the consumption, appropriation, or destruction of, or damage to, personal property by the military authorities or troops of the United States, where such claim originated during the war for the suppression of the southern rebellion, in a State, or part of a State, declared in insurrection by the proclamation of the President of the United States, dated July first, eighteen hundred and sixty-two, or in a State which by an ordinance of secession attempted to withdraw from the United States Government: *Provided,* That nothing herein contained shall repeal or modify the effect of any act or joint resolution extending the provisions of the said act of July fourth, eighteen hundred and sixty-four, to the loyal citizens of the State of Tennessee, or of the State of West Virginia, or to any county therein. (14 U. S. Stats., 397.)

Your first question is this: Does the act of March 3, 1871, repeal, displace, or supersede, so far as the State of Tennessee, and the counties of Berkeley and Jefferson, in West Virginia, are concerned, the acts of July 4, 1864, and February 21, 1867, and the joint resolutions of June 18 and July 28, 1866?

If there had been no previous legislation on the subject of claims arising in Tennessee, and the counties of Berkeley and Jefferson in West Virginia, the act of March 3, 1871, would undoubtedly have been construed to embrace such claims. It sends to the board such claims of the defined classes as originated in States (including, by fair construction, parts of States) proclaimed in insurrection. Tennessee and the part of Virginia then embracing said counties were so proclaimed.

But the act contains no express words of repeal; and are its provisions so repugnant to the prior legislation in relation to that State and those counties, as to work a repeal by implication? Repeal by implication is not favored; and a later act does not repeal a prior act by implication unless there is a positive repugnance between the two.— (Dwaris on Statutes, p. 533; Dr. Foster's Case, Rep., Pt. II, pp. 62–64; Wood *vs.* The United States, 16 Pet. Rep., p. 342; Bowen *vs.* Lease, 5 Hill's Rep., p. 221.)

The act of July 4, 1864, as extended by the resolutions of June and July, 1866, provided for settling in the Departments claims of the defined classes arising in said State and counties. The act of March 3, 1871, provides that all claims considered by the board shall be reported to the Speaker of the House for submission to Congress, a provision which would be nugatory if the claims might meanwhile be settled elsewhere. It shuts out from any Department all claims within the act which but for this prohibition some Department would entertain.

What claims can these be except claims from Tennessee and the said counties? Claims from the loyal States are not within the act. Claims of the classes in question from the disloyal States, except from Tennessee and said counties, are never entertained by any Department; hence these words of exclusion can have no operation except upon claims from said State and counties.

Here, then, is found the repugnancy between the act of March 3, 1871, and the prior legislation in relation to Tennessee and said counties, which the rule requires in order to work a repeal by implication.

An additional argument in support of the same construction is derivable from the act of February 21, 1867, above quoted. In that act Congress placed a restricted construction upon the act of July 4, 1864; and having used general language, which would extend this restriction to Tennessee and the counties in question, took care to reserve said State and counties from the operation of this general language by special provision. In passing the act of March 3, 1871, Congress must have had in mind all the legislation upon the general subject, and the omission to make, in favor of that State and those counties, the exception which was made in the act of 1867 signifies that such exception was not intended.

I am therefore of opinion that the act of March 3, 1871, repeals the act of July 4, 1864, and the joint resolution of June 18 and July 28, 1866, so far as Tennessee and said counties are concerned, and places that State and those counties upon the same footing, in respect to these claims, as other insurrectionary States.

Your second question is as follows: If the first question be answered in the affirmative, when did or will such change in the law become operative, and how will such claims from the said State and counties submitted under the former law of March 3, 1871, be affected thereby?

The act of March 3, 1871, as to the matter under consideration, taking effect immediately, all such claims have been improperly submitted to the Departments since the 3d day of March, 1871.

The additional question which your letter presents relates to a supposed distinction between property "taken" and property "furnished," as those words are used in the act of March 3, 1871.

These words are not new in statutes upon this subject. They are found in the act of July 4, 1864, and also in the act of February 21, 1867.

The act of July 4, 1864, indicates the different senses in which these words were used by Congress. The property for which the proper officers gave receipts is described as "furnished" to the Army, and that for which the officers did not give receipts is described as "taken." In the latter part of the second and third sections of the same act the word "received" seems to be substituted for the word "furnished," but referring to the same transactions, the former word describing the act of the officer and the latter the act of the owner who delivered the property.

The difference intended by Congress between "taken" and "furnished" seems to be this: that while both words signify such appropriations as were essentially involuntary on the part of the owners, there was an exertion of force in cases of *taking* which did not exist in cases of *furnishing*. The giving of receipts in the latter, and the failure to give receipts in the former, indicates, in the one case, a ready submission by the owner to the caption of his property which is wanting in the other.

Attorney-General Evarts construed these acts (of July 4, 1864, and February 21, 1867) not to comprehend accounts founded upon express contracts for the purchase of supplies for the Army made by the proper agent of the Government within the scope of the Army appropriation acts. (12 Opins., 439.)

Following that opinion, which I believe to be sound, I think that none of the acts which I have cited forbids the payment of such accounts.

The claim of John T. Lee, to which your letter refers, is reported as a case of appropriation by the officers, and not of ordinary contract between the Government agents and Mr. Lee.

Hence I am of opinion that it falls within the scope of the act of March 3, 1871, and must go before the board of commissioners, for which that act provides.

Very respectfully, your obedient servant,

A. T. AKERMAN,
*Attorney-General.*

This was followed by the act of April 20, 1871, (17 Statutes, 12,) which contains these provisions:

That the jurisdiction conferred by the joint resolution of June eighteen, eighteen hundred and sixty-six, in regard to claims from the counties of Berkeley and Jefferson, in the State of West Virginia, and by the joint resolution of July twenty-eight, eighteen hundred and sixty-six, in regard to claims from the State of Tennessee, and by the joint resolution of December twenty-three, eighteen hundred and sixty-nine, as amended by the act of March three, eighteen hundred and seventy-one, in regard to steamboats and other vessels, shall not be withdrawn or impaired by any construction of the law creating commissioners of claims to examine claims arising in States proclaimed to be in insurrection, and the jurisdiction upon all claims presented by loyal citizens from said State of Tennessee, and from said counties of Berkeley and Jefferson, to the proper Department before the third of March, eighteen hundred and seventy-one, shall remain as before the passage of said act creating said commissioners of claims.

This gave construction to section 4 of the act of March 3, 1871, chapter 116, section 2, (which is found on page 322 of the foregoing report.)

Under these laws the Quartermaster's Department held that *it had* jurisdiction to receive, examine, and report to the Third Auditor of the Treasury, claims for quartermaster's stores originating under the act of July 4, 1864, and acts amendatory thereof. The Commissary-General *held otherwise*, and took no jurisdiction until in June, 1874, when a new Commissary-General took jurisdiction of and paid the famous Sugg Fort claim, for which see the report of the Committee on War-Claims made in the House of Representatives, March, 1875.

It is proper to say, however, that this was after the act of June 16, 1874, which is found on page 311 of this report, where it is by a typographical error inserted as "Approved June 17, 1874;" it should be June 16, 1874.

### THE PROPER MODE OF EXAMINING CLAIMS.

This subject was elaborately discussed at the 2d session of the 30th Congress. (Globe, vol. 20, pp. 38, 139, 144, 159, 172, 178, 188, 198, 203, 302, 303, 307, 378, 492, 543.) The discussion also refers to a valuable report made on the subject during that Congress, which shows a large proportion of all claims presented to Congress without merit.

### THE ACT OF CONGRESS OF APRIL 9, 1816.

For a discussion of this act, and for a report of proceedings under it see Annals of Congress, 14th Congress, 2d session, 1816–1817, pp. 245, 299, 462, 1028, 1035, 1040, 1051, 1211; debates on pp. 382–426; Senate proceedings, pp. 20, 65, 67, 78, 89, 96, 106.

In the House debates, Mr. Clay discussed the duty of the Government to repair losses by the ravages of war. Mr. Calhoun declared the Government was not liable for damages inflicted by the enemy; that the Government was not an *insurer;* that if it would become such "the enemy would make war on you in that way which will most affect your Treasury;" that it would invite the enemy to destroy property of citizens, &c.

### INTEREST.

Cases in which allowed on revolutionary claims, Annals of Congress, 2d session, 14th Congress, 1816–1817, pp. 1250–1254, &c.

### CLAIMS FOR COTTON CAPTURED AND SOLD BY UNITED STATES GOVERNMENT DURING THE REBELLION.

The United States Supreme Court, in Sprott *vs.* United States, at October term, 1874, held that a purchaser of cotton from the Confederate States, who knew that the money he paid for it went to sustain the rebellion, cannot, in the Court of Claims, recover the proceeds, when it has been captured and sold, under the captured and abandoned property act. The cotton was sold to the claimant by an agent of the confederate government for the purpose of raising funds to purchase munitions of war, and the cotton was understood by the claimant to be the property of the confederate government. The claimant was a resident of Claiborne County, Mississippi, in March, 1865, the date of the purchase, and the cotton was captured in May, 1865, by the Federal forces, and afterward sold by the Government. Miller, J., who delivered the opinion, said: "The claimant now asserts a right to this money on the ground that he was the owner of the cotton when it was captured. This claim of right or ownership he must prove in the Court of Claims. He attempts to do so by showing that he purchased it of the confederate government and paid them for it in money. In doing this he gave aid and assistance to the rebellion in the most efficient manner he possibly could. * * * A clearer case of turpitude in the consideration of a contract can hardly be imagined, unless treason be taken out of the catalogue of crimes. The case is not relieved of its harsh features by the finding of the court that the claimant did not intend to aid the rebellion, but only to make money. It might as well be said that the man who would sell for a sum far beyond its value, to a lunatic, a weapon with which he knew the latter would kill himself, only intended to make money and did not intend to aid the lunatic in his fatal purpose. This court, in Hanaver *vs.* Doane, 12 Wall., 342, speaking of one who set up the same defense, says: 'He voluntarily aids treason. He cannot be permitted to stand on the nice metaphysical distinction that, although he knows that the purchaser buys the goods for the purpose of aiding the rebellion, he does not sell them for that purpose. The consequences of his acts are too serious to admit of such a plea. He must be taken to intend the consequences of his voluntary acts.' This case, and the succeeding one of Hanaver *vs.* Woodruff, 15 Wall., 349, are directly in point in support of our view of the case before us."

Field, J., delivered an elaborate opinion, dissenting from the view of the majority of the court, and maintaining that the claimant had the benefit of the proclamation of pardon and amnesty made by the President in December, 1868. He said: "That pardon and amnesty did not, of course, and could not, change the actual fact of previous disloyalty, if it existed, but, as was said in Carlisle *vs.* United States, 16 Wall., 151, they forever close the eyes of the court to the perception of that fact as an element in its judgment, no rights of third parties having intervened. In legal contemplation the executive pardon not merely releases an offender from the punishment prescribed for his offense, but it obliterates the offense itself. * * * And I submit respectfully that the eloquent denunciation of the wickedness of the rebellion contained in the opinion of the majority is no legal answer to the demand of the claimant for the proceeds of his property seized and sold by our Goverument, when that Government long since pardoned the only offense of which the claimant was guilty, and this gave him the assurance that he should stand in the courts of his country in as good plight and condition as any citizen who had never sinned against its authority."

# TABLE OF CASES CITED

AND

# INDEX.

# TABLE OF CASES CITED.

A.



B.



C.

# INDEX.

A.



*THE ACT OF APRIL 9, 1816.—For a discussion of this, and for report of proceedings under it, see Annals of Congress, 14th Congress, 2d session, 1816–'17, pp. 245, 299, 462, 1028, 1035, 1040, 1051, 1211; Debates on, 382–426; Senate proceedings, pp. 20, 65, 67, 78, 89, 96, 106. In the House debates, Henry Clay discussed the duty of the Government to repair losses by the ravages of war. Mr. Calhoun declared the Government was not liable for property destroyed by the enemy. He said the Government did not become an insurer, and that if the Government would "the enemy will make war on you in that way which will most affect your Treasury." It would be an invitation to the enemy to destroy property. (See foregoing report, 285.)

## D.



## E.

*In the debate in House of Representatives on the bill to provide for the security of elections, February 27, 1875, General Butler argued that war *ipso facto* suspends the writ of *habeas corpus*. He stated generally the effect of suspending it.

## J.



## K.



## L.

## Q.

Page.

## R.

# APPENDIX.

House Executive Document No. 100. Forty-third Congress, first session.

GOVERNMENT OF UNITED STATES ARMIES IN THE FIELD.

*Letter from the Secretary of War, relative to "Instructions for the Government of Armies of the United States in the Field." January 29, 1874.—Referred to the Committee on War-Claims, and ordered to be printed.*

WAR DEPARTMENT, *January* 24, 1874.

The Secretary of War has the honor to transmit to the House of Representatives, for the information of the Committee on War-Claims, in reply to letter of said committee (by its clerk) of the 19th instant, a copy of General Orders No. 100, dated April 24, 1863, from this Department, publishing "Instructions for the Government of Armies of the United States in the Field," prepared by Francis Leiber, LL. D., and revised by a board of officers, of which Maj. Gen. E. A. Hitchcock was president.

The suggestions regarding the same, desired by the committee, will be submitted in a future communication, the matter being now under consideration.

WM. W. BELKNAP,
*Secretary of War.*

---

[General Orders No. 100.]

WAR DEPARTMENT,
ADJUTANT-GENERAL'S OFFICE,
*Washington, April* 24, 1863.

The following "Instructions for the Government of Armies of the United States in the Field," prepared by Francis Lieber, LL. D., and revised by a board of officers, of which Maj. Gen. E. A. Hitchcock is president, having been approved by the President of the United States, he commands that they be published for the information of all concerned.

By order of the Secretary of War.

E. D. TOWNSEND,
*Assistant Adjutant-General.*

---

## INSTRUCTIONS FOR THE GOVERNMENT OF ARMIES OF THE UNITED STATES IN THE FIELD.

### SECTION I.

*Martial law—Military jurisdiction—Military necessities—Retaliation.*

1. A place, district, or country occupied by an enemy stands, in consequence of the occupation, under the martial law of the invading or occupying army, whether any proclamation declaring martial law, or any public warning to the inhabitants, has been issued or not. Martial law is the immediate and direct effect and consequence of occupation and conquest.

The presence of a hostile army proclaims its martial law.

2. Martial law does not cease during the hostile occupation, except by special proclamation, ordered by the commander-in-chief; or by special mention in the treaty of peace concluding the war, when the occupation of a place or territory continues beyond the conclusion of peace as one of the conditions of the same.

3. Martial law in a hostile country consists in the suspension, by the occupying military authority, of the criminal and civil law, and of the domestic administration and government in the occupied place or territory, and in the substitution of military rule and force for the

same, as well as in the dictation of general laws, as far as military necessity requires this suspension, substitution, or dictation.

The commander of the forces may proclaim that the administration of all civil and penal law shall continue, either wholly or in part, as in times of peace, unless otherwise ordered by the military authority.

4. Martial law is simply military authority exercised in accordance with the laws and usages of war. Military oppression is not martial law; it is the abuse of the power which that law confers. As martial law is executed by military force, it is incumbent upon those who administer it to be strictly guided by the principles of justice, honor, and humanity—virtues adorning a soldier even more than other men, for the very reason that he possesses the power of his arms against the unarmed.

5. Martial law should be less stringent in places and countries fully occupied and fairly conquered. Much greater severity may be exercised in places or regions where actual hostilities exist, or are expected and must be prepared for. Its most complete sway is allowed—even in the commander's own country—when face to face with the enemy, because of the absolute necessities of the case, and of the paramount duty to defend the country against invasion.

To save the country is paramount to all other considerations.

6. All civil and penal law shall continue to take its usual course in the enemy's places and territories under martial law, unless interrupted or stopped by order of the occupying military power; but all the functions of the hostile government—legislative, executive, or administrative—whether of a general, provincial, or local character, cease under martial law, or continue only with the sanction, or, if deemed necessary, the participation of the occupier or invader.

7. Martial law extends to property, and to persons, whether they are subjects of the enemy or aliens to that government.

8. Consuls, among American and European nations, are not diplomatic agents. Nevertheless, their offices and persons will be subjected to martial law in cases of urgent necessity only: their property and business are not exempted. Any delinquency they commit against the established military rule may be punished as in the case of any other inhabitant, and such punishment furnishes no reasonable ground for international complaint.

9. The functions of embassadors, ministers, or other diplomatic agents, accredited by neutral powers to the hostile government cease, so far as regards the displaced government; but the conquering or occupying power usually recognizes them as temporarily accredited to itself.

10. Martial law affects chiefly the police and collection of public revenue and taxes, whether imposed by the expelled government or by the invader, and refers mainly to the support and efficiency of the army, its safety, and the safety of its operations.

11. The law of war does not only disclaim all cruelty and bad faith concerning engagements concluded with the enemy during the war, but also the breaking of stipulations solemnly contracted by the belligerents in time of peace, and avowedly intended to remain in force in case of war between the contracting powers.

It disclaims all extortions and other transactions for individual gain; all acts of private revenge, or connivance at such acts.

Offenses to the contrary shall be severely punished, and especially so if committed by officers.

12. Whenever feasible, martial law is carried out in cases of individual offenders by military courts; but sentences of death shall be executed only with the approval of the chief executive, provided the urgency of the case does not require a speedier execution, and then only with the approval of the chief commander.

13. Military jurisdiction is of two kinds: First, that which is conferred and defined by statute; second, that which is derived from the common law of war. Military offenses under the statute law must be tried in the manner therein directed; but military offenses which do not come within the statute must be tried and punished under the common law of war. The character of the courts which exercise these jurisdictions depends upon the local laws of each particular country.

In the armies of the United States the first is exercised by courts-martial; while cases which do not come within the "Rules and Articles of War," or the jurisdiction conferred by statute on courts-martial, are tried by military commissions.

14. Military necessity, as understood by modern civilized nations, consists in the necessity of those measures which are indispensable for securing the ends of the war, and which are lawful according to the modern law and usages of war.

15. Military necessity admits of all direct destruction of life or limb of *armed* enemies, and of other persons whose destruction is incidentally *unavoidable* in the armed contests of the war; it allows of the capturing of every armed enemy, and every enemy of importance to the hostile government, or of peculiar danger to the captor; it allows of all destruction of property and obstruction of the ways and channels of traffic, travel, or communication, and of all withholding of sustenance or means of life from the enemy; of the appropriation of whatever an enemy's country affords necessary for the subsistence and safety of the army, and of such deception as does not involve the breaking of good faith, either positively pledged,

regarding agreements entered into during the war, or supposed by the modern law of war to exist. Men who take up arms against one another in public war do not cease on this account to be moral beings, responsible to one another, and to God.

16. Military necessity does not admit of cruelty; that is, the infliction of suffering for the sake of suffering or for revenge, nor of maiming or wounding except in fight, nor of torture to extort confessions. It does not admit of the use of poison in any way, nor of the wanton devastation of a district. It admits of deception, but disclaims acts of perfidy; and, in general, military necessity does not include any act of hostility which makes the return to peace unnecessarily difficult.

17. War is not carried on by arms alone. It is lawful to starve the hostile belligerent, armed or unarmed, so that it leads to the speedier subjection of the enemy.

18. When the commander of a besieged place expels the non-combatants, in order to lessen the number of those who consume his stock of provisions, it is lawful, though an extreme measure, to drive them back, so as to hasten on the surrender.

19. Commanders, whenever admissible, inform the enemy of their intention to bombard a place, so that the non-combatants, and especially the women and children, may be removed before the bombardment commences; but it is no infraction of the common law of war to omit thus to inform the enemy. Surprise may be a necessity.

20. Public war is a state of armed hostility between sovereign nations or governments. It is a law and requisite of civilized existence that men live in political, continuous societies, forming organized units, called states or nations, whose constituents bear, enjoy, and suffer, advance and retrograde together, in peace and in war.

21. The citizen or native of a hostile country is thus an enemy, as one of the constituents of the hostile state or nation, and as such is subjected to the hardships of the war.

22. Nevertheless, as civilization has advanced during the last centuries, so has likewise steadily advanced, especially in war on land, the distinction between the private individual belonging to a hostile country and the hostile country itself, with its men in arms. The principle has been more and more acknowledged that the unarmed citizen is to be spared in person, property, and honor, as much as the exigencies of war will admit.

23. Private citizens are no longer murdered, enslaved, or carried off to distant parts, and the inoffensive individual is as little disturbed in his private relations as the commander of the hostile troops can afford to grant in the overruling demands of a vigorous war.

24. The almost universal rule in remote times was, and continues to be with barbarous armies, that the private individual of the hostile country is destined to suffer every privation of liberty and protection, and every disruption of family ties. Protection was, and still is with uncivilized people, the exception.

25. In modern regular wars of the Europeans, and their descendants in other portions of the globe, protection of the inoffensive citizen of the hostile country is the rule; privation and disturbance of private relations are the exceptions.

26. Commanding generals may cause the magistrates and civil officers of the hostile country to take the oath of temporary allegiance or an oath of fidelity to their own victorious government or rulers, and they may expel every one who declines to do so. But whether they do so or not, the people and their civil officers owe strict obedience to them as long as they hold sway over the district or country, at the peril of their lives.

27. The law of war can no more wholly dispense with retaliation than can the law of nations, of which it is a branch. Yet, civilized nations acknowledge retaliation as the sternest feature of war. A reckless enemy often leaves to his opponent no other means of securing himself against the repetition of barbarous outrage.

28. Retaliation will, therefore, never be resorted to as a measure of mere revenge, but only as a means of protective retribution, and, moreover, cautiously and unavoidably; that is to say, retaliation shall only be resorted to after careful inquiry into the real occurrence and the character of the misdeeds that may demand retribution.

Unjust or inconsiderate retaliation removes the belligerents farther and farther from the mitigation rules of a regular war, and by rapid steps leads them nearer to the internecine wars of savages.

29. Modern times are distinguished from earlier ages by the existence, at one and the same time, of many nations and great governments related to one another in close intercourse.

Peace is their normal condition; war is the exception. The ultimate object of all modern war is a renewed state of peace.

The more vigorously wars are pursued, the better it is for humanity. Sharp wars are brief.

30. Ever since the formation and co-existence of modern nations, and ever since wars have become great national wars, war has come to be acknowledged not to be its own end, but the means to obtain great ends of state, or to consist in defense against wrong; and no conventional restriction of the modes adopted to injure the enemy is any longer admitted; but the law of war imposes many limitations and restrictions on principles of justice, faith, and honor.

## SECTION II.

*Public and private property of the enemy—Protection of persons, and especially women; of religion, the arts, and sciences—Punishment of crimes against the inhabitants of hostile countries.*

31. A victorious army appropriates all public money, seizes all public movable property until further direction by its government, and sequesters for its own benefit or that of its government all the revenues of real property belonging to the hostile government or nation. The title to such real property remains in abeyance during military occupation, and until the conquest is made complete.

32. A victorious army, by the martial power inherent in the same, may suspend, change, or abolish, as far as the martial power extends, the relations which arise from the services due, according to the existing laws of the invaded country, from one citizen, subject or native, of the same to another.

The commander of the army must leave it to the ultimate treaty of peace to settle the permanency of this change.

33. It is no longer considered lawful—on the contrary, it is held to be a serious breach of the law of war—to force the subjects of the enemy into the service of the victorious government, except the latter should proclaim, after a fair and complete conquest of the hostile country or district, that it is resolved to keep the country, district, or place permanently as its own, and make it a portion of its own country.

34. As a general rule, the property belonging to churches, to hospitals, or other establishments of an exclusively charitable character, to establishments of education, or foundations for the promotion of knowledge, whether public schools, universities, academies of learning, or observatories, museums of the fine arts, or of a scientific character, such property is not to be considered public property in the sense of paragraph 31; but it may be taxed or used when the public service may require it.

35. Classical work of art, libraries, scientific collections, or precious instruments, such as astronomical telescopes, as well as hospitals, must be secured against all avoidable injury, even when they are contained in fortified places while besieged or bombarded.

36. If such works of art, libraries, collections, or instruments, belonging to a hostile nation or government, can be removed without injury, the ruler of the conquering state or nation may order them to be seized and removed for the benefit of the said nation. The ultimate ownership is to be settled by the ensuing treaty of peace.

In no case shall they be sold or given away, if captured by the armies of the United States, nor shall they ever be privately appropriated, or wantonly destroyed or injured.

37. The United States acknowledge and protect, in hostile countries occupied by them, religion and morality; strictly private property; the persons of the inhabitants, especially those of women; and the sacredness of domestic relations. Offenses to the contrary shall be rigorously punished.

This rule does not interfere with the right of the victorious invader to tax the people or their property, to levy forced loans, to billet soldiers, or to appropriate property, especially houses, land, boats, or ships, and churches, for temporary and military uses.

38. Private property, unless forfeited by crimes or by offenses of the owner, can be seized only by way of military necessity for the support or other benefit of the Army or of the United States.

If the owner has not fled, the commanding officer will cause receipts to be given, which will serve the spoliated owner to obtain indemnity.

39. The salaries of civil officers of the hostile government who remain in the invaded territory, and continue the work of their office, and can continue it according to the circumstances arising out of the war—such as judges, administrative or police officers, officers of city or communal governments—are paid from the public revenue of the invaded territory until the military government has reason wholly or partially to discontinue it. Salaries or incomes connected with purely honorary titles are always stopped.

40. There exists no law or body of authoritative rules of action between hostile armies, except that branch of the law of nature and nations which is called the law and usages of war on land.

41. All municipal law of the ground on which the armies stand, or of the countries to which they belong, is silent and of no effect between armies in the field.

42. Slavery, complicating and confounding the ideas of property (that is, of a *thing*) and of personality, (that is, of *humanity*,) exists according to municipal or local law only. The law of nature and nations has never acknowledged it. The digest of the Roman law enacts the early dictum of the pagan jurist, that, "so far as the law of nature is concerned, all men are equal." Fugitives escaping from a country in which they were slaves, villians, or serfs, into another country, have, for centuries past, been held free and acknowledged free by judicial decisions of European countries, even though the municipal law of the country in which the slave had taken refuge acknowledged slavery within its own dominions.

43. Therefore, in a war between the United States and a belligerent which admits of slavery, if a person held in bondage by that belligerent be captured by or come as a fugitive

under the protection of the military forces of the United States, such person is immediately entitled to the rights and privileges of a freeman. To return such person into slavery would amount to enslaving a free person, and neither the United States nor any officer under their authority can enslave any human being. Moreover, a person so made free by the law of war is under the shield of the law of nations, and the former owner or state can have, by the law of postliminy, no belligerent lien or claim of service.

44. All wanton violence committed against persons in the invaded country, all destruction of property not commanded by the authorized officer, all robbery, all pillage or sacking, even after taking a place by main force, all rape, wounding, maiming, or killing of such inhabitants, are prohibited under the penalty of death, or such other severe punishment as may seem adequate for the gravity of the offense.

A soldier, officer, or private, in the act of committing such violence, and disobeying a superior ordering him to abstain from it, may be lawfully killed on the spot by such superior.

45. All captures and booty belong, according to the modern law of war, primarily to the government of the captor.

Prize-money, whether on sea or land, can now only be claimed under local law.

46. Neither officers nor soldiers are allowed to make use of their position or power in the hostile country for private gain, not even for commercial transactions otherwise legitimate. Offenses to the contrary committed by commissioned officers will be punished with cashiering or such other punishment as the nature of the offense may require; if by soldiers, they shall be punished according to the nature of the offense.

47. Crimes punishable by all penal codes, such as arson, murder, maiming, assaults, highway robbery, theft, burglary, fraud, forgery, and rape, if committed by an American soldier in a hostile country against its inhabitants, are not only punishable as at home, but in all cases in which death is not inflicted the severer punishment shall be preferred.

## Section III.

*Deserters—Prisoners of war—Hostages—Booty on the battle-field.*

48. Deserters from the American Army, having entered the service of the enemy, suffer death if they fall again into the hands of the United States, whether by capture or being delivered up to the American Army; and if a deserter from the enemy, having taken service in the Army of the United States, is captured by the enemy, and punished by them with death or otherwise, it is not a breach against the law and usages of war requiring redress or retaliation.

49. A prisoner of war is a public enemy, armed or attached to the hostile army for active aid, who has fallen into the hands of the captor, either fighting or wounded, on the field or in the hospital, by individual surrender or by capitulation.

All soldiers, of whatever species of arms; all men who belong to the rising *en masse* of the hostile country; all those who are attached to the army for its efficiency, and promote directly the object of the war, except such as are hereinafter provided for; all disabled men or officers on the field or elsewhere, if captured; all enemies who have thrown away their arms and ask for quarter, are prisoners of war, and, as such, exposed to the inconveniences as well as entitled to the privileges of a prisoner of war.

50. Moreover, citizens who accompany an army for whatever purpose, such as sutlers, editors, or reporters of journals, or contractors, if captured, may be made prisoners of war, and be detained as such.

The monarch and members of the hostile reigning family, male or female, the chief, and chief officers of the hostile government, its diplomatic agents, and all persons who are of particular and singular use and benefit to the hostile army or its government, are, if captured on belligerent ground, and if unprovided with a safe-conduct granted by the captor's government, prisoners of war.

51. If the people of that portion of an invaded country which is not yet occupied by the enemy, or of the whole country, at the approach of a hostile army, rise, under a duly-authorized levy, *en masse*, to resist the invader, they are now treated as public enemies, and, if captured, are prisoners of war.

52. No belligerent has the right to declare that he will treat every captured man in arms of a levy *en masse* as a brigand or a bandit.

If, however, the people of a country, or any portion of the same, already occupied by an army, rise against it, they are violators of the laws of war, and are not entitled to their protection.

53. The enemy's chaplains, officers of the medical staff, apothecaries, hospital nurses and servants, if they fall into the hands of the American Army, are not prisoners of war, unless the commander has reasons to retain them. In this latter case, or if, at their own desire, they are allowed to remain with their captured companions, they are treated as prisoners of war, and may be exchanged if the commander see fit.

54. A hostage is a person accepted as a pledge for the fulfillment of an agreement con-

cluded between belligerents during the war, or in consequence of war. Hostages are rare in the present age.

55. If a hostage is accepted, he is treated like a prisoner of war, according to rank and condition, as circumstances may admit.

56. A prisoner of war is subject to no punishment for being a public enemy, nor is any revenge wreaked upon him by the intentional infliction of any suffering, or disgrace, by cruel imprisonment, want of food, by mutilation, death, or any other barbarity.

57. So soon as a man is armed by a sovereign government, and takes the soldier's oath of fidelity, he is a belligerent; his killing, wounding, or other warlike acts are no individual crimes or offenses. No belligerent has a right to declare that enemies of a certain class, color, or condition, when properly organized as soldiers, will not be treated by him as public enemies.

58. The law of nations knows of no distinction of color, and, if an enemy of the United States should enslave and sell any captured persons of their Army, it would be a case for the severest retaliation, if not redressed upon complaint.

The United States cannot retaliate by enslavement: therefore death must be the retaliation for this crime against the law of nations.

59. A prisoner of war remains answerable for his crimes committed against the captor's army or people, committed before he was captured, and for which he has not been punished by his own authorities.

All prisoners of war are liable to the infliction of retaliatory measures.

60. It is against the usage of modern war to resolve, in hatred and revenge, to give no quarter. No body of troops has the right to declare that it will not give, and therefore will not expect, quarter; but a commander is permitted to direct his troops to give no quarter, in great straits, when his own salvation makes it *impossible* to cumber himself with prisoners.

61. Troops that give no quarter have no right to kill enemies already disabled on the ground, or prisoners captured by other troops.

62. All troops of the enemy known or discovered to give no quarter in general, or to any portion of the army, receive none.

63. Troops who fight in the uniform of their enemies, without any plain, striking, and uniform mark of distinction of their own, can expect no quarter.

64. If American troops capture a train containing uniforms of the enemy, and the commander considers it advisable to distribute them for use among his men, some striking mark or sign must be adopted to distinguish the American soldier from the enemy.

65. The use of the enemy's national standard, flag, or other emblem of nationality, for the purpose of deceiving the enemy in battle, is an act of perfidy by which they lose all claim to the protection of the laws of war.

66. Quarter having been given to an enemy by American troops, under a misapprehension of his true character, he may, nevertheless, be ordered to suffer death if, within three days after the battle, it be discovered that he belongs to a corps which gives no quarter.

67. The law of nations allows every sovereign government to make war upon another sovereign state, and, therefore, admits of no rules or laws different from those of regular warfare, regarding the treatment of prisoners of war, although they may belong to the army of a government which the captor may consider as a wanton and unjust assailant.

68. Modern wars are not internecine wars, in which the killing of the enemy is the object. The destruction of the enemy in modern war, and, indeed, modern war itself, are means to obtain that object of the belligerent which lies beyond the war.

Unnecessary or revengeful destruction of life is not lawful.

69. Outposts, sentinels, or pickets are not to be fired upon, except to drive them in, or when a positive order, special or general, has been issued to that effect.

70. The use of poison in any manner, be it to poison wells, or food, or arms, is wholly excluded from modern warfare. He that uses it puts himself out of the pale of the law and usages of war.

71. Whoever intentionally inflicts additional wounds on an enemy already wholly disabled, or kills such an enemy, or who orders or encourages soldiers to do so, shall suffer death, if duly convicted, whether he belongs to the Army of the United States, or is an enemy captured after having committed his misdeed.

72. Money and other valuables on the person of a prisoner, such as watches or jewelry, as well as extra clothing, are regarded by the American Army as the private property of the prisoner, and the appropriation of such valuables or money is considered dishonorable, and is prohibited.

Nevertheless, if *large* sums are found upon the persons of prisoners, or in their possession, they shall be taken from them, and the surplus, after providing for their own support, appropriated for the use of the Army, under the direction of the commander, unless otherwise ordered by the Government. Nor can prisoners claim, as private property, large sums found and captured in their train, although they had been placed in the private luggage of the prisoners.

73. All officers, when captured, must surrender their side-arms to the captor. They may be restored to the prisoner in marked cases, by the commander, to signalize admiration of

his distinguished bravery, or approbation of his humane treatment of prisoners before his capture. The captured officer to whom they may be restored cannot wear them during captivity.

74. A prisoner of war, being a public enemy, is the prisoner of the Government, and not of the captor. No ransom can be paid by a prisoner of war to his individual captor, or to any officer in command. The Government alone releases captives, according to rules prescribed by itself.

75. Prisoners of war are subject to confinement or imprisonment such as may be deemed necessary on account of safety, but they are to be subjected to no other intentional suffering or indignity. The confinement and mode of treating a prisoner may be varied during his captivity according to the demands of safety.

76. Prisoners of war shall be fed upon plain and wholesome food whenever practicable, and treated with humanity.

They may be required to work for the benefit of the captor's government, according to their rank and condition.

77. A prisoner of war who escapes may be shot, or otherwise killed in his flight, but neither death nor any other punishment shall be inflicted upon him simply for his attempt to escape, which the law of war does not consider a crime. Stricter means of security shall be used after an unsuccessful attempt at escape.

If, however, a conspiracy is discovered, the purpose of which is a united or general escape, the conspirators may be rigorously punished, even with death; and capital punishment may also be inflicted upon prisoners of war discovered to have plotted rebellion against the authorities of the captors, whether in union with fellow-prisoners or other persons.

78. If prisoners of war, having given no pledge, nor made any promise on their honor, forcibly or otherwise escape, and are captured again in battle, after having rejoined their own army, they shall not be punished for their escape, but shall be treated as simple prisoners of war, although they will be subjected to stricter confinement.

79. Every captured wounded enemy shall be medically treated according to the ability of the medical staff.

80. Honorable men, when captured, will abstain from giving to the enemy information concerning their own army, and the modern law of war permits no longer the use of any violence against prisoners, in order to extort the desired information, or to punish them for having given false information.

## Section IV.

*Partisans—Armed enemies not belonging to the hostile army—Scouts—Armed prowlers—War-rebels.*

81. Partisans are soldiers armed and wearing the uniform of their army, but belonging to a corps which acts detached from the main body, for the purpose of making inroads into the territory occupied by the enemy. If captured, they are entitled to all the privileges of the prisoner of war.

82. Men, or squads of men, who commit hostilities, whether by fighting, or inroads for destruction or plunder, or by raids of any kind without commission, without being part and portion of the organized hostile army, and without sharing continuously in the war, but who do so with intermitting returns to their homes and avocations, or with the occasional assumption of the semblance of peaceful pursuits, divesting themselves of the character or appearance of soldiers—such men or squads of men are not public enemies, and, therefore, if captured, are not entitled to the privileges of prisoners of war, but shall be treated summarily as highway robbers or pirates.

83. Scouts or single soldiers, if disguised in the dress of the country, or in the uniform of the army hostile to their own, employed in obtaining information, if found within or lurking about the lines of the captor, are treated as spies, and suffer death.

84. Armed prowlers, by whatever names they may be called, or persons of the enemy's territory who steal within the lines of a hostile army for the purpose of robbing, killing, or of destroying bridges, roads, or canals, or of robbing or destroying the mail, or of cutting the telegraph wires, are not entitled to the privileges of the prisoner of war.

85. War-rebels are persons within an occupied territory who rise in arms against the occupying or conquering army, or against the authorities established by the same. If captured, they may suffer death, whether they rise singly, in small or large bands, and whether called upon to do so by their own, but expelled, government or not. They are not prisoners of war; nor are they, if discovered and secured before their conspiracy has matured to an actual rising, or to armed violence.

## Section V.

*Safe-conduct—Spies—War-traitors—Captured messengers—Abuse of the flag of truce.*

86. All intercourse between the territories occupied by belligerent armies, whether by traffic, by letter, by travel, or in any other way, ceases. This is the general rule, to be observed without special proclamation.

Exceptions to this rule, whether by safe-conduct or permission to trade on a small or large scale, or by exchanging mails, or by travel from one territory into the other, can take place only according to agreement approved by the government, or by the highest military authority.

Contraventions of this rule are highly punishable.

87. Embassadors, and all other diplomatic agents of neutral powers, accredited to the enemy, may receive safe-conducts through the territories occupied by the belligerents, unless there are military reasons to the contrary, and unless they may reach the place of their destination conveniently by another route. It implies no international affront if the safe-conduct is declined. Such passes are usually given by the supreme authority of the state, and not by subordinate officers.

88. A spy is a person who secretly, in disguise or under false pretense, seeks information with the intention of communicating it to the enemy.

The spy is punishable with death by hanging by the neck, whether or not he succeeded in obtaining the information or in conveying it to the enemy.

89. If a citizen of the United States obtains information in a legitimate manner and betrays it to the enemy, be he a military or civil officer or a private citizen, he shall suffer death.

90. A traitor, under the law of war, or a war-traitor, is a person in a place or district under martial law who, unauthorized by the military commander, gives information of any kind to the enemy, or holds intercourse with him.

91. The war-traitor is always severely punished. If his offense consists in betraying to the enemy anything concerning the condition, safety, operations, or plans of the troops holding or occupying the place or district, his punishment is death.

92. If the citizen or subject of a country or place invaded or conquered gives information to his own government, from which he is separated by the hostile army, or to the army of his governmant, he is a war-traitor, and death is the penalty of his offense.

93. All armies in the field stand in need of guides, and impress them if they cannot obtain them otherwise.

94. No person having been forced by the enemy to serve as a guide is punishable for having done so.

95. If a citizen of a hostile and invaded district voluntarily serves as a guide to the enemy, or offers to do so, he is deemed a war-traitor, and shall suffer death.

96. A citizen serving voluntarily as a guide against his own country commits treason, and will be dealt with according to the law of his country.

97. Guides, when it is clearly proved that they have misled intentionally, may be put to death.

98. All unauthorized or secret communication with the enemy is considered treasonable by the law of war.

Foreign residents in an invaded or occupied territory, or foreign visitors in the same, can claim no immunity from this law. They may communicate with foreign parts, or with the inhabitants of the hostile country, so far as the military authority permits, but no further. Instant expulsion from the occupied territory would be the very least punishment for the infraction of this rule.

99. A messenger carrying written dispatches or verbal messages from one portion of the army, or from a besieged place, to another portion of the same army, or its government, if armed, and in the uniform of his army, and if captured, while doing so, in the territory occupied by the enemy, is treated by the captor as a prisoner of war; if not in uniform, nor a soldier, the circumstances connected with his capture must determine the disposition that shall be made of him.

100. A messenger or agent who attempts to steal through the territory occupied by the enemy, to further, in any manner, the interests of the enemy, if captured, is not entitled to the privileges of the prisoner or war, and may be dealt with according to the circumstances of the case.

101. While deception in war is admitted as a just and necessary means of hostility, and is consistent with honorable warfare, the common law of war allows even capital punishment for clandestine or treacherous attempts to injure an enemy, because they are so dangerous, and it is so difficult to guard against them.

102. The law of war, like the criminal law regarding other offenses, makes no difference, on account of the difference of sexes, concerning the spy, the war-traitor, or the war-rebel.

103. Spies, war-traitors, and war-rebels are not exchanged according to the common law of war. The exchange of such persons would require a special cartel, authorized by the government, or, at a great distance from it, by the chief commander of the army in the field.

104. A successful spy or war-traitor, safely returned to his own army, and afterward captured as an enemy, is not subject to punishment for his acts as a spy or war-traitor, but he may be held in closer custody as a person individually dangerous.

## SECTION VI.

*Exchange of prisoners—Flags of truce—Flags of protection.*

105. Exchanges of prisoners take place number for number, rank for rank, wounded for wounded, with added condition for added condition, such, for instance, as not to serve for a certain period.

106. In exchanging prisoners of war, such numbers of persons of inferior rank may be substituted as an equivalent for one of superior rank as may be agreed upon by cartel, which requires the sanction of the government, or of the commander of the army in the field.

107. A prisoner of war is in honor bound truly to state to the captor his rank; and he is not to assume a lower rank than belongs to him, in order to cause a more advantageous exchange; nor a higher rank, for the purpose of obtaining better treatment.

Offenses to the contrary have been justly published by the commanders of released prisoners, and may be good cause for refusing to release such prisoners.

108. The surplus number of prisoners of war remaining after an exchange has taken place is sometimes released either for the payment of a stipulated sum of money, or, in urgent cases, of provision, clothing, or other necessaries.

Such arrangement, however, requires the sanction of the highest authority.

109. The exchange of prisoners of war is an act of convenience to both belligerents. If no general cartel has been concluded, it cannot be demanded by either of them. No belligerent is obliged to exchange prisoners of war.

A cartel is voidable so soon as either party has violated it.

110. No exchange of prisoners shall be made except after complete capture, and after an accurate account of them, and a list of the captured officers has been taken.

111. The bearer of a flag of truce cannot insist upon being admitted. He must always be admitted with great caution. Unnecessary frequency is carefully to be avoided.

112. If the bearer of a flag of truce offer himself during an engagement, he can be admitted as a very rare exception only. It is no breach of good faith to retain such a flag of truce, if admitted during the engagement. Firing is not required to cease on the appearance of a flag of truce in battle.

113. If the bearer of a flag of truce, presenting himself during an engagement, is killed or wounded, it furnishes no ground of complaint whatever.

114. If it be discovered, and fairly proved, that a flag of truce has been abused for surreptitiously obtaining military knowledge, the bearer of the flag thus abusing his sacred character is deemed a spy.

So sacred is the character of a flag of truce, and so necessary is its sacredness, that while its abuse is an especially heinous offense, great caution is requisite, on the other hand, in convicting the bearer of a flag of truce as a spy.

115. It is customary to designate, by certain flags, (usually yellow,) the hospitals in places which are shelled, so that the besieging enemy may avoid firing on them. The same has been done in battles, when hospitals are situated within the field of the engagement.

116. Honorable belligerents often request that the hospitals within the territory of the enemy may be designated, so that they may be spared.

An honorable belligerent allows himself to be guided by flags or signals of protection as much as the contingencies and the necessities of the fight will permit.

117. It is justly considered an act of bad faith, of infamy or fiendishness, to deceive the enemy by flags of protection. Such act of bad fuith may be good cause for refusing to respect such flags.

118. The besieging belligerent has sometimes requested the besieged to designate the buildings containing collections of works of art, scientific museums, astronomical observatories, or precious libraries, so that their destruction may be avoided as much as possible.

## SECTION VII.

*The Parole.*

119. Prisoners of war may be released from captivity by exchange, and, under certain circumstances, also by parole.

120. The term parole designates the pledge of individual good faith and honor to do, or to omit doing, certain acts after he who gives his parole shall have been dismissed, wholly or partially, from the power of the captor.

121. The pledge of the parole is always an individual, but not a private, act.

122. The parole applies chiefly to prisoners of war whom the captor allows to return to their country, or to live in greater freedom within the captor's country or territory, on conditions stated in the parole.

123. Release of prisoners of war by exchange is the general rule; release by parole is the exception.

124. Breaking the parole is punished with death when the person breaking the parole is captured again.

Accurate lists, therefore, of the paroled persons must be kept by the belligerents.

125. When paroles are given and received there must be an exchange of two written documents, in which the name and rank of the paroled individuals are accurately and truthfully stated.

126. Commissioned officers only are allowed to give their parole, and they can give it only with the permission of their superior, as long as a superior in rank is within reach.

127. No non-commissioned officer or private can give his parole except through an officer. Individual paroles not given through an officer are not only void, but subject the individual giving them to the punishment of death as deserters. The only admissible exception is where individuals, properly separated from their commands, have suffered long confinement without the possibility of being paroled through an officer.

128. No paroling on the battle-field; no paroling of entire bodies of troops after a battle; and no dismissal of large numbers of prisoners, with a general declaration that they are paroled, is permitted, or of any value.

129. In capitulations for the surrender of strong places or fortified camps the commanding officer, in cases of urgent necessity, may agree that the troops under his command shall not fight again during the war, unless exchanged.

130. The usual pledge given in the parole is, not to serve during the existing war unless exchanged.

This pledge refers only to the active service in the field, against the paroling belligerent or his allies actively engaged in the same war. These cases of breaking the parole are patent acts, and can be visited with the punishment of death; but the pledge does not refer to internal service, such as recruiting or drilling the recruits, fortifying places not besieged, quelling civil commotions, fighting against belligerents unconnected with the paroling belligerents, or to civil or diplomatic service for which the paroled officer may be employed.

131. If the government does not approve of the parole, the paroled officer must return into captivity, and, should the enemy refuse to receive him, he is free of his parole.

132. A belligerent government may declare, by general order, whether it will allow paroling, and on what conditions it will allow it. Such order is communicated to the enemy.

133. No prisoner of war can be forced by the hostile government to parole himself, and no government is obliged to parole prisoners of war, or to parole all captured officers, if it paroles any. As the pledging of the parole is an individual act, so is paroling, on the other hand, an act of choice on the part of the belligerent.

134. The commander of an occupying army may require of the civil officers of the enemy, and of its citizens, any pledge he may consider necessary for the safety or security of his army, and upon their failure to give it he may arrest, confine, or detain them.

## SECTION VIII.

### *Armistice—Capitulation.*

135. An armistice is the cessation of active hostilities for a period agreed upon between belligerents. It must be agreed upon in writing, and duly ratified by the highest authorities of the contending parties.

136. If an armistice be declared without conditions, it extends no further than to require a total cessation of hostilities along the front of both belligerents.

If conditions be agreed upon, they should be clearly expressed, and must be rigidly adhered to by both parties. If either party violates any express condition, the armistice may be declared null and void by the other.

137. An armistice may be general, and valid for all points and lines of the belligerents; or special, that is, referring to certain troops or certain localities only.

An armistice may be concluded for a definite time, or for an indefinite time, during which either belligerent may resume hostilities on giving the notice agreed upon to the other.

138. The motives which induce the one or the other belligerent to conclude an armistice, whether it be expected to be preliminary to a treaty of peace or to prepare during the armistice for a more vigorous prosecution of the war, does in no way affect the character of the armistice itself.

139. An armistice is binding upon the belligerents from the day of the agreed commencement, but the officers of the armies are responsible from the day only when they receive official information of its existence.

140. Commanding officers have the right to conclude armistices binding on the district over which their command extends, but such armistice is subject to the ratification of the superior authority, and ceases so soon as it is made known to the enemy that the armistice is not ratified, even if a certain time for the elapsing between giving notice of cessation and the resumption of hostilities should have been stipulated for.

141. It is incumbent upon the contracting parties of an armistice to stipulate what intercourse of persons or traffic between the inhabitants of the territories occupied by the hostile armies shall be allowed, if any.

If nothing is stipulated, the intercourse remains suspended, as during actual hostilities.

142. An armistice is not a partial or temporary peace; it is only the suspension of military operations to the extent agreed upon by the parties.

143. When an armistice is concluded between a fortified place and the army besieging it, it is agreed by all the authorities on this subject that the besieger must cease all extension, perfection, or advance of his attacking works, as much so as from attacks by main force.

But as there is a difference of opinion among martial jurists, whether the besieged have the right to repair breaches or to erect new works of defense within the place during an armistice, this point should be determined by express agreement between the parties.

144. So soon as a capitulation is signed the capitulator has no right to demolish, destroy, or injure the works, arms, stores, or ammunition in his possession during the time which elapses between the signing and the execution of the capitulation, unless otherwise stipulated in the same.

145. When an armistice is clearly broken by one of the parties, the other party is released from all obligation to observe it.

146. Prisoners taken in the act of breaking an armistice must be treated as prisoners of war, the officer alone being responsible who gives the order for such a violation of an armistice. The highest authority of the belligerent aggrieved may demand redress for the infraction of an armistice.

147. Belligerents sometimes conclude an armistice while their plenipotentiaries are met to discuss the conditions of a treaty of peace; but plenipotentiaries may meet without a preliminary armistice. In the latter case the war is carried on without any abatement.

## SECTION IX.

### *Assassination.*

148. The law of war does not allow proclaiming either an individual belonging to the hostile army, or a citizen, or a subject of the hostile government, an outlaw, who may be slain without trial by any captor, any more than the modern law of peace allows such international outlawry; on the contrary, it abhors such outrage. The sternest retaliation should follow the murder committed in consequence of such proclamation, made by whatever authority. Civilized nations look with horror upon offers of rewards for the assassination of enemies as relapses into barbarism.

## SECTION X.

### *Insurrection—Civil war—Rebellion.*

149. Insurrection is the rising of people in arms against their government, or a portion of it, or against one or more of its laws, or against an officer or officers of the government. It may be confined to mere armed resistance or it may have greater ends in view.

150. Civil war is war between two or more portions of a country or state, each contending for the mastery of the whole, and each claiming to be the legitimate government. The term is also sometimes applied to war of rebellion, when the rebellious provinces or portions of the state are contiguous to those containing the seat of government.

151. The term rebellion is applied to an insurrection of large extent, and is usually a war between the legitimate government of a country and portions or provinces of the same who seek to throw off their allegiance to it and set up a government of their own.

152. When humanity induces the adoption of the rules of regular war toward rebels, whether the adoption is partial or entire, it does in no way whatever imply a partial or complete acknowledgment of their government, if they have set up one, or of them as an independent or sovereign power. Neutrals have no right to make the adoption of the rules of war by the assailed government toward rebels the ground of their own acknowledgment of the revolted people as an independent power.

153. Treating captured rebels as prisoners of war, exchanging them, concluding of cartels, capitulations, or other warlike agreements with them; addressing officers of a rebel army by the rank they may have in the same; accepting flags of truce; or, on the other hand, proclaiming martial law in their territory, or levying war-taxes or forced loans, or doing any other act sanctioned or demanded by the law and usages of public war between sovereign belligerents, neither proves nor establishes an acknowledgment of the rebellious people, or of the government which they may have erected, as a public or sovereign power. Nor does the adoption of the rules of war toward rebels imply an engagement with them extending beyond the limits of these rules. It is victory in the field that ends the strife and settles the future relations between the contending parties.

154. Treating, in the field, the rebellious enemy according to the law and usages of war has never prevented the legitimate government from trying the leaders of the rebellion or chief rebels for high treason, and from treating them accordingly, unless they are included in a general amnesty.

155. All enemies in regular war are divided into two general classes; that is to say, into combatants and non-combatants, or unarmed citizens of the hostile government.

The military commander of the legitimate government, in a war of rebellion, distinguishes between the loyal citizen in the revolted portion of the country and the disloyal citizen. The disloyal citizens may further be classified into those citizens known to sympathize with the rebellion, without positively aiding it, and those who, without taking up arms, give positive aid and comfort to the rebellious enemy, without being bodily forced thereto.

156. Common justice and plain expediency require that the military commander protect the manifestly loyal citizens, in revolted territories, against the hardships of the war as much as the common misfortune of all war admits.

The commander will throw the burden of the war, as much as lies within his power, on the disloyal citizens of the revolted portion or province, subjecting them to a stricter police than the non-combatant enemies have to suffer in regular war; and, if he deems it appropriate, or if his government demands of him that every citizen shall, by an oath of allegiance, or by some other manifest act, declare his fidelity to the legitimate government, he may expel, transfer, imprison, or fine the revolted citizens who refuse to pledge themselves anew as citizens obedient to the law and loyal to the government.

Whether it is expedient to do so, and whether reliance can be placed upon such oaths, the commander or his government have the right to decide.

157. Armed or unarmed resistance by citizens of the United States against the lawful movements of their troops is levying war against the United States, and is therefore treason.

www.ingramcontent.com/pod-product-compliance
Lightning Source LLC
LaVergne TN
LVHW021139110826
845150LV00005B/1072

*9781425549381*